To

Norman

The Delightfulest
Friend I have
ever had!

FROM -:

Richard Blake Brown

...

January 28th 1931.

NORMAN HARTNELL

THE BIOGRAPHY

Norman Hartnell (1901-1979) Portrait by Madame Yevonde c 1930

NORMAN HARTNELL

THE BIOGRAPHY

MICHAEL PICK

ZULEIKA

First published 2019

by Zuleika Books & Publishing

Thomas House, 84 Eccleston Square
London, SW1V 1PX

Copyright © 2019 Michael Pick

The right of Michael Pick to be identified
as author of this work has been asserted in
accordance with sections 77 and 78 of the
Copyright, Designs and Patents Act 1988.

British Library Cataloguing in Publication Data

A catalogue record for this book is
available from the British Library

ISBN: 978-1-99-962328-9

Designed by Euan Monaghan
Printed in England

For Eiji and in memory of my mother, who in the 1950s showed me her 1930s Hartnell dresses and explained pre-war glamour.

HENRY VAUGHAN (1622–1695)

The Garland

Thou, who dost flow and flourish here below,
To whom a falling star and nine days' glory,
Or some frail beauty makes the bravest show,
Hark, and make use of this ensuing story.

When first my youthful, sinful age
Grew master of my ways,
Appointing Error for my Page,
And Darkness for my days;
I flung away, and with full cry
Of wild affections, rid
In post for pleasures, bent to try
All gamesters that would bid.
I play'd with fire, did counsel spurn,
Made life my common stake;
But never thought that fire would burn,
Or that a soul could ache.

Glorious deceptions, gilded mists,
False joys, fantastic flights,
Pieces of sackcloth with silk lists,
These were my prime delights.
I sought choice bowers, haunted the spring,
Cull'd flowers and made me posies;
Gave my fond humours their full wing,
And crown'd my head with roses.
But at the height of this career
I met with a dead man,
Who, noting well my vain abear,
Thus unto me began:
Desist, fond fool, be not undone;
What thou has cut to-day
Will fade at night, and with this sun
Quite vanish and decay.

Flowers gather'd in this world, die here; if thou
Wouldst have a wreath that fades not, let them grow,
And grow for thee. Who spares them here, shall find
A garland, where comes neither rain, nor wind.

CONTENTS

A Tale of a Safe and a Dress 1

1. Crown & Sceptre 5

2. Academical 27

3. Not if . . . but when 49

4. When London was lovely 77

5. Paris follows . . . the very essence of youth 105

6. '. . . Dropped them on the floor' 123

7. Don't miss this one! 147

8. Happy days 173

9. Regal renaissance 193

10. Swank London dress salons carry on 223

11. Aren't I smart? 263

12. Inspired my . . . new look 281

13. Increasing indignation and resentment 315

14. A crowded hour 335

15. The top of success 347

16. Hartnell puts it right 365

17. Another go at it 379

18. But never mind! 399

19. A few yards of satin 423

Appendix I 453

Appendix II 463

Notes 469

Index 487

Bibliography 503

A TALE OF A SAFE
AND A DRESS

After a busy day poring over ledgers and invoices in her bookkeeper's office at Norman Hartnell Ltd, a homeward-bound, quietly dressed businesswoman hurried out of the gloom of a foggy 1948 autumn evening into the misty brightness of the mainline terminus. Miss Ivy Godley had worked later than usual and now joined a thinning crowd of commuters hurrying to their platforms, eagerly looking forward to warm homes and escape from another inhospitable work day in Austerity Britain.

London was far from post-war recovery, yet the city was coping as usual with the effects of the recent war. Miss Godley was one of millions of working women who had experienced bereavement, the dire economic situation at home and the familiar sight of slowly disappearing bomb sites, rationing of food, fuel, materials and clothing, all tightly controlled by the government's strict Austerity regulations. These affected her daily existence in more than domestic terms, for although she was surrounded by luxury in her workplace, it was generally in short supply, even to those of moderate means.

But Miss Godley was fortunate in retaining her position as bookkeeper in the luxurious setting of Norman Hartnell Ltd, albeit with the attendant complications involved in running a luxury business, one hedged in by fuel and material shortages, extra taxes and the necessity of applying the scarce coupons to clients' orders. This was in addition to the many other complications of administering daily life behind the scenes at 26 Bruton Street in Mayfair, the glamorous setting for Britain's leading dress designer and his large workforce. The huge business existed on five floors in a building extending back a whole block deep to face Bruton Mews at the rear. It was an enterprise solely dependent upon the world-famous talent of Norman Hartnell, aided by his indispensable and highly skilled workforce; not least of whom was his trusted bookkeeper Miss Godley, privy to most of the secrets behind the facade of the successful enterprise.

About to board her train to the suburbs, Miss Godley paused with a heart-stopping thought. Had she locked the safe and, furthermore, where was its vital key? Automatically, she opened her bag with a jolt. Keys to her front door, keys to the Bruton Street door, but no key to the safe. It was a nerve-wracking moment. In the safe were not only cash and cheque books together with various ledgers, but also the private information on the accounts of Hartnell's most highly valued clients: the various ladies of the Royal Family. Mentally she retraced her usual actions. Leaving late had caused her to perhaps rush her procedures. There was no alternative; she sped back to Hartnell.

Miss Godley was now more than ever acutely aware of her position of trust as she hurriedly returned to Mayfair. In such straitened times, criminal gangs were notoriously targeting the premises of the vendors of luxury goods, including dress houses and furriers. Hartnell was all these things and had extremely valuable stock. Security was tight – there was even night security – but an open safe could tempt anyone.

On arrival at the Hartnell building's imposing entrance, Miss Godley passed between the famous marble obelisks supporting the lanterns illuminating the marble flags and huge double doors, with their impressive lion's-mask handles. Miss Godley pressed her key into the lock but was aghast when the door swung ajar. She was certain that it was locked when she left. Should she call a policeman? Hartnell with its royal and famously affluent clientele was a prime target, not least for copyists seeking information on the latest designs. But Miss Godley was made of stern stuff; she had survived the blitz and the rocket attacks, which had demolished a huge, now vacant corner site at the Bruton Street–Bond Street crossroads. With other Hartnell employees, she had witnessed the famous chandeliers of the large first-floor salon swaying in the bomb blast and had seen falling glass and the famous mirror cladding crack in places. She was not afraid but cautiously pushed the door slightly open, peering through the opening.

The pale green, marble-floored, mirrored lobby was bright. The chandelier was gleaming, which was unexpected; she had switched if off upon leaving. The next set of doors being of clear glass, there was no one visible beyond, only more chandeliers and the Hartnell green carpeting of the floor and stairs. The intrepid employee ventured to push open the heavy glass doors and walked forward into the wide hall at the foot of the impressive staircase. She heard and saw nothing more until she softly walked further inwards to look up the stairwell. Then came a surprise – in fact a shock such as Miss Godley had never expected.

Sitting towards the rear of the hall near the telephonist's table was a figure resplendent in a sparkling evening dress. The silhouette of the wide embroidered crinoline skirt was familiar as the one devised by Hartnell in 1937 for the Queen of England and popularised by her into a worldwide fashion, now also worn by her daughters Princesses Elizabeth and Margaret and made even more popular with all clients after 1947 by Christian Dior's New Look version. Miss Godley wondered for a moment. She thought of the reported sightings of a ghost within the building, but her anxiety was swiftly brought to an end. The figure moved. It spoke. It was Norman Hartnell himself.

In that moment Miss Godley realised two things: her employer was expecting a visitor and the conundrum of the dresses ordered by a woman in the Midlands, so out of keeping with that location, together with curious measurements and equally unusual clothing coupon and payment arrangements, must relate to Mr Hartnell's fancy dress, as she perceived the situation, which was shortly explained to her.

Miss Godley, already warm from her rushed return, felt red hot on explaining her presence and swiftly became intent on her duties; she walked up the stairs and then made her way to her office, discovering that the safe was locked and secure. She felt relieved yet perturbed and left pondering first the fact that the safe was indeed locked and then the unusual appearance of her employer, 'Bossie', as she and others knew him. He was no longer visible to her. She did not mention the supposed fancy dress partygoer to anyone for many years. Nor did he ever mention her safe-locking quandary to her.

However, the unknown client in the Midlands sporadically continued to order elaborate evening dresses for many more years.[1]

CHAPTER ONE

Crown & Sceptre

Of all the arts, that of the dressmaker and designer is the most ephemeral. Few sights are as sad as an old dress hanging on a dummy: no matter how well cared for, fabrics change colour, textures disappear and the sheen of fine silk grows dull. There is a sadness about old clothes. The more fashionable the dress, the sadder it appears without the human form bringing it to life. If re-worn, it becomes a piece of fancy dress with inappropriate embroideries or trimmings. It is a tiny piece of history, a lost moment in time that cannot be recreated. The successful designer is acutely conscious of this and must constantly recreate a new personality and look to be fashionable and reinvent success. Few achieve this but for six decades Norman Hartnell did. Always equivocal about the exact status of the designer as an artist, he was unequivocal in his rejection of the term 'dressmaker' for himself, as he could neither cut nor sew. Yet he proudly displayed two Royal Warrants above his premises, on his stationery, scent and packaging: 'By Appointment Dressmaker to Her Majesty the Queen' and 'By Appointment Dressmaker to Her Majesty Queen Elizabeth II'. He considered himself a designer and firmly explained his views in his autobiography *Silver and Gold* and elsewhere: 'I regard the design of dress as an art.'[2, 3]

This opinion of his own talents is an indication of the straightforward no-nonsense character which he projected to the world at large, albeit often with a touch of whimsy. Hartnell inhabited the glamorous world of haute couture from the Jazz Age to the Age of Rock, adapting himself like a chameleon to all the dramatic changes of taste in the twentieth century, constantly reinventing his own taste to suit several generations of women seeking elegance. From all over the world clients sought his creations, visiting his glass salon in Mayfair, where the multifaceted mirrors and chandelier drops refracted the light into the rainbow of colour which inspired him and flattered the young and old.

All Halls of Mirrors are deceptive in their distortion, whether in the fairground or in a palace. They all hold secrets, reflect falsehoods and true reality becomes distorted or disguised. Could Sir Norman, the first English couturier to be knighted, be quite as pleasant, diffident, cosy, charming, thoughtful, kind and, to use a favourite word of his, 'jolly' as he seemed? Could the man with the look of a ruddy-faced 'country squire' be the urbane genius behind six decades of designing, the worldwide fame of his name emblazoned amongst acres of newsprint, many pasted into the thick volumes of press cuttings that, at the end of his life, mouldered in his decaying premises? His chameleon nature subtly reflected his complex and constantly adaptable personality. Above all he was a self-invented, self-made man in an era which gave qualified promise to those of lesser social standing making their way to the top. When it became fashionable to boast of humble beginnings in the 1960s, it was too late for Hartnell to climb down from his earlier vague versions of his origins, even when the chameleon was cleverly pinned to the ground by the same press which had trumpeted his success for decades.

It was an aborted edition of one of the BBC's most popular programmes *This is Your Life*, filmed for Monday, 15 February 15 1960 as a quintessentially period slice of popular glamour, which brought forth the truth of Hartnell's own origins and provided the key to so much of his character. The programme was always made with the assistance of the star's friends and colleagues, all sworn to secrecy – the star being inveigled as a guest to a specious theatrical performance and then being surprised live by the host, Eamonn Andrews, with his large red book. This edition was withdrawn at the last moment when Hartnell discovered that he was to be the subject. The poised Hartnell was, in truth, the shy Normie, who was anxious before any appearance in front of complete strangers, and especially unwilling to talk about his private life and origins. A convenient excuse was found in his status as a Royal Warrant holder: it would be improper for him to appear on television as this would constitute an unseemly form of advertising and breach the regulations governing the behaviour of Warrant holders.

The life story of Hartnell had actually emerged five years earlier as *Silver and Gold* was serialised in *Woman's Day* and had firmly set out his own official version of his life; it was chatty, self-deprecating and as lacking in hard dates and facts as possible to the point of jumbling events out of sequence. It remains a typically glamorous biography of the period, leaving out far more than is necessary and projecting the image of the young gentleman genius creating success from nothing in the cut-throat world of fashion, leading eventually to the creation of one of the most famous garments in the world – the Coronation Dress of Her Majesty Queen Elizabeth II.

Yet why did Hartnell publicly make a point of his television non-appearance and stress to the popular William Hickey, columnist of the *Daily Express*, 'I should have been most apprehensive. I am most deeply relieved it never happened.'[4]

All autobiography is partly an exercise in ego-massaging, but *Silver and Gold* is remarkable and charming in its diffidence. Barely three pages cover the first two decades of the young Norman's life. His mother and father are barely mentioned; it is as though he wished us to believe that he had appeared under a gooseberry bush, small but perfectly formed. The very stuff of which glamorous fairy tales are made tinges the pages of his life story, which begins: 'My interest in Fashion began with a box of crayons . . . perhaps because I was in revolt against the emphatic ginger cows varnished on my night-nursery walls . . . soon I was given a box of water-colour paints and with it sketched my first dress design.'[5] His cousin Constance Barnett had it made up by a local dressmaker and she won first prize at a New Year's Eve fancy-dress ball. Like the young Mozart, the young Hartnell was a virtuoso in his chosen medium, progressing from wallpaper designs to workable sketches. Alas, we have no date for this event and no indication of the location of the 'night nursery' with its comfortable suggestion of solid turn-of-the-century prosperity. Today, when background seems to be of no importance to a celebrity, as Norman Hartnell was to become, lineage, education and even attainments often count for nothing. But until the 1950s this was not generally the case in Britain and most certainly not so in Britain before the First World War. The Hartnell family was acutely aspirational and, after the birth of Norman, the family moved several times, always being upwardly mobile in occupation and location.

It seems unlikely that the prophetically named Crown & Sceptre public house located at 2A Streatham Hill, London SW2 should be the birthplace of such an extraordinary designer as Norman Hartnell, but it is so. On 12 June 1901, Henry Bishop Hartnell and his wife Emma Mary Hartnell, late Coulson, formerly née Polley as stated on Norman's birth certificate, became the parents of their last child, to be known to family and friends as Normie and later to devoted employees as 'Bossie'.[6]

The Crown & Sceptre still stands at a considerably enlarged crossroads, the solid early-nineteenth-century building with two angular bays of windows facing Streatham Hill originally a coaching inn on a major London–Brighton route. Small balustrades embellish the bays, and the roof line was embellished with carved detailing suggesting the detailed ends of rafters. In the 1930s the whole aspect of the building was changed with a form of polished ceramic cladding, but Norman's father, known as 'Bish', had long ceased his connections with the business.

In later years, Norman Hartnell press releases stated that he 'came of an old Devonshire family' which is indeed partly the case and seems to have been first publicised by Richard Fletcher, described by Hartnell as 'my old friend'[7]; an intriguing figure of an older generation who was known in the 1920s as a publicist and 'fixer'.[8] The basis for Fletcher's PR background story is based on the origins of Bish, Henry Bishop Hartnell, who was born on 8 February 1872, the son of George Hartnell and Elizabeth Hartnell, formerly Clegg. The birth was registered on 12 February 1872 at Honiton, in the county of Devon. Bish's own father seems to have been more interested in registering his son than Bish was to be with baby Norman. George was a farmer at Roebuck near Honiton, famous for lace production, yet still remote from London in spite of the relatively recent railway connections.

Writing to an adopted 'cousin' in 1977, Norman explained something of his family's background:

> I also enclose a card which results from my discovery of where my father was born. It is a pleasant family house on the main road, near to Honiton. Years ago, it lay right back in its own grounds, but now the new motorway has got its nose in there and it is only a few yards from the little old house. It is quite pretty, still attractive and even something to be proud of. I only saw the wife Mrs Underdown, who did not know much about me . . .[9]

Young Bish was clearly an enterprising young man, for by 1896 the London Directory lists him as a landlord of the Lord High Admiral at 89 Church Street, NW8 as well as The Cock, 12 Stanhope Street, NW8, with an associate known as Dare. The Directory also lists a Henry Hartnell carrying out the business of beer retailer at 871 Old Kent Road in conjunction with a Timothy Lockett. The similarity of the two Hartnells seems unlikely to be coincidental and implies that the 24-year-old Bish already had established family connections in London. The 1894 Directory implies that these were probably extensive for a Dare and Bishop are listed at The Kings Head, Essex Road, N1 and a Henry Bishop at The Mitre, 68 St Martins Lane, WC, as well as at The Tooke Arms, 165 West Ferry Road, E14.[10] One can only assume in the absence of firm documentary proof that the Hartnells and Henry Bishop mentioned were either related by marriage to Bish or possibly godparents. They possibly gave the farmer's son an early entrée to late-nineteenth-century London, the bustling, prosperous imperial capital full of lucrative prospects for the level-headed man Bish was to prove himself to be.

Norman's father's ancestry does extend back over many centuries of West Country history, latterly predominately in Devonshire. The Hartnells were mainly attached to the land in various occupations, not least in keeping inns. The use of the unusual Christian name Bishop clearly had a family significance and is recorded as early as 1733. Remarkably, his son was then christened Bishop Bishop Hartnell (1774–1817), and he was father to seven children including George Bishop Hartnell, who married Elizabeth (1809–63) and then Elizabeth Clegg (1836–63) at Colyton. This George had the Greyhound Inn at Ferry Bridge, Ottery St Mary, Devon. By his first wife he had three children and by his second, much younger wife four more, including Norman's father Henry Bishop Hartnell (1872–1945). Henry was born in Honiton, as George had moved his family from the Greyhound Inn to Roebuck Farm, Honiton. As we shall see, this remarrying and fathering of many children by both wives was not unusual. Divorce was virtually unknown outside the most rarefied and monied circles at that time, death brought the necessity for new spouses, and children were a natural result of this reaffirmation of life and existence.

Norman's father Bish was himself to marry twice, firstly to Lucy Kate who died in 1897 and has no further part in this narrative. His second wife was the widowed Mrs John Coulson, Norman's mother Emma Mary, née Polley. It seems only natural that her grandfather Henry Killick Polley (1804–68) should have been a victualler at The Lord Northbrook in Lee, Essex. His wife, also Emma Mary, the grandmother of Norman, was born in Poplar c1838. This family were also publicans or licensed victuallers involving generations of the family in the business, which began with Miss Harriet Hambrook, hence the middle name of Norman's mother's first husband. By 1867, the date of Norman's mother's birth in Bromley, Kent, the Polleys had proved, in common with the Hartnells, the Victorian ethos of upward social mobility.

Norman's descent from the Polleys was of no obvious interest to him. Norman's mother and her family were clearly intimately connected with the publicans' trade, and into the 1960s, at the time of the ill-fated *This is Your Life* episode, Norman was still in contact with many relatives on both sides of his family, though he was usually unwilling to be too involved with them, as correspondence reveals:

> Mrs E. Payne to N.H. 'It is imperative that I see you to discuss your Uncle Edward Polley.' 20.2.62.

> 'Regarding to [sic] the matter of your Uncle's welfare of which I have written to you on several occasions. The position is such that I must now seek further advice, regarding to his case.' 16.03.62.

Even though the letters were sent by registered post they remained unanswered.

At least one member of his former employees stated that Hartnell's grandmother had a public house near Seven Dials, which indicates a member of her first husband's family. Miss Emma Mary Polley (1867–1921) was born in Bromley and married John Harmston Coulson. His family were originally Lincolnshire farmers but like her own had been drawn into the vibrant expanding world capital of London, finding their livelihood by running public houses. It was to stand both sides of Norman's family in good stead and they eventually benefitted from their fortune and London's expanding railway network to move away from their public houses and live in more peaceful or leafy locations.

Emma Mary, Hartnell's mother, was left a widow in 1894. Bish must have known the Coulsons, perhaps through George Coulson of The Talbot, later co-owned by Towers and Coulson, at 64 Tottenham Court Road and 2 Goodge Street, W1T, though it could also have been via the Crown & Anchor at 24 Neal Street, Long Acre, WC2H, next to Covent Garden, which was owned by Hartnell's mother's first husband John Harmston Coulson (1847–94) from 1873 to 1882 and then by Samuel John Coulson from 1899 to 1921. Coulson was not a widespread name, so he was almost certainly related. The widowed Mrs Coulson would have met and become impressed by the enterprising young Bish with his slim build, dark hair and full moustache.

In 1893 the pub had been in the possession of Miss Betsy Coulson, so the life of a publican was familiar to Norman's mother, who at the time of John Coulson's death had three daughters and a son to bring up, and so a bargain was clearly made with Bish for she apparently brought a reasonable amount of money to the marriage, as well as her professional experience. Even in the happier days of plentiful domestic servants, the landlord's wife was an important figure in creating the character of a popular public house, especially when she served behind the bar and had a striking personality and looks. There is no doubt that Emma Mary's own family felt that she had married beneath her in some way, for Norman's great-niece remembered that 'no one could understand what she saw in Bish'; he was considered 'jumped-up' and 'vulgar'. His stepchildren considered that he was 'spending their mother's money' and he was usually known as 'Old Man Hartnell'.[11]

In 1898 Mrs Coulson is recorded as the licensee of the Crown & Sceptre, 2A Streatham Hill, which had belonged to Truman, Hanbury, Buxton & Co. Ltd since June 1894. The next year finds Mrs E. M. Hartnell the licensee following her marriage to Bish, who then took over the licence. Bish also took leases on 32, 32a and 34a Streatham Place in May 1901 and June 1908, assigning these all to Emma Mary on 25 August 1908. These were later left to her two children by Bish: Norman and Phyllis. As Emma's own four children were born in the 1880s, they were all in their teens when their mother remarried and rather resented this event and subsequent developments.[13,14] Some of Bish's character was often spotted in the older Norman, for although Norman presented an amiable face to the world, his teenaged second cousin Angela Goldsbrough, who worked for a short time at Norman Hartnell in the 1960s, remembered him as an intimidating, even frightening man when annoyed, with off-putting mannerisms even when amiable.[13] Those alive in the 1990s from pre-war days remember Bish as a natty, check-suited, energetic figure with a rather coarse, florid face, fond of racing and possessing a forceful manner.[14] It seems that he fitted the mould of the ageing Edwardian Masher at a time when Victorian and Edwardian men naturally still abounded. All of the pub buildings and the later hotel associated with the Polleys and Hartnells still survive, although the Crown & Anchor was rebuilt in 1894 and the Lord High Admiral in the 1960s following war damage.

Emma Mary, Norman's mother, had a brother named Alfred Polley. He emigrated to South Africa in a move at first sight as firmly entrepreneurial as Bish's, but it was actually to seek a cure for tuberculosis – or TB as it was generally called. His marriage produced two cousins for Emma's children: Harry and Jim. When cured, Alfred became a hotelier in Pretoria. Their youngest sister was the mother of Angela Goldsbrough (subsequently Angela Loudon), but a family rift occurred when Harry and Jim tried to break a trust set up by Alfred for their young sister, Margot.

With this complicated family background, the young Norman found himself in an interesting circle of a stepbrother and stepsisters when growing up in Streatham. Perhaps this was not too unusual at the time, and in any case children are very accepting of their home surroundings and circumstances, especially as young Norman was the baby of the family and apparently cosseted by everyone. In the 1960s, the viewing public embraced the fairly ordinary origins of public figures, and after the Second World War running a country inn or pub was often a peaceful career change for many ex-officers.

William Hickey's then famously chatty newspaper column attempted to recreate all that Norman feared from the cancelled episode of *This is Your Life*. It painted an interesting picture of 'Mr Henry Bishop Hartnell, the popular licensed victualler, pulling pints in the saloon bar, while your [Norman's] mother . . . busied [sic] herself in the kitchen. A far cry from the elegant salons, the Royal Warrant, the fame and the fortune . . .'[15] In fact, one contributor had been at hand to reminisce about Norman's mother cutting sandwiches behind the bar and about Norman's childhood.

Phyllis Maude was the first of the two children Emma had with Bish, and they were to be the parents of Norman in 1901, adding to Emma's existing son and three daughters by Coulson, so there were six children to bring up in a fairly rough area around the Lord High Admiral in Church Street.

The street had a peculiar mixture of small shops and businesses with dwellings above interspersed with the large furniture shop of Marsh and Eland on the corner with Edgware Road.[16] The present public house of the same name dates from wholesale redevelopment in the 1960s and replaced the bomb-damaged original. It is difficult to imagine the glare of the gas and new electric lighting, the bustle of crowds and rumble of carts and carriages on the Edgware Road as traffic flowed from Marble Arch past Church Street into Maida Vale and Kilburn on a major route north out of London. In 1890, the railway terminating in Marylebone Station had been cut through from Swiss Cottage, obliterating the once elegant Blandford Square, though nearby Dorset Square remained as a partial reminder of the 'genteel' nature of Lisson Grove.

On Edgware Road, the elegant, disused wrought-iron gates of Peter Keevil

& Sons provision merchants are still visible just around the corner from Church Street and would have been passed often by Bish. The dairy, along with its cowshed, was, in turn, around the corner from his pub and this area, Malthouse Mews, also contained lecture rooms, stables, and van and wheel works with a smithy also close at hand. The area was full of horses; the smell and dirt must have been considerable.[17] The Salvation Army was particularly needed in the area around Lisson Grove, and the poverty map collated by Charles Booth (not related to the General of the Salvation Army) shows that mews just off Church Street also held what he termed 'semi-criminals' or 'a small and declining percentage' or 'a horde of barbarians'. Nearby, in 1885, W.T. Stead 'bought a child of thirteen from her parents for £5 for immoral purposes'.[18] As editor of the *Pall Mall Gazette* he was attempting to prove how easy such an action was and how degrading the lives of many poor people were.[19] As J. Whitehead points out, George Bernard Shaw must have known of the case when writing the part of Eliza in *Pygmalion*, for the child Eliza Armstrong of the case is transformed into Eliza Doolittle of Lisson Grove. Emma and Bish Hartnell would eventually move their family from this dubious area to the leafy, suburban Streatham Hill.

Although Streatham is today an unremarkable and poorly rebuilt suburb of South London following massive Second World War bomb damage, this was clearly not so around 1900. It was a flourishing, even partially elegant area connected to London by regular trains. A tram terminus existed outside the then town hall down the hill from the Crown & Sceptre; a bus service became motorised and central London was easily reached by those for whom the flourishing plenitude of smaller shops or the grand department store, Pratts, were not enough.

There were many people who had money: Sir Henry Tate, benefactor of the Tate Gallery and main subscriber to the building of the unpretentious lending library, which surely the young Norman must have known as it is close to the house his parents later owned, was one such figure. Mr and Mrs Derry of Derry & Toms department store in Kensington also had a large house in Streatham, for although a distinct suburb the place had begun as a village and was already semi-fashionable in the seventeenth century: there were 'negro servants' of the affluent, even 'one named Pick, a negro man at Mr Chaplin's was buried in 1694' in the churchyard, according to the Parish Records.[20] Steen Eiler Rasmussen, the great pre-war delineator of London's architectural history, illustrated the beautiful Regency houses, villas set in their own fine gardens and redolent of the spa which flourished in Streatham into Edwardian days and just beyond, for the Curtis Brothers Dairy also advertised mineral water into the First World War.[21]

If the department store Pratts lingered on as part of the John Lewis group into the 1990s, very little else has. The large houses and gardens were already disappearing before the arrival of the Hartnell family. Streatham Hill, formerly a beautiful, curving tree-lined road bounded by gardens and houses, was just disappearing under red-brick buildings housing shops to become traffic-bound and part of a long major London–Brighton route. After the war, further development by the local council and an ethnically mixed population have completely changed the area, but the Hartnell house Elsmore, 12 Days-brook Road, SW2, can still be gauged by the fine quality of the remaining houses in the street. (It was demolished by 'Bomb 33' at midnight on 22 July 1944). Occupying a sunny corner site, the detached house had a long garden along Wavertree Road.

Bish is last recorded at Church Street in 1897.[22] In 1905 he was still at the Crown & Sceptre, but by 1908 this was in the possession of Mrs J. Austin.[23] Clearly the industrious Bish had taken the seven-year-old Norman and his older sister Phyllis to Elsmore and was reinvesting his money. He even added to his financial investments from 1910 to 1915 by taking on the London pub The Pindar of Wakefield at 328 Grays Inn Road, WC1. He was indeed the true son of his father and, indeed, father of his son when it came to resource-fulness and imaginative planning. His wife was undoubtedly keen for her husband to prosper, but her early death indicates her more fragile health, something Norman inherited and did not mind stating publicly. 'I was a sickly child,' he later stressed in his autobiography.[24] By this time, Emma Mary's children by Coulson were all of marrying age, and had a family connection with Hassocks, then a house at Clayton in Sussex was taken where they lived in a roomy villa called 'Royston'. This connection lasted with Norman beyond death, for he is buried next to his mother and sister in Clayton churchyard.

The Hartnells' neighbours at Elsmore, itself a whimsical name, inhabited the unpretentious recently completed terracotta and brick-faced villas with small front gardens, vaguely Arts and Crafts glass in the front-door and larger gardens at the rear. The young Hartnell at no. 12 would have been aware of the Reverend Professor Archibald McCaig B.A., LL.D. at no. 8 and Professor of Music Sydney Usherwood at no. 14. For Bish and Emma there could scarcely have been a greater contrast between these new neighbours and those of the Lord High Admiral some ten years earlier.

One of the attractions of Streatham must have lain in the great number of scholastic establishments and colleges in the area for the 'sons of gentlefolk'. Phyllis was sent across the road to Streatham Hill High School and young Norman was also educated locally at the same school from 1908–11, which was in new buildings (1897) at the Wavertree Road junction with Daysbrook Road, opposite their house. At the age of eleven he went to Belmont School, Streatham from 1912 to 1914. Belmont was also the name of the prep school for Mill Hill to which he was sent in the autumn of 1914, entering School House.[25] Hartnell usually dissociated himself from Streatham contacts in the days of his fame, although he was remembered by churchgoers as a former Sunday school member. In 1960 the *Streatham News* recorded that Norman had attended Sunday School at Christ Church, notable for the beautiful Walter Crane-designed windows, the best Arts and Crafts work for many miles around: 'Last year the people of the church, some of whom had known him as a child, wrote asking him to open their bazaar. He refused.' (19 February 1960).[26]

Sunday School was almost certainly the first place that Norman heard serious music. Music was a lifelong passion of his, and it is inconceivable that he never heard singing in his parents' pub, as it was a usual accompaniment to an evening in a public bar. He would also have heard the popular music of the day when taken to theatres or even from street barrel organs. For the rest of his life Norman was typical of his generation in also listening to the dance music of the period in all manner of locations, and as fashions in clothes changed, so were they in symbiosis with the evolving dance and popular music.

As Hartnell never publicly reminisced about his pre-Mill Hill Streatham days, we are left with the memories of his sister's friends. If he had any of his own, they were abandoned on entering Mill Hill, which evokes the first vivid memories in *Silver and Gold*.

At this point we should consider the young Norman in the context of his home life. Photographs show a sombre little boy with appealing eyes and fluffy curls. His early life in the Crown & Sceptre was undoubtedly marked by the sights and leathery smells of the horses delivering beer and supplies to the better-off customers in their horse-drawn carriages, as one of his later friends wrote: London 'smelt of malt as the train passed a brewery in slowing down and then there were the frightening horses clattering in herds, it seemed, over the cobbles, and the smoky air and the giant policemen.'[27]

Streatham Hill formed part of the well documented and illustrated *Brighton Road*,[28] a bustling route that undoubtedly fascinated Norman. In 1960, the landlord of the Crown & Sceptre showed the *Streatham News* the room in which Hartnell was said to have been born: 'In those days the family lived in what is now the saloon bar . . . Great changes have taken place since then. What is now the off-sales were stables.' A further glimpse of the infant Norman is given: 'As a child, Norman played on the grass outside the pub and watched the horse buggies and trams passing and made infrequent visits to Streatham Village [sic].' [289]

The bicycling boom of the 1880s was marked by the invention and introduction of both the 'safety' bicycle and pneumatic tyre, for which Dunlop took out a patent in 1888, and 'its influence on fashions, manners and morals had been disconcerting to upholders of The Little Woman Tradition.'[29] Hordes of cyclists took to the Brighton Road and would have been a familiar sight swooping down through Streatham and even in the Crown & Sceptre.[30]

'Bloomers in the Bar-Parlour' (the *Streatham News* was stressing the female cyclists' independent spirit) 'you may well envy those who enjoyed the unrepeatable charm of cycling on roads frequented only by an occasional farmer's gig, a fine lady on horseback of a wagonette-load of excursionists drawn by a couple of spanking mares.'[31]

Bish was a farmer's boy and would have known all about the tending of the horses calling at his premises, and the gilt lettering of Hartnell's Crown & Sceptre became a familiar landmark. A visit to London was an adventure indeed, where a ride in a hansom through the gas-lit streets could be so touched with high romance. There was something elegant about these unhurrying vehicles with their slender wheels and gentle curves, their leathery smell and jingling harness, the driver perched loftily behind – some quality of breeding which the motorcar failed to inherit. [32]

Motor cars were just making their appearance as Norman toddled around his parents' home, as were more Tube lines and motorbuses. It was an exciting time to be alive in Britain between the Boer and First World War. The short Edwardian period ended with the death of King Edward VII on 6 May 1910 and the accession of King George V, aged forty-five with his consort, Queen Mary. Hartnell was barely nine years old, a sensitive child who, like his contemporary Cecil Beaton, was an avid reader of the Society and Theatre pages of newspapers and illustrated journals, which his mother and four sisters also read.

As the baby in what was then termed a respectable middle-class home, he would have observed the female dress, as remembered by Mrs Florence Ingillson: 'when I was dressed in my finery for a dance or the theatre I wore three petticoats, the under one of white flannel beautifully embroidered, then a moiré one, and the third of silk with five or six rows of frills – and didn't they take some ironing. The frills had to be goffered with a special iron like a pair of curling tongs, but when you walked they sounded lovely, they went *fru fru*. Underclothes were of silk or wool or cotton, for of course there was no artificial silk or nylon. Most girls wore black cotton stockings at sixpence or a shilling a pair; real silk were anything from 10s.6d. (55p) or £5 a pair . . .'[33]

At this time a maid cost 2s. 6d. to 3s. a week, whilst a cook generally cost £15 a year – and to set this in context, butter was a shilling a pint and milk ¾d. Grapefruit were unknown, Messrs Fyffes only imported bananas on a large scale after 1901 and 'tomatoes were rare and reported to be bad for you.'[34]

Public houses were great centres of self-made entertainment with songs sung around the piano, mainly songs made popular in the music halls and often taken from operettas. Norman would have heard these, although his growing taste for the exotic Gaby Deslys points to an over-sophisticated taste at an early age,[35] a taste he again shared with the young Cecil Beaton up in Hampstead.[36]

Partly due to the bicycling craze, the bustle of the late Victorian era had ceased to be fashionable. Women playing tennis, women cycling and women riding all caused a redesigning of women's day-to-day clothing. Exoticism came via Paris and the stage in equal measure; this might be evinced by the Gibson Girl, a curvaceously laced stage phenomenon popularising a silhouette with a wasp waist. This too waned as designers were influenced by dress reformers and Russian ballet – as Paul Poiret was, liberating women's forms from tight lacing – although the hobble skirt formed from a tightly fitting tube of fabric was also popular. Norman absorbed all these details.

Bish and Emma Mary decided to send Norman to the famous non-conformists' school Mill Hill in 1913, and Norman was thirteen when he entered the junior school Belmont in 1914. After two terms, he entered the main school as a member of School House.[37] He has little to write about this in *Silver and Gold*, but it proved to be the most formative period of his life, on which he built his subsequent success at Cambridge and then in London.

One incident not included in the final text of *Silver and Gold* is indicative of Norman's personality at the time and his subsequent creation of a stolid designer and businessman: 'I did possess a rather singular singing voice.

Instead of having the usual chalky quality of a boyish treble, my voice would trill throatily.' New boys were stood on the table and told to sing. Most boys sang 'Rule Britannia' or 'God Save the King'. Not Norman:

> I foolishly thought it would please the bigger boys and probably save me from further humiliation if I sang the theme song from *The Chocolate Soldier*. As I reached the last stanza, I opened wide my larynx and fairly let go on the top C . . . shouts, shrieks, laughter and even ruder noises greeted me, while lumps of rubber, pencils, rulers and old slippers were flung at me.[38]

His sister Phyllis enjoyed a wide circle of friends and was as popular in Streatham Hill High School as his parents were in Streatham. Decades later, an unidentified school friend wrote:

> I lived almost next door to you at Streatham Hill (alas many years ago). My father's business was at 306 Brixton Hill (two doors from the Crown & Sceptre) – Sidney Williams by name, a shoe shop. I knew your mother very well, also one of your sisters when you lived in Daysbrook Road. We then lived in Wyatt Park Road. It seems a terrific time ago. [39]

It is in the few surviving letters referring to this time that we see how Norman's mother was clearly popular with young people outside the family:

> I have just finished reading your book *Silver and Gold* . . . Your references here and there to Phyllis brought back memories of our school days together at S.H.H.S. when my name was Helen Passavant and she and I were in the same class – I spent many happy times at your house. Your mother was always most kind to me and I was very fond of her. The last time we met was a year or so before I married and left England for Canada. Mrs Hartnell was trousseau shopping with Betty in Bourne & Hollingsworth and we visited for quite a little while.' [40]

The Mill Hill Register recorded Bish's address at Elsmore and Heathfield, Hassocks, Sussex. The burial place of Emma Mary at Clayton (and later

Norman too) has a Bishop connection, for the publican of the Cricketers Arms in the last quarter of the nineteenth century was a John Gilbert Bishop. Norman's stepsisters were still renting houses in Hassocks into the 1940s, and he often referred to his happy holidays there, from Mill Hill during the increasingly depressing days of the First World War and later into the 1920s.

Some forty years later his former friend Marjorie Allen (née Albery) was to write:

> For twenty years, I have meant to write this letter to you . . . It is really only to tell you what pleasure, and almost pride, my family, friends and I have taken in your quite brilliant career because we were 'in' at the very beginning of it! Do you remember life in Hassocks when we were all teenagers? Tennis in the garden, piano playing in the evening and a most extraordinary concert we gave in the village for which you designed some very magnificent butter muslin costumes? You sang the number 'I beg your condescension, your most august attention, to what I now relate . . .' while Phyllis played? . . . I am still friends with Molly Rutter and Kathleen Evans and so, with my sisters, we often talk about you and your family . . .[40]

These early forays into design – and that mentioned earlier for his cousin Constance Barnett – form the earliest recorded executed work of the future world-famous designer. They also reveal a more extroverted Norman than he would have us believe at this time. His artistic efforts were not confined to the holidays from his school, then presided over by the great headmaster Sir John David McClure LL.D.; a former fellow pupil of Hartnell commented on 'the memory of another Mrs D. who encouraged me to concentrate on my sketching. . .[41] (something he had begun during his infancy) On the other hand, H. S. Sly in a letter to the school magazine later demonstrated how deceptive memories of schooldays may be in response to an earlier letter mentioning an H. C. Dudman, '(he) is certainly wrong when he says that Hartnell was with him at Mill Hill from 1919 to 1923. I was there from 1913 to 1917 and Norman Bishop Hartnell was certainly there then. I don't think he even played rugby well enough to get into the Third XV. He was not interested in sport, unless you call it sport to doodle on blotting paper all through the lesson and produce lovely ladies in lovely frocks. Also the story about Hartnell setting fire to another study's bin is a bit far-fetched. It was not *Norman Bishop* anyway – perhaps some relation.[42]

It was not. Norman himself writes of his 'doodlings' but selectively omits any mention of his sharing a study with H. Curtis Dudman, who later distinguished himself during the siege of Tobruk when he organised the oil installations. He and Norman must have had amusing times as they both took part in O.T.C. and play readings together. Dudman seems to have been more interested in organisation than Hartnell, who was a prefect by 1919. Dudman was a more superior monitor and also editor of the school journal, *Mill Hill Magazine*, whilst also being on the Musical Society Committee.

Although most memories of Norman Hartnell at this time recall his artistic efforts, none recall his membership of the Third XV in 1919. Only a faded photograph shows this to have been true and that the chameleon-like Norman looked every inch the part. He was also a lance corporal in the O.T.C., something he might have relished as his interest in military uniforms began at an early age and was to become increasingly marked in later years, assisting with his designs for Royal Family members' clothes, so correct for each specific occasion. But at this time, he also had the normal appetites of a normal boy – less so with advancing years, but certainly not the appetite of an effete young man. Hartnell was ever the robust trencherman delighting in British fare:

> I remember as a boy – young man – I used to go up north in various houses in Cumberland and Yorkshire and everything, and the meal I enjoyed the most then was known as high tea because in that high tea you got everything that a boy could think was lovely. Started off with tripe, mixed grill, potted shrimps, smoked salmon, hot toasted scones, jam and honey, everything you could think of, and I thought that was an ideal meal.[43]

In later years many of his contemporaries wrote to him with their memories of Mill Hill: '. . . I refrain from using our nicknames. I came across these snaps when throwing things away and thought you might be interested in one of your earlier efforts of dress designing. Yours May Plummer.'[44]

Norman replied:

I am refraining from using our nicknames. I must keep those snaps . . . I well remember the occasion. It was performing *Twelfth Night* in the gardens of the Master's house opposite the main school building. At this stage I certainly did not know what was ahead of me.[45]

In fact his father Bish had been so alarmed by his son's artistic and thespian learnings that he presented him with a pair of boxing gloves in a remarkably misguided attempt to change his ideas. Another school friend, later recalling a shared passion for the many musical stars and productions of their youth, wrote to him some thirty years later and Norman responded:

When I heard you broadcast, last night, my mind went back long ago to the days of Doris Keane and *Romance*, remember?[46] Did you approve of the wedding dress (for H.R.H. Princess Elizabeth) and the bridesmaids? I saw them in the Abbey and was very pleased that I had started doing my dress designing years ago at Mill Hill School.[47]

Hartnell certainly remembered *Romance* and mentioned the effect Doris Keane had on him together with Miss José Collins and Gaby Deslys. The first page of *Silver and Gold* mentions his mathematics, geometry and algebra books covered with their likenesses, studied from the picture postcards then on sale. Doris Keane's dresses were by Jeanne Lanvin, 'a name unknown to me then, but later to mean magic'[48] and 'the majority of my sketches depicted her in a dress of swaying black velvet, white ermine jacket and cascades of limpid pearls weighted by a diamond cross.'[49] The familiar Hartnell style was already evolving, although the early drawings and sketches are a remarkable pastiche of the highly influential designers Bakst and Erté with something of the sinister flavour of the illustrations by Alistair. [50] Hartnell was fascinated by the posters influenced by Bakst and 'the rest of the Diaghilev School' seen in the underground stations.[51]

The early schoolboy admiration and understanding of the influential artists and designers of his childhood is made very clear by another letter to a friend, H.J.C. Whitmee:

Of course I remember you – actually quite clearly. You were the funny little thing with gold curly hair, pimples and a squint! So, I was really quite pleased to hear from you after all these years. However, to be serious I must firstly say how deeply sorry I am to hear about the death of Mrs Whitmee. I remember her so clearly at Mill Hill when she used to come down to the school in lovely dresses and rivalling my own sisters, Nimbo and Betty. I have always had a special regard for her, added to the fact that she was one of my original customers when I first started here.[52]

Whitmee was a Mill Hill contemporary of Norman's and was with him whilst studying for the school play reading of John Galsworthy's *Strife* in autumn 1919. He read David Roberts, Norman acted Enid Underwood, one of his first female roles, whilst H. Curtis Dudman was Oliver Wanklin, although seven weeks of term passed and none of the plays rehearsed by the 'chosen few' were read in public. The group also rehearsed Bernard Shaw's *You Never Can Tell* with Norman as Dolly Clandon, and Whitmee and Dudman in other male roles.[53]

All these theatrical roles were a clear indication of Hartnell's increasing fascination for both dress and the stage, which he explains at length in *Silver and Gold*, with emphasis on a sighting of Gaby Deslys at Maidenhead during his last school holidays before going up to Cambridge in 1920. But before this, Norman could enjoy the O.T.C. Field Day of 27 November 1919, arranged by the staff of the Eastern Command at Ampthill.

In one of Norman's most sweeping phases of amnesia he was to write:

> I was still too young to appreciate the grimness of the years between 1914 and 1918, and those years linger in my mind today as great theatre-going times, much as they must have done in the minds of countless thousands on leave from the Flanders mud. There always seemed to be dozens of delightful musical comedies . . .[54]

It is difficult to reconcile this 'memory' of those horrific years with their many hardships and wholesale bereavements, also recorded in the school magazine. Norman chooses to remember one small meeting and a trivial incident from those days when he and his school friend Edward Higham met Kate Day, later a royal milliner, for an illicit tea at The Green Man. Kate, 'short, smart, plump, white and dimpled', led him to show off by carrying a cane to which only prefects were entitled. He was spotted by his housemaster:

> on the cinder path that leads up by the playing fields . . . the curly end stuck out between the back buttons at the top of my trouser. The master removed the cane and administered punishment on the spot. Miss Day has not led me into any similar misbehaviour since![55]

In fact, they worked together professionally on and off from the date of Hartnell's first opening in 1923 and even before. When she was at Wentworth Hall, the boarding school next door, her first contract was signed: they produced 'intermediate' theatrical evenings with 'gowns by Norman, hats and dancing by Kate'. Kate states: 'My hats were extraordinary, my dancing had gusto . . . and I was completely overshadowed by Norman.'[56,57,58]

It is clear that Mill Hill was quite advanced, even enlightened, for its day and that Norman had a huge personality, which, like his father's, was put to use whenever required.

Another Mill Hill friend, Ginette Spanier, later became right-hand woman to Pierre Balmain a friend and Parisian couture rival of Norman in later years,[59] whilst Teddy Higham, perhaps his best friend at Mill Hill, was still in touch with Norman in the 1960s:

> To me you're still 'Bish' Hartnell, the best friend I've ever had. You were always elegantly dressed. You never became a prefect, you weren't very brilliant at sport (though you once won the three-mile cross-country) but you were popular for all that. I once tried to crib your Latin and found you were drawing pictures of pretty actresses.'

But none of this essentially frivolous activity explains why Hartnell fails to mention the dramatic announcement of the Armistice by the head master Sir John McClure received in silence, after which the pandemonium was then let loose.

But even David Williamson (a pupil from 1918 to 1922), realised that for McClure and the senior masters the moment was too poignant for prolonged noise: 'Boys were left to their own – very mixed – reactions. For some, there was unbounded excitement and hilarity. Others wept quietly.' [60,61]

Norman noted in *Silver and Gold* that 'A few went off . . to be alone with their thoughts.'

We shall never know how Norman reacted, but everyone must have felt the moment.

A year later, as Norman entered his final term at school, P.C. Hubbard, a member of the Musical Society Committee and 'stage manager and costumier', wrote the following poem dedicated to Norman:

De Profundis to N.B.H.

O BARD, whose hand of late did touch
Thy lyre to tones of sweetest joy,
Fair Spirit, speak, – Hast lived? Hast known
The Evil that our lives doth cloy?
Methinks that in thy parting words
Some sign of grief I did discern,
But 'twas a grief thou namedst sweet,
A grief that only love can earn.
A more propitious, kindlier star
Upon thy joyful birth did shine
Thou that which, for the common herd,
But shows th' indifference divine.
Kind providence thy steps hath kept
Upon a path o'erstrewn with flowers,
Thou never hatedst thine own life,
Nor cursed the never-ending hours.
Thou hast not deemed that life is void,
That heaven is empty, God a lie,
Nor knowing this hast rent thy soul
With one long piercing hideous cry:
Life? What is life but dust –
Dregs of Olympian Wine?
Love? What is love but a dream –
One kiss, and a long repine?
God? What is God but a fable
Told by the Priests of ill?
Hell? but a craven fear,

A curb for man's lawless will.
So let us live in silence,
Sullenly cursing the light,
Then with a cry of anguish
Spring into endless night.

P.C.H.[62]

Mill Hill was clearly an extraordinary school and Norman no ordinary pupil.

CHAPTER TWO

Academical

C ambridge in the early 1920s remained in mourning for the lost generation epitomised by its most famous poet son Rupert Brooke. Whilst
the academic establishment was emotionally scarred by the war,
the physical appearance of the university was marred by late Victorian and
Edwardian expansion and rebuilding. King's Parade, the Senate House and
King's Chapel were overshadowed by the impertinence of the Caius Water-
house-designed tower, a permanent reminder of the remarkable academic
achievements of the pre-1914 generations. The 'fearless, uninfluential Cambridge that sought for reality and cared for truth', as E. M. Forster succinctly
put it,[1] was what awaited Hartnell. The Cambridge evoked by a member of
the Cambridge Darwin clan, Gwen Raverat in *Period Piece* was essentially just
that: a community devoted to thought, research and study with 'hearty' activities on the playing fields and river as physical recreation. For Forster, who went
up to King's in 1897, had a Cambridge life that mirrored that of successive
generations, including Hartnell's throughout the subsequent century:

> As Cambridge filled up with friends it acquired a magical quality.
> Body and spirit, reason and emotion, work and play, architecture
> and scenery, laughter and seriousness, life and art – these pairs
> which are elsewhere contrasted were there fused into one. People
> and books reinforced one another, intelligence joined hands with
> affection, speculation became a passion and discussion was made
> profound by love.[2]

But the academic world embraced by Forster, which encompassed the
London Bloomsbury Set, touching, for example, the social circle around
Sir Edward Marsh, was one forever outside the orbit of Hartnell's star. His

reading remained limited to romantic novels, whilst his taste in music was for operettas, revues and musicals and some opera, such as Wagner, or ballet when taken by friends. The theatre in all its manifestations gripped him with its design possibilities:

> As far back as I can remember, I have been designing. I started with wallpapers, in revolt against the hideous brown cows on my nursery walls. I crayoned feathers and ferns, hearts and shells, pigeons and pearls. These continued to entwine my school books, which were later embellished with theatrical costumes, depicted in drawings of the leading ladies of the day.[3]

As might be expected of someone who was later a friend of Beverley Nichols and Godfrey Winn, the solid academic life of Cambridge had very little positive effect on Norman, who was to be interested in living people and design for the rest of his life, with little time for books or thoughts of an abstract nature. Norman's own memories of his Cambridge days barely cover one and a half pages of his autobiography and are mainly centred on his designing triumphs for the Footlights, the university's amateur theatrical club. Thirty-two years after leaving the university without a degree he returned at the invitation of the then Master Sir Henry Urmston Willink and wrote a characteristic letter of thanks:

> Dear Master (This appellation sounds like addressing Noël Coward) –
>
> Anyhow, dear Master, I am writing to thank you for the most enjoyable evening last week.
>
> I was most honoured to sit next to you in Hall, and most charmed to be taken to your private house afterwards to meet Mrs Willinck and your nice daughter.
>
> Cambridge revisited brings on a violent attack of nostalgia, with all its dreamy beauty and the mellow warmth of Magdalene itself.
>
> Of course, Master, if I had known you would all be moving about in beautiful silk gowns, I could also have brought a gown of my own!
>
> But there, two years at the University, could in no way entitle me to a degree, and I would like to explain again that, back in

1922, I removed myself voluntarily from the College. The force of circumstances at that time being that my mother had died, my father had hastily remarried and cut off my allowance.

With alacrity, thereupon I seized a job at three pounds per week as a dress designer and have always wondered since if the authorities of Magdalene College are proud or ashamed of me.

Again, I must thank you for an enchanting evening, and assure you that I am your grateful undergraduate.[4]

The reply, if any, from Willinck is missing, but if this was a subtle hint that a degree of some kind might now be forthcoming it fell on stony ground. For all of Norman's later success it must have always annoyed him that his near rivals in stage-costume design Cecil Beaton (St Johns 1922–25) and stage-costume and dress design Victor Stiebel (Jesus 1926–29) had travelled the same route he had initially opened when up at Cambridge and still had the aptitude and means to at least finish their three-year degree courses. In later years, Hartnell attended both Magdalene and Footlights dinners, whereas he seldom bothered with Mill Hill. He invariably returned with his lifelong Magdalene friend Richard Blake Brown, the only close friend he retained from his youth, both seeing and corresponding with him on a regular basis until Blake died. Blake and Bish, as they called one another, returned together for the 1954 visit detailed above. Hartnell originally only went up in 1920 after a struggle.

***

In his Application for Admission Norman filled in the place and date of his birth: 2 Streatham Hill, SW obfuscating the suburban location by omitting the exact London area number of the period; his father's details are given as 'Henry B. Hartnell (Shipper) Royston, Hassocks'. The given profession of Henry, the older Bish, is also intriguing, as he could only ever have been a 'shipper' of wine, spirits and beer.

From 1917 until 1920 Hartnell's Warrington Hotel at 93 Warrington Crescent, Maida Vale, was the focus of his entrepreneurial gifts. At 91 Warrington Crescent, from which Norman was writing in 1922, William *Bishop* Page was listed as the owner, another link to the Hartnell clan. The Warrington Hotel still famously stands with a remarkably intact Victorian bar in the best Gin Palace style, and the during the First World War must have provided a good living for the Hartnell family. Interestingly, the hotel is a mere ten minutes' walk from the Lord High Admiral, father Bish's former pub in Church Street, and at no. 103 in this street a cheesemonger named Henry John Hartnell was trading whilst Bish was at the Warrington, another link to the Hartnell family.

Due to its location, Maida Vale had attracted many West Country migrants arriving by train at Paddington Station: in the nurses' institution at 37 Warwick Avenue, a Miss Maud Hartnell was listed in the Post Office Directory.[5] Phyllis Maud Hartnell was the name of Norman's sister and so one may assume that the area contained several relatives and friends. All this was ignored by Norman as he prepared to enter Magdalene to read Modern Languages (or Architecture) in October 1920.[6]

To the Tutor   Feb 1920

Dear Sir,

I beg herewith to submit an application to your college for October next. I am quite aware of the present abnormal rush for the 'varsities and also that colleges are no longer a matter of choice, nevertheless I apply to Magdalene first, for it is my particular wish to enter it, and I should be deeply grateful if you could find room for me.

I left Mill Hill School last term, and having decided that I should go to Cambridge, my headmaster Sir John McClure entertained some thought of taking me back; in any case I have arranged for private tutorage preparatory to my taking the 'Little Go'.

If I am fortunate enough to be able to come up in October it is my intention to read Modern Languages with the ultimate aim of becoming an architect.

Sir John desires me to refer you to him for further particulars of myself, which I sincerely hope you will find satisfactory.

Yrs very faithfully,
Norman B. Hartnell

This well-poised formal letter from the eighteen-year-old Norman met with a positive response for his application and on 13 February he wrote to A. S. Ramsey Esq.:

Dear Sir,

I enclose the character certificate from my Headmaster which I hope you will find adequate.

If it is not now too late, I would like to enter for Part I of the Previous Examination in March, and would be very grateful for further information as to the date of and particulars of the fees.

Yrs very faithfully.
N.B. Hartnell.

In spite of Norman's warm words for McClure, his former headmaster, in *Silver and Gold* the latter's note of 10 February 1920 is terse: 'I have pleasure in certifying that Norman Bishop Hartnell was a pupil at this school from May 1914 until December 1919: that his conduct and industry were satisfactory and that I believe him to be a youth of sound moral character.'

Exactly why the eighteen-year-old Norman should have completed only one term of his final school year remains unclear.[6]

***

In March 1920, Norman sat Part I of the Previous Examination: Latin (*Plantas* & unprepared) and French (composition and translation), and had rooms in the College for the event; his first taste of Cambridge life.[7] On 22 May he wrote to A.S. Ramsey Esq. again asking to be entered for Part II of the Previous Examination: '. . . if you would let me know particulars of the College Entrance Examination, as to what subjects it comprises, and when I am required to arrive in Cambridge I should be very grateful.'

Having paid his fee by cheque and stating that 'I wish to take Paley's Evidences' he then sat the exams in June. The letters not only reveal the formality of the period but already have a distinctly 'Hartnell' look in the elegant handwriting, with one word frequently joined to another by a flourish of the pen. The spacing and layout of the sentences shows an element of design and the handwritten address of his letter dated 22 July 1920 is beautiful: Villa L'Eté, rue de Paris, Le Touquet-Paris-Plage, France.

Norman Hartnell had a love of France and French holidays throughout his life but was undoubtedly supposed to be learning French on this holiday. To A.S. Ramsey Esq. he now wrote:

Dear Sir,

    Thank you very much for your letter which I received some days ago. This was the first intimation of my success in the Previous Examination, and my people are very pleased.

    I shall return to England soon, and shall await the particulars of the lodgings which you purpose to send me.

    I am looking forward with great pleasure to my University career and hope to gain great benefit thereby.

Yrs sincerely
    Norman B. Hartnell

The style of this letter seems almost a parody of an Edwardian young man writing to his tutor, and it is doubtful if the 'great benefit' Norman gained from his Cambridge days was ever contemplated by Mr Ramsey. He might have taken a cue from McClure, for Norman was clearly a capable student when he applied himself, but academic studies were not for him, as become clear in the following two years.[8]

***

After an initial mix-up over rooms, Mrs Chapman at 10 Castle Street preferred to Mrs Hough at 19 Victoria Park,[8] Norman Hartnell went up to Magdalene and became close friends with Richard Blake Brown. Their lifelong correspondence reveals the undying undergraduate enthusiasms of both for Ouida, King Ludwig of Bavaria, the Empress Elisabeth of Austria, Wagner, Daisy, Princess of Pless, Mrs Patrick Campbell and Edwardian society. Had Hartnell remained for his third year, 1922–3, Cecil Beaton's first, it is interesting to speculate how the two personalities with similar interests and enthusiasms would have got on. With Norman's remarkably adept techniques at winning over difficult people, Beaton might not have written of the Christmas cover of *Granta:* 'done by that horrid N.B. Hartnell. It's the worst thing I've ever seen!'[9]

    At this stage Beaton was more interested in designing dresses for the stage or for society women, and a photographic career was barely considered, so feelings of rivalry were to the fore, especially as Beaton would have heard of the opening of Hartnell's business as a designer on St George's Day 1923.

Beaton also attempted to make friends amongst the academic establishment of Cambridge, and his own impressions of Cambridge are recorded with hard detail in his diaries, not through the romantic afterglow of success which colours Hartnell's recollections:

> In 1921 I went up to Magdalene College and fell instantly in love with the narrow streets of Cambridge, the grey colleges huddling close to one another, and behind the velvet lawns stretching down to the quietly flowing river. Mirrored in the still ribbon of silent water were the weeping willows that swayed like cascades of soft green feathers in the stifling breeze, and clusters of lilac and pendant wisteria bordered the verdant banks, which in the Spring became carpets of close lying daffodils.[10]

Of course, it was autumn when Hartnell first went up; leaves were falling, and the damp Fenland mists and fogs were a preliminary to the biting winds which would soon strip the trees of the last leaves before the ice and snow of winter set in. Richard Blake Brown, who could be equally whimsical – as his many novels prove – corrected Bish:

> You say you went up to Cambridge in 1921, when of course it was 1920, *1920*, so that when you go down in 1922 it looks as if you'd only been there ONE year, though you were there TWO: but this trifling error could be corrected in the next edition . . .[11]

He also notified Hartnell of changes in Cambridge noted on his visits, of Magdalene: 'the Coat of Arms below the oriel window are *now* vividly painted. The heraldic dogs are vividest scarlet, and there is much brilliant goldleaf. The old-rose brick in *our* day was covered with dirty plaster.'[12]

In these much drabber surroundings the two young men dreamed of their future successes and undoubtedly discussed colour in aesthetic terms allied to their mutual sense of drama and mood. Both in his autobiography and novels, Blake describes the colour of things. His letters are even written in inks of varied hues and the letter headings are printed in scarlets, turquoises, and even mauve and purple. Blake's childhood fascination with religious ceremony has been described by Rupert Croft-Cooke and an almost obsessive preoccupation with colour is detailed.[13] Both pupils at Tonbridge (also E.M.

Forster's school), Blake had invented a religious service with Croft-Cooke as acolyte in a small room of Blake's parents' house. As a clergyman in 1929 he was to write in his diary:

> Sunday, June 23rd . . . to Penshurst Rectory after lunch for there the Bishop of Rochester was spending part of the day. How odd it all was! Rupert Croft-Cooke and I, filling a big part of our hectic boyhood with playing at *Church* and dressing up as bishops, had often looked with care-free mirth to explore Penshurst Place and the Church. And Dr Reginald Hammer, the Bishop of Rochester was the very first Church of England Bishop that I ever saw in my life – here he was sitting opposite me in the dining-room of Penshurst Rectory. A strange little comedy.'[14]

Comedy was another bond between Bish and Blake and they continually reacted to any absurdities of character or situation they witnessed. Blake later found tragedy in his failed marriage and the disturbing 'doubts' that came to him as a clergyman. Hartnell was to experience grief and unhappiness throughout his troubled life, but their early Cambridge days appear unclouded by any great problems. Hartnell's own nostalgically tinted impressions of Cambridge are echoed in the mature Blake's later reminiscences of 'the incredibly happy hours spent in King's College Chapel on Sunday afternoons when I was a dreamy, absurd undergraduate at Cambridge'[15] - 'Adorable Cambridge, the home of picturesque energy and idle happiness.'[16] Sentiments shared by Hartnell and countless undergraduates alive today.

As Hartnell's first term of Cambridge went by he made friends: Harold Warrender, whose mother and sisters were amongst his first clients in 1923, and M.D. Lyon, who became a judge and was well known in the 1920s and 1930s as a Somerset cricketer.[17] Hartnell was later godfather to his second daughter. Others with rooms in his lodging house were David Ogilvy and Lord Burghley.[18] Magdalene was a small college with an interesting mixture of undergraduates, but it was clearly Blake who was most in sympathy with Norman, both becoming members of Footlights, then a mixture of undergraduate performances somewhat in the manner of talented popular revue. After Norman had also joined the more serious Marlowe Society, which had specialised in the late nineteenth century in reviving Shakespearean productions in Cambridge and then the works of neglected Elizabethan and

Jacobean playwrights. By Bish and Blake's time there existed considerable collaboration between the two societies, which interested both men.

As autumn turned to the biting Fenland winter, Norman would share Blake's experiences:

> That curious winter-feeling came over me again paralysing my senses exquisitely as I sat there: the exciting street noises of Cambridge sounded in my ears deliciously, like that curious sea-shell ringing one used to have in one's ear as a child. I thought of King's College Chapel and of 47 Garden Walk, and I thought of God and love and life and sorrow, just like any sentimental school master or chambermaid.[19]

As all Cambridge men know, it is impossible to remain immune to the place and certain things can trigger Proustian memories: 'How well I can recollect, and almost can re-taste, the fine dark brown sherry obtainable from the Buttery at Magdalene.'[20] However busy Norman was in later life, and Blake wrote this a mere six years after going down, he always found time to see Blake or visit him. Magdalene brought them together and their tastes echoed each other's, although Blake was incomparably more erudite and became the author of a fascinating autobiography and thirty whimsical novels, of which only a mere handful were published.

Blake was one of three sons of affluent American parents, Donald, Richard and Lincoln, who later motored American visitors around England in a succession of glamorous limousines. All appreciated Norman, as did Rupert Croft-Cooke, who was Hartnell's predecessor in Blake's perpetual dressing up and play-acting, meeting him often throughout his life. Suitably, Croft-Cooke was asked home from school for tea and asked to take part in an adaptation of the popular novel *Trilby*. As Blake described it, there were hitches at first 'because Richard, an unusually beautiful boy of thirteen, wanted to be both Svengali and Trilby, the former role because he had then (and has retained throughout his life) a passion for wearing beards, the latter because he . . . would obviously make the best girl'.[21]

The parallels with Norman's school stage career are obvious. The result was to be unforgettable performances in Footlights productions, which began to absorb far too much of Norman's time at the expense of his studies of the French and Spanish languages he was supposed to be reading before taking up architecture. At no time did his doodles ever conjure up buildings. He was firmly and utterly obsessed with painting and exhibited his work in a university art show, winning a prize.[22]

His intentions were good for he made his first Cambridge stage appearance in the serious Marlowe Dramatic Society production of Swinburne's *The Duke of Garcia* in 1921. As he wrote:

> I graduated, or descended, to the Footlights Dramatic Club which had broader and more popular tastes. It was a club largely made up from the current polo-playing, gambling, sporting set to which I did not belong. Nearly all of them had money: I had not, but my enthusiasm made up for it.[23]

More than this, the rather raffish milieu was something that intoxicated Norman. The very masculine world of horses, drink and sports combined with a taste for glittering, rather comic entertainment was not too far removed from that enjoyed by his father, Bish. It remained slightly Edwardian, and Bish remained a man about town – or in the period terms of the music-hall song 'Gilbert the Filbert the nut with a K', a 'knut', albeit a shrewd one – until his death as a councillor in that most appropriate of places for him: Brighton.

Cambridge undergraduate life of Norman's period had very little of the more dissolute life enjoyed by the Oxford set later immortalised by Evelyn Waugh in *Brideshead Revisited*. Although George Rylands was referring to Cecil Beaton, the following words also apply to Norman: 'Oxford would have been very bad for Cecil . . . He would have gone straight down the Evelyn Waugh drain. They drank champagne at eleven in the morning, while we drank beer at night – or occasionally Burgundy. We lived in a rather poverty-stricken, priggish way.'[24] But Rylands and Beaton were not like Hartnell and clearly did not appreciate him. They were of the next generation, better bred and read. They had more interest in ideas and in academic life in general. Of the two, Rylands preferred Blake to Norman and his reminiscences of Hartnell were based on his later experiences:

> Richard Blake Brown called on me several times after he went down; the opposite of Hartnell in every way – quite clever, energetic . . . positive – N.H. negative . . . I met N.H. once or twice when I went down . . . I knew Cecil Beaton (a year junior) – a

friend then and after. Doubtless he was jealous of N. and saw him as a rival. (Cecil designed for the theatre.) He was malicious and had a sharp tongue.[25]

As Rylands did not know Hartnell at Cambridge, but did observe him on stage, his opinion is formed on distant impressions and undoubtedly clouded by Beaton's observation, summed up in the 'horrid Norman Hartnell' comment already remarked upon. For although Norman showed very little intellectual curiosity, he was generally known as a most amusing companion, with a quick wit sadly difficult to capture, and he had an engagingly diffident manner. He was astute enough to keep his opinions of people to himself and so avoid offending them. With the exception of Angela Loudon (née Goldsbrough), a younger generation member of his family, we must remember that no one interviewed for this book had an unpleasant thing to say about him. His public face was impeccable and his former business and domestic acquaintances also stressed this, as he did too in later life: 'You have got to have patience with the clients and the staff – all very trying, and tact.'[26]

Hartnell always had this quality. No doubt it was ingrained from his earliest days in a large family with four older children, three of whom, at least, did not care for his father, Bish. Then at school he must have kept quiet about his father and mother's early livelihood in public houses. Like many children who grow up in rather unusual circumstances, he learned to look and listen, retreating often into his fantasy world of drawing and doodling.

In answer to the question: 'Are you temperamental?', put to him at the height of his career in 1963, he replied:

Well, I don't think I am. About once every eleven years I may get cross about something where I'm usually in the wrong and I feel ill for two days, so I try to overcome these very rare fits of temper *and I only allow temperament in those nice very talented people that I employ here. French ladies* that go up in the air like a sky rocket *and fall down dampened afterwards and everything goes on screamingly.*[27]

It is indicative of the man's personality that the italicised parts of this statement were deleted by Norman before the broadcast. He hated to offend or confront people face to face, a diffident trait that was to lead him into many disastrous situations.

Although his mother died in February 1921, a momentous event for Norman, he chose to adjust the dates in *Silver and Gold* and so alter the circumstances surrounding his departure from Cambridge without a degree. As the baby of the extensive family, he was distraught at his mother's untimely death but makes little direct reference to it in his biography, nor elsewhere in interviews throughout his long career. It immediately affected his Cambridge academic life and he sought escape from the trauma by devoting himself to furthering his stage interests, both as an actor and costume designer.

Elected to Footlights on 7 March 1921 he was in the June 1921 Footlights production entitled: *What a Picnic: A New and Original Caricaturistical Farce* by H. Rottenburg, who was a stalwart of the club and involved with all three of the productions in which Norman had a leading part. Blake was also involved and had joined almost as soon as he went up, in November 1920. His impersonations of Miss José Collins as Miss Cosy Jollins at 'Smokers' evening club 'revue' performances, were highly acclaimed.

Bish also impersonated leading revue stars of the day. The farce included typical lyrics – the chorus performing 'May Week is a Source of Exasperation' and two songs by Claude Hulbert: 'Rose' and 'The Bolshevik', indicating that current events did just impinge upon Norman's life. The final chorus of 'I've Got to Say Goodbye to Cambridge' was to prove almost too accurate for Norman however, as his academic work suffered abysmally following his mother's death. However, as Kitty Fenton, niece of Philiberta Foodle, Norman showed his talents to advantage, as did Blake as her friend Violet Burton. Women were not then allowed to progress to degrees, and the *Granta* reviewer was overcome by the bizarre spectacle as witnessed in all its grotesque splendour by a photograph of the cast in full, lit by cruel daylight: 'The girls are excellent; Norman Bishop Hartnell and Richard Blake Brown make extraordinarily charming maidens. ("Are Newnham and Girton to Go?" Well we can really do without them if Magdalene can produce damsels like this.)'

The Times was more level-headed:

> After the established custom, the female characters were played by members of the club. There were three of them – Mr F. Gorell Barnes, Mr N.B. Hartnell and Mr Richard Blake Brown. One was obviously a man. The second was a rather masculine lady and the

third, even when he spoke, was almost perfect. It would be invidi-
ous to say which was which.

This was a review of the London matinée performance and *The Times* critic
chose one gem out of the dialogue: 'A characteristic pleasantry was the remark
that a Labour leader resembled the cox of a boat because both did no work,
had lots to say and all the time was carried along by the others.' If not wholly
true, this was at least amusing.[28]

For Norman, the production meant that his costume-design talents were
highly visible. He appears monstrously regal in a photograph, with neat
crossed ankles emerging from pale high heels, the mid-calf shirt with a fashionable gathered band of a hem and the décolletée square neckline banded
by smocking carried around the short sleeves. Graduated beads fall over his
chest and above a lantern jaw the rouged lips are slightly parted, his eyes just
visible beneath a large hat with osprey plumes – virtually an identical model
to one he was to design for H.M. Queen Elizabeth the Queen Mother when
she made a State Visit to Paris in 1937.

Blake sits in the manner of Mrs Patrick Campbell, head tilted beneath a
large circular hat with an ostrich plume and a haze of lace draping in the
manner of an old lampshade. In a 1982 broadcast, Dr Rylands remembered
Blake as an excellent female impersonator. The effect of the thick-necked
men is more pantomime dame than soubrette: 'In the May Week Footlights
revue 1921 which I saw he [Norman] was no singer, no actor, but appeared in
a succession of remarkable GOWNS of his creation – matronly, I think. The
Footlights Show was amateur to a degree – under-rehearsed and alcoholic – a
RAG in fact.'[29]

Dr Rylands may have confused his revues, as he went up in 1922 just as
Hartnell went down, and Norman was still involved in the 1923 production,
but the message is clear. In a 1982 broadcast Dr Rylands reminisced about his
experience of this Footlights production. He stressed that Norman designed
and displayed his marvellous dresses to perfection, but his voice was too soft
for the stage.

There is no doubt that Norman would have liked to be an actor, and that
his greater love was designing for the stage or for State occasions full of colour
and pageantry. Asked once if he would have liked to become an actor instead
of a designer he replied, 'An actor . . . yes. I'd have been rather good only my
head's too big, you see . . . that limits the parts I think.'[30]

Apart from his typical self-deprecation we gain further insight from another interview when asked about his childhood passion for drawing 'beautiful ladies in beautiful dresses' as Norman put it: 'So when it came time to think about a job was that the first thing you thought of?'

Norman replied:

> It was always at the back of my mind that I wanted to do that really, but there was no means of doing it. So, my mind turned to the theatre. However, that was sort of stuffed up by my family and I was sent off to school and to Cambridge; all the time I was drawing and designing . . .

The interviewer continued: 'You say that your family objected to [dress designing] because it was a bit beyond the pale in those days?', to which Norman replied, 'Of course.'[31]

The apparent fantasy of *What a Picnic* was more real to Norman than his studies. In the January before the production a letter was written about his academic attainments after his first term:

> I am rather disappointed to find that there is doubt about . . . Hartnell being able to take the Tripos . . . I have discussed the matter with . . . Hartnell . . . I find [him] to be quite willing to go on with Tripos work for the present and to do his best to get through the Mays. I gather from him that he would have found time for a fuller programme of lectures and classes than he had last term and I should be glad if you will kindly arrange for him to attend as many lectures and classes as you think will be useful to him.[32]

This was not entirely adhered to by Norman. During the exciting days of *Picnic* he was out late on very many nights: due to be back in his lodgings at 10 pm it was reported that he was out late every night for the week of 10 June, returning at 7 am one morning: 'Mr Hartnell appears to have been out without leave after 12 am . . . and Mr Ramsay wishes to know why Mrs Hough did not report this in accordance with the rules of the Lodging Houses Syndicate.'[33]

Soon afterwards Norman was home for the summer vacation at Royston, Hassocks in Sussex.

The letter continues: 'The result of the Mays Examination is rather surprising for you passed in Spanish and failed in French . . . I cannot understand how you can have done so badly in French. It is a serious comment on the amount of work you have been doing.'

The letter ends with the well-known words: 'I hope that you will make the most of your opportunities for improving yourself in both languages during the Vacation.'[34] There is no record of a reply.

***

Those hopeful years following the First World War allowed young men and women time to dream of a peaceful new world. For Bish and Blake, fantasy was created out of a romantic past; dashing King Ludwig of Bavaria, Richard Wagner and the Empress Elisabeth of Austria obsessed Blake, who infected Bish with his enthusiasms. They soon worshipped the memory of Gaby Deslys:

'I'm Gaby the Baby
The Pride of the stage
In London the fashion
In Paris the rage . . .'[35]

Hartnell devotes more pages in *Silver and Gold* to a description of her than he does to his family. The Marseilles-born star of light musicals and revues lived a life of conspicuous luxury, her clothes, headdresses, houses and cars put her into the illustrated magazines such as *The Sketch* and *Tatler*. The designer Erté described her succinctly as 'indeed the greatest star of the musical hall . . . she originated the elaborate feathered costumes of music hall revue: Mistinguett and all who came later were but imitators of her unique allure.'[36] She died tragically young in 1920 and formed a topic of conversation between Blake and Bish, as they both loved extravagance, especially her hats – as Erté noted 'vast cart-wheels of feathers, flowers, fruit and veiling were balanced on top of piled-up hair.'

The clothes and hats in *Picnic* were but a prelude for their extravagant plans for the next Footlights production.

***

Norman's next surviving letter to his tutor shows no sign of contrition, nor any embarrassment at his poor academic performance, undoubtedly already expressed in person:

8 September 1921

I have lately received from Messrs Eaden Lilley & Co a valuation of the furniture in the College rooms which I am to take over next term.

It consists only of the carpet, washstand, bedstead etc., whereas I understood I should be left the desk, table, sofa and chairs. I thought it advisable to consult you before buying anything new and to ask you if the above-mentioned things are the only pieces of furniture available with the rooms.

With apologies for troubling you on these matters.[37]

Moving into the College should have put Norman into a more controlled and studious environment, but it did not stop his plans for an even more adventurous production with Footlights – the now famous 1922 production of *The Bedder's Opera*. Neither Blake nor Bish were to gain positions on the committee but were highly visible and no doubt forceful participants in planning the design of scenery and costumes, whilst also befriending actors at the ADC theatre and spending time with friends.

A 'bedder' is the Cambridge term for one of the small army of women who appear each morning to clean and make beds. Nigel Playfair's revival of John Gay's *The Beggar's Opera* was a talking point of the London theatre-going public for three years in the early 1920s and the awful pun on the name proved ideal for a Cambridge revue. The title is in complete contrast to Cecil Beaton's later 1925 production *All the Vogue* and so were the designs, which have more wit than Beaton's. The distinctive programme cover of *The Bedder's Opera* by Hartnell is peculiarly interesting, resembling the silhouette of an ogreish conductor, more pantomime dame than 'bedder'. The dress with huge skirt, hat sprouting feathers and a hand with long fingers of virtuoso flexibility – a feature that was to remain a Hartnell touch in his more fanciful sketches. The lettering is redolent of the 1890s and Beardsley, as is the technique of the silhouette. The cover of the lyrics is also Beardsleyesque: a sweet little girl in a vast crinoline dress, embroidered with flower heads and trimmed with fur, peeps out from inside a vast beribboned bonnet. From this a ribbon falls over an open book held by the impossibly crooked fingers to form *The Bedder's Opera*. A heart pierced by an arrow is indicated by a pointing finger, and a bangle hangs from a very limp wrist. These covers are highly accomplished and remarkably nostalgic, albeit an amusing parody of Lovat Fraser's costumes.

As with the design of the crinolines, Norman was already asserting his own style, only paying attention to other trends and not copying them. He was preoccupied with being original, and if his attention to his French and Spanish studies was negligible, he was assiduous in creating a stir through the Footlights productions. In retrospect, his designs were fashionable, if slightly démodé, but Norman was not; he was completely of his time in his attitude to life as succinctly expressed by a contemporary commentator: 'The younger generation of the British people have come to love the jazz step, as it typifies "pep", energy, push, advancement, the love of living, and the things that go with an up-to-date and modern world.'[38]

Against this should be set the phenomenal success of Playfair's Hammersmith production of the 1728 *Beggar's Opera*, which ran for 1,463 performances from 1920 to 1923, often to family audiences. Whilst 'Tiger Rag' and 'Yes! We Have No Bananas' were current popular hits, audiences were entranced by John Gay's evocation of a Hogarthian world peopled by an array of characters also encountered during the amoral times of post-war life, although vicariously on stage for most of the audience. Prostitutes, thieves, rogues, vagabonds and tricksters abounded on stage and off. In London, nightclub after nightclub sprang up to cater for them.[39] The socialite and the parasite existed in a night-time world, which Norman certainly experienced after Cambridge and quite possibly even before then.

The Bedder's Opera was written by H. Cecil Leon, Brian Davies and N.B. Hartnell. Their talents were later variously expressed – the former became a judge and remained in touch with Norman until his death. The music was by Norman's cricketing chums M.D. Lyon, A.C. Ferguson and Brian Davies. Leon also wrote the lyrics of the piece, which was followed by *The Living Dead – A Drama in One Act* by H. Rottenburg, a Footlights member since 1902, and in turn this was followed by *The Warmth That Kills – A Turkish Drama in One Act* by M.D. Lyon, Eric Maschwitz (later to be a celebrated scriptwriter) and the ubiquitous H. Rottenburg, who became a Footlights legend. The presentation ran from Monday, 5 June to Monday, 12 June 1922, covering the period of Norman's late returns to his lodgings delineated the previous year. As one production began at 8.45 pm, they become understandable.

A surviving 'Annual Supper' menu card records the names of members attending at the Club Rooms, Corn Exchange Street on Saturday, 10 June 1922 after *The Bedder's Opera*, with Norman B. Hartnell, M.D. Lyon, H. Rottenburg and others signing in pencil above the flourish of 'Love from Richard Blake Brown', obviously affected by the five toasts on the 'toast list' and his role as 'Desirée de Menthe (an Actress)'. Norman was 'Sylvia Somers (an Actress)', but Blake had an extra role to play in *The Warmth That Kills* as 'The Wife'. The programme records: 'Messrs Hartnell's and Brown's dresses in the last act by Myra Salter, Hanover Square. Other dresses by Miss Lane, Cambridge. Mr Hartnell's dresses executed from original designs by himself.' Other dresses were by Cambridge dressmakers except for A.M.B. Schofield as 'Senorita Tim (a Spanish Dancer)' which was by 'Marcel, Paris'.

So Bish and Blake wore Hartnell, Norman gaining his first insight and experience of a larger West End dressmaker when visiting Myra Salter. As to the *Opera*, it was a spoof of a satire, for the 'May Week Play' was its subject with scenes in 'The Garden of the Limelight Club' and 'The Novelty Theatre' in which the two playlets emerge as plays within the *Opera*. With wonderfully dreadful songs performed by Bish and Blake such as 'The Autograph Book', the play was a riot:

> Desirée: I've some autographs here:
> Penny: How remarkably queer!
> D: Well some I admit read queerly,
> For I've 'Nicky with love'
> And oh! Heavens above!
> Here's 'Horatio very sincerely . . .'
> Sylvie: Margot Asquith I swear!

The pantomime style spread to a duet between Sylvia and Desirée quarrelling:

> Desirée: You cat, you!
> I know him –
> I know he doesn't love you!
> Yes, drat you!
> I'll show him

44

How far he is above you.
Sylvia: You, no doubt, look
Quite refined, dear!
I don't mind dear!
You're a dud.
To his outlook
You're unsightly,
Put politely,
Your name's mud
etc etc.[40]

As Dr Rylands put it, 'a RAG in fact!'[41]

However, this was the production which propelled Norman on his way. 'Appearing as the principal lady in the Footlights Review . . . with a large picture hat and sporting a foot-long cigarette holder he dominated the performance with a seductive voice.'[42] The whole production then transferred for a matinée performance to Daly's in London, and on the following day Norman drove down to stay with his friend M.D. Lyon and his brother Beverley at Doddington Park.

Hartnell later wrote that after dinner Mrs Lyon came over to him with a copy of the *Evening Standard* in her hands.

'Did you see what they say about you?' she asked me, pointing out a paragraph in a feature written by one 'Corisande'.
'Is the dress genius of the future now at Cambridge? I'd hate to presume to advise an undergraduate on his future career, but the frocks in *The Bedder's Opera* given by the Footlights Dramatic Club yesterday set me thinking as to whether Mr N.B. Hartnell wasn't contemplating conquering feminine London with original gowns.'
That was enough for me. I could hardly wait to get back to London to take up the quill pen which I then affected![43]

Affirmation of his success was also marked by the inclusion of a whole page illustrating *The Bedder's Opera* in the 14 June 1922 edition of the influential illustrated periodical *The Sphere*, amongst the first to publicise his talents in the context of a stage production.

Meanwhile in Cambridge, examination papers were being marked as the life of the university moved on its usual course. Barely a week after Norman's appearance in the *Evening News*, his father, Bish, received the following formal letter from Magdalene:

> Dear Sir
>
> I am sorry to report that your son failed in his examination. This means that of the four examinations necessary for a pass degree your son has passed only one by the end of two years of residence. This is very unsatisfactory, and I am instructed by the Governing Body of the College to say that if your son does not pass another examination by December he will have to be superannuated. I am afraid that his main interests are with matters altogether outside his work.
>
> Yours very truly[44]

'I was simply idling and Cambridge is an ideal place to do that'[45] was how Norman glossed over an important phase of his life. His dedication to the Footlights productions, his dress designing and his friendships were all aspects of his beginnings. As a famous dress designer he may have forgotten that he applied himself to the things which mattered most to him and were 'work'. He was quite correct in his opinion when he stated that, 'If I wanted to become an architect I was not going the right way about it. If I had wanted to become an actor, then I should have been in Gower Street at the Royal Academy of Dramatic Art.' He skipped lectures and neglected the career he had been pushed into choosing by his sensible parents with their own preconceptions of how to get on in life, perhaps omitting to acknowledge that they had no intellectual training or skills beyond sound common sense and drive.

***

According to his own version in *Silver and Gold*, there then came a terrible moment for both Norman and his family when his mother, not a robust woman, suddenly died. However, she died on 3 April 1921, a month after he was elected to Footlights and threw himself into the designs of *What a Picnic*. Later in his autobiography Norman writes that after his first professional dress show in March 1924, he paid a visit to his mother's grave in Clayton to mark the third anniversary of her death. Work was always to be the antidote to any unpleasantness in his life from which he sought to conceal both himself and his feelings. The pressure of work was both a useful excuse and a truthful one in the years to come, when he relied increasingly on those around him to form a shield between himself and any unpleasant reality.

By September 1922 Norman was still in Hassocks and received a letter from the College reminding him that his account was two months overdue for payment.[46] This letter received an answer from Bish, badly typed on paper without a letterhead from 91 Warrington Crescent, Maida Vale, W9, already seen to have belonged to a relative, next to his former business Hartnell's Warrington Hotel.

19 September 1922

I am sorry to state that I wish to withdraw my son from Magdalene College. Owing to his having failed his recent examination and the fact that his main interests are outside his academical [sic] work, I do not think it advisable that he should return to Cambridge next term.

I am sorry not to have been able to inform you of this earlier, but it has been very difficult for us to come to a decision.

Yours very truly
H.B. Hartnell[47]

With term only a few weeks away, the decision was some three months in the making. A letter of reply dated 22 September, to Bish, from Magdalene signed by Ramsey, merely states: 'I am sorry your son will not be returning into residence here. I hope he will soon find a useful sphere.' There then follows a request for the money owing, which Bish was probably unaware of as it amounted to £71.12s.1d. and was a considerable sum for one term's expenses in 1922! It was still unpaid a month later, and on 1 January 1923 a letter was sent to Norman at Hassocks requesting payment: 'As it is now more than six months since you left the College I think you must agree that it is not unreasonable to ask for an immediate settlement.' Ramsey unbends a little and adds: 'I was glad to hear that you have got a good post and do hope that you find the work interesting. With all good wishes for the New Year.'[48]

If the hope expressed was in the belief that Norman was incapable of either working or finding it interesting, then he had failed to comprehend the energy with which his former pupil was to pursue his career for the next fifty-five years, and the true genius which he possessed as a designer. However, the existence of these letters in the College archives would undoubtedly have been known to a later Master when Norman wrote a flattering letter of thanks for dinner in 1956. The full facts of the situation are obviously at variance to the version he gave. Nevertheless, an Honorary Degree would have been a much-merited gesture to one of the university's most talented and famous sons. Designing anything but machinery or buildings seems to have been dismissed as a facile occupation, but it was at Cambridge that Hartnell honed and first practised his talents before a reasonably sophisticated audience. This led to Cambridge showing itself at Daly's, and indeed to the name of Hartnell and dress designing being fortuitously coupled in a London newspaper. The fuse had been lit.

CHAPTER THREE

Not if . . . but when

In 1907, when Norman was first leafing through illustrated weeklies, gazing at photographs and drawings of the latest fashions worn by society and actresses, there were some 125 court dressmakers in London and about 725 dressmakers.[1] Some of the latter were the 'little woman round the corner', as he would also laughingly describe himself later on. Others had grander premises as ready-to-wear clothing was seldom bought by any woman with pretension to being well dressed, even if altered to fit, nor were the current fashions particularly suitable for easy copying. By 1966 when Hartnell's fireworks were fizzling out 'Court Dressmakers: see Dressmakers' was the category marking the sad end to a once flourishing business. Of the 123 or so names listed under 'Wholesale', virtually all were for ready-to-wear or for the wholesale trade. Three hundred and twenty-five names appear under 'Court and manufacturing', famous names and small businesses all mixed together.[2]

In his lifetime, Norman witnessed the rise of a distinctive British couture and its decline to near-extinction. Its twentieth-century rise and expansion was largely due to his own extraordinary talents and energy, which propelled his name skywards through the 1920s. His fame exploded on to the international fashion scene at the end of the decade. The colourful glitter was to last for four decades and it drew in its wake a remarkable group of London designers whose fame faded with his, but for a couple of exceptions – most notably the younger Sir Hardy Amies.

When Norman took up his quill and wrote to 'Corisande', it was not solely to thank her but to ask her advice. Few can resist the implicit flattery of being asked for advice, especially from the young. 'Corisande' – Miss Minnie Hogg – was no exception and was swift in her response, sending on a letter from a court dressmaker who was looking for 'any young designer wanting a trial'. This was an extension of what Norman termed 'the strange twists of Fortune's finger', a typical Normie expression. On the day of the Daly's performance Miss Hogg had been in the editor's office of the *Evening Standard* looking for a storyline, and saw 'a pair of tickets and, since there was nothing better to do, decided to drop in on the show'.[3]

Writing forty-four years later in 1966 to:

> 'Dear Norman Hartnell, Excuse this form of address!! I always think of you as when I first met you . . . I would just like to add what I have often wanted to say, and that is I do so much appreciate the generous way you have always in interviews and so on, brought in my name as helping you to start. I've had cuttings sent me from overseas – thank you *very* much. I may add that I sometimes give myself a little pat on the back for having very indirectly helped to dress two queens and several princesses of England.'[4]

Norman never forgot her prophetic remarks as 'Corisande'. The dress genius of the future was always generous with his thanks. In 1922, in the aftermath of his mother's death and the failure of his Cambridge academic career, he was heartened by such a public expression of faith in his distinctive talents.

Madame Desirée, a court dressmaker of Hertford Street, W1 catered specifically for Mayfair mothers and debutantes in need of the right sort of dresses for presentations at Court and other social activities such as dances, racing and holidays. On 7 July 1921 the first postwar Court at Buckingham Palace since 1914 took place with few horse-drawn broughams. Most of those invited queued again in The Mall, but in motor cars, and the throng of people gawping was enormous. Queen Mary wore a dress of sapphire blue brocade and an array of diamonds. Bish and Blake had absorbed this news as the Queen was a favourite obsession of Blake.

The owner of Madame Desirée catered for such occasions and turned out to be 'an impressive lady charming and beautiful with a large black velvet hat set on silvery hair and with ropes of pearls dangling to her knees.'[5] She also turned out to be really Mrs Hughes, French names having more cachet, but after examining Norman's Cambridge designs offered him £3 a week, not 'the thousand a year I rather expected . . . shocked at the insult I thought it would be impossible to accept her offer, but that I would let her know'.[6]

Hertford Street was and is not the grandest street off Park Lane and there were very many better dressmakers in the West End. But Norman wanted to design for the theatre and with Madame Desirée there was a chance of this. Miss Hogg obviously knew this.

Although money was tight, the Hartnell finances were not too shaky as both Norman and Phyllis were left a joint interest by their mother in a row of shops with living accommodation above at 44 to 48 Morrish Road, Brixton Hill, SW2. These were not far from their previous Streatham homes, and gave them a small income of their own. Streatham was a genteel suburb and sought after by city clerks and their families at a time when renting was more usual than owning, so the income was steady. Normie, as the family called him, and Phyllis were living in Maida Vale 'in two rather drab, big rooms' in the Warrington Crescent house next to Bish's former gin palace, Hartnell's Warrington Hotel. But his father had other plans. He was told by his doctor that if he wished to live longer, then he should move to the seaside and escape the choking fogs and coal-fired pollution of London. Nowhere was more suitable for him than Brighton, albeit with a less raffish and more solid business future in front of him.[7]

Meanwhile, his two children had the rooms in London and it was but a twopenny ride on the no. 16 bus from Park Lane to Maida Vale for Norman to discuss matters with Phyllis. 'Luckily my sister was practical.' She was to be practical with him until the early 1950s when she gave up the unequal struggle and resigned from the board of Norman Hartnell Ltd. She pointed out to her brother that he had a good education with nothing at all to show for it except his proven talent as a designer. 'Here is something you can do, and do well.' So 'it was twopence on the bus or the dusty pavement of the Edgware Road, a sausage or more rarely a chop for dinner, and without a shilling to spare or a friend in sight . . .' or 'tea and toast at the Express Dairy in Maida Vale'.[8]

Not surprisingly, Norman's friends, including Blake, were beginning their last years at Cambridge, and Norman was forced to make a new life for himself and approached a freezing cold garage belonging to Mrs Hughes in which he found a rickety table for his box of paints. 'I am not lightly depressed, but there seemed little to look forward to.' Then, as Miss Hogg had expected, theatrical work came his way, for Jack Buchanan had to produce *Battling Butler*, a musical comedy starring himself, Phyllis Titmuss and Sylvia Leslie.

After meeting Buchanan, one of the most glamorous stars of light comedy with an engagingly grating voice, Norman found himself responsible for designing over 200 costumes. All dress houses have or had uncredited designers and sketch artists producing drawings which might be used by the house or adapted in the hands of the main designer and given the 'house' style. Madame Desirée clearly employed Norman for this purpose on the strength of his glamorous sub-Bakst–Alistair–Beardsleyesque Cambridge designs. Although he wrote that he knew nothing of fabrics and less about the techniques of dressmaking, this cannot be entirely true. He had enough knowledge from childhood on, through school and university theatricals, to both design and wear dresses and to examine and discuss the fabrics they were made of. Blake was especially interested in fabrics, as Croft-Cooke explains in his memoirs – Bish and Blake were great chatterboxes on their favourite themes. Nevertheless, Norman gained a great deal of knowledge whilst designing the costumes and a lifelong resentment of Jack Buchanan, only agreeing reluctantly to participate in Alan Melville's wireless retrospective *The Jack Buchanan Story* in 1958.

> Jack was my first customer – my very first. I'd been working for exactly two hours . . . I started at nine a.m. . . . and at eleven a.m. I was told to go downstairs to the salon where Mr Jack Buchanan was waiting, and find out what on earth *he* wanted. I had the most terrible attack of schoolboy nerves, but down I went – and there was Jack as immaculate as ever. I may as well confess that at that stage in my career I honestly didn't know the difference between Scotch Wool and French tulle . . . but I had just enough common sense or intuition to realise that Jack was almost as nervous as I was, and obviously didn't know any more about ladies' dresses than I did.[8]

Apart from typical Normie self-deprecation, his mention of 'nerves' is a clue to what could be a nearly crippling problem for him at times. Norman continued:

> After a little jockeying for position, he announced to my amazement that he wanted to order 300 dresses. I seem to remember there were three scenes in the show – a Garden Party, a ball, a scene at the Albert Hall [the following was cut by Norman from the script] . . . and I thought the dresses we made were out-of-this-world. They may not have been: at any rate Jack never came back

to me for any of his other shows. But he *was*, I'm proud to say, my first customer.[9]

Each design for Buchanan was different and Norman went to the theatre eagerly awaiting their reception. His name was not printed in the programme and he was upset about this; for the rest of his life it rankled . . . 'but my good friend "Corisande" gave me a tiny mention in her column which I read gratefully!'

The play appeared at the New Oxford, of which the chairman and managing director was Charles B. Cochran, one of the most enterprising theatrical producers of the century. Norman worked for him in the 1930s. In 1925 'Cockie' was declared bankrupt and the New Oxford showed losses of £98,000, so not surprisingly *Battling Butler* is not mentioned in his autobiography.[10] If the designs had been truly spectacular, there seems little reason to doubt that Norman's name would have been mentioned in many reviews, but *Battling Butler* was a mediocre production on all counts, only of interest as Norman's first commercial undertaking. After two further months of waiting for the Friday-night pay packet 'tactfully placed on my rickety table' Norman was called to Mrs Hughes' office and sacked. 'It was Christmas Eve'[11] he added for extra drama.'

At this time plans for the 1923 Footlights production of *Folly* were already well advanced and although no longer an undergraduate, Norman was still a member of the club and not forgotten by his friends, especially Blake and M.D. Lyon. His designs for *Battling Butler* were seen by his friends and he was asked to both design for and perform in the June production. The £3 was probably well spent over his weekends away from Mrs Hughes and Norman was convinced that 'I did not want to be a dressmaker. I never considered myself one . . . I am a designer and in 1923 I wanted to be a designer of dresses for the Theatre.'[11]

Whilst designing and working on *Folly*, which required rehearsals and fittings, he was also busy looking for work. Nothing was too modest for him and he had various typically near misses:

You were interested in designing dresses for the theatricals in 1923 or 4. At that time I was managing a small exclusive shop in Regent Street (Myra Salter) and I recall how you came in to see me with a well-drawn sketch and beautifully coloured (a crinoline in frills

53

and shading from deep fuchsia to very pale) you offered me 8 gns –
I thought it would be a good advert! I was unable to comply apart
from the price!! My small workroom was full up, but I remarked
to my fitter 'What a flair that young man has and should go a long
way – how right I was . . . I have been a fashion buyer for 28 years
and advisor and as a girl model at Jay's and Revel [*sic* – Reville]
and Rossiter.'[12]

The most significant detail here is the mention of the crinoline, for which
Hartnell became world famous in the late 1930s as a result of royal patronage.
It is clear that such a dress was unfashionable in 1923, although Lanvin floated
the idea in Paris, when Paris-led styles in dresses were generally increasingly
svelte and understated in line, although often encrusted with luxurious
embroidery.

The wedding of H.R.H. the Princess Royal to Viscount Lascelles on 28
February 1922 had attracted huge publicity, not only because it was the first
truly joyful state event since the Great War, but also because it was the first
sight of a major Royal bride in a post-war wedding dress cut on straight
'up and down' tubular lines. This was the most fashionable silhouette and
was mainly produced by compressing the female form, the bust with a tight
binder and the rest with corsets, which remained a major fashion ingredient
until the miniskirt of the 1960s. Underwear became at best 'wispy' even if it
consisted of the popular wartime innovation of cami knickers, which combined two pieces of underwear into one. The waistline was 'disguised' and
legs became increasingly visible in new types of stockings.

Norman could hardly be unaware of all these dramatic changes towards
a greater simplicity. He loathed the fashions of the 1920s and the 'dreary
creations of Mlle Chanel'[13] as he described them. They were the antithesis
of his desire to create glamorous dresses for beautiful, feminine women. The
impeccably dressed Yvonne Arnaud, a leading musical comedy star in the
1920s and future client of Norman's, described the look:

as flat as a herringbone! – and d'you know where the waist was?
Just above the knee – and there was a little fringe attached to the
skirt and I thought I was fabulously beautiful. I had bobbed hair
and a fringe and a hat like a flower pot inverted on my head. And
a very flat chest – many poor women must have suffered torture to

have the body flattened so. Really when I look back at the fashions
I wonder whether human intelligence did not go away in 1920.

She also pointed out that 'we wore hideous jumpers in ghastly colours, with
long strings of beads and long sleeves, the whole thing terrifically long and
loose fitting. It was, if I can use that word, a loose fitting era!'[14]

During the decade hems crept up and down around 1923, then as the
modern girl got into her stride in a general craze for 'youth', it went up to
its fullest extent worldwide in 1927, so much so that a fashionable Japanese
woman was named a '*moga*', and a boy a '*mobo*'. As James Laver put it: 'For
probably the first time in history the flapper was free, and it was she who was
to dictate the fashion of the next decade.' This was not confined to Britain.[15]

Norman's designs were at variance with this theory to a considerable degree,
yet he became a trans-Atlantic success in the 1920s. Perhaps this variation to
the Parisian rule of the period did not appeal to Mr Laver, as he was to make
scant reference to Norman, or any other London designer apart from Victor
Stiebel in his books, although the two certainly met and corresponded from
time to time.

Robert Graves was surely closer to the truth when he wrote that the sack-
line, the boyish appearance, short hair and skirts were 'a symbol of female
independence'.[16] C. Willet Cunnington went further and wrote of 'a wave of
psychological homosexuality . . . the schoolboy figure became the structure on
which fashions were built and young women sought by every physical means
to obliterate their feminine outline and assume that of the miniature male'.

Because of the 1921 slump and tougher economic conditions, the young
men back from the war who were faced with a larger female population did
not particularly want large families or 'the maternal type of woman'. It was
now a world which 'wished to cut itself adrift from all elderly obsolete traditions'.[17] This was not a world in which Norman felt entirely at ease. He loved
theatre, glamour, pageantry and traditions; although he was also keen to
innovate his own style in both the design of clothes and interiors, he wished
to reinterpret the best ideas of the past and fuse them with all that was best in
the 'modern' world of the 1920s. As his future patron and client Noël Coward
put it in the finale of *The Vortex*, 'It doesn't matter about death, but it matters
terribly about life' and Norman proved how deeply he felt this in his own life
and subsequent career.

Early in 1923, Norman wrote to impresarios Charles B. Cochran, John

Murray Anderson and André Charlot in turn, asking for interviews, for he was convinced that his own fantasies would find a home in any one of their lavish productions, crinolines and all. At Cochran's office, 49 Old Bond Street, WI he was received by the impresario's stage director Frank Collins, who 'had a tongue that became bitter for me that day as he looked at the Hartnell designs'. Norman's entrance had been ruined, because he snagged his portfolio and all the carefully arranged designs had cascaded over the floor. Collins' response: 'This is the sort of thing we have been supplying to Delysia for years. It would be pointless to waste Mr Cochran's time by showing him these.'

He had no more success with Charlot and decided that his 'throbbing talent' was not wanted on the London stage. But as a direct result of his meeting with Collins, Norman was recommended to Gordon Selfridge and began what was also to be a nearly lifelong connection with the Oxford Street department store. His lift girls were then a novelty and Selfridge wanted a 'smart new costume' for the famous beauties.

The link to Selfridge was undoubtedly through the Dolly Sisters; Cochran promoted Jenny and Rosie Dolly in revue and Selfridge housed them in the rented Lansdowne House at the foot of Berkeley Square. Norman thought he had twenty well-drawn 'pretty little pictures' to show Selfridge, who said, 'Go away, my boy, and learn to draw.'[18] Although Norman could dismiss them thirty years later as more suitable for 'amateur waitresses in Nell Gwynne's Tea Rooms', he always insisted that his designs *were* well drawn. Looking again at the lyrics cover for *The Bedder's Opera* one can immediately see that Selfridge's evolving taste radically included the Edgar Brandt bronzed lift cages at Selfridges. It was hardly likely to be sympathetic to Norman's presentation of romantically fluffy creations. Norman quickly achieved the fashionable svelte, commercially-viable line, leading to the future commissioned designs of several uniforms for women. When he had successfully asserted his name with this change of direction, Selfridge himself sent him many clients.

With Bish installed at 6 Eastern Terrace, Brighton, taking the sea air and regaining his strength, Norman began to visit the town together with his sister and make firm acquaintances there amongst many types of the inhabitants:

Dear Mr Norman . . . you may not remember me, but I was in your father's employment about 34 years ago (1923) . . . you used to visit there with Miss Phyllis at the week-ends and I used to see you had your breakfast and caught the train for Town on the Monday morning. You used to have breakfast in the kitchen. How proud your Father would be of you now you have achieved your aims . . . you are marvelous [sic].[19]

Part of Norman's lifelong success as a designer depended upon his innate charm, his sincerity, lack of pretension and his ability to be at ease with almost anyone.

Brighton was infinitely more pleasant than Maida Vale's leafy staid avenues and the breezy, smartly raffish nature of the place suited Bish, who soon began to carve out another career for himself. This invariably included some aspect of inn-keeping, whilst Norman's London life certainly included the rounds of the many nightclubs which sprang up around Leicester Square and Soho in the 1920s, and were visited by Society and lowlife alike, a combination Norman found fascinating.

Friends clearly sought him out and came down for outings whenever possible. Pierre Balmain's famous head vendeuse Ginette Spanier later recalled the mores of the time for a good middle-class girl:

Man was a crafty, inconstant beast, ever ready to attract, make a fool of and drop the maiden who 'cheapened' herself. Cheapen was the operative word. And oh how easy it apparently was to cheapen oneself.

You could cheapen yourself by leaving your underwear visible in a bathing cabin. You could cheapen yourself by not squashing your bust down flat. I cheapened myself finally and beyond recall because one evening after having dined at the Berkeley Hotel with some young men from Cambridge, a whole lot of us went back to the flat of a young man called Norman Hartnell and he gave me a drawing he had just done.[20]

It was Minnie Hogg ('Corisande') who again came to Norman's aid by writing to tell him that she had arranged for him to meet the famous pre-war designer Lucile – Lucy, Lady Duff-Gordon – famous for her dress salons in London and Paris and her success in New York. The Anglo-Irish Paris-based designer Captain Edward Molyneux had once worked for her, as had the

Hollywood film costume designer Howard Greer. Both were to be amongst the most talented and internationally known designers of the century. Apart from her own fame, Lucile was the sister of Elinor Glyn, a bestselling romantic novelist and scriptwriter.

Lucile should have given Norman his most important lesson as a fledgling designer before he even went to meet her in her small flat in Park Place, St James's, SW1. Her fame had barely survived the First World War and her finances were in tatters. She was a product of the epoch of conspicuous consumption, 'La Belle Époque', in both Edwardian London and New York; it proved impossible for her to truly adjust to the age of the modern woman.[21] But her style was, of course, exactly right for the rather dated posturings of Norman's early 1920s designs, which veer between the decadence of Alistair and the sentimentality of Kate Greenaway, sometimes managing to combine both in unnerving colours and intricate pen work.

Miss Hogg had clearly thought them a good match, but Norman was also unprepared for what he found:

> [a] celebrated lady . . . rather advanced in years. A green and silver tissue turban surmounted by a wealth of bright red hair which draped down on either side of her face, 'like a couple of fire-escapes,' I thought to myself. She pulled down the rather ugly lampshade of stretched green silk until it was only a few inches away from the beetroot-red chenille cloth that covered a small circular table. Then she whipped out horn lorgnettes and closely examined my dress designs under the glaring light. 'These are exactly the sort of thing I need', she said and, in one breath, 'I trained and made Molyneux. I can train and make you. Are you free? It would mean, of course, your travelling to Paris and New York to work with me.'

It was as though a whole new world had been opened to Norman, who strolled off swinging his umbrella and imagining himself in a silver aeroplane bound for Paris or aboard a gilded liner crossing the Atlantic – 'Adieu, Edgware Road!'

Having left his designs with Lucile, he was then amazed to see one illustrating her weekly column 'Dorothy' in *The Sketch*. He had been told that she would consider the amount of his salary and then be in touch with him. After two fruitless attempts to contact Lucile, who had actually fled Paris as a bankrupt in 1923, Norman was amazed to see yet another article with an accompanying sketch clearly reproducing his signature. Lucile's first piece had included the words 'My dear Dorothy, I've designed this lovely dress just for you.'

Consulting Phyllis and Bish, Norman decided to sue Lucile and borrowed a grey suit from his brother-in-law, Hew Kilner, as he could not then afford to buy a new one. Phyllis went with him 'her face half-hidden in a black cloche hat and wearing a discreet black marocain dress draped to the hips à la Dame Clara Butt in order to assume the appearance of maturity'.[22] His solicitor advised settling for £50 and costs, and Norman left the court with merely 'a promise of £50 and nothing in view for the future'.

Writing in 1955 he wished that he had demanded a considerably larger sum as he felt that it would have created a valuable precedent for future actions against those pirating designs. It is clear that had a greater amount been demanded, then 'Lucile would have been unable to pay as she was not just financially broken, but also emotionally and physically near collapse'. She would struggle to write her 'Dorothy' column and go out to Pontings and Barkers with her granddaughter to root out ideas for her 'working-girl' readers, but the sight of the fabrics upset her:[23] 'I was like an artist shut away from his colour, or a violinist deprived of his violin.'[24]

Norman could not have known this but might have guessed at the truth from the miserable surroundings he experienced in her flat. If so, he conspicuously failed to heed the experience in later years. But he was never so overbearingly arrogant to anyone seeking a job with him. Whatever he might have felt, he became famous for his courtesy and kindness towards the young.

Seen through the eyes of Beverley Nichols, a contemporary and friend of Norman, 'Lucile was a rather tiresome woman who used to trail around in mauve tulle talking about the "dress of temperament". If she had dressed to match her own temperament she would have worn sateen shorts.'[25]

At this point Norman was helped by one of the many older men who were to play a critical role in his young life. Facing the former Hanover Square premises of Lucile was another grand court dressmaker named Reville – 'a vast dressmaking establishment' was how Norman described it. His 'faithful friend Richard Fletcher' was able to gain Norman many star clients in the years to come and he now thought that he could introduce Mr Reville to Mr Hartnell, on the basis of some chance meeting with the great owner of one of the grandest British Houses. Fletcher was then in his fifties and had clearly encountered Norman, and possibly Blake, in his social wanderings. He was to become an intimate of Norman's and to write press releases and publicity articles for him.

An imposing bearded Edwardian in appearance and manner, he was still remembered in the 1990s by Hartnell employees working for Norman in Bruton Street during the war. His impecunious grandeur became an embarrassment to Norman, who nicknamed him 'Old Beardie' in a 1944 letter to a friend, but he loyally supported him until and beyond death, for he paid the funeral expenses.

In 1923, 'Old Beardie' was influential enough to be courted by many. Croft-Cooke termed him 'a very odd character', which must mean that he was extraordinary, given Croft-Cooke's own temperament.

> He was an American who had emigrated to London in his youth
> and become more English than the English, with a deep resonant
> English voice and the style, the clothes, the appearance of an
> English man-about-town. He was then in his fifties, tall, imposing,
> handsome with thick silver hair and a neat moustache. He was
> to be seen only in the most expensive places and quite often with
> distinguished people. He was arrogant and intolerant, indeed no
> one would have thought he lived only by his wits.[26]

For Norman, the moustache attached to a handsome face was always alluring.[27] The combination often proved irresistible in later years and Fletcher must have acted as Norman's mentor to the fringes of society on which he plied his wits. 'This he achieved by securing for ambitious hostesses those most coveted things, paragraphs in the gossip columns, but acting as a go-between in delicate matters, by hushing-up scandals, obtaining apologies and by such polite blackmail as these activities made possible.'[28]

If Fletcher had kept diaries they would be of great interest. However, Croft-Cooke was writing in 1963 so no connection is directly made with Norman, who had in any case dealt with Fletcher's effects on his death. In 1991, a battered suitcase was still mouldering in Bruton Street with Fletcher's prayer book amongst the decayed rubbish. There are and always will be figures such as Richard Fletcher bluffing their way on the telephone into gatherings and events and attempting to arrange advantageous meetings. With Norman eagerly listening, squeezed into a public call box in the Haymarket, the call fizzed out into a rejection without Mr Reville ever speaking personally to his supplicants, gazing hopefully at the 'old-fashioned instrument' with 'a mouthpiece like an unhealthy black lily'.

> In the Carlton Bar Richard extinguished the stump of his now acid cigar and ordered me a brandy and soda.
> We walked into the cool air of the Haymarket and entered the quiet of St Martin-in-the-Fields where we stayed for a while. As we came out Richard murmured, 'Never mind, one day you will walk out of here with a high heart.'[29]

These words were to be proved prophetic in 1927, when Norman attended the wedding there of Daphne Vivian to Lord Weymouth and the Hartnell-designed wedding dress caused a sensation. But there were years of great struggle before Norman was able to achieve this position.

Partly because of the Reville rebuff, Norman wrote that 'my courage failed me' when it came to approaching the grandest of the establishments: Worth in Hanover Square.

Charles Frederick Worth had left England for Paris in 1846 and founded the business in the 1850s, which still exists as a name on scent bottles. He had a great understanding of line, the handling, cutting and embellishing of fabrics allied to superb colour sense. In the early 1920s, the London House produced sublimely elegant embroidered sheaths or 'flowing draperies of snow-white chiffon'[30] for Edith Evans and Marie Löhr respectively, who were reproducing fashionable society on the stage.

Norman was an avid playgoer and also would have known of the clientele Worth attracted, but he already had the idea of aiming at Paris. Worth had done it and so had Molyneux.... 'Famous old Worth must not be bothered by unknown young Hartnell . . . I must prepare a special collection of sketches for Paquin,' he thought and tried to create designs that were 'truly French, but nevertheless British! In Maida Vale, where no birds sing and nobody seems very French or even very British, I scratched and dabbed at ten sheets of paper.' Artistic licence was applied to the birds of leafy Maida Vale, but he conveyed that Maida Vale then had a sizeable Jewish community.

There were five evening dresses in the French taste, as he saw it, and five frock coats forming the British taste. Looking back at his drawings in 1955, he could see that his evening dresses were more Eastern European 'goaded on by Poiret's Oriental leanings and bedizened with the jewelled titbits of Aubrey Beardsley's Salomé.' He also thought that 'the day-dresses were the very epitome of Swan and Edgar's contemporary catalogue'. At the time, he thought them marvellous and was furious when at Paquin's London house 'a mere unimportant lady' told him to go to the trade entrance and show his sketches to the manager – 'Not that we ever buy any.'

His dreams of life in Paris shattered, he stalked off feeling his artistic status maligned. Not surprisingly, he records that his spirits were 'low' and Phyllis then agreed to accompany him on his next visit to 'Madame Esther's' in Grafton Street. Typically, for Norman, he had gone to Paquin, which had seen its biggest successes after its founding in 1897 until 1914, but had continued with new svelte lines and a fashionable clientele. The French name had deeply infiltrated his consciousness in a way that Madame Esther was unlikely to do.

On the floor of their rooms in 91 Warrington Crescent, a red-brick building diagonally across from the synagogue, his sister attempted to give her youthful looks dignity with the remains of her mother's wardrobe. A cartwheel taffeta hat was enhanced by black osprey feathers and the hem of her black coat was given 'a well-balanced hunk of black monkey fur' to create a very 'femme du monde' ensemble that became 'an overwhelming toilette'. Madame Esther offered Phyllis a job as 'social sales lady' and Norman a place in the stockroom. It was back on the no. 16 bus, Norman holding his 'Elegant Esther' and Phyllis (known in the family as 'Topsy') clutching one brass rail in one hand and hat in the other 'like Queen Boadicea'. It must have been a miserable time for them both, Norman taking his sketches to various dressmakers, as we have seen, and Topsy without a job. However, a later wartime press release states that she was involved with dressmaking even before Norman opened his own business.

One final attempt was made by his friend Harold Warrender's mother, the distinguished Lady Maud Warrender, who sent him to her own dressmaker with a business proposition. Norman had about £300 left from his mother's bequest – about £15,000 today. Named 'Miss Harper' in *Silver and Gold* the business sounded like 'Hartnell' and could be changed with an infusion of Norman's capital with him as designer. 'Miss Harper was a large Irish woman with a mouse-grey husband and drab. Dislike was instant and mutual,' Norman wrote.

Norman explained his plan and Miss Harper candidly told him she had no proof of his talent and his name was unknown. 'Mr' Harper was delegated to write to Norman with her decision and the letter arrived 'one evening in Maida Vale'. She was 'not willing to renounce the substance for the shadow'. The crisis had come. 'I faced myself in the mirror of our lodging house bathroom. And then the worm turned. It turned sideways and said to its sister:

"'I'm going to start on my own."

"'If you do," she answered, "I will help you."'

It was St George's Day, 23 April 1923.[31] Topsy was to prove she had a remarkably clear head for business, more so than Normie, for she not only brought her determination and drive but also truly understood and quickly learned the business of a top court dressmaker. She was to remain a director of Norman Hartnell Ltd until the early 1950s and it was to prove one of a series of unbusiness-like moves of Norman that he forced her resignation. In 1923, none of this could have been dreamed of, for it was to father Bish that Topsy and Normie now turned for the financial help and business acumen they urgently needed.

It can be imagined that Bish was not easily persuaded that the son on whom he had pressed boxing gloves as an antidote to alarming tendencies should now have more money spent on him. Mill Hill, Cambridge, holidays in France and a year running around London in pursuit of his stage-designing career had done little for Norman's prospects and nothing for his sister. Normie and Topsy could not have seemed much of a business proposition, yet Norman could at least point to the execution of his designs and their appearance on stage, as well as the encouragement of Miss Hogg, Richard Fletcher and Lady Warrender. Others were to claim later that they also had a hand in the success of Norman's designing career. Although unacknowledged in the published version of *Silver and Gold*, both Beverley Nichols and Dame Barbara Cartland are in the draft and influenced his life for the better, the former both before and after he opened his business and the latter up to his death in 1979.

Nichols met Norman:

> in whose launching I played a minor role . . . at a party in Cambridge and was so impressed that I whisked him off to the house of a lady called Gracie Ansell . . . an unforgettable figure of the Twenties . . . an Edwardian, with all that goes with that word. 'My dear,' she would hiss in her curious throaty voice, 'I used to be able to sit on my hair. And when I know you better, my dear, I shall tell you what King Edward said about *that* at Goodwood!'

When Norman and Beverley arrived, a mah-jong game was being played by Gracie Ansell, Lady Diana Cooper, Olga 'Oggie' Lynn and Tallulah Bankhead.

> The game of mah-jong rattled on and young Norman sat in a corner, clutching his portfolio of sketches with trembling fingers, and nobody – least of all himself – suspected that one day those same fingers would be drawing the design for a dress that was to play its part in the world-famous pageant of history – the Coronation Dress of Queen Elizabeth II. But when the game was over, they gathered round and they said the designs were marvellous – (pronounced 'mahvlz') – and Tallulah said, 'Dahling, you'll go to the top' and – well, he did.[32]

Norman undoubtedly mentioned this encounter and others to Bish: Tallulah Bankhead became an immediate sensation in London when she first appeared on stage at Wyndham's Theatre in *The Dancers* in February 1923, and Lady Diana Cooper, one of the great beauties and wits of the century, was seldom out of the newspapers. On 5 March 1923, for example, she was fined for one of her famous motoring misdemeanours. Beverley Nichols had already established his reputation as a leading journalist, having been President of the Oxford Union. It is clear that Nichols had met Norman during one of the many trips he was making to Cambridge in connection with his last Footlights extravaganza *Folly* in June 1923: his business opened in July and was advertised in the programme.

In *Silver and Gold* Norman writes at length about the problems surrounding the opening of his first business venture: 'the capital was £300, a box of paints and the enthusiasm of ignorance'. Even in 1955 he was writing 'a precise warning of what not to do'. At the height of his powers and fame during the 1950s, he had already sensed the decline of 'couture' as a profitable venture without diversification into any area of merchandising based on his name that would be profitable. In 1923, some Parisian designers were already capitalising on their names through the sale of scent, but it is doubtful if any of the three Hartnells had any concept of such a profitable area for the future exploitation of Norman's name. Only in the following decade did Hartnell become a world-famous name and they then acquired the necessary advisors.

Suitable premises were the initial priority and 10 Bruton Street, Mayfair,

W1 was found. At the time, this short street connecting Bond Street and Berkeley Square had a mainly fashionable residential character. It was on 15 January 1923 that the announcement of the forthcoming marriage between the King's second son, H.R.H. the Duke of York to Lady Elizabeth Bowes-Lyon had been announced and on 16 January they had lunch with her parents, Lord and Lady Strathmore, in their London house, 17 Bruton Street. This significant fact cannot have escaped the founders of Norman Hartnell Ltd. Nearby No. 10 already housed tailors, but the upper floors were to let with an L-shaped drawing room and two more floors above 'without the lush parquet of the first'.

Norman stresses his lack of business acumen:

'The rent is £850 exclusive.'

'Oh, very,' I agreed. 'It is a very exclusive neighbourhood.'

'Exclusive of rates,' corrected Mr Bradley. 'By the way, have you two young people anyone – *responsible* – acting for you in this matter?'

Amusing and typically whimsical Normie, we need not believe this to be a verbatim account. Both Normie and Topsy owned property in Brixton Hill and their father's profession is given on legal papers of the period as 'property owner'. We can be sure from the tone of the letters between the two men, albeit of a later date, that everything was fully dissected before the siblings set out on their search. Topsy was to prove a formidable businesswoman with a remarkable grasp of the development of Norman Hartnell Ltd and she was to be appointed a lifetime director together with Normie.

Whatever the exact background to the negotiations, father Bish met the landlord and stumped up the rent in advance with the following advice. 'Try and make this last for twelve months. It is not a case of if you go broke, it is when,' he said grimly.

Whether the hard-nosed Bish exactly said this or not, there is every reason to believe that without Topsy he would not have given his blessing.

As Norman stated: 'My sister had volunteered to oversee everything and I imposed upon the poor girl the combined duties of manageress, receptionist, saleswoman, bookkeeper and stenographer. Her office was a table and a chair behind a grey velvet screen, which kept falling over, revealing her in all her capacities' – or, as a 1950s press release called her, 'Jill-of-all-Trades'. In a 1946 press release we read that 'his sister was already creating dresses which gave Hartnell the opportunity of joining her in this business'.

As some of this release has been deleted in pencil leaving the preceding sentence intact we must assume that Topsy had indeed accepted a job else-where and learnt about dressmaking.[33] With an experienced older sister in charge, Bish's compliance in their scheme seems more explicable: in 1923, £800 was a considerable amount of money at a time when a chauffeur earned £3.10s a week or an indoor servant £2 per week, already double the pre-war rates of pay.[34] The explanation for the screen surrounding Topsy, although rooms were available above, is also explained in a 1940s *Tatler* article drafted by Norman:

> The top floor was my private floor. My father's advice was 'Better to live over your shop than over your income' . . . I sat there in soli-tude until my friends brought in their mothers, sisters and fiancées to see out of curiosity this friend of theirs who had started a shop of women's clothes in London.[35]

Again, this is partially true, partly whimsy and was preceded by a Hartnell success.

Folly burst onto a well-conditioned Cambridge audience at the New The-atre on Monday, 4 June 1923 and ran for seven performances. It was called *A Farcical Foolishness in Three Acts Entitled 'Folly'* (*not* being a sequel to *The Bedder's Opera*) by F.A. Rice and with 'Saul Blackman and his Band' per-forming before Act II. No doubt Dr Ryland's summing up of previous annual productions applied: 'a RAG'.

This revue was set around 'St Tibb's College', 'Rooms, Johnson's Lane' and 'Dibson Paddock', and the musical numbers included 'Why Can't You Love Me?', 'It Ain't the Dons', the inevitable 'May Week', 'The Love of a Boy', 'A Girl in Love' and the intriguing 'Ku Klux Klan', with a ballet thrown in for good measure.

Norman was in the leading female role as 'Gwendolen Bentley (the Dean's daughter)', Blake was 'Miss Blewstock (a Newnhamite)', which reminds us that both Girton and Newnham could have provided adequate females had they been allowed to perform. In the all-male surroundings of Footlights at the time, such an idea would have caused the leading ladies a certain amount of hysteria, and possibly many of the men too. Harold Warrender, whose mother had been so helpful to Norman, was 'Mrs Wroxton (Hugh's mother)', Hugh being 'an Undergraduate'. The hero of the piece was played by C.G. Pilgrim. 'Nada Navarre (an Actress)' and 'Mrs Filcher (a Bedmaker)' were both played by C. Hildyard, and Blake also had a quick change as 'Mrs Dole (a Landlady)'. Chris Hildyard remained a friend of Norman's for the rest of his life and became, like Blake, a clergyman, except that he rose quickly to hold the position of Chaplain at Westminster Abbey. He proved himself an elegantly witty caricaturist, drawing the well-known sketch of:

Mr Hartnell as Gwen
Looks quite pretty now and then.
You will agree that his dresses are divine
Made from his own design!

Wrongly attributed to *The Bedder's Opera* of the previous year in subsequent publications, the drawing has a greater significance for the production obviously occurred at the end of Norman's missing third and degreeless academic year. It is a measure of the friendships he had made and the consideration for his talents that he was so prominent a member of the production. There were perhaps others, like Cecil Beaton, who resented Norman's apparent popularity and success.

The programme notes credit 'Mr Hartnell's costumes, Mr Brown's costume in Act II and Mr Hildyard's [sic] costume in Act III designed and executed by Hartnell, London', the first public appearance of what became a world-famous trademark. This is not of minor significance, for the whole production transferred again to London for a charity matinée performance on 15 June in aid of St Dunstan's at the Strand Theatre. Norman's clothes now received their first London showing from his new London base and the first of his successful charity shows was made – the first of scores. The following day's reviews were led by *The Times*, which remarked on the 'women . . . all good as three different types of womanhood'. Norman's London career as a dressmaker had now been publicly launched.

Back at 10 Bruton Street staff were engaged. From Madame Desirée came the fitter who 'usually wore a moleskin coat, had moles on her face and, believe it or not, her name was Madame Mole'. Emanating from Muswell Hill, she brought some clients with her and was the first of the army of Norman's subsequent employees – over 500 in his heyday. She was joined by six others: Mrs Leach, the Misses Holliday, Griffin, Violet Durling, Mabel Cox and 'little Nellie Todd', who was 'only half a girl' as the regulations allowed only six and a half people to the cubic capacity filled by Norman Hartnell:

'thus only half of her was permitted in the workroom. *In toto* she was against the law' which led to amusing incidents when an inspectress appeared to examine working conditions.

In 1953, Ethel Griffin wrote to Norman 'having very happy memories of those early Bruton Street,'[36] and remembered a Mrs Evans also working there. What were they working on?

In his 1946 press release Norman endorsed, as he did repeatedly, the opinion that 'at this time women's fashions were extremely ugly'. Hartnell did much to restore them to grace and beauty. The photographs of his earliest creations reveal clothes that are of the period but have a style of their own. Expensive fur and embroideries are already apparent, as is a fuller, more flowing line than usual. The silhouette chosen by Madame Lanvin to promote her own business, with its full skirt based upon a truncated crinoline, was one utilised by other designers, and it also intrigued Norman. It had a slightly inflated outline, always layered, fold on tuck; an outer garment drawn over frock.

As a boost to the finances of Norman Hartnell Ltd the famous wartime pin-up Miss Gladys Cooper was granted the lease of the second floor for her newly-launched Beauty Preparations: an immediate example to young Norman of how a successful merchandising policy based on a personality could make money. He also noted that she was dressed by Lucile's former protégé Captain Edward Molyneux, an increasingly successful Paris-based Anglo-Irish designer. Annoyingly, Norman was unable to lure her into his tiny salon as a client.

As Norman was often inspired by fabrics and patterns, like many designers, it was probably no hardship for him to leave Madame Mole and 'her girls' at their work whilst he acted as 'matching boy', looking for the correct materials for his creations. For decades, there existed:

> a wonderful race of women, mostly small girls, who haunt the West End every day in search of correct materials, of the right shade and texture, for the big dressmakers . . . I joined the queues of jostling matchers at Peter Robinson, Bourne & Hollingsworth and John Lewis . . . Not knowing the protocol of the matching world, I would wander up to the head of the queue.
>
> 'Here, what are you doing? – and who do you think you are?' a little Cockney would ask.

'Oh, I'm Hartnell,' I would say with a sickly smile.

'Never heard of you. Anyhow, get to the back of the queue and wait your turn. Go on, do the bird's trick and hop it!'

Forty years later one of the John Lewis staff wrote to Norman reminding him of the days when he had regularly used the shop as a source for fabrics and trimmings. He clearly stood out from the 'matchers'.[37] His designs also stood out, becoming more striking as he sketched

> . . . unwearable dresses. My sister would look over my shoulder: 'Norman, dear, I know that a band of magenta coq feathers stitched across the stomach of an apple-green satin dress is most original, but wouldn't a simple little dress of black wool or brown tweed, or even a grey flannel suit, be . . . nice?'
>
> 'No, it would not! I despise simplicity. It is the negation of all that is beautiful,' I said haughtily.

In the following years some of his most beautiful and acclaimed designs were often the simplest, but for the moment he revelled in colour, texture and intricate workmanship. His salon reflected his taste in clothes: cornflower blue and yellow, it had no hint of any of the modernism already sweeping fashionable Europe. On the floor were large French nineteenth-century marble vases embellished with ormolu mounts and candelabra. The furniture was also in the same taste and the whole atmosphere was French in spirit, just like the other London dress Houses. France was the undoubted leader of fashion and the Ritz style was virtually de rigueur for the best clothes shops. Both ideas were soon to be upset by Norman.

Meanwhile, Blake had come down from Cambridge intent on a career in the theatre. Norman was tired of sharing his private home life with the restrictions of an older sister and in spite of father Bish's flat refusal to finance his son's idea of rooms in St James's, Bish and Blake so arranged their finances that they shared rooms in Bury Street together, just off St James's.

Phyllis and Norman had meanwhile employed a stock-keeper who inhabited a room above the former mews reached by a glazed gangway. With a supply of blank cheques signed by the gullible Norman, the woman helped herself to the firm's cash, instead of paying suppliers for some months. One Friday she disappeared having telephoned everyone to say that Hartnell was nearly bankrupt. Luckily for Norman, clients, suppliers and even Gladys Cooper were all helpful; War Bonds and savings were virtually exhausted and Norman contritely sat down to design 'lots of little black dresses and numerous flannel suits' to appease Phyllis.

Another woman appeared on the scene, another link with Molyneux. 'I am Miss Doherty. I have just left Molyneux in Paris. You, they tell me, are the new genius. I made Molyneux. I can make you.' Lucile had said the same thing to him. 'I reserved the thought that Molyneux might have made himself!' However, she soon found that there were no business books and set up an efficient system. Madame Mole was dismissed and the knowledgeable insistence on a French fitter resulted in the employment of Madame Germaine Davide 'the famous Mam'selle who started with me at £4 a week and soon rose to a salary of £2,000 a year.'

Miss Doherty had not only a clear vision of the running of a successful couture House, but knew that only a truly experienced French fitter could correctly interpret every nuance of the couturier's design. Hartnell needed garments that were well made, on a par with the best French clothes so eagerly sought by discriminating monied British women, who could not imagine anything as good emanating from a British House. This bias did not include tailor-made coats and skirts, although some women thought that Paris was also the only true source for the most elegant and beautifully fitted of these garments. It was ingrained prejudice, largely based on second-rate products in London, which was truly an accepted leader in male clothes.

It should be remembered that Norman could not cut or sew, much less fit a garment. Although he grew to understand and evaluate all the processes involved in the creation of a magnificent dress and thus employed competent experts, in the workrooms he relied on them to interpret his ideas. This was more usual amongst leading designers than is supposed, but his drawings were more exact than most, his embroideries quite often set out by himself from stocks of paillettes, beads or spangles, and his knowledge of how fabrics handled grew all the time. Sometimes he and his assistants painted designs onto fabrics by hand, and always there was the knowledge of how clothes should move, which began with amateur theatricals at home and Mill Hill and was enhanced by his Footlights appearances in his own creations. Many of the famous designers of this century have produced little more than a few strokes of the pen or the brush to delineate a new idea in women's clothing.

Part of Norman's appeal to his clients, Royal or otherwise, lay in his obvious love of producing a delightful sketch including some witty personal touch, at a time when women living far from London often ordered from a selection of sketches. Only Victor Stiebel at this pre-war period had a similar ability, but whereas Stiebel sketches usually have an element of moody stage drama, Norman's are always crisply bright as though under an arc light, as he put it: 'I did not want to be a dressmaker. I never considered myself one, neither do I now. I am a designer and, in 1923, I wanted to be a designer of dresses for the Theatre.' It was the fantasy inherent in theatre that drove him to create his finest clothes for special occasions, not for the everyday clothes that brought in the steady income, the bread and butter. For Norman, it was the jam and honey he was interested in and this could veer dangerously towards a penchant for treacle.

With Blake and other friends, Norman made the rounds of the nightclubs, increasing his circle of acquaintances and knowledge of London Society. Blake was certainly disquieted by his life in London, and he wrote in his diary three years later:

> 23 June 1927: I have been in the throes of reading a really killing, clever and loathsome novel called *Crazy Pavements* by Beverley Nichols, with whom I had the august honour of once supping in Oxford. The novel is about a nice, clean, gold-haired Public School type, called Brian Elme, who becomes contaminated by decadent members of a bad set in London. The book has revolted me but it makes me wonder about my own experience of London when I was careering about there from September 1923 to March 1924. I cannot help contrasting my own experience with that of poor Brian. I shall send this stupid book to my friend, Denis Partington, in Burgos, in order that he may have the satisfaction of sinking it in a Spanish stagnant pool at midnight.[38]

Having been ordained and hating his life in Portsea, Blake was then 'having doubts'. *Crazy Pavements* is a torrid, if not melodramatic, novel in which the writer of a gossip column shares a dreary Marble Arch flat with a faithful friend, clearly in love with him. This friend stands by him as he rushes round London with Bright Young People including 'Lord William', who is as depraved as possible within the limits of a 1927 novel. He is also seduced by a rich girl: 'I'm going to dance with you now. Like a good old lounge-lizard. For hours and hours and hours. Oh, Julia, isn't this priceless.'[39]

Croft-Cooke, whose own sexual predilections led to a spell in prison and inconvenient escapades abroad, wrote that whilst Blake and Bish were sharing rooms, the former 'gained himself a small reputation for extravagant dress and highly unconventional behaviour' At the time, he 'spent a season or two at the Old Vic where . . . he learned little but to do hilarious impersonations of Lilian Baylis'.[40]

Richard Fletcher was firmly part of Norman's milieu and he suggested in late 1923 that Norman should hold a press show. Business had failed to boom and the siblings were depressed. Fletcher and Minnie Hogg made the arrangements, after Fletcher had boasted, 'Norman, you have been dressing Muswell Hill. I will bring you Mayfair!' What this cost Norman is unknown, but when Croft-Cooke and Blake's brother Lincoln went to see Fletcher in a 'highly upholstered' bar in the Haymarket 'he was concerned in gauging our own capacity for immediate disbursement'. They had written a book, wrapper designed by Norman. '"I will *launch* the book," he asserted grandly and with such conviction that we could almost see a royal personage breaking a bottle of champagne over its bows.'[41] They were disappointed, but Norman was not.

As the creation of dresses for the March show proceeded Norman Hartnell Ltd acquired two new ingredients of polar opposites. The first was another threat of extinction, when one of the large fabric suppliers unpaid by Norman's thieving magpie demanded payment in full. The second was a remarkable 'busy little body called Louie', who was to stay with the firm until she left him to assist Norman's former right-hand and consummate sketch artist Ian Thomas, shortly after he set up by himself. Christened Louise, the typically Norman name of 'Louie' stuck. Her mother may have hated it, but she was to become 'Miss Louie' and remain so in spite of subsequent marriage.[42]

Norman's creations for 1924 – 'some were frightful, some were beautiful' – literally hung by a thread as he kept the terrible threat to the fledgling business secret. His father was roaming around in the South of France and could only be contacted with difficulty. Topsy and Normie were children again, anxiously awaiting a letter from their father, and none came. The show had to go on and Norman, who had been given ten days' grace, worked to complete the forty-seven models: 'In some schizophrenic way I managed to split and freeze the one half of my mind that was in the grip of financial terror and apply the active half to the creative effort.'[43] Sadly, this was to be the foretaste of many similar crises he was to face over the next fifty-four long years in which he remained in business. It can now be seen as an inoculation against fear of failure.

The day of the show was actually in February 1924 (Norman's dates were again out – numbers were not his favourite thing) and was notable for several momentous events for Norman and Phyllis, as well as Miss Doherty, Mam'selle and her girls. Sidonie Goossens plucked her harp strings and a small black boy tricked out like a carved Nubian figure, then a fashionable drawing-room object, opened the grey velvet draperies on the grey velvet stage. Long-stemmed lilacs filled out the corners of the room and the Fletcher–Hogg invitees trouped in and began to drink tea. Norman began his habit of avoiding his public and peeped through the draperies and screens that concealed the mannequins changing area.

The introduction of Epstein's famous model Dolores as one of the mannequins was newsworthy in itself and she wore the more 'statuesque' models of the amazing variety Norman provided. Although his day clothes were attractive, it was the evening clothes that invariably caught the attention of everyone.

As Miss Goossens deftly plucked away, a parade of 'tea gowns of pink satin and pearls or lilac lace' alternated with

> a foaming band of shaded blue grey . . . stitched onto the hem of periwinkle blue velvet, rose ostrich fronds to pale pink lace and one outrageous garment was emblazoned with a gilt thread dragon. The colour beige was everywhere . . . Silver tissues were hung with cascades of crystal fringe that fell from a girdle of diamonds and sapphires.

Printed sketches depict the trailing velvets edged with sables caught up at the side, often with trains lined with gilt tissue or caught in bows at the base of the rear décolletage.[44]

Hauled out from behind the screens by his sister, Norman met Lady Kimberley, Lady Massereene and Ferrard,

> the lovely Lady Lavery and the unforgettable Lady Oxford and Asquith – taut and slender – dressed in grey and the colour of cigarette ash all over. Her intelligent face in profile was a piece of fine

fretwork. She spoke in a deep mellow voice: 'My dear young man, you've had a beautiful day and your future should be beautiful too. The golden ball is at your feet – now kick it!' I promised to kick it as hard as I could.

Whilst escorting her to the door, as if by magic the reprieve came by post from his father with 'a small letter of admonishment', which one longs to have survived.

The next day Norman visited his mother's grave in Clayton, Sussex with lilacs from the salon and saw his name in the papers at Victoria Station. From Magdalene to Mayfair 'light' and 'blue' were dancing in front of his eyes as the train sped out of London into the countryside.[45]

Ever ready for novelty, Norman found himself in demand by the newspapers and journals for the rest of his life and he seldom disappointed them. Dolores was not slow in giving her own opinions: 'Women are Clothes Hangers' she told the *Daily Sketch* on 29 February 1924, 'the average society woman dresses very badly . . . London business girls dress neatly and carefully . . . because they have little money and so cannot overdress . . . short skirts are hideous. Legs are never pretty after a girl has left childhood days behind.'

All this is a perfect reflection of the Hartnell dress philosophy:

> Dresses should be a part of the woman and not the woman a part of the dress. When one meets a woman, one should first see how beautiful she is, and then note how perfect a setting she has in her dress. My favourite woman's dress is the sari . . . It is simply wrapped around the body and then on to the head.

Norman was to say much the same thing over the succeeding decades, although he was to indulge many clients in skilful camouflage too. No doubt he particularly appreciated Dolores's parting blast: 'Shingling is hideous, and reminds me of nothing on earth more than of a female impersonator with his wig off.'[46]

Success came literally overnight, but a throng did not appear immediately clamouring for beautiful dresses, although a steady trickle of well-connected women began to order from him. He also had good links to the journals widely read by the fashionable and rich. For example, *The Bystander,* an established magazine long before its amalgamation with *Tatler,* profiled him and his collection on 12 March 1924 and included two sketches, whilst noting that 'he was a prominent member of the Marlowe Society and a caricaturist and poster designer of skill'. This was at least a variant on the 'young Cambridge graduate' tag that lasted for well over a decade.

Although orders for Ascot and the autumn accumulated, Norman was to be found in Brighton on Saturday, 20 December. An advertisement announced discreetly to the readers of the *Sussex Daily News* that 'Norman Hartnell – The Young Cambridge Undergraduate Dress Artist – will present a small collection recently designed for Christmas at the Metropole Hotel.' Bish was not taking any further chances with his investment and undoubtedly encouraged his Brighton friends to turn up. The owner of the Metropole was a good friend of his, but the 'Cambridge Undergraduate' touch two years after his son had ceased his academic career seems more than overanxious.[46]

Yet, Norman's career did flourish throughout 1925. Blake left London life for Oxford determined to take Holy Orders – 'I was then youthfully eager to preach to bring gaiety, as Christ did, into the stale and dreary corners etc.'[47] –the Bury Street rooms were abandoned and Norman was now free to cast off the undergraduate tag and kick the 'golden ball' hard.

CHAPTER FOUR

When London was lovely

Whilst Norman had been struggling to establish himself as a successful designer and businessman, several events which were to affect his future life in dramatic ways occurred. A few doors away from his Bruton Street premises, on 26 April 1923 a future Queen of England, Lady Elizabeth Bowes-Lyon, left her parents' house at no. 17 and was driven to Westminster Abbey, where she and the Duke of York were married. Unknown to all of them, one of Norman's most illustrious future clients was already living in the street that was to continually bring him good luck.

Whilst he was agonising over his future, he naturally noted the bride's dress, which came from the well-established and dignified Court Dressmaker, Handley-Seymour Ltd, holders of a Royal Warrant to Queen Mary. The firm of Reville-Terry, another of Queen Mary's dressmakers, had supplied the Princess Royal's wedding dress the previous year. This had revived the ancient custom of using silver tissue as the basis of the garment, which Reville then embellished with embroidery worked in a trellis pattern of roses. This was on an overskirt of marquisette, using pearl beads highlighted by paste beads, enclosed in a girdle encircling the waist. The satin train was embroidered in India with silver lotus flowers, the Royal family links extended to the use of the veil formerly used by Queen Mary. The dress could scarcely be termed in the vanguard of fashion. However, the line was modern and it embodied a symbolic traditionalism with echoes of fifteenth-century depictions of dress.

Similarly, the dress of the future Duchess of York echoed the past with some deference to current fashion. The loosely fitted line of the straight-up-and-down skirt was gathered at the waist with a few tucks in the chiffon moiré around the natural waistline. An historic, slightly medieval girdle effect was created by embroidering a band of worked silver lamé around the waist and down the front of the skirt. This was also embroidered with seed pearls

77

on bands of horizontal 'smoked' strips across the bodice. The dress had short sleeves and, as an unusual innovation, two trains – one of which was from the waistline in the same fabric as the dress; the other of floating tulle from the shoulders. It is the wearing of the veil in the form of a soft cloche clamped down with flowers and leaves which now most dates the design.[1]

These two royal weddings and clothes worn by Queen Mary on a State Visit to Italy in May were followed by the marriage of Lady Mary Cambridge (a niece of Queen Mary) to the heir of the Duke of Beaufort. This focused attention on royal dress and glamorously unusual wedding dresses, particularly as the year 1923 also witnessed the marriage of the future Queen Louise of Sweden (1889–1965), Lady Louise Mountbatten, to the widower Crown Prince of Sweden in the Chapel Royal. Her wedding dress was startling: beautifully cut from the squared neck to the fashionable dropped waist decorated with faux orange blossoms formed as a lover's knot to the wrap-over skirt made of Indian silver gauze. The orange blossom motifs in silver thread descended down the dress with a twelve-foot-long train, covered at the top by an ermine capelet. As another modern interpretation of historic dress, the tiara – worn low as a bandeau – was made from a wired lattice shape incorporating orange-blossom buds, anchoring the heavy Honiton lace veil. Cape and veil were family possessions and the silk tissue was a family present. The originality and symbolism of the apparently simple design of this modern interpretation of earlier dress was not lost on the public, nor on Norman Hartnell.

Undoubtedly, Norman must have longed to design for the illustrious ladies of the Royal Family, then an unattainable goal for a new name and type of business amongst the established London dress Houses and designers. In *Silver and Gold* Norman wrote that the star wedding dress of his first 1924 dress show had been bought by Daphne Vivian. Had this been so, he would have earned more clients far sooner. With his propensity for muddling dates, the dress was in fact in his 1927 collection and 1924 proved to be a tough year.

Norman could eye Noël Coward's continuing success on the stage in *The Vortex* after his *London Calling!* of 1923, which included rows of chorus girls, none of them dressed by him. The London theatre was alive with successful, lavishly dressed productions, none of them particularly interested in young Hartnell's creations. This was partly because, although Norman's clothes were innovative, they were too different for those wishing to be in the Parisian mode.

As Norman said to Beverley Nichols in 1958, whilst looking at tubular-shaped women in his albums, 'If Sabrina had lived in those days, she would have been obliged to stay indoors'. (Nichols explained to his readers that Sabrina was the young lady with 'a highly developed chest', the attribute of much popular 1950s fashion.)[2]

Most of Norman's new clients seemed on the verge of fading away with his dreams of lovely wedding dresses and trousseaux until, by luck, someone alerted Miss Barbara Cartland to the shiny new dressmaker in Bruton Street. Already known as a novelist and journalist, Miss Cartland was one of three children left with their war-widowed mother in rather unfortunate circumstances. Miss Cartland used her brains and beauty, coupled with great vitality, to extricate herself and her family from the financial difficulties they were in and by 1925 was famously succeeding as an innovative 'modern' woman.

It was rapidly becoming a period of pageants and semi-amateur theatricals in aid of charity. If a duke's daughter, Lady Diana Cooper, could tread the boards in *The Miracle* then the home charades of pre-war days could clearly take to the public stage, albeit in controlled circumstances. Miss Cartland's 1924 appearance was in a huge show, *Chiquita*, at Covent Garden. She then appeared in a three-legged dance at Daly's and later became involved with *The Mayfair Revue* of 1925, which was held in the Hotel Cecil on the Strand. Norman's talents were sought: 'He was good-looking, enthusiastic, eager and so charming that everyone wanted to help him. He certainly produced the most attractive clothes and he was delighted to make gowns for the cast very cheaply.'

One talented fighter recognised another, as she later wrote: 'Norman, can you design dresses for Lord Bethell's daughters? They are doing a song and dance.'

'Of course, will they pay?'

'Yes, a reasonable amount and they are certain to send you their friends.'

'Splendid, I'll draw something for them to see. Do you think £8 for each dress will be too much?'

The dresses turned out to be so beautiful that they were stolen after the dress rehearsal and all the girls had to rush out to buy replacements, so Norman's clothes had still not achieved a return to the public stage since *Folly*. However, Miss Cartland and her mother soon ordered clothes from Norman for their Presentations on 22 May 1925 at 9.30 pm. That of Miss Barbara Cartland was to the mid-calf with a fashionable dropped waist, and whilst conforming to the regulations governing correct 'Court Dress *with* feathers and trains' it had bands of embroidery in a V from the shoulders to a large motif at the waist where the fabric was gathered from all directions. Her train was edged with chinchilla, whereas Mrs Cartland had the prescribed flimsy drapery from her shoulders, Miss Cartland's white dress had a trellis pattern of paillettes and diamanté, the pleated dropped skirt embellished with diamanté loops. Some favourite decorative devices of Norman's were already being used. Sadly, Mrs Cartland complained that the £12 she paid Norman for her dress was too much and all the way to the Palace she told her patient daughter that Norman had overcharged her. Norman's path was not easy at the best of times.[3]

Miss Louie remembered that the Hartnell 10 Bruton Street house was a happy, close-knit environment in which Phyllis had extra assistance from Constance Barnett, the cousin for whom Norman had produced a pantomime-prize dress as a child. She would also model Hartnell clothes for shows and photographic shoots for newspapers. Their hours were from 9 am until 6 pm and Saturday mornings. Norman and Phyllis often had a sandwich with the workroom staff and later in the 1930s, when there was a staff canteen, he would sometimes have a cup of tea or coffee there, but he would say sternly, 'Never in the stockroom!'[4]

Norman was always jolly and hardly ever seen in a bad mood. He would joke with Miss Louie, once saying of her to a visitor, 'Sorry she's so short, but she's intelligent.' Miss Louie observed that 'he did not realise how clever he was'; similarly, he did not perhaps fully understand just how much he owed to his father, who was always 'very helpful'. Both seemed ashamed of each other. Bish of Norman 'because he was gay' and Norman of Bish 'because he was quite loud . . . a man's man.' When the 1960s episode of *This Is Your Life* on him was cancelled, Norman remained sensitive about his origins and expressed his relief to Miss Louie that his early days would remain nebulous. She told him that 'he should be grateful for his parents.'

Obviously fond of one another, their working relationship proved highly successful. It had only begun when the fourteen-year-old Louise had taken the place of Winnie, a young girl who had fallen ill. Louise went along 'to keep the job free'. Sadly, Winnie died so Louie stayed on and did everything. However, as a sewer who turned out to be left-handed in a time when everything was done right-handed, she did not carry on sewing but busied herself around the place. She became a matcher and then, by the early 1930s, was in charge of the stockroom and the costings that went towards the making-up of the all-important invoices. She was able to observe the business growing and the way in which an experienced fitter such as the famous Mam'selle Davide would become a crucial part of the process in creating a perfectly cut and fitted hand-made garment.

'She was wonderful – a sewer *and* fitter', Louie stressed, but Mam'selle knew her worth for when she had family trouble in Paris and then left, the business slipped, and when she came back she made Mr Hartnell pay much more money. With one leg shorter than the other, work could not have been easy for Mam'selle, but she remained with him for three decades in spite of attempts by others to lure her away.[4]

When at no. 10 (until 1934), the business expanded so that extra rooms were taken either side of Bruton Place, the mews running behind the future building across the street at no. 26. One was for the fitter and the other for embroidery, which increasingly absorbed Norman – 'he half lived there and would direct the girls on the frames'. If there is one thing for which Hartnell stood out above his rivals it was the quality and variety of the embroideries, always produced in house.[5]

Given the London competition and the weightier design lead of Paris, it was imperative that Norman achieved his own look with a fashionable clientele as swiftly as possible. This was as much of a problem in 1925 as in 1924. One source of effective free publicity lay in the descriptions of his designs and those of others as worn by those presented to Their Majesties. Brief descriptions accompanied these in the newspapers and fashion editors combed them for potential copy. Illustrated fashion magazines were also influential, but Norman had no extra money to take advertising at this stage and so could not buy his way into them. But if his photographed designs of 1925 as worn on mannequins showed little to knock out Parisian competition, this was as much the result of the static poses and the often-generous nature of the mannequins' figures. Poiret, Patou, Chanel and Molyneux were then the *Vogue* stars, with others such as Lelong, Lanvin or Worth not far behind. The point has to be stressed that no matter how the readers' taste ranked the French competition, it was better trained, better organised, more innovative and thus more influential, also having more immediate access to the latest fabrics and accessories. It also had the ambience of Paris.

Paris breathed fashion and drew the most fashionably elegant clients to its products from all over the world. As Mam'selle snapped one day at a worried

Norman: 'Every English lady wishes something that is French. If it were not for the pure beauty of your dresses you would not sell a single one.'[6] By which she also meant 'my fitting brings the whole darn thing together and makes it wearable, so don't forget it'. Norman no doubt kept an eye on any potential opposition in Paris and closely at home and would have noted the undergraduate Cecil Beaton's accomplished designs for new Cambridge productions, and his publicised twenty-first birthday dance in his parents' house at 3 Hyde Park Street, W2 in January.

Suddenly, almost in spite of the opposition, orders came in. The Earl Beauchamp, a notable figure of the period with beautiful daughters, appeared at no. 10 in order to choose dresses for his wife and daughters as 1925 Christmas presents. A delighted Norman told the press, 'Dresses were shown him and displayed by the mannequins and he selected all three, and even chose the shades of the material with which they are to be made.'[7] Some months before, his wife and daughters had visited the salon and Lady Lettice Lygon, the eldest daughter, had already ordered clothes so measurements were on hand for the garments.

This was to be the beginning of Norman's fame. In July 1926, for a costume ball held at Hampden House given by the Duchess of Sutherland, Lady Lettice Lygon appeared in 'the marvellous c18th frock . . . of Romney blue taffeta, the skirt had been lavishly printed with bouquets of lilac roses, cornflowers and daises and the lace underdress had little pink ribbon bows and roses'. Norman had painted the designs himself at night 'and it is quite the fashion to have clothes designed and painted by him in his dress salon in Bruton Street.'[8]

Before his sensational costume design appeared, Norman had created a whole series of dresses for Court and Ascot. Lady Lettice, now one of his main supporters, appeared as the first to wear 'a new greenish silvery blue shade' created by Norman from studies of the blue used by Leonardo da Vinci 'and which is so becoming to red gold hair and high colouring'. His Ascot dresses and colourings were all arranged in the open air and with verdure for a background. These were not designed in a showroom, the first intimation of Norman's love of a quiet countrified setting as a workplace for designing and inspiration, later achieved at Lovel Dene, his house in Windsor Forest.

For summer 1926 he favoured picture dresses and large hats. 'Mannish modes are being gradually swamped by the attractive young women,' he said, and it was to them that he turned his attention.

Amongst many new innovative photographers to click with Hartnell was Madame Yevonde, and a photograph of hers from late 1925 was published in *The Bystander* of January 1926. It shows Lady Lettice in a satin-sheathed bodice held by tiny straps with fabric flowers, repeated on the net overskirt, which hangs over a full pleated skirt. Norman has played down the trimmings and concentrated on the line, so that when *Vogue* (UK) finally gave him a full page in early May 1927 his design was captured by another talented portrait photographer Hugh Cecil in semi-profile. 'A bouffant *robe de style* of pale blue taffeta' is a curious way of describing a knee-length 1920s creation, but it is covered with hand-painted flowers in shades of orchid, blue and white with a taffeta surplice ending in a bow above a pine chiffon bodice. This is a sophisticated design, preceded by his use of new Bianchi fabrics in autumn 1926, in which the red, black and white velvets are on a chiffon ground and the outline is simple, although trimmings of flying fox add weight.

Innovative photographers were always attracted to Norman Hartnell and he to them throughout his long career. It was a fascination with the latest printing techniques that led them all to utilise the many illustrated magazines in a period when even the most modest person might go to a studio for a photographic portrait. These were not only displayed at home but given to family and friends. The journals encouraged such portraits of personalities – Madame Yevonde, for example, provided journals and subjects with fascinating studies of women and men, especially fashionable women wearing the latest fashions.

Norman had studied, indeed devoured, such magazines since boyhood and by March 1926 was attracting considerable press publicity – 'to hold a collection at the private view of a dress parade is an original method of benefitting charity. It is the idea of Mr Norman Hartnell, who is soliciting funds for the Royal Northern Hospital today at his salon'[9] and 'those attending the show included Lady Asquith, Tallulah Bankhead, Athene Seyler, H.G. Wells and Norman's Cambridge friend M. 'Dar' Lyon. His stepsister's daughter Suzanne Kilner, aged four, was attired as Little Red Riding Hood and collected the money in half-crowns.'[10] and by May:

> although he is so young Mr Hartnell has a genius for designing and personality, and chic is expressed in every one of his models, the lines of which are perfection. Every gown shown was expressive of the Englishwoman at her very best and all were designed by Mr

Hartnell alone and made by British workers. Miss Barbara Cartland in mauve, with furs, was greatly interested in the display.[11]

All the elements of his future success seem encapsulated in this item: Norman was young, personable, talented, with beautiful admirers, and *British*. He must have been a breath of fresh air in the London fashion world so dominated by the older Houses, department stores and the innumerable 'Madam' shops catering to so many 'little women round the corner'.

Norman was also aware of every nuance in fashionable life by now, as seen in one of his earliest surviving evening dresses to be found in the Museum of London. It is the outer covering of a mid-1920s two-tiered waistless evening dress with a tabard-like effect. The inner fragile silk dress has not survived, but the outer sections forming the tabard are decorated by luxuriously beaded chinoiserie-inspired panels of embroidery. Sadly, the client is now unknown, but perhaps played the fashionable mah-jong or owned an Oriental inspired room. Like other surviving Hartnell dresses of the period, it evokes the Jazz Age and gives the lie to his own later dismissal of his early work and the 1920s.

By June 1926 *The Sphere* determined that Norman was 'a Dreaming Galahad' with a photographic portrait to bear witness to this and a résumé of his bold thoughts on British and French fashion:

> to redeem English dress from the thraldom of France may be set down as the mission of Mr Norman Hartnell, the threshold of whose dressmaking establishment – he would gnash his teeth were it described as a salon – no French model has passed from his workshop to a client. Just as French women look best in French frocks, so he maintains Englishwomen must look better in frocks designed by English hands. He is probably the only English university man who has taken up dressmaking, and is the youngest in the direct line of succession to Worth, who astonished the modern world as its first male modiste. Although he has never had a drawing lesson in his life Mr Hartnell makes all his own designs.

The interviewer then mentioned *The Bedder's Opera* 'which ran for one hilarious afternoon at Daly's Theatre' and gave further insight into young Norman's attitude to dress: 'the secret of his remarkable success partly lies in dyeing fabrics specially to colours he sees in his imagination.' As we see, by 1926 Norman was considered an original and successful designer by the established press.

By this date Barbara Cartland was already a considerable celebrity, beloved by journalists looking for stories based on good-looking, enterprising women. She designed her own long tulle wedding dress made by Hartnell for her wedding on 23 April 1927, exactly four years to the day since Norman and Phyllis had decided to join together as a business partnership. Dame Barbara claimed that hers was the first tulle wedding dress to be made since the war but also wished that Norman had designed it. The tier on tier of tulle ruffles hung limply in repose but appear to advantage in photographs of her walking on the arm of her first husband Alistair McCorquodale, with the bevy of bridesmaids in shaded pink.

Norman's other wedding commission of importance in that year was for some of the trousseaux of Miss Jean Brooke's niece of the Rajah of Sarawak, who married Lieutenant T.E. Halsey, RN, nephew of the Prince of Wales' Treasurer and Comptroller. Weddings were always to prove a spectacular outlet for his creative energies, which were let loose in unlikely ways:

> He was showing yesterday a frock trimmed with melon seeds. He had seen a string of melon pips round the neck of little niece . . . so he had them painted and stitched on to his gowns as trimming. Steel and brass nail tops . . . and a collar made of plaited string ironed out flat, which had the appearance of heavy beige lace.[12]

It was around this time that Norman sat out a dance on the stairs with Oliver Messel's beautiful young sister Anne. 'Yes, when I first met you, you were exquisitely pretty' he wrote to her in 1977[13] and she returned the compliment in 1985 when she wrote a foreword to the Brighton retrospective devoted to Norman's life and work. 'Dear, kind Norman never made a client feel anything but a fairy princess.'[14] She was to wear some of his best 1920s dresses and Norman remembered them all fifty years later.

By now Norman had a small Mayfair flat in Clarges Street. Photographs were taken of him there for press interviews and there is little sense of interior decoration, apart from heavy curtains and pelmets. The drawing room resembles early 1920s college rooms, almost a set for a Footlights revue, as it includes reproduction oak furniture, a Knole settee and little else of interest. It is the flat of one who is usually out, as Norman was, only using it to sleep in.

Despite these triumphs, his lack of full success rankled. It was scarcely enough to read in the papers the list of those presented in his dresses and the meagre attentions of the fashion press. It still rankled that women would come to his salon, admire the clothes and even order something before asking the name of the designer.

It was quite usual for London dressmakers and shops to buy models from the more famous Paris Houses. Then would come the question: 'By the way, whose model is it?' Norman would tell them his own and interest would fade away – 'Not a French model . . . Good afternoon.' As he put it: 'I suffered from the unforgivable disadvantage of being English in England.' He also realised that American buyers went to Paris in February and August for the new collections: London was scarcely on the map, but he was virtually the only young independent British designer.[15]

Furthermore, 1926 had been a particularly bad year because Britain had been rocked by the General Strike, when it seemed as though the whole nation would be paralysed and members of the middle and upper classes manned transport and helped with deliveries of supplies. This escaped Norman's notice in *Silver and Gold*, but it must have badly affected his business in common with others.

Apart from this, the appeal of London to the influential editions of the journal *Vogue* was slim. *Harpers* gave Norman some good publicity with de Meyer photography, but as for *Vogue*: 'It may be the climate, it may be the English cooking, but whatever the reason, members of the American staff have never clamoured to work in the offices of British *Vogue* as they clamour for a shot at our French colleague,'[16] wrote the doyenne of *Vogue*, Edna Woolman Chase, in 1954. English *Vogue* under Dorothy Todd in the 1920s became more of a literary and arts journal than a lucrative fashion journal, so Englishwomen took French *Vogue* for fashion news. There were certainly other journals and papers, but *Vogue* had superb production values and more cachet. It was not doing its job properly in Hartnell's view, but in the 1920s, with the exception of young Norman, there were *no* other young original London designers at work in the couture sphere until Victor Stiebel opened in 1932. As we have seen, Norman was a lonely trailblazer, which also helped him. Even the wholesale houses were thought to be half a generation behind those of America in design and manufacture.[17]

Norman therefore decided to follow his nineteenth-century predecessor

Worth and hold a show in Paris. If Worth and Molyneux could do it, why not he? Lucile and Creed were also examples of English taste transported to French soil, the latter firm flourishing in the 1920s. It must have cost Norman sleepless nights in obtaining the agreement of both Phyllis and Bish to his scheme: 'It was a flashy but brave little gesture actuated by complete ignorance of what lay ahead of me . . . I flew to Paris . . . to make arrangements for my first show . . . and I landed up to my neck in trouble!'[18]

This trip was well orchestrated with Richard Fletcher. Newsreel showed Hartnell and the plane setting off for a Norman Conquest in reverse. In Paris, Monsieur Armbruster, director of the new Plaza Athénée, arranged for Norman to have a small room for his displays off the central flower-filled courtyard. Armbruster agreed to arrange all the necessary details, and Norman returned to London to finish his collection for a show on 5 August on the same day as Worth, Champcommunal and Brialix.

Norman was placed with some good competition. Elspeth Champcommunal (a native Scot) would later work in London, notably for Worth. Brialix, on the other hand, was formed from the small Maison Anna and faded away in the 1930s.

Yet Trouble Came, the title of one of Blake's novels, could be the title of the indignities to which the Hartnell group of partners and mannequins were subjected after their eventual Channel crossing. Norman had asked the French Consul's office in London to tell him of the necessary formalities for the import of his clothes into France. 'None,' he had been told, only to be faced with French Customs demanding his '*patente*', a licence permitting temporary trading in France.

He had one day left before his show and went to the Ritz, where he met by chance Evan Morgan, future Lord Tredegar, who managed to make an appointment for Norman to see his cousin Sir Eric Phipps, the British Minister, the following morning at 11 am. Sir Eric made the necessary arrangements and Norman returned to Customs: 'They had apparently received a telephone call which had not left them in the most amicable of tempers. Our trunks were opened out on the damp, dirty floor, which looked as if a herd of cattle had been the last passengers through the customs. Out poured . . . our precious models.'[19]

These were whisked by taxis to the Plaza Athénée, and there ninety-five dresses appeared on his two mannequins – Eileen, a brunette, and Shirley, a blonde. The press was kind.

Capt. Molyneux and other English dressmakers have established themselves amid a Parisian environment. Mr Hartnell, however, is making a more direct attack on the citadel. There is in his titles no compromise with French names 'Country Cousin', 'Forty Winks', 'Up-to-Town' and 'Tinker Bell' – the last mentioned an evening gown in ripe peach satin, veiled with gold lace appliquéd tulle to match the peach foundation. Only at the sides is any effort made to reach the ankle and these flowing draperies give the uneven hem that is fashionable and the longer skirt-line that some English and Parisian dressmakers are now encouraging.[20]

An American journalist wrote: 'He also considered several different patterned fabrics in one ensemble, as plain angora and satin . . . plain and patterned velvets and fancy velvets.'[21] Another noted: 'Fitted Bodices Appear . . . black Ciré Spanish lace dresses . . . ostrich . . . sports costumes of Scotch tweeds . . . fur with a stole-like end around the neck.'[22] Yet another noted, 'Mr Hartnell told me that being short of a mannequin he naively appealed to a big dressmaker to lend him one! She nearly went through the floor! The Parisian dressmaker despises English clothes and is a little afraid of them as well.'[23] The latter comment is most intriguing and significant.

Much was made of Hartnell's names for his models, which were to be a feature of his shows for the next fifty years. 'All Aboard', 'Follow Me' and 'Highland Lass' were coat, skirt and jumper designs. 'Rosy Posy' was a pink taffeta and leaf-green tulle dress. 'Goosey Gander', 'Miss Muffet', 'Jam Slice' and 'Little Pickle' were other typically Norman names, often dreamt up by him and sometimes by girls in the workroom. These dresses also had something his French rivals lacked: the small lead *plomb* of the customs officials!

One thing became clear: insufficient advance press coverage had resulted in a small turnout of buyers, the Americans scarcely aware of any 'English fashion'. But one buyer, Herman Patrick Tappé, bought a copy of a wedding dress Norman had made for a forthcoming autumn 1927 wedding and a tweed suit, 'Country Cousin'.

After the show, an American approached Norman and told him that 'Goosey Gander' was the best black lace dress in Paris. He was Main Bocher, later famous as the designer of the wedding dress for the Duchess of Windsor, but then as editor of Paris *Vogue*. Norman was flattered as 'it is hard to invest a black lace dress with any quality of novelty. Here is the criterion by which women unconsciously judge a true designer's skill.'[24]

The other important part of the advice Norman was told over dinner by the man (later to be famous as a designer in his own right and not only for their mutual client Mrs Simpson), echoes back again and again in Norman's career: 'I have never seen so many incredibly beautiful dresses so incredibly badly made.' This was one in the eye for Mam'selle and her girls but should also have taught Norman to keep a closer eye on workmanship. Unlike Chanel, he was not versed in dressmaking, nor in the habit of pulling garments to pieces. Certainly, he could not have correctly placed misaligned sleeves, nor did he have a prop in the form of Vionnet's celebrated wooden doll. Draping fabric on furniture, dummies or pinning it on curtains or across mannequins was the limit of Norman's physical capabilities as a 'dressmaker'. He was foremost a designer and as such he returned home to notable press acclaim, which also impressed clients and American buyers. Whilst determined to pay a return visit to Paris, he now had two full-scale glamorous weddings in hand, both of which were minor sensations during the autumn of 1927.

Back from Paris, Norman set off for a walking tour of Devon, sketchbook in hand 'going back to Nature' to inspire his autumn collection. 'I have no use for dresses chiefly for the young and pretty set, that includes Lady Lettice and Lady Sibell Lygon.'[25]

The marriage of Miss Daphne Vivian to Lord Weymouth, heir to the Marquess of Bath, had secretly taken place in 1926 but a public ceremony was timed for 27 October at St Martin-in-the-Fields. Her great-aunt Susan Holford 'lent me Dorchester House for the reception, and Norman Hartnell who had made many clothes for her friend Lady Lettice Lygon, asked her to visit him to look at his wedding dresses. At the final fitting Cecil Beaton took photographs in Norman's salon of the bridal gown.'[26,27]

This may well have been Beaton's first visit to the 'horrid Norman Hartnell's' salon, although he was to photograph Norman's creations on many occasions in the future. There was little rapport between the two and barely a mention or a word of praise from Beaton in his diaries or writings. Beaton clearly professionally chose to ignore most English designers in favour of Paris and his life was certainly made interesting as he executed this policy. However, jealousy seems to have burst out of Beaton's being whenever he saw success, as he noted in his unpublished diary for 26 February 1926: 'Lady Doniville . . . was lunching with that awful young Barbara Cartland whose housemaid novels of Mayfair are such a success. I think B.C. is one of the most awful snobs. Thoroughly precocious and ugly.'[28]

As Beaton was almost three years younger than Barbara Cartland, his remark seems even more spiteful and it seems as though the two men did not meet on this occasion. Norman 'was laid low by flu and was in bed when he should, by rights, have been attending the conference on satin and orange blossom', as the final details were discussed over the wedding dress of white net over a silver sheath, with gold and silver fleur-de-lys and garlands of laurel leaves scattered over it.

Norman designed medieval-style doublets of red velvet and gold for the pages, and the bridesmaids wore gold dresses with wimples and crimson roses. The *Evening Standard* loyally wrote that it was 'one of the loveliest bridal ensembles that has ever left 10 Bruton Street'[29] as though Norman had been in business for more than three short years. Norman undoubtedly remembered his visit to the same church with Richard Fletcher after their unsuccessful attempt to storm the doors of one of the grandest of the older Court Dressmakers. Now he was listed amongst the guests, as was Mrs A. McCorquodale (Barbara Cartland) and a varied cross section of well-known names (amongst whom were Nancy Mitford and Lady Cunard), including Lady Sibell Lygon and also Lady Mary Thynne, Norman's next 'bride', the sister of Lord Weymouth. [29]

This wedding was held in St Margaret's, Westminster, and it was noted that Lady Mary, who was engaged to Lord Nunburnholme, had been a brides-maid of both the Princess Royal and the Duchess of York. Norman now pulled out all the stops. 'From an early 14th Century picture in the National Gallery [he] derived the inspiration which enabled him to design one of the most picturesque gowns ever worn by a bride.'[30]

Norman stated:

> .....The picture of *The Marriage of the Virgin* by an Italian master gave me the idea for the bodice of the wedding dress. The design for the rest of the gown is, however, entirely original. The dress is made in ivory panne velvet, with a very full skirt attached to a long plain bodice. The long sleeves and the high neckline are outlined with embroidery of pearls and silver. The skirt touches the ground, but there is a very long train of velvet in which there is a design of Gothic arches in silver tissue.

The painting by Niccolò Buonaccorso (no. 1, 109) was suggested to Norman as a source of inspiration as he sat 'chewing his pencil' trying to think of a better design than the one 'lavished' on Lady Weymouth's dress.[31] The bride was photographed in her dress before the wedding and the pictures were widely published. Eight hundred guests were asked so that this wedding was an even grander affair than Lord Weymouth's. The bride received a ruby and diamond pendant from the King and Queen, the Princess Royal sent an antique clock and the Duchess of York a diamond brooch. The Duchess could have hardly overlooked the design of the dress with its attendant publicity and had returned as a Hartnell neighbour to Bruton Street, where Princess Elizabeth, now the Queen, was born on 21 April 1926.

The spectacle of such a wedding was treated as a form of street theatre by the public in those days. 'Thousands of women and a great many men stood four and five deep round the railings of the church in the hope of catching a glimpse of the bride. Extra police were called into service, and mounted men helped to regulate the crowd.'[32]

This was indeed the best street theatre and Norman must have been gratified to see his design finally at the centre of such an event. Although he makes no mention of his design in *Silver and Gold*, the faithful 'Corisande' produced a full-length sketch by Dorothy Thatcher and mentioned the silver dresses of the bridesmaids and tabards of the pages emblazoned with their family arms, all designed by Norman. Other headlines included 'A White Bride on a Grey Day', 'Police Find Difficulty in Making Path for Bride', 'Several Women Faint', 'Court Mourning for the Marquess of Cambridge Prevented Queen Mary from Attending', no doubt a blow to Norman, who could be consoled by 'Crowds Cheer a Beautiful Bride – Almost a Royal Ovation for Lady Mary Thynne!'

Public, press and Norman had a field day, even if the *Sheffield Independent*'s correspondent brought things down to earth by writing of the private view of the dresses beforehand: 'It occurred to me how many snacks one gets on a really busy day of meetings, private views and parties in London during the Little Season. There really is no need for any solid meals at all.'[33] It was not simply a struggle for Norman to attract overseas attention; the standard of provincial fashion reporting was also due for a shake-up.

With the dress for Lady Mary Thynne, Norman had established himself primarily as a designer of wedding dresses. Virtually all the newspaper reports mention this 'speciality', but they also dwell on the fact that he was virtually a lone male in a female world – 'quite the dress oracle of the ultra smart set.'[33]

He seemed to be the best alternative to the older established houses: Daphne Vivian had been taken to Ospovat, also used by Lady Diana Cooper, as well as to others such as Reville. Apart from all the listed 'court dress-makers' and the larger department stores with their own alteration services and a certain bespoke element to orders, such as in Debenham, Son & Freebody, Swan & Edgar, Harvey Nichols or Harrods, there was no young designer in business like him. Norman Hartnell was rapidly becoming the most fashionable new London House, with youth on his side and a growing professionalism.

> An Oxford man, Captain Phillips, has struck out on still more novel lines, for he advises women on how to dress in order to make the most of themselves and also undertakes to find the right garments for them . . . Baron d'Erlanger's son, Robin, has designed all the beautiful dresses representing the 'signs of the Zodiac' to be worn at a ball on December 17 in aid of a Lewisham hospital.[34]

Apart from a few stage designers, Norman had a clear field for kicking the golden ball, as Lady Asquith had famously urged him to do.

In September 1927, Norman wrote the short article 'New Modes at Last':

> The present season is particularly interesting, in that the essentials of dress have undergone a change. At last we dressmakers have tempted women to change from that shapeless, lazy tube-dress, cut off at the knee, to the graceful, rhythmic lines which will be affected by every smart woman before Michaelmas.

He then underlines the fact that dress had become international: 'With the artificial aid of cosmetics and hair dyes, these women of the world obliterate their national and natural traces and demonstrate a universal uniform of "chic" . . . new ideas and fads influenced by Wimbledon or Lindbergh's flight have a brief span of popularity spread and ended by press coverage.'

In view of his later career, some of his comments are interesting as part of the 1920s view of fashion:

To call even the most celebrated dressmaker in the world 'a creator of fashion' is today an exaggeration. The best of us are like the exchange of a telephone service – to connect the fashionable women with her beholder and in the end she calls the number . . . illustrious women who can launch a fashion. Queens like our Elizabeth or Marie Antoinette of France were in this exalted position, and the Empresses Josephine and Eugenie from their thrones in France dominated the sphere of dress.[35]

Writing to Captain Basil Liddell-Hart on 4 January 1944 Richard Fletcher stressed:

As I was present in Venice in 1927 at the Lido's celebrations in honour of the late King Fuad of Egypt, I was a witness to the excitement caused by a Hartnell dress called 'Goosey Gander' and worn by Mrs P.G. Kennedy, the widow of the well-known art-critic of *The Observer*, at the time this was a version of the long skirt . . . At once Mr Hartnell was recognized by the international society who gathered on the terrace of the Excelsior Hotel at the Gala, as the one Englishman of inventiveness and courage. I think this point should be a matter of historical record, as people fairly stood on their chairs to see the graceful skirt of this Hartnell creation.

In the following decade, film again changed the impact of fashion on the viewing public worldwide, as did greatly improved printing techniques and a growth in the circulation of women's illustrated journals. Film stars and stage actresses maintained a highly fashion-conscious image for most of Norman's professional life, and he could not have foreseen the roles to be filled by the younger members of the British Royal Family.

The watershed in Norman's search for an international reputation as a designer of genius occurred as a result of his Paris show in the spring of 1927, as we have seen. His success was an undoubted delight to old friends, and when his old school friend Edward Higham married in 1927, his wife wore a dress specially designed for her by Norman. An intricate cut, the satin *beauté* interleaved with two layers of net and embroidered with silver and pearl leaves, as was the eight-foot-long train lined with ice blue. It was exhibited in Accrington in 1954 and then modelled for an enthusiastic audience!

By January 1928 Norman's views were increasingly sought by the press and his younger clientele was growing steadily. He planned his second assault on Paris, and the American buyers who could bring him into direct contact with the thriving, pre-1929-crash, fashion-hungry women of the USA. During this time, Norman revealed his own ideas on fashion, elaborating the themes of his earlier *Sunday Express* article:

> A good deal of nonsense is talked, not without some encourage-ment from dressmakers themselves, about the creative genius of great dress designers. The dress designer is and always will be, the servant of the smart woman who chooses what she likes from his many ideas. Hers is the instinct that says the last word. Through her good taste modern fashions develop.

This pragmatic view of the designer's role was novel at the time and gave a youthful, vigorous impression of the young designer, not unlike the opinions he was to express throughout his life, but lacking the later whimsy. He has no doubts in stating: 'Chanel is the outstanding genius of today. To her we owe the simple sports suit, the shingled head and most of the simple elegance of dress. It is hard to imagine modern dress without her. Vionnet is another designer of genius.'

Years later he deprecated Chanel's repetitive designs as 'dreary', but the genius of Vionnet's construction and use of fabric remained objects of admi-ration forever. In writing the article, Norman candidly admitted that 'great dress houses show several hundred designs at the two great opening displays in spring and autumn. If ten out of that number are successful, then the house may be counted lucky.'

This was to be a problem throughout Norman's career – how to sell enough of his designs to keep a large House in business? It explains everything about subsequent business developments within the business and why every possible exploration of the Norman Hartnell name was attempted over the subsequent five decades, as he explained:

> Dress always is a reflection of the mentality of the times. The remaining hundreds of models are simply scrapped. It is obvious that the smart woman who sets the seal of her approval on certain designs sets the fashion of what will be worn by the many. The

discriminating client was necessarily given exclusive designs by a talented designer; it was and still is the creation of an individual style for a particular client that marks the genius of a designer. It was never easy: I designed recently three special dresses for a very smart client. They were something out of the ordinary in line. They were all turned down by her with the remark that she would not become a silhouette to show off new fashion ideas. This is typical of the chic modern woman. The dress designer simply must please her or she will search elsewhere for that she wants . . . Successful dressing today depends on cut, material, design and workmanship. It no longer depends on being unique. The word exclusive now excites nothing but derision in the world of fashion. It has become intensely suburban.

This is an extraordinary remark, for in retrospect exclusivity would seem to have been an advantage for anyone with a great establishment, such as Norman later created. His explanation also gives a different perspective on 1920s dressing:

The designs of the great Paris houses have become universal. A new model is copied in all grades of material and at all prices within a month or two of its debut in Paris. That is the successful smart model that some smart women have given their approval to. Another significant fact is that the smart woman will buy her clothes where she likes. Last spring I took a collection of my own designs to Paris to show . . . Against the wishes of many I showed my entire collection of afternoon things and I was entirely justified. For amongst the visitors to my collection were the most astute and famous of American buyers. They told me that the English version of dress had an elegance of naturalness and an innate dignity which the well-dressed women of America – famed for their taste – wished to acquire . . . I confidently hope the day will come when people believe that not only French houses can produce beautiful fashions for the world.[36]

Of the French designers, Jean Patou had already publicised his clothes to the USA with a show using only American mannequins; Chanel went further and designed for Hollywood. Travis Banton and Howard Greer, both former protégés of Lucile, were to have long contracts with major Hollywood studios, so Norman had his almost unique essential Englishness to exploit. He had one curious asset – Britain was so unlikely a source for fashion in the eyes of the Condé Nast establishment that a determined talent such as his was newsworthy, and Norman predicted that fashion would not change much for some time:

> It cannot be improved on as regards comfort and practicability and it certainly is beautiful. It cannot go back to the black ages of tight waists, bustles, bones and coifs skewered with a vicious fancy pin. Dress today must find its novelties in cut and decoration that in no way interfere with the simple line woman has taken to her heart and will not relinquish.[37]

In early October 1927 Norman was at the wedding held at Brompton Parish Church for the former captain of the Cambridge University golf team, Rex Hartley, to Muriel Stewart. He had designed her satin *beauté* dress and those of the bridesmaids. With this and the Weymouth wedding in the offing he had held his autumn dress show featuring the 'peacock line'.

'I think it suits the English figure. The French are rather too short and squat – a hint to those of us not exactly slender,' wrote the correspondent of *The Lady*.

At this point, one should stress that much surviving couture of the 1920s and 1930s was made for women who were equivalent in size to many of today's twelve-year-olds. Back then *The Lady* highlighted 'No Nonsense', 'Trot Along' and 'High Tea',[38] as well as 'Goosey Gander', which had a ruff of feathers at the waist and two long tails of them sweeping the floor behind, and 'Mrs Midas' – a shimmer and clank of gold-lined fringes.[39]

Within a year, British *Vogue* was reporting his October 1928 collection:

> This clever young designer has a new and youthful attack. His clothes express the vagaries as well as the careless chic of a wayward smart generation. The dance dress for important occasions in lace or tulle is his speciality. The runabout dress in crêpe, wool or even printed velvet (so casual a quality does he give this fabric) and the little dress of satin and lace for restaurant wear are equally

important in his scheme of things, however. Coats he cuts beautifully, but is more interested in cutting them of velvet and trimming them luxuriously with fur than in severely tailoring them of tweed. One superbly smart leather coat – in three-quarter length of green – with a green and red jersey dress he includes in his collection just to show he can do that sort of thing when he has a mind to.[40]

This is typical of British *Vogue*'s view of Norman; the stress on fine stuffs and the quality of the craftsmanship, allied to the stressing of the simplest of his creations. In August 1927, British *Vogue* published a full-page photograph, slightly tongue-in-cheek, entitled 'To Paris and the Continent by the Golden Arrow', with a model dressed in a 'three-piece costume' of coat over a blue, red and white jumper suit and worn with a cloche hat. By 5 September 1928 'Printed Velvet is a Matter of Great Importance' was illustrated by four black-and-white illustrations: 'Hundreds of Thousands' and 'Workaday' by Norman Hartnell, and 'no. 50' and 'no. 16' by Molyneux. The juxtaposition is as significant as the different methods of naming the models, yet in this instance those of Molyneux are the more elaborate of the two. Norman's had a svelte line that is echoed in a full-page advertisement in British *Vogue* of 19 September 1928 for a bias-cut evening dress of chiffon with handkerchief printed skirt touching the floor to one side, and bodice and hips encrusted with paillettes. Molyneux was already well established in Paris at this date, whilst Norman was still battling in foggy London. But between the autumn of 1927 and early 1928 Norman established his reputation with significant work for the stage, as he had always planned to do.

By now it is apparent that the attitude to women's dress at this time and for some decades to come was as fastidious, if not obsessive, as it had been amongst the rich and fashionable for some centuries, probably since the time of Cleopatra. Every detail of a dress was carefully pored over in salon, shop and publication. For those bemused by the wealth of detail given to descriptions of Hartnell's creations, this is exactly what appealed to women and many men at the time, and it recreates the period and taste of the era. It was not only a widespread interest, it was the driving force of Norman Hartnell's very existence and what he lived for. Until the end of his life he was capable of turning out an apparently unending stream of innovative designs capturing the latest fashions and giving them a different and highly original twist. By 1928 this was an established and well-known facet of his genius.

On 29 March 1928 Norman's design for an all-pink wedding dress was worn by Mrs Carl Bendix at Claridge's for the pageant 'Dream of Fair Women'. The dress excited much press comment; it was of palest pink satin with a wide hem of pink net, the ruched layered edge of the embroidered train a distinctive touch, as was the wide star motif appliqued to the cuffs of the arms and the band of embroidery extending from the hips to the knees.

A reporter in the *Yorkshire Post* wrote of Norman's contemporary at this time: 'Very weird and wonderful are the forecasts of dresses of the future, which have been designed by Mr Cecil Beaton. For instance, a bride of the future is attired in a trouser suit of white oilcloth, a material which makes many of these costumes.'[40] Beaton seems to have been forty years ahead with his intriguing visions. Yet it was no doubt old hat to Norman, who had included lounging trousers in his 1924 collection, naturally of chiffon with fox cuffs. Furthermore, the Bendix wedding dress was accepted by the London Museum as 'a perfect nuptial robe of the period, to be preserved in an air-tight compartment until 1960 when it would then be exhibited.' There is no record that it was, but is now in pristine condition in the collections of the Museum of London.

Nevertheless, Beaton was clearly impressed by Hartnell's work and reputation, for when his sister Nancy was presented at the Fourth Court of the 1928 season on 12 June she wore a Hartnell 'gown of white silk tulle in graduating flounces embroidered with miniature silver paillettes, the entire dress worked over an underdress of gleaming silver tissue, [with a dainty] train of white tulle spangled with silver embroidery'.[41] The tulle represented thirty yards of extraordinary workmanship and Beaton's photographs of his sister evoke the fairy-tale quality of her appearance.

That evening, eleven women were presented wearing Norman's creations. The financial rewards for his business were small, but the publicity brought more orders and the Courts brought in a steady income, which few of the Paris Houses could directly compete with, as it became gradually the habit to patronise British dressmakers for these occasions. Handley-Seymour, Reville, Madame Isobel were all well represented – as were some no doubt interesting designs run up by 'little women' and designed by their owners to incorporate antique fabrics and, more usually, lace – the sort of thing which gave Norman alternate fits of shudders and giggles. He likened the colour of old lace to old dentures, and in *Silver and Gold* gave a macabre example of one valiant old girl out of many, who turned up in Bruton Street wearing a frightening assemblage of odd fragments 'inspired by you, Mr Hartnell'.[42] Such grotesque behaviour was largely confined to correspondents; in later years large files of letters marked 'Maniacs' were stored away by Norman's secretary Ann Price.

There was nothing grotesque about Norman's designs for Frances Doble playing the part of a young married woman falling in love with a young Anglo-Italian in *Sirocco*, again at Daly's, where Hartnell had himself appeared in the Footlights production that first recommended him to Minnie Hogg. Ivor Novello played the gigolo and the play was by Noël Coward, so it should all have been a huge success. Sadly, only Norman's designs received favourable criticism: the play was a fiasco and the cast and author booed off the stage. Norman had already designed dresses for Jane Wood in Coward's *Easy Virtue*. She was accorded choruses of 'ohs', when she appeared in more and more glamorous creations. Whether this antagonized Coward and whether the success of Norman's designs for Frances Doble formed too great a contrast to the flop of *Sirocco*, Coward remained a firm adherent of his friend Molyneux for great couture elegance. Gertrude Lawrence became a good if notoriously non-paying client of Norman's and he created the sensational dresses for her New York appearance in *Tonight at 8.30*. But there was little warmth between Noël Coward and Norman Hartnell. They were too dissimilar in their tastes and, as with Cecil Beaton, both remained wary of one another until old age mellowed them and a remembrance of shared youthful experiences reunited them.

In his private life, Norman was no more settled than he had been on leaving Cambridge. He had his own flat and Miss Louie remembers that he seemed to 'share' it with someone. His love of the masculine horsey world brought him into contact with those who rode in Hyde Park, and he also took up riding and even running in the morning. There is little evidence that he was amongst those looking for sexual contacts in the Park, but if so, based on contemporary accounts he would not have found it difficult. He was slim, good-looking and beautifully dressed, as always throughout his life, in quiet business clothes usually with a buttonhole. During the Oxford and Cambridge Boat Race he would appear in his Cambridge blazer clutching a large teddy bear of Cambridge blue colour and if Cambridge won, cakes would be bought for all his staff. In the 1930s he would take parties by horse and carriage to the Derby. Those who worked for him at the time were particularly won over by the same friendly and sympathetic manner which appealed to his clients.

His unforced natural charm and sense of humour remained with him throughout his life. One of his workroom girls at that time imagined that he would not wish himself acknowledged or recognised on the street and was amazed to see him stop and repeatedly wave to her with a smile on his face across a crowded Mayfair Street. At first, she thought he was waving at a friend or client and so ignored him until she realised he was waving at her and she waved back. Social attitudes have so changed that this seems an implausible occurrence, but the impression remained over sixty years later.[43]

Many of his original staff from no. 10 were to remain with him until past official retirement age: marriage was one of the few things which dragged 'his girls' away from him, to his immense regret. As with many essentially kind-hearted and sentimental people, Norman found it often difficult to cope with strong personalities, to say 'no' and, as time went on, even to say 'goodbye' to those leaving Hartnell after decades of service. At no. 10 he had a bell near the showroom door which he would ring so that he could find out if clients were in the salon. There were few that he would gladly meet often, particularly those known to be difficult about making final choices or arguing about alterations during fittings, all of which helped, of course, to fill clients' empty hours in those halcyon leisured days, when social conduct was so much easier. There were many social rules to be followed, some written as with the exact form of clothing to be worn by debutantes on presentation to their Majesties; these were known and followed so that life progressed more smoothly for those both 'in' and, indeed, 'out' of Society. As Lady Bracknell crushingly advised an earlier generation: 'Never speak disrespectfully of Society Algernon, only those who cannot get into it . . .'

By the end of 1927, Norman was a familiar figure in London Society. *Eve's* correspondent caught him leaving a relative novelty, the first night of the film *Uncle Tom's Cabin*, the audience divided on what the correct wear should be, 'the range of sartorial exhibits varying from advanced or, rather, retarded evening dress to models suitable for wearing with caps'. One thing all were agreed upon – the content of the film was gruelling. 'Mr Norman Hartnell confessed at the finish that he was quite worn out.[44]

Norman was rather more enamoured of the light musical stars such as Miss José Collins; doodles of her adorned his school exercise books. She also exercised a spell over Blake Brown and whilst he was 'having doubts in Portsea', Norman, ever the kind friend, cheered him up by visiting Blake at weekends and introducing the two. Norman had already designed dresses for her, but Blake had impersonated her in Footlights' *Smokers* as Miss Cosy Jollins. He was now able to go to her dressing room and entertain her, with a dun-coloured toque on his head and a black silk petticoat stuffed into his dinner jacket, as 'all the better known crowned queens of Europe'. She responded by giving her famous final impersonation of Queen Victoria 'until Lord Robert Innes-Ker took her away'. This friendship lasted for some time, with Bish and Blake dining with the Innes-Kers in London and Blake striking up one of his typically eccentric correspondences with Miss Collins.[45]

Norman was also noted by the nightclub owner Mrs Kate Meyrick, often called 'Ma' Meyrick, the nightclub queen of the 1920s, as a patron of her better establishment, the Silver Slipper in Regent Street. 'I see it so clearly crowded out night after night by the world of beauty and fashion,' she wrote in 1933 and listed as patrons Tallulah Bankhead, Jack Buchanan, Lord Sefton with Lady Louis Mountbatten with 'priceless jewellery, her arms covered with diamond bracelets', Dorothy Dixon and Norman Hartnell, 'London's cleverest dress designer, scrutinising with the eye of a connoisseur the frocks of the dancers as they pass'.

All three women named were clients of Norman, as was the principal artiste, Frances Day, who made her name in the club as a platinum blonde with the New York Revellers. She had been one of Texas Guinan's girls and was to become not only a friendly client, but a friend who helped Norman to advertise his clothes over the succeeding decades. Mrs Meyrick was a clever Irish widow of respectable if impecunious origins, who used the turbulent nightclub scene of the 1920s to bring in a sizeable income for herself and her daughters, who in turn made excellent marriages. She was a 1920s version of the Edwardian Rosa Lewis of the Cavendish Hotel, 'modern' in as much as she also went to prison on several occasions for breach of licensing regulations. This did not stop her popularity amongst the smartest of London's Bright Young Things. Her 43 club attracted Norman, as well as the Dukes of Leeds, Manchester and Norfolk, Prince Christopher of Greece, Prince Nicholas of Romania, Norman's friend Sir Anthony Lindsay Hogg, who married the ill-fated star of *Sirocco* Frances Doble and tragic Brenda Dean Paul, and then a whole new post-Bright Young Things generation including a star Hartnell client Margaret Whigham and her friend and rival Rose Bingham.[46] The illuminated glass floor shone on Norman and his friendly clients; he saw and was seen. It remained now for him to plan his own mammoth party to cap all the pageants and fancy-dress balls which so absorbed the frenetic fun seekers of the period. His famous Circus Party of 1929 was the result.

Whilst the planning went on, Norman's career advanced steadily. His designs were increasingly sought by the smarter women and his salon seemed to be too small for his needs, as were his workrooms. Several successful American weddings were graced by his reworkings of gowns first produced for English brides, but refined and redesigned for trans-Atlantic tastes, so that by 1928 B. Altman & Co. of New York's Fifth Avenue could advertise his 'Tulle Frock – a New Version' in pink and blue tulle, shirred and flaring ruffles emanating from what they termed 'a side sweeping, bouffant silhouette'. The bodice remained quite plain, but the sweeping sides of the dress flowed on the floor whilst being swept up to the knees back and front. This silhouette was unlike those of other designers in Paris or London and Norman was written about in *The New Yorker* September fashion report on equal terms with Molyneux, Chanel, Chéruit, Patou and Lelong.[47]

It is a fact that at this time Hartnell garments had become the equal of Paris in their construction, the insides of the dress as finely finished as the exterior embroidery. The selvedge of hems and seams was quite usually oversewn, the pinked edges having a fine cobweb of stitches running along as a design motif in themselves. Fastenings with hooks and eyes and press studs were straightforward to use. As with all good clothes, the dresses usually opened and closed up the side from the waistline to the arm, sometimes including the shoulder straps of the particularly svelte dresses of the late 1920s and early 1930s. None of this was directly Norman's work, but he and Phyllis now knew exactly what good clothes consisted of and insisted on the finest workmanship. With Mlle Davide and her influence, the workrooms went on to produce clothes as good as any available to women in this century. Embroidery, tailoring, fur and hats were all included in Norman's repertoire. His sketches were more detailed and complex than most designers. They had the personal artistic look lacking in the more slickly commercial sketches of a house such as Reville, or in the few lines of doodling seen in many other houses, where a great deal of extra discussion was necessary to interpret the exact intentions.

Most former employees remembered that Norman's sketches were easy to work from, his immediate wishes clear, and although the construction might have to be discussed, line and decoration were all included, and sometimes the back of the dress and accessories were drawn in. The latter were a constant source of irritation to Norman as his suggestions were usually abandoned by clients and his concept thus muddled by mismatched bags, shoes, gloves and hats. Later on with Queen Elizabeth the concepts were more coordinated, as his collaboration with the shoemaker Edward Rayne turned out to work extremely well. But in the late 1920s, the Duchess of York was largely a client of the older and established Houses; indeed her wardrobe for the 1926 Royal Tour to Australia and New Zealand even included svelte items by the Paris House of Lanvin.

It was always Paris that seemed to thwart Norman's ambition. An Englishman through and through, he relished his life in the buzzing excitement of 1920s London, yet had he followed the example of the designers Worth, Creed, Redfern and Molyneux by living in Paris then his rise might have been meteoric with greater financial gain. After discussions with his father and sister, he decided to go one better and keep London as his base but open a Paris salon and attract the private and commercial attention of the world by hopefully operating two lucrative bases. He would have a terrific show in Paris and follow it with a huge Society party in London, followed by yet another show. One can only guess at Richard Fletcher's role in this, and at his father's reaction. But all were involved and, perforce, totally committed to the idea. When Lady Oxford advised Norman to kick the golden ball at his feet, she could have had little idea that he would boot it over the moon.

CHAPTER FIVE

Paris follows . . . the very essence of youth

With typically nonchalant bravura Norman condensed six years of his life (1928–34) into barely three pages of his autobiography *Silver and Gold*. Nearly thirty years later his view of these years was undeniably overshadowed by his extraordinary success as a designer and internationally known Dressmaker to three English Queens (by Appointment to two) and other members of the Royal Family, as well as most of the world's famous and rich women. Yet his Paris years form a fascinating if forgotten period straddling the ills following the Wall Street Crash in 1929, and the initial years of the 1930s Great Depression. The world's press was quick to accord him the status of a youthful genius. Not yet thirty, he dared to compete with Parisian couture directly on his own terms. As we have seen, his initial foray into the complex world of French couture revealed him as a sort of Candide, oblivious to most of the obvious disasters awaiting him, but young enough to rely upon his youth, the goodwill of others and his genius. This second venture was more carefully planned and had the backing of the press. Norman made news with his designs for newsworthy women; his opinions were sought and now reached an even wider public through the medium of both stage and film.

The famous Edwardian star Lily Elsie, about whom Cecil Beaton wrote at length in his diaries, had captured the hearts of the theatre-going public. If Gladys Cooper had offices in 10 Bruton Street, then Lily Elsie starred in the Hartnell salon modelling the clothes he designed for her appearance in *The Truth Game* starring opposite Ivor Novello and Lilian Braithwaite at The Globe in October 1928. Newspapers and magazines regaled their readers with fulsome descriptions of the clothes worn, all mentioning Norman's name. The *Daily Mail* went to the heart of Norman's success:

Angora and moiré silk in the same sports suit is one of the interesting ideas materialised in the charming clothes . . . 'Why not moiré in a sports suit? It is no more dressy a material than crêpe de chine, which we use so lavishly,' said Mr Norman Hartnell.

After a description of the suit he went on:

> The geography of this beige satin and lace negligée is interesting. The belt, which passes over the right front panel, goes through a slit in the seam under the left arm and then round the back to tie with the other end which passes over the left front panel. This ensures the negligée staying in place much better than with an ordinary tie. The lace that extends up the sleeves, through the yoke round the neck and shoulder, and then right down the front is, you may notice, all cut from one piece. In addition to cutting it carefully to shape, we persuaded it to fit at any awkward corners by steaming, stretching, pressing, and shrinking it where required.[1]

The sophistication of this design and the craftsmanship involved mark the transformation of Norman's work from the beautifully decorative and original to the couture garments in which construction and workmanship are also touched with the genius redolent of that word.

Norman had no other competitors of his own age in London, with the exception of Peter Russell (calling himself 'Peter's Studio') and Philip Brookes.[2] The former had success later especially with his more tailored garments and the latter never had success under his own name.

In October 1928, Best & Co., then one of Fifth Avenue's leading retail merchants of dresses situated next to St Patrick's Cathedral, took out full-page advertisements in the *New York Herald* and *New York Evening Post* asserting that 'England was the place to watch for the latest developments in fashion'. The *Daily Express* correspondent wrote, 'England Leads Fashions of the World – Striking Praise From New York – Paris Follows'.

Although Best & Co. were to form a lucrative relationship with Hartnell, their comments were unlikely to be ridiculed and stressed that English stodginess had been brushed aside. With a clear reference to Chanel, the influence of English sports clothes on her ideas is remarked upon, as is her use of English tweeds and jerseys, and that she 'controls the output of the finest North of England mill today'. Best & Co's ad asks:

> Do you know that an English firm is second only to hers in Paris in making sports clothes . . . that one of the most sensational successes among Paris openings was scored by a young Englishman, who had his first showing in Paris this season . . . that he gowns many of the most beautiful young women in London society: that his debut and presentation frocks are much sought after . . . the finest gauge sweaters in the world are made in England . . . and supply the majority of French couturiers with sweaters?[3]

Heartening propaganda for British Empire products was fine and enhanced Norman's chances at home. The nationalistic tone to promoting British or Empire goods above anything 'foreign' was increasingly seen in the press. This also included the fashion press. A typical piece of editorial from the pen of Madame X (the irony was perhaps lost) in the *Graphic* of 12 January 1929 asserted: 'It was Molyneux and Chanel who brought in dull grey and browns and practically forbade anything brighter than flesh or putty, but the younger dressmakers Lady Victor Paget, Mr Hartnell and Mrs Fox-Pitt (Elspeth Phelps) are brave and have started out on the campaign of red and green.' This could have emanated from Norman's own pen.

On 12 March 1929 he held his dress show at the May Fair Hotel. The arresting programme of grey card is embellished with red type and an applied gold foil design of three women, one behind the other, in red outlines. Remarkable red cupid's-bow lips pout at the viewer, and the foremost figure, in typical Norman style, has long tapering fingers bearing elongated red nails and a ring with an enormous stone emanating glittering red rays. His prize dresses included 'Daisy Chain', bought by many – including Lady Evelyn Guinness and the actress Edna Best. The dress had long chains of silver daisies sewn over 'an airy cloud of white tulle', but for the more sophisticated there was 'Dracula', photographed for *Vogue* by Hoyningen-Huene, worn by Lady Ashley and described as 'an outstanding event in the history of taffeta'. It had a low sleeveless scalloped bodice held by fine net over the shoulders, and the front of the short skirt was an inverted apron with shirred and scalloped gathered taffeta ruffles echoed in the full-length skirt to the floor at the back. It could also be worn with the ruffles turned down on one side to give a one-sided effect. Paris could offer nothing quite like this sophistication: the dress was a must for sophisticated young London and American women viewing the successive shows at no. 10 Bruton Street, where a huntsman and two negro pages ushered in other models such as 'Garden Path', 'Ghostie', 'Father's Fancy' and 'Aunt Ethel's Ready'.

Norman wrote that his Paris show, which swiftly followed the London one, could not be held in a hotel like the Plaza Athénée as before. He could find nothing suitable until a friend of his, Miss Archibald, came up with the 'magasin d'antiquités' formed from rooms once lived in by Madame de Pompadour in an old Paris *hôtel* or town house. Miss Archibald was to remain a lifelong friend and client of Norman's and became Lady Clark Minor, her husband later head of British War Relief in the USA. She also introduced clients to Norman for 10% commission, a usual arrangement of most French Houses with a few of their most distinguished clients, who then wore discounted or free clothes to notable social events. Miss Dezengremel, to whom the rooms belonged, dealt in a variety of goods and Norman had to sleep amongst them to guard his dresses in accordance with some clause in the lease. 'Dollars poured into my lap,' he recorded. This was in the months before the Wall Street Crash.[4]

The whole trip was carefully planned this time and the premises set up well beforehand, possibly by Phyllis, who had begun to travel regularly with Hartnell Collections out to India, where she and a friend maintained a successful dress shop in Calcutta. She usually landed at Marseilles, where Norman often met her.

Certainly the address of the new French salon, 33 rue de Ponthieu, Champs-Élysées appears in newspaper and magazine reports from March 1929, and it also appeared in Norman Hartnell advertisements. The former Miss Bell remembered that the salon appeared very like the 10 Bruton Street one, and an illustrated report in *Fairchild's International* stressed 'the fresh English atmosphere' of his Paris salon. It was in some ways a dress rehearsal for his later famous premises at 26 Bruton Street. The colour scheme was entirely in 'soft pistache green', even to the background of the chintz curtains with pink and white bouquets of flowers. The two rooms had been modernised by removing the large double doors and fitting art-deco wrought iron and glass doors by Courtois and Detrois. The geometric framework was covered by wrought iron, simulating vines with bunches of glass grapes, amber, green and amethyst, lit by electricity from within.[5]

The *New York Herald*[6] reported the showing of the new Hartnell collection in these rooms, and his evening dresses and day clothes were equally praised. Polka dots and spots of contrasting colour were considered to be especially interesting; although Bettina Bedwell writing in *Liberty* noted that Norman (now nearing thirty years old) was 'the wonder child of fashion creation', 'making long and short dresses, according to the occasion'. Many dresses were both long and short, but he was a believer in width and length for skirts and the 'older and more experienced Paris houses' were backing him.[7] In general the trend was for longer below-the-knee skirts, but Norman was dropping them mainly to the floor, with what was still termed a 'peacock silhouette'.

There is also no doubt that Hoyningen-Huhne's innovative, less stylised photography brought clothes to life on the page as no other photographer had done in fashion journals before. The impact and influence of these photographs was both profound and extensive. If one style brought about an inspired or new wave of photographers, including Beaton and Horst, so dresses such as Norman's appeared before a wider audience. The German-speaking press was also soon publishing his more streamlined frocks that appealed to suntanned, sporty, pleasure-seeking girls in the rocky last years of the Weimar Republic.

Paris kept a weather eye on the young Englishman muscling in on the dollar income so avidly fought for. The prestige of French couture was not simply a matter of national pride, it was a matter of economic importance, for couture and its allied industries formed one of the greatest sources of revenue whilst employing huge numbers of people. Norman himself approved of the regulations which insisted that a viewer of a French couture show must purchase at least two models from the collection. The codification of behaviour and the beneficial status conferred on couture houses were of great interest to Norman, and were frequently discussed by him in interviews and later with colleagues in the Incorporated Society of London Fashion Designers, which he co-founded from 1941 until its official creation in 1942.

The Sphere of 6 April 1929 included a photograph of a stunning dress from the Hartnell collection promoting the return of the long skirt – it was tiered and had pearl embroidery over the white tulle. Norman not only showed Paris the way in the all-important annual dress lengths battle, but could also show Miss Cartland just how he could design and make a white tulle dress.

Even whilst he was in Paris selling his latest collection, manufactured in England, *The Garey Divorce Case* opened at the Court Theatre starring Isabel

Jeans wearing clothes designed for her by Norman. The *Daily Telegraph* commented on the simple black dress she wore in the divorce scene: 'the tragic frock . . . expresses the deepest sadness'. Whilst showing that he could produce beautifully simple clothes, he let himself go to newsworthy excess: 'Women who admired the beautiful lemon-coloured coat . . . little realised what a terrible weight it was, for, being entirely made of beads on a satin foundation, it is heavier than most furs.'[7]

The luxury of extravagant workmanship ingeniously used was good business: it caused a sensation and the garment was expensive. On the stage, it also reached a wider appreciative audience than a static photograph. The effect on buyers from abroad was also beneficial: T. Eaton, one of Canada's leading department stores, began buying Hartnell models, including 'bridal gowns'.

Yet none of this is remembered in *Silver and Gold*. It was his old friend Beverley Nichols who first dragged out of him his real feelings about 1920s dresses – that they 'involved the designers in an arduous and exhausting struggle against nature'.[8] Looking at photographs of the period, one realises that only sleek youth looked well in those skimpy shapeless clothes. Most women resemble Cecil Beaton's cruelly accurate famous contemporary sketches for *Vogue* in which lumpy older women sit uncomfortably compressed and bulging in an unfortunately conspicuous manner.

This is what Norman was rebelling against in his most sophisticated clothes, with their hints of eighteenth-century decorative fullness in panels and scallops, frills and trains forming part of the skirts. His clothes were adored by the young smart women in society. 'And so to Another Party', an article written by Nancy Beaton includes the obviously Cecil-inspired line: 'The star-spangled tulle dress from Hartnell is laid on the bed, looking like a piece of sea foam.'[9] As Anne, Countess of Rosse was to write, 'receiving a Hartnell box and opening it gave enormous pleasure, particularly as his dresses were simple to put on and front or back immediately identifiable', which was apparently not always the case with the products of other designers favoured by her, such as Charles James.[10]

Norman was back in London for April. His workrooms hummed as they produced dresses for the Courts in May, and Lady Bridget Poulett and Mrs Bryan Guinness, two of England's most beautiful women, wore dresses designed by Norman, Mrs Guinness also wearing a tiara of diamonds and pearls. *The Times* commented on the 'delicate colourings' of fabrics used and noted the new French and bouffant skirts.[11] One of Norman's creations used fifteen yards of tulle cut on the cross. *Women's Wear Daily,* then as now with the most influential fashion news, illustrated three day dresses of Norman's on the front page. They had the new flared skirts, and one was embroidered with white beads suggesting lace, a favourite motif on Hartnell dresses throughout the next fifty years of Norman's career.[12]

De Meyer photographed 'Dracula' for a page in *Harper's Bazaar* in May 1929 with the caption 'Black Faille flares in Aggressive Chic suggesting a Bird's Plumage'. Norman dressed the current star Edna Best again, now for her role in *Paris Bound* at the Lyric, another wedding dress adding to the apt title of the play, as far as Norman was concerned. Helen Ford also wore Norman Hartnell dresses at the Apollo in *Coquette* during June, although she wore models from the latest collection including 'Daisy Chain' and 'Garden Path', and the publicity was excellent. The *Paris Times* illustrated one of Norman's typically elongated sketches of an evening dress with 'tiers of 1920s sun-ray pleating' – 'Girlish and Gay – Hartnell has won phenomenal success during the past year by the distinction of his costumes.'[13]

There then came a major heart-stopping moment for London designers in particular, with the rumour that neither the King nor Queen Mary would attend Royal Ascot, for the King had been seriously ill. 'The successful society dress-maker Norman Hartnell' told the *Daily Mirror:* 'Ascot frocks have already been ordered . . . I think they will be worn whether there is a royal procession or not. The King and Queen would not wish any difference to be made, even if they were absent.'[14] They were, but: 'It is the one occasion on which English women let themselves go in the matter of dress. If the dresses are not worn at Ascot they will certainly be worn at garden parties.' Many were worn and illustrated, the most elegant being a coat hemmed by smoke fox fur, the favourite fur of Norman's which he also began to dye to the colour of the fabric to which it was attached.

June not only contained Ascot but also one of Norman's most imaginative and beautiful wedding dresses on show when worn by Miss Oonagh Guinness for her marriage to Mr Philip Kindersley. One of three lovely sisters, daughters of Ernest Guinness, Oonagh was almost doll-like in her size and beauty. Norman dressed her and twelve bridesmaids with even greater ingenuity than seen before. The emergence of what American journals termed a return to the Louis XIV line, and others called the new 'Princess' line, meant that Norman's preference for full skirts was integral to the design, again based on paintings of the Madonna studied by the designer in the National

Gallery. As St Margaret's, Westminster was again the setting and a vast crowd expected, Norman turned his client into a radiant figure.

The pale parchment-coloured satin of the dress encases a naturally positioned bosom and waist, and the dress flows out from the hips, again in their natural place after a decade of 'tubism'. Viewed from the front, the centre of the hem of the skirt is gathered up to allow the wearer some space to walk, for the triumph of the design is not in the embroidery but in the train formed out of the skirt and extending back along the ground for four yards. The precursor of many other famous designs, this train has silver tissue lilies with gold leaves and pearls along its length, an extension of the design for the tight sleeves with their long, trailing, open-pointed cuffs. The tulle veil was held by a halo made of bones of gold tissue embroidered with seed pearls which completed the effect. The bridesmaids' dresses were a reflection of the design for the wedding dress, but with full long tulle skirts. Although the wedding dress is now ninety years old and, in common with many dresses of the period, would only fit a twelve-year-old girl, the design is as astonishingly original and wearable as in 1929. It is only when such a garment is worn that it lives again and moves in sympathy with the body inside.

The bridesmaids included Lady Honor Guinness, soon to be married to the now famous diarist Henry 'Chips' Channon and the Hon. Anne Hill-Wood, daughter of the Viceroy of India. Eight hundred guests admired the scene and once again Norman could congratulate himself on a remarkably innovative design excellently made, the subject of great admiration.

Now came his moment to be a part of 'the gay twenties' and almost one of the 'Bright Young Things' before they faded away. His Circus Party was held in the first week of July 1929 after extensive planning. Phyllis, Richard Fletcher and father Bish must all have been consulted. Fletcher was possibly the instigator of almost the last of the odd fancy-dress parties of the period, which included Baby Parties, Sailor Parties – in fact parties on any theme likely to cause a frenetic diversion and some mild scandal.

No. 17 Bruton Street, a few doors away from Norman Hartnell at no. 10, was the former house of Lord Strathmore and birthplace of the present Queen. It was empty and so leased for the evening. The clever young designer Ronald Fleming was hired to design and produce the decorations for the main reception rooms. A designer successfully combining elements of modernism with antique furniture, Fleming went into business with Mrs Dolly Mann, a respected decorator with a knowledge of Regency furniture that she used in her schemes and sold in her shop near the Ritz. Norman later used Mann & Fleming Ltd. to decorate his own houses.

It was not until Marie-Jacqueline Lancaster wrote her biography of Brian Howard and Barbara Cartland her autobiography of the 1920s, *We Danced All Night*, that Norman began to 'remember' his party of forty years ago. As he wrote to Miss Cartland in 1969 in typical Normie 1920s E.F. Benson manner:

I feel very much a naughty Norman in not having answered your nice little letter before, but I have been a very busy boy as a bright girl like you probably realises.

Anyhow I am terribly sorry I really have no books like Eleanor Smith's, or any of that period with which to help you.

Yes, I did give the Circus Party . . .

Ferraro of the Berkeley did all the food and the buffet table was decorated with pale green ice animals. The Ballroom was hung with scarlet and magenta drapes. The Supper Room in gold tissue, and the Breakfast Room for kippers and cocoa was done in huge checker [sic] design of silver and emerald metal.

Lord Northesk and Nelson Keys were the two Barkers.

Lord Hardwicke and Sir Anthony Lindsay Hogg came as cowboys.

The Ruthven twins garbed themselves as gorillas, Lily Elsie and Ivor Novello came as a couple of sailor boys in blue velvet. Lady Carisbrooke left her horse outside, wearing a wonderful riding habit and top hat of violet cloth (Irene was wearing it, not the horse). But Eleanor Smith brought in her white pony jingling with golden bells and scarlet saddlery and cantered up the circular white staircase.

The date was in late July.

It had been the Wedding Day of Oonagh Guinness and Maureen Guinness the head bridesmaid arrived with a bevy of other bridesmaids in gold gauze (by Hartnell) and complained that I had not put up over one of the tents 'Guinness is Good For You!'

There were masses of members from the 'Bright Young Things'. Countess Babe Bosdari, Valerie French, Dorothy Plunkett, Doris Castlerosse, etc.

That's enough for now.
All my love to my dear, beautiful Barbara.'[15]

In fact the party was on 1 July and the Guinness–Kindersley wedding had been solemnized a week earlier, but the bridesmaids did turn up in their Hartnell dresses. Fletcher had orchestrated the pre-party publicity and Norman's invitations were printed on a strip of pink paper half a yard long, according to newspaper reports the text read:

A renic spectacles
nimals
crobats
nd so forth

C hic
ircus
ontributions
hosen by
aptions
onnoisseurs

and requested guests to come dressed as a circus character. The *Daily Mail* correspondent, clearly a woman, wrote that she telephoned to complain that men were getting the best of it. Having called the party a 'freak' the *Daily Express* was more snide:

I feel sorry for Mr Norman Hartnell . . . He is, you see, a successful dress designer. And anyone who follows such a calling professionally becomes instantly suspect if he chooses to entertain his friends in a novel and expensive way. 'Huh!' say disgruntled people who have (it maybe) not been invited. 'Doing it for publicity, of course.' And echo answers: '*Of course.*'[16]

Nevertheless, the party was a huge success: 'The Lions of Mayfair: Queer Menagerie Party'; 'Amazing and Marvellous Circus Party'. Even the *Brooklyn Daily Eagle* reported it: 'Circus Game Popular in London Smart Set'. Other guests included Tilly Losch, Mr and Mrs Bryan Guinness, the famous

Ruthven twins (who *were* clad as monkeys), Nancy Beaton, Lord Rosse, Nancy Mitford, Ernest Thesiger 'in grotesque pink tights' and Miss Elizabeth Ponsonby, who was another 'Hartnell bride' a week later.

A live and alarmingly hungry big black bear was perhaps the star of the evening, although Norman looked superb in a ringmaster's outfit and Phyllis the epitome of Hartnell chic, as was the ill-fated Brenda Dean Paul. The guests could all have been part of an evening at the Silver Slipper and Ivor Novello, Beverley Nichols with Lady Duff, all entered into the spirit of the evening. Many of the guests had come on from other parties and found a huge crush of people when they arrived. *The Sketch* reported that a near disaster was averted when a flashlight set some of the decorations on fire, and the two snakes writhing on Miss Olivia Wyndham's neck caused a fright to someone who only just recovered his balance in time to prevent him falling on the Siberian wolves.[17] Everyone had a good time: not least the journalists, who wrote up the event at length, one describing Norman as 'a famous, fashionable and expensive creator of dresses; his salon is always crowded with beautiful women' which, as he might have written, was not bad considering that less than ten years previously he had been a busy boy trudging the streets trying to sell his designs.

The fact that his clothes were so highly praised by 1929 meant that Mrs L. Hart of Toronto would write to Norman in 1966 and ask for original designs of two dresses bought in his spring sale of 1929 by her mother Mrs H.E. Rawlings as presents for her. Norman could remember that '"Flower Afloat" was white satin and green lace with a water lily. And "Airy Fairy", I believe, was of many layers of white tulle, vandyked with silver thread.'[18] The dresses were given to McCord Museum, Toronto, one of many in the world to contain an interesting selection of Norman's work.

To another correspondent enquiring about the price of a dress ordered at this time by his mother, Mrs Ann Price, Norman's secretary, replied on his behalf that it would have then cost 'about 20 gns. Today (1977) it would cost *320* gns in similar style and with pleating forming the long skirt.'[19]

Today's sterling equivalent is calculated at £1300, however, wages and overheads are not accounted for and the true cost would be probably fifteen times more.

In the warmth of the 1929 summer there were more Hartnell weddings: Mr Dennis Pelly married Miss Elizabeth Ponsonby, who afterwards danced at the reception with Brian Howard whilst Hutch performed at the piano. Her bridesmaids 'like dainty fairies from a hoard of wild flowers' wore leaf-green tulle dresses and the wedding dress had leaves appliqued all over it onto the silk net, the veins of the leaves being worked in seed pearls. Again, bust, waist and hips were all in place as nature intended, as with Lady Victoria Haig's dress when she married Mr Claud Andrew Montagu Douglas Scott. Her dress most clearly points the way to the narrow, figure-hugging dresses which displayed Hartnell workmanship to great advantage through the first half of the 1930s.

Norman had but a short holiday before returning to Paris with his autumn and winter collections. The *Daily Mail* considered that his collection of hand-woven tweeds was 'well worth seeing apart from his graceful evening clothes'.[20] His choice of the princess line and use of new fabrics such as a virtually untearable net caused comment, as did his sleeveless pullovers. Bettina Bedwell, writing for the *Chicago Tribune*, termed him 'the youthful marvel from London . . . [his] models . . . justify his reputation as one of the first prophets of individualism in dress'. This perceptive comment will have pleased Norman as he sought to create and be known for his own style, rather than as a flash-in-the pan innovator of just one style.

For example, whilst Patou used Van Cleef & Arpels necklaces of diamonds with his models, Norman used ones of Venetian glass and china. Of the fifty or so firms showing, Norman Hartnell received many compliments and was discussed in the same terms as Lanvin, Vionnet and Worth. As a comment on the times Norman was living through, it should be noted that the amazing Paul Poiret was still designing, the former comet now a waning star. *Women's Wear Daily* illustrated several dresses by Norman and his black and white dresses were praised, whilst a bridesmaid's black dress created the stir intended and both his 'A Trifle' and 'Stuff and Nonsense' had full skirts touching the floor. The latter evening dress had sweeping horizontal bands and a large taffeta bow on the skirt. As it happens this was the collection shown in the '*magasin d'antiquités*' in the rue Saint-Honoré, formerly the town house of the Marquise de Pompadour. There was nothing shabby about the premises or the location, and the press reports were all flattering and enhanced his reputation.[21] He also produced designs for Mary McCord, a cabaret artiste appearing at the fashionable Château de Madrid au Bois.[22]

More fashionable weddings in London during the late summer were turned into grand occasions by Norman's designs for the brides, and he designed dresses for Renee Kelly in Percy Hutchison's *Miss Adventure* and *The New York Times* featured a full-page advertisement with three of Norman's latest dresses:

It's grand to be young and wear a Norman Hartnell evening gown! Norman Hartnell is the designer who de-flapped the flapper! He took her out of her fly-away 'little rags of things' and made her a creature of mysterious loveliness and slim, elusive charm. He is the debutantes' very own designer – and the designer of the woman who holds the gift of youth.

Russeks' (of Fifth Avenue at 36th Street) page was another coup for Norman: they even printed a facsimile of his 'letter' to them of 6 July:

Gentlemen,
   I take great pleasure in sending you today our dresses 'Rambling Rosie', 'Lily Pond' and 'May Day'.
   These dresses were greatly admired at our opening and I feel sure that by showing them to your distinguished clients you will meet with the same remarkable success.[22]

The letterhead is printed with both London and Paris addresses, and beneath the NORMAN HARTNELL is printed 'Robes Manteaux' (in the 1930s to be lengthened with 'Chapeaux') proving that whatever Norman might feel about the Englishness of his craft, the language of great couture, like that of great haute cuisine, remained French.

This undoubtedly indicated something to American buyers too, and as proof of his success the even more prestigious Best & Co. of Fifth Avenue at 25th Street devoted a whole window to five of Norman's dresses on stylised figurines surrounded by smart Norman Hartnell dress boxes trailing tissue paper. A photograph of the young star designer peered out at the passing elegance on New York's smartest street, as his contact at Best & Co. wrote to Norman,

The window practically stopped the traffic – people were three deep around it and it received much favourable comment. And I am sure that everybody in New York knows who Norman Hartnell is now. All the young things who can't afford a Norman Hartnell party frock are probably reduced to tears.

On a more intensely practical point the writer goes on:

> Our copies are very well done and would please you, I am sure. They are going nicely and I do want you to know that I appreciate your cooperation in the matter of prices. P.S. Gimbels of Philadelphia asked me to recommend a house for a '1940' wedding gown to be used in their anniversary displays. I told them there was only 'one person in the world who could do it' and that was you![23]

The letter illustrates the usual purchase by a copyist of a model from a collection for reproduction. In this case, it seems unlikely that much more than the price of the dress was paid, and although there were guidelines laid down for the Paris couture it was finally in the hands of each house to battle with tough buyers representing such powerful stores as Best & Co. The publicity was clearly to Norman's advantage in this instance, as was the recommendation for the '1940' wedding dress. One fascinating detail lies in the date of the letter, for the very day before on 29 October 1929, 16,410,300 shares were traded on the floor of the New York Stock Exchange. The normal 300,000 to 1 million shares a day had been grossly surpassed and 'for three days and nights Wall Street looked like Broadway with the lights in offices blazing all night, the pavements jammed with people.'[24] Norman's American goose had laid him a golden egg and then expired – dramatically.

Throughout his life Norman had a great deal of luck on his side. Business might be terrible, opportunities lost, ideas and income misappropriated or stolen, but until he died in 1979, Norman remained a respected figure in his profession. In his early days talent was allied to a capacity for hard work, and charm obviously won him friends and clients. Behind him stood his capable sister Phyllis and tough father Bish. It is a reflection of the capabilities of all three that Norman Hartnell Ltd was incorporated on 18 October 1929, the primary object asset out in the Memorandum of Association:

> 3. To acquire from Norman Hartnell the goodwill and other assets of the business heretofore carried on by him at 10 Bruton Street . . . and elsewhere . . .

1

1 Norman Hartnell exudes elegance, charm and style c. 1955

2

3

2 Norman Bishop Hartnell, early elegance in lace with a big hat c. 1905
3 NH top right standing Mill Hill Rugby 3rd XV c. 1918

4

5

6

4 NH as 'Kitty Fenton' in 'What a Picnic' 1921. NH fourth from left.
Richard Blake Brown seventh from left.

5 NH as 'Gwendolen Bentley' in 'Folly' cartoon by C Hildyard 1923

6 NH. a cast member, possibly 'What a Picnic' 1921

Harry from Dick May 12. 1932.

Yours incorrigibly, Richard Blake Brown

1929 - To be laid at the base of the Tonbridge War Memorial — !!

7

9

10

7 Richard Blake Brown in clerical garb. 1929
8 A typical Hartnell evening design 1928
9 NH, architect Gerald Lacoste centre. Salcombe c. 1934
10 NH, Gerald Lacoste centre. Salcombe c. 1934

12

11 NH, sister Phyllis 'Topsy' at 26 Bruton Street, Mayfair c. 1940
12 NH, Miss Louie in the stockroom c. 1965
13 Richard Fletcher 'Old Beardie', 26 Bruton Street, Mayfair c. 1942

14 NH 'fishing' with Swan & Edgar, Lovel Dene c. 1964
15 John Pleydell rides out. Lovel Dene c. 1936
16 'Mam'selle' Davide fitting an evening dress c. 1938
17 Lacoste's glass chimney-piece, culmination of art-moderne
interiors designed for 26 Bruton Street, Mayfair. 1935

18 Margaret Whigham, a 'Hartnell Bride,' as Turquoise in Hartnell. A Jewel Ball 1930.
19 NH, Alice Delysia and Mistinguett in the new salon. 1936

23

22

20 Alice Delysia wears Hartnell at home, Biarritz, 1936
21 NH, John Pleydell, Delysia, Biarritz, summer 1936
22 Gertrude Lawrence c. 1937
23 NH, last working holiday August 1939

5. The Share Capital of the Company is Twenty thousand pounds, divided into shares of One Pound each . . .

The subscribers were Norman, 'Designer', with 4,000 shares, Phyllis, 'Spinster', with 4,000 shares and Bish, 'Property Owner', with 1,700 shares. The Directors were Norman, Phyllis, Bish and Francis Walter Smith, the last three to be paid £125 a year each plus travelling expenses. Norman, as Managing Director, was to be paid £1,200 a year and Phyllis £400 as joint Managing Director. Norman's business capacities were known to need reinforcement and it was impossible for him to carry the whole burden of the business.

Phyllis was no back-room figure. She had proved herself a resourceful saleswoman with the Hartnell collections she took to India, was an attractive adornment on social occasions, including the Circus Party, and was amusing enough as compère at Norman's Paris shows to attract press comment and praise.

Norman was now allowed to charge his business entertainment expenses and travel to the company. He was seen more often at the most fashionable night spots and restaurants, as well as smart places abroad, so this represented a substantial increase on his salary. Furthermore, additional salary was to be paid to him 'in any year when the net profits of the company (after deduction of the extra salary) exceeded by more than £2,000 the amount required for payment of a dividend of 20% upon the capital paid upon the shares of the company' with provisos for changes in the share structure.

As long as Norman and Phyllis remained directors they were entitled to be managing directors. Both Norman and Phyllis sank virtually all their capital into the business, knowing that it relied entirely upon Norman for its continuing success. He was just twenty-eight years old, but for Phyllis, still unmarried and over thirty, it must have seemed an act of faith to put all her money into a one-man show.

Bish had a second wife to consider, but his business contacts were extensive and he had brought Fred Smith into the business. Owner of The Bow Foundry, Preston, the reason for his interest in a couture business is not known. However, Bish retained his interests in public houses and was associated with The Pindar of Wakefield in the Farringdon Road near Kings Cross until the late 1930s. A substantial pub with rooms to let above, more on the lines of his Warrington Hotel, it is not too far-fetched to imagine that useful business connections were made there. Bish was owner in conjunction with Mr and Mrs Kagi, who were permanently in the pub, whilst Bish was based in Brighton. He was also involved in the wholesale wines and spirits trade and later on also dealt in timber, both before and after he became a councillor in Brighton. In other words, whilst the Depression loomed and share values dived in 1929, a steady background income from the continuing sales of liquor buoyed up the Hartnell family finances. Phyllis and Norman also knew that they could just survive if necessary on the income from their South London property.

Shortly after Norman's KCVO was announced in 1977 an elderly Brighton acquaintance of Bish wrote that whenever she saw Bish in the late 1920s and asked him about Norman he would simply reply 'he's doing very well'. As Miss Louie pointed out, father and son were rather embarrassed by each other, but the support Bish gave to his son never wavered and it is thanks to him and Phyllis that a solid financial base was established.

In later decades, the name Norman Hartnell immediately meant gorgeous evening wear. Ian Thomas, his assistant from 1952 to 1969, was amused that Norman found day clothes so dull to design: this was not so in 1929 when he used tweeds in his Paris shows and was credited by *The New York Times* with the 'intricate detailing' applied to tweeds. Chanel and Molyneux had already popularised new uses of a 'male' fabric for women, but Norman softened the outline and made tweed clothes less 'sporty' and more 'feminine'.[25] His 'sleeveless pullover', worn over a crêpe dress, was illustrated by the *Herald Tribune*, and an advertisement for autumn opera capes showed a tiered and flounced trailing velvet example with a deep fur collar: this caused outrage at Hartnell as it was uncredited and no one knew if a manufacturer or the store had actually bought the model or copied it. However, the *Herald Tribune* also showed two of his best evening dresses 'through . . . [the] . . . entire collection runs, like a bright ribbon, the very essence of youth'. His dresses were now to the floor and some with a short train, the first return to long dresses creating the new evening silhouette, which became the international look of the 1930s.

In November 1929, the Hartnell new look was well publicised by the press. A fashion show at the new Park Lane hotel Grosvenor House emphasised that his day clothes were as short as ever, *The Shanghai Times* and the *Calcutta Englishman* stressing the point, whereas *The New York Times*, *Vogue* and *Harper's Bazaar* concentrated on Norman's more glamorous evening dresses.

Norman Hartnell had now seriously put English fashion on the world map. His ideas were as interesting and commercially viable as most emanating from Paris. Young girls and matrons bought his clothes. He was *news*.

CHAPTER SIX

'. . . Dropped them on the floor'

The 1930s began well for Norman. The New Year's Day edition of *The Daily Telegraph* featured a photograph in their series 'Art Gallery of Fashion' headed 'The Charm of Black Tulle'. The floor-length evening dress given such prominence was made of horizontally tucked satin ciré to the knees, and then of large graduated frills of tulle to the floor. The very high back depended on invisible shoulder straps from which long, draped scarves floated. This new silhouette was a variant on Norman's 1929 Paris success and underlined his facility at dealing with fabrics in unusual ways and colours. It expressed the increasing sophistication of Norman's ideas and his workrooms.

Mam'selle was an asset to his work, as were his embroiderers and cutters. His inspiration most often came from the English countryside, but on 2 January an *Evening Standard* correspondent wrote that she had been to visit him in his Paris salon and found him designing there. He said, tactfully, that he preferred designing for Englishwomen as they were 'more easy to dress'. The implication is that his London January sale was full of models from Paris, although he had no great workroom there. Dresses were usually sent from London to Paris, and if unsold they were sent back.

With the important change in silhouette, the previous year's Norman Hartnells were as outdated as everyone else's. Both Patou and Molyneux were also quick to design floor-length evening dresses in early 1930 and soon Paris designers all took up the theme.

One of Norman's finest dresses shown in Paris in early 1930 used his favourite pale leaf green, later known as Hartnell Green, but above the tulle flounces of the skirt he used solid embroidery of paillettes on hips, bodice and three-quarter-length jacket. A similar idea appeared in another glittering evening dress in which the sheath silhouette makes its first appearance and sets the scene for the most elegant and popular line of the 1930s. The arms and body of the jacket are encrusted with shaded and horizontally banded paillettes to just below the hips, where a deep band of white fox encircles the body over a slender band of black fox to the knees, from which a burst of black-and-white net sweeps the floor. Part of the sophistication of the image is due to the lighting of the scene by the incomparable de Meyer and the apparent depth and movement he instils into it that creates his New Look. Apart from the existing London Houses, Paris models were still eagerly sought by London women: in 1930 they could buy Vionnet from Maison Arthur in Dover Street and a Chanel copy in Gamages for 9 gns.[1]

But whereas the Chanel copy was simply 'No. 19', Norman's pre-Paris January show included models with the usual exotic names such as 'Laudanum Loo' a sinuous, yet voluminous skirted model of black chiffon printed with dull red poppies. 'Dresses not only *sweep* the floor, but they well-nigh cover it! Mannequins have to be acrobats as well as navigators,'[2] the *Evening News* reported. Most evening dresses were as tightly fitting as gloves to the knees, with flounces beneath to the floor. The American newspapers quickly reported this and the *Daily Telegraph* noted Norman's role in changing the design of women's clothes back to something based on a natural figure with the lines broken by the salient points of the body.[3]

The 'Gallery Girls' and London public in general saw the new line on the stage in *The Man in Possession* by H.M. Harwood at the Ambassadors Theatre, in which Isabel Jeans wore a coral pink chiffon dress with a yard-long train designed by Norman. Under his name in the programme credits appeared an acknowledgement for the loan of telephones from a company on Streatham Hill, SW2. If Norman noticed this, he must have realised his fortune even more keenly. As another coincidental touch, the next line reads 'Books by W & G Foyle, Ltd'. A quarter of a century later Norman would be the guest of Christina Foyle for the launch of *Silver and Gold* at one of her Foyle's Literary Luncheons; one of many subsequent attendances at these gatherings.

Interviewed after the play, Norman said: 'Women will have to learn again how to manage trains. They have forgotten too long.' He stressed that they had better learn quickly as Ascot clothes were bound to echo his new fashion. They probably found it simpler to apply the brilliant red-lacquered nail polish his mannequins wore.

All of his new 1930 dresses went with him to Paris later in January to show to the American buyers. Ever up to date he described them in his period cut-glass tones for an early sound newsreel film before setting off with his mannequins and models such as 'Circus Cissie', a favourite with many English clients, including Lady Weymouth. The young novelist Mollie Panter-Downes, later famous for her 'Letter from London' for *The New Yorker*, set off for America with a her own wardrobe of Norman Hartnell clothes, including 'Back to Nature' and 'Water Babies'. It was a trip taken to publicise her new book *Storm Bird*, and she was to fly from New York to Hollywood, then a journey of two days. This was all welcome publicity for Norman.

Whilst British and American newspapers applauded Norman's successes and credited him with having anticipated the '1930 mode', he was increasingly asked for his opinions on women and dress. On trousers for women he 'emphatically disapproved of the fashion',[4] in spite of having designed exotic 'lounging pyjamas' for his collections in 1924. He also predicted 'talkie' fashion shows, although doubting that they would ever be as popular as his live parades – 'Most women are not content to order dresses until they have handled them or tried them on. Such shows might be given by society hostesses.'[5]

Increasingly seen as the latest of 'British Brains Behind British Frocks'[6] in a group of four – Worth, Redfern, Molyneux and Hartnell – Norman was seen as a new fashion despot so that when the *Daily Express* launched 'A British Fashion Jury' he was included with the tennis player Eileen Bennett, the actress Isabel Jeans, painter C.R.W. Nevinson, illustrator Lewis Baumer and impresario Charles B. Cochran, for whom Norman had so desperately wanted to design a few years before. The other designer, Peter Russell, was making a name as a designer of day and sports clothes.

Both Norman and Charles B. Cochran thought that women should 'study fourteenth-century fashions' for the simplicity of line, Norman pointing out that modern life had introduced into dress 'stern plainness, dullness and even ugliness' which he sought to combat. On Englishwomen in general, he stated: 'It is probably her lack of intuition as to how to dress appropriately to the occasion that is the Englishwoman's greatest fault'[7] - yet he continued, 'We only notice an American when she is badly dressed.'[8]

This general espousing of American good taste was partly because all dress designers saw the advantage of gaining dollars from a market still rich enough to buy and reproduce models for profitable resale. Molyneux, particularly, sold well in America, and fabric manufacturers hit by the Depression were equally keen to sell their fabrics for the reproduced models. The longer skirts inevitably used more fabric, and most fabric houses extended credit to designers able to sell abroad and gain publicity. Some of the Norman Hartnell advertising of the 1930s was paid for by the producer of fabric used in the model illustrated. For Norman, expansion into other areas of the British Empire was an option under investigation for exploitation as soon as practicable.

A more pressing need was new premises. At the first meeting of directors of Norman Hartnell Ltd on 19 October 1929 it was agreed that a French company should be established. By 1 November Norman's father Bish had bought 250 more shares, his wife doing the same. Fred Smith bought 400 and Percival Parker, auditor of the company, also did so. Loans of 8% pa were given to the company, Smith and Parker loaning £350 each and Bish £1,600, his wife loaning £1,000, so that all capital came from family and friends, other than the Westminster Bank, which was to provide a fluctuating overdraft facility.

Norman Hartnell Ltd also took over the leases of 18 and 18A Bruton Place as well as 22 South Bruton Place, all housing workrooms which saw 800 models a year brought into existence. As an advertorial in *Harper's Bazaar* put it 'some wonder if even his present premises are big enough'. It was a question which began to exercise the new board, whilst they rearranged the finances and kept the Paris and London houses going in the teeth of the recession. Furthermore, a young Cambridge graduate who had approached Norman for advice on his career and joined Reville-Terry was now about to open his own business nearby. A former Footlights designer and performer, the young Victor Stiebel gave Norman uneasy moments as he realised that he would not be the youngest newsworthy designer in London for much longer.

From one point of view Norman had no need to worry. His success was such that at his May Show in the May Fair Hotel, there was not a spare seat in either of the two large hired rooms nor in the hall. Lady Diana Cooper, Lady Louis Mountbatten and the Hon. Mrs Richard Norton were amongst the guests, the latter two clients of Norman.[9] He was also called on to design a variety of dresses for some of the year's most distinguished weddings. The sister of the former Oonagh Guinness, now Mrs Philip Kindersley, Maureen Guinness, married the Earl of Ava, son of the Marquess of Dufferin and Ava. Although the bride's dress was inspired by Botticelli with a train some twelve feet long all embroidered with raised white satin lilies and gold leaves, her eleven bridesmaids wore the nearest design to a full-skirted crinoline 'Victorian' dress seen for many years. The tulle dresses as reported had 'applied shirred, large, circular overlapping applied panels to the skirts', a development of the decoration on the 'Vampire' model some seasons past. The posies they carried were made of silver and gold glass.[10] Hartnell's love of glass grew with the years, as seen in his houses and the large salon of his next premises, but had begun with the discovery of a discarded glass ship model designed in France as a light fitting. Decades later the veteran fashion journalist Alison Settle was to remember this unusual mascot in his first salon as a good-luck talisman.[11]

In the spring a niece of Lady Diana Cooper, Deirdre Hart-Davis, had married Ronald Balfour wearing one of the new sheath dresses in soft gold lamé with a golden veil, and her bridesmaids were in gold tulle. Their headdresses were described as 'uncomfortable' – '"Hold these, Randolph," said Miss "Baby" Jungman, as she took off hers, handing her lilies to Mr Churchill, who forthwith dropped them on the floor.'[12]

As a contrast in style – and all the wedding dresses were completely different or variants – as in the case of the Hon. Eileen Berry, who married Mr T. Thistlethwayte on 3 July 1930, the train was cut as part of the skirt as with Oonagh Guinness's and she also had a halo headdress but made of three bands of satin. The well-built bridesmaids all had figure-hugging dresses which swept out below the knee. But all these dresses were quite eclipsed by the wedding of Maysie Gasque to John Robinson at St Margaret's, Westminster. Miss Gasque was the daughter of the former company secretary and a director of F.W. Woolworth, and known as 'the wealthy American heiress'.

There were twelve bridesmaids and a thousand guests. It was a wedding attracting huge crowds of sightseers and they were not disappointed by the sight of Miss Gasque. Indeed, the crowd tried to follow her into the church, whereupon the mounted police sprang into action to protect the sixteen feet of the embroidered satin train, which fell as an overskirt from the waist, her veil hanging from a mantilla-like headdress. Like Miss Berry, who ordered twenty-four Hartnell models for her trousseau, Miss Gasque ordered all of hers from Norman, including her going-away gown of Cambridge blue taffeta trimmed with pale grey fox fur. Norman's preoccupation with the use of fur was becoming a lucrative hallmark of his finer designs. A black-and-white dress illustrated in British *Vogue* with the sheath outline was of white net with a sunburst arrangement of silver paillettes centring on the waist and shading into black on the black tulle below-the-knee spreading skirt. The loose three-quarter coat was encrusted with paillettes and weighted with a deep band of white fox. Again and again, these elements occur in Norman's designs over the years, varying as the line developed throughout the 1930s.

The income and publicity from such weddings was very necessary for Norman Hartnell Ltd. In addition to stage and increasingly film clothes, Norman also participated in a touring display of British fashion which travelled the country backed by the *Daily Sketch*. He was also probably the first British designer to donate a dress for a raffle at a charity ball in 1930 – an evening dress then worth a colossal 42 gns. A fashion show in Manchester with other designers participating was also agreed to and proved a success as it brought in some rich clients. Nevertheless, the Directors' minutes of this period reveal the scramble behind the scenes to accommodate the business within the recession. The Circus Party had cost over £285 and was written off by the company as publicity.

In February 1930, the question of closing the Paris premises was discussed, and in London Gladys Cooper's Beauty Preparations had left the second floor of no. 10 so Norman moved his offices into them, with the idea of letting the top floor as a flat.

Fred Smith and Bish travelled to Paris to investigate the state of business in the rue de Ponthieu and eventually decided that it would be better to let Phyllis take on sole responsibility for it. She was to move over to Paris and run the business and also operate workrooms. She became engaged to James Stuart of the Ordnance Section in the Indian Army, so this plan came to nothing in 1931.[13]

In May, Miss Margaret Whigham had been presented at Court wearing her latest Hartnell dress of white tulle embroidered over the hips and bodice of the sheath outline with silver flowers and carrying a Victorian posy. Her mother had also been expensively dressed for the occasion. Already much written about and illustrated by the press, Margaret Whigham was to be the most famous debutante not only of the year or decade but ultimately of the century. She was to become a client of Victor Stiebel too, but she and Norman were made for one another. Many voices whispered crossly that Miss Whigham employed a press agent in order to achieve the publicity she did, but her looks and enigmatic personality were enough to achieve her success. Although fond of Norman until his death and a client for decades and through both her marriages, theirs was strictly a business relationship and it would never have occurred to her to 'ask my dressmaker to dinner'.[14] It was fine to meet socially at parties, but in those days, that was that, an opinion independently shared by Dame Barbara Cartland.[15] Norman could hardly have cared less. Apart from meeting prospective brides and some actresses, he shunned most contacts with clients, though glad to benefit from their publicity, especially if they were in films or on the stage.

By September 1930 a decrease of 11% in profits was noted. Madame Denise, the vendeuse, was to fix prices in the salon and stick to them if she and her colleagues wanted any commission, and this would only be paid when the clients paid for the orders, not at the time of ordering. Nor could any employee order more than £10 of goods without the permission of a director. The problems of internal management were to be dealt with by decreasing all salaries by 10% and cutting down on advertising, repair and travelling expenses. Cash payments to achieve larger discounts and an overall saving of 5% on the previous year's buying were all indications of the Depression biting. Norman was to be sent to America as a PR measure. But financially things did not get better for some years, a typical symptom of the times. However, Norman devoted much thought to the design of lucrative and elegant day clothes, much as he found them boring. *The Sphere* was one of many journals in March 1930 to illustrate his day clothes: fashionable tweed coats and skirts given a less countrified appearance.

A revealing interview took place between Norman and Baron de Meyer in 1930. The Baron insisted that he was alone in believing many Paris fashions begin in England, although, as we have seen, few of the major papers or journals of the time would have agreed with him. He wrote that Norman:

> holds me responsible for his not having moved as yet. 'You said unless I found an entire house suitable for business, I was not to leave Bruton Street. I haven't found anything yet . . . My skirts are all of them even-lengthed . . . don't insist on the theme – "Hartnell is particularly successful with spangles and net". Acquired reputations are so hard to live down. All my clothes are made simpler.'[16]

De Mayer demurred.

Norman then stressed how in 1928 his evening dresses were to the ground and de Meyer agreed that he was on the right track then. Norman was interested to know what de Meyer would write about London fashions. De Meyer put the problems of a London designer into focus by saying that a Parisienne discards a style before it goes out of date, whilst an Englishwoman only accepts it just as it is out of date, and that coming from an active fashion centre such as Paris it is extraordinary to see 'an accumulation of outdated fashions'. There was then a small number of women in England caring to be 'a la mode' and it is not yet quite correct to be 'too actively interested in clothes'. De Meyer then interviewed Lady Juliet Duff, Lady Diana Cooper, Lady Curzon and Lady Mountbatten. Lady Diana Cooper dressed at Ospovat, as did Lady Curzon. Lady Mountbatten liked Lady Victor Paget's and Kay Norton's dress shops, sadly not mentioning Hartnell, but remarking that Englishwomen simply had not the interest or elegance of French or American women in their clothes, although looking good in British tweeds for sporting events. Clearly Norman's battle was still on for London as a fashion centre.

José Collins helped. For a Bristol appearance, she ordered a variety of dresses including one model called 'Venusberg' – shades of his shared love of Wagner with Blake. A now forgotten American film star, Jacqueline Logan starred with Ivor Novello in *A Symphony in Two Flats* and bought a variety of dresses from Norman, as did Alice Delysia, who became a friend of his. Captivated as a child by Gaby Deslys, Norman found himself enraptured by Delysia. 'She seemed then the very essence of naughtiness which existed for me in some kind of adolescent fairy tale.'[17]

Norman was on the PR trip in 1930 to New York when a vendeuse in the salon, Miss Paula Knight, sent a long cable telling him that Delysia had been in and wanted Norman to dress her for her role in the musical comedy *A Pair of Trousers*. The cast included Harold Warrender, but for Norman the star's desertion of Jean Patou for him put him into a frenzy of designing. The designs were sent and approved, so that he arrived back in time for the first fittings with her: 'She wore high silk stockings and a hat with tall feathers sprouting out like fireworks.'[18]

Over lunch at Quaglino's she invited Norman to accompany her on a short holiday to Marrakesh before the opening of the play and he accepted, before thinking it over for a day or two and deciding to have a diplomatic cold. Norman's memories of Delysia telescope five years into two pages. Although the play was not the success hoped for, it caused a sensation, having a trial run in Birmingham and then Southampton before moving to the Criterion for its short London run.

'Alice Delysia stood in the centre of the stage in one of the most fascinating long coats I have seen' began the *Daily Express* review, which was largely about Norman's clothes, as the review confessed to not understanding what was going on in the play. Delysia became a firm friend and even brought

Norman a new client – Mistinguett, the great Parisian star with the world-fa-mous legs and for a time the highest-paid entertainer in the world.

In January 1931, Norman was highly visible at the Chelsea Arts Ball with Lady Portarlington, Oliver Messel and Colonel Moore-Brabazon in a slouch hat and big brown beard. He also designed the dress for Lady Perdita Asquith's wedding to William Jolliffe. Lady Diana Cooper had advised Sir James Barrie, who bought the dress for his goddaughter for a 'pink' wedding. The dress was described as having the colour of the centre of a pink tea rose and had the now familiar fourteenth-century sheath line with long trailing lace sleeves. The pink fringe of the satin was in a shade to be repeated in a few years for Lady Alice Montagu Douglas Scott on her marriage to H.R.H. the Duke of Gloucester, Norman's first royal commission.

As a slight foretaste of these royal commissions, the comedy *The Improper Duchess* required that the Anglo-French comedienne Yvonne Arnaud be given some imposing dresses for her equally imposing figure. As the improbably named Stella Stallite wrote of Norman's designs for the skirts, 'they are immensely full, even voluminous'. Pink, rose and cinnamon were the main colours, and heavy borders of dyed or white fox weighted the regal beaded confections.[19] This was a new side of Hartnell's talents, for the bared back had become his latest twist to the beaded dresses he now designed for his youngest and most glamorous clients.

In his January show Norman had sixty models, *Women's Wear Daily* term-ing him 'most fashionable' but noting that three-quarters of the models were for girls only, with lots of lace and net, and one black net model named 'Nicely Thanks'. He also put brides into satin berets and thought up as many novelties as today's aspiring designers, making a wedding dress of a white cobweb lace. De Meyer was again amongst the spectators lending a connois-seur's approval to the show, and American buyers still turned up; Norman Hartnell models sold to several American department stores.

In 1931 the young architect Gerald Lacoste (b. 1907) opened his own prac-tice at 14 Bruton Street. Of a younger generation and the son of an Eastbourne businessman, he had been educated at Brighton College and was the youngest ever associate of the RIBA. At a tennis party attended by Norman in Frinton, the two men met and, apart from being Bruton Street neighbours and fans of Brighton, found that they had much in common. Norman had initially worked towards becoming an architect but had become a dress designer. Lacoste had been attracted to dress designing, but had found a talent for innovative architectural design. Both men were interested in modern design, particularly in the increasingly sophisticated use of glass. Norman had used glass jewellery in his shows in preference to valuable stones and had unusual cut-glass lights in his showrooms. The two men and their mutual friends occasionally spent weekends together and apart from discussing clients and Society, the future development of Norman Hartnell Ltd and the pressing need for a complete new large building was discussed. Both men had active, sociable fathers prominent in their local seaside communities and had their eyes set on glittering futures.[20]

One of Lacoste's future clients appeared through Norman when Miss Valerie French married the 21-year-old Lord Brougham and Vaux. One of the bridesmaids was Miss 'Baby' Jungman, and the Whigham and Beaton families were amongst the guests. At a preview of the dresses in Norman's salon, 'a man with a Guard's moustache, in the corner of the room, volunteered the observation that the dress worn by a tall mannequin was "too sweetly pretty".'[21] Somehow there was always to be a big man with a moustache in Norman's life until he died, for reasons later to be discussed.

As the reporter noted on watching the parade of clothes, a hundred years ago it would have been a parade of the groom's clothes that would have attracted attention. Huge crowds again watched the wedding party arriving and departing. The bride was in a satin sheath with a flared below-the-knee skirt, the forerunner of many other heavy satin wedding dresses, and it was said to be the tightest dress of the season.

Jessie Matthews, another elegant leading actress of the 1930s, was photographed by Hoyningen-Huene wearing Norman's 'Slide', a white 'peau d'ange' skirt worn under a long black fox-trimmed coat. She had recently starred in *Ever Green* and several of her later films were dressed by Norman. She also modelled a chainmail all-paillette-covered evening dress for a British *Vogue* feature. This was as nothing compared to the First Court of 1931, in which a dozen women wore Norman's clothes, including Lady Victoria Scott, whose Norman Hartnell clothes impressed Lady Alice Montagu Douglas Scott.

At the next Court Miss Behar was presented wearing one of Norman's dresses. The Behar family were to prove one of Gerald Lacoste's greatest clients, with Mayfair flats and other properties requiring architectural and interior design. The list of those present also included several of the recent Hartnell 'brides', now settling into married life, with all the social round this then implied. For Hartnell it meant orders and income. By the Third Court it was reported that more spectacular frocks had been made by Hartnell for London debutantes than by any other dressmaker. For the June Courts, he recorded twenty-five new dresses, but for Norman a great upheaval loomed in his business and private life as his sister Phyllis, known to him as Topsy, married in mid-July with the intention of leaving for India in September.

Topsy's decision was undoubtedly a blow to both Norman and their father Bish. Used to her absence in India or Paris, she was nevertheless a good solid influence on Normie's more extravagant lifestyle. She was his only sister; the stepchildren of his parents were never as close to him or as important in his life.

In March, it had been decided to close the Paris salon and let it, with the promise that it would be vacated for two weeks each year for dress shows. In fact, the address was maintained in this way until the war. Bish's new wife wanted the money she had invested in Norman Hartnell Ltd returned and so Norman bought her shares. Topsy wanted a dress allowance, which was refused. As a sign of the situation it was decided by the directors of the company to insure Norman for £5,000, enough to cover everyone's financial interest in the company should he meet with a fatal accident. But as the months passed it emerged that neither sibling had paid income tax and the company loaned the money, to be repaid in two years. No more such loans were to be made and everyone must have wondered whether Topsy had been the restraining influence on Norman they had thought her to be.

By September the company was also asked to pay for Topsy's wedding, which was usually the problem of the father. In this instance, Topsy and Normie paid 50% and the company the other half owing. Even the cost of Topsy's wedding trousseau was discussed and the company paid over 50%, Topsy agreeing to pay the rest. The £200 income tax each owed by Norman and Phyllis was to be borne entirely by the company, as were their debts to the company. Norman owed some £423 and Topsy £304.

During the September meeting it was also decided to pay monthly salaries to Normie and Topsy at the end of each month, so that they could manage their affairs more comfortably in the difficult times they were all experiencing. Topsy went further: she asked Norman to buy 1,000 of her shares at a guinea each within six months, and a further 1,000 at a later date. Norman duly paid for 1,000 shares in October. Soon Topsy had left for India, where she still carried on a business selling Hartnell creations and was later remembered as a vivacious, elegantly clad officer's wife, so dark in her colouring that some people thought she must be Jewish, particularly as she was involved in a clothing business and wore black often. Such were the typically naive attitudes and prejudices of the expatriate community at a period when the new film star Merle Oberon hid her Indian roots and kept her own mother hidden from sight.

'The new Rolls-Royce drew up on the south side of Bruton Street in front of the famous Salons of Norman Hartnell, about whose success as the leading dress-maker of Europe, Gertrude had read greedily . . .'[22] So began many a visit to Bruton Street. Some clients came every few days to fill time: 'And Gertrude took to the fashions of circa 1902, and paid poor Norman Hartnell absolutely fabulous sums of money for jeopardising his impregnably precarious position by turning her out like a positive Cochran revue, only better, of course.'[23]

Blake had seen enough at the salon to compress his knowledge into a few telling lines, but in this novel dedicated to his friend he could not resist the sort of joke they both loved: 'She and Norman Hartnell, after putting their heads together, concocted a new and jolly uniform for the poor dark blue Girl Guides, which was instantly sanctioned by a grateful nation, for it consisted of dainty tailor-mades patterned with sprightly hollyhocks, honeysuckles and fig-leaves: and saucy sun bonnets to match.'[24] This was typical of the nonsense which made Blake and Bish roar with laughter. In 1944, Norman *did* design a uniform for the Girl Guides. It was not a patterned dainty tailor-made design.

In the October *Vogue*, a survey of London fashions with witty drawings by Cecil Beaton urged readers to consider the reduced prices on some of the Norman Hartnell day clothes. The desire to maximise returns was clearly in full swing, as was his publicity machine. Photographs of Margaret Whigham at Ascot in a long puff-sleeved and smocked afternoon dress were reproduced in almost every major American newspaper, attention focused on her smocked muff. She was increasingly photographed wearing his dresses.

Many commentators remarked on the new 'Victorian' or 'Empire' line, without bothering to check just what they meant. This nonsense extended to Norman, who was credited with reviving the bustle and stated in an interview: 'I abominate the bustle – I have never seen a smart woman wearing a bustle. No house of repute is showing frocks with bustles . . . I am delighted with the new silhouette, broad shoulders, slim hips and a reasonable fullness in the skirt.' He espoused 'the Princess line' and in view of his earlier success and later developments interestingly opined, 'There is no point in reviving bygone fashions.' His own autumn collection was based on colour inspired by cathedral windows and included 'jacket suits in corduroy, velvet and velveteen – British materials shown in Paris'.[25] *Harper's Bazaar* remarked on his 'Magpie' dresses of black and white, a design he reworked continually to great effect over the decades, as well as a new idea of using coloured gloves with evening dresses.[26]

One legal case that had great relevance to all in retail business occurred in November 1931 when traders obtained a court ruling that made a man free of the responsibility for his wife's debts if she was extravagant. Until the 1960s it was still quite usual for Norman's clients' accounts to be sent directly to the husband of the woman ordering items. In the 1930s, many women neither asked nor discussed the price of things they were ordering and simply assumed that their husbands paid the account. Norman said of the court result 'that he has not had such good news in years. At last,' he said, 'I shall know where I am. It has been the bane of my life having to ask customers insolent questions about their matrimonial relations with a view to finding out what credit to allow.'[27]

Norman's stage and film work attracted more publicity when Isabel Jeans appeared in some striking black-and-white clothes in *Counsel's Opinion* at the Strand Theatre, and Edna Best and Anne Grey, two promising young film stars in English films, wore some of Norman's latest collection. The work involved in choosing appropriate clothes for films became a matter of increasing interest to women in general throughout the country, and they had to be chosen with the release date of a year ahead in mind.

To crown his achievements in an emotionally and financially difficult year, Gertrude Lawrence, a unique star of the period, wore a series of Norman's clothes in the comedy *Can the Leopard?* at the Haymarket Theatre 'in which she swooped and swooned, floated around and flirted with Kim Peacock, her leading man'.[28] Her evening dress of lamé coloured chiffon had a horizontal tucked bodice and sunray pleated skirt with a pleated cape. Norman discussed at length in *Silver and Gold* a difficult elderly duchess who wasted an afternoon discussing the shades of red which might suit her, interrupted by continual put-downs of Norman and his suggestions. As an illustration of exactly why he avoided most clients and the showroom, the story is unsurpassed. The next day the dress was ordered in black and the services of his vendeuses and his time had been again wasted.

The year 1932 already augured well in January: Norman dressed the bride and bridesmaids at another huge wedding at St Margaret's, Westminster where the 21-year-old Earl of Jersey married the 19-year-old Patricia Richards from Australia. The bride wore a supremely elegant simple ivory satin gown embroidered with pearls with a full skirt and train, all a foil to the lace veil said to have belonged to Marie Antoinette. Due to cold weather, the eight bridesmaids wore slim dresses of flame-coloured velvet. Of the villagers bussed in for the ceremony from the Earl's Oxfordshire estate, one old boy replied without any timidity to the London journalists, 'Been to London afore? I dare-say as I have. I dare-say as I was here afore you was born. I dare-say as I have seen more weddings than you.'

In a move to generate more business in London, Norman joined with Reville-Terry and Isobel to put on a combined dress show, the first time major London designers had dared to emulate Paris on even this minor scale. Norman was reported as saying he had no doubt that London would eventually be recognised as a major fashion centre.

Whilst film star Jeanette MacDonald became his first Hollywood client, the London Fashions Group held a lunch at the Savoy to begin a big promotion of British wholesale fashion houses. They also applauded the decision of the British Colour Council to decide on 'the fashionable tones for women's clothes' and so free themselves from the dictates of the French and Austrian manufacturers. Although smitten by flu for some weeks, Norman was well enough to welcome an invention that had caught on in America and Europe, but not in Britain. ICI had a new 'improved Lightning Fastner or Zipp [sic]' of a new lightweight construction, so ever in the vanguard of novel new design, Norman designed 'Real Estate', a model of silver lamé with diamante embroidery and a zipper fitted up one side to replace all the former studs and hooks formerly used to achieve an absolutely flat line at the opening.

Although this and the joint exhibition brought him a great deal of publicity, he had to beware of his rivals. A new Abnormal Importations Act of autumn 1931 which potentially raised import duty to 100% on certain quantities of goods, combined with the falling value of the pound had an adverse effect on Paris exports to Britain, particularly of silk or artificial silk garments. Thus Captain Molyneux appeared swiftly in London in January 1932 to inspect buildings suitable for a potential London branch of his business. Over the next few years, various other new tariffs added to the attractions of a London business for other Parisian designers.

Although the managing director of Reville-Terry made a brave show of being part of a new London world-fashion base, the arrival of Molyneux created some unease. His reputation and clientele were so great that it was feared he would take away a good deal of established London business. The combined dress show at Claridge's, attended by Princesses Helene Victoria, Marie Louise and 'Pat', as well as Mrs Stanley Baldwin, also attracted Queen Mary's attention and she was sent a sample of the models on view for a private view. Molyneux, one of Gertrude Lawrence's designers, was neglected again by her when she chose to wear an ultra-sophisticated selection of Norman's slinkiest clothes for the Elstree film of Frederick Lonsdale's *Aren't We All?* so that British fashion design, and Norman especially, received an accolade from a popular star. Norman then went to Paris for his spring show.

It is impossible to disentangle Norman's memories as condensed in *Silver and Gold*, for he showed his collections regularly in Paris until 1939. One of his early mannequins, Mrs McKillop, remembered that for the spring 1932 showings she was one of five girls who went with Norman and Phyllis.[28] They flew down from Croydon aerodrome in an Imperial Airways machine with Captain Dudley Travers, one of the Royal Mail plane's pilots usually flying to Cape Town. The party was seen off by Bish, no doubt anxious about the whole venture, although Travers was a friend of Norman's. Not unnaturally, the publicity surrounding the flight was extensive, with photographs of the elegantly hatted and coated girls forming an interesting background to Norman in a vast travelling coat and large peaked flat cap.

Norman bravely said:

> I shall make Americans buy English frocks in Paris. All repeat orders are telephoned back to my Bruton Street salon and every dress is thus made in England. They are then sent out to North and South America and Spain . . . I am flying over with my special staff. My British models will be shown by beautiful English mannequins and will be made of British materials.

Apart from blowing the trumpet for British goods and so coercing wavering society women to 'Buy British', Norman then commented on his four years of showing in Paris in his salon:

   . . . it was a great struggle to keep it on in the face of the severe
   opposition I have encountered from the Parisian firms. I expect
   they will be more antagonistic now, but I have established myself
   on their doorstep and I shall make overseas buyers purchase my
   models on French soil.

Hanging on to his cap, Norman and his girls boarded the plane.

In Paris, he showed the versatility of ICI's lightning zip fastener on many
clothes, but even as he was there Molyneux was in London supervising the
decoration of his first London House in Grosvenor Street. *Women's Wear
Daily* reported the characteristics of the main twenty Paris Houses of which
Norman Hartnell was considered to be of equal status by now with Molyneux, Mainbocher, Chanel, Lanvin, Patou, Vionnet or Schiaparelli.[29]

It was fortunate that his London business was so well established, because
a month after his return he found that he had acquired a new neighbour. The
Durban-born Victor Stiebel

   is what the Americans call 'a hustler'. In less than three weeks he
   acquired the premises he wanted, had them decorated, and completed all the models he had decided to show. I liked particularly
   his chic and serviceable tweeds, his exquisitely artistic evening
   dresses . . . All the jewellery . . . was real . . . the furs of a rare
   quality and beautifully worked.[30]

The settings of the new Stiebel concern were designed by the redoubtable
interior decorator Syrie Maugham with floral displays by the equally distinguished Constance Spry, in itself a newsworthy event.

Bish immediately arranged with Revillon for the loan of a hugely expensive fur coat which was placed in a showcase in the hall at 10 Bruton Street.
Having 'lost' his sister Phyllis, Norman might well have envied Stiebel his
elegant sisters from Surrey.

The Stiebel clothes were immediately popular, made on svelte young lines
of beautiful fabrics and just right for the slim debutantes so courted by
Norman.

   He was selling clothes rather like mine, only more cheaply . . .
   Edward Molyneux . . . sold dresses not at all like mine and much

more expensively. Quite frankly, I could with pleasure at that time have packed Victor and Edward into a wheelbarrow and tipped them both over Beachy Head.[31]

With the initial panic over, Norman soon realised that neither of them had his unique eye for embroidery, that most sophisticated of the dressmaker's arts; nor did they have his established clientele. Even though fickle, his clientele knew enough about clothes to recognise the virtuoso capacity of Norman for creating a major dress for every grand occasion. Both Stiebel and Molyneux, especially, made superb evening clothes, but their forte lay in day clothes, something never very dear to Norman's heart, although he recognised the financial merits.

As the decade rapidly progressed, all this became clear. For the moment the cost of materials, which had prompted the directors of Hartnell to issue stern instructions to their employees, remained a major problem. The cost of fine silk stockings doubled as imported silk attracted heavy new import duties. The use of British fabrics became both a patriotic and economic necessity. 'English printed silks are the Cinderella of the textile world,' an Oxford Street wholesaler told the *Yorkshire Post*. 'I can show you patterned fabrics from France where there are fourteen colours. The Englishman only makes his printed silks in three colours.'[32] If Britain really aspired to 'world leadership in fashion' then changes were overdue. They came quite rapidly from manufacturers quick to see the financial incentives.

By May 'Nottingham laces and satins have been the first choice of the majority of those ordering court gowns. In cases where a dress has been hand-embroidered, customers invariably insisted that even the beads should be British made,' Norman told the *Daily Mail*.[33] Molyneux also confirmed that their dresses 'were patriotic down to the last detail', revealing that they were fully in business.

Norman now dressed Jeanne Stuart and the other actresses for *It's A Girl* and went overboard with a riot of expensive white fox and fashionable tucks to the dresses, drawing loud applause from the Depression-battered audience of the Alhambra in distant Glasgow. He then gave a fashion show in the Café de Paris for which Gerald Lacoste designed the background of a two-sided disc, one side silvered and one black, reversing for light or dark-coloured dresses. The girls gave a good show under the lights 'with arms extended . . . like butterflies impaled'[34] against the disc. Mrs

Wooley-Hart, an extravagantly kind client of Norman's, was present as were Lady Brougham and Vaux, Isabel Jeans and Lady Ashley. Lacoste was a keen guest at Mrs Wooley-Hart's parties, some of which he designed for her, and he became Lord Brougham and Vaux's architect. The *Daily Sketch* noted that Lacoste wanted people to 'go all modern'[35] in their homes, something at which the British were rather backward. Under his influence, Norman's thoughts of new premises for his business were easily turned to ultra-modernistic elegance, for was he not considered to be the epitome of the most modern of young designers?

Stiebel and Peter Russell had fashionably austere backgrounds for display in their salons. Molyneux had a surprisingly imaginative faux Louis XVI look to his building, which he later vacated when Norman moved to reopen in his large new House at 26 Bruton Street. Molyneux was so impressed by Norman's new premises that he hired Lacoste to both build and design an even larger building for him, one of three remarkable Mayfair dress Houses created by Lacoste in the 1930s, at a time when he was much in demand as an innovative young architect.

Lacoste studied the Hartnell salon and workroom for two years and observed the workings of a top couture Jouse. He also travelled to Paris with Norman and together they saw the most advanced designs utilised by the greatest couturiers. There was nothing that Norman left to chance, including the presentation of his clothes.

'Page', Mrs Robert Nesbitt, was the most successful and sought-after mannequin and she explained how a dress should be worn: 'go on strike and pretend that you have come straight out of one of those so-called schools for mannequins'. Norman relayed this to his Sonia, who then snaked her way across the room, making the dress look like an exploded paper bag.[36]

Nothing just happened at Norman Hartnell: Norman had to control everything and as the strain mounted with the years, so did the tensions and his bouts of ill health grow more frequent.

In 1932, he was still young, highly energetic and his clothes were fun: Cecil Beaton's photographs of his sister Nancy, wearing the latest Hartnell dress, appeared as a full-page announcement on her engagement to Sir Hugh Smiley in *The Sketch* (no more references to 'horrid Norman Hartnell') whilst he was useful, and similar prominence was given to Lady Eleanor Smith in British *Vogue*, all fading away in the face of vast press coverage for Alice Delysia in *Mother of Pearl* produced by C.B. Cochran. She wore a blue-violet evening dress of sheath outline and with a fish train, with over 4,000 beads sewn on by hand.

Norman told the press,

> It is really very simple. Mlle Delysia told me the character she was to play, and I sat down and thought out a few frocks, which I sketched onto this paper. Delysia approved. Then we got some fine white net, with which she was fitted. That was the basis of the frock. After that we chose the colour, the choice being made on the stage, with the foot-lights and 'limes' full on, so that we should know exactly what it would look like.'

Norman also told an unidentified reporter that Delysia had duplicates of all her clothes, as they became dusty and worn on stage. The sophistication of Delysia, her figure and the allure of her movements took London by storm yet again. Girls and young women aspired to the elegance she encapsulated: callow youth was not sought after. Girls wanted to wear make-up and cover themselves with beautiful clothes as sophisticates.

A consummation of this desire, the wedding of Norman's star debutante client Margaret Whigham to Charles Sweeny, a golfing friend of the Prince of Wales, had no equal. Held at the Brompton Oratory it was the public 'Hartnell Wedding' of the decade. Until he dressed members of the Royal Family, neither the dress nor the scale of the theatre surrounding the event were to be replicated. In February 1933, the wedding captured the attention of press and public in a manner none of his competitors managed to do for their clients.

In her autobiography *Forget Not*, Margaret, Duchess of Argyll (as she became later) was quite candid about her two near marriages before this one. The daughter of a rich and successful businessman with a fortune based on British Celanese, Margaret Whigham was clearly a desirable heiress and a stunningly beautiful one too. She almost married Prince Aly Khan and then the Earl of Warwick, famously breaking off her engagement to him. He magnanimously gave her a green shagreen cocktail cabinet as a wedding present, moved to America and later had a contract with MGM as an aspiring film star, marrying Lady Rose Bingham, one of the bridesmaids. The Prince later married Miss Joan Guinness née Yarde-Buller.

Quite late in life the Duchess was justifiably proud of her first wedding dress, although she erroneously and somewhat typically thought the design was a precursor of Norman's for Princess Elizabeth in 1947.[37] Norman thought 'her perfection of appearance recalls the pink and white of camellias, and her hesitant stutter adds one more charm to this beautiful person who showed the women of her age how to use cosmetics, how to dress, how to be a success, and how to behave whilst becoming one'.[38]

The width of the aisle of the Oratory made a wide train possible and the 28-foot-long train of embroidered tulle and satin duly astounded everyone who saw it. When it was shown in the salon, it stretched nine feet wide right across the main room and curled around the corner into the next. Thirty workroom girls spent six weeks on the ensemble. The dress is rightly considered a major example of twentieth-century dress in pearl white satin embroidered with a large star motif cut out on net and sewn with seed pearls and silver glass bugle beads. The close-fitting skirt sweeps out in a burst of tulle at the knees, and the long sleeves have long folds of hanging white tulle.

Over 2,000 guests arrived, but 1,000 or so spectators forced their way into the church; women using elbows and umbrellas scuffled with police and the Knightsbridge traffic stopped.

If the bride's dress excited admiration, then so did her going-away dress and glorious trousseau, all shown at the salon on Miss Whigham beforehand, and including five ingenious evening dresses. An astute journalist caught Norman typically in an alcove at the end. He cast an eye over each model and then added a brooch or a bracelet, took off a scarf and substituted a fur, or tweaked a hat to a different angle! 'He has an eagle eye for just the little thing that makes the hair's breadth between success and failure.'[39]

Possibly as a gesture towards the new Mrs Sweeny's father's financial success with British Celanese, Norman also showed some day and evening models in rayon and caused a stir at the White City Fashion Show promoting British clothes and fabrics on 20 February 1933, two days before Miss Whigham became Mrs Sweeny.

Both the bride and her mother were enthusiastic patrons of Norman Hartnell and Victor Stiebel, but with the great success of the wedding dress, Norman realised that he had again asserted his pre-eminence as the leading London designer. He also had the promise of more such successes, for his young clients also included a bridesmaid at the wedding, Lady Bridget Poulett, as lovely in her own way as Mrs Sweeny and with the added mystique of being an aristocrat with ancient lineage. Other friends of the recent bride included Jeanne Stourton, also a bridesmaid, and Baba

Beaton, Cecil's other sister. All were and remained Hartnell clients to a lesser or greater degree.

Already in April 1932 the directors of Norman Hartnell Ltd were considering a letter from Wilson & Co., estate agents, offering the premises of 26 Bruton Street, diagonally across the road from no. 10. It was decided to offer £1,000 a year rent and the remainder of the lease of 10 Bruton Street.

The leases of the scattered workrooms were a constant irritant, as were the scattered rooms themselves. No. 26 is a large building, a substantially George III town house given an imposing staircase around 1800 and then redesigned about 1890, and the greatest practical advantage lay in the completed redevelopment of the mews house at the rear of the building. This had been reconstructed with an eye to the local dressmakers, for it now consisted of large workrooms with large steel-framed windows and the garden area between mews and main house had also been built over so that a business such as Norman's could easily expand within its walls. As it happened, the premises were later to prove too small and extra workrooms still had to be hired nearby in the decades to come.

Although the move had been thought about for at least two years previously, it was not to happen until 1934. As the company minutes reveal, the negotiations dragged on through 1932 and 1933. In his account of this period in *Silver and Gold* Norman mentions other possibilities investigated: Sunderland House – 'too overpowering'; Grosvenor Street – 'I also scorned'. Although the rents were a third of Bruton Street, Molyneux, of course, was already a large presence there.

Mrs Syrie Maugham advised Norman to take an Adam house in the grand-looking Portland Place, however Norman 'feared that my clients would not care to take their limousines northwards across the hubbub of Oxford Street'. Curiously, he thought that Belgravia was the place to be as 'the wind was blowing westward'. Neither Belgrave nor Berkeley Square were suitable. The former had no use for trade,[40] the latter was about to be vandalised by the elephantine Berkeley Square House, which entailed the demolition of almost all the interesting old houses on the east side of the Square together with most of the south side of Bruton Street. Neither no. 10 or no. 17 survived for longer than five more years. Berkeley Square House has itself been replaced since Norman's death.

It was, as always, a question of finance. Phyllis had written from India suggesting that monies in the Hartnell Paris account should be transferred to London. Norman again owed income tax (£256.9s.8d!) and the company paid it. Things were marginally better so the 10% decrease in salaries and commissions was abandoned (although Fred Smith disagreed) and by the following December (1932) Miss Eileen and Madame Andrée were given salary increases, whilst Mlle Davide was given a generous new contract. Everyone realised just how much the whole success of the business depended on her supreme fitting skills.

By November 1933, the Sweeny wedding having come and gone, finances were still difficult. Bish's wife offered a £500 loan and Phyllis was prepared to accept an annual salary of £125, 'this matter to be revised when the trading figures improved'. She was, of course, married and living in India, so it was not with her that Norman eventually sat down to discuss schemes for the redecoration of 26 Bruton Street, as he wrote later.[41] This was largely done with his young architect Gerald Lacoste and a forceful friend, John Pleydell, with whom Norman was to share his life for the next five years.

Commander Pleydell, as he became, was the type of man Norman was attracted to. Tall, well built and rather menacing, all who remember him as manager of Norman Hartnell Ltd testify to his disturbingly menacing presence.[42] In May 1934, he became a director of the company, having bought a good chunk of the shares. Phyllis proposed him and Norman seconded his appointment as a director. How the two men met is unclear, but the mutual attraction was clear. Pleydell's dynamic personality resulted in the pushing through of the move to 26 Bruton Street, the acquisition of a country house, Lovel Dene (also remodelled by Lacoste), ostensibly Norman's but financed by Pleydell (in the 1990s the servants' bells of the rooms were still marked with their names), the gradual winding up of the Paris house, the move into wider American markets and the establishment of the necessary merchandising venture into scents.

Both men shared an interest in horses and horsemen, but whereas Norman had a sure instinct for design, Pleydell had a grasp of business that was applauded in the company minutes and probably came to frighten the less sophisticated Bish and Smith, who had a far more cautious approach to matters. None of these men were referred to in *Silver and Gold*. Lacoste, who gave the salon its look; Pleydell, who built the business up into a 1930s success; or Smith, who was to faithfully attempt to steer Norman on a rational course through the 1940s, and Bish is barely mentioned. He is altogether omitted from the index, whereas Lady Clare Hartnell is put in: she was 'discovered' by Blake during the war and soon adopted as 'my distant cousin by marriage', although she was only married to an unrelated Hartnell. Norman could always be relied on to dump uncomfortable family or friends and to retreat into his own world when anything disturbed his way of life and designing.

In May 1934, the minutes record that negotiations for no. 26 should be completed 'providing that the alterations to the premises could be carried out to the complete satisfaction of the company'. There is never a mention of any other premises and negotiations had been long and hard-fought, so that by the end of May everything was agreed between Town Investments Ltd and Norman Hartnell Ltd. Pleydell was voted £20 for his troubles over the negotiations since March, which shows how he had pushed the deal along, for business was better, but only just. He also produced accurate weekly reports on all aspects of the business. By July he was signing the company cheques, although not authorised to do so. He was then empowered to carry on and explained why he had taken the decisions on the appointment of contractors for the new building using Lawrence for the structural work at £1,558.19s.0d. not Trollope's, as the former were less expensive and the latter were to carry out the interior works at £1,295.10s.0d. Both Smith and Phyllis proposed that £4,000 should be the limit for the move and redecorations, which was agreed. For the first time in the minutes a vote of congratulation and thanks was then proposed for the increase in profits, which made the move possible, and Norman's work was praised.

Hartnell had poached Madame Banti for the workrooms and received a letter from her previous employer asking that they send her back. They did not, which made the company's protests at the proposals made to Mlle Davide seem hypocritical at the least. Pleydell also employed Mr Elisack as tailor and he proved excellent.

A new accounting system was discussed and Pleydell congratulated on his achievements, which included getting rid of the secretary Miss Mulholland, who had proved unsatisfactory. As further proof of his dynamism, Pleydell then brought forward the Associate Company to deal in furs for which he had Mr Bauer offering to subscribe £5,000 if Mr Stanley Blaxhall of Paris could be obtained. This was certainly a scheme from Mars for Bish, who had obtained the loan of a showcase fur from Revillon!

Mr Blaxhall consented to join the company and offered to subscribe £2,500 whilst enjoying a salary of £1,000 a year. An injection of £7,500 capital was most welcome: London matrons had long bought their furs at Bradleys,

Chepstow Place, Bayswater, W2 or the London branch of Revillon Frères, but the furs designed by Norman were of an elegance and style beyond them and most others. He claimed to be the first to dye furs to the shade of the clothes they adorned, and also made them as integral a part of the dress or coat as possible, so that one without the other became impossible. Furs were big business and brought in a good income; about an eighth of all sales came from furs in 1934, and one fifth in 1935 after the new arrangement.

By February 1935, Norman was showing that furs were an integral part of his designs: 'not a single fur cape' was on show in his new salons, according to *The Fur World*. The momentous move to 26 Bruton Street had been accomplished in time for the Jubilee Year of King George V and Queen Mary, with all the extra pageantry and social events which that created.

The construction and redesign of the advanced modern building's interiors were sensational and much discussed. The entrance, stairs and salon remain one of Britain's greatest commercial inter-war interiors with Lacoste's and Norman's use of glass in their unusual modernistic forms. There next came the planning of the sensational opening show with all the theatrical mastery that Norman could muster. Even *Vogue* was impressed.

CHAPTER SEVEN

'Don't miss this one!'

In 1979 'The Thirties' exhibition at the Hayward Gallery included the unique facetted plate-glass fireplace designed by Gerald Lacoste as the centrepiece of the new Norman Hartnell salon and focal point of the design of the building. (Given to the V&A, it was later restored to its original location by the author.) The planning that went into the remarkable new interiors and exciting move from no. 10 to no. 26 Bruton Street had occupied most of 1934.

If Molyneux and Stiebel's London competition caused pangs of discomfort, worry set in after a *Vogue* favourite Elsa Schiaparelli opened a London House in Upper Grosvenor Street and the equally chic Parisienne Maggy Rouff planned her opening near The Dorchester, the recently opened luxurious hotel attracting a rich clientele.

This move of the Paris-based couturiers to mop up extra business in London was soon augmented by the appointment of Elspeth Champcommunal to head the London branch of Worth, after her own Paris House closed. Her attempt to create a mainly American market foundered because of the Depression, which was a particular source of anxiety to the French designers. On the positive side, these openings were partly due to tax and customs tariffs, partly to the allure of the English pound and Court, but also partly because North American buyers were treating London as a serious fashion capital, often viewing the London collections even before those of Paris.[1]

Hartnell can certainly be credited with most of London's success and there is no doubt that in spite of Molyneux's talents, Norman remained the star of London fashion. Schiaparelli's eccentricities were worn by few Englishwomen, so her main London models were interesting but lacking the English qualities and attributes that made Norman's so popular. The same was true of Maggy Rouff's clothes. They had a distinctively French look and verged on being too chic, which was fine in the highly fashion-conscious Paris milieu, rapidly changing clothes each season, but not in England where new clothes were not generally expected to be totally out of fashion in one season. Madame Champcommunal was another matter; her quiet designs for Court dresses became popular in a business known for understated elegance and superb craftsmanship, but luckily there were enough debutantes and mothers, as well as others, to go around. Norman concentrated harder on his collections and building plans.

In planning the new House, Gerald Lacoste and Norman went to view the Paris Houses of the major designers. Molyneux's faux-Louis XVI style (copied in his London House) was a somewhat dated if timeless backdrop, with the grey tones giving a neutral background for the display of his models, although the large chandeliers caught the eye. Paul Poiret, still existing as a swan song of a great pre-war era, had new backers and updated his salon to include complete walls of mirror plate, curved cornices with no mouldings and some of the first indirect cove lighting. His Corbusier–Bauhaus-inspired decoration extended to tubular steel armchairs and a vast shagpile rug running down the centre of the salon. In retrospect, the room seems thirty years ahead of his time and it impressed the two young Englishmen with its individuality.

The most interesting House and salon for Lacoste proved to be that of Chanel, with a modernistic curving staircase, walls lined with cleverly cut plate mirrors, as at Poiret, but in a less austere manner. Lacoste had spent some months in the architect Oswald Milne's office, when Milne was redecorating Claridge's in his stripped 1920s neo-classical style fused with elements of art deco, and Lacoste's first design for the salon was a weak 1920s pastiche of a Georgian room of no specific date but with some modernistic touches. This had prompted the visit to Paris and on their return, he and Hartnell had decided to create not only the House with the largest salon in London but the most super-elegant, using as much glass as possible.

Glass was particularly in favour in Paris during the late 1920s, when the revolutionary Polish-born hairstylist Antoine had astounded *tout Paris* with his all-glass house in which everything possible was of glass; he famously slept in a glass coffin. Norman did not go so far, but Lacoste's scheme includes the famous cut and facetted glass fireplace, which is the culmination of the House decoration and the focal point of the salon, replete with a glowing electric fire shining through a louvred metal screen.

When the new flush double doors of no. 26 to the street with their imposing circular lion's head handles finally opened to the public, the impressed visitor crossed a hall floor of pale green Swedish marble slabs, contrasting with dark green veined Italian marble surrounding the impressive exterior entrance. Lacoste's frameless glass doors were the first of their kind by Pilkingtons and connected the hall past a lift tower to the staircase, the walls of which are still lined with mirrors reflecting cut-glass chandeliers given to Norman by American heiress Mrs Corrigan, an admiring client.

When she first visited Norman 'she stepped out of a sumptuous grey car. . . flinging two priceless chinchilla capes on the floor; one short, one long. "No, I just don't need any special designs – just join them up into one lovely big rug for my car, dear."'[1]

The main salon, formed from an L-shaped drawing room, retains a screen formed by two tall pillars covered with panels of facetted mirror reflecting the colour of the rainbow showered across the room by two vast Regency chandeliers of the best English glass ever made. Another pair of similar columns merge at their base into thick plate-glass shelves with typically 1930s curved ends and drawer units. Even the radiator grille is of glass – thick rods of it shield the gaze from the radiators' unlovely form.

Norman wrote:

> All this was costing me a great deal more money than I had antic-ipated. I despaired at the cost of it and once even wanted to tele-phone the landlord in the middle of the night to stop it all. I had nightmares of toppling crystal columns and chandeliers crashing into a chaos of marble and carpet. There was, of course, no turn-ing back. I set to and produced a luxurious and expensive collec-tion. Everything now hinged upon the success of my presentation, which was fixed for one evening in September 1935.[2]

As so often, whimsy leads to inaccuracy, for the house opened in September 1934 and not only was the whole project strictly controlled by both the archi-tect and John Pleydell but also by the directors, including Bish, who kept very close control over the budget of £4,000.

Norman may well have felt anxious about the quality of his dress designs for such a conspicuous show, but his only recorded major irritation occurred when trying to obtain the 'Hartnell Green' paint which gave the walls a warm 'creamy tone'. There were the inevitable problems when it came to mixing the colour: 'When a firm delivered a lorry load containing 600 gallons of green paint the colour of a faded bicycle shed, I promptly returned the lot.' [2]

'Hartnell Green' is difficult to replicate:

> The body colour is white, into which I tipped hooker's green, meridian green, a touch of gamboge and mid-grey. This mixture produced a subtle tone of green resembling lichen, celadon green or that elusive shade that gleams on the back of the leaves of the silver willow when softly stirred by the breeze . . . When displayed in great areas on the staircase and on the showroom walls, it seemed as one of nature's natural backgrounds to every colour of flower or rainbow.[2]

That this should be the 'Hartnell Green' came as no surprise to his clients. As early as 18 March 1931 *The Bystander* described a dress show attended by de Meyer featuring the 'Hartnell . . . green favoured shade, his "pussy willow, being a softest most adorable tone of green which instantly brought to mind the soft burrs that dapple the brown stick of palm".'

Curtains were made of velvet dyed to a special green in Paris, and a large banquette and a day bed were covered in this velvet. Low glass tables were made by Pilkington to Lacoste's designs with thick circular tops on double U-shaped glass bases. Notably, there was a special place for the lucky cut-glass galleon model formed as a wall light over the entrance door to the salon. Hartnell had found this discarded in a shop and believed that it was his lucky talisman.

Lacoste later installed what was named the 'Hat Bar' consisting of three fitted, lit mirrored alcoves to the right on entering the main salon, millinery being an essential part of many ensembles designed by Hartnell and later various famous milliners. Streamlined fitting rooms were accessed through a passage leading from the salon to the right of the mannequin entrance and connecting the front and rear buildings forming 26 Bruton Street. One side of the passage had a long built-in showcase for the display of accessories and later Hartnell merchandise.

The passage led to a series of comfortably equipped fitting rooms containing a mixture of elegant modern and faux antique pieces of furniture offset by a large mirror edged with a series of light bulbs behind obscured glass roundels which concealed the bulbs, reminiscent of a Hollywood film star's dressing room. No effort was spared in order to inculcate the feeling of luxurious stardom to the client.

In the same mood, a simple booklet of Hartnell Green paper contained a full, if selective, biographical account of Norman's career and the creation of the new building by Richard Fletcher with an introductory message signed in facsimile by Alison Settle, already a highly regarded fashion journalist with a long career ahead and then editor of British *Vogue*: 'At every new collection his rooms got more and more crowded – to be able to take a friend was truly a feather in one's cap.'

P. Joyce Reynolds, then the influential editor of *Harper's Bazaar* included her praise:

> With London setting the pace for chic cosmopolitans throughout the world, the English traditional genius for pageantry has permeated every phase of dress. . . At 26 Bruton Street women can choose Hartnell gowns against a background as glamorous as any in England and see your [Norman's] artistic achievement rounded to perfection.

Fletcher's long adulatory essay includes a neat explanation for the Hartnell business retrenchment in Paris. 'Gradually foreseeing the eclipse of Paris as the sole nerve-centre of fashion he withdrew his activities from the French capital to concentrate on his English interests and to prepare for the eventual aggrandisement of the house of Hartnell in London.'

This sounded confident about the future and was partly true, as were the credits for the new salon: 'Norman Hartnell, who conceived the plan and decorations of the house of Hartnell, acknowledges with thanks the co-operation of the many experts involved such as: Interior Decorations by Trollope & Sons [then the leading decorating establishment in Belgravia], Glasswork by Pugh Bros [of a quality now impossible to replicate], Curtains and fittings by D.S. Mann.'

Mrs Mann was one of the several famous inter-war women antique dealers and decorators and her then assistant Norris Wakefield was sent out by her to various male clients, including the surrealist Edward James. Wakefield reported all to Mrs Mann and formed a lasting friendship with Hartnell, continuing to work for Norman for the next three decades.

Last in the list came 'Architectural Supervision by Gerald Lacoste ARIBA'.

As with his later assistant, Ian Thomas, Norman thought it important to be seen as the one genius of Norman Hartnell Ltd, a tactic that worked well and was the usual practice in all dress Houses.

The building was ready in August, and on the opening evening every space was crammed to inspect the latest Hartnell collection. At last a truly large number of clients, press and well-wishers could be incorporated under Norman's own roof.

Rehearsals had gone well; both Pleydell and Norman had drilled everyone concerned. The unexpected then happened when just after the third mannequin had emerged from the model room and paused in the dramatic spotlit entrance to the salon framed with bevelled mirror, all the lights failed. Many considered this to be a clever publicity stunt and applauded, but Miss Louie confirmed that it was not and '"The Boss" was very cross'. Although the show continued with the girls carrying candles, the press could scarcely see anything to write about, although the clothes were ravishing and Norman had 'developed into the ultra-sophisticated designer predicted, something for women who were almost dangerously too chic'.[3]

Over time, minor modifications were inevitably made to the salon and the building, not least to the glass entrance door of the salon itself, which was subsequently engraved with stars, as he explained in a 1968 interview: 'We added them because ladies used to bump their noses against the transparent glass. They did, you know, they were very silly.' A world-weary comment on his pre-war clientele made in less extravagant days to come.[4]

A rare example of Norman's heightened designing skills and the consummate workroom skills practised at Norman Hartnell at this time is now in the collections of the Museum of London. A figure hugging dress of clearest pale 'Hartnell Green' silk. The design depends solely upon the finest pleating and tucking in geometric shapes to form a virtuoso display of decoration without any embroidery, but clearly echoing Lacoste's mirrored interiors. A note from the donor states that the dress was bought at a Hartnell sale shortly after with the opening of the new building, which remained for him the base of his business until he died in 1979. He not only remained attached to his House but also the memory of what it represented after a long career, stating when interviewed in 1968 with no intention of retiring, 'Mine's a Cinderella story, you know. Out of the drab of Maida Vale to this. (Though of course I'd been to the university where one's treated like a lord, with servants and everything).[4]

Hartnell's ever imaginative design skills did bring him four more films to dress in 1934, One, *Brewster's Millions* he shared with Schiaparelli and Motley. It was also in 1934 that Delysia brought the French star of revue Mistinguett by aeroplane to be dressed in sequin sheaths trimmed with fur. She later flew back for two fittings. This was news, as were Norman's increasing links to the film world. Joseph Schenck brought his new star Merle Oberon to be dressed by Norman, and much was made of her new designer.

A familiar name now to audiences of theatre and filmgoers, each new celebrity added to the publicity given to Norman Hartnell Ltd, Norman's name associated with the great allure of beautiful women and the sinuous lines of his evening clothes, often offset by lavish furs, which were in tune with the equally sinuous dances and music of the period.

The valuable furs sold in the salon were actually from the Paris House of Jacques Heim. 'Voo-Doo,' a black velvet model trimmed with five silver foxes, became popular, and twenty expensive copies were sold. Merle Oberon posed for photographs in the salon wearing some of her new clinging, heavily sequined dresses, a Hartnell speciality necessitating intensive craftsmanship and many hands. 'From four to four hundred,' Norman was quoted as saying about the workforce in his new building. By December he stated that he had already achieved two thirds of his previous year's turnover.

All this was heartening in view of the worry caused to Norman at the end of August. An announcement was made from Buckingham Palace that the Duke of Kent was to marry Princess Marina of Greece. It was known that the Princess was a client of Molyneux and the wedding preoccupied the press with copious accounts of Captain Molyneux's career, not surprisingly dwelling on his position as a leading Parisian designer. The royal couple married in Westminster Abbey on 29 November, the Princess (later Duchess of Kent) wearing a simply draped, classically inspired masterpiece by Moly-neux. It was the epitome of restrained elegance, which was the essence of the Princess's style, whether dressed by Molyneux or as later by Norman. There is no doubt that this event really boosted the fortunes of Molyneux both in Paris and London, for the Princess was beautiful and photogenic. It also boosted the place of London as a fashion centre but was a huge put-down of Norman's leading position as a London designer. At this stage Norman had no such royal client, though he did have friends amongst and contacts to the Royal Family, and his work was seen at Courts and on the stage or in film. Housed in his glamorous and imposing new art moderne surroundings, anything seemed possible. A journalist caught the mood of the House and the man:

> In a high, greeny-grey Mayfair room, a-glimmer with discreet mirrors, slender mannequins willowed past the appraising eyes of half-a-dozen women. There was a rarefied velvety atmosphere about the room – the atmosphere that makes you feel rich just to sit in it. And suddenly, out of nowhere, Mr Norman Hartnell appeared sitting by my side – talking of women and their ways.
>
> 'Women are adorable,' he said. 'Of course, they're difficult about fittings and things and why shouldn't they be? Their whole appearance is at stake. Sometimes they make a dreadful fuss about nothing. And then they ring up next morning and say the dress is divine and I refrain from saying "I told you so".'
>
> Hartnell speaks in little bursts of words, in a rich and pleasant voice, but half his attention is on the gowns that go by on the long-limbed, self-possessed mannequins. 'If only they wouldn't be so dogmatic about what suits them. The young ones are much more difficult about that than the older ones. Women are not at heart artists. Their husbands usually have a much more selective eye for beauty. A woman will look at a frock and say, "No, that won't suit me. I don't want to see it." But her husband will say, "That's a beautiful dress, try it on, it may suit you." And very often he is right. But their wives are seldom persuaded.'
>
> He clapped his hands and looked round the room. 'Do you like my room? It's nice isn't it. It shows up the colours so well. But Englishwomen are so afraid of colours. Englishwomen are nearly always afraid of anything new. Americans never are. That's one of the reasons they're nice to design for. But I like designing for Englishwomen best. They can wear the "grande robe" better than any woman in the world.'[4]

Norman's views on women, dresses and his clients remained constant until he died. In an interview thirty years later he stated: 'The truth is that decorating a room gives me *more* pleasure than designing for a lovely woman,'[5] going on to explain that he can do exactly as he wishes with a room and the result is not changed.

He also held uncompromising views on women dress designers:

> Most dress designers are men. It may sound highfalutin of me, but
> I regard the design of dress as an art; and most experienced of art
> [sic] if you reflect – have been men.
>
> It wasn't Mrs Wagner or Mrs Mendelssohn who composed the
> music . . . or Mdme Rembrandt or Mdme Renoir who painted
> pictures . . . neither was it Lady Tennyson or Anne Hathaway who
> wrote the beautiful words . . . their husbands did.[6]

Apart from his own contradiction of his usual opinion, that dress design
is not an art, both Paris and London had of course talented and successful
women designers, disposed of by him with one causal swipe. 'Although I
admire Jean Lauvin [sic] the dress designer, Madame Grés for her sculptured
drapery and of course the eternal Madame Chanel for her monotonous miracles . . .'[4] Written in the 1960s, it is doubtful if Norman would have been
quite so forceful publicly in the 1930s. However he never forgot the attempt of
Madame de Rivoli to spy out his creations by infiltrating one of her mannequins into a Paris show he gave in the early 1930s. The spy clearly came from
Chanel. Yet Norman also sent out girls to 'look around'.

When it came to the artistry in making Norman's clothes, he was delighted
with the many expertly trained women who served him in their various
departments, of which the embroidery room was always his favourite. Apart
from his sketching and embroidery design, he would also select all the con-
stituent parts of the completed design; the paillettes, bugle beads, glass sparklets, pearls, metal studs, stars, crescents – all these and more were bought in
every variety of colour and shape. Each design was kept in a small cotton bag,
all clearly labelled and kept in boxes, the contents of which formed part of the
annual stock check. When the House finally closed its doors in 1992, there
were hundreds of thousands of sad little reminders of glorious dresses of the
past in their marked dusty boxes extending back to the 1920s.

A visit to the embroidery room by Norman was always a pleasurable activity as he observed the designs growing on fabrics stretched across embroidery
frames. It obviously appealed to the embroideresses too, as many stayed on
for decades. Sometimes when one did retire Norman was too upset to say
goodbye.

After the Second World War, extra room had to be found for an increased number of embroideresses when the combined influence of Norman's own full-blown crinoline style, the New Look and Royal patronage made the exclusive embroidered dresses highly sought after. In the mid-1930s, the remodelling of the old town house of the Viscount Hereford (Premier Viscounts of England) had created a great stir and placed Norman firmly on or above the same status level as the older London Houses of Reville or Worth. But he was younger and had designs more attuned to a younger clientele, whilst being able to dress older women sympathetically in fashion, and thus he extended his worldwide fame.

Together with John Pleydell he embarked on a different phase of his career, which he curiously terms in *Silver and Gold* 'the phase of dressing the stage.' As we have seen, this had been constant in his career for many years and formed the basis of his first success.

Pleydell now used his own energy and a considerable amount of his own income in harnessing Hartnell's name to merchandising, exploiting the fame and name of Norman by producing Hartnell scent. In France, this was an established pre-First World War method of generating extra income for designers, and in the 1920s, Lanvin and Molyneux, for example, produced bottles of ingenious design in novel packaging, extending the purchase of part of a famous couturier to any woman with even very slender means. Norman went to Grasse and the flower fields, then *the* place for natural flower-essence extraction, before synthetic formulae dominated the expensive end of the business. Chanel had her 'No. 5' and was to find the profits a satisfactory substitute for lost income during the time her House was shut (1940–54).

In 1934, Norman launched 'Hartnell No. 6' (light), 'Hartnell No. 16' (medium) and 'Hartnell No. 26' (heavy). The complexities of the financing, manufacture, packaging, promotion and retailing of this scent were no less difficult than any of the subsequent scents to be promoted under the Norman Hartnell name.

Surviving thick files of business papers connected with the complexities of manufacturing and marketing scent reveal the twists and turns of endless negotiations. Each scent promotion involved heavy expenses and legal costs at each stage, so although a large income was eventually generated from sales, over time Norman saw very little of it personally. In the case of 'No. 6', '16' and '26' he was initially lucky, for Pleydell was an astute businessman, tougher than Norman and never going into a project without thorough investigation. Yet he too failed personally, if only because Norman's affections for him changed. In 1934, this was unforeseen.

In anticipation of projected extra income from scent sales and as a result of the acclaim for his move and accompanying success of his collection, Norman and John Pleydell sought a country house throughout the winter months.

Whilst looking, Norman's address was Basmore Cottage, Shiplake-on-Thames, a convenient place for searching out a house in the Windsor area. He also announced that he would show his spring collection in London at the same time as the Paris collections, having already sounded out American buyers and journalists. Partly because of the Kent wedding, London was even more newsworthy, but the burgeoning interest in the Silver Jubilee Year of King George V was also a factor. London expected a large number of foreign visitors from the Empire and other countries for a great variety of events and parties.

American *Vogue* had been excited by the royal wedding and featured a Molyneux sketch of Princess Marina in her wedding dress, which caused a certain amount of disapproval at Buckingham Palace. The influential magazine, under the formidable eye of Mrs Chase, geared up for more coverage of royal events, fanned by both Mrs Chase's eye for a good story and Cecil Beaton's perceptive accounts of what was in store. In the event the *Vogue* delegate John McMullin typically witnessed proceedings from Schiaparelli's suite at the Carlton Hotel.[7] Even at this stage the informed taste was taken to be for things French or Parisian (as 'Schiap' was Italian), and were accorded first place.

But English *Vogue* at last paid attention to the major fashion Houses emerging on its doorstep. In April 1935, a comprehensive account of the London Collections was given with more serious attention to the evolution of London fashion. Special attention was paid to Norman's position and his new House full of pink arum lilies; the clothes were likened to bouquets and everything, including the accessories, termed 'feminine and glamorous'.[8] By partly closing his Paris House and concentrating the minds of his American clients on London, Norman now established himself as the 'King of the Romantics' in any capital.[9] His skirts were already fuller than those of any other designer, his designs already leading to the romance of the large skirts he preferred. His special showing of dresses for the Courts incorporated this new facet of his designs together with dyed fox fur of every colour emphasising this newly expanded part of his business.

Whilst his neighbour Victor Stiebel was concentrating on a '1910 Jubilee' line, Norman had other ideas:

> This year women will rustle through the ballrooms with wide skirts, swishing around their feet . . . Low décolletés are definitely back. These will make the ear and throat important and jewellery will be indispensable . . . big cabochons. Aquamarines and amethysts for the pinks and greys . . . rubies . . . with pale blues. Diamonds, of course, will be 'right'. I cannot imagine them being out of place on any of my dresses.

Just how he imagined his designs is clear: 'Coiffure and head ornaments should have a *Merry Widow* touch about them. By that I mean that the hair should be short, tightly curled and jewelled slides . . . worn on the crest. Certainly it is to be a year of grace.'[9]

This innovation was epitomised by the lovely Lady Bridget Poulett and Norman's in-house mannequins. The five floors of Norman Hartnell buzzed with activity and the large popular staff canteen in the basement, visited by The Boss (or 'Bossie' to his closest employees), dispensed sustenance at moderate prices to his workforce. They coped with ever-expanding order books and discussed how Norman was now increasingly seen in all fashionable places: at Aage Thaarup's hat show with Fay Wray, who wore an enormous Chinese coolie hat, for instance.[10]

One of Norman's brides, Lady Weymouth, a favourite of the vendeuse and fitters (who rather disliked the often over-demanding actresses), appeared at Court on 28 March in one of Norman's designs covered with silver and sea-green crystals over pale green net. The green velvet train was shot with silver and held by silver straps, while British *Vogue* in April termed Gertrude Lawrence a 'mermaid in sequins', wearing a Hartnell sheath of brown sequins with a tulle wrap. She had just filmed *La Bohème* for BIP and was part of a fashion panel with Norman, Oliver Messel and a clutch of fashion editresses to judge the '£1,000 Best Dressed Girl Competition'. 'Fashion' in those days could conceivably be worn by *any* woman, with minor adjustments for varying figures and to the quality of the fabrics employed.

With the publicity he was getting and the intermittent services of Richard Fletcher, Pleydell clearly thought that a more aggressive approach was needed, particularly to promote the scents, and in April the newly founded publicity specialists headed by the 24-year-old Lord Selby announced that Norman Hartnell Ltd had become a client. It is difficult to understand how much extra publicity was required, for when Lord Birkenhead married Miss Sheila Berry in May the coverage and photographs of the wedding filled all the newspapers. The bride wore a pearl-white satin dress cut on simple lines, with the train again formed from the rear of the skirt in the best Norman Hartnell fashion. The only embroidery consisted of tiny gold beads at the neck and wrists, these beads also forming part of the halo-headdress holding her veil. This dress proved that Norman's clothes could, without any doubt, rely on a superb simplicity of line achieved by his famous fitters and cutters. Norman had now more than followed the advice of Main Bocher given in Paris a few years previously and the result was conspicuous worldwide fame for his own creations.[11]

The services of Richard Fletcher were again put to good use in 1936 when he wrote an illustrated piece for the then lavish journal *Decoration* about Lovel Dene, Woodside, Windsor Forest, the house found after a long search by Norman and John Pleydell in 1935 and bought by Pleydell himself. A relatively small, albeit rambling, building dating from the 1830s and said to incorporate an early-eighteenth-century cottage, the house had stabling, a cottage, and flower and kitchen gardens together with a lake. The ornamental garden stretched to the lake and woods at the end of the property.

Surrounded by trees and close to a bend of the rural road, the L-shaped house had the defect of having the sun all day only on the stairs, drawing room and the smaller bedrooms. The entrance was in the corner of the L with the hall and staircase to the right; the kitchen and what was later Norman's studio also had sunlight, but the dining room, study, main bedrooms and bathroom all had cold north-west light, albeit with attractive views. This possibly accorded with the new owner's own taste for subdued lighting.

In early spring, with daffodils nodding on the lawns, the house is still idyllic in its wooded setting and at the time gave Norman the chance to practise his own ideas on decoration with Gerald Lacoste again asked to be the architect and open out the cluster of small rooms. He also designed a summer house 'The Peacock Pavilion' in an amusing if debased form of early-eighteenth-century neo-classicism. It has echoes of Alexander Korda's London Films production of *Knight without Armour* starring Marlene Dietrich (a client of Norman) and made in 1936, and a similar Russian flavour to the pavilion is found in the Korda film with the design of the Grand Duchess's country house. Norman later claimed that the design was suggested to him by Rex Whistler, but the suggestion was a far cry from the finished designs of Whistler's own work and his was completely Lacoste's design.

The house, with its Gothick windows and cosy-looking charm, was treated inside as though it were a Mayfair house of the period. Remodelled and decorated over the years, it gained in fantasy through the decades. Fletcher termed the finished product, again achieved with the firm of D.S. Mann and the young Norris Wakefield's services, 'a paragon of practicability and beauty and, to the bow of a window curtain, Mr Hartnell's unerring touch may be seen'. He pointed out that this former Rangers house had been on the market for years as a 'squat hideous building' until Norman spotted the possibilities and had the staircase moved and drawing room cut across the end of one wing with windows on three sides, creating a spacious modern house with eighteenth century spaces.

For this, Norris Wakefield, 'Wakers', as Norman called him, provided soft furnishings throughout to Normans' specific instructions with much colour co-ordination. The drawing room carpet was dyed 'Vaseline Yellow' and, as Fletcher lyrically put it, 'Mr Hartnell plays on the rainbow as Heifetz does on the violin.'

The turquoise blue and silver hall gave way to the lilac mauve of the drawing room with white grand piano and white-lacquered radiogram. The dining room was filled with mahogany Regency furniture and was, as Fletcher entitled his article, 'Regency Revival'. This was the famous speciality of Wakers' employer, Mrs Mann.

Doors of squared mirror glass led to the 'den' with curtains of a gay chintz, quilted by hand and producing a peculiar effect of depth and detail. Norman's bedroom of chocolate brown and white ('purely Regency') was designed around the bed with a brown buttoned velvet head and footboard. Two shell chairs were said to have come from the Royal Pavilion, Brighton.

Given the tiny proportions of this room, not much more than a dressing room, it seems improbable that the vast blue bedroom, termed the 'conjugal bedroom' with its adjoining bathroom, should have been neglected by Norman and Pleydell and given to an infrequent visitor:

> a vast bed is covered with sapphire velvet, overhung with a canopy
> of pale Roman satin caught by the chubby hands of a white por-
> celain cherub . . . The mahogany furniture, Wedgwood plaques

and Venetian mirrors made it the most glamorous room in the house . . . Adjoining, the blue bathroom is luxurious, spacious and modern.

Possibly because Lovel Dene in various phases of updated decoration featured repeatedly in magazines over the years and was a useful publicity tool, there is very little about the house in *Silver and Gold*. It is mentioned always as a source of creative energy and the inspirational backdrop to the realisation of many thousands of Norman's designs.

In the 1920s, Norman went off for weekends or country holidays and took along his sketchpads. Nature inspired him, colour excited him and the way in which light changed the appearance of colour and fabrics challenged the artist within him. There is no doubt about his need for the privacy he prized within the relative seclusion of Lovel Dene, nor of his love for it as his first true home since his mother had died.

If the decoration of Lovel Dene seems elaborate to modern eyes, it was scarcely so at the time. Norman had become a star to the press and general public, so he lived in the style of his contemporary stars – creating new interiors to reflect their personalities rather than inhabiting inherited historic houses, as the featured members of Society usually did. Recent writing on Norman's taste and his burgeoning collecting of 'antiques' or curios attempts to describe this as a manifestation of his sexuality in the terms of what is known as Queer Studies. However, this completely misunderstands the fashionable design trends of the period at home and abroad, whilst also negating the considerable achievements of old and new decorating companies. Lovel Dene followed a fashionable pattern with a Georgian dining room, a male-orientated study and a lighter drawing room suitable for entertaining men and women. The specious label of Queer Taste also falls away with the decoration of the bedrooms – distilled from the style of redecorated grander houses of the period and designed to flatter guests of both sexes, as did Lovel Dene in its entirety. That is, of course, how it was received by the public reading the lavish new publication *Decoration* – it fitted into the general pattern of new developments in interior decoration as seen in the pages of very many journals such as *Country Life* and most visibly in films of the time.

If Norman ever felt that his full life lacked anything, it was probably the separation from his capable sister Topsy and her husband Jim, known as Jugs, who were now based in distant India, although Topsy returned at least once a year (paid for by the company) and kept her interest in the business. Letters reveal the complexities of her accounts managed for her at Hartnell, relating also to her role as a selling agent in India.

They were a friendly, popular couple participating in all the usual ex-pat social events: expeditions with swimming and picnics or dances and dinners. Norman had seen his half-sisters often during the 1920s at Hassocks, but contact slackened from the 1930s onwards. Norman became simply too busy. He did maintain his friendship with Blake, who had moved to a cottage in Kent, decorated with his usual bright colours and eccentric individual taste. Here he wrote amusing novels; *My Aunt in Pink* of 1936 is full of colourful descriptions for absurdly overblown decorative schemes and names: "'The bath-room is beyond, Miss Maud,' declared Mrs Hoose . . . she turned herself about and glided – like a black mechanical swan – from the room.'[12] Just the humour to amuse Norman, as was Blake's scheme for the cottage staircase walls: 'royal blue velvet, embroidered brilliantly with wools of orange, lime-green, yellow, vermilion and cochineal pink'.[13] Although Norman's palette was wide, this was perhaps too much for him, although the professional 'dress' description is nicely done.

Blake was to stay often at Lovel Dene over the next thirty years of Norman's life there. When Norman was forced to leave in the 1960s, it was as though his life had been torn to shreds, and he was never the same man again.

In his mid-thirties with a strong and dynamic close friend in Pleydell to fulfil his personal life and manage the business, these were happy days for Norman. In spite of the continual pressure to pull another dramatic collection out of nowhere but his own inspiration, there were apparently limitless possibilities for his business throughout the world. Britain was weathering the Depression, whilst the major countries of the old British Empire including Canada, South Africa and Australia were emerging as profitable markets for his collections in addition to the valuable market of the USA. Summing up the position of London as a fashion centre at this time he wrote:

> When a dress is made, evolved and bought completely in London,
> it avoids the model-copying complications of a Paris-bought dress.
> The London dress is sold to you at a price and is the same to all
> your friends, but a foreign dress is sold to you at a certain price
> and is the same for all your friends, but a foreign dress you can buy
> for 80 gns and your friends can buy it on the other side of Regent

Street for 8 gns – hence the bitter words and difficulties. The quality of the few London designers is as excellent as the Paris designer, unfortunately however, the quantity is pathetically inferior.

Norman then wrote:

> Proofs of the quality of London designer number one: An offer from Fox Films to go to Hollywood, as they considered I could design clothes better than the ones they had got there. I spoke to my friend [Mr Travis Banton] the designer for Paramount – he advised me not to go, I took his advice and lost the dollar.

Later on, Norman, who kept a keen interest in films and went often to the cinema, adapted some of Banton's ideas utilised in dressing stars for Queen Elizabeth. The heightening of a client's personality through the strong line and beautiful detail of Norman's designs were ideally suited to films, as can still be appreciated. Norman also stressed that Mistinguett paid for her designs with 'her treasured French francs' and that

> ...a month or so ago [she] visited me again, would I make all the dresses for her new Revue in Paris, (she gets them free in Paris) however, she was willing to pay me for them, however, I was unable to do it as it meant leaving my lovely business in the height of the Season.

Most strikingly he related how

> ...Marcelle Rogez, the dazzling blonde Parisian star was at Deauville this summer in a beautiful nacre paillette dress and cape I had made her. Up came the French reporters and sketch artists and all described her dress as the most lovely dress in the room that evening at the Casino Club. However, when they learnt that it came from me, the descriptions were torn up and the sketches rubbed out. Isn't that proof? Whenever a really beautiful dress of mine appears in the paper, that nice shop near the 'Berkeley' always copies it.

This was Paris Trades from which Daphne Vivian had ordered her dress, before Norman persuaded her to change. He then mentioned his three favourite clients of the moment: Lady Louis Mountbatten, 'one of the nicest people I have ever had the honour of making sketches for'; Isabel Jeans, who made the author alter the text if a dress she liked failed to fit the plot ('I call that being an actress'); and Gertrude Lawrence, who was then in a state of financial shock and arranged to wear Norman's clothes, which she did to acres of publicity as she 'cannot fail to look lovely, especially with the guidance of Noël Coward with his unerring good taste'.[14]

As a direct contrast to all this high glamour, Norman visited the Handsworth School of Dress Design on 10 May and gave some ideas to the pupils whilst admiring their ability to make the things they designed.[15] As one former employee of his remembered, he once tried to cut out something and the performance ended in laughter.[16] Norman was probably not a stranger to Birmingham, as his stepmother's family were living there.

He then plunged into his mid-season Jubilee Collection showings, and Ascot dresses were sold together with many cartwheel hats and Court dresses. He attended the Mammoth Cabaret and Ball at Grosvenor House, in aid of the Actors' Benevolent Fund at which he had a ringside seat, as did Alice Delysia. July, which was hot, also saw the Royal Garden Party and clients kept Hartnell busy with increased orders for new clothes. Fixed American and European buyers came to view Norman's Autumn Collection on 26 July - arranged for several days before the Paris collections. Victor Stiebel took his own collection to show in Paris for the first ten days in August, copying Norman's previous policy of becoming part of the major fashion scene.

Novelty was ever in Norman's mind and he now used expensive fur in parallel bands around the hips and thighs of an evening coat in silver which brought the desired publicity. Following this publicity he left with John Pleydell for a holiday with Alice Delysia in her villa near Biarritz where they were all photographed for *The Bystander*, Norman wearing a dashing dark shirt with matching shorts, Delysia in a striking horizontally striped beach dress reaching to the ground. At the height of its popularity, Biarritz contained a great number of fashionable women to watch Delysia's carefully timed entrances and exits with Norman from the various restaurants and night spots.

Isabel Jeans and Heather Thatcher carried on in London in September where Delysia left off in France: Ivor Novello's *Full House* at the Haymarket was a riotous comedy in which the women were not only dressed by Norman, but they also mentioned his House (with the address) in the dialogue. This and his even greater popularity later in 1935, as a result of his designs for the wedding and bridesmaids' dresses for the marriage of the King's third son Prince Henry, Duke of Gloucester, to a daughter of the Duke of Buccleuch, Lady Alice Montagu Douglas Scott, brought Hartnell a considerable income that year, and for Norman a salary of: £4,530.6s.6d. including commission.[18] In terms of purchasing power today, this equates to roughly £315,000, marking the success of Norman's designing skills coupled with the business skills of John Pleydell.

Although Norman initiated the idea by letter that the wedding dress should be designed by himself, Princess Alice, Duchess of Gloucester remembered that she had been aware of his clothes because her sister-in-law Mary, Duchess of Buccleuch had visited his premises and ordered clothes from him.[19]

Norman scrutinised the clothes worn by the ladies of the Royal Family during the Jubilee Celebrations. Queen Mary had remained true to her set style, as had the Princess Royal, something of a disappointment to the English designers as she became the embodiment of everything meant by the 'English country lady' in terms of fashionable dress. The Duchess of York had evolved her own style, very largely drawing on the services of the well-established House of Handley-Seymour and selected their designs, usually in their own version of the latest fashionable trends. It was Princess Marina, the Duchess of Kent, who continually filled the fashion pages wearing her Molyneux creations, although her large platter hat gave her obvious problems during the drive to and from the Service of Thanksgiving in St Paul's Cathedral.

The prospect of a new royal bride was too good an opportunity to miss and so *the* letter was sent. It seems unlikely that Norman would have boldly written this without Pleydell urging him along. After Daphne Vivian's wedding, he was 'too shy to go to the reception at Dorchester House' and just walked happily away from the church exhilarated that his 'nets of silver and gold' had been such a success. When Lady Mary Thynne was married and pictures of the dress had been leaked to the press by some untrustworthy person, definitely *not* him, he had again felt too shy to go to the reception but

> I saw the new Lady Weymouth (formerly Daphne Vivian) at the church, lovely and exhilaratingly gay, wearing ink blue velvet and flamboyant furs. As I was about to go away again, she said:

'Nonsense! Of course you must come. Come with me. Maybe you missed the reception, but I'll see you don't miss this one.'[20]

Such kindness and firmness were qualities Norman needed from those who loved and understood him, as he remained intermittently shy to the end of his life with his grander clients. Although, some times were better or worse than others, and he positively glowed in the company of stage and film stars or those reflecting aspects of his family background.

However, the letter was written and the designs sent. They were not met with disapproval but certainly interested Lady Alice Scott, who had spent a great deal of time in East Africa, being a keen outdoors woman. At this time, she had little interest in clothes, borrowing some from her sister Lady Angela Scott when invited to stay at Balmoral.[21]

Norman did not have to wait long.

> The answer came back from Drumlanrig Castle in Dumfriesshire. It was written with a directness which I found later to be charac- teristic. The letter which I still cherish said that Lady Alice would call and see me when she returned to London the following week. She came with another sister Lady Sybil Phipps. Hartnell wrote – 'I noticed her beautifully moulded cheek bones and the smile which someone has described as like that of a forest gnome . . .' Having selected some dresses from the collection for her trousseau she dis- cussed the wedding dress – 'to be of a strict simplicity'.[22]

This was not difficult for Norman, although a display of inventive embroidery would have pleased him more, but he could now show the world that Moly- neux was not alone in being able to produce an elegantly simple, yet grand, wedding dress for a royal bride. Sadly, as so often in his career, circumstances altered and dashed his expectations, for when the wedding day approached he was robbed of the stage-set surroundings of Westminster Abbey. Lady Alice's father sadly died, a period of mourning began and so the extensive festive wedding with public processions were considered inappropriate and the cere- mony was scaled down and transferred to the private chapel in Buckingham Palace. This was a relief for the naturally reticent bride, who even found the crowds watching her progress by coach to Buckingham Palace a strain, but Norman and the status of British fashion would have undoubtedly benefitted from a full airing of his latest masterpiece processing up and down the aisle of the Abbey.

At Norman's suggestion, 'pearly pink' satin was used for the wedding dress, as hard white was considered unsuitable for the then dim lighting of the Abbey in the days before film and television, with their necessary bright lighting, were utilised. The softer tone was approved and he was relieved that old family lace for the veil was considered unsuitable. 'Crisp tulle' is what he always advocated rather than some lank old treasure kept in a chest and discoloured with age 'like old false teeth' as he described it.

As Lady Alice had not previously used any one particular source for her clothes, she had certainly found the best designer to assist her with her own style. The nature of both the fabric and design of the wedding dress produced Norman's first problems, with the nosy press clamouring for details of an important royal dress. Strict secrecy was insisted upon then, as in the future, and all infringements brought stern warnings from the Palace. Norman had already been upset over the breach of confidentiality with Lady Mary Thynne's wedding dress; elaborate precautions were now taken and Norman's usual availability to the press curtailed.

A mass of misinformation concerning him, his career and clients was the result. Photographs of models examined by Lady Alice were reprinted in some papers with the claim that they were chosen for the trousseau, for which, it was claimed, 400 girls were hard at work. Oddly Norman was termed 'a kind of Raphael of dressmakers' by the normally staid *Manchester Guardian* although Victor Stiebel was compared to Tiepolo. [23,24]

Norman had, of course, great experience in dressing elaborate and grand occasions and in costuming films and plays, so he could envisage how a dress would appear amongst widely disparate garments. For a Royal princess-to-be it was also vital that he study the uniforms to be encountered by the dress on its triumphal path. This was to prove a remarkable gift in his future dealings with all royal events, State Visits and Royal Tours. It was also a pleasant task because of his love of uniforms and fascination with their design, as well as the colourful decorations and orders that might be worn by their interesting wearers.

Britain's worldwide status was still suffering from the after-effects of the traumatic loss of life and economic consequences of the financially expensive First World War, closely followed by the upheaval of the Wall Street Crash and then the Great Depression. At this time Norman naturally envisaged a truly romantic and fully royal, imperial celebration of the wedding in the ancient symbolic setting of Westminster Abbey. The music would be as sublime as the setting, in which the bride, dressed of course by Norman Hartnell, would be the focus of all attention, perhaps even more so than King George V and Queen Mary with all the members of the Royal Family.

The announcement of the names of the bridesmaids drove the press and Hartnell workrooms alike into a state of near hysteria when it was learned that both of the daughters of the Duke and Duchess of York would be amongst them. Interest in Princesses Elizabeth and Margaret Rose was intense to the point of mania and mounted as the fittings for the wedding dress and trousseau proceeded. A special fitting room was equipped for the use of Lady Alice and her friends in the rooms beyond the salon in the new building facing Bruton Mews. Not yet a member of the Royal Family, the fittings for the wedding dress and extensive trousseau were held at the Hartnell premises. Lady Alice was even photographed outside, with press photographers and journalists laying siege to both the entrance and rear of the building, Pleydell giving firm instructions to make windows and staff immune to all hint of what was being made within.

As the 'Little Season' proceeded, the *Daily Express* termed the future Princess the 'heroine of the Little Season'. Concurrently Norman was photographed in his role as godfather to the baby daughter of his old Cambridge friend M.D. Lyon and was quoted as saying 'the key-note to all my ideas for women is Simplicity in the daytime and Romance for the night,' which gave nothing away. John Pleydell displayed his inherent managerial skills and merely stated 'we are delighted and honoured to be participating in this completely all-British wedding'[25]

As the wedding day of 6 November grew nearer, there were ominous reports of the Duke of Buccleuch's poor health. However, the dress and trousseau of fourteen items, including a going-away ensemble of *ardoise* grey velvet 'especially approved of by H.M. the Queen',[26] were finished and invitations then issued to the press to view the wedding dress and bridesmaids' dresses. The former was worn for pre-wedding photographs by the distinguished Madame Yevonde in her studios at 23 Berkeley Square, four days before the wedding. Norman went to the studio to arrange the veil and had to change it completely as it was too dark for the colouring of Lady Alice.[27] Madame Yevonde (like Norman also born in Streatham) was a pioneer of colour photography using the complicated 'Vivex' process, which gave glorious results.

Her photographs of the future Princess Alice and her dress are a fascinating and powerful historic record of one of Norman's most perfect simple wedding dresses, with an integrated skirt and four-yard-long train, most akin to early Regency dresses. Unfortunately, the dress has not survived as it was later altered to form an evening dress.[28] However, one of the girls who made it kept a piece of the offcuts as a memento of the delicate colouring of the masterpiece and a great royal occasion.

Norman's designs of the bridesmaids' dresses were meant to make up for the simplicity of the bridal gown by forming a decorative background with long dresses 'of a sophisticated Empire style'. King George V wanted his granddaughters in girlish short skirts. 'So the frocks were made short' of pale pink satin and overskirts of tulle with three graduated rows of fine ruched tulle. If the King was adamant about seeing their pretty little knees, as reported to Norman, then Norman was visibly upset. 'They'll look like bloody little fairies,' he said.[29] He seldom lost his temper, but this final frustration of his ambition for a truly sophisticated tableau of his designs was too much for even his equable temper.

His forbearance, talent and tact obviously impressed the Duchess of York on a visit to view her daughters' dresses, although her daughters 'then both very young, seemed more interested in the scintillating cars in the mews than in their frocks'.[30] Needless to say certain journalists termed them 'fairy frocks'. Miss Louie remembers that there was a rumour going around 'that Princess Margaret was deaf and dumb, a rumour soon put to rest in no. 7 fitting room.'[31]

Writing twenty years later, Norman could remember clearly just what the Duchess had been wearing when she first entered his salon. He studied her as she appreciated the points of various dresses in the collection shown to her, a small figure in elegant 'silver grey georgette clouded with the palest grey fur and her jewels were dew-drop diamonds and aquamarines'[32]

This meeting marked even more of a turning point for his future than his design of Princess Alice's wedding dress might have suggested. It was almost unthinkable then that the Duchess would become Queen Consort on the unexpected abdication of King George V's eldest son, King Edward VIII, who was still Prince of Wales, unmarried and in the public's mind inclined to marry one of several women with whom the press continually linked his name.

Almost as another omen of his future career, the wedding itself brought

Norman into the Throne Room of the Palace, where so many of his earlier creations had been seen at a variety of Royal Courts and other events. Norman was there to arrange the veil again, this time for Hay Wrightson the photographer. 'As I stood up a deep voice said to me: "We are very pleased. We think everything is very, very pretty."'[33] Norman was also to design dresses for Queen Mary, who had been complimenting him. In fact, she had also had her own input into the designs submitted for both the wedding dress and the trousseau, to which she gave her full approval.

The heightened excitement occasioned by the events surrounding this wedding and the prospect of future new royal patronage added to the stressful time experienced by Norman. He was also designing for his next collection, attending to special requests from clients for exclusive designs, decorating Lovel Dene and costuming plays such as *Seeing Stars* at the Alhambra, Glasgow. Florence Desmond tried out the production wearing breathtaking new Hartnell clothes, including ivy-green satin pyjamas worn under a heavily quilted iris-blue coat.

John Pleydell was undoubtedly a strong, comforting presence in Norman's life at this time relieved him of most of the worries inherent in administration and finance of what had become a large company based on satisfying the tastes of rich women for the very best of fashionable clothes. All of this was at a time when each season brought changes of line, colour, fabric and accessories. The success of Hartnell depended entirely upon the genius of one man, Norman, who apparently endlessly resourceful was not known for his strong constitution. This was an enterprise demanding much skill in very many delicate areas and relationships that did not apply to the majority of successful businesses.

In addition to the day-to-day workings of the company, the rebuilding of 26 Bruton Street required a considerable profit to be made to enable repayment of the investment, for the original quotation was unsurprisingly superseded by Norman's desire to add more elaborate furnishings to fully stamp his personality on his rooms. More chandeliers, curtains, carpets and other luxurious items were bought, and the £4,000 budget went up to £5,298.16s.11d.

The Loan Interest Company Accounts at this time also reveal that Mlle Davide, the much coveted and admired fitter, loaned the Company £250, on which she was paid 6% interest half yearly and was therefore given a keen personal interest in the progress of the business, which had finally paid Norman a salary of £3,755.11s.4½d at the end of 1935 and provided him with his Humber motor car. By contrast, John Pleydell earned £1,742.1s.7d. including his commission and director's fees.[34] He had truly put Norman Hartnell Ltd on a sound financial footing and provided for the future happiness of his friend, particularly with the purchase of their shared refuge in Windsor Forest, Lovel Dene, with its sylvan setting, stables, horses and above all the quiet privacy essential for Norman's contemplative relaxation and creative inspiration. For the next thirty years Lovel Dene was considered by Norman his refuge from the inevitable stress of maintaining Norman Hartnell Ltd. and his growing status through war, economic upheavals and the permanent challenge of ever-changing fashion.

CHAPTER EIGHT

Happy days

A s Norman fully enjoyed the just fruits of his labours by the mid-1930s, it is fair to ask how his employees fared under his roof. None of his employees earned huge amounts, although Mlle Davide was known to be well paid, justly so it was thought in view of her remarkable and visible talents. As we saw, the salaries of all staff were to be cut at the onset of the Depression, a short-term measure soon overturned. Although paid a matter of pounds a week, when the pound earned was worth roughly £70 in 2019 terms, the skilled and less skilled workforce consulted in the 1990s all remembered their days with great pleasure and satisfaction in the end product. Considered as an attractive alternative to working in a factory or a shop, employment in the structured, clean and comfortable surroundings of a well-run dressmakers also brought a feeling of pride in their communal achievements.

Wages and hours were regulated by both unions and government. Premises were regularly inspected to ensure that the facilities came up to the legal requirements. In the light and airy workrooms and large canteen of the new building, the necessary lavatories and a small restroom had all been incorporated by Gerald Lacoste. They were not luxurious, but they were all new, although there never seemed to be enough of them![1] Miss Louie had her stockroom with her own telephone line and was besieged at times by the number of representatives wishing to see her. She was known to many a fabric representative, including Miss Louie's later husband, who remembered not only the great number of Houses he visited daily, but also the truly amazing quality and quantity of the goods on offer. Most firms gave credit, especially to a House with the clout of Norman Hartnell Ltd. Miss Louie was necessarily firm with both representatives and staff alike; she was entrusted with a major expenditure and the control of the many items forming a company investment. She had to cost a whole model so that the profit margin could be worked out and the materials used could be exactly calculated.[2] Norman had trust and faith in her skill and loyalty, which was reciprocated for over forty years.

At this time an assistant to a fitter, or 'second', had a good chance of a further career in a House such as Hartnell's and when the young Mrs Muriel Monson joined she was able to observe just what went on in the workrooms and fitting rooms. She observed Madame Madeleine de Casteele, formerly with Worth and head of the workroom in which Mrs Monson worked. Casteele had been in charge of Princess Alice's wedding dress and would go down to the fitting rooms to attend to clients, and as she spoke little English was also reliant on young Mrs Monson to assist her with any linguistic difficulties. The two women would cover their black working clothes with an overall of a similar lichen-green colour to that of the salon and then descend using the back stairs. The largest fitting room at the rear of the building facing Bruton Mews was reserved for wedding or Court dress fittings as well as for the most important clients. It was from the window there that the two Princesses Elizabeth and Margaret had watched the cars being manoeuvred in and out of garages.

Madame Jeanne Normand Habans, known to everyone as Madame Jeanne (variously appearing in the press as Madame Haban or even Raban), was the Directrice of the salon and was always immaculate in Hartnell green; she would discuss the client's needs and then assign a vendeuse to her. To her, as to all those who met them in the House, the theatrical stars were considered the most difficult of all clients, especially two superstars of stage and screen, Cicely Courtneidge and Evelyn Laye. Other clients such as Barbara Cartland were particularly popular, and when she once appeared with her daughter Raine, Mrs Monson remembered that there was 'such a commotion that Mr Hartnell came down and it was like a party'.

John Pleydell was always saying how difficult it was to make the workroom pay, but he was considered a good manager, as we have seen, and was undoubtedly responsible for the three interviews Mrs Monson had to endure before she was accepted. She had decided that Molyneux and Hartnell were the best dressmakers in which to work, having wanted to become a Court Dressmaker since playing with her doll's house as a child.

Mrs Monson found that although the pay was not enormous, she could easily afford to visit the hairdresser once a week. She was interested in the embroidery room headed by Mrs Jackson but most fascinated by the way clothes were created from the fabric by 'cutting straight into the cloth the French way', without any patterns of any kind and thus requiring great skill and dexterity. The embroideries were created 'after the cutting, with very big turnings, the fabric shrank with cutting and everything was finished on the stand, each workroom having its own clients and ten to fifteen stands all padded to the shape of the client's figure'.[3]

Beverley Nichols gives something of the atmosphere of the vast House and its empty rooms as he toured it after hours in the late 1930s.

> I found myself in a large deserted work-room filled with busts. On each bust was a label 'The Countess of X', 'Madame de P', 'The Hon. Mrs Q'. (Mrs Monson was particularly struck by the fact that Madame Emilienne, the famous head of a work-room, had a small husband called Cézard who could make 'feminine suits *with a bust*'.) Here . . . were the corporeal likenesses of the great ladies of the town . . . they were all roaring off to Ascot. So these ladies had their busts copied and when they wanted a new frock they just rang up and the bust got all the boredom and the pin-pricks . . . My eyes wandered around and hit upon a bust standing by itself . . . reverently wrapped in brown paper. It looked the sort of bust that would stand no nonsense. It had an aura – yes – an aura of majesty. Then Norman came into the room. And suddenly I realised who the bust was. I turned to him. 'That bust in the parcel,' I began, 'is it Queen Ma—?' But the second syllable froze on my lips. It was, of course, but Norman never discusses his royal clients.[4]

Amongst these busts was also that of Mrs Ernest Simpson, who had dressed at Eva Lutyens' small but inventive House, before her new position in the circle around the Prince of Wales brought her to both Schiaparelli in Grosvenor Street and Norman Hartnell. Mrs Monson remembers that she was always 'a most immaculate and well groomed person, who gave the most praise of anyone who came and ordered clothes', although her 'very grating voice' was considered a defect.

So the two women who were to propel Norman into the position of dress-maker to Her Majesty the Queen, unwittingly and eerily met him and each other at 26 Bruton Street. Other insights given by an astute employee of the period into Norman's great success indicate that Norman could be depressed if designs failed to sell. On one occasion his fur coats sold badly, but 'the dear little man who made them reconstructed them in the most refined manner so that the wearer seemed slim, yet the coats also moved; they were *very* expensive'. She also noted that because of the way the Madame de Casteele cut dresses straight from the material she always asked for extra fabric; Miss Louie, who could read Norman's precise sketches (and those of his sketch artist Kathleen Street) as though they were accurate engineering plans would give less – and she was always correct. As a small insight into the girls' working day, a three-course lunch was 1s.9d. at the Ariston near the Palladium or a little place in Davies Street before the canteen was up and running.[5]

Although no. 10 Bruton Street was smaller and cosier, with Norman in closer everyday contact with his staff, he had no difficulty in transferring the same feeling of bonhomie to the larger premises and in making his workforce feel part of a large and rather cosy family. His secretary Cressie Armelin and bookkeeper Miss Ivy Godley stayed with him and were a reminder of the happy days when Topsy had also been there to confide in.

Inevitably he could trust a large workforce less than a small one. The *Daily Express* of 1 November 1935 had published a sketch of 'Lady Alice's wedding dress' that caused more consternation at the Palace than *Vogue*'s behaviour over Princess Marina's. Norman furiously pencilled 'wrong' over various of the major details, but it was a warning to him. Someone had talked enough to give away the basic outline and some of the detail.

As an indication of the gossip possible in such a large House, 'about a year before England knew of the 'Simpson Affair, Marguerite came into the workroom and told us that the future Queen of England was in the salon. How wrong she was!'[6] Mrs Mary Dubury, who began working with Norman Hartnell at this time was aged sixteen and had trained in dressmaking at a technical college in Shoreditch for two years, where she received a thorough grounding. She was two years older than the apprentice starting age, then the school leaving age.

> Naturally I was very excited but soon found the work very exacting – long hours – low pay – the latter accepted for the opportunity of being in such an establishment. I found strict discipline and most of all cleanliness – white overalls a must and all work covered with

white sheets within the limits of working. I found the girls nice and friendly which made a good working atmosphere.

Apprentices naturally did all the menial tasks including taking dresses to fitting rooms. If they met or saw a client then they would return with 'a garbled version – enlightening and funny at times' There were girls like herself next in the pecking order doing a variety of jobs. As she was in the great Mlle Davide's workrooms, of which she had two, she could observe her at close quarters. She was 'a nice person – very fair – but being French temperamental – the girls all liked her'. When Mlle Davide married at Marylebone Registry Office 'we all went along to see her as she came out – she was deeply touched'. Mlle Davide also had the useful idea of fitting clients' clothes on girls of similar size, which saved time and helped to give the clothes a better fit.

Another skilled employee, Mrs Taylor, specialised at first in making sleeves, which were then very varied in style and often came to a point over the wrist with a great deal of buttoning. Whenever a girl left to get married, then 'we all went up the "scale"'. Mrs Holiday held the highly responsible position of cutter, handling the superb silks, velvets and wools, 'before synthetics'. Patterns were made from Norman's design 'mostly under his supervision, so we saw quite a lot of him'. They also saw mannequins such as Louise and Gina, particularly during the hectic behind-the-scenes activity of the shows; 'and then we had to sit back and await orders – this was always trying – as with most big Houses we were laid off for short periods and found ourselves at labour exchanges because we were not paid.' Mrs Tofield was then in charge of the embroidery workroom, and the neighbouring workroom of Mlle Davide's was the millinery one where the matching hats were made for all occasions. Silk flowers, initially bought from France, were later made in the House.

Mrs Taylor stressed that the canteen and restroom were really established in 1938 as a result of an Act of Parliament. Before that the girls shrouded their work and then ate in the workroom, if they stayed in for their one-hour break. The working hours were from 9 am to 6 pm and from 9 am to 1 pm on Saturdays (half-day working Saturdays were then usual). Overtime of an hour or two was worked in the busy Court Season when all apprentices went to 'the nearby Beaux Arts Café to buy super bread and dripping' eaten with all the gorgeous gowns around. 'It went down very well!'[6]

It should be remembered that at this date there were four dressmaking workrooms, each with its own French fitter and assistants. All the best Houses had French fitters; the superiority of their training and experience made the prospect of a truly 'All British Couture' especially remote, and there was and is no adequate English word that encapsulates the word couture.

In addition, there was also the tailoring workroom, embroidery workroom and later the furrier's room. Interestingly, Mrs Monson remembers that at this date Norman *did* have a dress stand in his studio on which he could 'drape materials to see the "hand and handle" of them *before* sketching'.

When the large royal orders came in, Madame de Casteele was put in charge of them as she had been used to members of European royal families at Worth in Paris. As a footnote to Beverley Nichol's visit to the busts, Mrs Monson padded a dress stand for Queen Mary 'to her special shape from newspaper photos plus her measurements. It was very good and Mr Hartnell used to show it to his visitors. Our workroom was outside his studio.'[7] Although Norman was devoted to his royal clients, and always quite discreet, he could relax with those he trusted and Queen Mary was a particular favourite topic of conversation and correspondence for Blake. Indeed, Blake could never hear enough of her and was one of many at the time who did remarkable impersonations of 'the august lady', as he frequently termed her.

Norman's sense of fun was extended to those he felt most comfortable with. Grace Gray, who started with him in 1931 aged fourteen and a half, was very shy and always blushed when he spoke to her.

> That really amused him . . . he was a very gentle and sincere man, always interested in his employees' progress in carrying out his designs. He had the habit of giving one the name of a famous person or a film star if he thought there was any resemblance, he would call me Ruby [Keeler]. If he saw you on the street he would wave frantically until you waved back . . . he was never snobbish and would introduce us to whoever he was with. Once he introduced me to a brigadier and said this is Ruby, and what a lovely hat you are wearing . . . During an air raid we went into the basement one day. Evelyn Laye was there. Mr Hartnell introduced us saying meet Miss Laye, doesn't she look nice, she is forty-two, you wouldn't think so, and she never pays her bills on time. He said these things in such a way nobody ever took offence.

His concern was genuine. 'Once an apprentice named Vicky was taken into hospital with septicaemia . . . Mr Hartnell offered to pay for any special treatment.' Sadly, she died.

Mr Gray was called up into the Air Force in the war, when the House changed continually. 'I look back with nostalgia; they were happy days.'[8]

Another member of Madame Madeleine's workroom, Margaret Donaldson, began there in 1936 and remembers that Madame Jeanne was the vendeuse who accompanied Norman to the Palace for royal fittings. In addition to all Norman's attributes she thinks he was a good employer as he gave two weeks' paid holiday a year, taken when the whole House closed for the summer break.

> We received a bottle of port or sherry as a Christmas present and girls were allowed to make their own wedding dresses in the workroom (this was a parting gift as a girl always left work when she got married) . . . His was the first couture house to have a staff canteen where a hot midday meal was provided for 6d. However, he didn't encourage other breaks, although unbeknown to him we secretly made tea using a gas ring hidden in a cupboard and crept out two at a time to drink it . . . My starting salary (as a 'junior') was £1.2s. and when I left (in 1939) it was £2.7s.6d. Increases were given according to the standard of work.

These amounts were slightly above the pay at less prominent establishments, regulated by statute.

Mrs Donaldson was a 'hand' with two assistants working under her from 1938 to 1939.

> Working practices were traditional – all zips were put in by hand and electric irons were never used (there was a rank of gas rings in the workroom with irons constantly ready for use, these being removed as required with a metal hook). It was the custom for a dressmaker to sew one of her own hairs into the seam or hem of a wedding dress for good luck . . . on many occasions we were allowed downstairs to see the final fitting of dresses we had worked on.[9]

Other significant employees included Sergeant Green, the doorman indispensable to such an establishment in his frogged uniform and huge umbrella to hand, ready to protect some of the world's most beautiful and influential women as they made their way in and out of Norman's glittering House. Rarely did they leave with boxes – these were the days of delivery either by the Hartnell van around central London or by registered post to the provinces.

If his employees admired and respected him, then clients might also love him; Alice Delysia thought of him as 'Mon Petit Pet', as she both called him and wrote to him. His close relationship with John Pleydell was of no importance to a Frenchwoman at the top of her profession in the theatre. Photographs of them and friends at her villa on the Plateau de Bidart, Biarritz, overlooking the shoreline towards Spain, reveal a fantastically eccentric group of four assorted men and their hostess in her best 'Hartnell Beachwear'.

No less striking are photographs of her surrounded by yet more men seated in the depths of a sofa in the fashionable setting of the Regency drawing room at Lovel Dene. Norman told of his embarrassment when another star client, Florence Desmond, came over to them at the Café de Paris one night and said casually

> 'Hello, my dear, I hear you two are engaged.'
> 'Yes,' said Alice. 'Isn't it wonderful.'
> I agreed it was wonderful. The next day the papers announced our engagement and soon the house was in a state of uproar, for she immediately drove down to Ascot [sic]. It was a trying evening.[10]

There is no doubt that Alice was very fond of Norman, however a publicity stunt was clearly manufactured, wittingly or not. Alice knew that Norman had no sexual interest in women and that an 'arranged marriage' would be of no interest to him either. He both enjoyed the friendship and publicly benefitted from his time with her in Biarritz. Unlike his rivals Patou and Molyneux, who both had salons in this highly fashionable resort, Norman was there as a guest of a great star, not ostensibly on a 'working' holiday. Patou had successfully shown the 'new' long dresses in 1930 and Norman had been the one to instigate their Paris introduction to wide acclaim in 1929. Norman could well have thought it worthwhile to show his face in Biarritz society, but he could not match Molyneux, who had a third salon in Monte Carlo. According to John Cavanagh, Molyneux's assistant in the late 1930s, money had come in so fast in 1930 that the Molyneux bookkeepers 'hardly had time to count it'.[11]

The pay-off for Delysia now came in fabricating an unusual alliance. Barbara Cartland remembers: 'Delysia was a superb cook, she would walk in the rain, darn Norman Hartnell's socks and look seductive, entrancing and very "naughty" in the first solid-sequin dress he ever designed,'[12] but Norman 'was obviously "gay" in the way he walked and talked'[13] and as he aged these mannerisms grew more pronounced, especially the way in which he smoked and held his cigarette, which most people remember vividly, and as he archly underlined by writing, 'I was seduced by Madame Nicotine at an early age.'[14]

This was the only seduction of Norman by any Madame, but it was a life-long and ultimately fatal love affair.

The Delysia affair was not improbable in an age of extravagant public-star behaviour when reported by a press insatiable for gossip and a public reliant on the press in those days for most of their news. Under siege at the normally quiet Lovel Dene, the 'lovers' decided that there would be no peace until Delysia returned to the Savoy, and the next day they placed denials of the 'match' in the papers. Had the true picture of Norman's life with John Pleydell emerged, then his business would have certainly been drastically cut, if not ruined. But the papers were then most reticent on such subjects.

The Lovel Dene–Bidart alternate weekends and holidays went on for some years, until the newspapers finally became too intrusive into the true state of 'the romance'. Norman then began to take summer breaks in Aix-les-Bains, a thoroughly 'proper' place full of Edwardian relics and quiet money.

As if the 'romance' with Delysia was not enough, he then became embroiled in the life of Gertrude Lawrence, whose pre-war existence contained all the pace and drama of an off-stage Noël Coward play. Coward was a friend and fan of the more intellectual and older Captain Edward Molyneux, who had designed the ravishing dresses for Miss Lawrence in *Private Lives* of 1930. However, there came a moment when he would not or 'could not' make the clothes for Gertrude Lawrence to wear in Ronald Jean's *Can the Leopard?* (1931), a play in which she played an extravagant wife whose husband could not change her ways. This was a success tailor-made for Miss Lawrence, who looked stunning in her Norman Hartnell dresses, and her ruinously extravagant behaviour is described at length by Norman and explains why she was declared bankrupt in 1935. His visit to her flat resulted in him being physically sick at the combined effect of the overpowering scent sprayed onto the curtains and given off by huge vases of lilies placed amongst the sumptuous decoration, including a glass table and glass plates.

In 1968 he told Francis Wyndham, writing an article for the *Sunday Times* magazine under the title 'The Pearly King':

> I adored that woman so much that I wanted to get away from her! She made me *ill* with fascination, I couldn't be in her presence. But she wasn't all sugar and spice, you know. No, Gertie was like a little serpent: she would tremble with temper and shiver with chic! (I say, that's rather good!) But she was so delicious, nobody minded.

Having been one of Molyneux's star clients on and off the stage, she shared her patronage with Norman from 1930 and by 1935 her press announcements stated that she was dressed exclusively by him. Today no one would care about such an accolade, but in 1935, popular fascination with Miss Lawrence turned even elderly club men into 'gallery girls'. Those hordes of fans watching and copying her every movement and dress foible, just as millions also copied film-star fashion seen at the cinema and epitomised in their own way by Coward, Lawrence and Hartnell. The three South London-bred children, who had escaped their modest backgrounds by the use of their outstanding talents and entered into worlds they first aspired to, and then helped to mould in their own image.

Miss Lawrence's image received a recharge when Norman designed an extensive number of glamorous dresses for her 1936 London opening in the playlets forming Coward's *Tonight at 8.30* starring 'Noël and Gertie', as their fans called them, and partly devised in an effort to revive her depleted fortune. Norman then designed another even better mini-collection for the New York run of the play later in the year. These designs received extraordinary publicity, as did the play, because at a special benefit evening held in the Waldorf Astoria's Starlight Room she modelled the complete collection. The publicity went further, as programmes on the theatre seats contained a fully descriptive list of each garment worn as though it were part theatre, part dress show.

Could Norman have been surprised when Miss Lawrence repeated Delysia's performance as a woman ostensibly infatuated with him?

> Gertrude Lawrence entered the showroom and walked with her nimble legs across the greensward of the velvety carpet . . . I went towards her and taking her hand in mine brought her to where she

hesitated about two yards from the banquette in my showroom and then without preliminaries she murmured, 'Will you marry me?' I answered, '..whatever for?' . . . and she replied, 'Because nobody else will.' I realise that my answer to her, put in print now, may sound discourteous. I really meant, 'For whatever reason would an irresistible creature like you want to join your brilliant life with mine?' But I knew that she was not speaking seriously and that nobody could have been more perturbed than Gertie herself if I had countered, 'Yes, when?' I think that her casually posed question was simply a cry of loneliness from the heart.

The fittings for dresses then went ahead: 'Thus was killed an unborn tenderness that never would have brought to her the happiness that she might have given to me.'

Miss Lawrence was not the last woman to make the suggestion of marriage to Norman, who could have given each one a pleasantly quiet private life had he been blessed with the stamina to cope with the heavy demands of all his career entailed. Of Gertrude Lawrence, he wrote: 'Since her swift death, I have thought of her constantly. There was no one like her and there never will be. In the distress of the moment I wrote to Noël Coward and he replied thus in a letter which I keep.'

> My dear Norman,
> I was touched by your letter about our darling Gertie.
> I want you to know that Gertie was truly and deeply fond of you.
> I know this because she has told me so many, many times and I am pretty sure that she knew how much you loved her.[16]

His mother, his sister, Delysia, Gertrude Lawrence – they were all strong women he loved and respected. The first two were the strongest influences on him as a young man, whilst the third and fourth revealed how they raised stage glamour into a form of living that also formed an escape for him from many of the unpleasant realities of life. This escape was one into a world where he was surrounded by strong protective personalities, though his own strong personality was exercised exactly as he wished. But the strongest personalities he came to appreciate most were all male. Norman created his own world, a situation granted to few and he was to pay for it, sometimes willingly but often not.

It will not surprise the reader to learn that Norman was homosexual from his boyhood on. There is no evidence that he was ever sexually interested in women, and his own sexuality was early expressed through his love of wearing women's clothing in school plays and then in the justly famous Cambridge Footlights productions. These of course gave him a true sense of what women expected of their clothing and how it could be worn, within the confines of his own male body. The taste for wearing women's clothes was not a form of high jinks left behind at Footlights, and his evolving sex life was as inventive as his designing. It extended beyond cross-dressing to fetishism. In later life, he explained to the designer Kenneth Partridge 'that as a boy he had been excited by a young male relative, possibly his missing half-brother, who used to dangle him on his knee and slide him up and down his riding boots'.[18]

We have no knowledge of his boyhood habits beyond his brief history in *Silver and Gold*, but presumably he enjoyed dressing up in old clothes, as most children still do. At Cambridge, he continued to find it amusing to dress up in women's clothing and he was attracted to sportsmen and older masculine men, who were also attracted to him. No doubt he was also popular with them because of his fresh boyish good looks, fair hair and blue eyes. He was slightly built with an impish look accentuated by his larger-than-average-sized head. But that is all that can be said about him at that time.

Soon after he first opened his business in 1923, he shared rooms in St James's with Blake Brown, and when Blake left to take up his religious studies, he shared the flat before moving to another flat within Mayfair. Blake suffered from a crisis of identity and was married for a short time. Like Mr Prendergast in Evelyn Waugh's slightly later novel *Decline and Fall*, Blake renounced marriage and also suffered religious doubts for a time. Norman did not appear to suffer any doubts, and perhaps his reported daily runs in Hyde Park were made in an effort to find the anonymous male company he enjoyed throughout his life.

Norman's relationship with John Pleydell was based both on his greater social standing, combined with hearty masculinity and his business acumen, all of which were familiar to Norman from his childhood on, his home life dominated by his loud and hearty father exuding forceful Victorian entrepreneurial drive. His mother was naturally quieter but no less entrepreneurial. She was used to controlling a pub and bar, as we have seen, so had no qualms about subduing obdurate men. Her death was especially traumatic for Norman, the baby of this bustling family. He never ceased to mourn her and visit her grave on significant dates.

Norman's private life was known to very few, as actively practised homosexuality remained a criminal offence until the Sexual Offence Bill of 1967 became the Act which decriminalised homosexual acts between two men over twenty-one in private in England and Wales. Norman enjoyed sex at home, where it became part of a fetishistic ritual.

His private behaviour was known to very few, as was usual with homosexuals at the time, called by a variety of sneering derogatory names by many. Blake certainly knew of Norman's secret passions and, as witnessed by the prologue, others amongst his employees also knew but were naturally reticent in keeping the secret.[21] His former butler and handyman in the 1960s was another and some thirty years later still complained at having to clean the collection of riding boots housed in a special cabinet at Lovel Dene, although The Boss had not ridden seriously since the 1930s.[19]

The boots formed a significant part of the rituals evolved by Norman over the years in which the cross-dressing Norman was transformed into 'Miss Kitty', a character played by Norman in Footlights, menaced by a large male sexual partner with a riding crop and then finally violated with considerable force. Later on, an array of some of the objects used in the violation were discovered abandoned with other items in the outbuildings of George Mitchison's country house by the recent purchaser. He did not return them.

This form of sexual behaviour probably began as a playful romp when Norman was a young undergraduate with rooms of his own, but as he further explained to Kenneth Partridge, Miss Kitty became closely associated in Norman's mind with the character of Flavia in Anthony Hope's novel *The Prisoner of Zenda*, a favourite novel and film of Norman's. He assumed the character of the imprisoned heroine and wearing a wig of corkscrew curls and a crinoline dress made at Hartnell to measurements purportedly 'sent in by a poor crippled woman, who can't travel'. In fact, the making of garments to precise measurements sent in from a distant client was not unusual. The *mise-en-scène* naturally required at least one enthusiastic partner clad in boots and uniform to enter the dimly lit bedroom, always at night, and then undertake the role of rampant gaoler.

Both Kenneth Partridge and Ian Thomas were aware of the unusual activities going on when they were attractive young men staying at Lovel

Dene. Kenneth said that he would leave for a bike ride once the large cars of middle-aged men began to arrive. Ian had his own bedroom slightly apart from the others – Ian's Room – and would retreat in there for the night, wedging a chair under the doorknob. This suited Norman. They were not his type.[20]

However, Kenneth Partridge was told by other visitors that whenever Miss Kitty had readied herself upstairs, a number would be displayed on a note informing the lucky man just which uniform should be taken out of the collection and worn for the event, which presupposes that the invited men were roughly of similar size. They were typically tweedy pipe-smoking men seeking a release from wives and families.[21]

For a professional psychiatrist today, part of the diagnosis of Norman's condition lies in whether Norman had gender issues or if the matter was more fetishistic, so that once he had achieved the level of pleasure he sought, this would lapse until he peaked again. There is no evidence that Norman wore women's underclothing during the day during his business activities, but the forms of outer clothing, fur and feathers clearly excited him and certainly often occurred in his designs throughout his career.[22]

Although Norman confided that he did not like pain, it certainly interested his partners. For Norman, the main thrill came from his costume and the suspense of waiting for the arrival of his partner. His fantasies did not lessen with age; they became a habitual part of his life at Lovel Dene, though his world there would be cruelly shattered in the 1960s. His passions even encompassed some of his decorative fantasies, which were usually in the most sophisticated taste of the day. However, Wakers was marginally surprised to be commissioned to design what was known to many as the Black Room at Lovel Dene, ostensibly part of Norman's display of militaria but furnished with black patent-leather-covered furniture set on a fake leopard-skin carpet. The respectable front was maintained by another small room exclusively displaying more militaria as a small personal museum.[23]

After John Pleydell's departure, Norman never had another full-time, live-in lover with the exception of George Mitchison for a very short time after he had met him in 1938, when he was stationed at the Regent's Park Barracks, a mere stone's throw from Norman's Regent's Park house, The Tower House. This encounter with the good-looking, moustachioed soldier was undoubtedly part of the reason for the end of his relationship with Pleydell. Miss Louie was often sent from Bruton Street with notes to George at the barracks and resented being the 'front' for Norman, as she understood that he was just an ordinary man from Northumberland with a background no different to hers.[25]

George left the army and became an employee of Hartnell until called up for war service. As will be explained, he returned as Major, but aroused surprise at Hartnell, for he was married to Doris and then began a family. His subsequent lifelong role in the life of Norman and existence of Norman Hartnell Ltd will be narrated later.[26]

Norman's private life may well have been suspect to many but was effectively kept quiet during his lifetime. It was the era of illicit homosexuality, when poorly paid young men could be bought for the night or longer, as J.R. Ackerley's memoirs describe. For anyone versed in fetishism, Norman's professional hands-on embracing of textiles, furs and feathers was no doubt revealing, especially his predilection for monkey fur. But to most people this was a foreign country, and Norman was considered a slightly eccentric artistic type with an engaging character, not unlike the confirmed bachelors found in many families at the time. It is hardly likely that Norman himself ever deeply pondered his tastes and occupation until late in life. He simply enjoyed himself in the daily whirl of his changing activities, and the repetitive nature of his deeply personal pleasures made them necessarily an obsessive routine at the root of his existence, though they would come to severely handicap his personal and business fortunes after the Second World War.

However, in 1936 Norman remained outwardly the same youthful, slim and pleasant-looking young Englishman, whom even then would often be referred to in the press as 'the Cambridge graduate designer' – the 'under' had at least been dropped. But the season of that year was overshadowed by the death of King George V on 20 January 1936. After the glories of the London season of Jubilee Year now came the usual period of Court Mourning and the public realisation that the new King Edward VIII was apparently to be crowned without a spouse at his side, a lonely figure, unlike his younger brothers and sister. The presence of Mrs Simpson was known to a wider circle, although the newspapers were responsible for muffling the issue. Mrs Simpson, as a client of Norman Hartnell, *might* have become the first Queen Consort to be dressed by Norman, as Molyneux was so famously Princess Marina's designer. No doubt the thought had occurred to Norman.

The year progressed with a sense of unease, not simply about the new uncrowned King, but also political developments abroad. The consequences of the German reoccupation of the Rhineland; Mussolini's campaign to found an Italian Empire and the sickening reports of the Civil War in Spain were a dampener to the spirits, as were Stalin's policies in Russia. An increase in German Jewish citizens fleeing the revolting repression and continual legalised theft of their possessions meant that some highly skilled workers in the clothing industry swelled the numbers working in London dress Houses as well as in the wholesale manufacturing and retail trades. Berlin had long been noted for the excellent finish and design of mass-produced clothing, and in London competition from the wholesale dress firms increased, as under the influence of immigrants versed in the latest mechanised techniques, their products improved in quality and appearance. This was carefully watched by London designers and the numbers of immigrants were watched by the immigration authorities with an eye on the large numbers of unemployed still prevalent in Britain. There was also some feeling of unease and resentment at the capabilities of the new arrivals.

As for couture, Joe Strassner was one of Berlin's leading designers for elegant women, including the star Marlene Dietrich. He opened his own Mayfair House on the corner of South Audley Street and Grosvenor Square, proving to be highly successful in attracting both publicity in British *Vogue* and new clients. His own genius was also transferred from the Berlin UFA film studios and notably utilised by Alfred Hitchcock in his 1930s British films. His work was regarded as an addition to London's fashion status.

Norman in turn dressed the German star Brigitte Horney in the British-made film *The House of the Spaniard*, at a time when the 1936 Berlin Olympic Games were a temporary propaganda coup in representing Germany as a civilised 'normal country'.

There were other rivals amongst the dressmakers. A young man appeared ('Is this the second Norman Hartnell?' as the papers blared) and opened in Berkeley Square under his own name: Derek Skeffington. The smart American women's 'sportswear' shop of Marjorie Castle full of useful coats, shirts and blouses opened nearby and at Lachasse the young Hardy Amies was already introducing his own carefully restructured women's tailor-mades and then evening and wedding dresses. His predecessor Digby Morton had left in 1934 and begun his own successful business. London was by terms anxious or elated, but it fizzed with varied fashion talents.

By November, when the uncrowned King Edward VIII opened Parliament,

London was in a state of high anxiety as rumours about him and Mrs Simpson were widely discussed. Norman's clothes for Miss Lawrence's New York appearance in *Tonight at 8.30* accompanied the star and John Pleydell on the *Queen Mary*, where passengers were hoping for a 'private preview'.[27] Plans for the Coronation Collection at Norman Hartnell were far advanced; after the Earl Marshall had issued full details for the regulation robes of peers and peeresses, every House produced collections of dresses which could be worn and seen to advantage beneath them.

Norman further showed 'Winter Cruisewear', with a full complement of day and evening wear, whilst Schiaparelli, always to the fore with novelties, included 'deck suits' in her London collection. Norman's own collection – on which girls worked almost all night on the day before the show – was an extraordinary display of versatility in expensive time-consuming tucking used on all fabrics, even velvet. It was a superbly finished coronation gown embroidered virtually all over with graduated pearls on a fern-frond design over silver lamé.

In addition to this collection, the House was busy on a number of exceedingly elaborate costumes for impresario C.B.Cochran's *Coronation Revue* which was due to open at the Manchester Opera House on 23 December, starring Hungarian Gitta Alpár wearing clothes by Norman. Norman certainly felt a nostalgic pang of déjà vu when his dresses appeared at the Streatham Hill Theatre on 5 December 1936 adorning Diana Wynyard in *Heart's Content*; the director Raymond Massey was a fan of Norman's and used his services several times.

Hartnell designs were seen to advantage in a bewildering number of settings at this time. On 2 November 1936 Adele Dixon wore a pale blue sequined dress with a bird of paradise over one shoulder for the opening programme of the new BBC television service at Alexandra Palace, which attracted great publicity. The King abdicated on 10 December, so the impact of the new BBC service was overshadowed, whilst the staff of Norman Hartnell wondered about their former client Mrs Simpson and the fate of their extensive Coronation Collection which had been featured in so many publications. Cochran swiftly changed the name of his revue to *Home and Beauty*. It opened as planned with the *Manchester City News* opening its review: 'The hero of C.B. Cochran's newly christened *Home and Beauty* is never seen on stage at all; his name is Norman Hartnell; he has designed the dresses of the principals and in total he gets more applause than any star of the show.'[28]

Although Norman attributed this production to one of the biggest losses on his books for 1935, he was mistaken; the financial loss was Cochran's and in 1937, when the star developed problems with her throat, the production was as ill-fated as the Coronation it had been intended to celebrate.

The revue provided Norman with three other irritating leading ladies to dress; everything wanted by Gitta Alpár was then requested by Binnie Hale, Iris March and Sepha Treble, be it extravagant furs, feathers or frills.

For Norman, there were also memories of his first production for Cochran, when a whole series of beach costumes were required as part of a Noël Coward revue set in the south of France. His designs were so overdone that they seemed like fancy dress rather than chic girls on the beach at Cannes, so Coward rejected them all. This probably explains Noël Coward's wariness of Norman, who frequently attempted to prove that more was less – as Michael Sherard, one of his later colleagues in Inc Soc said, 'he could gild the lily in more ways than anyone else would have thought possible'.[29] (Norman was not so miffed, as he managed to sell all the costumes to Elizabeth Arden for her New York shop). Nevertheless, in Noël Coward's *Mademoiselle*, produced at Wyndham's at the end of 1936, Isabel Jeans wore Molyneux and Greer Garson Norman's designs in 'a lavish display of gowns'.

One of the sights of London in 1936 was Marlene Dietrich 'resting' from her triumphant self-imposed Hollywood exile and making the film *Knight Without Armour* for Alexander Korda's London Films at Denham. She bought several of Norman's tailored suits (as did another visiting Hollywood star Miriam Hopkins), evening dresses, including a cloak, whilst finding her friend Strassner's and Victor Stiebel's evening clothes even more to her taste. She was disliked by theatre casts and audiences, because she usually made her own staged entrances by arriving at theatres in the middle of the first act and causing a commotion.

She was also joined in London by other non-emigre and émigré German stars, such as Brigitte Horney who made a British film in 1936 with a former Footlights luminary, Peter Haddon, whose best if few films were dressed by Norman. Hartnell film dress designs were more frequent than generally recognised.

But much as 1936 was a year packed with incident for Norman and Britain alike, and as suddenly as the work for the Coronation Collection of King

Edward VIII had ended, so that of the Coronation of King George VI and Queen Elizabeth, his Queen Consort, began. It was to prove a momentous occasion for Norman in particular.

CHAPTER NINE

Regal renaissance

When the Duchess of York and the 'Two Little Princesses' had visited Norman's House in 1935 for the fittings of the Princesses' bridesmaids' dresses to be worn at the wedding of their uncle, the Duke of Gloucester, their host was overwhelmed by the personality of 'The Smiling Duchess'. Born Elizabeth Bowes-Lyon, a daughter of an ancient and noble family, the Duchess had for ten years dutifully carried out her royal duties to universal acclaim. She was a near neighbour of Hartnell when he was at no. 10 Bruton Street and subsequently he was briefly a tenant of her parents' former house for his Circus Party, thus Norman was more attuned than most to the frequent newspaper coverage of the Duke and Duchess's engagements and many photographs showing her current clothing.

The first commissions from the Duchess for Norman's designs came in January 1936, three months after the wedding of the Duke and Duchess of Gloucester. An embryonic rapport was clearly felt, as Norman said afterwards to one of the fitters, 'She's a dear girl.' They were of the same vintage, the Duchess born in 1900, and Norman in 1901, so with her lovely delicate features and fine colouring, her beautiful small hands, feet and sparkling eyes, Norman was won over to his own perennial devotion of the woman who was to become his remarkable lifelong patron and forever saw in her the powerful romance which a Queen Consort could bring to the institution of the British monarchy.

His earliest designs for her were cautious exercises and not too dissimilar in outline from those of her established dressmaker Handley-Seymour, clearly a style the Duchess herself favoured. Madame Handley-Seymour had her own style and an extensive clientele, including work for the stage, producing elegantly detailed sketches and for the Duchess, often with a vignette of the design detailed from the rear in a corner of the main sketch.

One of the advantages of studying Norman's royal dress designs lies in the plentiful photographic material showing clothes from all angles and allowing one to judge the details of side and back, for which Norman was famously inventive. His own early sketches for the Duchess show greater care, as might be expected, but also amusing details that must have entertained his client. The angle at which a bag is held, a fur clasped or hat worn sometimes veer towards a theatricality that stops short of being outrageous but required a certain regal demeanour from the wearer that few could get away with. Indeed, some of Norman's 1940s designs seem almost outrageous in their suggestions of detailing within the fashionable silhouette of the period and were worn with such élan by his royal client that they became as regal as Queen Mary's imposing outfits.

The first orders included black ensembles which were beautiful yet befitting Court Mourning. In some drawings, the shadow of the model and facsimile of the Duchess cast a remarkably evocative shadow across the paper. All designs were set within a pencilled and washed framework, a small rectangle at the foot of the design reading 'specially designed for . . .' followed by the name of the client.

If the Duchess had been happy wearing the long-established Handley-Seymour's designs, she must have been happier in those emanating from Norman's hands. Two people of the same age and both with a clear understanding of what was required for her role, which represented a dramatic change after the Abdication of King Edward VIII. From the existing correspondence, it is quite clear that there was great empathy between royal client and designer. For the rest of his working life, forty-two years, Norman Hartnell devotedly committed himself to finding ingenious ways of sustaining the individual images of both Queen Elizabeth and her family. Furthermore, with the exception of some 'casual' or country clothes, he remained the only designer for Queen Elizabeth until his death. Her loyalty to him and satisfaction with his workforce ensured her patronage until the House closed in 1992.

Norman's experience of designing for the stage and films together with his interest in historic fashion were indispensable for this new evolving phase of his career. From the earliest days of film-making, clothes worn in costume pictures had all shown a rare disregard for all but the most superficial resemblance to the correct date of the happenings portrayed. By 1935, Alexander Korda's London Films in particular had made some rare strides in attempting accuracy and some of these designs, together with then current stage designs, undeniably affected Norman, who was a particularly keen cinema-goer.

In March 1935, British *Vogue* noted evening dresses by Norman in the 'Nell Gwynne' manner, the 1934 film of her life being a box-office success and starring Anna Neagle, another favourite client. The evening dresses noted in his House collection lifted in front to show a white petticoat and tied at the shoulder line; not for the first or last time he repeated historical detail, so often an inspiration for his grandest wedding dresses.

Possessor of a photographic memory prompted by an ever-growing collection of books on costume history and old fashion plates, he also subscribed to the latest international fashion journals. Norman was thus able to assess the changing line of fashion and almost by osmosis interpret the trends and integrate the salient features into his own individual designs. He more than once influenced world fashion, but his vision as a great designer, which he certainly was, primarily depended on clothing his clients individually in a manner uniquely expressive of their personalities.

Of course, he produced grand collections each year, yet he did not necessarily expect to sell the models directly to his clients as they viewed them. He was pleased if he did, particularly delighted if a foreign store buyer bought models for copying, but models could be reproduced in different fabrics, with varied details or embroideries for a client willing to pay. Such women often asked for designs to be made especially for themselves and a sketch artist would work up Norman's design, attach a few swatches and consultation would begin. This would often all happen by post until fittings were required.

One former pre-war employee remembered a client buying everything in the Cruise Collection, only to return and demand a quantity of extra designs from Norman just for her. When modern killjoys turn green with envy at such a woman's lifestyle, they fail to remember the employment her expenditure generated as a tiny part of the orders taken to keep 400 Hartnell employees in work. This is in addition to the fabric producers, the suppliers, the button, zip, cotton, leather, fur and hat workers, together with those producing the necessary accessories.

In the same way, the dazzling Evening Courts kept a host of caterers, limousine-hire firms, florists, photographers and many others gainfully employed. In retrospect, everyone involved with the elevated world forming Society during those days recalls them with pleasure. Pay for the humbler employees may have been low, but it was more pleasing to work in a 'glamorous' trade than in a smelly, noisy factory or stand in a shop, and there was a buzz and excitement in the continuing social round of the clients and the employment it created. As British *Vogue* pointed out in its 20 March 1935 issue, 'the sport' of the moment was for fashionable women to do the rounds of the daily dress shows, often given with as much panache as a private party and the 'dress parades' were then considered better than anything in Paris.

By the time of the 1937 Coronation Collection, consisting of 143 models, Norman Hartnell Ltd had been so far advanced by Pleydell's management that all of the models were registered in Great Britain and 'no other house has the right to sell reproductions or copies'. A new department was opened to further promote the selling of suits, those necessary bread-and-butter components of the Hartnell success always of less interest to Norman's creativity. Even if Norman preferred designing evening wear, competition – particularly from Digby Morton, Hardy Amies at Lachasse and Peter Russell – was too intense to be ignored, so large and exclusive ranges of Scottish and French tweeds were kept in stock. At 16 gns a suit, fitted by expert tailors, the suits were competitively priced and sold well. Day dresses were also designed as part of a separate collection within the main collection, so that the idea of 'separates' was promoted. This particular 1937 Coronation Collection cleverly grouped such clothes under names and groups with one letter of the alphabet in the dress card or programme, so that the models made sense:

> 36 kodak black dress trimmed fringe
> 37 ladies club black dress trimmed fringe
> 38 lattice sage-green dress and jacket
> 39 little lamb black and white hand print
> 40 lunch bar black silk dress

And so on. It proved to be one of the most financially rewarding collections of Norman's career and out of the 143 models only sixteen were embroidered or sequined; which no doubt kept the otherwise very high production costs down.[1] As Barbara Cartland wrote at the time:

> What will Edward give us new? •
> Norman has a frill or two.
> Schap is sure to be surprising
> Let's hope Coco's price ain't rising.

Round and round the shops we go,
Mayfair must be chic you know.[2]

As it happened, Norman had a model no. 18 named 'Coco' – a white piqué suit and brown skirt, as a not particularly friendly gesture to Mlle Chanel and 'her monotonous miracles'.[3] One facet of the expanding business was the 'extensive stock of Canadian mink, Russian ermine, silver foxes and blue foxes etc.',[4] which were particularly suitable for the image of his latest great and royal client.

The confidence felt by this client in Norman is reflected in the newspaper reports that the Queen had ordered outfits from his Coronation Collection. Some papers put the number in the twenties, others at forty, but all were guesses as the information was not given out. Russeks, then a prominent New York store, gave Norman a whole window display for an embroidered evening ensemble as a foretaste of what might be seen.[5]

As *Tonight at 8.30* was still being discussed in the February papers, it was a good season for Hartnell in New York. In January's *Tatler* he was photographed at a Grosvenor House charity dinner-dance with Marcelle Rogez, the latest of his French actress admirers. By late March, American newspapers were carrying an interview with Norman on the subject of his royal designs, angled to suggest that 'a court dress in cream satin richly embroidered with gold' was his 'pièce-de-resistance which the Queen will probably wear beneath the purple velvet train'.[6]

In fact, Madame Handley-Seymour provided the Coronation dress; after so many devoted years of designing for the Duchess of York, it would have been unthinkable for her not to have made clothes for this important occasion. Norman may have felt slightly disappointed but not surprised, and he was favoured with the design of the dresses for the Maids of Honour, created on the 'princess line' with panels of embroidery in a flowing-wheat design adding to the overall design of the Queen's Coronation Dress. The details of these were announced well in advance, as was the design of the Duchess of Gloucester's dress. Details of the Queen's and Princess's dresses were to be kept confidential until the actual event took place. This was apparently a problem for all involved, as the press made assumptions and asked angled questions. Norman had excellent relations with the press and knew how much business depended on them, but he had learned not to discuss his clients and their taste without permission.

In February 1937, he was given the distinction of being pictured with Molyneux and Schiaparelli in *Time* magazine and described as the third-most-important designer in the world, the report stressing the shift away from the Paris couturiers as sources of great fashion. Interestingly, Rudolf Lanz of Salzburg was named after Mainbocher, the new Duchess of Windsor's favourite of the time, as the next great influence for his 'dirndl-based' designs, capitalised on by Hardy Amies in London. Christian 'Bebè' Bérard was also mentioned as an important influence on a younger generation of assistants in the older Houses. These included Pierre Balmain and an embryo Christian Dior, both post-war successes. Bérard worked for *Vogue* and was consistently photographed and written about by Cecil Beaton, rapidly becoming an influential contributor to American *Vogue*. For Norman, this was affirmation that he was an international designer of standing.

As the weeks progressed towards the Coronation so press fever for any information inevitably mounted. Norman revealed that he produced 1,600 sketches a year. Photographs of the workroom making dresses to be worn by the Maids of Honour appeared, whilst Norman dressed two West End plays and sent clothes to a fashion display in Sheffield. Madame Berthe was intercepted by Helene Gordon on 29 April as she returned from Windsor after a fitting with the Queen and, as Norman merely said, 'We are trying to stress the Queen's personality' she interrupted:

> She has simple tastes. Look. This is the dress the Queen likes best, the one I have just been trying on her. It is turquoise blue. The Queen adores turquoises. There will be a whole stream of them embroidered the full length of the dress. She will wear it for one of the first dinners after Coronation Day.[7]

With such garrulous employees, Norman might as well have pasted his designs on the front door, but then he himself gave a radio interview relayed to New York in which he described various dresses ordered and the pastel colour preferred by the Queen, who ordered from his submitted sketches. As there were no recorded repercussions, one can only assume that he had been granted permission to give out some useful information to appease the press without describing any of the important dresses for state occasions. In any case, his client would have borne in mind her own innocuous press interview at the time of her marriage in 1923, after which she had been firmly requested not to grant any further such interviews, a request verging on a command, emanating from King George V.

On 5 May 1937, the King and Queen held the first Court of their reign, with the Queen resplendent in a gown of gold brocade with an Indian embroidered train of gold lamé embellished with coloured paillettes. She also wore the Order of the Garter conferred on her by the King in the New Year's Honours List, which made a fine contrast with her dress, as Norman intended. He became the expert at regarding orders and the decorations worn at state events as part of the tableau when designing a dress.

At this Second Court, the Duchess of Gloucester was an outstanding figure in a pale turquoise and silver lamé dress, also designed by Norman, as she stood with the Duke behind the King and Queen. Almost 200 debutantes made their curtsies.

Others to wear Norman's designs included the wife and daughter of the Brazilian Ambassador Regis de Oliveira, the Marchioness of Milford Haven and Lady Tatiana Mountbatten, the Marchioness of Ely and Countess of Airlie. Altogether, some fifteen Hartnell dresses were visible on those presented and ten were worn at the Second Court on 6 May. The number of Hartnell dresses worn by other women amongst the general evening company present may well have been substantially greater, as the newspapers only reported the attire of women presented to the King and Queen.

For Norman, regular visits to Buckingham Palace had begun early in the year, after the Royal Family moved out of their London house, 145 Piccadilly.

'One becomes immediately aware of a sense of well-ordered calm, kindliness and courtesy which permeates down through every member of the staff of the Royal household,' he later wrote.

The design of the Maids of Honours' dresses was discussed by both the King and Queen with Norman, after they had together examined the painting *Coronation of Queen Victoria* by Sir George Hayter and the King pointed out the headdresses of gilded wheat worn by the train-bearers. Norman used this 'as the leitmotif' for his design of a short-sleeved long dress with a high corsage. The embroideries of wheat ears were then carried out in pearl and crystal beading with gold thread.

It was on that afternoon that the King, 'cigarette in hand', invited Norman to view paintings in the picture gallery and state apartments, drawing his attention to paintings by Winterhalter who endowed his women, particularly the lovely Empress Eugénie of France and the yet more lovely Empress Elizabeth of Austria with such regal and elegant grace . . . His Majesty made it clear in his quiet way that I should attempt to capture this picturesque grace in the dresses I was to design for the Queen. Thus, it is to the King and Winterhalter that are owed the fine praises I later received for the regal renaissance of the romantic crinoline.[7]

The King was notably interested in Queen Victoria and helpful to those seeking accurate historical information. When Anna Neagle researched her subject for the film of *Sixty Glorious Years* she was given access to Windsor and the King gave her introductions to the last surviving Lady in Waiting, Lady Antrim, and Princess Helena Victoria, a granddaughter.

At this time, there were also film and stage productions depicting nineteenth-century topics and employing crinoline dresses in their designs. Norman had already utilised the crinoline shape in earlier publicised designs, such as the Oonagh Guinness wedding dress. Furthermore, as a riposte to the enormous publicity surrounding the former King Edward VIII and his marriage to Mrs Simpson, who became ever more famous for her angular chic, the idea of reintroducing the fully romantic crinoline as an adjunct to the new Queen's image was a masterstroke. For Norman, it was pure joy to be able to produce designs of full, feminine dresses on which his favourite embroideries could shine. This was better than designing for the theatre, because he was aware of the crucial importance of the British monarchy in the highly charged political atmosphere of the late 1930s.

The Queen was renowned for both her charm and tact, and added to her innate intelligence and natural dignity were her formidable diplomatic skills. These were well known before she was Queen and a single example will display just what Norman was called upon to live up to. At the Paris Colonial Exhibition of 1931 Maréchal Lyautey, who had virtually given France an empire, conducted the royal couple around, before they sat down for tea, during which the Maréchal seemed tired and withdrawn.

The Duchess had asked that André Maurois be invited to join the party. 'Monsieur le Maréchal,' she said, 'you are so powerful, you created the beautiful country of Morocco and you have made this fine exhibition, would you do something for me?'

'For you, Madame?' Lyautey said in surprise. 'But what can I do for Your Royal Highness?'

'Why this,' she said. 'The sun is in my eyes, Monsieur le Maréchal. Will you make it disappear?'

The Marshal was looking at her in stupefaction when suddenly the sun went behind a cloud.

'Thank you, Monsieur le Maréchal,' said the Duchess with perfect equanimity. 'I knew you could do anything.'

He smiled and relaxed.[8]

Of course, she had seen the cloud coming as she whispered to Maurois.

But how was Norman to enhance her personality and project that undoubted charisma? Given that he could 'gild the lily' it became apparent that he found a solution partly through the Winterhalter-inspired evening *robes de styles* and an adaption of current fashions to the taste and status of his client, who was also Empress of India. In practical terms, the new Queen was a client such as he had been dealing with for many seasons. In the workroom, the dresses were just that but given extra care and attention, as well as secrecy, after Coronation on 12 May.

The press leaks almost ceased before the state visit of King Carol of Romania occurred.

> I provided a dress of pearl grey satin, *bouffant* and trailing, embroidered with grey pearls, silver and amethyst. This dress was never worn. For, on the morning of the day of the banquet, there appeared in a newspaper a detailed description, though with no mention of the designer's name, of this important dress. His Majesty was most displeased and the dress abandoned. Although innocent of offence, I had to make deep apology and can only think that some overzealous member of my staff must have let slip, or given away, the news before it was delivered to the Palace.[9]

As intimated, a constant stream of 'leaks' and inventions filled the press. For the next four decades, there were intermittent leaks and apologies, the point being not simply client confidentiality and the real risks of tawdry ready-to-wear copies appearing, but also the fact that each dress was something personal to the wearer, and intended as a compliment to whoever might see it amongst the invited guests. A monarch is not a film star and the furore over the Queen's wardrobe could strip an occasion of its proper dignity and endanger its purpose by undue emphasis on the incidentals, dresses, hats and jewellery. Of course, the ban on publishing details of dresses until they were actually worn tended to heighten speculation, but once the event was over any press coverage could hardly affect a fait accompli. From then on, written comments or descriptions of Hartnell royal designs were submitted to the Palace for approval. In due course, Norman was awarded a Royal Warrant as Dressmaker to H.M. the Queen with its strict regulations concerning publicity, and aided by these, he became doubly careful.

The Coronation Dress created by Madame Handley-Seymour for the Queen was a distillation of late 1930s slim-fitting fashion and was simple in line with sparing use of trailing foliate embroideries from the shoulders into the skirt and train. With it the Queen wore elegant high-heeled shoes embroidered on the toes. Norman was obviously privy to that design and so his agreed design for the Maids of Honour dresses perfectly complemented the major dress. The Coronation focussed worldwide attention on London, which became a city of pageantry and jubilant celebratory events.

Madame Handley-Seymour did her own research into the emblematic history of earlier coronation dresses, so that the embroidery on the Queen's dress emulated her predecessor as Queen Consort, Queen Mary, in using the emblems of the British Isles. The rose, thistle, shamrock and leek, and in addition those of the Commonwealth of Nations united under the British Crown including the maple leaf of Canada, the wattle of Australia, fern frond of New Zealand, protea flower of South Africa, lotus flower of India and, embroidered around the border, English oak leaves and acorns. It is virtually forgotten now, and not mentioned by Norman in *Silver and Gold*, but the four canopy bearers of the Queen – the Duchesses of Norfolk, Roxburghe, Buccleuch and Rutland – all wore dresses to a design by Molyneux of heavy white and gold faille with a large rose pattern. The Duchess of Kent also wore a Molyneux dress of gold brocade with a feather design embroidered with gold and silver paillettes and cabochons diamanté. Thus, Princess Marina's designer, Anglo-Irish Molyneux, was given due acknowledgement for having his own London House and everyone was content.

Norman had absolutely no reason to complain, for in the spring of 1937 he was asked to submit designs for Queen Mary. That she should vary her patronage by trying a young designer of smart clothes was remarkable in itself, for Queen Mary's style was individual and strikingly her own updated pre-war elegance. As Norman said of himself: 'I know that it is wise, having once gained a reputation for something, to stick to it.'[10]

Norman was visited by Miss Weller, the Queen's dresser, who amazed him by choosing 'Fish Out of Water', a shimmering sheath of green and mother-of-pearl worn by his young mannequin Fritzi, said to have been a former Berlin beauty queen, and hardly likely to be worn by the ample Queen Mary. However, Miss Weller suggested how alterations could achieve the desired result and also asked for it in aquamarine blue, and an additional silver brocade dress as well as one in mauve lace. Once a halfway solution to the problem of how accurately Norman was to depict Queen Mary's face on the sketches had been overcome, the completed designs were sent off. Queen Mary was by now fully aware of the craftsmanship of Hartnell's employees; she had observed plenty of examples at Courts and those worn by her two daughters-in-law, the Duchess of York, now Queen, and the Duchess of Gloucester. In spite of this, Norman was unconvinced that he would gain the patronage of Queen Mary.

When Miss Weller telephoned him to say that the Queen approved of his sketches, but not the price of 35 gns 'my heart's hopes drained through my shoes'. In fact, the admiration of the Queen was being expressed, for she wished to pay 45 gns a dress.[11] In his unpublished version of this event, which occurred just before the Coronation, Norman stated plainly that the Queen paid 55 gns a dress, which was more in keeping with his prices at the time. Chips Channon later described Queen Mary's appearance at the Coronation as 'ablaze, regal and overpowering'; Norman saw her rather differently and as his memories have never been published, they are reproduced here. They give both an interesting insight into his new role as an approved royal designer and the then current feeling of how the overlapping of Queen Mary's nineteenth-century world with that of his own time flavoured the period. They also show his own unedited style and give a flavour of his speech and quick wit:

> The staff at Marlborough House must surely have found it necessary to bestir themselves at exceptionally early hours, for the House of Hartnell had to deposit its representatives there at 8.45 am. Madame Jeanne, my *Directrice de Salon*, the vendeuse in charge, and Madame Madelaine, the Baronne de Casteele, who had joined my staff from Worth of Paris, as fitter.
>
> The accustomed French maquillage had not, it seemed, been

correctly applied to the French ladies' faces. In other places had been completely forgotten in the haste of the hurried morning departure, which was probably just as well, for a modicum of make-up and modesty of dress is always advisable when visiting palaces and royal homes.

We were received and taken to a small reception room. At 9 am precisely my staff were ushered through a big door and into the presence of Queen Mary.

On this first occasion I did not oversee the first preliminary fittings for they were not sufficiently advanced to warrant the observance of the male eye. When the fittings were over, however, I was received by the Queen, who expressed her approval of the dresses as far as they had gone.

Returning for the second fittings in about ten days' time, however, I was permitted to view the advanced stage of the dresses I had designed.

The upholstery and curtains of Queen Mary's bedroom were of carnation-pink satin brocade. Soft pink net curtains flapped and fluttered in the morning breeze and all the windows were wide open. Pink carnations and roses of every pinkish hue leaned their heads out of silver vases. There were many photographs and on the dressing table was a little rosewood rack holding a succession of 'hare's feet', tinged with the pink of rouge, shaded from pearl pink to clear carnation.

There she stood, with diamonds a-glitter at her ears and throat, her silver hair immaculately coiffured – and all this, mind you, at 9.05 am!

There she stood in a gown of shimmering blue paillettes, the first gown I had made for her.

Then Miss Weller brought out the Garter collar and the Garter riband; the brilliant ribbon of peacock blue and the circlet of embroidery with '*honi soit qui mal y pense*' in flashing diamonds. Both decorations were affixed to the sea-blue gown, and then the great diamond star.

I retired and then returned to see the silver brocade dress, with its pattern of magnolias, marguerites and ferns strengthened by pearl and rhinestone embroideries.

Next it was the turn of the mauve lace dress to be fitted.

There it was, lovely as lilac and from each arabesque of Nottingham thread cascaded a fall of mauve crystal. Each pendant fragment of threaded crystal fringe sewn on in varying lengths – short round the corsage and graduating longer and longer upon the skirt, like fronds of wisteria twinkling with dew.

The Queen was standing at her dressing table with the window on her left and myself – at a distance – on her right. She walked up and down the room a little to ensure that the length of the skirt was right and that the train trailed gracefully behind her.

Then she asked me, the better to see herself in profile, to open a long mirror door that was part of a large rosewood wardrobe on my left.

I turned a gilt handle and inclined the door at right angles towards me. Thus she could view the dress from a different angle, while I was half confronted by the contents of the wardrobe. There, separated by five mahogany shelves were the beautiful toques that had adorned her through so many years.

Not one toque, but forty or fifty!

The Crown Jewels, the Chelsea Flower Show, branches of hydrangea, any herbaceous border, the prisms of a chandelier, the stained windows of Chartres Cathedral, or the colours of the rainbow itself. None of these in all their glory could have equalled the gamut of exquisite colour that dazzled my wide-open eyes.

They were mostly in shades of blue.

Bluebell-blue velvet was swathed and secured with a sapphire ornament; harebell-blue tulle twisted softly round a wiry foundation and exploded with a little puff of upstanding tulle on one side.

Gentian-blue and silver brocade composed another more solid one.

A mist of tiny forget-me-nots formed a floral crown and all the celestial tones of delphinium and larkspur clustered closely together on another.

Then the cool blue of aquamarine-tinted soft tulle; turquoise-blue crepe and peacock and silver tissue.

Royalest blue velvet, purple panne velvet, orchid and cyclamen chiffon and one trenchant tone of petunia velvet contrasted side by side with a gleaming affair of white dripping with crystal dewdrops and tufts of white ostrich feather.

The sweet mauve of wisteria, delicately pruned by the modiste's scissors, nestled in one corner accompanied by its lilac sister, and on a small cloud of gathered grey tulle sparkled an amethyst jewel that pinned into place a pouf of shaded grey and mauve ostrich feather.

The ladies of the royal family, when needing any feather trimming in their hats, make it a rule to choose ostrich feather or coque feather, or any plumage which does not necessitate cruelty to the bird during the extraction of the plumage.

Even when, to the onlooker, it seems as though the aigrette, the osprey or the paradise feather has been used – this is merely an optical error, for it is the feather of the heron, cleverly treated by the plumassier that is employed.

Another lovely affair, this time of palest pink and silver, was trimmed – like so many of the others – with a downy plume of, again, pink ostrich fronds. This toque attracted me especially, for it was, I recollected, this lovely hat that graced Queen Mary's noble head when, with King George V, Her Majesty drove through the streets of London in celebration of Their Majesties' silver jubilee in 1935.

One dramatic but unwelcome toque of black velvet, clamped with cabochons of funereal jet, glowered from the lowest shelf.

'You may now shut that door, Mr Hartnell,' I was commanded by that soft and deep voice, and I am sure now that my roving eyes had not gone unnoticed.

The fittings for that day were over, and as I retired towards the door the Queen spoke again.

'Mr Hartnell, I suppose you have visited the exhibition at the Royal School of Needlework to see the coronation dress on display?' (For the coronation of King George VI and Queen Elizabeth in 1937.)

I explained that in my eagerness to do so I had twice travelled up to Kensington but finding on arrival there an infinite queue of waiting spectators, I had been obliged by the short time at my disposal to return disappointed.

'What a pity,' was all Queen Mary said.

I bowed myself out.

The next day I received a card of invitation to the needlework exhibition and across the top were written the words, 'Kindly allow Mr Hartnell to view the Exhibition without delay' and the signature was 'Mary R'.

***

Not so long ago, at Christmas time I visited the tomb of Queen Mary in St George's Chapel at Windsor Castle.

Her effigy by Sir Reid Dick is tenderly and gracefully carved in cream marble.

There it lies to receive the homage of those who wish to pay it, and all the beauty of her blameless life lies there beautifully still.[10]

The style evolved by Queen Mary changed very little from the time of the coronation of King George V until her death in 1953. Only a slight simplification of line and detail together with a shorter hemline after the King's death updated her appearance. The toques were her hallmark; like her appearance, they remained unchanging at the request of her husband, who wished for the appearance of continuity and stability: he even disapproved of her attempt to wear larger brimmed hats.

Her great presence as Queen was as difficult to follow as Queen Alexandra's had been for Queen Mary. This was the same for Queen Elizabeth. As James Pope-Hennessey wrote in his biography of Queen Mary, the role of Queen Consort is largely undefined and difficult; it is up to the occupant to make something of it using her own resources. Hence the decision of King George VI to personally conduct Norman around the Royal Collections in the Palace, and for his particular emphasis on the dresses of the nineteenth century. What better for another Queen of small stature than a modern interpretation of the elaborate dresses of Queen Victoria's reign, an age unassailably associated with Britain's Imperial might, a sense of duty, morality, industrial and economic strength representing progress? All the values which King George V and Queen Mary sought to foster, having been turned topsy-turvy by the conduct of their son and heir to the throne, were to be re-established as quickly as possible.

After the separate State Visits of the Kings of Belgium and Romania, the jubilant weeks surrounding the Coronation subsided in the face of the undeniable force of the events in Germany. If Belgium and Romania felt relieved by the consideration shown to them by Britain, Britain needed to reinforce her own position abroad. The State Visit to France by their Majesties should be seen as part of the display of friendly mutual support as a riposte to the aggressive plans of Hitler and Mussolini. The Visit was arranged to occur in July 1938, giving Norman time to ponder just how the Queen should appear in Paris under the most hyper-critical eyes in the world. He had to consider every aspect of the itinerary and envisage the settings, the uniforms and colours of buildings and interiors. He also had to consider all manner of weather possibilities, but naturally knew Paris well, and the Parisian designers and press knew him.

In addressing the Queen's image during his consultations, he now stressed both her soft femininity and small features; anything but the Parisian chic of Mrs Simpson. Platform shoes later worn by the Queen were only just becoming fashionable as beach or casual party wear, so the Queen wore higher heels than usual on occasion, her own charisma framed by Norman's remarkable designs. They were even more breathtaking than intended, for with the death of her mother, the Countess of Strathmore, three weeks before the event, Court Mourning ensued, for which black clothing was usual. There were even rumours that the Visit might be cancelled, but at this critical time it went ahead, postponed for just two weeks.

Norman's research luckily revealed white to be an historically permissible precedent as a possible colour for women's clothing during royal mourning and so, as the Parisian July weather was likely to be hot, the situation was gracefully saved at the cost of remaking eleven major outfits in white or ivory. The two weeks given over to this task were made slightly easier as matching trimmings were all white and no special dyeing was needed. In those days of embryo colour printing, the new collection possibly benefitted from the enforced monochrome image of the Queen without too many of Norman's colourful embellishments.

After leaving Victoria Station in an ensemble of soft black romaine, the next appearance of the Queen was in white crêpe rosalba at the Bois-de-Boulogne Station. Norman had designed a 'Napoleon hat trimmed off the face with feather mounts of shaded black and white Paradise plumes' and carefully specified 'Black velvet handbag and gloves'. At the State Banquet on the same evening of 19 July, the Queen dazzled the company in 'a lovely Pompadour dress with crinoline skirt entirely covered with bands of silver Valenciennes lace mounted on tulle, the lace re-embroidered with paillettes and "diamonds". The *berthe* shoulder cape and skirt hem bordered with finely pleated tulle, wonderfully re-encrusted with silver paillettes. Crimson order. Jewels: rubies.'[12]

The influence of Worth, the great Anglo-French designer, the references to French history and use of French lace were a flattering renaissance of ancient diplomatic practices. As the Visit unfolded, the French and then the international press became more ecstatic as the days wore on about the King and Queen and their unassuming charm, and the Queen's clothes and her designer drew many compliments. The decorations put up in Paris were as lavish as for the coronation and the Queen more than did them justice as she shimmered in organza in the Galerie des Glaces at Versailles. Her cobweb lace wafted in across the green lawns at Bagatelle, in an osprey-trimmed hat, outshining even Garnier's Opéra in 'a white duchesse satin crinoline panniered with draperies of white satin and flounced with silver lace entirely embroidered with diamond and silver pailettes'.[12] Clusters of white camellias were strewn on the skirt, which was later depicted in a memorable portrait of the Queen by Sir Gerald Kelly.

Not all the dresses were of crinoline form; some were virtually in the fashion of the day, having slim skirts and loose jackets weighted by fur, giving an impression of greater height to the wearer.

Norman joyfully noted a newspaper headline 'Today France is a Monarchy again. We have taken the Queen to our hearts. She rules over two nations.'[13]

The State Visit certainly cemented Anglo-French relations in the face of the belligerent fascist neighbouring governments. Norman's role in enhancing the Queen's image was particularly noted by the international press, the *New York Herald Tribune* giving over its front page to a photograph of the Queen in a dazzling white Hartnell creation, the report of the visit mentioning Norman and his workroom staff.[14] The sumptuous French journal *L'Illustration* produced one of its special numbers with an especially commissioned colour portrait of the King in his coronation robes on the cover, photographs and drawings showing the extent of Norman's creative genius, whilst the text drew parallels with the grandeur of the visit of King George V and Queen Mary in 1914.[15]

Norman had obviously arranged to be on hand in Paris with a fitter and six assistants, and the visit was a glorious vindication of his small beginnings in 1923 and his desire to once again bring innovative British fashion into the heart of Paris. The Queen's dresser, Miss Catherine MacClean, was in charge of the Queen's wardrobe and perfect appearance, as well as arranging the jewels.

The effect of the Queen's unique crinoline line for the major dresses of one visit had a profound influence on designers. Later on, in a 1951 press interview, Christian Dior was not simply being polite when he stressed that 'whenever I try to think of something particularly beautiful, I think always of those lovely dresses that Mr Hartnell made for your beautiful Queen when she visited Paris'.[16]

The line was also taken up by Molyneux, who by the next year had created a ruched form of the crinoline line for Princess Marina, less bell-shaped and using an experimental 'support system' for the underpinnings. He too had been influenced by seeing Winterhalter portraits at a Rothschild party and 'his cage support of jap silk and artificial whalebones resulted in a typically Molyneux *svelte* line with no folds or exterior bands'. This was the basis for his black velvet dress, which Princess Marina refused to wear, no doubt not wishing to impinge on the Queen's own style. However, her sister, Princess Paul of Yugoslavia, wore one from the winter collection in velvet and satin.[17]

Norman also set his girls to work on creating a flexible crinoline and produced a lightweight version that 'came out at the front, but the sides and back touched the hips and it was specially boned and structured with stiff net over a special tape on the frames. Each crinoline had a petticoat made to go with it.'[18] There were ample opportunities for designers and the public to view crinolines in the costume films of every country in the world, not least in the forthcoming blockbuster *Gone with the Wind*. But in 1938 they were seen by huge Parisian crowds and then on newsreels as worn by the Queen of England and designed by Norman Hartnell.

Norman treasured two particular memories of the State Visit. He was summoned to the Quai d'Orsay to be received by the King and Queen wearing her white, gold and silver crinoline dress, with the vermilion sash of the Legion of Honour. He was then thanked for his creation of the Queen's wardrobe. His second memory was of receiving the official French accolade for his talents in being created an *Officier d'Academie,* awarded to those making major contributions to French national education and culture. However, there was no official British recognition of his skills, which is perhaps a reflection of the difference in attitude of the French and British governments to the promotion and support of a prestigious industry. Norman was gratified to receive warm congratulations from critical French dressmakers themselves.[19] The young Pierre Balmain, who then worked for Molyneux and was invited to the reception for their Majesties at Bagatelle, was befriended by Norman at this time, and was later the French designer most closely to reflect Norman's own taste for embroidered dresses.

In his book *News of England*, Beverley Nichols described Norman's designing origins and an occasion when Norman bumped into him at a party and 'asked me if I knew any nice women. "What do you mean by nice?" [I asked.] "Rich," he said. Just like that.'

Nichols was surprised by the clarity of the sketches shown to him for he 'could draw . . . had a charming sense of colour. Also, most important of all, the dullest dressmaker could have seen, to the last button, how the design was to be transformed into a reality. "They're very good," I said. "Yes," he replied, "they are."'[20]

The proof of this statement was both unassailable and highly visible. James Laver, the noted Victoria and Albert Museum curator and acknowledged expert on dress, took on loan to the museum a selection of Norman's designs for the Queen, where they still glow today with all the vibrance of his colourful artistry. They are designs for a variety of private and public appearances.

As a final comment on the success of the State Visit there can be no better source than the eminent courtier Sir Louis Greig, who met Norman at the time and later told a mutual friend, 'He is our great ambassador. He has put the Queen on the map of the world.'[21]

After a short holiday in Paris and then in Provence, Norman was back home supervising the creation of the next collection. He was also looking for a London home, as 11 Clarges Street no longer suited his enhanced status. Eventually he settled on The Tower House, 12 Park Village West, Regent's Park, part of the Nash development he admired. Negotiations began for the remainder of a lease granted in 1922, including the adjoining studio. Meanwhile the status of his salon shows was enhanced by the Australian-born mannequin and actress Margaret Vyner (known to Norman as 'Bunch of Flowers', 'Bunch' or 'Michael').[22] Widely photographed in Norman's clothes from the mid-1930s until the war, she epitomises Norman's non-royal clothing of the period, best captured in movement in the film *Sailing Along* (1938) in which she was second lead to Jessie Matthews, both of whom wear their

Hartnell dresses in as individual a manner as their imposing co-star Athene Seyler.

The other great mannequin of the period was the former Berlin beauty queen Fritzi or 'Fritzie', as she signed herself to 'Normie'. 'The best mannequin I ever had . . . tall, lissome and lovely, a symphony in tones of brown.' Norman designed his 1937 brown collection around her, which gave women the 'further opportunity to wear their cherished brown mink . . . at night'.[23] Both women married playwrights and Margaret Vyner successfully co-authored and acted in plays with her husband Hugh Williams. 'Fritzie' became Mrs Hilde Lincoln Leven and her husband was later in the Army of Occupation in Germany, but on 11 July 1951 his play *Storks Don't Talk* starring Mischa Auer opened at the Comedy, Haymarket. The vital importance of a mannequin adept at displaying garments in the salon was stressed by Norman, for they could make or break a collection.

'Dolores' was certainly the most famous of them all, named after Epstein's equally famous model used by Norman in his first show. Miss Stephenson was a South London girl, who lived with her parents until she left home and Hartnell in the 1950s to open a models' school in South Africa and to marry. For some twenty years she would arrive

> looking almost frightening without a speck of make-up, to emerge at ten o'clock in full rig like a butterfly escaped from its chrysalis. Her funny face becomes heavy with cosmetics, and the wisps of black hair have been augmented by a strapping plait and a hefty bun of jet black hair, which I bought for her at some expense. She is a dress actress . . .[24]

No one who saw her has ever forgotten the 'Latin look' nor the sideways measured gliding walk, arms extended fore and aft like a somnambulist to show off fur-cuffed or heavily embroidered well-cut sleeves, and she was apparently a great hit with royal spectators.[25]

Averil Anstruther was another favourite mannequin 'with her wide-set eyes, cream skin and coffee-coloured hair'. Norman was able to use his favourite purples and violets on her with names such as 'Violent Violet', 'Ultra Violet' and 'Purple Past'. The former proved too accurate: as an elderly woman she was attacked and robbed, never recovering from the injuries she received.[26]

Norman loaded her with specially designed modern jewellery, fox furs and heavily embroidered dresses with coats encrusted with all manner of beads, often suggested by herself, but Norman was later to complain bitterly that women did not like his favourite purples or violets.

'Page', the first Mrs Robert Nesbit, was 'as thin as a toothpick . . . moved with the agility of some fleet-footed deer. She scraped back her tinted golden hair into a huge cluster of curls and had violet eyelids powdered with silver dust'. She formed a contrast to the 'blazing blonde . . . Suzanne Platt, a natural platinum blonde. She had square shoulders and the figure of a young athlete, and to all the pastels I made for her she added her blonde brilliance.'[27]

The square-shouldered line had been gradually introduced throughout the 1930s, notably worn on screen by Joan Crawford in designs by Adrian. Other designers gave prominence to the line, which hinted at the 'leg of lamb' sleeve silhouette of the 1890s. Norman introduced the look in 1937 and also used it for the loose coats and jackets worn by the Queen. It may have been a reflection of the militarism increasingly seen in daily life, but it also gave a useful shoulder platform for the ubiquitous fashion accessory of the 1930s and 1940s, the fox fur.

When settling back to work in London, Norman enjoyed his Bruton Street room:

> Wedgwood blue velvet curtains, blue carpets, crystal chandeliers and tall tapering candles are reflected in tall mirrors behind a large business-like desk on which lie tidy sheaves of sketches, patterns and papers and an enormous pile of well-sharpened pencils. Here, too, are books of sketches that hold a thrilling record of designs.[28]

His clients displayed his latest creations in a variety of locations. At the Ritz, Alice Delysia lunched wearing Hartnell's black-and-white stripes with a shoulder-wide black hat trimmed with veiling and white pom-poms and she rubbed shoulders with others 'in Hartnell' amongst them House clients Lady Oxford and Lady Mary Lygon whilst Signorina Schiaparelli was dressed 'by Mama'.[29]

Another interviewer found that Norman was at his desk early every morning and downstairs behind the curtains every afternoon in the model room beyond the salon whilst the daily show was staged from three to four thirty. 'But you don't actually see him.' He believed that evening dresses would become more and more romantic and 'day clothes will get simpler and simpler – I think they'll be of the kind you can practically play golf in and lunch immediately afterwards at the Ritz!' Of course, events were to prove him spot on. Norman then believed that Englishwomen lacked the flair of the Frenchwomen in wearing the 'little dinner dress' or cocktail suit with which she wore a silly, jaunty little hat. The author was struck by the friendly atmosphere, the smiling secretary and Norman's extreme attention to detail.[30]

This publicity occasioned by this interview helped to counteract the extraordinary publicity given in the press to a case brought by Mrs Marguerite Seadom Marks against the company for 'ruining' her fur coat during remodelling: 'The manageress said, "The man that did that has been sent away. He made a fine collar for his wife out of your coat."'[31] As ever, journalists were happy to build a reputation and then attempt to debunk it. Norman was unfazed and highly visible with Margaret Vyner 'the loveliest Australian ever exported' in a white Hartnell at the opening of *Maritza* together with Lady Rosse and her brother Oliver Messel enjoying the London season,[32] whole contingents of women having had a break in Paris for the State Visit, including Ladies Chamberlain, Diana Cooper, Elizabeth Paget, Ursula Manners, Dashwood, Derwent, Bessborough, Mrs Winston Churchill and the Duchess of Westminster.

In August, the House was closed for a time for redecoration under Pleydell's direction to include the new Fur Grill and Hat Bar on the ground floor, whilst Norman worked on his designs for Gracie Fields in *The Fleet's Lit Up* with Adele Dixon and Frances Day (also wearing Norman's clothes at the Hippodrome). Norman refused to comment on the rumour and say who was spending £4,000 a year with him on clothes, only saying, 'She is very well known in society, not very tall with dark hair and eyes.' The new Fur Grill had the invaluable windows to the street and had formerly been occupied by an antique dealer. In the couture recessions of the 1960s, this ground floor with street windows was short-sightedly reverted to the same use and so Norman Hartnell lost the impact of a street presence.

When opened, the Hat Bar included a novel collection of fur hats and others using fur. As the figures prove, fur was then a major source of income. The Edwardian hair fashions of piled curls brought small perched hats into vogue and Norman produced these in his September show, consisting of over 200 models, which featured many embroideries based on Indian motifs on both day and evening dresses with flat jewelled belts. The fitting rooms were now lined with satin and adorned with decorative 'crystal' trees as exotic as the newly introduced platform-soled shoes, the soles varying from half to one-and-a-half inches and in contrasting colours to the shoe itself.

Norman's father Bish had meanwhile withdrawn his name from the pub called Pindar of Wakefield on the Grays Inn Road, leaving it in the hands of the Kagis, and was by now well established as a councillor in Brighton. His wife was noted at the closing day of the August races as 'one of a party of racegoers visiting Tattersall's during the afternoon from the Sussex Motor Yacht Club's private enclosure [Bish was a leading member] . . . [she] wore a Liberty fabric frock and a navy blue hat'[33] designed by Norman, as were all her striking outfits on successive days. Bish retained interests in a variety of businesses, although the wholesale alcoholic drinks industry was his prime source of income.

In October, the new Vicereine of India, Lady Linlithgow and three daughters left for India with a huge wardrobe designed mainly by Norman, who provided similar Indian-inspired embroideries as seen in his collection, as well as many ostrich-feather trimmings, popularised by the Queen on her State Visit to France in order to promote the South African ostrich farmers. As a sign of Norman's popularity, he was appointed a new director of the Royal General Theatrical Board at the same time as Lupino Lane and John Gielgud. Norman also agreed to sit on the board of the new Bath Festival, an attempt to create a 'British Salzburg'. Gielgud was again on the committee, as were C. B. Cochran, Somerset Maugham, Oliver Messel, Lord and Lady Weymouth, Lady Diana Cooper and Lord Berners. The coming war killed this large project.

The 15 October 1938 issue of *Picture Post* gave a well-written and illustrated account of 'Back-stage at a Paris Fashion Show' which attempted to dilute the mystique of 'haute couture – there is no English equivalent of the expression – but we shall be needing one soon . . . the American buyers, gilded weather-cocks of the fashion trade-winds have been pointing more and more in the direction of London'. The House of Paquin was featured and on 19 November it was the turn of 'The Queen's Dressmaker', a résumé of Norman's achievements. This included illustrations of Lovel Dene, as well as his latest designs, whilst stressing the State Visit to France and subsequent wide-spread appearance in the Paris collections of a 'Scottish vogue' for Scottish tartans 'in honour of the Scottish Queen'. By this time plans for the Royal Tour of Canada and Visit to the USA for 1939 had been announced and Norman was continually 'fashion news' as *W.W.D.* affirmed in October.

The Queen's all-white crinoline and ermine ensemble for the State Opening of Parliament and the silver-grey satin crinoline worn with the Garter and diamonds for King Carol's banquet at the Romanian Legation, Belgrave Square as part of his November State Visit set the seal on the Queen's style as executed by Norman Hartnell. (Norman wrongly dated this to early 1938 in *Silver and Gold*.) The press reported increased fabric production and sales as a result of the Queen's dresses and lace production, a flagging industry, was similarly encouraged. The silver-grey crinoline embroidered with grey pearls was over a taffeta underskirt and measured forty-five feet around the folds of the hem; it was worn by the Queen with 'the sliding walk of the Victorian woman, a trait inherited from her mother, the late Lady Strathmore' in the opinion of one journalist.[34]

Norman at thirty-seven, reportedly with 'a slight lisp in his speech. It's incongruous and amusing'[35] had only the genius of Molyneux in London to consider as a near rival. At Lachasse, Hardy Amies 'thin, energetic and shrewd . . . a very live wire indeed' was establishing his own reputation largely based on the materials he often commissioned for women's suits, the construction of which he had reinvented. Apart from the older Houses, Denis Glenny, a former medical student, was also inventive with the tailoring that also fascinated him. Peter Russell and Digby Morton were similarly best known for tailoring, whilst the Russian-born Anna de Wolkoff (a name subsequently connected with fascist wartime spying) and Polish-born Eva Lutyens, a daughter-in-law of the famous architect, specialised in unusual evening dresses. These were some of the more individual personalities at work in London, together with Victor Stiebel, who came a close second to Norman in popularity amongst younger women.

Gerald Lacoste had redesigned a huge Grosvenor Street House for Molyneux in 1938 featuring a streamlined Louis XVI interior and Lacoste's own 'Queen Anne' style for the reconstructed exterior. He also designed the imaginative Rahvis House in Upper Grosvenor Street where the sparring South African sisters, Raymonde 'Rae' and Dora Davis, nagged their staff, mannequins and themselves into fits of fury and high temperament for the next three decades. None of this especially bothered those at the House of Hartnell where a 'representative' felt able to smack down a journalist with a stinging correction:

We don't call it a crinoline. We call it a modern picture gown. For the average person thirty-five to forty yards of tulle would be necessary, about three times the amount needed for the ordinary evening dress in the same material. There is much intricate work involved in making up the dress, calling for more expert labour, more machinists, more seamstresses, more work all round.

The gowns encouraged wholesalers to export 'large quantities' to Africa, New Zealand, America and the Continent. 'At first our customers gasped: not now.'[36]

Even Pleydell had not managed to create a wholesale-based ready-to-wear option for Norman Hartnell, who remained decidedly haute couture, although this was subsequently achieved with Berkertex under wartime conditions when the time for negotiating substantial peacetime fees and royalties for Hartnell had temporarily passed. Norman was not alone in this and even tried to patent his designs, but no one can patent a fashion trend, as opposed to a direct copy. Even the line of the Duchess of Gloucester's heavy satin dress for the Romanian banquet with wide flares of tucked spreading skirt was a first and only taken up in the 1950s, not least by its inventor.

For Norman, December 1938 saw the consummation of his London success with the Beau Geste Ball at Claridge's in aid of the British Homeopathic Association. He designed all the dresses for a fabulous display of jewellery shown on such beautiful women as Mrs Charles Sweeny, Lady Bridget Poulett in crinolines and Madame Jeanne Normand Raban, directrice of the salon wearing black pearls on a grey chiffon sheath gown sewn with grey steel beads, and the floating panel over the front of the left shoulder emanating as a crossed corsage. Madame Jeanne was already becoming a legendary figure of elegance for decades in the Hartnell salon with her mauve-tinted hair, tinkling bracelets and elegant cardigans pinned with brooches.

The 1938 Anschluss with Austria and the threat of German occupation of Czechoslovakia clearly foreshadowed events in Europe. The Munich agreement and news of the Reichskristallnacht with the savage victimisation of Jewish citizens in German territories were self-evident as refugees attempted to enter Britain. The Royal Tour of Canada and the short Visit to the USA in 1939 was a last-minute reaffirmation of Britain's ties with the free trans-Atlantic English-speaking world.

Norman was asked to provide some twenty-six ensembles and a detailed itinerary was provided so that he could familiarise himself with dates, events, movements and particularly the weather to be expected. The itinerary is ominously headed 'snowshoes and dark glasses essential'. As Norman wrote, 'For each day there would be six or seven occasions demanding a change of costume and the populace of each stop on the tour would *not* expect to see the same clothes worn previously.' Photography and newsreels had changed this aspect of Royal Tours, for news pictures appeared almost simultaneously, well reproduced throughout the world.

Notes to the itinerary mentioned that the overland train had seven bathrooms, five for those in attendance with wardrobe and pressing rooms (fitted with electric irons). Two baggage cars, one kept clear for pressing, were available, empty trunks being stored on the pilot train.

Norman was particularly pleased with his ingenious solution to the problem of a suitable garment to be worn by the Queen on a stopover at four in the morning: 'a long flowing négligée dress in nectarine velvet with a narrow band of sable'. This was not the least of a glorious collection of picture dresses; one worn for the State Opening of Parliament in Ottawa of white satin and embroidered with gold pearls was later presented as a memento to Canada at the request of the government.

The Queen's now famous use of a parasol in Washington and New York, including the World's Fair, caused a fashion rush to buy equivalents, and months after her return the American press was still writing about her impact on design. Mrs Wooley Hart, Mrs Joseph Kennedy and Bea Lillie were all reported to be in less regal versions of Norman's designs. 'Queen Gaining Fashion Leadership' was a typical headline and Margaret Vyner was tipped as a future Hollywood star dressed by Hartnell.[37] The general consensus was that the Queen's 'graciousness and beauty . . . elegance and femininity' were about to produce a 'lady-like' approach to dressing. The same mixture of 'picture gowns', long straight skirts and slim-line day dresses worn with simple accessories all enhanced the wearer as they had previously in Paris.[38]

A return State Visit to London by the French president in March 1939 had given Norman the opportunity to create some 'fairy-tale' dresses for the Queen, particularly for the Covent Garden Royal Gala performance. At the Royal Gala she wore the spangled tulle and net triple-tiered crinoline, famously photographed later in the year by Cecil Beaton, as he gave his own touch to the serene charm of the Queen's personality. He remarked in his diaries that the Queen had mentioned Norman's curiosity at seeing him in the Palace – no doubt Norman hoped for the same treatment of his designs that Beaton gave to other designers.

Curiously, after the previous year's reported wide variance of dress lengths at the daytime public meetings between the President's wife Madame Lebrun and the Queen, little if any liaison now occurred and so on several daytime occasions one was in a long dress and the other incongruously in a short dress.[39] These minor details of dress took place against the background of the German invasion of Czechoslovakia, a grim reality which turned the Visit into something more symbolic of Franco–British democratic institutions. Similarly, the Tour of Canada and Visit to America involving over 7,000 miles of travel was an immense propaganda triumph, which paid dividends when aid was desperately needed during the war. The German press were instructed by Goebbels to lampoon these events, a sure sign of disquiet: Hitler was said to have termed the Queen 'the most dangerous woman in Europe' having seen newsreels of the popular acclaim accorded the royal couple. Norman modestly made no comment on his own small role in this, but his designs for the Queen were a major success in creating the right ambience for the Queen's winning personality.[40]

As a foretaste of his talent, Norman entrusted Margaret Vyner with two collections of his models, one for America and one for Canada, and sent her over the Atlantic with them for sale. She had begun her career as a model for Jean Patou and gained fame by her work in films and for Norman. She made a successful trip. Needless to say, few of the Queen's clothes bore more than a passing resemblance to these collections. With all the work involved in this Royal Tour (Norman had been awarded a Royal Warrant following the State Visit to France) it is astonishing that he should have found the energy to create a new collection to be shown in Paris in the late summer.

His new London home, The Tower House, the lease of which was signed in September 1938, also absorbed some of his time, although he used his former builders and decorators to create his own modern Regency fantasy. The house is not large but has an interesting floor-plan. Entered through the small octagonal tower forming a lobby, there is a narrow hall with an oval staircase leading to a panelled study at one end and the drawing room on the other, a curving terrace outside connecting the French windows of both. The tall windows and good proportions of the mainly north-east-facing rooms were, like Lovel Dene, most suitable for Norman's evening entertainment. They are notably better proportioned than those of Lovel Dene and were decorated by Wakers in a less flamboyant style. In fact, The Tower House was as countrified in London as Lovel Dene was Mayfair in the country. The only drawback then was the basement dining room. It was prone to dampness, because of the Regent's Park Canal extension then outside. This was drained and blocked up in the war, but the empty canal bed and towpath gave burglars easy access to The Tower House on several occasions.

The drawing room is not atypical of a fashionable room of its time; Wakers contrived to include an eclectic mixture of furniture styles from George III to Empire, and Norman ordered elaborate pelmets carried on as a frieze around the room and above trellised ivy-patterned curtains and upholstery set against cream walls. The panelled study was more successful and contained a solid upholstered sofa and easy chairs. Against the pine-panelled walls were eighteenth-century tables and chairs set on a tawny orange carpet. Display cabinets contained an array of Norman's collected militaria. The house was then near the former barracks in Albany Street and it was here that Norman first entertained his new friend from the barracks, George Mitchison, whilst his friendship with John Pleydell waned.

Upstairs, Norman's brown satin-lined dressing room was connected with a bathroom and his bedroom. It was soberly furnished, with another eclectic mixture of satin-covered furniture, a chaise longue and a low table formed from a military drum next to some remarkably elaborate William IV mahogany furniture, including an enormous cheval glass framed with undulating carved dolphins. Silver-gilt shell chairs and a French Restauration dressing table were all offset by the Wedgwood wall plaques, scalloped pelmets and curtains painted with Wedgwood motifs. One great asset of the house, which only had two other tiny bedrooms, was the large adjoining studio that had two good rooms in addition to its own bathroom and kitchen. Although Norman kept the house on for some years into the 1950s, when it was let furnished first to the painter Vasco Laszlo and then Norman's friend, the shoemaker Edward Rayne and his wife, he never regarded it as the home Lovel Dene truly became, nor did he use it for publicity purposes in the same way.

As the ties with Pleydell were loosened, so Miss Louie, Norman's oldest and most trusted employee, found herself taking letters from Norman to George Mitchison at his barracks and presents of flowers to Leslie Hore-Belisha, Minister of War, who was in Aix when Norman holidayed there in 1939. It is clear that Norman sought the help of his father in breaking the relationship with Pleydell and that the latter bitterly resented this. He had not only shared Norman's life as a close friend but had also been a major reason for the sound financial basis on which the business now rested. Perhaps The

Tower House was partly Norman's way of loosening the ties that bound them together at Lovel Dene, for whereas Pleydell had paid for the latter, it was Norman himself who bought the lease of the former. Before the final break, Norman went to Paris with his Autumn-Winter Collection.

At the end of July 1939, Schiaparelli closed her London House with the public excuse that Englishwomen wanting her clothes were going to Paris for 'sensational fashions', the others being too conservative for her style. In fact, she was aware of the international situation and looking to America, where she spent most of the war.

At the Hôtel de Crillon, Norman showed some crinolines amongst his designs, but the full impact of these was waning in Paris. Most of the collection consisted of dresses reflecting slenderising lines for the evening, with a new pencil slim silhouette applied to vivid cineraria blue, lichen green and sage-coloured outfits often trimmed with rolled fur sumptuously applied to coats and tweeds. He showed at the same time as Chanel and attracted lucrative American orders. Before leaving for Paris, Norman had been received by the Queen, who expressed her gratitude for his work and presented him with cufflinks bearing her cypher 'ER'.

It had been a momentous year for many, not least Norman, and a particularly fine one for debutantes: Lady Elizabeth Scott, Lady Sarah Spencer-Churchill and Miss Elizabeth Leveson-Gower were launched by three Duchesses with grand London balls. The Courts, Ascot and other events had been almost despairingly brilliant as the country prepared for war whilst hoping for peace. Norman had overcome arguments with his directors about the expense of his glorious Lagonda touring car and now took it with him to France, driving south before heading for Aix-les-Bains, where he took a well-deserved rest and was photographed in a dark short-sleeved shirt patterned with white stripes.

Pierre Balmain was one of those he saw there. His mother had a little boutique in the town, then still fashionable with the English.

> I was invited to a big reception given by N.H. in a large house called 'La Maison du Diable', where Queen Victoria had spent some summer holidays. The ball was magnificent but it took place under the shadow of the hurried departure on the eve of the festivities of Mr Hore-Belisha, one of the guests and the then Minister of War, who had been called back urgently to London for a Cabinet meeting.[41]

This was to Norman the equivalent of the ball on the eve of Waterloo. The next day, Germany marched into Poland and Norman sped back to London in his Lagonda FXN 603. On 4 September 1939, the day after the declaration of war on Germany, employees arrived at the staff entrance at 26 Bruton Place to find a notice on the door announcing the closure of the House for the time being.

CHAPTER TEN

Swank London dress salons carry on

That last 1939 summer of peace is encapsulated in Cecil Beaton's photographs of the Queen in a wide variety of dresses designed by Norman mainly for the State Visit to France in 1938. Those taken in the empty spaces of the gardens at Buckingham Palace have a special poignancy as the wind moves the skirts of the dresses and sunlight dapples the scene. Although Beaton's diaries are detailed in descriptions of the dresses and of the Queen and Norman's interest in the photography, he is never praised for his achievements.[1] In spite of all the praise within the three separate editions of *Vogue* whilst he was making news in Paris and New York, most leading press commentators were then all highly pro-French and gave French designers preference in their pages.

At the outbreak of war, the uncertainties for the future of Europe were soon mirrored in their own way by the fashion press anxiously looking for suitable and new wartime fashions. It was clear that excess would be 'out', as were the bustles of recent seasons and crinolines; décolletés went up and sleeves down. Norman's immediate thoughts were that 'women will want sober frocks at such a time as this. My new dinner frocks will have long sleeves and high necklines with tailored lines replacing feminine frills. There will be little embroidery and narrow skirts.' Black, navy and grey were the expected autumn colours and no shortages were expected of fabrics and furs as stocks had already been bought.[2]

For Norman, the uncertainty of being a creator of luxury goods was an acute worry. During the summer of 1939, his reputation at home had been further enhanced by the Queen, who had returned from America and, with the King, reaffirmed the solidity of the monarchy. The Queen's new slim line of her dress worn at a charity garden party in the gardens of Sigismund Goetze's house in Regent's Park occasioned quite a gasp of surprise and admiration . . . to see that with her [long] frock of pale orchid-mauve the Queen had a long ostrich feather boa; dress, shoes, pochette and gloves all of the same pretty shade – the boa reached almost to the knees and she wore a 'new style of hat' . . . [the] high turned-up brim adds height and halo to the face.[3]

By 13 September, after the outbreak of war, it was reported that 'like Queen Mary in the last war . . . the Queen is going about London in her prettiest clothes – pastel georgettes and soft silks with hats which go with them – and the psychological effect is most heartening.'[4] For Norman, it was clear that his royal clients would still require clothes, as well as some of his richer clients. It was to be some time before the restrictions of clothes rationing became severe; he had time to realise that some frivolity of detail and overall design would still remain high priorities amongst all women, not simply his clients. Meanwhile, Hartnell's foreign orders proceeded and brought in desirable foreign currency.

In July 1939, matters between John Pleydell and Norman had reached crisis point and they had terminated their relationship. George Mitchison had succeeded him in Norman's affections; the holiday in France following the fashion show at the Crillon had postponed Norman's return. Pleydell left Lovel Dene and soon joined the Navy. Norman had literally no contact with him for twenty years, and when he called at Bruton Street in the hope of seeing some of his former colleagues during the war, Bish sent him a threatening letter telling him not to call again, no doubt at Norman's request.

In February, Norman and Pleydell had entered into an agreement with the *Sunday Graphic* whereby a ghostwriter would write six articles about the Queen's dresses and £500 would be paid to them, of which Norman was to receive 75% and Pleydell 25%. Pleydell was also negotiating a deal for republication in America, Canada and South Africa.[5] The first article was sent for approval to the Queen's Press Secretary, but the Queen herself refused to allow publication and made it clear that she did not like such publicity. On top of previous leaks, this could have been no surprise but may well have been part of the irritation felt between Norman and an assertive Pleydell.

There had also been major problems over the scent production. At a board meeting on 25 July 1939, Norman had explained that John wished to show scents at the 31 July Paris dress show in the Crillon. The apprehensive Bish and Smith refused permission unless Pleydell produced a copy of the letter addressed to Les Parfums Hartnell by the chairman. It then emerged that the company had been left in a weak position in relation to the scent-distribution company set up by John Pleydell in which he and Mrs Miller Mundy had a considerable stake. The problem was to last for years.

In 1962, John Pleydell wrote to remind Norman that he still possessed 'various Hartnell shares' and further mentioned in his letter that he still had an interest in Hartnell Perfumes Ltd.

> I spent a great deal of time over this. The matter of Lovel Dene is solely a matter for your conscience. We are both aware that under duress, I conveyed the property to you and as far as I am concerned the matter is closed. Life for us both now is rather short, so please let us continue with only pleasant thoughts and no bitterness.'[6]

Norman had consulted his usual solicitor David Jacobs and had sent Jacobs' reply which prompted Pleydell's reaction: 'From the facts as I remember them, Lovel Dene was purchased for £4,000 provided by you in 1935. A sum of £4,000 was subsequently paid to you and in addition, thereafter, a further sum of £1,000 (in the 1930s) by me and the property was conveyed to me.'

Clearly, something dramatic had happened to completely change the relationship between the two men, but in the late 1960s John Pleydell magnanimously attempted to help an ailing Norman financially and letters were again signed by him to Norman with 'My love to you'.[7] But in December 1939, Norman and his ever-forceful father Bish were attending solicitors together and they agreed to pay John Pleydell's fees as Director to 8 November. A new manager, F. Ward, was then appointed.

On 2 October, Hartnell staged a fashion show featuring a 'blackout' evening dress and the mannequins carried gas masks in holders matching their outfits and shaped like opera-glass cases, so it was 'Business as Usual'. Special elaborate crinoline or picture frocks with elaborate trimmings were sold to America.

> When the Yankee Clipper arrived in New York recently . . . little did the American designers realise that would be the last shipment of creations from the Old World for perhaps a long time . . . the last clothes to arrive from Paris (by air) . . . The handsomest of the

entire collection (Molyneux, Maggy Rouff, Schiaparelli) are the frocks from Norman Hartnell.[8]

This was so typical of Norman's fate; to have his commercial dreams almost fulfilled and then dashed. For there was little prospect of capitalising on this publicity and it had been the same during the 1939 London Season when the loveliest women such as the Countess of Rosse wore his creations to the Osterley Georgian Ball held in July, but events in Europe depressed hopes of good sales. What would wartime trading conditions now bring to his luxury market?

One thing Norman was determined to avoid was conscription. His health, as already noted, had been poor from childhood. Urgent letters were sent, and medical reports gathered to prove that he was not only unfit at thirty-eight but also doing vital work in keeping open a business employing many people and upholding prestige abroad. He also stressed his role in dressing the Queen. For the time being he was successful and allocated to Mayfair fire-watching duties, as were others from Hartnell, such as Averil Anstruther. On 8 November, it was announced by most newspapers that Norman would be actively engaged as an honorary member in designing costumes for Basil Dean's NAAFI entertainment branch in France, whilst fulfilling orders from the Queen (who had readjusted orders made for a cancelled State Visit to Belgium) and 'making tweed suits and embroidered wool dresses'. For the moment, he had his wartime role affirmed, whilst other designers such as Hardy Amies and Victor Stiebel were both conscripted.

Norman's health was truly a cause for concern. Never physically strong, he had several prolonged bouts of ill health and was to suffer from nervous exhaustion as the months wore on. He began to diet at this time, with little success. His great concern for the fate of George Mitchison was also acute. Variously referred to in 1939 as 'chauffeur or assistant' on Hartnell's insurance forms, George was posted with his regiment to Suffolk in 1941. In 1939, Norman's petrol-guzzling Lagonda was superseded by an Austin 7 and a Vauxhall, both driven by George.

By December 1939, Norman had fulfilled his first NAAFI work: Gracie Fields, Binnie Hale and the Debroy Somers quintet had been costumed by Norman and were raising morale in France, which rightly felt uneasy behind its Maginot Line and was finally invaded in June 1940. Paris fashion also continued until then; if there were no debutantes in London or grand Courts, there were still American debutantes waiting for glamorous European models to be reproduced and sold in the better stores. At home, there were various fashion shows, such as one steered by Frances Day's Penny Fund to organise games for the forces. Norman's December collection reflected military styles with warmer fabrics and swathes of fur, whilst his hats were defiant displays of trimmings or upturned plain saucers. As 1940 dawned, clothes became simpler in cut and had fewer trimmings.

Many of Norman's unmarried girls were about to be called up and his workforce of over 400 had dwindled to less than half this number. In February, Madame Jeanne bravely accompanied a special collection to New York, where Arundell Clarke arranged a special show on 20 February at the British Empire Building on Fifth Avenue. The show featured glamorous evening dresses with superb embroidery, the 'Sweetheart' dress having an elaborately detailed 'lover's knot'. Gertrude Lawrence in New York loyally wore Norman Hartnell at fashionable nightclubs and the news was syndicated nationwide. Madame Jeanne stressed that the Queen was wearing simpler, sensible clothes: 'she is a busy woman with little time . . . wartime is the time of sensible clothes not of frills and no one knows this better than the Queen'. Of Englishwomen in general she said that when war began 'they never dressed for the evening. They thought nothing of wearing an old work dress to dine. Now they realise it is their duty to dress so as to liven the atmosphere.'[9] Back in Bruton Street, a foretaste of more economies was apparent as Norman began using plentiful ribbons for trimmings and his designs for 'tubular' skirts for the evening which used less fabric.

Ivor Novello commissioned Norman again to dress *Ladies Into Action* starring Isabel Jeans and Lilli Palmer, whilst Jane Welsh wore his clothes at the Shaftesbury in *Good Men Sleep at Home*. Norman's personal income was rapidly dwindling, and although he had a small income from royalties on scent sales and some press articles, the cost of maintaining Bruton Street, Lovel Dene and The Tower House was becoming a drain on his account. In April 1940, he dressed George Black's *Black Velvet* at the Hippodrome with 500 lavish costumes commissioned by Robert Nesbitt from Norman and Alec Shanks and made in Norman's workshops. Some film costumes brought in fees and so did a dress for Macy's in New York, his conception of what 'Rebecca' would have worn in the film version had *he* designed the clothes.

Concentration on winning more British aid from America resulted in wide publicity for Norman's view that the King was the best-dressed man in the world, followed by Sumner Welles, 'the essence of the perfect diplomat'.[10] The list was longer and ended with 'Geo. Mitchison, one of Hartnell's friends, who is somewhere in France with the Grenadier Guards',[11] which was a typically Normie touch.

By May, the concentration on stage work was bringing more stars to Bruton Street, such as Evelyn Laye and Cicely Courtneidge. Norman made news with his feminine trouser suit formed of a long, divided skirt with voluminous trousers. A forerunner of culottes, it was worn by Mrs Franklin Delano Roosevelt Jr in a show put on in New York with eighteen models by Norman, Digby Morton and Victor Stiebel. Again, Syndicated Press Releases, put the picture into most US newspapers.

The invasion of France resulted in what *Time* described as 'the US dress business with US$1,000,000,000 of business (wholesale) headed without a rudder toward the open sea' as for the first time the usual 300 buyers were unable to reach Paris. *Vogue*'s Francophile Edna Woolman Chase and *Harper's Bazaar*'s Carmel Snow were enthusiastic about current American fashions and, of course, the two old snobs omitted to mention Britain.[12] This soon changed as the Blitzkrieg shocked them into action: 'Buying a British suit is as much a contribution to Britain's defense as a sum of money . . . – London Collections Undimmed.'[13]

By now Norman had augmented his slender income by letting Lovel Dene to Lord Rothermere and was living in The Tower House, thus also avoiding difficult travelling conditions and being near his work. He was often seen in fashionable restaurants, such as The Dorchester, or in nightclubs, usually with an actress or well-dressed woman friend wearing Hartnell. Air raids did not diminish the number of American buyers now ready to trade with London, and Molyneux said that his sales exceeded those he would usually have made in Paris, which was also good news for fabric manufacturers. Charles Creed had moved to London and was looking for premises, and amongst those still showing and taking orders were Hartnell, Stiebel, Russell, Worth, Paquin, Digby Morton and Lachasse. The shows at Hartnell were held in spite of the destruction by bombs of a chunk of Bruton Street only eight doors away, flying glass in the glass salon being everyone's fear. The Queen was reported to be out shopping wearing a horizon-blue ensemble over a 'necklace' dress by Norman featuring silver beads around the neckline. A crowd waited to see her set off during an alert in an armoured camouflaged car, which she changed after the All Clear to one with glass on all sides so everyone could see her. She wore a Canadian maple-leaf brooch in diamonds.[14] Norman contributed to morale boosting through his activities and was to become involved in more propaganda work.

Work went on in spite of raids. Mlle Davide, for example, carried out her immaculate work. Dockets reveal the extent of alterations clients wanted, and the Queen took the publicised lead in remaking existing clothing wherever possible.

An Export Collection to South America was planned as part of a governmental charm offensive against the prevalent Axis influence in the region; Norman agreed to participate and send both models and mannequins. He was often out of London for weekends with military friends. Yevonde wrote to him, 'The bombs have made you frightfully stand-offish . . . I don't want to pursue you, if you are feeling coy but as I made an appointment once and you came not and I telephoned you twice and you are not, I am seeing what the old-fashioned Post Office can achieve.'[15] Presumably he just walked round to her in Berkeley Square. He also asked for special tuition from Pitman's in shorthand and typing, perhaps in case he was left without a secretary or so that he could be put into a desk job if called up; this came to nothing. Lovel Dene became a nuisance when let, as it caught fire, not for the last time, and Norman had to put his dogs in kennels with his friend Rex Sherren, unable to keep them in London.

Money remained a constant worry. In April, he was told by the Inland Revenue that unless he paid £485 owing in surtax, he would be sued. Yet every time he went out of London an antique shop was visited and items were sent up to London. He also kept his Lagonda in store with Follett's, managing to get enough coupons for six gallons to deliver the thirsty beast to Bish for a short time, whilst keeping the two other cars for George, who was now back in England. Yet he refused offers from prospective purchasers for Lovel Dene. In August, he went on holiday to Suffolk and The Tower House was burgled. He had to shoulder the upheavals in common with the rest of the country and carried on working as normally as possible.

He designed a new collection for New York and obtained permission to leave England, booking a large suite in the Pierre for his showing. English designs were selling well to New York manufacturers starved of Paris ideas, Molyneux's rayon dresses proving a hit, and *W.W.D.* had reported in March that Norman was making his first dress for Princess Elizabeth since her bridesmaid's dress in 1935. The South American collection with eighteen mannequins had passed through New York with the girls reportedly saying, 'We don't want orchids – give us onions!' as they paraded what became known as the 'Hush-Hush' collection. The show was a success in Rio de Janeiro and São Paulo, and textile orders came to Britain whilst Norman's large straw-hatted beach outfit of white shorts and long split overskirt fastened with copper buttons made the fashion headlines.

The June enforcement of clothes rationing caused initial confusion, with everyone wondering exactly what constituted a scarf or handkerchief for coupon allocation. Sixty-six coupons a year were available to the housewife; a scarf needed two coupons and a handkerchief one – so why not buy a large handkerchief? This debate was extended to other items. Harrods and Selfridges were besieged by women buying chintz or linen suitable for making into clothes. In August, Norman showed a small collection of forty models, his simplified designs enhanced with embroidery and with an emphasis on warm travel clothes for the endless wartime journeys often undertaken in the blackout.

Norman was not the only designer with his sights on American dollars. In October, Raemonde Rahvis was there and rumoured to be filling the position of designer at MGM, about to be vacated by the highly talented and influential designer Adrian, who was leaving to set up his own dress company. The basis of this report lay in the fact that Rahvis had dressed various Hollywood stars, including Norma Shearer, the widow of MGM's Irving Thalberg. Norman remained at home. He was occupied with Mrs Ashley Havinden, an account executive of Crawford Advertising Agency and others including Colonel Pay of Worth London, in discussions with the Board of Trade. These discussions concerned the long-overdue creation of a form of British designers trade association, which in mid-October 1941 resulted in the formation of The Incorporated Society of London Fashion Designers. IncSoc, as it came to be known, was created in order that British designers could come together as the Parisian designers had long ago done for themselves in promoting their products and protecting their skills and interests. Norman, Peter Russell, Bianca Mosca (then at Paquin), Digby Morton, Worth and Hardy Amies were amongst the first members with Mrs Havinden as the first chairwoman and the internationally known chic former *Harper's Bazaar* French editor Mrs Reginald Fellowes as President.[16]

During 1941, Norman began negotiations with Leslie Berker of Berkertex to produce ready-to-wear 'Utility' dresses for mass production. At first, he was dubious of the effect this would have on his image as a royal and couture designer. The Board of Trade was keen to promote the idea and allowed specially produced fabrics at a low price to be used for garments sold at controlled prices. The name of Hartnell was sure to sell whatever effective designs he might contribute. The Board asked him to reconsider his first refusal and he eventually asked for the Queen's own opinion. 'You have made so many charming things for me,' she counselled, 'that if you can do likewise for my countrywomen, I think it would be an excellent thing to do.'[17] He now had to study the precise requirements of the housewife and assess the effect on the price of each button, seam or dart. The rationed fabric allowance was small, but with the aid of his workroom staff he managed to produce elegant and colourful garments that sold in their hundreds of thousands at home and for export abroad. The fee, which was negotiated at length, proved 'that such a collaboration between couture and wholesale was feasible and so Norman was the first British designer of note to go into ready-to-wear'.

A letter to Bish written at this time is revealing, for it not only shows his tacit reliance on his father, but also his attitude to many other matters.

28 November 1941

Dear Bish,

I have already answered your question about calling at the back door Bruton Place on Sunday.

You will be glad to know that I have been working like a grain solidly, ever since Monday morning and three and a half days' work have brought in about £700, for George Black's new Palladium show. These are all special sketches the result of my shilling paint box and expensive brains. But as the week's takings from this building amount to roughly £1 it is a good job that the directors employ such a clever designer (underpaid though he is!).

Incidentally my cheque from the firm for last month was £13 and I hear from the Income Tax today that they expect me to pay a monthly sum of £100, so every month in the future now I shall be a minus quantity!

Another thing. About the Lagonda. I think I should tell you that I have decided not to sell it. I certainly did have an offer from Follett's but over a whisky and soda he told me that in his considered opinion it was foolish to part with it, although it was against his business interests, Medlam [solicitor] also agreed. I have had it jacked up and stored away in the private, newly built centrally heated garage of a lady friend of mine (also a client), who lives in Stanmore. I thought I had better tell you this because I do not care to go on 'play acting' in the pretence of selling it.

Also Berker has approached me again. As you know the contract in America never fructified because all exports abroad were stopped by the government. He now wishes to change that contract so as to apply to England and the mailing of utility clothing, which all the women or at least 85% will eventually be wearing in this country.

Of course, I realise the danger is of standardising the name of Hartnell with ready-made clothes, which might effect [sic] this business, but at the same time it will be a tremendous country-wide advertisement and Berker wishes to make a very high-flying story about how I am helping the women of this country to dress in correct style and by assisting in the design of these dresses which they have all got to wear, I shall thereby be doing my country great service etc., etc.!

It certainly is a big thing and although my enemies might use this as a weapon against me, at the same time they would do it themselves if they had the chance and it can be written up certainly as a big and important good work to help the cloth-starved women, through this war crisis.

The money is slightly different, instead of 7%, I can only receive 4% but as he estimates a yearly turnover of £100,000 per annum, according to his generous and Jewish estimation I receive thereby £4,000. I realise that it is much more lucky to come up with 4d.!

Berker's angle to me is that as my exclusive business will become blooming exclusive, within a few months it will practically cease to exist. I might as well take the big money in a big thing rather than try and remain exclusive and get excluded from business entirely – get it?

I have said that I will not do it unless I have the Queen's permission and approval. He has, therefore, asked Mr Hevren who is at the Board of Trade and the head of the National Woman's Clothing Department to write to me, requesting my co-operation. This letter I have received and will show it to Her Majesty when next I go to Buckingham Palace. Of course, Berker wants to start soon. I have stalled him off until I get my directors' reaction and the royal approval – also the contract legally altered to my satisfaction.

Incidentally, the cloth manufacturers are soon to be allowed to serve the dressmakers including people like Harrods, Bon Marché Brixton, Molyneux and myself with only 10% of their entire cloth output, so you see what little material there will be available for anybody to do any business at all, even taking for granted that the women have the wish to buy and the coupons and the money and if we even have the staff to carry out these frail orders.

90% of the manufacturers cloth has to be devoted to utility clothing so it seems to me in the balance I might as well risk the jealous criticism of others in preference to a regrettably small business here.

Well that is something for you to think about. All the best to Jane and the same to you.

Yours[18]

Apart from the obvious attitudes of the period, it should be realised that Norman was not a keen businessman and that the strain of dealing virtually single-handed with every aspect of his own business in the middle of the war was steadily undermining his health.

Exhausted or not, Norman was certainly in no worse a situation than anyone else; indeed, he was in a better one as he had a large degree of influence over his own future. Edna Chase received a letter from Harold Yoxall, head of British *Vogue*: 'I am trying to assist as a kind of midhusband at the birth of an Incorporated Society of British Designers, but it is a pretty hard delivery, as all the limbs, so to speak, are kicking in different directions.' He felt that the unity achieved over the South American collection might soon be dissipated. But, in a now famous quote he wrote, 'You know enough of the London fashion trade to realise what it means when I say that Hartnell, Stiebel, Digby Morton and Miss Campbell of Lachasse were fraternising like buddies round the bar.'[19]

Mrs Chase was, as ever, condescending about British fashion, as she was about anything not French and it did not help that Mr Yoxall was born unknowledgeable about fashion in general and dismissive of English fashion in particular. Having worked at Condé Nast for forty years, he could still make mistakes in his later autobiography – for example that Hardy Amies had been a 'pupil' of Molyneux.[20] Although Norman took the fashion press seriously, he did not take it too seriously, especially not the 'glossies' – ever fair-weather friends.

A contract with the International Calico Printers' Association of Manchester signed in the spring of 1941 brought Norman a useful £49 a quarter. He advised on colour and designs of printed cottons for export with the help of Princess Vera Galitzine, who produced exquisitely detailed watercolour designs. This money helped him personally, but not the business. Nor did it help that Hartnell perfume sales were earning precious dollars but were being produced under licence as increasingly cheaper and flashier products. The 'number' scents had been succeeded by the registration of 'Sculpture', 'Gravure' and 'Peinture' just before the war. Names such as 'Bright Star' were used in America as a tangle of licensees battled between themselves and over the profits abroad.

By December 1941, Lieutenant Mitchison of the Suffolk Regiment was stationed at Gibraltar Barracks, Bury St Edmunds using Norman's Vauxhall. Norman wrote to the insurers Norwich Union that as a 'gesture of personal friendship . . . I would like to make this patriotic gesture to a member of his Majesty's Forces.'[21] George had a terrible driving record with an accident in France and one on the Southend road: 'My shocking record' as he wrote to Miss Godley in Bruton Street, but his London address remained The Tower House and Norman personally insured George's 'jewellery' for £245 and his personal effects for £105. As it was understood by everyone that he had been penniless on meeting Norman, this was some advancement. By August 1942, the car was in the garage and needed the front beating out and a complete respray, but George had been posted to Lahore and a constant stream of telegrams and presents were exchanged. '24.7.42 thanks for lovely presents and letters. Have you yet received ring and disc. Always thinking of you. Fondest love from Clare and Norman (Hartnell)' is typical.

Blake had been instrumental in suggesting 'Clare' as an alibi for Norman's correspondence, as the censor would undoubtedly have wondered at the correspondence between the two males, one a famous designer and the other a recent officer. This was a time when homosexual relations were illegal and Norman could not afford any hint of scandal. He sent a newspaper clipping mentioning Lady Clare Hartnell, hitherto unknown to Norman. He was later to claim her variously as 'an aunt' or 'distant cousin', when she became Mayor of Chelsea and later on when he opened the Chelsea Antiques Fair in the 1960s and had found out more about her, 'my aunt'. What began as a typical piece of Bish and Blake fun took on the guise of a typically Normie secret joke.

Norman kept in touch with George's friends 'Doris and Fiddler', as well as 'Auntie Agnes Masters' of Erdington, Birmingham who came to see Norman in London.[22] By November 1942, George was promoted to captain. There might be Captain Molyneux, but Norman how had his own Captain, and whilst he also befriended other military types and spent weekends away, his own Captain was safely away from the front in India. Old Hartnell hands still maintained that Norman's client Lady Wavell, Vicereine of India, was at least partly responsible for George's movements.

But Norman had worries of his own, for his deferment was being questioned and he eventually had to appear and explain himself and his position. He had left fire-watching and become a member of the Home Guard. John Pleydell had also been writing to him:

8.xi.42

My dear Norm, I am sorry you were not in London the weekend before last – I wanted to see you – however I took out one or two of the 'young' ladies . . . I wrote a long letter to you in reply to your last one to me and was very disappointed that you did *not* answer it. My address is still H.M.S. *Corfu* . . . Drop me a line.

It is typical of Norman that he should leave the answering to someone else. The tougher father Bish replied:

27 October 1942

Dear John,

I am leaving this letter for you in case you should visit these premises, to point out frankly that we find your renewal of contact with the firm is very unsettling and undignified.

Your invitations to members of staff do not make for the smooth running of the business and however well meant your interest may be, I assure you that hearkening [sic] back to the past is foolish at this moment.

It is difficult enough to keep going and I hope you will understand.

At the same time, we all wish you good luck in your war work and a safe return to civilian life.

Norman and John were now to remain separated until almost the end of their lives.[23]

Apart from his threatened call-up, Norman was worried by an action brought against him by the Board of Trade for exceeding the fur quota in his business. A fine of £200 was imposed, obviously an embarrassment. His deferment was then much debated, and requested by his manager on the following grounds:

1) because he has the honour of attending to the needs of her Majesty Queen Elizabeth, also the two Princesses, the Duchess of Gloucester and several other royal personages
2) his stage and screen work on three productions and one for MGM
3) export trade work
4) designing utility clothing

The Manpower Board was not convinced. By September 1942, Norman wrote personally to A.S. Frere at the Ministry of Labour that he was 'the life and soul of this established business . . . original and sole designer . . . organiser and production manager . . . since 1923 . . . My staff numbered 400 . . . now 80 and shortly to be reduced to 37.' He then stressed his achievements and the fact that the business would collapse without him. Also, he was now a trained fire watcher and 'zealous home guard' and that at forty-one this was more useful than wrecking a reputable business which had brought credit to the prestige of Britain's overseas trade.[24] This brought about his deferment (reviewed in March 1943) and exemption. He remained in the Home Guard until he was retired on 7 March 1944.

Just what this all cost Norman Hartnell Ltd and Norman's nerves can be seen in the weekly company reports. For example, at 31 April 1941, cash in hand amounted to £2329.1s.11d. Orders received amounted to £1,112.3s.8d. (the same period in 1940: £1,437.0s.8d.). Orders in hand stood at £7,310.19s.0d.

in 1940 and at the same date in 1941 £5,624.15s.5d. revealing the impact of rationing, less spending by clients and the tougher war conditions generally. By 30 August 1941, the company had an overdraft of £1,322.5s.7d. and the value of orders received had declined by almost £8,000 over the previous twelve months. Wages had declined from £249.16s.9½d. a week, reflecting the loss of both orders and manpower. The overdraft, which began in the last week of May 1941, was to fluctuate in the 1940s and eventually become one of the major problems in keeping the House of Hartnell going throughout the rest of Norman's life. The 1940 figures were also enhanced by the American venture resulting in orders worth £300 from the shows. After this time, such orders were minimal and formed part of the usual trading figures.

Both for his own good and that of the company, it was clearly necessary for Norman to find some form of patriotic work and preferably something which netted him the profits so necessary for both the continuation of his business with its dependants, not least himself, and better cash flow.

Tamara Talbot Rice provided him with a sure solution by asking him to cooperate with her own Ministry of Information propaganda offensive aimed at the neutral Middle Eastern countries, for which Turkey was a usual source of goods and information.[25] Germany had a head start in these regions, by means of beautifully produced journals, such as *Signal*, aimed at seducing readers into admiration for German achievements and modernity and appearing in many language editions. As Austria had been a traditional Turkish trading partner and their progressive architects had been commissioned under Atatürk to produce the major public buildings in the new government capital Ankara, the influence was entrenched. Britain's tangible answer was the journal *Réalités* produced as a superior broadsheet with Anglo-Turkish features. The British Ambassador, Sir Hughe Knatchbull-Hugessen, wrote a short foreword graced by a portrait of himself as the quintessential Englishman wearing a Homburg and with a clipped moustache. Articles on the 1943 Izmir Trade Fair stressed Anglo-Turkish trade links featuring modern glass, culture and the BBC, as well as a photomontage of journals likely to interest those in the whole Middle East.

According to Tamara Talbot Rice, the Egyptians and Iranians were particularly interested in fashion – as were the Lebanese and Turks. Two pages featured elegant London Utility day clothes, including a woollen trouser suit. Norman's contribution for several issues rested in his eight-page supplements on women's fashions. The Izmir Fair had a show of models from

Hartnell, Molyneux, Creed (by now established at Fortnum & Mason), Peter Russell and Hardy Amies, Norman showing the largest number of models, photographed by Cecil Beaton. In another issue, paper and print quality were improved to include colour for specially drawn designs by Norman in a modern adaptation of 'Arabian Nights' glamour, evening shoes with colossal platform soles in yellows, turquoises and pinks all given heavy coverage.

Embroidery was increasingly sparsely applied to English couture clothes as rationing controls became stiffer. A certain amount using glass and china beading was allowed and used by Norman. For export, controls were eased in the cause of earning valuable foreign currency, so his designs naturally featured some lavish designs likely to appeal to the Middle East, where strong light and harsh monochromatic natural surroundings make more extravagant patterns and colour a necessity. Latin America was similarly targeted as an area desperately needing more British propaganda and the earlier showing of London collections had been of use in winning over women's minds to Britain through the elegant clothes given much publicity.[25,26] The largely dictatorial governments were not too ill-disposed to the Axis powers, so a charm offensive was necessary. Paris had been a natural source for the more flamboyant clothes worn by South American women.

Although Paris was still producing collections under the Vichy government, France was increasingly starved of natural resources by Germany. The collections therefore operated under strict controls every bit as stringent as Utility controls, except that leather and the best fabrics were to become not only difficult to find but eventually unobtainable. The clients for French couture were drawn from French Society, commerce, banking and war profiteers. There were also German clients and others from neutral countries who might also supply their own fabrics. Lucien Lelong, as head of the Chambre Syndicale, fought a difficult battle to prevent the French Houses still in business from being moved to the envisaged European capital of Berlin, justly famous pre-war for the quality of ready-made clothing and with an active couture industry. German women's magazines of the war were full of designs and photographs of elegant models, but like *Vogue* in London they were increasingly filled with ideas for turning old outfits into new by ingenious methods. Germany's racial legislation had forced the many innovative Jewish designers and wholesalers out of Berlin in the 1930s, with the couturier Strassner setting up in London in the late 1930s and becoming a favourite of British *Vogue*'s pages throughout the war.

If Germany was selling itself to South America, so could Britain. In February 1943, Hartnell received a letter from Madame Gyliana B. Gerson of the France Libre Department Latino-Americain, who was to write an article for the MOI entitled 'In what consists the iron effort of the big London dressmakers?' Richard Fletcher was immediately brought into action. He had already been present with Norman for a showing of the current collection in the salon to a party of important Turkish women. Norman astutely wore his Home Guard uniform for the publicity photographs and Fletcher wore his famous beard.

Madame Gerson met Norman and they discussed fashion. In her article, she pointed out to him how his crinoline designs had set a Parisian fashion after the State Visit in 1938, but there had been an unfortunate result for all those ordering crinoline wedding dresses 'using forty metres of tulle, lace or satin for the skirts, because on entering modern cars there was difficulty in squeezing in. I reminded Hartnell of this detail and he laughed and was proud of his influence on Paris fashion.'[27]

He then discussed Utility fashions with her, she stressing how beautifully finished the machine-made garments were. He pointed out the difference between these clothes and the Austerity collections made by hand as 'couture' collections. She was interested in the simple cut and beautiful colours and decorations. Hartnell stressed that the latter were not *part* of the dress but produced separately and were in essence detachable, therefore allowable under Board of Trade regulations. He also stressed how much he admired South American women with their own style and 'the eyes that light up their clothes'. He also mentioned his plan for an exhibition of six centuries of British fashion, including dolls dressed to represent each of the South American countries. He then asked Madame Gerson in his timid voice why she was writing in Spanish: she was Chilean. Fletcher chipped in to tell her that Mr Hartnell was really a poet, a poet of dress. The most immediate result was the request from Madame Gerson for the loan of a black velvet evening dress for her March 1943 recital of Victor Hugo's 'A ceux qui sont morts pour la Patrie' at a great ceremony 'pour la France Combattante en honneur du milliénne jour de la Résistance à l'oppresseur'.[28]

The long-term positive result was to be found in Hartnell's newly expanded links with all the South American republics, as Norman dropped the historical British fashions from his planned exhibition. With the support of Richard Fletcher, he set about creating the famous exhibition of Latin American costumes in miniature which was to tour the British Isles raising money for the Soldiers, Sailors and Airmen and Families Association, whilst also helping to foster better relations with the twenty countries represented. Until his death, enquiries about this show regularly came in, as it was seen in every major British city and many minor towns. It involved Norman, Fletcher and Norman's loyal secretary Ann Price in visits up and down the country, often in the worst wartime conditions, and it became a worrying drain on Norman's always frail constitution.

In May 1942, Norman wrote that he had been compelled to have a short holiday 'under doctor's instructions',[29] and in June Miss Godley wrote from Bruton Street to his old Mill Hill friend Edward Higham that 'Mr Hartnell has been ill . . . away from this House for some considerable time.'[30] But by 8 June he was returning from the Angel Hotel, Bury St Edmunds to The Tower House and was well enough to cheer up the wartime gloom by looking through Selfridges windows with the sales manager Ernest Gillard and expressing an interest in two sets of mirrored Venetian blinds, which he bought for £1 each for himself.[31] By the end of the month he felt so well that he wrote to the Classic Cinema, Baker Street asking for a rerun of Garbo's *Anna Karenina* at a time when Anglo-Russian relations were being actively supported by the government 'as this was by a famous Russian author it might have a certain appeal' he hopefully explained.'[32] It certainly appealed to himself for he was a great Garbo fan and later in the early 1960s took his assistant Ian Thomas to a Garbo festival.

The sight of Adrian's lavish dresses must have been a tonic in the grim days he was living through. When Mrs Neville Allan (his old school friend's wife) ordered a dress in November 1942, her chosen design 'Japonica' cost 20 gns and 2 gns tax and then necessitated eleven coupons, including the allowable Parma violets embroidery, whereas another client buying a black day dress 'Rapunzel' had to pay 18 gns with silk tax of £3.15s.7d. and give seven coupons. The restrictions called for great ingenuity in Norman's designs.

Royal clothes were not exempt from these measures and coupons were surrendered for new orders, although much remodelling continued, as with other clients' clothes, hats and furs. Norman even resurrected his early 1920s technique of hand-painting decorations onto the Queen's dresses.

Weekend visits to friends in the country – such as Captain Heneker in Taunton, Lady Crane at Lapworth, Colonel Oldfield in Wiltshire or the Streets in Oxfordshire – helped to restore his spirits, and he usually roamed local antique shops buying furniture, china or prints. With Lovel Dene let he concentrated on The Tower House interiors. Surprisingly stubborn he clung on to his expensive Lagonda in storage, whilst selling the more utilitarian Vauxhall damaged by George.

In October, Norman steeled himself to do the thing he most loathed in public life – make a speech at Selfridges to launch a show of Utility clothes.

> I am a bit shy of making speeches, and I assure you that it is not my usual role to appear personally at dress shows. Today is . . . unusual . . . as I appear not only on behalf of my own work, but in support of a comprehensive collection of clothes made by many well-known manufacturers . . . (Incidentally, I have never spoken through a microphone before nor did I expect such a magnificent set-up as Selfridges have provided; or such a large crowd!!)

Although he was well versed at public speaking and had used a microphone in the past, he affected this timidity and went on to explain his link with Berkertex Utility dresses and how he had to be persuaded away from 'luxury' . . .

> to change one's mind is the privilege of an artist as well as sensible men . . . I decided to devote a lot of my time, much time to the production of good dresses for good people. It was pleasing to be identified . . . with helping the National effort. England should never be without beauty for there is no evil in beauty . . . An artist can often produce his best work when times are hardest and the darkest. That is what I call facing up to the challenge.

He then compared pre-war days with utility. 'It is like bidding *au revoir* to the ebbing tide of yesterday, and then changing one's mentality to welcome the new and inflowing tide of today.'

Next, he repeated his experiences of being sacked on Christmas Eve 1923 and his interview with Gordon Selfridge when the waitress and lift-girls sketches he had made were 'put into his waste-paper basket'. On handing over to the journalist Alison Settle to compère the show, he ended in pure Normie-ese '[she will] . . . explain to you in detail the points of each model, and supply that woman-like, workman-like and common-sense angle which I in my embarrassment may have lacked'.[33]

There were two results of this speech: one was a complaint to Berker that it seemed as though his company were the only manufacturers of Utility garments and that Norman was their only designer. The Chairman of Selfridges, H.A. Holmes, wrote to Norman deprecating such a misinterpretation: '[your] services . . . apart from being of assistance to us, are doing much in the national interests to create general acceptance by the public of garments which conform to the saving the government is anxious to effect in the use of materials and labour'.[34] For not everyone wanted to wear what they were told they should wear and it was the glamour behind the name of Norman Hartnell that helped to sell the Utility idea and products. The other result came in the form of a present from Selfridges: a fitted travelling case.

In November, Norman was unwell again and due to 'undergo a slight operation which may interfere with my duties' in the Home Guard. He wrote to his commander, the Hon. R.H. Vivian Smith, explaining that he had been unable to attend parades and had to go to the new Hippodrome Show for which he had designed the costumes and regretted his absence:

> As a matter of fact, I so enjoy serving under you that I hope you
> will call on me for any extra work, such as cleaning in the armoury,
> to compensate for my regrettable absences during the past fort-
> night. In every way and at all times I hope you will call on me if I
> can do anything for you.[35]

There exists no answer.

Norman had become involved with The Soldiers, Sailors, Airmen and Families Association by November 1942 and had asked Lt Col V. Vivian, Deputy Acting Chairman to approach the Lord Chamberlain's Office to arrange a Sunday licence for afternoon concerts in aid of the charity. A reply came that the LCC were responsible as he was only concerned with stage plays 'and these I never allow on Sundays – even in wartime!'[36] The Queen was asked if she would allow Norman to state that the concerts were 'under her patronage'. Unsurprisingly, she had to refuse or she would have been inundated with similar requests, but as a patron of the society her name could be used under patrons – H.M. The King and H.M. Queen Mary.[37]

The development of the Latin American Exhibition of Costume was thus enabled by Norman's connections. His agreement with Berkertex ensured a minimum commission for him of £1,000 a year, with an option to cancel if he did not receive at least £3,000 a year in the following three years, when it was envisaged he would be designing 'ready-to-wear' garments, and a minimum of £5,000 a year in the sixth and subsequent years. Most of this was the result of lengthy correspondence between solicitors. Later post-war wrangles were hardly foreseeable in 1943, but Norman had become the first world-famous designer to earn substantial amounts on mass-produced ready-to-wear clothes and in wartime conditions; a feat largely attributable to the negotiating skill of his co-directors Fred Smith and father Bish.

As the Queen had cancelled all her orders in June 1941 for summer and autumn clothes, there had been a 'patriotic' note to *not* wearing new clothes. 'Utility' and 'Austerity' helped to reverse this trend. Through 1943, the desire for glamour reasserted itself, and in June, *County Life* reported a renewed interest in long evening dresses seen at charity balls: Molyneux and Strassner showed them and Norman showed a black marocain model, short for day and adaptable to ankle length for evening, it was low and square around the front neckline and high at the back with folds over the shoulders. He also showed a simple wedding dress in duchesse satin with a train. In the same month, he designed the costumes for a Robert Nesbitt–George Blair show *We're All in It* featuring Elisabeth Welch in a variety of numbers for the Blackpool New Opera House audience. By October *Harper's Bazaar* featured the leading London designers, and Norman was credited with designing and renovating the Queen's wardrobe as an encouragement to other women to do the same.

By this time plans for the Latin American Exhibition were finalised. The idea was Norman's and hinged on his December 1942 loan of his premises for the sale of toys and presents in aid of the Soldiers, Sailors, Airmen and Families Association (SSAFA). He called on a pre-war holiday acquaintance in Aix, Marie, Dowager Marchioness of Willingdon, and wrote: 'I am now loaning my one-time fur department to the SSAFA for an exhibition of miniature costumes, historic and national to be called the British Latin American Relations in Costume Form. It is now my hope that you will aid me.'[38] She duly became President.

But Norman had already written to Mrs Marie Louise Arnold of the Latin American section of MOI three weeks earlier, as a result of talks they had held to discuss Norman's propaganda work: 'I believe that a miniature exhibition might be the nucleus of a wide-spread plan to make better known to the British those sunny countries of the New World, whose people I have always admired for their charm, romance and dignity.' He offered free use of the ground-floor salon, staff cooperation, heat and light if the MOI wished to put on a pictorial display.

'I am sure that my clientele will welcome so unusual and instinctive an exhibition, and as I am much engrossed in 'post-war planning', I foresee a favourable development of friendship and understanding between the Latin American Republic and Great Britain through this enterprise, spontaneous and timely.'[39] Mrs Arnold replied in grateful terms but pointed out that the MOI could not organise the exhibition. In fact, the MOI were reluctant to help in practically every way put forward to them over the next year but were happy to send out press releases and photographs, especially if it meant entertaining the diplomatic corps of the countries involved.[40]

Quite what Norman's 'post-war planning' was, beyond Berkertex contracts and fabric designs, is difficult to imagine, unless it meant keeping in regular touch with George Mitchison in Lahore. With Richard Fletcher exploiting every contact he had ever made in the course of his interesting career, Norman now assembled a collection of influential vice-presidents, all of whom were flattered and impressed that Lady Willingdon had 'asked' for their patriotic services. She had already been helpful in promoting the collection sent to South America as a result of which Her Excellency Doña Isabel Moniz de Aragão, wife of the Brazilian Ambassador, had wondered if Norman might make his collection reflect Latin American costumes in his designs. She was partly responsible for the famous collection of figurines that now followed.

Apart from having all the Vice-Presidents drawn from the Ambassadors, Ministers and Chargé d'Affaires of the twenty republics, Norman included the Marchioness of Donegal, Baroness Ravensdale, Lady Juliet Duff and Lady Clare Hartnell 'my distant cousin by marriage', so distant that although they began letters 'Dear Cousin', she always signed her name Clare Hartnell to be sure that the joke remained just that. It was Blake who in 1943 jokingly sent Norman a newspaper clipping about 'Mrs F.S.Hartnell (Mayor of Chelsea) a sister of Earl Manvers.' Her 'kinship' to Norman became a shared private joke. Sir Shane Leslie, a cousin of Winston Churchill, was included on the selection committee, as was the established authority on dress from the V&A Museum, James Laver, an acquaintance of Norman and Richard Fletcher. The latter stirred up everyone he could, old friends or acquaintances from the social, such as Antonio Gandarillas and Enid, Lady Kenmare, to the more intellectual such as Osbert and Sacheverell Sitwell. When it came to touring the country, every local dignitary from duchesses to mayoresses became involved.

The work involved in organising the exhibition became so intense that in August, Fletcher, then in his seventies, was recuperating in the country from ulcers. The work was to last until after his death in 1945 and had begun with Norman suffering from recurrent sinus problems in January 1943. It could not have helped his condition that he was a very heavy smoker.

In June, he had commissioned Miss Helen Lee Barclay, an attractive American sculptress, to sculpt the arms and some of the heads of the figurines, as Norman called them. He became irritated when they were termed 'dolls'. At 4 gns a head and 30 shillings per pair of arms they were not cheap and Norman (or Hartnell) was paying for twenty of them. He was on good terms with Miss Barclay and occasionally took the pretty artist to the theatre and dinner until she went back to New York in the spring of 1944, having angrily refused an offer by Goldscheider to produce a porcelain series of figurines based on the originals.[41]

The design of the costumes was based on considerable research, usually by a retired diplomat's wife, such as Lady Effie Millington-Drake, who, having lived en poste in Argentina and Uruguay, used her contacts to produce illustrations. They and the diplomats showered Norman with photographs and material, and he also used the library of the V&A. He then produced beautiful designs and Mlle Davide cut the costumes for the figurines based on the ones worn only by women of the highest rank. He also cut out the torso shapes himself in canvas and stuffed them, putting them on bamboo supports, next painting the faces of white plaster in warm skin tones and the lips and fingernails with crimson nail varnish.[42] Bernard Tussaud helped with the special rouge for 'the high-moulded cheekbones' and the famous perruquier Madame Gustave made the tiny wigs in varying styles. Cloth of any kind was difficult to obtain for the dresses, so that even Norman's famous patchwork quilts from Lovel Dene containing scraps of all his finest designs were sacrificed to be embroidered and embellished in the workrooms. Strangely, the face of every figurine resembles that of Marlene Dietrich, a favourite pre-war client.

The beautifully printed booklet had a colour cover designed by Norman in a glorification of the patron saints of England and America. St Rose of Lima, the subject of an article in the booklet by the biographer and historian Sir

Shane Leslie, was linked to the Rose of England with national emblems intertwined with stars and draped pearls. The booklet became the subject of an enquiry into 'waste of paper' by the usual official busybodies, but this enquiry was soundly rebuffed by the scale of the exhibition's success. By December 1944, when Fletcher wrote to Sir Shane and Norman was visiting his terminally ill father in Brighton, he could report that it was taking 'Scotland by storm'.[43] The historian Philip Guedalla was induced by Fletcher, at the instigation of Lady Willingdon, to write the preface and he immediately did so, concocting a suitable and flatteringly fanciful 'history' of South America and colourful poetic style. Fletcher also tried to use his conversion to Catholicism by asking the Father Provincial of the Dominican Order to give his 'imprimatur' to Shane Leslie's 'St Rose of Lima'. This was tactfully refused.[44]

In order to help with the expense of the project, the MOI having declined, Norman asked The Calico Printers' Association (with whom he had a fabric-designing contract) to assist. They replied that they did no business there and apparently were not interested in ever doing so: 'It so happens Latin America does not come into the picture.'[45] So Norman went ahead alone but augmented the Bruton Street opening by showing the historical costumed figures made by Miss Richards of Nottingham. The British Colour Council helped in this and with the maintenance of the sixty-nine figures, as well as insuring them for £5,000.

The exhibition then opened on 6 October. The figurines were shown on plinths loaned by the Tate Gallery or made of plywood from Norman's kitchen fittings taken from his studio. There were several events connected with the opening involving foreign diplomats and the Queen paid an informal visit, followed by the Duchess of Kent and then the Duchess of Gloucester, as Norman narrated in *Silver and Gold*. Queen Mary paid a visit when the exhibition was on tour in the West Country and all expressed their pleasure and delight. In spite of three invitations, the two Princesses Elizabeth and Margaret were never able to see it even when it was in Aberdeen and they were at Balmoral.[46] In mollifying the Paper Economy Committee, it was pointed out that by the end of December 1943 the exhibition had raised £1503.9s.10d. for the charity. The Committee could hardly have been unaware of this, given the columns of newsprint nationwide as the show moved on. The photographs of the figurines and distinguished or famous visitors went out worldwide and Canadian and American stores enquired about borrowing them, as did South American countries.

Such was the interest that Lee Miller contributed a rare colour photograph to *Vogue* in January 1944 of a dull-grey satin evening dress by Norman worn against a display of the figurines, the floor covered in a rainbow riot of dyed sheepskins. By 1944, Norman was writing to Hans Juda of the influential *IT* (International Textiles):

> I enclose my original sketch as I warned you the other day.
>
> It has turned out rather heavy and dreary and not very well drawn or painted, so that if you don't want to use my original painting, then don't. And, if you want it re-sketched by your brilliant Miss Ettinger, then do so.
>
> It is a fantastic use of the Cuban print. It is supposed to be a jacket of [a] cigar-brown crêpe skirt skirt, in front only; the back of the skirt being of the print, gathered up in ample fullness.
>
> As it gets very chilly out in Cuba in the evening, the print scarf is wrapped around, economically bordered with smoke blue fox . . . a broad belt of grey pearls; a new kind of necklace in lattice work seed pearls, and some nice light evening shoes, carved out from a solid block of cork and festooned with grey seed pearls and large blister drops.
>
> I can send you another small sketch soon for a little 'austerity' model, using up the same print for home consumption.[47]

How Norman must have loved the chance to design for his imaginary Latin ladies when now usually faced with what he termed 'dreary little day dresses'.

The figurines were photographed in colour on a more exact basis than Lee Miller's shot by the Hon. M.W. Elphinstone for a special exhibition in the spring of 1944. He had also taken some royal portraits in Ektachrome intended to be shown with them to the diplomatic corps and other guests. Norman turned this idea down as Batsford were trying to gain subscribers for a luxurious book showing all the figurines and 'they would transcend my other interest, such as my little figurines, and we do seriously want to get this book launched. Another point which has arisen is the inability of Gunter's (who are catering for the tea and eatables) to provide any good drink'. At this stage of the war shortages were rife. 'Do you have any odd bottles of whisky to donate?' Norman asked. The answer came that there was no whisky but sherry or 'if you want *tea* then telephone me – I can let you have all you can want of tea' and he then suggested that six colour photographs of Princess Elizabeth taken at Windsor could be put in a glass case.[48] The show was a huge success on 23 February with all the Latin American diplomatic missions represented.

Although this exhibition was to run into 1945, Norman found time once it had been pushed out of London to visit it as a 'star' turn and to refresh the figurines' make-up and dresses. Fletcher or Mrs Ann Price, by now Norman's loyal secretary, would also take turns in following it during the packing and unpacking. In November 1943, Norman saw more of his stage costumes in George Black's *Black Vanities*, for which both Cecil Beaton and Doris Zinkeisen also designed. His 'Jewel Print' fabrics were also featured and Miss Robert Nesbitt was photographed in colour wearing an 'Arabian Nights' turquoise hat with an enormous amethyst paste decoration. The mood for such extravagance was captured by MGM's *Kismet*, a lavish musical colour production of Edward Knoblock's fantasy as popular on screen as it had been on stage during the First World War: the fantasy was a form of escapism and Norman was the perfect exponent.

Norman proved his versatility by designing the new Girl Guides uniform seen in February's British *Vogue*. The design was naturally in keeping with Utility guidelines. Norman was determined not to make it too military look- ing and evolved a jaunty large peaked cap with a high crown in front to which the smart badge was affixed. The squared shoulders are typical of the period, as is the slight tucking of the shirt-waister dress with neat buttons to the waist encircled by a trim belt. The gathered and cuffed long sleeves display Norman's virtuosity, for they unfasten at a point halfway from shoulder to the elbow. Nothing could be further from the glittering evening dresses for which he was so famous, yet with his 'Utility' and 'Austerity' designs Norman had reinvented himself as a designer for women of all classes and ages.

In 1961, he was to write:

> All my working life I have lived on women. Doesn't that sound an awful thing to say and it sounds even worse if I add that I have loved every minute of it. Of course, it's not really awful at all because as a designer, women have always been the mainstay of my business and the subject of my constant attention. I have flattered them, bullied them, and been entranced and infuriated by them, praised them and criticised them . . . To me a woman is the finest piece of design there ever was.

There is never any doubt that women adored Norman, especially his clients. With his innate empathy for their desires and his asexual interest in them, he knew how to make a woman feel and look a glamorous object of desire. If he ever thought what women other than his clients thought of *him*, he does not seem to have put his thoughts on paper. In any case, he would always be able to defuse a potentially difficult situation with an absurdity: 'One final tip . . . Please, don't have your clothes too tight. They make you look like a sausage bursting out of its skin.'[49] This sense of humour put him apart from other colleagues, who had a tendency to take themselves and their work with enormous seriousness.

Many newspaper columns were devoted to Norman's success with Utility designs, for in the spring of 1944 there was no end in sight to shortages, although the war was steadily being won by the Allies. 'Utility' applied to a wide variety of items apart from clothing and these were exempt from Purchase Tax (except pencils and wedding rings) in order to encourage their use. Even if Norman had been able to produce clothes of unparalleled luxury, he would have found difficulty in recruiting staff to make them. For the Latin American Exhibition, he had just been able to employ the necessary embroideresses on the two-and-a-half-feet-high figurines' elaborate clothes. But one of them, Mrs Clare-Clare had already been making clothes for Queen Alexandra in the previous century and had been transported to London from the West Country to augment the depleted workforce.

When Brenda Naylor joined the House as Norman's new assistant and sketch artist in the spring of 1944, she found herself producing designs and sketches for distant clients unable or unwilling to make the difficult journey to London and risk suffering renewed air raids and sleepless nights. Londoners were tired and uneasy about the V-1 and later V-2 rockets that managed to penetrate the air defences around London and which would then cause huge devastation to a small area. In this way, many areas surrounding Norman's earliest home in Streatham disappeared into dust. Brenda Naylor also remembered the danger from falling shrapnel as guns targeted planes or rockets and also vividly recalled being machine-gunned on a Lewisham street by a fleeing German plane.[50]

Writing to Miss Godley from the Victoria Hotel, Wolverhampton, Richard Fletcher sympathised:

I do pray that the raids are less agonising. Here one thinks constantly of what you in London are enduring. I am glad that Mr Hartnell is away from it for a bit as I don't think his health satisfactory. He is taking a new tonic so let us hope for an improvement.[51]

Miss Godley replied that she was also glad Norman was with him touring the Latin American Exhibition. Fletcher's very extensive network of 'friends' was expanded to include relatives of mere acquaintances with whom they often stayed. His own health declined from the winter of 1943 onwards and he had barely two more years to live. Norman was indebted to him, as with all his older counsellors, for Fletcher constantly drummed up business for him and had introduced him to Major and Mrs Cecil Wills, who were to become a source of invaluable finance to Norman Hartnell Ltd.

Norman's wartime mood and preoccupations are obvious from the following sent to his office:

Wednesday 10 o'clock

Dear Busy Bee,
    Thanks so much for forwarding on letters, jewels, etc. Arrived first post this morning.
    As I am staying on here till next Monday – mainly to go and stay with Lord and Lady Dudley on Thursday night – you might continue to send on any important mail to me here up to Friday. I particularly want the mail from India (Tower House) so either ring up Mrs Fisher daily or tell her to ring you directly any arrives. Also ask her to expect me back on Monday. Must dash off now to the show.[52]

Mrs Fisher was his sometimes temperamental housekeeper and Norman was wanting news of George and his sister Topsy out in India. The strains were mounting.

On 6 July 1944 Lady Dartmouth wrote to Ann Price: 'First of all let me say how much we think of you in the midst of the very terrifying conditions under which all Londoners live daily, and I really feel ashamed of bothering you with a letter (about the exhibition catalogue).'[53]

Norman's indefatigable secretary replied three days later:

I am delighted to hear that the exhibition has made such a wonderful start. Life in London at the moment is not particularly pleasant – as I write this letter the bombs are exploding but, of course, this dying kick of a defeated foe must not be allowed to interfere with the various jobs we have to do.'[54]

As Norman's 'girl-novelist' client of an earlier decade, Mollie Panter-Downes, made clear in her 'London War Notes' for *The New Yorker*, Londoners were 'taking it' again with increased shortages and disruptions.[55]

One of those who famously did not allow the enemy to interfere with her 'various jobs' was Norman's most distinguished client, The Queen.

> The war brought a new dress problem to the Queen. What could she wear when visiting bomb sites and the devastated areas all over the country? How could she appear before the distressed women and children whose own kingdoms, their small homes, had been shattered and lay crumbled at her feet?
>
> In black? Black does not appear in the rainbow of hope. Conscious of tradition, the Queen made a wise decision in adhering to the gentle colours, and even though they became muted into what one might call dusty pink, dusty blue and dusty lilac, she never wore green and she never wore black. She wished to convey the most comforting, encouraging and sympathetic note possible: and the world knows how well she succeeded.

Norman had noted how the visibility of a royal figure is a pre-requisite for a design:

> the figure may be seen head and shoulders only in a slow car or a carriage and the face must be framed by a hat, not obscured. One further point in this matter of nobility: it is always a part of tradition that all the hats worn by the royal ladies must turn up and away from the brow, or at least reveal the face. The hats made for Her Majesty by Mr Aage Thaarup were always innocent of veils.
>
> Many ordinary women, in times of personal distress, find comfort behind sheltering veils, but to the women of whom I write, except at a royal funeral, they are not acceptable.[56]

Cecil Beaton has also left on record his impressions of a professional visit to photograph the Royal Family in the freezing fortress of Windsor Castle in 1943, when the Queen received him in a gloom-dispelling private outfit of banana yellow with fox trimming.[57] Colour photographs by Studio Lisa around this time show the Queen and the two Princesses wearing colourful summer dresses apparently of very British Liberty fabric. A formal group with the Queen wearing a tailored day dress, is more dated but not in absurd period style for it reflects Norman's careful creation of a personal, fashionable style is not ridiculous in later years, as it is not 'of extreme fashion, which is vulgar'.[58] This accords with his successful designs for films in which future fashions were predicted or created particularly in an idiom that does not quickly become out of date in consideration of the extended release dates of films.

One of the obvious 'props' in the Queen's Hartnell wardrobe as recorded by Beaton remain her favoured shoe styles. In the posed photographs, extremely high heels are worn, no doubt accounting for Chips Channon's remark in his diaries that the Queen had developed a new walk, leaning slightly backwards.[59] Norman augmented the illusion of greater height and her presence by devising floating panels hanging from the shoulders and often weighted with fox-fur or ostrich feathers. The Queen was quite capable of carrying off such ensembles, enhanced by her slow progress and the necessary twists and turns of her progress, often through a crowd. The effect was intensely regal and the style was subsequently evolved with the lighter fabrics used in subsequent decades.

Norman was naturally aware that the Queen's clothes also had to blend with the King's uniforms during the war years. The Queen herself chose not appear in uniform and so stressed the feminine role of mothers in wartime, a welcome respite. The Duchesses of Kent and Gloucester and the Princess Royal all appeared in uniform from time to time as Patrons or heads of organisations. Norman's House did make uniforms, but the royal ladies usually went to specialised military tailoring establishments for these.

It is well known that the Royal Family shared most of the general restrictions in force, except for some official entertaining. The baths of the compartments of the Royal Train in which they travelled or took tunnelled shelter in during the worst raids were painted with a line indicating the permitted amount of hot water to be used. The Queen showed publicly exactly how limited rationed resources and the restricted decoration of clothes could be turned to elegant advantage when designed by Norman. This was an Austerity fashion that gave a stamp of approval for 'Utility' clothes produced to Norman's designs with the Queen's blessing. The two Princesses were often clad in altered versions of their mother's pre-war clothes, and later on, the evening dresses of an earlier period were also reworked for them.

Norman's progress around Britain was often followed by misplacement of his ration book, as he so often stayed in hotels. George was in Lucknow with his regiment for most of 1944 and had been promoted to captain. Norman cabled to him anxiously when letters failed to arrive: 'Thanks sympathy cable. No letter for 3 weeks. Anxious news of you. Health category – address and any other particulars. Usual greetings. Hartnell (30 words pre-paid reply).'[60]

Of all his wartime stage commissions, few gave him as much pleasure as those for Elsie and Doris Waters; part of their act included the two Cockney 'chars' – 'Gert and Daisy':

17 July 1944

Dear Girls – Elsie and Doris,
    With great artistic pleasure – while dodging the 'Doodle Bugs' – I spent my Sabbath afternoon drawing these two sketches for you.
    No, don't be cross, it is not meant to be a portrait likeness – it looks more like Miss Gertrude Lawrence with toothache, and if you do not like either of these suggestions there is no obligation whatsoever to think you have got to order them.

The letter forms an extra insight into Norman's own ideas of his artistic worth and to his design methods.

The colouring is slightly crude but I think it has great value as a stage dress. Anyhow I enjoyed doing it.
    In the *Tatler* I have seen a grand picture of you two photographed in India with the Auchinlecks and I have straightway sent it off to George Mitchison in India. I know that he will be most amused to see a picture of two ladies whom he regards as his best friends.

George was to remain friends with them in the succeeding decades.
    Norman continued:

If you should see Robert Nesbitt in Blackpool (George Black's famous revue producer) do have a chat with him on my recommendation.

Tomorrow I am going up to Edinburgh . . . should you want anything done about these dresses urgently, it is better to communicate here with Madam Jeanne.

My best wishes and love from Norman.

On 14 August 1944 the 'girls' wrote to him:

Dear Mr Hartnell,

What you must think of us we daren't think . . . we were so terribly busy . . . (we were in the throes of deep conversations with Lady Louis Mountbatten and Capt. Bellenger MP about the awful conditions in the hospitals out in Assam and also had to make reports on what we saw while visiting said hospitals). It was very kind of you to give up your leisure Sunday time to us – especially with the flying blastards overhead – and we liked the designs of the dresses very much – but thought the embroidery was too bold a pattern for our work. We like to dress on the stage as we would at home – having an eye on 'a little bit of sparkle for the gallery'. We know how difficult it is to get exactly what you would like us to have in the way of embroidery and are wondering whether a mixture of gold and silver beads in a small design would be better. The blue is such a lovely shade that it doesn't seem to want an awful lot on it. What do you think?

Also do you think we could have the neckline more décoletée [sic] or isn't it à la mode ('Ark at our French, blimey!')

We were sorry not to see you . . . and . . . shall not be in London an awful lot . . . all the Provincial dates we should have played [whilst] in India have been [re-] arranged . . . In the meantime, we are struggling on with the coral and white beads – they look none the worse for their soaking in mud and clay – 'Vive l'Hartnell'

Have you heard from George and is he well? We should love to know – Isn't the news wonderful – you'll be designing court dresses before you know where you are. Yours very sincerely,

Elsie and Doris Waters

To which Norman replied in turn:

23 August 1944

Dear Sisters,

Your jolly letter was forwarded on to me at Glasgow and then forwarded back here.

. . . I agree with you about the yellow embroidery on the blue frocks, especially as you intend to wear these for genteel dining and not so much to impress the gallery. Therefore, your idea of delicate silver and gold embroidery on the blue shall be done and maybe a little pattern will be sent to you through the post, just for fun. Also, of course, you can have the décolletage made lower to suit your own figures. [The sisters dressed alike on and off the stage very often.]

Yes, isn't the news wonderful, but this does not blind me to the necessities and hardships of the 'Forgotten Army'. Our friend George, through continuous attacks of malaria due to inadequate medical supplies, inferior doctors and blimpish organisation, has now contracted his *fourth* attack of malaria (inexcusable I think) and has lost three stone in weight. As he was as slender as a hatpin to start off with, I cannot think where the three stone has fallen away from! Isn't this wicked? Why on earth cannot they send the poor fellow home? He volunteered at the first moment of the outbreak of war, has done two and a half years in India; wounded in Burma; was in both campaigns of Arakan and Assam – so why on earth cannot he be invalided home, like the sensible Americans do with their men.

The sisters were by now probably a little cross that they had mentioned Assam in their letter, however more followed:

When a certain high politician was ranting in Parliament about beer being cheaper over there than in the NAAFI here a letter from George from India arrived saying that if you *could* get any beer, which was very rare, it costs you 3/- a bottle, and in today's *Daily Mirror* a man writes from Burma, saying you cannot get any whatsoever!

It seems to me that if you want to do George a good turn, you could ask Lady Louis Mountbatten, as a favour in return to you for all your help and information, to have George transferred to Lord Louis' Command and do an ADC job properly, instead of leaving it to a gigolo hand-kisser!

Perhaps the sisters had other ideas and Norman also realised something of his blind fervour.

I am sorry to get so heated and political but the unfairness of this world gets my goat at times – and this is one of the times.

Furthermore, instead of wasting his time and physique out in that evil country, he could be doing a much better job with me here, helping me organise this business for import and immediate post-war organisation, enlargement and export.

Could Norman really have been so blind to the meaning of what he was writing? He ends this extraordinary letter to two women he barely knew as the whimsical Normie again:

I do hope that I shall be able to come and see you perform soon and have a good talk and a laugh, and perhaps one weeny little lemonade and water!
Yours devotedly

No reply remains on file from the 'dear sisters'.

Theatrical work often took Norman's mind off the war and his many friends occupied him.

What do you mean about me – being a one never telling anybody? Is it that Mr Fletcher has sent you my GLORIOUS poems, because I remember seeing a fat letter addressed to you in his handwriting, and I gather it must have contained poetic contents? Anyhow, I am very cross with him for having worried you, and I feel embarrassed, because I do not think my efforts are very good. In any case, I do not want anyone to recite them anyway. They are not half 'sheik' enough for the Barker couple!! . . . I am so pleased you are pleased with your dresses. You always look nice whatever you wear, and with your beautiful figure etc., you could not help looking otherwise in anybody's clothes.[61]

This was not the first or last time that the pitilessly zealous Richard Fletcher embarrassed Norman; his illness seemed to make 'Old Baldie', as Norman crossly referred to him, worse.

Mrs Lew Stone remembered Norman having dinner at The Dorchester, often with a glamorous actress at his table. Jeanne Stuart was one he liked to accompany him for theatre first nights and he would often go on to a nightclub such as Ciro's, the Mayfair Club or the Caravella Club, of which he was a member. In between raids and trips, Norman would return to The Tower House, which was again burgled during the blackout in common with other neighbours as the then extension of the canal bed was now dry and concealed trespassers could suddenly appear.

Lovel Dene, let to Lord Rothermere furnished, suffered one of its periodic fires, when the curtains of his bedroom were blown over an electric fire, causing extensive damage to the soft furnishings. Norman sent a rug to cover the burnt carpet with the curious comment

I am so sorry that this regrettable fire has caused you such domestic discomfort . . . I should like to say how pleased it makes me feel to think that so charming a person as yourself is looking after my small home till the happy days when I can relieve you of that responsibility.[62]

Norman was always extra nice to the press and was also receiving a handy sum of rent from the house. The trivia of life went on even in wartime: 'Could you reserve one of those light felt sage green hats as I bought before, and which I have regrettably lost. I think my pumpkin size is about 7¼.'[63]

Working conditions were also restricted.

Things seem to be going very well except that we are all very cold. The heating ban is severe and not even an electric fire must be used anywhere outside the workrooms which are 'industrial'. However, I hope we shall survive without a batch of colds and our bills should be lightened considerably.[64]

The records show that Norman was now receiving £41.13s.4d. salary a month – leaving him with £20.16s.8d. with tax removed – apart from other sources or dividends.[65] Ivy Godley ('Confidential Clerk to Mr N. Hartnell') kept track of all his affairs and celebrated eleven years of service in May 1944 'so perhaps we can shake hands on it on your return'.[66] On 23 May Norman received notice that his military deferment was again under review:

> Dear Miss Godley
>   . . . Please explain to the authorities that I am down here (trying to regain my health?) as well as supervising the tour in the West Country of the Lat:Am Exhibition which without me fails to function. I thought we had gone through all this before – but do they think I am the same person as 'N.H.' of 26 Bruton Street – or not? Anyhow you might ring up – or go round to see Sir Adolph Abrahams – in any case it would be advisable to consult him. As you know, this tour goes on throughout August and the early autumn – and then provisionally to USA and Canada. There's an invitation in the post to go to Australia . . . I am rather disconcerted by this new development. Congratulations on your ten years of help to the House of Hartnell . . . get word to [Deferment Board] that I cannot appear on 26 May – I am *here* for health and business reasons.
>   In great haste.[67]

Deferment came: it is useless to speculate how Norman could have been of more use to Britain in any other sphere aged forty-three and in poor health. Miss Godley wrote to him on 3 July after bad air raids:

> Thank you for your good wishes for us all. We need them. Most of the people come in but some are missing. A few who are missing today have not yet been in touch with me but I am hoping all is well. I go round everywhere each day . . . Am wondering if Mrs Price is still with you. She is not yet in (noon Monday) and we cannot get a reply from her flat. . . . The raids are really bad and very nerve-racking [sic]. I am taking as much care of our staff as possible. Your father has been in . . . For myself I am blasted out – rather literally too as I must move my furniture before any repairs

can be done. Windows, ceilings, walls and doors. Rain pouring in . . . A large piece of the plane was brought down from the roof. This happened on Friday afternoon and again in the night . . . I have telephoned your father and asked permission to store my large furniture in our ground floor. I would rather have spoken to you . . . I felt sure you would give permission but I like to ask and remember my manners. I really am in a plight . . . Louie and Edie are already sleeping most nights here for company and safety (comparative) . . . one or two of the people here have been blasted . . . I am sorry your cold is still bad but if you are having weather like London I am not surprised.[68]

This was in response to an enquiry by Norman (together with detailed orders): 'I am wondering how all my wonderful staff are progressing, I am deeply sympathetic for them during these agonising raids. Both day and night. PS Mr Fletcher is always concerned about the welfare of you all.'[69]

Norman wrote again to Ivy Godley: 'I am so really distressed about your domestic disaster. Well now you are a war heroine! And I am glad that dear old "26" can harbour you for a while . . . My regards to Louie, Edie and everybody, of course.'[70]

Miss Godley was typical of so many raid victims and sent more news:

One or two more girls had blast yesterday but are clearing up and I am so glad this house has been so fortunate so far. We had another bomb in Pimlico last night and all our nice new linen windows etc. blew out and more soot, plaster and ceilings descended . . . I do not know whether I am a war heroine but I am a struggler against dirt – a constant struggler . . . I have a cook starting here . . . she thinks she is coming to see if she suits us but I know it is really if we suit her . . . I had an airgraph from Mrs Stuart and she seems very keen to be home and also most hopeful.[71]

This situation went on for some time, letters passing to and fro as the long-distance telephone service 'trunks' was very often out of action due to alerts all through August, as Mrs Price wrote on 11 August: 'We had a short noisy raid this morning but there was no alert during the night. Wonderful!'

Norman was then staying with the store owner Hugh Fraser in Scotland

and wrote in his letter of thanks: 'I heard from Beardie that you have called upon him with gifts, and he is inexpressibly grateful for your kindness and attention and I know he is sincere.'[72] Norman was hoping for some financially beneficial link between the Hartnell and Fraser businesses, and Fred Smith went up to Scotland to talk matters over. With the liberation of Paris foreseeable in June 1944 and the subsequent stirrings of a revival in French couture, Norman was thinking ahead. Fraser had housed the figurines exhibition and Norman was constantly seeking a more congenial partner than he personally found Berkertex, as the correspondence reveals.

Norman's original designs for his 1944 summer models made good use of his 'Utility' experiences with Berkertex. A classic suit in black-and-white checks with two tiny breast pockets and a crisp white yoke collar worn with a white hat and dark accessories was and is still chic. Asked his views on post-war fashion, he prophetically stated:

> Women will want a most drastic change. They will run riot in colour. I do not think that after this war they will submit to the monstrosities which were imposed on them after the last war by people who still wanted to make money out of the miseries of mankind.[73]

This contrasts with James Laver's reported view that simple styles would follow with scanty skirts, also pale Air Force blue and plain materials. Norman was still sure that Latin American influences would have a large role to play and, as it happened, they were enthusiastic about Norman's reworking of a crinoline look when he took a collection there in 1946. They were to be even more enthusiastic about Christian Dior's own romantic line now known as the New Look in 1947. Norman also thought that Princess Elizabeth and her friends would be a big fashion influence to be copied by young women.

It is extraordinary that any orders of value were fulfilled. Molyneux, Worth, Digby Morton and Hardy Amies were others showing collections, but *The Observer* of 2 April warned about delays due to lack of work hands and the fact that no merchant could supply more than twelve yards of any one fabric to a designer. In an interview in May, Norman admitted that there was now no chance of London becoming *the* fashion centre of the world, as he had once hoped. He foresaw several influential centres with a place for 'British individualism not totalitarianism'.[74]

The mood of the country lightened following the Normandy Invasion in early June, although attack came from the air in the form of the V2 rockets, and whilst Britain was suffering the V-rockets, the Allied Forces broke through Caen and were in the open countryside so that victory seemed nearer. By 9 August Bebe Daniels was 'radiant in her latest Hartnell creation' entertaining troops near St Lo, Normandy, and Brenda Naylor noticed Marlene Dietrich sitting on a table in the Bruton Street salon talking to Norman and swinging her famous legs.[75]

Norman attended a reception at Claridge's on 6 September for the marriage of Princess Irena Obolensky to Major E. Beddington-Behrens, an occasion graced by many of his clients such as Mrs Charles Sweeny, and he was not fazed by the later Paris fashions now illustrated in the papers. He considered them the result of severe oppression. 'No-one can take any notice of them . . . They are horrible.'[76]

On 31 October 1944 Miss Godley wrote to Norman, who was in York renovating the mannequins.

> I am writing because a very short while ago the French section of the BBC telephoned. They are very anxious for you to give a short talk (recorded) to France regarding utility and austerity clothes . . . next Tuesday. You alone would be talking on dress – none of your competitors . . . Miss Darnieres wanted to know if you felt sure enough of your French. I said you had a very good accent . . .

Norman had already spoken on the wireless in 1940 and was to speak again often – in 1947 he talked in French about the design of Princess Elizabeth's wedding dress for the Canadian Broadcasting Company.

Vogue in November 1944 stressed that although Paris was short of materials, dresses could be made of anything as they had no restrictions. Norman's answer was to dress Cole Porter's *Panama Hattie* with glorious clothes that were 'guaranteed to curl the palm leaves' as worn by Bebe Daniels.[77]

The end of 1944 found Norman worried by the increasing ill health of his father and Richard Fletcher. Both were failing fast. On 7 December, he wrote to a friend that he was prevented from coming to an Army Show:

> I have on hand a string of all my glamour girls . . . Miss Edith Day, Evelyn Laye, Frances Day, Ellen Terry, Marie Lloyd and Sarah Bernhardt . . . all aching to come with me on Saturday.

So you see what you licentious guards have missed! Anyhow, . . .
I can't come to the ball. You see my father is seriously ill and I have
to rush down to Brighton to hear the doctor's verdict. Nevertheless,
I shall be thinking of you on Saturday – you, Alick, and Geoffrey,
my two ugly brothers. Yours, CINDERELLA.[78]

The year ended on a more resigned note as Norman regretted being unable
to dress a Latin American doll for an *Evening News* charity auction: 'Urgent
orders are claiming the attention of my workrooms up to mid-summer – you
will understand how this added work cannot be done in time.'[79] But this at
last was the harbinger of peace and of new fashion directions.

24 NH, Aix-les-Bains August 1939
25 Princess Paul of Yugoslavia at the Hartnell collection, Paris summer 1939
26 NH designing in 1943

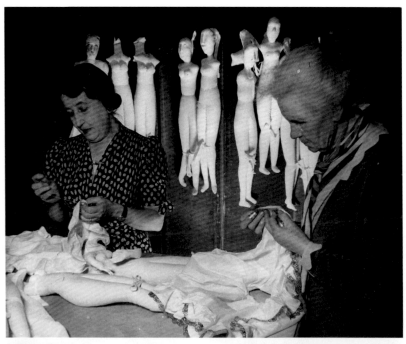

27

28

29

27 Mrs Clare-Clare, former needlewoman to Queen Alexandra and
Madame Vaegas work on costumes for the Latin-American Costume
Exhibition. Figures sculpted by American Helen Barclay 1943

28 Winnie Sexton, Hartnell milliner, fits 'Mexico' 1943

29 Madame Jeanne Habans, French Basque Directrice,
fits 'Chile' with emerald earrings 1943

32

33

30 NH, H.M. Queen Mary, Latin-American Costume
Exhibition, 26 Bruton Street, Mayfair 1943
31 NH with his collection Buenos Aires 1946
32 NH, George Mitchison, Tomas de Sancha left discuss **design** 1947
33 NH, George Mitchison, South American visit 1946

34

35

34 NH, 'Empire' furniture from South America 1947
35 London Fashion Club project l-r Charles Creed, Peter
Russell, NH, Lord Hollenden at Hartnell 1946

36 Hartnell Christmas Staff Party centre men l-r Leslie Berker, unknown, NH 1947
37 'The Fire Guard', NH depicts his male ideal 1945
38 NH, George Mitchison, Arnold Heckle UK Trade Commissioner,
Mont Gabriel Club, Piedmont Canada c. 1957

41

39 NH, Major and Mrs Cecil Wills and a daughter c. 1950
40 NH, Lovel Dene drawing room c. 1953
41 NH, 26 Bruton Street, Mayfair office c. 1950

42 The Tower House, Park Village West, Regent's Park, the study c. 1950
43 The Tower House, Park Village West, Regent's Park. NHs bedroom c. 1950
44 NH, black crinoline dress later worn by Barbara Cartland, Dolores (r) c. 1952

45

47

48

45 'The Soppy Old Queen' faces 'The Bitchy Old Queen' or
'Hardly Amiable', Amies. Unknown referee. c. 1952
46 NH, amiable IncSoc member Digby Morton, Lynn Fontanne 1952
47 NH signs 'Silver and Gold' 1955
48 Ian Thomas, Mrs Victor Riley, La Reserve, Beaulieu c. 1960

CHAPTER ELEVEN

Aren't I smart?

During the last quarter of 1944, Norman was able to see more of his old friend Blake. They spent many evenings together in London, when Blake could get away from his post as a Naval Chaplain with H.M.S. *Vernon II* in Portsmouth. They would dine and often go to the theatre, and sometimes Blake was able to stay at The Tower House, no doubt a welcome relief to Bish from his usual wartime worries. By 3 January 1945 Blake was still posted to H.M.S. *Vernon*, now at Roedean, Sussex, not too far from Brighton, where Norman's worries now extended to visiting his seriously ill father in hospital.

The older Bish had become a popular councillor nicknamed 'Farmer Hartnell'. He had shown proof of his earlier farm origins in Devon by instigating the ploughing up The Downs, a large area of scrubland, and was responsible for successfully turning it into much-needed agricultural land. On 3 January Blake received a telegram. 'Many Happy Returns of the Day, please contact me during your London visit. Urgent. Norman.' His father was now critically ill and so Norman needed friendly advice as he sped down to the coast to see his father and stepmother Jane.

By 15 January Bish was dead. It was some consolation that Phyllis was in England on a visit from India and had been in time to see her father – now they could console one another. Blake took the funeral service and Bish's ashes were scattered over his reclaimed Downs. As it was wartime, the service was mainly attended by local people, but echoes of his early London days resounded in the names of the mourners called Kagi and Sam Coulson, a reminder of the Victorian and Edwardian days that had formed the forceful Bish.

Norman now had the ailing Fletcher, steady Fred Smith and absent Topsy left as his immediate business advisers, but by 14 February he was wishing the former in hospital in Brighton 'Best Wishes for a speedy recovery. Hoping to see you soon.' Richard Fletcher had become a Roman Catholic in 1923 and was very devout, although mocked by Croft-Cooke for having a flamboyant crucifix and said by him to have only become a convert at the end

> with all the gratitude and ardour he felt for his more worldly host-esses. Loquacious and feverishly devout, he carried his rosary as ostentatiously as once he had carried a Cartier cigarette case and he died in the poverty which he had so long concealed under a magnificent ivory crucifix, the gift, he said, of a Cardinal.[1]

In fact, the impoverished Richard Fletcher died sadly at the end of February 1945 in hospital, when it was revealed to the surprise of many that he was an American and that his real name was Richard Fleckheimer. He had been of enormous help and was quite devoted to Norman, who was always loyal to him in spite of several irritations.

> My dear Nevvie,
> Do believe your old school chum when he says that he is most interested to hear of your criticisms and note the facts stated.
> It is no shock to me about Mr Fletcher, because I have already experienced his display of artistic tantrums, and know quite well that he puts a lot of people's backs up. Up to now, however, I have thought that the good points outweigh the bad, but as the poor man has collapsed three times with a serious complaint, necessitating nursing homes, etc., I am making plans for a nice commonsensical journalist woman to undertake the continuation of the Lat-Am. Tour.[2]

As late as 23 January Fletcher was writing to his friend Lady Kenmare (a good client of Norman's) about his typically ambitious plans for a colour film of Norman and his exhibition: 'Of course, the great Olivier would be the ideal commentator.' Writing from hospital he urged her to 'take the entire project under your wing and be assured that I shall cooperate when physically able'.[3]

By March, Richard Fletcher was dead and Norman once more journeyed to Brighton, organised the funeral and paid for this and the grave. Although few were untouched around him by wartime bereavements and Norman was not alone, he was already emotionally and physically exhausted – consequently his health weakened further.

In between the two deaths, he had written to Sir Adolphe Abrahams, his physician, on 13 February. 'In return for all the kindnesses you have done for me I am only too delighted with this opportunity of helping you.' This show of gratitude resulted in Hartnell making a dress for his daughter to wear at the March Queen Charlotte's Ball. 'All is well with me except that I want some thyroid pills for slimming.'

By 1 March, Norman was away from Bruton Street in a state of shock, no doubt made worse by his dieting and extra medication.

Old French friends and employees were now steadily making contact. Madeleine de Casteele wrote from Vichy to say that she was well and that 'you may believe that I have often been thinking of you and of all there . . . and miss dreadfully the activity of your firm'.[4]

Norman had little private time for mourning as the designing for collections and stage productions called upon all his energies. It proved impossible to take the figurines abroad in spite of invitations from the then prestigious department stores of Altman's in New York and T. Eaton in Canada, and two large stores including David Jones in Australia also keen to mount a big charity show there. In spite of everyone's efforts, official reaction was as depressingly unhelpful as ever, with only diplomats (both British and American) weighing in with their support. By November, plans were changed and Norman made a great effort to send the whole exhibition out to India accompanied by Topsy and another organiser. In spite of interviews with SSAFA, in which it was pointed out that £10,000 had been raised for the charity by the exhibition, the answer was unhelpful.

Part of the reason for this rather unusual exhibition of Latin American figurines being sent to India lay in Topsy's medical condition, as her husband Jug wrote to a friend:

> You will remember that in 1934–5 Topsy seized up solid with arthritis and was only cured with great difficulty . . . she has recently got stiff and ailing again . . . it was a considerable shock to Topsy and me [to discover that] she was suffering from a physical and nervous complaint.[5]

He then stressed that he had to reorganise his life entirely and could only go back to India if Topsy would go with them, accompanied by their seven-year-old son Charles. When all else failed, the former Vicereine of India, Marie,

Marchioness of Willingdon, GBE, CI, who had been the prime supporter of the exhibition all along, took up the matter with India House and asked for priority passages for two people organising the show and two tons of crates. Not surprisingly, a negative answer was received as there was a very long 'hardship' list to be cleared 'of ladies waiting for passages to join their husbands, fiancés etc'.[6]

The January edition of the popular weekly *Picture Post* examined whether London could ever become a fashion centre again. It stressed the fact that whereas most British House employees had been called up, all but 5% of the Parisian Houses' highly trained workers were still available with large stocks of satins and other stuffs available. Almost as a riposte, Norman produced some stunningly simple black satin evening dresses, illustrated in *Réalités* as well as in other journals worldwide. But Austerity still reigned and his silhouette was largely that of 1938, except for low square necklines in front. Parisian clothes luxuriated in folds, drapery and a newer, fuller outline. Luckily for Norman, his South American connections came to bear fruit in 1945 as he received suggestions from diplomat friends to show a selection of his current designs in Brazil; as he already had orders for special designs from businesses out there, the planning began at once.

With the end of the war in sight, Norman began to freshen the tired decoration of The Tower House and its contents. He bought various antique items because there was little new in the way of glass or china to be bought, but also because Lovel Dene would soon become vacant and he could profitably re-let it, so his main base remained in London. Lord Rothermere left and his agent Mrs Sibyl Tufnell relet the house to Lady Birkenhead, who even in those times was undecided until she found at least two servants. Norman waited patiently and wrote in March to his old school-days friend, the milliner Kate Day:

> It's no good – I cannot manage to come out next week. I have too much to do before Easter – I have to see many important people about important things and I really cannot spare an evening. I either have to go out on some semi-business occasion, or stay in working at the Tower House – (also it would not be fair for me to eat up your meat ration).[7]

The top bedroom in the tower of Norman's town house was used as a studio and his assistant Brenda Naylor often worked there with Norman, sketching the designs and filling in the colours under his direction, very often as he looked over her shoulder. The exterior of the house was spruced up and the interiors given the necessary cleaning – Mrs Naylor was particularly struck by the exotic leopard-skin pattern of the stair carpet. Not unnaturally, Norman itched to get back to Lovel Dene but needed the money from the rent and had to be content with nearby Regent's Park for sylvan inspiration. He inspected Lovel Dene in early May and wrote to Lady Birkenhead:

> As to the carpet in the drawing room, I did have an all-over fitted lemon-yellow carpet but I took it up before my first tenant Lady X moved in. This proved to be a most wise precaution in view of the subsequent shocking damage, vandalism and ill-mannered despoliation that I found in my small home when I returned to inspect it last weekend. This was nothing to do with Lord Rothermere, he was the perfect tenant . . . there is a large square of imitation leopard-skin, which I used to put down in front of the fireplace in the summer.

Norman then discussed ornaments and mentioned further depredations to his house.

> The blue drapery over the bed in the Wedgwood Room, which somebody for no reason at all wrenched off the wall, I am arranging to put back. The white pavilion at the bottom of the garden I see has been smashed into . . . I had to crawl in through the glass window on Saturday and I had to remove basketfuls of broken porcelain and crystal, things which I have had since my childhood and in my own home and which I naturally treasured.

He was also saddened by the state of the garden but admitted a vegetable garden was more necessary. He arranged for replantings but, 'Quite frankly, I was so disappointed with the appearance of Lovel Dene (which I now call Heartbreak House) that I think it is most kind of you to pay me what you are paying.'[8] Some days earlier he had seen a fitted dressing case with his initials on it. Two weeks later, although he felt sure his directors would disapprove, he spent £160 on it, no doubt to cheer himself up.

However, with the Liberation of France it was time for him to attempt a visit and find out what had happened to the French side of the perfume business that had so absorbed John Pleydell pre-war. Obviously, no monies had been received from Paris during the war; however, an agreement existed with the firm of Nanty Inc., New York for distribution of Hartnell scents in the USA. The last consignment from Les Parfums Hartnell was stranded in Bordeaux in October 1940. This company marketed 'La Peinture', 'La Gravure' and 'La Sculpture' so that new names had to be found for marketing anything under the Hartnell name in the USA. Mr Ward, business manager of Hartnell, participated in agreements, which led to such complications that even when a new consortium headed by Manny Silverman bought the business from Norman's heir George Mitchison in 1989, the tangle was never satisfactorily unravelled. Enormous promotions of Hartnell scent were made in America during the war, and Norman sent some dresses to be worn with them at Saks Fifth Avenue, Magnin's and Marshall Field. The names 'White Shoulders' and then 'Menace' were used and later disputed products included 'Bright Stars' and 'Gay Glitter'. The Hartnell income averaged US$35,000 a year and by March, Hartnell received 7% on sales and the promise of a new scent for Easter named 'Gay Diversion'.[9]

Another contract made by Norman during 1944 arose through his contact with Tom Gurr, then in London on behalf of Australian Newspapers Ltd, and related to a possible role for him as fashion consultant with the future formation of an Australian company – Norman Hartnell (Australia) Limited – with various provisos. In a letter to Bish in August 1944, Fred Smith thought the newspaper consultancy a good idea but not the idea of an Australian link-up: 'The population of Australia is not equal to that of Greater London.' He thought Norman should put his energies into America and South America where there would be only *one* Dressmaker to The Queen.[10]

Norman wrote Fred Smith a long letter explaining that he would only go to Australia once a year and that capital of £40,000 and a block of shares for himself were available with all expenses paid.

> As seasons alternate with the English it will be an excellent way of disposing of our elaborate peace-time collections at the end of each London season . . . it is another market for perfume. The only snag I can see is that I shall have so much to do when peace [comes] . . . that even one trip will be hard to arrange with my many activities here and connections with the Royal Family. Incidentally, Her

Majesty the Queen has given this Australian project her approval. Your contention that an American business would be preferable is like giving up the substance for the shadow, isn't it?

He then stressed that as yet no one in America had offered him a similar arrangement and ended, 'All the best to you, Mr Fred, sincerely and gratefully, Norman.'[11]

With this possibility at the back of his mind in 1945, Norman wrote to Leslie Berker in May asking for his help in getting over to Paris, and saying he liked the picture of Coral Browne in 'their' newest design. Travel and financial restrictions were difficult, but in September Norman eventually left by air to stay at the Ritz with his solicitor Isidore Kerman, who was also Secretary of the Anglo-Brazilian Society.

In May, the fur quota was lifted and fur coats were again sold at Hartnell, but there were only two remaining furriers employed on alterations. 'Austerity' ruled nationwide over everything else. By August, Norman was able to take two weeks' holiday in Branscombe and wrote to Mrs Price:

The place is somewhat ugly, but the food is good and simple – so are the X-family. The weather is dreary. Dull, black, overclouded and misty . . . . this morning I went to Church 2 miles away. And this afternoon I spent on the beach 2½ miles away! I walked there and back. It was *freezing* cold, but I feel better already. Now for a list of lovely jobs . . . arrange for yourself to have a holiday soon . . . N.H.[12]

Things got no better. 'It's blowing a gale here – rain and blizzards – terrible! I must take another holiday later. This one is not helping me at all. *Longing* to get back to The Tower House and bizz. Gratefully N.H.'[13]

By 22 May, a telegram arrived – 'Please send cigarettes immediately thanks' – crossing with a letter from Mrs Price, who thought that as he seemed to spend a lot of time walking, it was lucky it was not too hot and at least it was bracing: 'May I ask you to tell the good and simple X-family from me that they must take every care to see that you are made thoroughly comfortable.'[14]

Obviously, Mrs Price knew just how to deal with Norman, who was fretting for news from George. How he must have longed for his pre-war holidays. He was also fretting about the Paris expedition and wrote that he hated travelling and preferred to be at home: in the face of the arrival of much feted

'Le Théâtre de la Mode – Fantasy of Fashion' sponsored by the *Continental Daily Mail* he had need to look to his designs.

This was a showing of 'Lilliputian Elegance' on small figurines depicting the latest French clothes in miniature which was first shown in the Museum of Decorative Arts in Paris. It was to be displayed as a means of raising money for charities in France and the RAF Benevolent Fund of which the Duchess of Kent was Patron. It also included designs by Molyneux amongst the 181 items on display. If Norman saw this as a direct copy of his own successful exhibition, there is no recorded comment. However, after it opened on 12 September it made the arrangements of sending Norman's Latin American exhibition redundant to his South and North American clients – Paris designs were re-establishing their worldwide hold. Norman immediately pressed forward with his plans for a show of his latest designs in South America. By now, George had returned from service overseas and was settled in South London with the addition of a wife. He was appointed business manager, against Fred Smith's will, but with Topsy supporting Norman, who was now also supported by his 'sleeping' directors Cecil and Gladys Wills.

As Norman's health had been so poor, he now gladly made use of the influence of the wife of the Brazilian Ambassador to smooth his way into Rio de Janeiro. George's friend Captain Andrew Duncan was with the British Embassy there and so contacts were made and a full programme organised.

In April 1945, he had already written to Miss Arlow of *Latin American World* that:

> His Excellency Senhor S.J. Moniz de Aragão, who recently stated in the papers his desire for business between Great Britain and his vast country, did himself request me to accompany Her Excellency Dona Isabel back to Brazil to set about the inauguration of a Hartnell dressmaking establishment in Rio de Janeiro.

He then stressed that at their meeting in the Embassy he meant her to act on his behalf during a tour of the Latin American countries she was about to undertake. He was unable to finance the operation as draconian currency restrictions limited the taking of sterling out of the country. He thought those wanting his business would pay her and for his services in setting it up with a provision for him to visit once a year with 100 models a season. Part of Norman's attitude to the operation becomes clear:

I am trusting that by then I shall have the services of my working partner and business manager available. He is at present a Staff Captain in the Forces in the Far East, but I hope that the Authorities will permit this officer's release to support me in this essential business of vital National importance.[15]

It would certainly have been news to the staff of Bruton Street let alone to his directors that George was 'working partner and business manager', but Norman could be as manipulative as he chose when his own interests were at stake.

On 23 May 1946 Norman wrote boyishly excitedly to his friend Helen Street in Eire:

My dear, dear Nellie,

This is in great haste because tomorrow I fly off to Rio accompanied by George and Robert and Iris Nesbitt. Iris is to be the mannequin for 35 Hartnell glamour gowns, and Bobby is going to produce the show at the Golden Room of the Copacabana Hotel. A big dinner party is to be given for me by the British Ambassador and his wife at which I am to meet TRH Imperial Princesses of Braganza [sic]. Aren't I smart?

. . . As you know I was very ill and had to be in a nursing home for two months, undergoing terrible treatment and losing a stone and a half. This trip to South America is now a holiday according to Doctor's orders.

Norman's treatment included much exercise including log-sawing. He went often to Tempsford Hall for this radical treatment.

It was a twenty-seven-hour flight to Rio and the organiser, who had gone ahead to finalise all the arrangements, warned George and Mrs Price *not* to tell Norman how gruelling it was and that at least one day would be needed to recover. On Saturday, 25 May George and Norman arrived by 'Lancastrian' and the press photographs taken show a haggard, grim-looking Norman, but on Monday he was restored and meeting the Princesses of the former Imperial family and the wife of the Ambassador, Lady Gainer.

The climax of Norman's visit was the fashion show of his models at the Copacabana Palace with a dinner party given by the Ambassador, including

H.I.H. Prince Pedro de Orléans-Braganza, as well as Princesses Esperanza and Teresa. Norman's friends Mr and Mrs Robert Nesbitt were present, Mrs Nesbitt causing a sensation amongst the onlookers when she rose from the table and took part in the mannequin parade, as well-bred Brazilian women did not do such things and it took Lady Linlithgow a long time to calm their ruffled feathers and explain that Britain did things differently.[16] The shows were put on at the Copacabana for several days and also in the extremely lavish dress showrooms of Zulnie David, a masterpiece of 1940s Hollywood design with marble, wrought metal and satin upholstery to walls and furniture.

The lavish clothes now seem extraordinary to our eyes and were another manifestation of Norman's sure touch for knowing what the market wanted. If Zulnie David had satin-lined walls, it now housed satin-lined mannequins; none of the models did more than hint at a crinoline but relied on sleek sheath-like lines with peplum jackets and marvellous trimmings. A floor-length white fox cape was much admired when worn over a finely draped pale evening dress. Long reports from Miss Welsby to Frank Smith, Topsy (now firmly back in England) and Mrs Price followed and she replied:

> Mr Hartnell's inspiration never deserts him – each time he creates gowns and dresses, I think 'Well! These are just the best ever' – but when the next collection appears there is fresh delight and charm. I only hope the women-folk of Brazil are made to appreciate the things that will be set before them. They will hear from me if they don't!

She then laments the lack of 'nylons and the Arden, the drinks and the fruit. It must be lovely indeed . . .' Requests for lipsticks and nylons from others in the House were also posted, but Mrs Price then mentioned she was off for her first post-war visit to Paris.[17]

Topsy also showed her mettle in rounding up a press story, including the fact that Lady Linlithgow had returned to Rio just for the show, and she wrote that:

> I have concocted a sort of 'human' story for Miss Hogg, who as you know remembers my brother and I when we were 'Babes in the Wood' in Fleet Street parlance . . . anything is better than the milk and water nothingness they may get . . . *This is a story* if it's handled right.[18]

She was responding to Norman's telegram: 'Gala Show last night huge success models already selling. Have made arrangements to Harrods Buenos Aires to create new collection there for 27 June Love Norman.' Norman's ingenuity was quite remarkable for he was also on hand to design 'personal dresses' at £50 a time for the ladies of Rio 'just as he does for H.M. the Queen'.[19]

For Norman, there were two extraordinary highlights of his trip. The whole top floor of the hotel he stayed in, the Copacabana, was occupied by ex-King Carol of Romania and his beautiful mistress Elena Magda Lupescu, who wanted a dress from Norman's collection. Everything had been sold except

> the wedding dress, a wraith-like affair of flimsy silver gauze, falling softly as drapery around a Greek statue . . . some while later Lupescu, feeling her end was near, donned the bridal gown and lay on her death bed in it, surrounded by candles and lilies. As the candles burned low, King Carol pronounced her his queen. Soon afterwards Madame Lupescu stirred in her silver shroud, my wedding dress, and recovered.

In fact, Madame Lupescu had been suffering badly from anaemia, apparent in the wedding photographs of her wearing the wraith-like Norman Hartnell dress and in spite of her inimitable heavy dark lipstick.

Norman described the queenly 'corpse' as 'a most striking woman with orange hair and a flamboyant autumnal beauty'.[20]

From Montevideo came a letter from J. Henderson of Henderson & Cia emphasising the worldwide contacts available to Norman – 'You will perhaps remember that we were at Mill Hill together many years ago, and I remember you at Cambridge' – and he extended Norman an invitation to visit him and perhaps create designs for them.[21] However, Norman had virtually committed himself to an agreement for an 'in-house' salon with Harrods Buenos Aires by then, for on going to Argentina he had seen his 100 designs beautifully made up there within two weeks for a new show.

The oddity of the collection lay in Norman's usual infallible naming of the models, for with few exceptions all bore French names, including 'Chateau Margaux' 'Negresco' and inevitably, for Norman, 'Spahi' – 'Miss Mustard' and 'Scottie' seemed rather lonely amongst the forty-three models shown.

Norman later recorded that he was completely overshadowed and his collection show ruined by the arrival of Eva Perón, whom he met through her 'lady-in-waiting' Madame Alberto Dodero, formerly Betty Sudmark of London. Norman thought he had scored a coup by inviting her, but the Harrods directors were dismayed, fearing that all their great society guests would leave at the sight of her

> but by now it was too late to retract my faux pas. With the arrival of Madam Perón the entire working staff abandoned their posts of duty . . . 'Viva Evita,' they shouted . . . the great ladies had come but, as Eva Perón entered, not one of them moved, though all heads were turned towards her. With a calm and isolated assurance, she reviewed the entire collection . . . she chose . . . two black and jet embroidered dresses . . . every man and woman . . . gazed at her . . . Nobody looked at my dresses. Eva had killed the show.[22]

He was naturally exaggerating the incident. Writing to him admiringly afterwards, Dorothy Parrot said: 'Your show was positively breathtaking. Never have I seen such wonderful clothes nor such wonderful combinations of colour. Every detail of the accessories was perfect. And as for the hats!! I'm afraid your creations have left my poor pink feather very much in the shade.'

Norman however wrote: 'The whole thing was like something out of the Arabian Nights. I left Harrods wishing I could consign all my clothes to the incinerator – I was definitely not in the minority.'[23]

Norman telegrammed Topsy: 'Harrods show was best yet enormous resounding success. Congratulations pouring in. Financial offers to open house here. Very thrilled' contradicting his later, more entertaining memories. 'Now going Sao Paulo for similar show Mappin's. More work. What a holiday. Love Norman.'[24] He then created yet another new collection for Mappin, yet another leading department store, and on 12 July telegrammed Mrs Price: 'Arriving Monday afternoon alone. Please arrange large car Heathrow.'

Unsurprisingly, in April Norman had to rest in the country for over a month on doctor's orders, for he was exhausted again, but had the satisfaction of seeing the publicity he had gained. The *Tatler* of 17 July was quick to print photographs of his society women wearing his creations at the 'Copacabana Defilé'. He had also arranged with the David Company that he would be sent some 'Récamier furniture' which was sent to him from Brazil. But he was so tired that letters from Brazil went unanswered and it looks as though all the hard work was abandoned as Andrew Duncan vainly tried to make contact. Norman had been commanded to make the wardrobes of the Queen and the two Princesses for the Royal Tour of South Africa and Rhodesia to take place in early 1947. He first knew of this in early 1946, but time now rushed on.

This was a highly significant Royal Tour, the first since 1939, and it was a reassertion of Britain's ties to many countries around the globe at a time when the UK was still suffering from the effects of the war and the future status of India was under review. It came as Britain could celebrate peace, and the fact that the whole Royal Family, including the heir to the throne, was to set foot on African soil together was not simply newsworthy worldwide but also significant.

Norman was naturally planning the effects of his new designs for the Queen and the Princesses remembering that his designs of 1938 and 1939 had been seen as both fashionable and as the harbinger of new fashion styles.

A slight foretaste of the new styles to come in the Royal Tour was seen on the stand of the royal party for the Victory Day Parade of 8 June when the Queen stood beside the King. A week before, the ingenious Danish-born milliner Aage Thaarup had been summoned to Buckingham Palace and asked to design a hat for the Queen to wear on this occasion. Norman had designed the clothes and as the 'lovely pinky lilac colour' proved difficult to match, so Thaarup had the components of his hat specially dyed, finally making two hats, and took them along for a royal decision the day before. As he could not get the effect he wanted, he and his girls were up until two in the morning, whilst he tried to get the ostrich plumes to lie in a particular way. The Queen's dress had a typical bow tied over the left hip and a tight-sleeved rounded jacket, whilst Thaarup's hat was a masterpiece of side-tilted felt enhanced by crossed plumes of ostrich feathers running over the opposite side of the tilt across the Queen's hair. It stood out discreetly against the colour of the uniforms worn by the passing troops and formed a pleasing contrast to the King's naval uniform. Norman's mastery of setting and colour is clear for in the Parade marched

> the olive-green of the American helmets . . . the red tarbooshes of Egypt . . . red pompons of the French sailors; the blue tassels of the Greek 'Kilties', the khaki helmets and the silver spikes of the Trans-Jordan contingent, the wonderful Guardsmen, the blue and gold of the sailors and a host more.[25]

On one side of the King stood Queen Mary in one of her famous toques and to the other side the young Princesses Elizabeth and Margaret Rose in their own Hartnell-designed clothes, the Princess Elizabeth with a jaunty floral hat. Not surprisingly, Thaarup was commanded to design the Queen's hats for South Africa, a tour lasting ten weeks and requiring enormous preparations.

If 1946 was marked by great events in Norman's life, there were few developments in Blake's. He saw Norman when he paid a visit to his stepmother in Brighton and also went to see Richard Fletcher's grave on the anniversary of his death in February before going to Southsea to spend a Friday evening with George, who left the following morning. Norman wrote: 'All for the moment . . . I am so pleased to hear your dear Papa is mending – the same as my manners!'[26]

A letter to Blake from Mrs Price explains something of Norman's health after his return from Brazil: she said he was unwell suffering from a terrible cold and not certain if he was up to the theatre but could possibly go with him to Southsea where she had booked him a room – 'The change I think will do him a lot of good.'[27]

Major Timothy Tufnell, the son of Norman's former estate agent Sybil Tufnell and subsequently an equally adept businessman, wrote to Norman asking for help in providing costumes for a charity revue in Sunningdale. Norman wrote to him on 14th October 1946 explaining the situation:

> Dear Major Tufnell,
>   Yes, I will try and help you with your Charity Revue, but do not take what I said 'in gin' too literally because things like dresses, materials etc. are not so easily procurable as they used to be. I am sure you will understand what I mean.

In November, Blake was sent a ticket for *The Night and the Laughter* in which Norman's dresses once more aroused great acclaim.

Not unnaturally their designer was in agonies with the necessarily large orders for the forthcoming Royal Tour: seventeen dresses for the Queen, fifteen for Princess Elizabeth and ten for Princess Margaret were allowed to form a press preview. Norman cannot have been too displeased that Molyneux and Miss Ford were making some of the Princesses' clothes. Miss Avis Ford quietly ran a small court dressmakers in Albermarle Street and had made dresses for the Princesses from the time they were small girls. She also made some clothes for Queen Mary.

Press rumours were abounding that French dressmakers were likely to make the dresses for the Tour and George concocted a rambling press release, sent to the Palace for approval. A reply was sent that Her Majesty had no wish for the clothes to be photographed, but some models might be viewed by the press at a special showing if editors agreed to print nothing until 17 February 1947, the day of the Royal Family's arrival by H.M.S. *Vanguard* in Cape Town. The press view had first been practised with success for the wedding trousseau of the Duchess of Gloucester. For the views of the Queen's and then the Princesses' clothes every newspaper and journal involved signed an undertaking not to photograph or give out information before the appointed day. Captain Molyneux also showed his clothes on the same basis. Each newspaper and journal kept its word and so South Africans and Rhodesians were presented with a magnificent array of new clothes prepared for their eyes in accordance with the negotiated itinerary provided by the Palace and consultations between royal clients and designers.

As South Africa had for so long been 'fashion starved' and possessed an affluent stratum of society able to afford Norman's clothes, he had many great hopes of this tour. Australia had seen Hartnell clothes worn by the Duchess of Gloucester (as well as suits designed by Peter Russell) whilst there with her husband, who was appointed Governor General (1943–7), one reason why Norman was quite keen on the idea of a House out there.

Before H.M.S. *Vanguard* reached South Africa on 17 February 1947, the equivalent of a bombshell hit the fashion pages of the world's press. The nasty little imp on Norman's shoulder that allowed him to achieve just so much success and no more seemed to be at work again. With Christian Dior's first showing of his new collection featuring the 'Corolle' line in Paris on 12 February, the fashionable silhouette was now the very antithesis of 'Austerity' and its cousins. Carmel Snow remarked on the new look of Dior's full longer-skirted day-wear and so 'The New Look' it became.

Few designers ever achieve such worldwide status with the successful introduction of a revolutionary change in style. As we have seen, Norman had predicted romantic styles, while the acknowledged dress expert James Laver had foreseen the complete opposite.

The new Dior fashion was not immediately liked by many women faced with the huge costs involved in finding sufficient fabric for the huge skirts.

Not only was it a flamboyant assertion of conspicuous consumption in straitened times, but it also made all the preceding years' designs completely out of date overnight. There was no mere adjustment possible to hem lengths or skirt widths and vociferous protests arose amongst women, especially in North America and France, and inevitably from the British government, who seemed to revel in telling the nation what to do. Naturally, the style was the darling of fabric producers, stimulated French production of all dress-related components, and sold journals and newspapers worldwide, reasserting French fashion dominance.

Norman had famously reintroduced his own longer line in Paris some seventeen years earlier, just as he brought the 'crinoline' styles to Paris with the Queen in 1938, but he now worried that his own days of innovation were over. He was almost forty-six years old, firmly middle-aged at that time, and had been in business for nearly a quarter of a century. Of all the London designers showing their collections before Dior's 12 February show, only the clothes of Angèle Delanghe showed a silhouette that moved in the same direction as that espoused by Dior, and that only in her evening clothes. Whilst Dior was filling his order books, British designers were still compelled to make the officially sanctioned 'Export Collections', although as in Paris, London designers circumvented clothes rationing restrictions and adapted the New Look to their own House versions.

Norman's dresses for the Royal Tour of 1947 remained, completely in tune with fashions worn worldwide and by elegant women in South Africa and Rhodesia, who would scarcely order new clothes overnight. The royal clothes were also expressive of the individual styles and tastes of their wearers. The wide evening dresses of the Queen and the Princesses were based on his evolving concept of a glamorous *robe de style*, and they had the essential Hartnell elements of Dior's new line. Never had the Queen appeared so magnificent, from the arrival of H.M.S. *Vanguard* when she descended the gangplank wearing an 'afternoon reception dress in mist blue. Cross-over bodice, two long panels cascading down the back of the dress bordered with South African ostrich feathers to tone. Ostrich feather hat', as the official Hartnell description ran. Another bow to South Africa was formed by an apricot-pink ensemble made of native wool. For a ball in Durban the Queen wore a 'reception crinoline gown of oyster satin – Elizabethan quilted skirt in criss-cross design, re-embroidered with pearls and copper'.[28] The copper was another neat reference to local products, something Norman evolved as tribute to host countries through his many future designs for State Visits and Royal Tours.

Aage Thaarup, who was commanded to make first the hats for the Queen and Princess Elizabeth was also asked to make those of Princess Margaret as she observed the fittings. His problems were also Norman's: mosquitoes and tropical insects had to be considered, hot weather, strong sun and windy reviewing stands – 'it was quite a job'.[29]

The Queen's imposing appearance was enhanced by the heightening hats and fashionable platform-soled sandals she wore; all these items had to be packed for transport aboard the colossal White Train in which the royal party travelled for two months and which was a third of a mile long. All trunks were labelled, as was the jewellery to be worn with each outfit, a system already devised in 1939 for the tour of North America.

Thaarup wrote 'The young Princesses put up a sunshade or a tentative hand to shade the eyes. The Queen never loses her lovely smile. And on the King's brow barely a shadow of the illness which he must already have been feeling.'[29]

The King was also concerned that Britain was suffering one of the hardest winters ever experienced and had thought of going back to share the misery, rather than being seen in sunny climes. He was dissuaded by the Prime Minister, Clement Attlee, who considered that this particularly significant Royal Tour would also promote a rapprochement between the Boer and English elements of South African society.

It was also during this tour that Princess Elizabeth made her historic speech, dedicating her life to the service of her people and the Commonwealth. There was some petty domestic press criticism of the Tour occurring during the frozen weeks, but, as ever, photographs of the lovely Queen and her beautiful daughters superseded this and filled the newspapers and newsreels.[30,31]

Other details of dress received royal criticism. 'I recall,' wrote Norman, 'that from two similar yachting suits of white linen made for the princesses, His Majesty insisted that the brass buttons be removed, for they were authentic naval buttons, and replaced by plain ones.'[32]

Norman might later have remembered one of his most beautiful dresses created for the Queen and worn for the ceremonial Opening of Parliament in Cape Town at the beginning of the Tour. Both the King in his white naval uniform and the Queen wore their Garter ribbons, the Queen in a straight-cut dress with a short train all embroidered around the hem and the front up to the waist. With padded shoulders and elbow-length sleeves, the dress had a crossover detail in front cascading over the shoulders to form another long embroidered train sweeping the ground behind, but with an open centre to a point about sixteen inches above the point where it hit the floor. This ingenious open device enabled the Queen to sit without creasing the train, but this unique dress is not mentioned by Norman. Worn with a tiara of South African diamonds, it caused a sensation in the press, and had been carefully withheld from the press view in Bruton Street. It was worn again for the Opening of Parliament in Salisbury, Rhodesia as part of this Royal Tour.

In many ways, this dress points the way to the next phase of Norman's career – Dior might well have his New Look, but there was no one to touch Norman's genius at designing for the great occasions of state. The open panel of the Queen's train, allowing her to remain cool in the heat and seated without creasing the thin embroidered fabric, was a typical piece of ingenuity, the concept repeated in the skirt of Princess Margaret's wedding dress in 1960.

From the 1940s onwards Norman's designing career was heavily involved with designs for the many ladies of the Royal Family. Luckily there were several such royal clients, all perpetually ensuring that his name appeared throughout the media worldwide, for in the subsequent three decades all the attempts to merchandise his famous name resulted in little of the financial benefits accruing to him personally. He managed to save remarkably little in the years to come, so the time-consuming creation and sustaining of individual royal styles became not only a passion but also a consuming labour of love that sustained him and the glamorous House he had created.

CHAPTER TWELVE

Inspired my . . . new look

At the beginning of 1947, Norman accepted the invitation to become the third chairman of the Incorporated Society of London Fashion Designers. He had co-founded the society in 1941-42 as an expedient wartime publicity measure during the German Occupation of Paris, when the Chambre Syndicale struggled with both production and the retention of the physical status of Paris as a fashion centre. After the Liberation and Dior's New Look, Paris was busily effecting a successful reassertion of its pre-war status.

Norman's predecessor at IncSoc was Molyneux, who resigned in order to concentrate his energies on his far more productive Paris House and American interests. He would often be away from London and within a few years, also suffering from ill health, chose to close his large London House. In his letter of acceptance, Norman said that he hoped to be able to continue promoting British fashion. Compared to Paris, 'on the whole I feel cheated,' reported the correspondent of the *Evening Standard*. 'British fashion seems forever to hover on the fringe of something really quite lovely, but never quite makes it.'[1] Interestingly, this was written a week before the launch of Dior's New Look, and the journalist should have mentioned the great French government assistance to its luxury industries. The British government short-sightedly thought only in terms of added taxation and meagre supplies, coupled with virtually no government assistance in promotion at home or overseas for the great pool of fashion talent struggling in London.

Under the respected guidance of Lilian Hyder, the determined secretary of IncSoc, every effort was made to cajole or browbeat members into doing something positive. This not only included entertaining foreign press and buyers but also participating in showing combined collections abroad. It never achieved anything resembling the power and prestige of the Chambre Syndicale, but it made good efforts with whatever minimal and grudging government financial assistance was available with the addition of efficient Ministry of Information (MOI) press releases and photographic imagery.

Norman and George's friend Captain Andrew Duncan had been posted from Rio to the commercial section of the Brussels Embassy, and with the support of the Ambassador Sir Hughe Knatchbull-Hugessen now sought to interest them and IncSoc in putting on a fashion show for the Festival Bruxelles 1947 in the context of a British Film Week. The show took place with Robert Nesbitt again organising the fashion show, which included models from Hardy Amies, Charles Creed, Angèle Delanghe, Molyneux, Bianca Mosca, Peter Russell, Victor Stiebel at Jacqmar, and Worth.[2] Norman sent six models to be worn by Dolores and on his return, wrote to Captain Duncan:

> Better late than never, I always say. How useful that axiom has proved to me! . . . I somehow guessed you were a good diplomat, but now I know what a wonderful host you are . . . two charming English rosebuds to meet me at the airport – a big, beautiful, bustling English Rolls-Royce to whisk me off to the hotel – and unkind cameras to prove to the public my British bloodhound character.
>
> It was a real pleasure to be in your lovely apartment again and gaze out upon the market of birds and flowers . . . Both George and I hope to find some reason to come over to Brussels again for the sake of wining and dining – and seeing you.[3]

The aim of attracting the wives of rich Belgians away from Paris was a good one and press reports were favourable, particularly about Dolores, who was generally considered at home to be the London mannequin of the period – 'un Mélange de Mata-Hari de Dolores del Rio et de Josephine Baker'. Dolores lived at home with her parents in Sidcup![4]

Andrew Duncan was to be used again by George as a perfume representative and by Norman in his everlasting search for domestic staff. In despair, they tried to find some nice Belgians to replace the sulky home-grown versions, one of whom was sacked not because she was bad at her work (she was excellent) but because Norman was 'made to feel unwelcome in my own house'. In January, his young chauffeur Page died of pneumonia, valets came and went, and the sole mainstay was Mrs Fisher at The Tower House, who was also not infallible.[5]

Yet Brenda Naylor, who worked with Norman at The Tower House and Lovel Dene, and was known to him as 'Dear Girl', found him very easy to work with and appreciative, although given the age gap and their respective positions he was inclined to be quiet during the simple lunches they shared. She remembered the efficient Algar, butler at Lovel Dene, and Norman's consideration in having her collected and taken to the station at all times. She also remembered the behind-the-scenes forceful nature and 'domaines' created by the various senior women in the House at Bruton Street, getting on very well with Madame Jeanne in the salon. They sometimes went ice-skating together. The sketches of the mid-1940s to the early 1950s, when Ian Thomas arrived, are very often hers, although Norman would often work on them and sign them. She also worked with him on the designs of the Joint Indian Red Cross and St John Ambulance uniforms in April 1945, a commission that followed on from his interesting designs for the Girl Guides and Utility clothing. These designs also formed the basis for the 1948 design of nurses' uniforms for the General Nursing Council – innovative detachable buttoned sleeves included.

If good staff were hard to find, good burglars were not and the third burglary of The Tower House dispirited Norman, making the headlines as thieves ransacked the house, pickaxing and jemmying their way through locked doors. His cufflinks, a gift from the Queen, were overlooked, but '£3,000 of jewels' and his French decoration were taken whilst he was away staying with the Marquess of Bath in May. Sometime later, the night watchman was knocked unconscious by an intruder in Bruton Street. Given the losses amongst his possessions at Lovel Dene, Norman was dispirited by this and also the loss of his case against Berkertex, when he tried to enforce his reading of the contract, which he thought gave him the right to end it in any October given reasonable notice. He felt that he deserved more money for his work and he certainly needed it.

The costs of running the business and supporting two large spenders such as George and himself could hardly be supported by a slender couture income and the income from Berkertex. In America, Norman had a lucrative contract to supply models to the then prestigious Chicago store of Mandel Brothers, which gave whole window displays of his designs in autumn 1947. Leon Mandel, the president, had a beautiful wife who wore Norman's clothes and was much photographed, wearing a dress when pictured with Charles James, who was 'provoked' that American designers such as himself were overlooked. Norman also had another reasonably paid contract to design men's casual shirts in smart resort styles for the Californian firm of Thomas Shirts. Undoubtedly this helped to bring in useful cash, but one of the main reasons for his appeal was now attached to his world-famous designs for the ladies of the Royal Family.

The Mandel window displays were also attuned to the huge publicity surrounding the forthcoming wedding of H.R.H. Princess Elizabeth to Lieutenant Philip Mountbatten, RN on 20 November 1947; *Time* magazine stressed that: 'Austerity, coal crises, rationing and shortages faded from the news columns to make way for reports of the lovers.'

It was Norman's excuse of the amount of work involved in the design of the wedding dress, together with those of the bridesmaids, the Queen, other ladies of the royal family and his other clients – with the added burden of a new Hartnell collection – which led to one of Norman's most disastrous publicity and business gaffes. He was awarded the prestigious Neiman Marcus Fashion Award and accepted an invitation to the award ceremony in Dallas. A cable was received from Stanley Marcus stressing Norman's unique nomination for the 8 September award for America's most important recognition of fashion achievement. He needed Norman's acceptance within one week. Norman immediately wrote to Charles Rendigs of Nanty in New York swearing him to secrecy and asking him for his opinion of the necessity for an immediate trip:

> It does seem a pity to waste this golden opportunity to boost Les Parfums Hartnell which would have to pay for the trip because of currency restrictions. I have no idea what this award is, or what weight it carries in America. . . let me have the 'gen' . . . thanking you for the hams etc.

He then wrote to Fred Smith for his advice, who not unnaturally knew nothing much of fashion awards let alone Neiman Marcus and questioned the prestige of the award as set against the time and money involved in collecting it.

'I understand that the recent law action (Berkertex) has involved us in expenses of £2,000 and there is your Australia visit to consider,' he wrote on 3 July. Without much knowledge of the Neiman Marcus business, he thought it merely something to enhance the prestige of the 'House of Marcus' [sic] and that Norman should conserve his energies and remain at Hartnell to run things on a day-to-day basis. 'But the decision to go or not will now rest with you.'

Norman, who was to regret going along with Smith's uninformed advice at the last minute, replied, 'I feel that it would be very lazy and unenterprising to refuse this award.' He also mentioned that Hans Juda, publisher and textile expert, as well as Charles Rendigs had advised him to accept. He further wrote: 'I agree with you about taxing my energies too much. I do not want to go to America – much less do I want to go to Australia, but if I do not welcome these exceptional offers, somebody else will – and we, the directors of Hartnell's would wonder why!'[6]

His passage was booked on the *Queen Elizabeth* to New York for his onward journey to accept what was called the fashion 'Oscar' – 'because of your outstanding accomplishments over a period of years in the field of fashion you have been selected as the one person from England'.[7]

W.W.D. then reported on 25 August that he had cancelled his trip – 'the interpretation here is that he is detained by royal orders'. George was sent to deputise, but, good-looking as he was, this was an absurd move when the line-up included those who had undertaken the long journey Irene: world famous for her film-costume designs, Salvatore Ferragamo (already famous as the Florentine shoemaker) and, of course, Christian Dior from France. All gained immense added prestige via the media and Dior especially, as he was the one great couturier represented at the ceremony, which was also a reaffirmation of post-war luxury by one of America's most exclusive department stores in a country now ready to enjoy post-war spending power. His fame was already assured and widespread thanks to the noisy objections of groups of women protesting at the confining nature of his designs – 'Mr Dior we abhor' ran the placards of the anti-New Look women.

The loss of invaluable publicity and prestige for Norman in the eyes of the worldwide fashion press and consumers was marked, for no one had forgotten the reports that he could produce 100 designs in two weeks for the Buenos Aires show. However, Neiman Marcus generously bought three expensive Hartnell dresses for display, but how many more could he have sold had he appeared in person?

There was then further embarrassment when George returned to Britain carrying in his luggage a whole consignment of artificial seed pearls and told customs that they were '10,000 pearls, for the wedding dress of Princess Elizabeth'. Customs duly impounded the unpatriotic lot until duty was paid. In fact, although these tiny pearls were needed for embroidery of the dress, a London firm called Pompadour Products: 'Pearls for a Princess', founded by the innovative German émigré Otto Herrmann, provided most of the heavier approved larger ones for the train, and the omission of this fact caused even more embarrassment later on.

As the unremarkable IncSoc shows of September 1947 occurred, Norman was still preoccupied with clothes for the Royal Family and the wedding. Wedding dresses had been his pre-war *coups de théâtre* and he again searched picture galleries until he found inspiration in a Botticelli painting. The approved design was very much in the style of many of the embroidered evening dresses already worn by the Princess which reflected current taste for the princess line with fuller skirts beneath fitted bodices. The cut-out 'sweetheart' neckline of the top was given a more geometric outline and the incorporation of long sleeves was to counteract the November wedding in Westminster Abbey. Of ivory duchesse satin, the dress evoked a flattering description from James Laver:

> Mr Norman Hartnell has shown himself no mean poet, subtlety with seed pearls has always been one of the characteristics of his style and here he has no mere bodice or sleeve edge for his canvas, but a swirling skirt and a full court train. In a design based on delicate Botticelli curves, he has scattered over the ivory satin garlands of white York roses carried out in raised pearls, entwined with ears of corn minutely embroidered in crystal. By the device of reversed embroidery, he has alternated star flowers and orange blossom, now tulle on satin and now satin on tulle, the whole encrusted with pearls and crystals . . . the occasion demanded a poet and Mr Hartnell has not failed to string his lyre with art and to ring in tune.[8]

There were the usual snide remarks from the press – were the silk worms Japanese? No, they were 'Chinese worms – from Nationalist China, of course'.[9] The silk for the train came from Lullingstone Castle at the wish of the Queen, but the silk satin for the supple folds of the dress came from Dunfermline. The bridesmaids' dresses were of ivory silk tulle with full flowing skirts, and swathed over the shoulders, with a central bow, rested a tulle fichu with star-shaped flowers in pearl and crystal embroidery, reflecting those on the fifteen-yard-long train of the wedding dress. Norman drew this out alone one evening with Flora Ballard, the head embroideress, as he later explained:

I laid out fifteen yards of tracing paper flat on the linoleum floor. I rolled up my shirt sleeves and wore gymnasium shoes, so that I should not slip when running up and down both sides of fifteen paper yards secured by drawing pins to the shiny linoleum.

Graphite pencil in hand, I first marked out a long line from shoulder almost to the hem of the main backbone, a central line for the graduated satin syringa and orange blossoms. Similar pearl embroideries were to mark the edges of the train. Then, crawling on my knees, I marked in the more softly curving lines of the diamond and pearl wheat ears which feathered gracefully to the base of the train.

Norman's moments of agony and ecstasy were not over.

Sitting cross-legged and suffering from a severe cold in the head, I marked in circles the rich white roses of York to be carried out in padded satin and centred by strands of pearls threaded on silver wire and raised up in relief. All these motifs had to be assembled in a design proportioned like a florist's bouquet. Wherever there was space or weakness of design I drew more wheat, more leaves, more blossom of orange, syringa or jasmine.[10]

This work was not new to Norman and was in many ways a distillation of his designs seen on his wedding dresses throughout the 1920s and 1930s, but never had he worked on such a scale for one dress to be not only worn but also filmed, photographed and seen worldwide.

As with the Queen in her platform-soled gilt high-heeled sandals, the firm of H&M Rayne produced the Princesses' shoes to Norman's designs using a fabric supplied by Hartnell to match the dress. These shoes had wide banded ankle straps for warmth and support; the heels were of moderate height so that the hem of the skirt was at exactly the correct height to glide over the varied service leading from carriage to altar and back. A slow pace was in any case unavoidable due to the considerable length of the evil and perforce elegant. Princess Margaret Rose was later photographed in her bridesmaid's dress and suddenly it was realised by the press how truly beautiful she was. It says much again for Norman's flair that he could cater so well for the different tastes and styles of the two Princesses.

The collaboration with Rayne was also lucky, for it reaffirmed the long friendship between Edward Rayne and Norman, which had been cemented during Mayfair wartime fire-watching duties and later included his wife Mona. H&M Rayne were the holder of four Royal Warrants and Norman liaised often over shoe designs to complement his clothes for the Royal Family and those in his collections.[11]

No doubt Norman's worries over the immensely intricate embroideries and the vital fittings to ensure perfect weight distribution on the long walk down the aisle were the real reason for his cancellation of the visit to America, for the labour involved was intense and necessitated 350 women for seven weeks' work. However, it never again became feasible for him to break into the American market in any significant manner in the decades to come after his perceived snub of the Neiman Marcus Awards. His chance had been sacrificed. On the other hand, his fame was spread anew worldwide by the wedding and he appealed to younger women once more, and not just those of the Queen's generation. This was a generation that could not wait to grow up and appear both elegant and sophisticated in an adult 'dressed-up' way – now out of fashion.

Working on the dress proved such an experience that Norman began his own record entitled: 'Log Book – The Diary of the Dress'

Monday Oct: 13

Papers full of complaints that the Princess should say 'I obey'.

10.30 Call from Marlborough House. Queen Mary wants 1st fitting at 10 a.m. tomorrow. Mdme Jeanne, Queen Mary's vendeuse has poisoned her hand and cannot go. Spent hours redrawing design on tracing paper for the dress.

2.30 *News Review* – a catty paper – insists on interview. Too terrified to say 'no'. So give it with Yvonne as witness.

More hours on tracery. Pass Princess Margaret's ensemble for launch of ship in Ireland.

Evening News – still harping. Clive Duncan (?) Inc. Society a 'snob thing'.

***

Tuesday Oct: 14

Queen Mary's fitting.

Several papers call up to know when I'm going to Palace.

I think they want to take photos. I tell them 'no appointment yet'.

They don't believe it.

Lady Dudley says she too is suffering from hostile press because she was hostess to the Windsors.

Chose colour for the national glove makers to present to Princess.

Choose style and colour for woollen cardigans from press to Princess.

Visit embroidery room. The bodice design (on the tracing paper) is now almost correct. The motif of orange blossom and roses all in pearls has now been lengthened by the addition of sprays of wheat. I rub them out and redraw them in a graceful curved line, instead of sticking out like a depressed railway line indicator. Drop the design a further 1½ inches to keep the bustline. The design is now workable as a basis. It must now all be pricked through by hand with a sharp pin.

On fifteen yards of train this was an expensive undertaking in terms of time and money. Norman ends his description here mid-page; he had no Beaton-like aptitude for keeping a detailed continual diary, but one senses the work and strain involved.

For the Queen, Norman produced a slender-fitting long dress of glistening apricot and gold brocade with a draped train worn with the Garter ribbon, the Garter itself cleverly worked into the upper sleeve of the left arm. Norman also made his last ensemble for Queen Mary of golden tissue with sea-blue chenille. Crowned heads and heads of governments or their representatives attended: the news value was to prove immense for Norman.

The British press had previously reached a fever pitch of speculation as design and details were kept secret. Windows were whitewashed and attempts to hire neighbouring premises repelled by incensed owners. Norman was not too worried about plagiarists as the embroidery was so intricate. At last the 'four-foot box' was delivered and the Princess and family wore their dresses to great acclaim. For Norman, this work experience was invaluable in planning the Coronation Dress for Queen Elizabeth II in 1953.

If the nation was largely enthusiastic and cheered by the wedding, it was not the first time they had seen Norman's work on film. He had been included in newsreels and even a short colour film before the war. In the commercial cinema, he is credited from the 1920s onwards as the costume designer for many memorable films and provided stars on and off screen with clothes. By 1947 they were old news, as were the wartime films on which he worked, including *He Found a Star* and *Ships with Wings* (both 1941), and *The Demi-Paradise* (1943), the latter two with other IncSoc members. He memorably appeared in a 1946 film *Fashion Fantasy* in which a girl dreams of being de-mobbed and working as a mannequin at Hartnell.

Herbert Wilcox then put his wife Anna Neagle into the trio of popular Society themed musicals of the period dressed by Norman: *I Live in Grosvenor Square* (1946), *Spring in Park Lane* (1948) and *Maytime in Mayfair* (1949). The *Maytime* concoction included a colourful fashion sequence based on Hollywood films and each member of IncSoc was given a huge imaginary magazine cover out of which stepped the mannequin appropriately clad. Miss Neagle wore the star wedding dress in which she was then 'married', but all her other dresses in the film were by 'Miss Foster of Ships'. Stage work was as useful an income to Norman as film work, although both sources declined over the next two decades.

In March 1947, Norman became involved in the setting up of the Fashion Industries Club, an idea first put in 1944 to the main brain behind it, John Dannhom, by Arnold Hard of *The Maker Up*, a clothing professionals' journal. During that year, Lord Hollenden was acquired as president with Norman as the nominated 'couturier' on the 'committee of management' with J. Steinberg representing the wholesale side. George was on the General Committee, as were Edward Rayne and Sir Montague Burton. The Club was to be a meeting place for all those involved in every facet of fashion and as a focal point for overseas buyers, because there was no government department to help them or entertain them in a central well-informed centre. A building at 70 Brook Street, Mayfair was found and the distinguished modern architect Wells Coates produced the plans and perspectives.

Given the date, the designs for entrance hall, bar, dining room, smoke room and rear tea terrace have the excitingly spare look to be seen later at the Festival of Britain in 1951 and on into the 1960s, as much of their time as Norman's glass salon was. The Festival itself was hoped to bring in the necessary visitors to make the Club buzz when it was up and running, but it ran into difficulties early on. Norman had a horror of wasting time on committee meetings and scarcely attended, even those of IncSoc; furthermore, the fashion industry representatives were peculiarly slow to join as members. Lilian Hyder, the Administrator, was worried that IncSoc would be submerged if it joined en bloc and urged individuals to join, which negated the purpose as IncSoc had no such building in any case. A move to gain Princess Margaret as an honorary and fashionable figurehead foundered, as did the Club in 1952, the unhappy Lord Hollenden being sued for monies owed by the Club to suppliers. From the correspondence, George's role seems primarily to have been in taking good bar and kitchen staff from other restaurants to staff the new building. The FIC was a splendid idea into which the secretary Hugh Robinson poured all his energies, but it did make clear that if the industry was hardly prepared to pull together and back itself, then lukewarm government support would always be the most anyone could expect.[11]

Norman's January 1948 collection revealed that he too was moving along the Dior path in his own less extreme way. Unusually he gave his own commentary and described his voluminous scarlet wool top coat with its many folds 'like the tents of the Arabs before they are folded away'. Shoulders were less square and his skirts longer with nipped-in, tucked waistlines; he used draping on necks and panniered hips too on straight day dresses – even as the New Look evolved into different forms with Christian Dior.

Norman also revived a true haute couture note by showing hand-painted evening dresses of the type Brenda Naylor remembers helping to paint at The Tower House for some Royal dresses.[12] Norman said about the skirt-length question that occurred in every season of couture fashion through the 1940s and 1950s, 'I never bother about inches. Everything depends on the individual, but my model girls have theirs about fourteen inches from the ground.'[13]

In fact, the hemline was to remain a critical fashion point until the mid-1960s and the arrival of the popular miniskirt. During this time *the* wedding dress by Norman Hartnell was in an exhibition travelling around Britain. The exhibition drew in huge crowds whilst raising money for charity, at which time Osbert Lancaster contributed his first Hartnell cartoon to the *Daily Sketch* of an uncharacteristically behatted and soignée 'Miss Freya Stark explaining to a relatively unsophisticated audience the genius of Mr Norman Hartnell' whilst seated on the ground surrounded by a gaping group of Desert Sons. This was on view at the Redfern Gallery and was augmented by Heather Thatcher wearing Norman's designs in a Frederick Lonsdale comedy

Canaries Sometimes Sing at the Garrick, co-starring Jack Buchanan and Coral Browne with hats by Aage Thaarup.

There was also a spirited attempt to boost IncSoc with extensive government support when Harold Wilson, then President of the Board of Trade, received the overseas visitors to the collections at an evening reception in Lancaster House on 28 January. The Duchess of Kent also attended to give the evening added glamour.

The holding of the Olympic Games in London 1948 was similarly put to good use with special fashion shows for the official representatives held on Friday, 30 July and a buffet lunch for sixty-seven held at Lovel Dene the following day.[14] The buyers present included Norman's great fan Doreen Day of Canada's important T. Eaton Company. Colleagues included Hardy Amies, who had been the first foreign dress designer to arrive in America as the war ended and so continually reaped the rewards for this interest until he died.[15] These latter events were part of London Fashion Fortnight from 19 to 30 July with another Lancaster House reception. Apart from IncSoc shows, there were over 220 firms participating – all of whom might well have joined the Fashion Industries Club but did not. As Harold Wilson was a member of the Labour Socialist government it showed some clear thinking and vision for him to agree to Board of Trade sponsorship of the whole event on a hitherto unknown scale and Norman wrote him a warm letter of thanks.

Norman's domestic situation was now peaceful again. His Regent's Park neighbour Patricia, Countess of Cottenham, was even able to house a valet for Norman, having seen the last of her servants go:

> To be perfectly honest, I am enjoying a peace I haven't had in years, knowing that there are no drunken, dirty, snivelling, thieving people in the house. I have been the victim of such constant petty thefts for so long, that it is heaven to have harmony and peace in the house. The only drawback is looking at my hands which have not done kitchen work for 500 years . . . but even so . . . it is worth it. I am turning out to be a jolly good cook.[16]

This was a quite usual response to the new servantless age, which has been quickly forgotten. Norman's neighbour was a good friend, giving him little gifts, which he reciprocated. To another Pat (Buckley) he reminisced about pre-war days:

The dress you refer to was a three-tiered crinoline of white tulle with small gold stars scattered over it. It was worn at the drawing room courts at Buckingham Palace; also on the USA tour; also to receive the French President, Monsieur Lebrun and Madame Lebrun, that's enough, isn't it? It was so nice seeing you and dear Phil Monkman.

Blake, who had attended the firm's 20 December 1946 Hartnell Staff Dance 'in naval uniform and dinner afterwards' became a more frequent guest at The Tower House. 'What fun.' He was now obsessed with Princess Daisy of Pless's pre-First World War life at Fürstenstein. 'Certainly some distant day you and I ought to journey to sleek Silesia to see same if and when conditions in Europe permit though chaos may increase rather than diminish in *our* lifetime.'[17]

His somewhat affected otherworldliness and – to Norman – amusing eccentricities were not so amusing to everyone, however. 'I do agree with you (from your point of view) that "supper" at your own house would be FAR nicer than being stared at (or *ignored* by waiters: *worse*) in the Savoy Grill!!'[18]

In April, they went to a Footlights annual dinner in Cambridge at the invitation of D.C. Ordess, Norman writing to him: 'I thought the Club was defunct . . . I shall be only too happy to revive old memories.'[19]

Another Footlights friend, Eric Maschwitz, who also called Norman 'Bish', congratulated him on his designs for his play *Carissima* and on 20 May Queen Mary attended a gala performance with a show of Hartnell dresses included. His stepmother Jane continued to pursue him with orders for dresses and fur coats. 'So sorry I wasn't here – I think I was down at Lovel Dene working on the sketches for the future Australian tour, because the royal ladies – being very sensible – want to order their clothes as for export but wear them in this country before they go.'[20] He then explained that she was owed money from the company and sent a cheque relating to Bish's estate. Not surprisingly, she was rather lost without Bish and in common with many widows of the period spent time travelling around hotels on the South Coast and with relatives called Bockridge in Birmingham, who owned a dance school.

The Silver Wedding of the King and Queen on 26 April 1948 brought innumerable photographic tributes and glimpses of Norman's designs for the Queen, some of which were once more made of lace in the pre-war spirit of encouraging British manufacturers. A Service of Thanksgiving in St Paul's Cathedral entailed a drive in an open carriage and then the ascent of the long flight of steps outside the Cathedral. Both the King in uniform and the Queen wore decorations; the Queen's slim long dress, with a scalloped neckline, having a band of embroidery around it and three ropes of large pearls worn above. A light off-the-face hat was decorated with ribbons and the Queen's shoulders were swathed in an extra full and long boa of ostrich feathers. The Queen thoughtfully sent a garland of flowers to Norman and his staff to express her thanks.

Princess Elizabeth's five-day visit to Paris with Prince Philip at Whitsun in 1948 to open 'Eight Centuries of British Life' gave Norman a chance to show Paris how he could dress a beautiful young woman, as he had her mother the Queen ten years earlier. Although elegant and suitable to the Princess and occasion, there was nothing sensational about her wardrobe. Norman's designs for day clothes in his own full-skirted version of the evolving New Look had none of the *élan* of his Parisian rivals, except for some predictably magnificent embroidered dresses. However, Balmain was already echoing these and they were truly formal dresses compared to the quite extraordinary effects achieved at Christian Dior. Norman had to do better – they were already more sophisticated than the Princess's staid wedding trousseau – but he was also constrained by the fact that, unknown to the world, the Princess was awaiting the birth of her first child, Prince Charles, in October.

The Princess wore her Paris wardrobe back in Britain, wearing a lime-green coat, shaped at the front like a suit, when she opened the new Broadway in Coventry with a plea for good design, town planning and peace. Her clothes seemed to strike a note with the newspapers, as did the dresses Norman designed for one of his more eccentric clients, the extraordinary cat-loving concert pianist Avril Coleridge-Taylor. She hoped that the Leeds Town Hall would be cleaner than the Royal Albert Hall 'where the dust damaged a magnificent blue dress with a trailing skirt. Hartnell was distracted and implored her to take her own carpet with her.'[21] She now seems totally forgotten, unlike Eileen Joyce, for whom Norman designed memorable dresses in the 1950s. The larger skirts were increasingly demanded, but the press reported that there were no huge fabric stocks for the meagre coupon supply.

In August, George had to explain to the press that Filene's of Boston had bought out-of-date Hartnell-made dresses and that they were including them in their basement bargain sale, although when sold to Filene it was assumed they would be in the exclusively couture section of the store. This bungle was reported in every newspaper and did further harm to Norman's deflated prestige in America.

Too much attention had again been concentrated by Norman and George on Australia with their hopes pinned on the planned Royal Tour, and Norman was to have had concurrent collections shown at David Jones in Sydney and the Myer Emporium in Melbourne. Large sums of money were spent by George on attempting to resurrect the scent business, and over the succeeding years expenditure on entertaining crept up enormously, much to the dismay of the ever cautious and frugal Fred Smith. In 1947, Norman had finally sold his Lagonda for £2,700 cash, having kept it intact and garaged throughout the war in spite of Bish and Fred Smith's urging him to get rid of it.

The King's now frail health was causing concern and the Royal Tour of Australia was reluctantly cancelled. Lost revenue was the unfortunate consequence for Hartnell due to the abandonment of many orders and the now slim prospect of extensive business relations evolving in Australia. However, as ever he went on and his September collection showed his fullest acceptance of the Dior influence with the swirling skirts of his rather weighty New Look ankle-length coats weighted further by deep fur trimmings.

In direct contrast were his designs for the official uniforms of state-registered nurses and the simpler ensemble worn by the Queen at the Braemar Games. A feminine form of the kilt, the rounded lines of the jacket had lapels faced with the same Royal Stewart tartan, in direct contrast to the grey rayon satin dress Norman designed for the opening of the Rayon Design Centre at 1 Upper Grosvenor Street. Designed by even more radical modernists than Lacoste or Wells Coates, Maxwell Fry and Jane Drew created a spirited addition to the London fashion scene under the direction of another recent innovative architect, Dennis Lennon. The Centre had variable lighting to simulate climatic conditions in various parts of the world and was sadly as short-lived as the British Fashion Industries Club.

Whilst London buzzed with activity, so did Norman Hartnell. All was not well amongst the directors. One of them, Henry Medlam, was forthright in indicating the problems as he saw them: although he found Phyllis charming, he resented her interference and her treatment of him as if he was an office boy, believing that she had instigated the fuss with Berkertex whilst Norman was in South America. Since 1932, he had advised the board as an accountant. He also wrote that George had 'curious ways of doing business whilst trying to help Norman and seemed to think the flashy "throwing money about" approach as being the only one to succeed'. He was unsparing, if reticent on the complete lack of George's business experience:

> As you know, I fear that he encourages in Norman a natural apti-
> tude for extravagance and leads to the frittering away of resources
> which could otherwise build up Norman's capital position for his
> inevitable ultimate decline from the highest pinnacle. There is no
> doubt in my mind of his devotion to Norman or his sincerity . . .
> with regard to perfumes . . . my baby because I was the first to sug-
> gest producing in England and it was pooh-poohed by Norman . . .
> I feel I could build it [up] . . . or throw away all the work . . . to
> obtain for Norman the Paris business so cleverly given away by his
> late protégé Pleydell. . .[22]

Medlam clearly makes the point that John Pleydell was also never viewed as quite the successful friend and businessman as he chose to portray himself. One can only speculate that from the viewpoint of a professional accountant, Norman had been deceived and betrayed by Pleydell, hence his abrupt departure from Norman's life.

By 24 November 1948 Norman was writing to another experienced director, Frances Walter Smith, that because of the cancelled Royal Tour he was working entirely 'on the design of everything to do with bottles, packaging and, of course, the smell!' But the company was already 'heavily overdrawn' and was losing workroom staff in September, when the girls left for better-paid work elsewhere. The solution was applied by George – he raised wages and wrote: 'Norman took another large order from the Queen, which again means we lose a little more money. I will explain more fully when we next meet.'[23]

Hartnell made a modest profit on royal orders, but Norman was timid about sending invoices, even though all estimates for clothes ordered were always agreed in advance of work commencing on them. Smith was also worried about George's health: 'He did not look too well to me and when he was trying on his new dinner jacket, he looked considerably thinner. He wants to take care and not rush about so much.'[24]

At this time Mrs Price wrote to Smith's secretary; he was just going away on holiday and of his departure, she said, 'I am sure it is not such a pantomime as it is here when the two gentlemen decide to travel. Still there it is, it's all in a day's work.'[25]

Fred Smith's solicitude for George's health was to wane over the next two years, but in 1949 he was to loan Norman money for both a new car and travel to New York to attempt a solution to what had become the 'scent business'. He also involved himself in long discussions with Leslie Berker and the burgeoning retail fixer Eric Crabtree about Norman's remuneration from Berkertex. However, by April 1950, Smith was so far worried by the Hartnell financial plight that he refused to sign a company cheque sent to him and Norman sent a petulant four-page letter:

> To say I am extremely angry is putting it mildly . . . I have had just enough of this uncooperative attitude on the part of my directors, and as Chairman of the Board I take this as a personal insult . . . I have more than sufficient to do . . . I feel I must stress that I do most strongly object to this extremely unhelpful and hurtful attitude adopted towards me and should it continue, I imagine I may feel inclined to prefer direction from more quick-witted people, who have my interests at heart and are capable of taking properly reasoned decisions.[26]

This outburst was directed by Norman to an elderly experienced businessman, one of his mainstays throughout the 1930s and 1940s, whose sound advice linked to that of his friend Bish had kept Norman solvent and allowed the company to expand.

Norman's nerves had let him down before. In February 1948, Smith had written to George with the sound advice that Norman should take a short rest when necessary and so avoid the necessity of a longer rest later on.[27] Norman's letter later in the year on the subject of his new car reveals his curiously boyish excitement and a certain naivety as he reminded Fred Smith of his offer of a loan for this purpose:

> Did you really mean it, Fred? Because I would like to take advantage of your offer. You see I have been warned of the imminent delivery of the car within the next five days. It is not a super Rolls-Bentley or Daimler (which I would of course prefer!!!) but a quite good-looking Austin Sheerline, the price of which is about £1,800 (instead of a splendid six or seven thousand number).
>
> Would you let me know fairly soon please? When are you coming

to London again? Not Wednesday, because I've got the President of the Board of Trade coming down here at Lovel Dene – to discuss the perfume project (*one* instance when I need a decent car).

On Friday I have to go to Brussels (I don't want to) returning Tuesday so perhaps the week after next. . .[28]

This letter from Norman curiously resembles that of a small boy or flirtatious wife of the period, rather than a sophisticated world-famous man of forty-eight. In some ways, it resembles his friend Blake's less controlled behaviour.

In 1946, Blake had written to the young novelist Denton Welch, who recorded that he was more bemused than amused by all the coloured inks and odd headings on the writing paper that he affected e.g. 'No telephone on purpose.' In September 1947, Denton Welch's friend Eric Oliver met Blake and Norman, but Blake was at his most eccentric and urged him to talk about the cut of Princess Elizabeth's bloomers and continuously made every remark seem a double entendre. Norman remained 'good-natured and fat' and unresponsive whilst the other two men climbed the tower at Hadlow Castle.[29] Norman could be the chameleon character of all things to all men, but with some old friends or acquaintances such as Blake or Smith, his true character was often untrammelled, rather like an engine letting off steam.

The background to Norman's petulant letter to Smith now becomes clear in the reply to the effusions:

> My dear Norman . . . I agree that the acquisition of a car for a person of your presumed financial status should present no financial difficulty.
>
> On the other hand this request does not fit in with the financial position of the company.

He then outlined the necessity for a radical and 'drastic' reorganisation of the company but said 'at the moment I am quite willing to abide by what I have offered to do for you'.[30]

Smith considered the situation carefully – as a director he was also legally liable for the correct running of the company. His very long nine-page letter of 8 November 1949 to Norman marked a turning point in Norman's life. The 1947 success of Dior's New Look had clearly shaken him into the recognition that he might never again create a fashion innovation – after all, he had been in business since 1923. He even went so far as to suggest to the Queen that he might perhaps be too old to design the wedding dress of the much younger Princess Elizabeth. The response had been a royal command to undertake the work. Perhaps this review of his own talents was the reason for his late abandonment of a personal appearance at the Neiman Marcus award ceremony. He simply did not wish to appear with the new French fashion genius Christian Dior and be subject to the inevitable comparisons in the press reflecting on his royal patrons and his clients. The Royal Wedding rectified his setback in the world press and the subsequent patronage of Princess Elizabeth and Princess Margaret gave him new horizons and fame.

The restoration of Norman's faith in his talent and future, and his clinging to the person of George against all advice, was partly responsible for the rejection of the similar advice and warnings of *all* his solid advisors. This was to send his business into a roller-coaster ride ending stuck in the water dip as he approached his fiftieth birthday.

For an understanding of the public relationship of Norman and George one has to consider the following letter from Fred Smith. This letter is the most crucial, of thousands in the surviving files, for a concise understanding of the failure of the business to generate sufficient funds during the subsequent years of Norman's life until his death in 1979.

Bow Lane Foundry, Preston 8 November 1949
  Norman Hartnell, Esq.
  Lovel Dene,
  Winkfield,
  Windsor Forest,
  BERKS.

Dear Norman,

Norman Hartnell Ltd

I have just received from the auditors a report upon the trading for the year ending 31 July 1949, and the information contained in this report (which I presume you have also received) shows that the business is in a very grave position, and in this letter I am going to have no hesitation in putting forth my views upon how this business of yours, built up with such care during the past twenty-five years now appears to be heading for disaster, and from this letter you will see with whom I place the bulk of the blame for this unsatisfactory position.

Before going into details, I would respectfully refer you to my letter to you of 21 September last. In dictating this letter, I spent a great deal of time and thought in putting forward the views then expressed by me. I have not had the courtesy of a reply to this letter, but on 6 October I received a letter, from Mr Mitchison which he dated 26 September, in which he endeavoured to pin upon me the responsibility for such a very unsatisfactory trading result which I envisaged in that letter. The information for which he asked in that letter was available to him from day to day on the premises, and if he possessed an elementary idea of business matters he could have obtained this information, but, as he tells me in his letter that he is a mere infant in the business world, it is easy to understand his anxiety for other people to 'pull his chestnuts out of the fire'.

I will now proceed to deal with the information submitted to us by the auditors.

On 13 October 1948, following upon the receipt of the trading results for the year ending 31 July 1948, I pointed out to you the considerable loss in profits sustained in that year, and I indicated in that letter what I considered should be done to pull the company round. It would appear to me that no notice has been taken of my advice, because for the twelve months ended July 1949 the results are even worse than for the previous year.

I do not know when Mitchison returned from the army, but it was shortly after the accounts for the year ending 31 July 1945 were produced. On these accounts the financial position of the Company was as follows:

Cash in bank	£13,131
Investments	£4,000

For the year ending 31 July 1948, the investments had all been realised, and instead of our having £13,131 in the bank, we owed the bank £5,899. Today we owe them £14,444.

For the last year of the war, ending 31 July 1945 you will be surprised to learn that the sales were only £45,169, considerably less than half the sales for the year ending 31 July 1949, but in that year, with such a small output you were debited with a salary of £2,000 and commission of £4,440, and there was still a sum of £4,440 profit for appropriation. It appears that the accounts for the year ending 31 July 1949 are not yet completed by the auditors, but, from the information embodied in the report it would appear that the nett [sic] profit earned will hardly be sufficient to cover even your salary of £2,000 per annum.

It will be noted that the profits have been greatly reduced owing to the large amounts of taxation which we shall have to find. You might wonder why there is so little profit, but the Inspector of Taxes is empowered today to investigate cases of expenditure which he considers should not be charged against a company's trading accounts, and these amounts which he considers have been improperly charged are added back, and income tax must be paid thereon. These amounts which the Inspector of Taxes considers to have been improperly charged represent very large sums, and I consider that he has been very modest in his allocation of the writing back of the amounts which he considers reasonable.

The nett [sic] result of all the work you have put in for the year ending 31 July 1949 shows that the assets of the company have been reduced by the sum of £8,555. The only assets you have today are valued at £22,000 made up of money owing by customers and the stock you have on hand. This state of affairs has accumulated since the introduction of Mitchison to the company. Now we are in the hands of the bank, and if they like to put pressure upon us they can do so, and consequently our trading position would be gravely imperilled.

Some time ago I informed you that Mr Medlam and I would endeavour to get from the bank increased facilities, and you will also remember me telling you at that time, or in correspondence, that the accounts would show up in a very poor light to obtain the concession we required. We saw the bank manager a short time ago and asked for increased credit facilities, i.e. £15,000 for Norman Hartnell Ltd, and £7,500 for yourself. Mr Gilbert at that time insisted that before any decision could be made regarding increased facilities he would require to see the accounts of the company for the year ending 31 July 1949. It would appear that whilst the accounts have not been approved by the company, the auditors, in order to get the new credit facilities arranged, have provided draft accounts. The results shown in these accounts are so infernally bad that I am not surprised to learn that he has refused to give us any increased facilities, and it may be that, in due course, we shall receive notification from him to reduce our indebtedness. Then, you might say, alright, we will go to another bank, but no other bank would take on this large liability. You might say, alright, I will see some of my friends and get whatever money I want. I cannot envisage any of your friends providing you with funds if they know the true financial position of the company.

You might tell me, we have had two bad years, and things will change. Alright, what is the position so far since July 1949? Only three months have elapsed since the commencement of the present financial year, and our orders are already £14,000 down. The goods we have despatched are down nearly £4,000, but the wages and salaries in the workroom are up by approximately £150. There is no sign in these figures of any improvement whatever. On the other hand, it must mean that we are getting further into the mire each week, because, according to the auditors' report, it would appear that the expenses are continuing at least at the rate of last year.

The grave position in which we are now placed is attributable to several reasons.

The first reason, and maybe not the most important reason, is the fact that Mitchison is, according to his own admission, not a business man. I do not know his background, but putting his age at say thirty-two years, and his having spent several years in the army, this does not allow him to possess the business experience one would expect from his present position of General Manager. He is very extravagant, and his financial knowledge elementary.

The responsibility for his entering the business rests with you, due to your insistence upon it, and I assume that you accept the responsibility for your choice. His predecessor, Mr Ward, whilst not being satisfactory, did at least produce profits for you, and keep down expenditure, but the extravagance which is now rampant throughout the company is almost beyond belief. When Mitchison first started in the business, he was quite modest, but, with growing power and influence, he eschewed economy, and proceeded to spend the company's money upon travelling expenses and entertaining in an unjustifiably lavish manner.

During the year ending 31 July 1947, the following amounts were charged as follows:

Travelling	£1,571
Entertaining	£3,590
Motor Car	£433
	£5,594

I can hardly accept items alleged to be paid as tips and entertaining as being legitimately chargeable to the Company, of which the following are a few examples:

Tips

Prospective customer.	£10
Post Office workers.	£70 approx.
Wife of deceased doorkeeper.	£20

Entertaining

Tesse [sic] O'Shea & Mrs Bowes-Lyon.	£50
Lady Willingden.	£129
Duchess of Westminster.	£20
Mignon.	£25
Office Drinks.	£21

When the accountants presented the accounts for the year in question to the Inspector of Taxes I am assuming that the Inspector would query the amounts charged to travelling and entertaining, and at the moment I do not know the amount Mr Medlam got the Inspector to pass, but I have no doubt that he did very well in the company's interests.

Even then, with all these expenses and probably £2,000 in that year for wine and whisky, we still made a good profit. At the annual meeting when the approved accounts were passed I thought it incumbent upon me to let you and Mrs Stuart know what entertaining expenses were costing the company, and I read out the list of everybody alleged to have been entertained, which accounted for the figure of £3,590, but to my surprise, no comments were made regarding this expenditure which at the time I thought, and still think, was very significant.

The following year, i.e. year ending 31 July 1948, we got a bombshell when we saw the results of the trading for the year. In my letter to you of 13 October 1948 I set out at considerable length my impressions regarding that year's trading, which resulted in the cost of production being up over £9,000 on practically the same turnover.

I specifically indicated in that same letter of 13 October what should be done immediately to prevent a repetition of the loss of almost £10,000 in profits, but today I cannot find any signs that Mitchison has taken any cognizance of my remarks and reduced his manufacturing costs; in fact for the twelve months ending July 1949, the costs of manufacture are up.

For the year ending 31 July 1949 these expenses are still astoundingly high – I understand over £5,000. I have no details of how these are made up as yet, but I do know of one item which he has charged – i.e. £50 for tips to five porters at Buckingham Palace.

You will remember that before Mitchison came on the scene we entered into an agreement with Rendigs for the sale of perfumes, and in one year alone we received by way of royalties over £9,000. Something went wrong in New York with the wholesaler, and although we received approaching £29,000 from this source, it eventually ceased.

About two years ago Mr Rendigs attended a meeting of the board when it was suggested that a similar policy be repeated regarding the sale of perfumes in New York, but that the wholesaler with whom the arrangement would be made must be of the highest integrity. Has Mitchison carried out any investigations in this matter? On the contrary, he thought what a fine thing it would be if he could run the perfume business. Large sums have been spent in running over to America and Paris, but, as far as I know, we are as far from obtaining royalties for perfumes as we were. I do not know what the position is today, neither do I know what liabilities he has incurred, but I understand we have spent over £3,000 with more liabilities to meet. If the policy pursued by the board some years ago with Rendigs had been re-instituted we should have been receiving a very considerable profit from the USA today.

At Mitchison's request, I have been to London on two occasions, and met Mr Dyas of Messrs Grossmith & Sons. What arrangements have been come to with Mr Dyas I do not know.

A short time ago I was called to attend a meeting regarding the development of an Australian company. I went to considerable trouble to put forward my views, which were for the benefit of the company, but I have never heard anything further from Mitchison as to what has happened.

The next thing I hear is that you are having a dress show in New York. In a letter to me Mitchison tells me that you have been told by various visitors that you ought to break into the American market, and that arrangements have been made for you to do so, but in my last long letter to you I advocated this in specific terms, and I have also advocated this on many occasions when I have seen you.

About eighteen months ago, by what I consider irregular methods, a motor car was bought from funds which we had in New York. I presume that this is now worn out.

I am surprised a new car has been ordered for which the sum of £1,800 has been paid. I think you have assumed that I have given approval for the purchase of this car, as would appear from your letter of 14 October last. This is the first intimation I have received from you that you received my letter of 21 September last. It would appear from your letter to me of 14 October last that you have construed my remarks to approve of the purchase of the new car. If you will refer to my letter of 11 October last you will see that I said that the acquisition of a car to a person of your presumed financial status should not present any financial difficulty. On the other hand, I also stated that this request did not fit in with the financial position of the company as generally put forth in my letter of 13 September last, to which I still await an adequate reply. No other part of my letter to you of 11 October last is in relation to your request for a car. I should like to know how it is that the car has been produced in so short a time, and whether the sum of £1,800 covers the cost of the new car without any other inducements, allowances or exchanges being made to get the car in advance of other people.

There is the question of bad debts. It would appear that a considerable sum has been set aside for these, amounting to over £1,000. I have queried with Miss Godley what steps have been taken to make these customers pay up. Several of the amounts owing to customers were dealt with by Miss Godley.

From what Miss Godley tells me, some of our customers are very disgruntled people, and well they may be. A Mrs Adams asked for two buttons, for which we sent her a bill for 11/- and 4/4 Purchase Tax. Another customer is very annoyed about her suit, and although we are allowing her 5 gns, she is still dissatisfied. A Mrs Merrick's suit was really an awful failure, and another lady was charged £18 for alterations, and we considered it advisable to write this amount off.

Miss Godley referred me to Mitchison for some of the other items, and he tells me that he considers that Mandel Brothers should get away with £81.18.0d. He says these are extremely good customers, but they are not very good customers when we have to lose £81.18.0d. There is an account of £180 against Berthold David. They are Brazilians, and, I understand, Brazilians are notoriously bad payers. Should we have accepted their orders when we knew the circumstances? Mrs Powell Weill owes us £97.8.3d. I asked if she was satisfied with her clothes, and Mitchison says definitely not. He says it is advisable to write off the amount owing and trusts that his answers to my queries are satisfactory.

I must refer again to the auditors' report. They confirm in item 7 that there is considerable extravagance and unnecessary expenditure and lack of supervision. That is obvious. In paragraphs 9 it is apparent that the auditors do not feel disposed to accept Mitchison's charges to expenses as satisfactory, and it is very serious when Mitchison has forgotten how the expenditure was incurred. This is very significant.

It may not surprise you to know that one of the extravagances of the company is in the purchase of whisky and wines. You have spent several thousand pounds since Mitchison came on the scene on this item alone. It is always the same story – entertaining prospective customers. You will know that our customers are ladies of high standing, and birth, etc., and I cannot visualise them drinking whisky and soda and the like to the extent covered by the charges to the company. I noticed in the accounts recently sent to me for signature that there was one for £151.0.9d., for gin, whisky and Champagne. This was ordered from A. Cottle & Son, of Sutton, and I agree with the auditors in wondering where all the whisky etc., bought by the company has been sent. The auditors state that they have had difficulty in obtaining this information, and I must assume that it has not been delivered to no. 26 Bruton Street. In item 11 of the auditors' report they state that £170 of wine etc. was given away to a customer. I should like to know who this customer was, and why the gift was made.

I notice from the auditors' report that Mitchison owes the company £401. The bulk of this is in connection with a transaction which is far from satisfactory.

A year or two ago, we had many thousands of pounds in America. This has been dissipated, and at present we have no funds whatever there.

I do not know what steps you are taking with regard to the show in America. I do not know whether you can get anyone to finance this or not, but, even if you can, we will be liable for a considerable amount of the expenses. I am all for a show of this description, and it should have been carried out long ago. The most serious aspect of this business is the question of where the money is coming from to finance it. Our resources are almost exhausted, and I am not surprised to hear that the Westminster Bank will not allow us increased credit facilities. Today our overdraft stands at £14,444, and I have cheques on my desk for signature amounting to £5,362. These have got to be paid. There is also another £2,000 to be paid for rates and P.A.Y.E.

I have warned you on many occasions that the position of the company has been steadily deteriorating, but apparently no notice has been taken of any warnings, and no steps have been taken to mend the position. There is no cost system in your works. The cost of production has gone up £10,000 in the last two or three years, and this, with all the money which you have been spending has brought the company to this sorry pass. Every week your position will get worse, because the sales are falling, and yet all the expenses are still being maintained.

You must accept some responsibility for the position in which we are now placed, because you have brought in a man of your own choice, who has shown himself to lack the necessary business acumen.

I consider the auditors' report to which I have referred to be of a most disturbing nature. I have never seen such a report put forward by the auditors of a company, and their condemnation of the management of the company as it is at present conducted.

As a director and shareholder, I cannot allow such a state of affairs to continue, and I ask that the General Manager, who, in my opinion, is mainly responsible for our present position, and for the day-to-day management of the concern, be dismissed forthwith.

I have purposely avoided embodying in this letter many aspects of expenditure which I think it politic to refrain from referring to at the moment, but, if there is to be any resistance to my request for Mr Mitchison's removal, I may feel compelled to deal with such matters in detail.

In this letter, it has not been very easy to put in regular order the various points which I wish to make. It has taken a large amount of time to delve into the various matters which I have recorded.

I understand that my removal as a Director from the Company and also that of Mr Medlam may be anticipated. I hope that this is only a rumour, and I would advise you to shelve this idea for the time being. When I feel that the company's interests are secure and a certain amount of prosperity restored to it, I will not stand in the way of fresh blood being grafted into the business, but, for the time being, I hope you will not develop your thoughts on this subject further.

Kind regards,
F.W. SMITH[31]

The subsequent twists and turns of the correspondence fill many files and make sad reading. Suffice it to say that Fred Smith eventually resigned from the board and new accountants and lawyers were taken on. It is as though Norman had an urge to self-destruct. As with many rather immature and otherwise talented men, he was not prepared to take good advice if unpalatable to him, particularly if it impinged on his entrenched lifestyle. Even though the company paid endlessly for expensive alternative opinions, they were ultimately disregarded until Norman's business and professional life were completely in the hands of his bankers, as was George.

For George the situation was two-edged. On the one hand, he earned considerable sums of money, which later took him out of his small South London house near Sutton and allowed him to take his wife Doris to the large house he acquired in Ticehurst, Sussex. He was able to bring up his children Norman and Clare there in comfort and space. Had he left the army and gone into another business it is conceivable that he would have done as well, but having stuck to Norman for very strong personal reasons he had to protect his friend and provider as powerfully as he could. As outlined by Fred Smith, Norman was George's major source of revenue. Norman had his reputation as a designer and his talent to carry him on if disaster struck. George had very little to offer in the business after five years, ten years or even thirty years later. He simply was *not* a good businessman as the files sadly reveal; he could initiate schemes but he could not follow them through or negotiate coherently at the very beginning – and nor could Norman. They desperately needed good independent legal and accountancy advice, which they usually rejected if they appeared to be losing any control of the business, so many others ultimately profited most from the Hartnell name.

Norman's own problems in the late 1940s were also compounded by his work for the stage. In May, he had been designing clothes for Yvonne Arnaud in *Traveller's Joy* at the Criterion.

'The sort of obstacles that arise in the theatre are a joy and a stimulant to him, for he never admits himself beaten,' remarked a columnist as, '[he] returns to his first love: the stage.' To sum up: he had dressed too few plays in his career, which was considered a loss to the theatre as he had such a feel for line, decoration and colour and had dressed most of the major stars. But, no fault of his, he had been associated with two flops in a row: *Champagne for Delilah* starring Googie Withers (9 June 1949, ran seventeen days) and *Two Dozen Red Roses* with Evelyn Laye (25 May for thirty-two days). Inevitably the comment was, 'I'm no drama critic, but I know a well-dressed show when I see one.'[32] In attempting another variation of his skills and trying to tap a source of revenue, Norman became associated with flops, through no fault of his own.

Luckily, Norman was able to turn his hand to all forms of dress design. He was asked to submit designs for women's uniforms for the Women's Royal Army Corps (the former ATS) in 1947 and in 1949, after almost endless negotiations, a choice was to be made by the King from anonymously submitted designs by Norman, Creed and Molyneux (muddled in his dating in *Silver and Gold* this is put at a date before his Red Cross uniforms).

Dame Mary Tyrwhitt, acting head of the Women's Corps, gave him other necessary technical and military advice. Norman was fascinated by every detail and realised that, as with Utility dresses, his design must be adaptable to many shapes and sizes. The skirt itself had to be wearable in many conditions and was made with two panels cut on the straight and two side panels on the cross, and even the four seams were designed to keep the costs to a minimum. The design of the tunic was inspired by an Hussar's uniform, and Norman examined every potential detail. The deep bottle-green colour was to be a background for brass buttons and black or brown leather gloves and shoes. Tan was also used for a sash, borrowed from some Guards' regiments. In short, it was this carefully researched, highly practical solution that was chosen by the King. Norman Hartnell made the first one for the Colonel-in-Chief the Princess Royal – Princess Mary, Countess of Harewood (the King's sister). The design was also used in a different colour combination for the uniforms of Queen Alexandra's Royal Army Nursing Corps. Norman attributed this work as adding to the strain on his health at the end of the war – but in his memoirs, he muddled the Girl Guide uniform with this enterprise undertaken three years later.[33]

The 1948 Ascot had revived interest in grander summer daytime dresses as in pre-war days and although coupons and Austerity continued with restricted use of materials, Norman's workrooms were kept busy. Similarly, the summer Garden Parties at Buckingham Palace replacing the sumptuous pre-war Courts brought a demand for dresses from mothers and debutante daughters, as did the increasing number of dances and balls. The post-war levels of spending were still not such that Hartnell could make enough profit from these occasions, nor were the fur-coat orders sufficient, although profit margins were good. Restrictions on the import of certain furs added to the difficulties. Furthermore, the renewed attractions of Paris where shortages seemed invisible, drew many fashionable women to the couture Houses there in spite of draconian currency regulations.

Norman's appeal to younger women was enhanced by Princess Margaret's light wardrobe for an Italian holiday in 1949 when she wore a black tulle evening dress, although Molyneux was also designing for her. Nanty in New York copied the tiered dress for sale in Saks Fifth Avenue and aroused more interest in Hartnell. The press loved the idea of what was termed a 'fashion war' between designers and critically examined every aspect of the Princess's appearance; Mrs Peacock of H & M Rayne named Princess Margaret 'her favourite customer'. She wore half-inch platform soles and ankle straps in size 3½ although they were considered by some ladies as 'not quite nice', even though the Queen and Princess Elizabeth sometimes wore them.[34] To balance the resulting overall dress silhouette, elaborate hats by Aage Thaarup were worn.

Popular interest in changing fashions is emphasised by a topical *Daily Herald* cartoon published during Ascot week depicting a crowd of female race-goers with their backs to the track peering through binoculars, the caption reading, 'I make it Hartnell still leading with Victor Steibel [sic], Dior, Paquin and Schiaparelli all close up!'[35] Norman was indeed a household name and in his many-faceted role as an all-round designer, his design of a navy-blue light wool 'coat-frock' was worn by British women delegates to the Stockholm Second World Festival of Gymnastics in July 1949. He did, however, reject the offer of designing overalls for a large laundry chain, no doubt thinking of his Royal Warrant status. He received more worldwide publicity when being photographed in this salon with Hollywood film star Linda Christian, Mrs Tyrone Power, who commissioned a 'blessed event' trousseau of ten items for $2,400 from him and she received some wonderfully embroidered three-quarter 'tent' coats and one embroidered and paste-encrusted blue 'jewel coat' photographed for all *Vogue* editions.

The summer parade of the Hartnell autumn collection reflected practicality and included reversible coats; these also appeared in his winter collections, still an official 'export collection'. In temperatures of 90°F and with an eye to the shrinkages in private incomes and purchases of 'one occasion' dresses, Norman produced 'Turncoat' – a green, black and white check country coat that reversed into a black town coat – a 'chameleon act' as one journalist described Norman with more truth than she realised.[36]

By September 1948, Norman was still receiving headlines in the American press due to his use of the Pyramid silhouette. But the dress causing the most interest in America was an evening creation with a black velvet bodice, the enormous rose silk frilled skirt embroidered and decorated with 144 roses satisfying the enduring love of romantic full-skirted dresses.

Norman could so often be relied on to steal a fashion headline, when American papers were reporting an alleged 'Royal Row' between the Queen and Princess Margaret over the low décolletage (described as a 'plunging neckline') of a Dior white tulle evening dress ('Mom cries No!') which Hartnell reportedly 'hoisted. Whether Margaret pouted was not known here.'[37]

Clearly Princess Margaret and her fashion sense were big news from which Norman could profit as her clothes were widely discussed. The Dior mannequin who modelled the dress was interviewed and indicated just what the wearing of such a dress entailed at the time. 'I could hardly breathe, encased in whalebone and that hoop around the hips. I couldn't even sit down in the thing,' exclaimed Miss de Boisson. Norman seems to have managed things a little better, for the famous black velvet crinoline worn by the Queen for the 1948 sitting suggested by Cecil Beaton, who used a specially devised Winterhalter setting, was subsequently worn without any problem to an evening reception at the V&A. The Queen was photographed sitting comfortably, smiling and talking.

For the State Visit of President Auriol of France in March 1950, Norman was again at great pains to prove his versatility as a designer to the Queen and the Princesses, fully aware that the French and international press were poised for comment. He again proved his talent by designing coordinating dresses, the Queen appearing especially magnificent in a white satin crinoline with an irregularly petal-tiered skirt enhanced with topaz, silver and gold embroidery for the Covent Garden Gala. One journalist wrote: 'He'll be putting embroidery in the hair next!'

Norman was amused to learn from the wife of the French Ambassador, Madame Massigli, that Madame Auriol had telephoned to find out how long the Queen's dress would be for the President's arrival at Victoria Station; the incidents of contrasting lengths with Madame Lebrun in 1938 and 1939 had left an indelible mark on diplomats' minds![38]

Relations between the Palace press officers and Hartnell could be tricky. George was quoted in *The Observer*: 'Statements to the press have to be passed by Buckingham Palace. Their press attaché is a junior Molotov.'[39] George again proved his curiously unreliable nature, but Norman often had to smooth over lapses and leaks of information attributed to himself with Commander Richard Colville, an ably fierce defender of protocol.

Norman's old friend Blake came to the rescue when *The Music Teacher* asked him for his strongest musical impression of 1949.

> I have been charmed by Tchaikovsky's Third Symphony the 'Polish'; Eileen Joyce's interpretation of Grieg's Piano Concerto in A was a masterly performance and very much impressed me; and the book of music that has appealed to me most is 'Ten Composers' by Neville Cardus, more especially the chapters on Elgar and César Franck. Vaughan Williams' Sixth Symphony I found as fascinating as a rare tapestry.[40]

Over the next two decades of his life, Norman gave many similar 'choices'; in fact, he rarely found time to read much more than magazines or newspapers and the erudite Blake often received a useful cheque for his efforts.

Mr and Mrs Cracknell, Norman's housekeeper and butler-cum-odd-job-man remembered Norman listening to music with pleasure on his radiogram – usually a musical such as *South Pacific* and he also took many children's comics for the jokes, afterwards handing them on to their daughter. High intellectual pursuits were alien to Norman, although he wished to be thought well educated and certainly enjoyed his client Miss Joyce's playing and visits to the opera with Blake.[41]

An equally typical evening was suggested: 'Have just got two tickets for Hermione Sin-Bold (i.e. Gingold) for Monday. I expect to expect you sometime on Monday. We may stay at Tower House or I may whisk you off through the purple night to Lovel Dene cheerio, Bish.'[42]

Things went sadly from bad to worse for Blake through the 1950s. As a divorced man, he failed to obtain a country living and was for a time chaplain at Romsey College. 'The Headmaster's new secretary lacks a chin; she appears to have everything else, but *NOT* a chin! As ever (almost) Blake.'[43] Later, as Chaplain of Bristol Prison, he often found the depressing surroundings and his life almost unbearable and relied on friends, more especially Norman, to cheer him up, which they usually did.

By 1950, the fashion talking point revolved around a new version of 1920s dresses. Hermione Gingold thought they were 'wonderful, all my old props'.

Norman, of course, hated the thought. 'Extremes are unbecoming – the world may be foolish but British women are not.'[44] He cast a weary eye at the new Paris Collections and showed his latest designs at Ciro's nightclub at the end of March 1950, whilst Dior staged a London showing on 25 April, when the fashion historian and collector Doris Langley Moore organised the event at the Savoy Hotel.

The wife of the French Ambassador, Madame Massigli, had previously arranged for a private showing of the collection featuring the famous New Look at the French Embassy for the Queen, Princess Margaret, the Duchess of Kent and her sister Princess Olga of Yugoslavia. Dior wrote of the occasion and his impressions of the Queen, whose elegance made a great impression on him, mentioning that her mauve dress and draped hat would have been inconceivable on anyone else but were exactly right for her and that they were the best designs to enhance her. This was certainly also intended as a compliment to Norman, whom Dior admired. Dior also mentioned that Princess Margaret visited his salon in Paris at a later date. This was the cause of considerable press comment, when she bought at Dior.

However, there was some further embarrassment for Norman. He had viewed the collection as a guest on the day before and now went to see Dior to tell him how much he admired it. This gesture of friendship then backfired. On suggesting that he might mention to the Queen that she would enjoy viewing the collection, Dior had to explain what had happened. But Norman, remarked Dior, had 'extreme good manners' and the two enjoyed friendly relations until Dior's untimely death. (Strangely, Dior was also muddled with dates in his autobiography and thought this occurred in the autumn of 1947).

After viewing the Savoy show, Norman told journalists, 'Now I know why busmen are always taking holidays. This was a busman's holiday for me and I loved every minute of it. The show was sheer beauty.'

Dior later paid Norman a great compliment at the reception: 'It was the crinolines you designed for the Queen to wear in Paris in 1939 which inspired my evening dresses and the New Look.'[45]

CHAPTER THIRTEEN

Increasing indignation and resentment

T owards the end of 1950, Norman was interviewed in his salon by a Canadian journalist, who found him wearing 'a loose suit, aesthetic tie and soft suede shoes.'

> He talks about dresses with the aplomb of a society woman in accents that echo the cynical brittle London of the 1920s. Putting the tips of his fingers together or spreading his hands in effervescent gestures he patters, 'It's really *too* adorable . . . I think it's so funny!' He's not so vapid as he pretends.[1]

Norman was now approaching fifty and was certainly not vapid at a time when most men take stock of their lives and think about future retirement. In 1950, being fifty years old was no longer being young and scarcely still middle-aged at a time when living beyond seventy was considered unusual.

Whilst Norman battled with the financial problems besetting Norman Hartnell Ltd, he undoubtedly took stock of his life. Retirement was not possible, even if he had desired it, and he had to work hard on a variety of schemes to make the funding of daily life possible. At the end of 1950, newspaper criticism of his designs for the Queen had begun and were not confined to the English press. The Spanish and German press weighed in, as did *France Soir* with a photograph of the Queen in a quite remarkable wrap-over draped dress. The diagonal slant of this fringed to a depth of twelve inches and touched the floor beyond the hemline. With this she wore a feather hat, high platform-soled shoes and carried in her gloved hands a decorated clutch bag.

Norman's subliminal absorption of dress detail led to some interesting designs for the Queen, some apparently based on Travis Banton's pre-war film costumes, notably for Marlene Dietrich and Mae West, both of whom were clients during their respective visits to London, and both presented him with signed photographs of themselves in tribute to his designing skills.

Another variant of the side draped design arousing criticism of the Queen's appearance was a floral day dress with a long floating floor-length side panel and the *Sunday Pictorial* demanded, 'Who is dressing the Queen like this?' It was naturally no secret and Norman said, 'They deliberately picked out the worst picture taken that day. Everybody photographs badly at some time.' This was a new beginning to the subsequent regular tabloid journalism aimed at increasing circulation. It is still prevalent today in the twenty-first century.

Norman's advancing years were underlined by himself: 'Nowadays I'm so occupied with *people*, everybody from high society to the messenger boy at the back door, that all I want when I get home are a hot bath and a whisky and soda.' Of his designs for the Queen, he said, 'The Queen has no wish to be a leader of fashion. She dresses to please herself. She tells me what she would like and I make it for her,' although the process naturally emanated from Norman's response to requests from her dresser for various types of clothing, often for particular occasions. Norman always responded with a selection of sketches with fabric snippets attached for the Queen's selection and comments, most usually written in pencil on the returned sketches.

In 1949, Norman had spent large sums on redecorating Lovel Dene with Gothick details, especially to some of the windows. He now spent most of his time there and let The Tower House to Edward Rayne. The cost of two establishments was too much for him, as were the staffing problems. He also preferred to work in the peaceful surroundings of Lovel Dene and took pleasure in his boxer dog Sugar Ray, named after the boxer, and in his studio. New staff cottages had been designed for him by Gerald Lacoste, but building restrictions only allowed renovation of the adjoining stable block, not rebuilding as he wished. The gardens were put in order and the adjoining small lake dredged out for his swans, named Swan and Edgar, a jokey reference to the then famous department store at Piccadilly Circus. His summer post-racing garden parties during Ascot week became well known and attracted many friend and well-known clients, such as the then Begum Aga Khan.

During 1951, negotiations with possible Australian and South African licensees occurred and a new manager, John Coyle, was appointed to deal with such matters. A forest of paperwork was generated as Jack Barregar in South Africa and Tom Gurr in Australia both attempted to create mutually beneficial businesses. Norman and George spent enormous amounts of time and money on each aspect of every detail, and eventually received some financial remuneration for themselves and the company throughout the 1950s and 1960s.

George went on business to Australia in June and was immediately characterised by the press as 'sturdy mustached Captain Mitchison' and he stated, 'Australian girls seem to be especially designed by nature for showing clothes to advantage.'

Australian Judy Barraclough had been a Hartnell mannequin and it now became a clever press ploy to hire both South African and Australian girls, leading to extra press coverage in potentially valuable markets. George was in Sydney because the postponed Royal Tour of Australia was still planned; the Queen and Princess Margaret's clothes were already a cause of much speculation. George then unwittingly became the butt of a press commotion when he wore a silk scarf round his neck and was then asked to leave the lounge of an Adelaide Hotel for not wearing a tie. Seven university students read about the incident and turned up some days later at the hotel in shorts, but wearing ties, and were still refused service. One of them carried forty-seven ties, so the whole thing luckily blew over as a joke. In fact, George was actually there to secretly investigate the establishment of an Australian Norman Hartnell business.[2]

A transcript of just one boardroom meeting gives a complete picture of how matters were discussed at 26 Bruton Street and the personalities of those involved:

Notes taken at the Meeting held at 26 Bruton Street, on Friday, 13 April 1951, in connection with the Australian Newspaper Service, Sydney.

In attendance:
Mr. Norman Hartnell
Major Cecil Wills
R. Fearnley-Whittingstall
Capt. G. Mitchison

Friday, 13 April 1951

Mr Fearnley-Whittingstall. This Australian contract is now out of date, of course. We have seen the Australian letter just received, which confirms that they are still anxious to go ahead. (This letter is from the Aus. Newspaper Service.)

23 November 1944 set the scene – but it has lapsed.

We want to write to Kennedy (Associated Newspapers) and say that the matter has been discussed at a meeting of the directors and these are our views . . .

Hordern's appear to be suitable. Do we go into the 'Marble Arch' quarter of Sydney? If not, where?

Mr G. Mitchison. Property in Australia has become very expensive. If premises had been available, the Australian Newspaper Service would have taken them some time ago. This has been the stumbling block.

If we cannot have a building to ourselves, why should we not have space in a store?

Hordern's is downtown, away from the up-town smart area, and two or three blocks away from David Jones – a smart, modern store.

F.W. If we are agreeable to taking space in Hordern's, they would like to smarten up their place and get back the carriage trade they had. There is an excellent chance of getting into Hordern's. Are we going to take a chance and start there, or do we insist upon premises elsewhere?

Mr Norman Hartnell. This has been the cause of the delay – not being able to get premises.

F.W. In principle then, we are in favour of Hordern's?

Major Wills. It is something to be in an established building.

F.W. Hordern's will give us free publicity, and once we are established under their roof, it is up to them to do their best to see that Hartnell's get a good kick-off.

The next point is participation.

From my notes of the interview with Kennedy on 19 December 1950, I understand that one third of the equity goes to Hartnell's and finance from the Associated Newspaper Service to the tune of £60,000 or £70,000.

£60,000

30,000 Ordinary

30,000 Preference – 5% . . . 6% (?)

£10,000 for Hartnell

£20,000 for Financier Ordinaries

Equity buy 30,000 of Ordinary Shares.

You can insist that instead of getting one third of the Ordinary, you should get £10,000 in cash (so many Preference Shares). But they will probably not play.

Major Wills There is no trouble in payment of dividends from Australia to England?

F.W. No, not at the moment.

Now the basis on which the general approach is to be made. I think that if George is to go out to Australia, he should be reinforced from the beginning and he ought to take with him a drawn-up agreement – to be agreed upon and signed. If George goes out with no instructions whatsoever and he only has to listen, they are going to put over a number of varying schemes on which he will have to get instructions.

If he goes out and says – 'This is the draft of the agreement which Norman Hartnell wants to see concluded, although certain modifications may have to be put forward. If the agreement is to be altered, instructions will have to be obtained from England, so do not make more alterations than necessary as we shall never get anywhere.'

A minor point. It is only fair that George's expenses are paid by the other side, no matter what.

It is contained in the agreement of 1944, to which Mr Kennedy referred, that this question is in order.

Mr Hartnell can say – 'Referring to my letter of April, I am sending George Mitchison out on the understanding, of course, that your group will be responsible for his expenses.'

G. Mitchison Is that quite right? It is the principle of the thing. They really did dig their toes in and are quite likely to say – 'If this is the attitude, our people may think you are out for all you can get. After all, we are taking a chance and we may lose.'

F.W. I think we ought to be fair within the limits of cordiality and not leave it as an afterthought and cable – 'Of course you will be paying George's expenses?'

N. Hartnell The Australian people are spending £60,000. Cannot we spend another £100 or £200? We do not want to appear mean to start off with.

F.W. If we can avoid being landed with the expenses, so much the better. Hartnell's will be responsible for George's salary while he is out in Australia.

N. Hartnell It is crying rather poor if we cannot afford expenses while he is there, and not quite nice.

F.W. Terms of the letter will have to be approved, so let me carry my suggestion of expenses.

N. Hartnell We do not want to turn the Australian people against us.

Major Wills 'We understand that Mr Mitchison's fare will be paid out and back by the Aust. Co. which we much appreciate.' Could we put it like that? If nothing is said about expenses, perhaps they will arrange the question with George when he gets there. We do not want them to think we are out for all we can get – most certainly not.

F.W. If we send Mitchison out and pay his salary, this is a charge on us during the time he is there.

G. Mitchison I think the third is the limit to which they will go.

Major Wills Why not leave the question of expenses unmentioned, and it would be a nice gesture on their part if they will pay them.

G. Mitchison I do not like this attitude. I would rather not go with cap in hand. 'I am to be paid this' and 'We hope you will pay that'.

F.W. No such thing. You must have some understanding. The other side might say 'Who is going to pay him?'

This is because it is an ad hoc arrangement which must be set out in a letter, the forerunner of a draft agreement.

N. Hartnell Surely they will take it for granted that we are paying Mitchison's salary?

G. Mitchison They are taking a big chance and may lose it, so why should we haggle over a few pounds whilst I am there? I would much prefer not to go.

N. Hartnell I think the terms you suggest are niggardly and quite appalling.

F.W. Supposing no business resulted at all and you received a bill from Australia for expenses, say, £1200. Who is going to pay for them?

Major Wills I think they offer expenses in the agreement. We do not want to offend – you must be businesslike, after all.

F.W. I see the expenses are mentioned in the agreement.

Major Wills We now understand that Mr Hartnell, or his representative, will have his fare and expenses paid. Well then, we must repeat the phrases in the agreement, which is certainly a long time ago.

F.W. Rough outline of a draft agreement.
  Capital structure discussed and personnel angle to be gone into.
  Australia will have one director of the company, and we shall have one. The board shall not exceed five.
  As far as service is concerned, I assume that we shall offer to lend the services of George for a specified period, not exceeding one or two years, and they will have to put him on their charge.
  The Aus. company will say – 'You must let us have him for six months or a year' (or whatever it may be).

N. Hartnell I thought he would go for just a short time at first.

F.W. I cannot see the Aus. Co. will let George go until the King and Queen leave Australia. 'All the crescendo to build up – we must now organise ourselves. Do not take Mitchison away just yet. We want the benefit of his views. Where do we go from here?'

While the King and Queen are in Australia, people will go into the store. When the King and Queen leave, the Aus. Co., will be able to sit back and say, 'We sold so many dresses and made so much turnover. Now we want to keep the customers who came to us and we want George Mitchison to see us over our teething troubles.'

N. Hartnell I will not allow George to go for all that time. And it may not be convenient for him as far as his domestic arrangements are concerned.

Surely they will let their own manager take over?

Major Wills Norman may not be able to spare George, and they may suggest someone else.

F.W. I am not suggesting that we should specify the exact length of George's stay, but we must have some idea of our own.

N. Hartnell We will have to go out to Australia alternately.

F.W. Are there any other points we want to take particular note of?

We understand that Hartnell will not commit himself (or representative?) to a visit more than once a year. Any other visit optional.

This seems a reasonable agreement as it stands, but what of the set-up of the company; the engagement of staff for instance. The English Co. should have complete say as to who is to hold the key positions with regard to fitting and cutting, etc. It should be laid down that we have the choice of choosing our people for such positions as mentioned. This is important. [This ruling was endorsed by Major Wills who considered it a most important point.]

F.W. Any other points?

N. Hartnell The Australian Group are out to please me in every way.

F.W. I am sure they will welcome you setting out concisely what you want, and help you in every way to make the thing a go.

G. Mitchison Raised the perfume question.

F.W. The position is not too clear. We still have the French Co. to explore.

G. Mitchison Concerning Australia. You have a million and a half people at the moment, and right now a majority of them very rich. You get a small clientele who will pay any price, but you get the vast population paying about £25 to £30. I feel when we are firmly established, mass production can come into the picture. Myers and David Jones are interested and know there is a market for mass production. We ought to exploit that market as well. It is rather like Hartnell here with Frederick Starke (models at £35).

F.W. The Australian Co. can sell its name, but Norman, as a remedy, if he thinks that the Australian Co. is making too free a use of his name, can sever his name from the company. We must prove distinction between Norman Hartnell Ltd, and Norman Hartnell to Australia.
Suppose £90,000 in rent, wages and materials. To earn £100,000, your profit is £10,000, but if you load up with various managers etc. whose salaries total £7,500, your profit is only £2,500. After all, the company cannot declare a bigger dividend than is recommended and is available.

G. Mitchison. This is my own idea (following) and I do not want a big board meeting to take place on my return and questions asked, such as – 'Who is the fool who suggested that?' I would like various ideas now before I go out. Must royalty be paid on the turnover? etc., etc.
£60–75,000 Preference Shares bearing interest at 5 or 6% and the owners of the Preference Shares should be allowed to purchase the same number of Ordinary Shares at 1/- each. Mr Hartnell to be allotted one third of the ordinary Shares free.
If some better proposition does crop up besides Hordern's, what

shall we do? Does every little thing come back here? How much latitude are we going to allow in the organisation of affairs by the Aust. Co.?

F.W. Large responsibility to the man on the spot.

Major Wills They say they will find premises. If George approves them, surely that is alright?

F.W. Once the agreement is drafted and approved over here, yes. 'We have put in an equity of 40% to us here.' It is alright for him to settle for 33%. 'We must control the appointment of a head fitter and head tailor.' It is alright for him to settle for the appointment of the head fitter, only, etc., etc.

G. Mitchison Mr Hartnell to have the power of veto on the question of the engagement of executives. This clause should be embodied in any contract that may be made with employees.

The following snatches of conversation were also recorded:

Royalty on profit? George to have instructions and this should be included in the agreement.

In view of no dividend being distributed, royalty on an agreed amount will be payable.

Director's fee or designer's fee?

Should royalty be paid on the turnover and not on profits? This means something, as where there may be no profits, there will certainly be a turnover.

If the business does not run at a profit, we will have to pay out royalty on our losses.

Can you have a third of the equity and a small percentage of the profit?

Suggest one third of the equity and a guaranteed minimum dividend of, say, X pounds.

Australian Income Tax to be considered.[3]

Fred Smith clearly thought that George could be prised out of the London business and had no realisation of the strong emotional attachment between Norman and George, even at this date. The fact that George was married with a family clearly masked the real background to his presence at Hartnell.

Later in October, the fashion for square dance skirts began with great publicity for Princess Elizabeth and Prince Philip in Canada and then the USA. There was an added pang of worry for Norman, as the younger Hardy Amies was now also designing for the Princess. Most fashion writers were however more interested in Princess Margaret's five days in Paris in November; Norman was gratified to see some of his designs worn by her and one of his more unusual evening dresses for Princess Elizabeth worn by her for a photograph forming a *Life* colour cover. Norman himself went to New York in November to discuss perfume and design promotions.[4]

Apart from the opening of a belated boutique on the ground floor at Bruton Street, something French Houses had successfully initiated pre-war, the major event of Norman's year was the catastrophic estrangement from his sister Phyllis – Topsy. She had loyally supported him from the very beginning of his life, then in 1923 when he established his first House, and subsequently in all his endeavours. But as with John Pleydell over the question of scent negotiations and the ownership of Lovel Dene, so Norman had begun to question his own sister's financial interest in the affairs of both Norman Hartnell and his own personal finances. After some unpleasant exchanges, she wrote to him:

> If you honestly believe your statements as to moneys are the true facts, then you have a very legitimate grouse, and have for years, *must* have, felt a justifiable and increasing indignation and resentment at what has happened and is happening.
>
> But . . . they are not the true facts . . . if you have no objection I will ask banks, the lawyers and such gentleman to dig up, way back to 1921, records of what did happen. [1921 was the date of their mother's death and their inheritance of her property in Streatham.] It will then be seen clearly to what extent anyone is indebted to the other. That seems the only fair solution I think, don't you?

As far as these large war damage cheques I am supposed to have been paid, I am doing my best to trace them, they have never been cashed . . . that *I* can trace. Here is my most earnest promise to put right anything which I have done wrong or accepted without paying you your share. [They were now selling the properties as they both needed money.]

About the scent I quite agree its potentialities as a money-making idea and I have already told Fearnley-Whittingstall the exact position regarding your wishes in this matter and my promise to you *I want no part of your scent profits* and say again, here and now, take it, have it all, as you have asked and I have promised. But as a director of the firm supplying the funds to launch it, I am dragged unwillingly into discussions and must take at least an intelligent interest in seeing where the money goes – [but is] the game worth the candle?

I do agree with you let us keep board meetings amiable and constructive . . . [and] a little happier than at present. Because frankly you can't go on like this, Norman. *Somebody* must manage your shop, and try as you will, you cannot do it all yourself.

Decide with your advisors a policy to cope with the falling sales and let them cut ruthlessly. I do not ask for any say in this but will not shirk from giving it if required. . . . Somehow you must get your *facts* right before you evolve your theories. It is far better . . . our differences are aired outside board meetings. I do agree the clash of personal likes and dislikes and ganging up generally are deplorable and utterly defeating when the main idea is to run a business as efficiently as possible. We will iron out details, Norman, and the pundits will find out who owes who, and how much . . . Pick anybody you like . . . but it must be on record somewhere that my 'very sensible appetite for money' is not the prime reason for my actions, nor does it 'counter-balance' my affection for you. Get a referee, and see what *they* think, and see if *their* sister would have gone on sinking all they had, without question, until it had all gone. That's, of course, only *my* idea of what took place and I might easily be wrong. But it *must* be settled once and for all. Otherwise you are perfectly justified in all you do and feel. So long, dear boy, you're quite right, *we* mustn't quarrel, Love from Maude.[5] [Maude was also a nickname.]

Another crucial milestone had been reached in his life. He remained obdurate.

In August, Phyllis wrote again: 'I have found this, does it help you?' This was a basis for an agreement that Phyllis be an employee rather than a director at £200 a year plus travelling and hotel expenses as a representative, and have the right to reduced prices on clothes bought from the company.

> May I point out that it costs the firm considerably less than my commission on the sales I bring in, than you pay your chars, than you spend on cigarettes. I would suggest it's well worth the price and fulfils your dearest wish. And since you indicated some time ago so unmistakeably that my services could be dispensed with as director, I have every hope you will see the sense . . . I have sent cheques (for rents from Streatham owing from 1948). You may be agreeable to not cashing the one for £10.0s.0d. At the time, I asked you if you were willing that I should retain at least part of this amount towards the expenses and fuss of getting it *at all*. If you've now changed your mind, well life seems to be getting like that! (My battle in 1948 produced £50 p.a. extra ever since) . . . Love from Maude.[6]

By November a settlement had been reached and Topsy wrote:

> I am, as you asked, repeating my promise to you to send in no report (to the directors) and to take no further part in guiding your affairs. You have nothing to fear from me.
>
> All I ask is to be allowed to withdraw now with no further obstruction or refusal to my requests on retiring – I am hoping your advisers will decide that these are not unreasonable, and, in view of your promise that we should leave them to settle these terms and you would agree to any practical solution. I feel sure you will see that it is only fair to decide on them and carry them out now . . . this unpleasant business. Best love dear Phyllis.'[7]

By 24 January 1951, Phyllis had resigned her directorship in Norman Hartnell Ltd. After nearly thirty years, her relationship with the company was ended, except as an 'outside representative', her shares were sold to Major and Mrs Cecil Wills, and, most importantly for her, she was no longer a 'joint and several' guarantor of the Hartnell overdraft. The loyal Major and Mrs Wills were to help keep the House afloat for two decades, but the value of their shares was never fully recovered by their heirs at the end of their lives and dividends dwindled over the successive trading years.

One point in Phyllis's last letter to Norman on finances mentioned that she had a 'scheme for raising money to rescue Lovel Dene for you on the lines I discussed'. As Norman's own borrowings were outstripping his assets, his bank wanted him to sell the house and raise some capital, and eventually the company bought it and ran it for him until business losses were such that he eventually lost it.[8] But that was a distant event in the early 1950s, although far from inconceivable.

The February edition of British *Vogue* was entitled 'The Britannia Number' and at last the editors gave a whole-hearted clarion call for British fashion unusually heralding the London Collections as the most wearable in the world. Norman had himself described his life as designer-cum-businessman schizophrenic. His health was now constantly causing concern and the sanctuary of Lovel Dene was increasingly necessary for him. He relished the calm atmosphere in which he could design away from the hustle and bustle of Bruton Street. In spite of very personal upsets within the business, which recall the coldly intimidating Norman remembered by the young Angela Goldsbrough, Norman continued to pull surprising rabbits out of hats for his collections and for individual clients wanting exclusive designs, including the royal commissions. The early 1950s were marked by the fashion for increasingly close-fitting suits and skirts suitable for the slim women, who still used a wide variety of corseting, and the pencil-slim skirt was a popular alternative to the wider skirted styles on offer.

One of Norman's most publicised clients in that year was Mrs Denys Lowson, wife of the Lord Mayor of London, for whom Norman created picture dresses in a simplified version of his royal designs. The genius inherent in his varied designs was visible when the ten members of IncSoc put on a fashion show for the Queen and Princess Margaret at the London house of their President Lady Rothermere, the palatial Warwick House next door to St James's Palace. Whilst the six dresses of each member were shown in the drawing room, the designer concerned sat there in turn next to the Queen to explain the details. Hartnell's pencil-slim white tulle sheath of encrusted brilliants with floating tulle panels – 'Jack Frost' – was a predictable *coup de théâtre*, especially as the long-gloved mannequin wore a tiara and had Lenthéric 'Rocket Red' lips.

The State Banquet of November 1950 for Queen Juliana of The Netherlands had already displayed contrasting skirt widths, and this was repeated at a Palace State Banquet in May 1951 for the Danish King and Queen, the Duchess of Kent wearing a slim dress with a fishtail, and the Queen resplendent in a contrasting crinoline gown. Both dresses came from Hartnell, for the Duchess's favourite designer Edward Molyneux closed his London House in the summer of 1950 and thereafter the Duchess often patronised Hartnell.[9]

Norman had need of all his designing versatility. In 1950, Hardy Amies had made clothes for the Canadian Tour and USA Visit undertaken by Princess Elizabeth, after the Princess had admired Amies clothes worn by Lady Alice Egerton. After the tour both Princesses had a private showing of Hardy Amies' latest collection at his House in Savile Row.[10]

In his first autobiography of 1954, *Just So Far*, the young Hardy Amies stressed that he was most attracted to the style of Molyneux, and having trained in the steps of Digby Morton at the 'tailored House of Lachasse',[11] he was always most interested in the construction and cut of clothes, something that was not the first thing Norman chose to emphasise in his designing. Day dresses or suits were not Norman's first love, as his later assistant Ian Thomas stressed, and this was the first time the Princess had desired darker shades of fabrics from Norman. Hardy Amies had much success with his use of darker colours, especially for suits, and this made Norman nervous.

Whilst many day dresses for the Queen were elaborate, as we have seen, the two Princesses were of a younger and slim generation with an individual sense of their own style distilled from current fashion. For the Queen, unconsciously or not, Norman, the avid film-goer, reworked many ideas of his old friend Travis Banton, so that the dress worn by the Queen for the opening of Parliament in South Africa and Rhodesia in 1947 noticeably resembles in outline the hourglass creations Banton designed for his client Mae West in her films of almost a decade earlier.

Similarly, a comparison of photographs also reveals the Queen attending a late 1940s wedding wearing a version of a remarkably similar side draped dress designed for Marlene Dietrich by Banton in 1936 for the film *Desire*. Ian Thomas was not sure if this was a coincidence. Norman had a remarkable photographic memory for detail and could rework ideas lodged in his mind with great facility without necessarily remembering the context in which he had seen them, especially for his star client. As we have seen, he not only had an interest in historic styles and fashions, resulting in his later book

Royal Courts of Fashion, but also in the minutiae of military uniforms. He regularly visited picture galleries in search of further inspiration. A television documentary of the late 1980s showed the Queen looking at a Dutch seventeenth-century painting by de Hooch of a woman in a flowing dress and remarking that Norman Hartnell had once suggested something similar to her. He was a man who revelled in dress design of all eras, and the more elaborate or complicated the design, the more he felt tested and elated when he put his own design to it.

Some of his specially commissioned dresses of this period were made for use in fabric and lace manufacturers' advertisements, including a famous series of clothes for Atkinsons' scents and soaps. On these he lavished great care, particularly on the unique embroideries. For A.C. Gill & Co., manufacturers of Nottingham lace, he created a skirt so voluminous and stiffly encrusted with paillettes and beads that no one could have manoeuvred it into a car. Where are all these garments now? Although his clothes were usually worn by very thrifty Englishwomen until they fell apart, it was noted by a resigned Hardy Amies that his best friend was the moth. This was so unlike their European cousins that all London dressmakers included this amongst their reasons for fearing bankruptcy.

In August, Princess Margaret became twenty-one and gratifyingly posed for Cecil Beaton's photographs in one of the three evening dresses ordered from Norman. He was now successfully negotiating with the newsworthy Parisian milliner Claude Saint-Cyr to open a branch in 26 Bruton Street, for his old friend Kate Day had left to open her own business nearby at 99 Mount Street Mayfair.

The appeal of exclusive French couture is eternal as an article in *The Economist* of August 1951 made clear. 'Haute Couture in London' explained some of the problems peculiar to such businesses in Britain at a time when the Inland Revenue statistics showed exactly how miserably impoverished Britain had become. Although the figures and opinions given were all averages and perhaps highly debatable, they underlined the facts that manufacturing costs were much higher in London due to the unaltered shortage of truly skilled staff. A fully trained Parisian seamstress earned about £5 a week, her London counterpart about £8.10s.0d. and yet an evening dress in Paris cost roughly £300, whilst in London it was £125 plus 22.5% Purchase Tax for home consumption. Yet a Paris House was able to spend around £10,000 promoting each collection, while an English House could only spend about £2,000, and this disparity underlined why France could achieve so much more not least in publicity.[12]

The London shortage of highly skilled labour was acute. In April, Charles Creed with a London House and a Paris business underlines a problem common to both capitals when writing to Norman desperately looking for tailors and dress-hands.[13]

One way in which Norman was potentially able to increase Hartnell income lay in the sale of ready-to-wear clothing, and despite his court case against Berkertex he was still under contract to them. They had the astute headline-capturing notion of producing ready-to-wear garments and selling them in Paris. Au Printemps thus became the Parisian outlet selling dresses designed by the acclaimed Royal Dressmaker from £5 upwards. They were popular and made in trim styles using both corduroy and wool.[14]

Topsy wrote to him: 'Well done, ducks. And oh, these chic Parisiennes – I bet you're gloating!!! Maude.'[15]

Not unnaturally, French manufacturers soon ousted the British competition, but the publicity ensured successful sales through the Berkertex in-store departments of British stores. Norman now repeated the nationwide personal appearances that had proved successful with the Latin American Exhibition, the difference being that the income now benefitted him.

He often showed some of his current collection to the vast glamour-starved audiences; 2,000 women attended at Gardiners of Ipswich on 6 November, where Dolores, June Chorley, Thelma Cranston and Lana paraded his latest creations to thunderous applause. Over 12,000 local women were said to have attended his Norwich show at Garlands a week later. If the glamorous and affluent of Rio de Janeiro or Buenos Aires were lacking, the experienced presence of Leslie Berker and his managing director Eric Crabtree ensured profits. Crabtree became a wizard at organising profitable clothes retailers and was asked to do the same for Hartnell. His one condition was unacceptable to Norman; George had once again to be sacrificed. George remained, Crabtree would not agree on these terms and Norman Hartnell Ltd continued to scrape along, Norman always fearful of the emerging competition.

In 1952, John Cavanagh, who had trained in Paris with Molyneux, opened his own London House; the equally talented Ronald Paterson also opened one. Both joined IncSoc, the organisation still remaining unconvinced about the merits of the Fashion Industries Club, which finally opened in a blaze of indifference. Douglas Dick had replaced Wells Coates as architect and a dull interior was filled with a pedestrian pre-war taste for neo-Regency and Adamesque furnishings. The only part of Coates's exciting design to remain was the modern restaurant filled with all the abandoned furniture from the 1951 Festival of Britain's Regatta Restaurant. This was another opportunity lost for IncSoc members to meet and then truly collaborate with manufacturers and also promote British fashion within an exciting building.

The figures for Hartnell in 1950–2 make depressing reading. George vainly attempted to raise capital by selling The Tower House to Lady Mount Temple. Norman was forced to write to Captain Buckmaster of Buck's Club that he was not giving any Ascot parties that year, 'as I constantly tell people, who constantly disbelieve me, I find things these days very difficult financially'.[16] He was also reduced to writing to the interior decorators Kelso, for whom Wakers was now working, about his overdue account for the works Wakers had carried out at Lovel Dene, receiving four months' credit on the £400 owing. As an indication of how bad his finances had become, he later wrote to Kelso's owner:

> Dear Madam,
> I feel constrained to say that in all my twenty-seven years of business I have never been treated in such an unpleasant way as by you. Will you please, therefore, consider my account closed.[17]

It already had been.

By November, he wrote to his old friend Gerald Hervey cancelling another appointment: 'Frankly I have been so worried lately, the truth is the appointment with you had gone completely out of my head . . . when I tell you all about it you will hardly believe your shell-pink ears.'[18]

Norman saw some light at the end of his partly self-induced gloomy tunnel and embarked on the royal command to create a wardrobe for the anticipated four-month Tour of Princess Elizabeth and Prince Philip to Australia representing the King and Queen. The King's health had deteriorated and the rigours of such a Tour were considered inadvisable for his condition. For Norman, this absorbing work was all he needed to forget the harsh realities of his financial situation. It was to be a pattern established until he died in 1979.

On 31 January 1952, the press and newsreels reported that the King stood bare-headed in the biting wind as he waved the royal couple off at London Airport. Their Tour was tragically cut short in Kenya when the King died on the night of 5 February. Britain awoke the following morning to ponder the future reign of Queen Elizabeth II.

Norman naturally rushed into action, and whilst expressing his sorrow privately to the dressers of his royal clients, he also penned touching letters to them individually. On a practical note, he immediately suggested some black ensembles for the Queen, Queen Elizabeth and Princess Margaret. The gruelling period of the funeral ceremonies and burial led to the usual period of Court Mourning, plans for the Coronation soon being worked on as the constitutional processes ground remorselessly on.

In November 1952, Norman was still dressmaker to his royal clients, as though he would have doubted this, and was asked to visit the Earl Marshall's office in Belgrave Square. In charge of the arrangements for the Coronation, the Duke of Norfolk had several official assistants and advisors; Bluemantle Pursuivant of Arms explained that 'a new design was required for alternative dresses to be worn by Viscountesses and Baronesses at the Coronation'.

For anyone under the age of seventy, the memory of the Queen's Coronation in June 1953 will be quite blurred or non-existent, so the complex web of historically based ceremonial that encompasses every detail of procedure and dress are difficult to convey succinctly. This Coronation was visually to be more important because it was both filmed and televised, so no detail was too obscure to be considered at length.

In *Silver and Gold* Norman explained his redesigning of certain robes from a viewpoint only two years distant from the ceremony.[19] Suffice it to say that the Robes of State and Coronet had not been altered since the reign of Queen Anne and he now encountered the added problem of finding less expensive velvets and furs, as Austerity had not yet ended, particularly so amongst many peers attempting to keep ancestral roofs over their heads. There were then still alive a considerable number of peers and peeresses who had not only been present at the Coronation of 1937 but also that of 1911; some even remained alive from King Edward VII's in 1901.

Many existing robes of various vintages were brought out for reuse or refurbishment. For those wanting something up to date, Norman redesigned the kirtle and robe in inexpensive red velveteen trimmed with 'cheap white pelts of the humble rabbit' instead of ermine. He drew six designs and thirty Caps of State, reducing the price of these from £500 to £30. These were examined by the Garter King of Arms who also drew his own idea of what sort of temporary head covering might be used by ladies attending the ceremony in 'perhaps day clothes if the short-skirted fashion was permitted'. Tiaras were to be worn with long dresses.

Norman designed 'a few dozen more' types of headgear, including a form of shoulder-length veil leaving the face uncovered of any light fabric such as tulle, and any colour except black could be used with an appropriate comb, clip or flower attachment, but not feathers.

Once the Cap of State was made up it was shown to the most important person in the proceedings: 'Later I was granted the honour of an audience at Buckingham Palace. Her Majesty was pleased to approve of everything submitted to her notice and I retired feeling less guilty of having interfered with fashions favoured in the reign of good Queen Anne.'[20]

This was one part of his design role in this ceremonial on which the eyes of the world were turned, for the Queen was also a very beautiful young woman and her sudden accession to the throne aroused unprecedented interest, as Norman wrote: 'One October afternoon in 1952, Her Majesty the Queen desired me to make for her the dress to be worn at her coronation.'[21]

CHAPTER FOURTEEN

A crowded hour

The genesis of the eventual design for the Coronation Dress, surely one of the most famous dresses of the twentieth century, is detailed by Norman in *Silver and Gold*, but omits any mention of the role played by his new assistant, the late Ian Thomas. Norman wrote of his audience with the Queen and subsequent actions:

> One fateful day in October I received a message from the Palace, via Miss Macdonald, that efficient yet perfectly charming person who attends Her Majesty so devotedly, to say that instead of arriving at three o'clock would I be there a little earlier as the Queen wished to see me on some special matter.
>
> On being ushered into the Queen's presence, and having performed my little bow, the Queen said to me, 'Mr Hartnell would you be so kind as to make my coronation dress?' I was so overwhelmed by this great message, so simply phrased, that quite frankly, I have forgotten what I said in reply, but I know that I felt most peculiar inside and went a little white.

These were Norman's own notes on the occasion omitted from the published version of *Silver and Gold*, which carries on the great story.

> I can scarcely remember what I murmured in reply. In simple conversational tones the Queen went on to explain her wishes. Her Majesty required that the dress should conform in line to her wedding dress and that the material should be white satin. It was almost exactly five years earlier that I had put the final touches to the dress . . .

When my first exhilaration was over I settled down to study exactly what history and tradition meant by a 'coronation dress'. I visited the London Library and leafed through authoritative tomes . . . After gathering all the factual material I could, I then retired to the seclusion of Windsor Forest and there spent many days making trial sketches. My mind was teeming with heraldic and floral ideas . . . everything heavenly that might be embroidered upon such a dress destined to be historic.'[1]

Unable to design the Queen's dress for the 1937 Coronation due to her understandable loyalty to her long-serving dressmaker Madame Handley-Seymour, Norman now had the chance to create something truly outstanding reflecting the taste of the new Queen, a reigning Queen, and current fashion utilising his own famous taste for creating spectacular full-skirted dresses. The 1937 dress had been subordinate to the vestments of the King, for Queen Elizabeth was the Consort, not ruling monarch. Norman now completed his own research and designed nine versions for the Queen, who had indicated her preference for a dress reflecting something of the line of her own wedding dress.

The first eight designs were shown to the Queen, who rejected the idea of a white dress, as Queen Victoria, the nearest precedent for a young Queen Regent, had only been eighteen and unmarried at the time of her coronation, whereas the new Queen was older and mother of two children. She also considered silver and white embroidery representing the emblems for the United Kingdom to be too similar in colour to her wedding dress. Norman then coloured a design for another version of the dress.

> Later, at another audience, the Queen made a wise and sovereign observation. It was, in effect, that she was unwilling to wear a gown bearing emblems of Great Britain without the emblems of all the dominions of which she was now Queen . . . I then drew and painted the *ninth* design which proved more complicated than I had expected.[2]

His friend Gerald Hervey provided copious notes from sources in The London Library and the Victoria and Albert Museum. Norman was by now too busy to go himself.

Whilst this was going on there was no lessening of activity in Norman's other fields. He also had to create a coronation collection, his famous 'Silver and Gold Coronation Collection' and on 13 November 1952 the Commissioner of Police was told that there would be abnormal activity around 26 Bruton Street as some 550 people had been invited to the launch of Norman Hartnell's scent 'In Love', the product of so much personal drama, expense, heartache, ill will and many tantrums. Pink-flock printed hearts were sent out as invitation cards and both salons were filled with guests who received samples and women's handkerchiefs impregnated with 'something new, young and sophisticated for the glorious coronation year which lies ahead'.[3] A song was commissioned from Norman's friend David Heneker and sung by Joan Anderson wearing a shimming Hartnell dress, all being the epitome of early 1950s London.

> With feeling IN LOVE! Those words were just a
> phrase I'd read in books and plays
> until the day you came along like a song of love
> sung by a mill on chains
> breathed by a million flowers, a melody so sweet
> and strong – its perfume filled the air – seeming to
> foretell a love affair, beyond compare:
> beneath a strange and magic spell I saw,
> you and I fell in love – in love! IN LOVE![4]

No one in the fashion world of the time or since has ever forgotten the name.

Into all this walked a young Oxfordshire-bred man, Ian Thomas. He had been offered a job by John Cavanagh, but turned the offer of £3 a week down as he thought he could do better. Cavanagh generously suggested he try Stiebel, Hartnell or Hardy Amies.

> Not knowing London I asked him who happened to be nearest
> and he said Hartnell . . . I trotted forth and found myself standing
> outside a most impressive building covered in royal coats of arms
> with an imposing green marble entrance front – standing in front
> of that door was the tall figure of a doorman in dark green serge
> – black braid and silver buttons . . . somehow I found the courage

to open the door to the showroom. Inside sitting in a half-circle were the saleswomen and their assistants – dressed in their Hartnell green dresses. One of them managed to come over and talk to this nonentity – a male – who had suddenly appeared. No, Mr Hartnell was not in – he was with the Queen Mother – could I leave my sketches?[5]

It was undoubtedly these that clinched the job for Ian, as they have a brilliance and movement lacking in Norman's more idiosyncratic designs. Most of the sketches signed 'Norman Hartnell' in *Silver and Gold*, including that of the Queen in her Coronation Dress, were drawn by Ian, who would have designed the cover of this biography had he not sadly died prematurely. A simple comparison of styles distinguishes Norman's designs from those of his assistants, including Brenda Naylor, who was leaving to marry. Their dates overlapped at Hartnell, and such was the volume of work that Ian worked on anything he was given to do in an attic room shared with a 'man-hater' of a telephonist.

Norman and George having met Ian, he was then shown part of the collection of 'stunning glamour', as he remembered it. He found himself, a shy country boy, rather isolated, although he became friendly enough with Brenda and her new husband, who accompanied him out riding and furthered a love of horses inherited from his father, a former blacksmith. The tailor Mr Rossi (formerly with Lucile and Molyneux) befriended him.

Mr Hartnell – who I found out hated designing day dresses – left Rossi to his own devices with the tweeds and woolly numbers so essential for a fashion house's 'bread and butter'. Rossi would come up to my little room under the eaves and rifle through my sketches for ideas. I was always called 'Boy' by Mr Rossi and 'Boy' would be called down to look at his creations cut and fitted on one of the house models. In this way, we together created a good few selling numbers – one particularly good one 'Over my Shoulder' – a black coat suit with its detachable cape. With his almost lack of English Rossi got away with murder with his clients . . . he always told them that he would give them a bust – or 'buzzy' as he called it – that their husbands – or lovers – would be proud of! His assistant was a Miss Chambers – or Miss Potts as Mr Hartnell cleverly called her. Rossi had the peculiarity of only wanting criticism, if I had over-admired a garment it would straightaway be taken back to the workroom and ripped apart!

Miss Potts once threatened Ian with her shears when he forgot about this.

In this odd environment, Ian managed to make himself gradually known to the preoccupied Norman, who finally felt at ease with him after a particularly pleasing design of a white jersey evening dress embroidered with a line of gold embroidery. Ian remembered that coronation year was particularly busy and

> an enormous collection was made of mostly white and gold dresses, also suitable for peeresses to wear under their velvet robes. Perhaps for the first and last time I was seeing a luxury collection of clothes made up for the wealthy and luxury-loving woman. Evening dresses had fur-trimmed full-length coats – all day dresses had particularly stunning hats made by Claude Saint-Cyr.

In her own memoirs written in the early 1990s, Madame Saint-Cyr described her collaboration with Norman, commuting between London and Paris and creating hats for many clients including the royal ladies.[6]

As far as *the* dress was concerned,

> sketches galore were done mainly in white and silver or white and gold – and it was much later, after many discussions, that Her Majesty's own suggestion of using colours for the emblems of the Commonwealth was brought into play. About this time Mr Hartnell had a slight set-back – a breakdown – so it was left to me to get on with working on the emblems – working with the embroidery room and devising new ways of making the leek, the emblem of Wales, a thing of beauty![7]

Norman had initially put in a daffodil.

'A daffodil!' exclaimed Garter. 'On no account will I give you a daffodil. I will give you the correct emblem of Wales, which is the *leek* . . . No, Hartnell. You must have the leek!' said Garter, adamant.

In the end, by using lovely silks and sprinkling it with the dew of diamonds, we were able to transform the earthy leek into a vision of Cinderella charm and worthy of mingling with her sisters Rose and Mimosa in a brilliant royal assembly and fit to embellish the dress of a Queen.[8]

Samples of all embroideries were made and taken to Sandringham together with a selection of spring dresses for the Queen to view and possibly select for wear during the Royal Tour of the Commonwealth. This tour would follow the coronation later in 1953, with the samples and dressed 'all packed by the indispensable Florrie' – Flo Smith, who had been dispatched to Brighton in May 1944 to hurriedly pack up the Latin American Exhibition just before the area was sealed off in preparation for the manoeuvres necessary for the Normandy Landings. The Curator Clifford Musgrave had been furious because it had just opened, after endless nitpicking by himself. Each member of Norman's staff had their own stories to tell and more were to follow now.

Of the embroideries proposed for the Coronation Dress, only the Irish shamrock colour failed to please the Queen. After these discussions at Sandringham, Norman showed Queen Elizabeth, the Queen Mother and Princess Margaret their dresses. They had been sitting on a slender Victorian sofa at the foot of 'an enormous bedstead'.

The Queen Mother's dress had a crinoline with gold tissue border at the base of the white satin feather-embroidered dress enhanced with crystal, gold and diamante. With these she wore platform-soled sandals by Rayne. The border had been cleverly designed to give softness to the stiff crinoline and the overall impression of a majestically gliding figure. Princess Margaret's dress was of white satin with an open-work broderie anglaise design embroidered with marguerites and roses in silver thread 'and shimmering with pearls'.

Norman then presented his designs for the accompanying train-bearers of the Queen, the Maids of Honour.

Realising that . . . carrying the Queen's State Robes of imperial velvet would show the backs of the dresses almost more than the front as they followed her up the aisle, [I] had arranged for the embroideries of small golden leaves and pearl-white blossom to cascade down the backs of their billowing skirts of white satin.

This proven design technique had worked admirably with the Maids of Honour dresses he had designed for the 1937 coronation. He then explained the motifs on the dresses for the Duchess of Kent and Princess Alexandra 'so that there should be no clash or confusion of colour in the dresses' and he designed dresses of differently patterned white and gold brocade for the Countess of Euston and the Countess of Leicester, Her Majesty's Ladies of the Bedchamber. As he modestly wrote in *Silver and Gold*, 'It had in truth been a very crowded hour.'

The subsequent fittings of all these dresses followed one upon the other with increasing frequency, and 26 Bruton Street buzzed and hummed with activity. Madame Isabelle, Norman's best 'premiere' as he described her, found it very difficult to make the finished skirt of the Coronation Dress swing to the right balance on the model stand – it would fall sideways 'so it was entirely lined or backed with cream taffeta, reinforced with three layers of horsehair crinoline, which gave it a dignified and gentle movement'.

Norman came back from the Palace full of gloom from a fitting. Although the Queen had previously admired the extraordinary beauty of the design and workmanship, on trying it on she had told him it was very heavy – which it most certainly was. Later on, it was worn for the Opening of Parliament in hot climates during the Royal Tour when it was also discovered by the Queen, as she later stated, to resemble being encased in a radiator. But on the Coronation Day in June a typical English summer produced cold rainy weather, so the internal warmth was luckily appropriate for Westminster Abbey.

A similar problem was encountered by Madame Emilienne 'clever, quick and resourceful', as Norman described her. When she had finished the Queen Mother's dress, Norman described the effect: the weight made it 'hang in limp and disappointing nuance . . . the skirt was glorified into regal fullness by mounting it on an underskirt of ivory taffeta laced with bands of horse hair and further strengthened with countless strands of whalebone.'

Norman acidly remarked, 'Madame Alice found no difficulty with her dresses for the Maids of Honour, and throughout this period Miss Edie Duley and her wonderful young women were in control of all the great embroideries.'[9]

Ian Thomas provided an explanation: 'Emilienne Servat was a fitter that I worked with quite a lot . . . her tantrums were legendary, ending on one furious occasion by her throwing a dress she had been fitting at me – and I promptly throwing it back.'[10] Of Isabelle, who had come from Molyneux, he wrote: 'She would scream if I was spending more time in the other fitter's workroom, insisting I go to her room immediately! The jealousy for attention was rife.'

With so much temperament on display around him, Norman would have needed no nerves at all to survive unscathed. The rehearsals of the Queen and the Maids of Honour took place until they were able to perform all the stops and starts and folding of the State Robes; Norman sewed a small shamrock into the stunning Coronation Dress for luck and eventually the Queen pronounced it 'Glorious'.

Many remarked on the beauty and simplicity of his design for the belted white linen overdress made for the most sacred moment of the coronation ceremony, The Anointing. Most films versions now exclude this most significant religious moment, but photographs reveal a lawn garment with sun-ray pleating. Another problem was solved with the boat-shaped neckline, a deep collar hiding the short, embroidered sleeves of the main dress. No zips or tiny buttons could be used on the dress as Mary, Duchess of Devonshire, the Mistress of the Robes, wore white kid gloves during the ceremony, so large buttons and buttonholes were provided on this dress.

Norman left with his van driver, Ted Dane, to deliver the dresses in person. Noticing an interested number of onlookers and still carrying out so many orders at no. 26 in 'closed quarters' they used a taxi, Norman shouting out, 'Victoria Station.' Approved reproductions of the design were released to the press and Norman walked home on the eve of the coronation from the Savoy having seen the early editions, only to be threatened with arrest by a vigilant bobby for taking down part of his own house's external decorations of ermine tails.

In common with most major buildings, the facade was floodlit to show off the purple draperies and eight-foot-high metal court plumes. 'The crude scarlet of geraniums and golden fringes added a sharp note of contrast. At the windows of each floor were voluminous swags of curtain in white satin spotted with ermine tails.'[12] Each morning souvenir hunters had taken some of these and now he was detained for doing the same thing. 'I went quickly up to bed . . . anxious to snatch a few hours' sleep.'[13]

The events of Norman's own day are rightly left entirely to him. Others have written of their own impressions, most notably Cecil Beaton, but Norman's personal account, so unlike the more formal one given in *Silver and*

Gold eloquently brings to life the greatest satisfaction of his career as a dress designer:

NORMAN HARTNELL

At 5 a.m. on Tuesday morning, 2 June, the telephone jingled, warning me that the great day had arrived.

After a hurried bath, I started to don my black velvet court suit. I fastened up my stiff shirt cuffs with the lovely gold enamelled cufflinks which Her Majesty the Queen Mother had given me in 1939, clasped my shirt front with two pearl studs (2/9d a pair – 1/4½d each) and buckled on my sword with a glittering cut-steel hilt. Clasping the cocked hat under my arm, I got into a large Bentley to drive off to the Abbey.

I arrived at about half past seven and, politely ushered by gold staff officers, I reached my destined seat in the Queen's box.

I felt nervous and immediately ate a lump of sugar which I had secreted in my black velvet coat tails.

The scene was already brilliant as many other people, with a less privileged seat, had arrived earlier.

Behind on my left were the peers, magnificently attired in their masculine versions of white ermine and crimson velvet.

Opposite was the incredible sight of hundreds of peeresses. Row after row of them, mounted right up to the roof of the Abbey. They looked like a lovely hunk of fruitcake; the damson jam of their velvet, lined with clotted cream of ermine, and sprinkled with the sugar of diamonds.

Stretching towards the screen was a strip of lapis lazuli blue carpet. Over this strip of carpet flowed one lovely-looking human being after another. Graceful peeresses trailed their crimson robes; visiting royalties arrived and Eastern potentates, all taking their seats like semi-precious stones in a setting of carved wood. 'Oh! I thought, if only everybody, every day, would dress like this at breakfast time!'

I gazed at the lovely honey-coloured carpet that started at the stairs towards the throne and led up to the altar which was loaded with gleaming gold plate.

This beautiful coloured carpet in the brilliant lighting which had been especially installed in the Abbey was to prove a perfect base for all the dresses and vestments that were soon to people it.

The doors of the Abbey were closed at 8.30 a.m. and a hush of expectancy permeated the building.

The procession of Their Royal Highnesses, the Princes and Princesses of the Blood Royal had started.

The Princess Royal, looking strangely like her beloved mother, the late Queen Mary, then H.R.H. the Duchess of Gloucester, delightful in white satin. The first Hartnell dress I saw to be worn by a member of the Royal Family, appeared on H.R.H. the Duchess of Kent, tall and lovely in white satin embroidered gold. The Duchess was followed by H.R.H. the young and fairy-like Princess Alexandra of Kent in white lace and tulle, sparkling with golden thread.

H.R.H. the Princess Margaret followed in her all white dress of white satin, embroidered with silver and dripping pendant pearls – a snow white princess walking with measured gait and religious mien.

I was particularly moved by the procession of Her Majesty the Queen Mother for I thought, as did probably thousands of others, of the memories that must have been crowding in upon her, when she visited Westminster Abbey for a similar ceremony in which she was partnered by our late beloved monarch, King George VI. This time, however, she could take rightful pride in the great call to duty of her daughter.

The vivid blue ribbon of the Garter crossed the corsage of her white satin and gold tissue dress, and the glittering tracery of the feather frond embroidery – which I had had such difficulty in making light enough – sparkled delicately with every movement of her majestic walk.

It was at this point of nerve-strained tension and emotional expectancy, awaiting the arrival of Her Majesty, that there came a moment of comic relief. Four splendid people in crisp white overalls scampered up the nave with brand new brooms and swept away any bits and pieces that might encumber the appearance of Her Majesty. On reflection, one cannot help remarking what a most practical and homely arrangement this was.

I braced myself up for the arrival of Her Majesty. I half-closed my eyes and through my lowered lids I was seeing the Queen of England arrive for her coronation. There was the dress that I had worked on for months – there it was shimmering and sparkling, its gold, its crystal, its diamonds, and the muted colours of God's rainbow in the emblems which festooned her wide spreading skirt. Her Majesty had told me graciously that the dress was triumphant. To me, it seems to take on the Order of a holy vestment – both stood out and blended with that lovely honey-coloured carpet, and mingled sympathetically with the cloth upon the altar.

It is not necessary for me, a dressmaker, to describe the beauty of the holy moments of that great emotional and sacred ceremony. To me, the loveliest moment was when, shedding herself of all her jewels and cloaking her glittering gown with the simple shift which I had made to cover the coronation dress, in all simplicity Her Majesty knelt on the faldstool to kiss the Bible. And the second-most moving moment was when her husband, the Duke of Edinburgh, kneeled before Her Majesty, announcing his words of homage.

The solemnity of the Queen's coronation being ended, we, the people, stood and sang the Te Deum, Her Majesty wearing her crown and the purple Robes of State, and bearing in her right hand the sceptre, in her left hand the orb, proceeded in state through the choir and the nave to the door of the church and went out to meet her people.

We sang GOD SAVE THE QUEEN.[15]

CHAPTER FIFTEEN

The top of success

To complete Norman's joy at his successful designs for everything connected with the Coronation of Queen Elizabeth II, he was appointed MVO, a Member of the Royal Victorian Order, within the sole gift of the monarch, as a token of the Queen's personal gratitude to him for his outstanding services. The news was released prior to the day of the Coronation. Letters and telegrams poured in, and this is typical of the messages of congratulations:

> Birmingham 5 June 1953. How very proud your dear parents would be and dear Richard Fletcher would also have been delighted . . . May you, my very dear friend, be constantly in God's care . . . God bless you always for your kindness and goodness to me in days gone past, thoughts of which are sacredly kept by me; and for your wonderful help to our dear George; and for all the happiness he has been able to have through your devoted friendship. Always yours very affectionately, Auntie Agnes (Masters).

Friends and colleagues' messages included those from Edward Molyneux, Hardy Amies and Victor Stiebel, who wrote:

> Every congratulation in the world for the superb Abbey job which you executed with such brilliance. It must have been a hair-raising assignment. You must be absolutely exhausted, but oh! What a wonderful sense of triumph must calm you now!
> I went to Paris . . . I was lucky to have seats for the opening there of the coronation film. I wish you could have heard the sighs of pleasure that greeted the Queen (and also the rounds of applause

that greeted each contingent, each incident in the procession). You must be *very* pleased . . . Do hope you are much better. With affection, Victor.

As always, a perceptive and friendly colleague, Victor Stiebel, and as so often, an exhausted and unwell Norman.

If the Parisian audience at the film was enthralled then so was his old friend Pierre Balmain.

I just came back from the coronation, enchanted! I am flying tonight to New York but I want, first, to write you my congratulations about the decoration that Her Majesty has just given you – and may I congratulate you also for all the lovely dresses that you have designed for the Abbey. I particularly admired the magnificent dress that the Queen was wearing – also the Duchess of Kent's – I must say that you succeeded perfectly to combine the splendour of tradition with the most perfect sense of modern proportion.

All dress designers of the world are proud when one of them reaches the top of success.

Again, let me tell you my warmest greetings, very sincerely yours, Pierre Balmain.

Congratulations from the designers Mattli and Digby Morton were added to those from the designers at Lachasse, Worth and many others. Norman's stepmother Jane, now living in Sparkhill, Birmingham wrote of the MVO, 'Congratulations, I expected more – but as the old woman said, every little helps.' On 1 June, Topsy wrote:

Well, Normie dear, to say that I was terribly bucked to see the news about your decoration this morning is a bit inadequate. Also anything I can think of writing would be sentimental, slightly morbid or just embarrassing – so, among all the many people who will shake your hand and wish you well, are those who today are sharing your success and good fortune, I have sent you a telegram to your home.

We are very proud of you dear, and I shall think of you taking your place among the distinguished in the Abbey tomorrow. Good luck and congratulations, bless you. Maude.

Apart from the family greetings, milliner Kate Day sent a telegram – 'A thousand congratulations. Nobody deserves it more. From your oldest girlfriend. Kate.' The Headmaster of Mill Hill also congratulated him on 'behalf of the many who remember you here' and Leslie Berker summed up the general feeling amongst the fashion trade, 'Wonderful news – never was an honour more appropriate or truly earned.'

In the years to come Norman might have expected advancement from MVO as his work for the Queen and her family became ever more extensive. His next progression, a source of huge pride and pleasure, occurred in 1977 with his advancement to KCVO, the first Dressmaker by Appointment to be created a Knight..

Reminiscing about the early 1950s, Norman later wrote:

> Whenever I am asked by a journalist what is the most important dress I have ever made, I reply, unhesitatingly, 'Her Majesty's coronation dress, of course. Naturally I also hold great sentimental attachment to the pearl-strewn wedding dress I made for Her Majesty as H.R.H. the Princess Elizabeth. Both these dresses are destined to inhabit some solemn museum. It is strange how a few yards of satin can enjoy an artificial life of some hundreds of years.[1]

When the official announcement that he had been appointed the designer of the Coronation Dress was made on 10 March 1953 Norman had by then kept the royal command secret for over three months. He was good at keeping secrets; his whole life was one of open tact and diplomacy. If he had said that his head was made too large for him to be a successful actor, he was the perfectly modest designer in public with nothing apparently ruffling his outward ease. Of course, it was different at home.

As congratulations poured in from all sides, it was Victor Stiebel who again elegantly summed them up by writing 'nobody could do it better', an opinion echoed in a note from Hardy Amies and later in his second autobiography when he wrote of how much he also admired the cut of the skirt of the dress.[2]

Victor Stiebel remembered Hartnell's kindness to him, much as another designer with his own London House Michael Sherard did.

I first met Hartnell in 1928 . . . I had just come down from Cambridge. 'I want to become a dress designer,' I said to him. 'What do I do about it?'

'You don't,' he answered and then spent ten minutes in trying to dissuade me. However, I refused to budge and finally he gave me a letter to Mr Reville, at that time the czar of London Couture.

This was the same Mr Reville approached so unsuccessfully by Richard Fletcher on Norman's behalf some years earlier. Sherard continued:

That is Hartnell, sympathetic to the problems of others and constructive in his advice. Hartnell is a shy man, fastidious and difficult to know. He is withdrawn and appears to live in a world decorated with his own dreams, a world of Parma violet velvet, pearls, diamonds and shivering chandeliers, full-blown roses – a theatre world. But the décor is imposed on a background of hard common sense, of lively intelligence and courage.[3]

Courage was needed in the build-up to the Coronation for as Ian Thomas remarked, 'Mr H. had health problems and yet managed to pack into an eighteen-hour day – more work than he had known since pre-war days.' At the beginning of his August holidays in 1950, Norman had fractured his sacrum and this was to give him trouble physically and add to his mental strain.

Jane Chorley, one of his star mannequins in the 1950s, considered him in an interview 'patient, unflurried and considerate . . . his staff are devoted to him . . . many of them have been with him for years and just wouldn't be happy anywhere else.' Certainly, his secretary Ann Price was with him for forty years and was deeply attached to him..

A man of simple tastes, he is supremely happy in tweeds or flannels when enjoying rare leisure at his country house and farm. Most designers have a forte . . . [he] is equally at ease with a creation of dazzling brilliance designed to be the focal point of a great event, or when producing the discreet day dress of a well-groomed woman – or indeed the uniform for one of H.M. women's services . . . his generous disposition makes working for him an interesting and enjoyable privilege.[4]

This remarkable man was also the subject of attention by a New Zealander, who wrote for *The People* on why 'the higher they climb, the harder they find it to fall in love. Three famous men who can't find the right girl.' The hapless girl went to her three victims, Ivor Novello, Terence Rattigan and Norman, who 'was actually shy. But not shy enough to stress that a girl with a strong personality can be a blooming nuisance,' he said candidly. 'And very often the plain soap-and-water girl is the nicest of the lot. He, too, I sadly concluded was beyond our reach and that of all us lovely females of the species.' No doubt many smiled knowingly over their morning teacups at the thought of the three confirmed bachelors in those more decorous days.[5]

The months leading up to the Coronation had seen Norman's innovative and newsworthy cotton dresses worn by the Duchess of Kent on a visit to the tropical rigours of Malaya, a boost for the British cotton industry and for the boom in copies that quickly filled the shops. Copying of his designs was inevitably a problem during all of Norman's existence, more especially in the 1950s, for the clothes of the Queen and Princess Margaret were eagerly scrutinised for fashion hints. In the autumn of 1952, the young and as yet uncrowned Queen attended the Royal Command Film Performance. Norman reverted to his 1930s success of the black-and-white 'Magpie' design, so that when the Queen emerged from her car into the cinema she outshone everyone present in a halter-neck black satin with a gently flowing outline, a white panel to the front and halter-neck line. Not only were the press reports and viewers ecstatic; overnight cheap copies were made and on sale in Oxford Street next day, so that the Queen was never known to wear it again and afterwards chose less dramatic and less easily copied dresses for such occasions.

Television, which played its important part at the coronation ceremony, had already broadcast James Laver talking to Pierre Balmain in the London studio in December 1949. In 1952, the IncSoc show was also filmed for TV and Norman made his own TV debut in what was to become the greatest popular broadcasting medium of the period.

Norman's extensive Silver and Gold Coronation Collection achieved much publicity in addition to designs for the coronation and many members of his clientele. It also formed part of a British fashion show in St Moritz when the loveliest mannequins paraded in snow and ice snow under a brilliant sun. Nola Rose, Fiona Campbell-Walter and Marla Scarafia were amongst the first of the new international models as they paraded in a display of mid-century clothes. A similar show was put on in Le Touquet.

Norman continually toured Britain, making trips to Newcastle, Edinburgh and Nottingham to show new collections and in July 1953 was aghast at Dior's headline-snatching collection with skirts up to sixteen inches from the ground during Norman's moment of enhanced June glory as 'Back to the 1920s' headlines filled the newspapers. Dior announced:

> I expect the fresh approach to be just as successful as the New Look. They laughed then but pretty soon everyone was wearing it. My revolution is not just in skirt lengths, it is above all in the body. For the first time I have suppressed boning, even in some dance frocks . . . I have done away with corsets . . . I mean the 'battleship armour' type.

This radical change was as carefully and ingeniously planned as the introduction of his New Look. Everything was smoother in line and for younger bodies. Hartnell announced that he was not changing lengths back to the ugly shorter lengths of the despised fashions of the 1920s.

At what might be interpreted as a clear riposte to the worldwide success of Norman's – in fact all London couture's – designs, during Britain's June coronation forming a huge attraction to American buyers, Dior ended his interview: 'My short skirt is designed for modern living; after all, dresses are not made for a museum.'[6]

After this radical change in Paris couture lines, there was little hope that London could avoid the changes, especially when popular ready-to-wear manufacturers, with few exceptions, said they would follow it.

The following letter written to Dior by Norman explains the extent of Dior's influence and Norman's reaction to Dior personally:

8 September 1953

> I am writing to you personally, because I am more than personally distressed.
>
> Please let me explain.
>
> When I returned to England a week ago, I gathered there had been much publicity in the world's press purporting to describe a quarrel that had arisen between you and me.
>
> I ignored this, because one had to forgive certain inventions on

the part of hard-working fashion journalists, as you too must naturally understand.

When, however, my Madame Jeanne, who had visited your house in Paris, explained to me how upset you yourself were, I felt that something should be done to clear up this misunderstanding which has been forced upon us.

Dear Christian Dior, let me say immediately that I have always admired your beautiful work and always expressed my admiration of it to everybody.

When I first heard the news that you had decided to introduce the shorter skirt, my first remark was, 'How splendid! No, Madam Journalist, I am sure it will not be ugly. Whatever Mr Dior decided to do, he would do it beautifully.'

That was on the morning of 29 July.

After that, I heard no more until on my holidays the fashion representative of the *Telegraph* of Amsterdam requested an interview with me, and said that it had been published in all the press, that I had sent a telegram to Christian Dior, saying, 'I do not like your new line – I shall not copy your fashions.'

I was quite astounded.

Dear Mr Dior, you know as well as I do that no such telegram was ever sent by me, or received by you.

On Saturday morning last, 5 September, the *Evening Standard* telephoned to me at my country house, asking whether I had seen the French press and their attacks upon me. I replied that I had not.

This representative said that all the French papers were carrying an article saying that I was sneering at the Dior fashions; that my own fashions in London (as far as I know the French press have not seen my collection) were old-fashioned and frumpy; and that I called myself the 'English Dior'. You know quite well, dear Christian, that is a title which I would never adopt for myself.

All this distresses me very much and I am inclined to make a statement in the papers, yet I feel this would only continue the absurd controversy yet longer.

It upsets me very much that the French papers should be so hostile towards me, in view of the fact that I have always had the most delightful reception from the French press when I used to give my shows in Paris.

The big silk houses always supported me; my staff here is half-French; and after the state visit of Their Britannic Majesties in 1938, your French government saw fit to honour me with the 'Les Palmes Académiques' – a gesture which I will cherish throughout my life.

I also remember, dear Christian Dior, when at the press reception after your lovely dress show at the Savoy Hotel you said – in front of me to several women journalists – 'Dear ladies, when I want to think of anything particularly beautiful, I think of the beautiful dresses that your Mr Hartnell, here, made for the Queen's visit to Paris.' That I shall never forget.

Would I, therefore, now be so ungrateful as to criticise you in any way whatsoever? After that wonderful praise from you, would I say anything unkind about you?

I know an artist and a gentleman when I meet one. I also know good manners.

What upsets me most about the whole situation is that the report of antagonism on my part is not only untruthful, but the very complete opposite from the truth.

I hear that you may be visiting London quite soon. If that is true, how delighted I should be to see you if you would care to come and see me, and my little collection.

In the meanwhile, my dear friend, I give you my word as an Englishman and cross my heart as a Frenchman, that all the unkind things that have been said are absolutely untrue.

Sadly, no reply to this has apparently survived.

When the journalist and politician Tom Driberg interviewed Norman in January 1954 he found him in the throes of marking thirty years of designing with his latest collection and preparing for another north of England tour and one in Germany. Before his lunch of sausages and onions, Norman looked over a few mannequins – 'No, a bit too haystacky at the back' – and showed that he was a man of equable temperament. 'All that stuff is so corny, doesn't help anybody and only exhausts one,' he said of tantrums. At that moment, a girl carried past a dress he had asked to be treated with great care – and dropped it. 'Oh!' he said. 'Don't look. . .' and then showed a 1936 dress still being worn and in for repair, a typical occurrence at Hartnell.[7]

This was not as odd as the sight greeting Madame Jeanne when Norman's enthusiastic fans Elsie and Doris Waters came for their fittings one day. 'The Sisters', as they often signed themselves, remained two of Norman's favourite revue artists and George was a great favourite of theirs. Although they were hardly his ideal advertisement with their shapeless figures, they had a regal charm in the evening dresses designed by Norman for the first half of their act. On one fateful day, they were late for a show and had changed into the clothes of their famous Cockney chars 'Gert and Daisy', appearing in front of a busy salon unrecognised by Madame Jeanne as The Sisters with comical results. At Hartnell there was often an unusual event in the offing.[8]

By the time Ian Thomas had joined Hartnell, Madame Jeanne had ceased to wear the bouquet of violets on her shoulder that matched her pale mauve hair, but 'she had a marvellous, imperious walk and her attractive strut across a crowded showroom was a joy to behold'.[9]

It is the job of a good vendeuse to cosset her particular clients, advise them of new developments in colours, fabrics and line. Madame Jeanne was a highly knowledgeable and prized asset of the business, not only popular with her clients but also respected by them for her tact and taste in all matters of dress. She was the conduit between Norman and his clients. From her, he, in turn, learned of his clients' idiosyncrasies and taste, what was most popular amongst his designs and what was not. As we have seen, Norman was becoming content to create designs likely to catch the headlines but no longer necessarily to create a fashion revolution.

Of his most illustrious clients he was quoted as saying in New York in January 1953: 'It is never the intention of the English royal ladies to set fashions. If it happens that they do, it is unintentional. Their desire is to dress appropriately for all occasions.' This was an assessment made by successive designers over the years.

It was not entirely true of Princess Margaret, whose fashionable clothing was much copied and whose wardrobe included Dior evening dresses and a keen interest in Parisian trends. It could also not have been so rigidly applied by the Queen when she ordered the 'Magpie' dress, but both diversions were seldom repeated.

As for the Duchess of Kent, Ian Thomas saw her quite often in the Hartnell building. For some reason, she preferred to use the rear doors in Bruton

Place through which Hartnell employees came and went, 'picking her way through the dustbins and walking up the back staircase rather than coming in through the front door and possibly meeting other clients in the showroom'. Ian noticed that she was rather shy... 'She spoke to her saleswoman always in French and in that dark brown smoker's voice.'

Norman had none of the rapport with her that he enjoyed with other royal clients. 'Her dresses were always the same – a fitted bodice – dead plain, with usually a bateau neckline and either a plain or pleated skirt.' It irritated Norman that 'she designed most of her dresses herself or had them copied from *L'Officiel.*'

He was also aggrieved when the Duchess sent him a curt letter because a newspaper report stated that he had designed all her dresses for the tour of Malaya. He replied coolly stating that he had not said this and as he had previously been so accommodating with her, he would have to review their arrangements. The Duchess was not well off and often borrowed clothes; sometimes they were returned rather the worse for wear, as with Norman's famous white wool lace coat, one of the few exuberant models she ever borrowed. Needless to say, once his steam had been released, Norman never sent this letter.[10]

The Duchess used clothes almost as a background to her 'accessories that always made her so outstandingly well turned out – the choker of pearls, the ruckled-down gloves, small bag and well-chosen shoes.' It was the choice of appropriate matching shoes which so exercised the royal designers in their dealings with the Queen's devoted dresser Miss MacDonald, so often given the blame for 'ruining' a design. With the Duchess, no one else took decisions – 'she could wear a fur stole as well as or better than a model girl' and made a huge impression on Ian Thomas, who stored up information later put to practical use for *his* future career as a Royal Dressmaker by Appointment, independently of Norman.

The novelty of so many attractive royal ladies drove magazines and newspapers to ecstasy. It must have been an irritant that the true roles of monarch and family were so often blurred into a great romantic fantasy, but it was a delight for Norman and designs poured out of his studio. He was not the only beneficiary of royal patronage; with so many designs needed, Hardy Amies, Victor Stiebel, John Cavanagh and Ronald Paterson were also able to enjoy welcome royal orders.

Down at Lovel Dene, Ian settled into a routine similar to that enjoyed by Brenda Naylor before him.

The following years were happy ones. Before spring or winter collections we would both retire to his lovely home . . . where we could work all day and only be interrupted by a light lunch and the usual comment: 'You don't want a drink do you?' In the evening a cocktail was allowed! And we would sit by the fire and discuss the day's work.[11]

The accounts for the period 1 August 1953 to 31 August 1954 give an accurate picture of how Norman's variable finances stood. The Fashion Industries Club had folded and so the tiny debenture of £1 was written off as the least of Norman's problems. He received a salary of £3,500, but owed the company £1,319. The company paid for various expenses at Lovel Dene, his dress allowance and for £1,003 of drinks and cigarettes for entertaining, no small sum at the time, and something Fred Smith had complained of.

It also emerged in the accountant's report that 'Mr Mitchison . . . has been reimbursed for expenses well in excess of this figure' – £4,500 in fact. Further information was sought on the disposal of the Austin car, for which Norman had badgered Fred Smith, and its replacement – 'a Rolls Royce which cost £1,200 in February 1954'. Norman clearly loved expensive cars commensurate with his own style and perceived status, but they always came with a chauffeur as he hated to drive himself.

It should also be remembered that Lovel Dene, Norman's sole residence now, apart from a useful room at 26 Bruton Street, was now owned by the company and valued at £20,240. This had finally occurred in 1951 at the insistence of the Westminster Bank, whereupon they increased the overdraft facility to £14,000, an increase of £2,000. The bank managers were heartily unimpressed by Norman's financial status and his personal incapacity or willingness to plan or take good advice – in 1942 he had taken £2,000 away from his life assurance policy which had been carefully arranged for him by Pleydell and Bish.

We have seen how his spending on furnishings, antique items, cars and entertainment never slackened and how in 1955 he eventually turned against his sister and advisor R. (Bob) Fearnley-Whittingstall, as he had against 'Tito' Medlam whilst they wrestled with the bank.

As an indication of Norman's curiously naive attitude to the business, all his own extra efforts in the way of designing for magazine articles (£2,020), personal appearance fees of £787.10s., *News Chronicle*-commissioned design fees of £750 and other items amounting to £10,250.17s.10d. which could legitimately have been claimed as personal rather than company income *all* went into the company coffers. Just two half years of such fees and he could have easily paid off the company ownership of Lovel Dene, although outgoings there cost the company £3,411.2s.5d., almost the whole of Norman's salary as a director and this sum included nearly £1,000 of redecoration expenses.

At this time, the bank overdraft stood at £19,048.14s.11d. and after all other outgoings were accounted for, the company was left with £2,690.7s.8d. from gross profit of £41,527. Norman and George both lived in comfort, Norman apparently in great luxury, but behind the faceted reflections of his mirror-like existence was a truly *Alice in Wonderland* situation. He owned the clothes he stood up in and an interest in his company. His house, car, even some of his furniture, belonged to the company. His investments were remarkably few: the property in South London had been sold and was never replaced with another stable source of revenue. His valuable jewellery and other items had been stolen from the robberies at The Tower House and Lovel Dene, the resulting insurance compensation being spent in other ways rather than the reacquisition of comparable pieces as an investment. Apart from some life assurance policies and his undoubtedly great talent, Norman had really few tangible assets to show for his thirty hard-working years, except a few shares and the money in his bank account – only some £6,000.

Norman's whole existence depended on keeping the business going. His hand–to-mouth attitude seems to have been that he alone was the business and the business was him. There was an inner Micawber always daring him to spend recklessly.

Norman had made money from films since the 1920s; one major star and Hartnell client of the time was Anna Neagle whose husband the producer-director Herbert Wilcox wanted to make a film of Norman's life. One can only wonder at the role Anna Neagle would have played and how the fiction of his officially promoted early life would have been portrayed. Anna Neagle had made an early success of her roles as Nell Gwynne and Queen Victoria, so perhaps this was a Wilcox tease.

After a first-night party given by Anna Neagle, who remained one of Norman's greatest fans, he left at 4 am for Lovel Dene arriving to find that burglars had again visited him. 'They did not get away with much. I keep all my valuable things in London. I think that made them angry – they left the house in a bit of a state.'[12] The truth was, of course, that there was little left of his portable valuables, so his suits were also taken.

He attempted to shrug off the experience with the press. 'Oh, what do you pay for yours, about £40 or £50 isn't it. I had grown out of some of them anyway.' Some were left in the mud in the garden along with a mink rug, made from bits left on the furriers' benches – 'I've had a few made from time to time. I usually give them away as wedding presents to daughters of people I know socially.'[13] Other reports depicted him wearing a polka-dotted silk dressing gown. He was too depressed to say more and went to feed the ducks on his lake.

He must have also pondered the likelihood of his special 'Black Room' and collection of military outfits coming to light, but by playing the whole matter down, it was quickly forgotten. New fashions swept in, diverting journalists' attention to such innovations as the novelty of 'these new high-heeled shoes first shown in Rome . . . Unattractive and uncomfortable they have very high, very thin heels that spread slightly at the bottom and pointed toes.'[14] Rayne swiftly introduced this new stiletto heel and every IncSoc member showed them on their mannequins. The stiletto of Italian fashion was the beginning of strong Italian fashion rivalry to Paris and London. The fashionable serving of hot chocolate at the London shows was scarcely a substitute,[15] nor was the comment of the *Daily Sketch*: 'No Dior hemline rubbish for the Queen when she goes on her Commonwealth tour.'[16]

The Queen's clothes excited enormous interest during her 1953–4 tour. After forty years of State Visits and Royal Tours these events are bound to be of less interest to the Queen's subjects today, although so many of the elaborate evening dresses are of historic importance. From the Royal Tour of South Africa in 1947 onwards, the Queen has some eight decades of experience in these matters, almost paralleled by her mother, the late Queen Elizabeth, the Queen Mother. Others have written of these events and so it is not necessary to give a complete list of dates and descriptions of the Hartnell clothes worn, unless they have some very special feature.[17]

For the arduous six-month-long Tour of 1953–4, the Queen took a considerable wardrobe out to Fiji, Tonga, New Zealand, Australia, Ceylon, Aden, Uganda and Malta. The Coronation Dress was worn on occasion, notably for the first ever Opening of Parliament in Australia by a British monarch, and similarly elsewhere. Throughout the Tour, both day and evening dresses aroused great admiration, though these also included some designed by Hardy Amies and a few Horrockses cotton day dresses.[18]

Norman developed the idea first put into practice in Paris in 1938 and developed during the South African tour of 1947, whereby local motifs or elements were introduced into the design or decoration of the dresses as a compliment to the country in which they were worn. During the French State Visit of 1938, Norman had utilised yards of cobwebby Valenciennes lace in one of Queen Elizabeth's day dresses. Similarly in 1947 he had focused local attention on South African exports; one of the famous all-white dresses of Queen Elizabeth had 'copper' and 'diamond' beads and spangles embroidered onto a dress, and the Queen used local ostrich-feather trimmings in her hat and used a feather boa.

Local flowers were to form part of the embroidered designs on Norman's evening dresses for Royal Tours and State Visits until he died. They always provoked appreciative comment. For the 1953–4 Royal Tour the Queen's day dresses were certainly not long, nor were they short in the recent Dior fashion.

As already mentioned, the press of both Britain and France fuelled an imaginary Dior/Hartnell feud, *Paris-Presse* slated his September 1953 show during the Royal Tour as 'going back three years to a presentation in a provincial salon'.[19] Having gone out of his way to assure Dior of his personal friendship, he accepted an invitation from him and on 16 January 1954 the two lunched together in Dior's Paris house. Nevertheless, the story was too good for the newspapers to abandon, in spite of the embarrassment of the timing, and misinformation was spread during every subsequent Dior innovation. This was truly an instance of Fake News.

Norman had made his feelings about Parisian innovations and particularly the New Look clear in 1947: 'During the war I designed several million "utility" dresses, using just three yards of material. This threatened fashion will now demand anything from nine to twelve yards of material for each dress . . . it is not new, being a revival of the skirt length of 1930.' He then discussed British coupon controls and ended, 'It is women who set the fashion and it is up them to accept or refuse. But purely from the point of view of beauty in dress, the longer the better.'[20] He never wavered from this view.

The New Look had been seized on with gusto in the Germany of the Wirtschaftswunder and Dior's first essay on fashion 'Ich mache Mode' ('I Create Fashion') was published there during the fast developing Wirtschaftswunder.

At the instigation of the leading fashion journal *Elegante Welt*, Norman showed a selection of his latest collection to invited guests on 8 and 9 April

1954 at the Hotel Atlantic, Hamburg, traditionally the most Anglophile German city. There were the usual last-minute letters from George, who on 19 March was still insisting that Hartnell would pay for absolutely nothing to do with the show and on 24 March had only discovered that there were conditions on bringing foreign clothes into the country. The Hartnell show was supposed to go on to Düsseldorf and Munich and originally the invitation was also extended to Norman, if he so wished. He did not. Nor did he take up the offer of an extended tour of the collection through the major German cities.

Just as short-sightedly, affluent Düsseldorf was dropped from the itinerary, as was Munich. The fashionable Kurhaus at Baden-Baden was the only other venue. The usual Hartnell management indecision, incompetence and muddle prevailed and a week before the event Norman was forced to write to Dr J.K. Dunlop CMG, CBE, MD, TD, Land Commissioner and H.M. Consul General in Hamburg:

'You may wonder why I have not yet replied, and with my deepest apologies I beg to explain there was an element of doubt that the visit would ever be accomplished.' He then turned down an offer of accommodation at the house of Dr Dunlop, but had the nerve to write, 'However, it would be delightful if you would care to give a very small reception for me and my staff.'[21]

Arrangements had been negotiated since 1953: the German organisers were at a loss to understand George's indolence and prevarication on each minor detail. They must truly have thought, 'However did they win the war?' Yet, this was the man Norman insisted on as invaluable to the future development of the company from the time he tried to manoeuvre his release from the army. Fred Smith, Phyllis, Medlam, Fearnley-Whittingstall – all sound business brains – were ruthlessly negated and forced out of Norman Hartnell Ltd because of George's immense hold on Norman.

German newspapers, notably the large Stuttgart regional one, had already tipped English clothes and fashions as being more suitable to German dimensions and tastes than the French. The immense German press coverage of the show included photographs revealing the truth of this. 'The Queen's Designer' and his collection was a great hit with them, as were the Saint-Cyr hats and Rayne shoes; and when interviewed Norman said flattering things about Hamburg. Then suddenly he had gone, with no attempt to build up a design or production link, nor much later contact until he pursued menswear in the mid-1960s. Why did he spend so much time and physical effort? French fashions increasingly gained Germany as a market, especially after Dior shortened the skirts. Norman needed a detached, even ruthlessly efficient business brain in his House such as Eric Crabtree was for Berker, then Amies and subsequently Harvey Nichols, amongst his other commercial triumphs.

In 1953, Norman added to his workload by designing a new uniform for the Red Cross. He simply could not do everything alone, yet shrank from getting rid of George. Hardy Amies often summed up the fatal flaw in Norman and the difference between them, as he saw it: 'Norman was a soppy old queen and I am a bitchy old queen.' But Norman sadly was a bitchy old queen to many who had his best interests at heart.

Norman should also have worried more about his future, for as mentioned, the vast wardrobe of clothes worn by the Queen during the Royal Tour of 1953–4 also included designs by Hardy Amies and cotton dresses by Horrockses. Apart from that, Dior was keenly interested in the burgeoning Japanese market, where Moheitoh held her first all-wool show of Japanese fabrics modelled by Japanese women. Her audience of 32,000 was accomplished by showing in three major cities, and the Imperial Princesses were present together with working girls making up the huge audiences. George should have been gauging the market there too, but perhaps he regarded the former enemy with scorn, for Germany and Japan were left out of his schedule until the 1960s when Norman was 'old hat' and elderly, so that the links eventually forged were seen as an act of desperation rather than innovation. Japan was, and still is, fashion hungry but usually looks to Paris first.

As further proof of Hartnell business methods, a typical letter of Norman's to an American men's shirt manufacturer runs:

> Please do not think one too ill-mannered in not answering your letter dated 5 August before now [in September 1954], but as it arrived just the day after I left for my vacation, and I have only just returned, I could not send an earlier reply.
>
> I am most deeply interested to hear all you have to say about the progress of the Hartnell-designed shirts, and to realise that four of your chosen thirteen already look interesting . . . I look forward with excitement to receiving the first shirt and seeing the first Hartnell woven labels. I mentioned your name casually to Madame Schiaparelli a few weeks ago and her involuntary cry was,

'Oh, Thomas Shirts are the very highest mark in America – wonderful merchandise!'

The usual flurry of excuses for tardy contact was mixed with flattery and kept the relationship afloat for a few more years.[22]

Norman's wartime acquaintance with Hugh Fraser did bring tangible business success. One apparent symbol was the special fashion festival held as part of the Scottish Industries Fair of 1954. Held in September at Kelvin Hall, Glasgow, on 2 September there was a private showing for Queen Elizabeth, the Queen Mother of nineteen designs, the last four by Norman. The show was compèred by Michael Whittaker, who had a model agency, but who was also a talented stage and film-set designer, sometimes designing clothes for productions. (To Norman he signed himself inexplicably 'Dear Heart', as Norman did to him.) Such shows were good publicity but did little or nothing for the expansion of the Hartnell name overseas, which was largely delegated to Jack Barregar in South Africa and Tom Gurr in Australia, both far away from Bruton Street.

The Hibiscus Queen Festival at Margate near Durban included one such Hartnell publicity drive, largely for the promotion of the development of Margate as an idyllic sort of Palm Beach. Norman even had an option on a pleasant house there, contributing to its design and hopeful of a windfall retirement fund to be earned from merchandising. Jack Barregar's business empire eventually petered out, however. The wrong horse had been backed and had also been nobbled – the thousands of pieces of correspondence reveal a typical story of a situation out of the control of Norman and George's hands, whilst it was swallowing huge sums of money. Monies generated after everyone abroad had received a cut went largely to prop up the voracious in-House needs at 26 Bruton Street.[23]

In 1954, Hardy Amies published his informative autobiography *Just So Far*, an engrossing history of his origins and life including chapters detailing the technical and financial aspects of running a successful couture house.[24] Norman had by this date been in business for thirty-one years against Amies' twenty, so he now gave in to repeated requests to write his own memoirs and tell his own success story. He may not have realised that he would die still working twenty-five years later but at the age of fifty-four might have wondered if he was now at the pinnacle of his career.

CHAPTER SIXTEEN

Hartnell puts it right

S *ilver and Gold* was planned throughout 1954. It was commissioned by John Browning of Evans Brothers, publishers known originally for their educational publications, and now becoming famous for such best-selling works as *I Flew for the Fuehrer, The Dam Busters* or *Cheshire VC*, best-selling autobiographies or accounts relating to the history of the recent war. The major event of the 1953 Coronation and subsequent Royal Tour of the Commonwealth meant that the name of Norman Hartnell was known worldwide even to those most ignorant of fashion. A unusual lavishly illustrated book was planned and magazine serialisation to follow with J.W. Drawbell of Newnes and Pearson most concerned that it should achieve serial publication in *Woman's Day* by March 1955. Both Norman and George were ill in September 1954, causing the delay in publication. As he had little time to work on the book, the manuscript was worked on by other hands, which must account for some of the garbled dates and sequences of events, before its submission to Buckingham Palace so that all references to members of the Royal Family could be checked for their suitability.

The autobiography was a remarkable success; *Woman's Day* serialised it with excellent illustrations and the Evans Brothers' printers produced two versions. One was a fine leather-bound limited edition and the other cloth-bound with a beautiful blue watered-silk effect on the binding.

The bold concept of Evans Brothers' Managing Director paid off. The use of colour illustrations put the book into a visually superior league to the Amies biography; Ian Thomas reworked many of Norman's pre-war coloured sketches with great verve and helped with the finished design by Norman of the colourful dust wrapper.[1]

Of the very many pieces of information that were omitted from Norman's story, few have as much relevance as Mademoiselle Davide's memories told to the press. She stayed with him for thirty years and when interviewed considered that the Circus Party was what really 'put him on the map . . . a knockout even for the Roaring Twenties . . . The party lasted through the night. When dawn broke there were a good many broken windows in Bruton Street.'

She had then worked for him for five years, having come to England with the intention of learning the language before going back to Paris in order to open her own dress shop. Norman needed a fitter and she went to the 'small house in Bruton Street and I didn't think much of the place. And Mr Hartnell – he was nothing like a couturier! He wore a crumpled jacket, a shirt with an even more crumpled collar, awful Oxford bags and a shaggy woollen pullover.'

All this accords with early photographs of Norman fiddling with the dresses worn by mannequins in his first salon. Mam'selle then discovered, 'He was shy and nervous and chewed his lips while his white-haired saleswoman conducted the interview.' Mlle Davide then went to her job the following Monday 'without much hope or excitement. But I found things even worse than I thought.' The premises were just one floor with Phyllis and Norman in a flat on the top, the workroom was so tiny she felt herself

> in a padded cell . . . I made up my mind I would give Hartnell just one week. And then he gave me his first sketches. I knew in a minute that Hartnell was not just an ordinary dressmaker. The designs were fantastic, the colours were beautiful, there was grace and delicacy in every line. But the designs as Hartnell sketched them were quite unwearable. They needed a practical mind to turn them from paper fantasies into real clothes.

She learned to cope with the 'crush and the muddle' and decided to stay for six months, captivated by Norman's 'big blue eyes as I started to bring his sketches to life . . . He would go around the place with a look of wide-eyed admiration for anyone who could help him translate his dreams into practical reality.'

This look became too much for one of the girls, who fell in love with him and 'followed him round like a spaniel . . . Hartnell was terrified. He couldn't even turn to his sister Phyllis, for she was in India. Eventually he ran into his office and slammed the door. "Tell her to go away. Please make her go," he shouted.'

This insight into Norman's often mentioned shyness completely under-lines the dependency Norman always had on other stronger characters in his business and personal life. His father and mother were obviously strong characters; so were Topsy, John Pleydell and then most certainly George until Norman died.

Mam'selle did not shrink from her own more personal memories of her dealings with the royal clients. The Duchess of Gloucester was the most ner-vous bride she ever encountered and trembled so much it was difficult to fit her 'shell-pink satin wedding dress' as she recited all the long list of the Duke's Christian names, 'so that she could repeat them perfectly at the cere-mony. She murmured them so often that they stick in my mind today.'

The Queen, on the other hand, was 'the most solemn bride' she encoun-tered and she was astonished by her bedroom at Windsor when she went to fit the then Princess Elizabeth with her first long evening dress. The room 'did not seem suitable for a young girl. It was full of sombre portraits.' A particu-larly heavy one hung over the bedhead.

> I couldn't help hoping it was very securely fastened . . . When I first
> knew her, she had absolutely no interest in clothes. She refused to
> have anything new for her visit to Paris just after she was married.
> Then – a complete reversal, two days before she was due to leave.

Everything was pushed through at full speed and at Hartnell they were all eager

> to know what the French had thought of her clothes. But when she
> returned she didn't say a word. It was her mother who went out of
> her way to thank Hartnell and tell us what a success the dresses
> had been, and if you ask me which was Princess Elizabeth's favou-
> rite garment at that time I would say confidently it was the tailored
> uniform which she wore at Trooping the Colour. But now she has
> become much fonder of pretty, more feminine clothes.

Mlle Davide was drawn to Princess Margaret who 'is the most interested in clothes, even to picking up the pins I drop. She wears all colours except green, which she thinks is unlucky.'

Mam'selle was born with one leg shorter than the other and resolutely refused to let this interfere with her skills. Other glimpses of clients include two vignettes of the King's interest in Queen Elizabeth's clothes at the time of the Russian–German pact of 1939.

> Inside the Palace we were trying to impress the Queen with a new-style Russian hat, the kind of thing Cossacks wear. The King walked into the room and looked horrified.
>
> 'Take it off,' he said. 'It just won't do. It isn't at all opportune.' And off it came.

Another time Hartnell was showing the Queen a coat with fur-trimmed pockets. The King studied it for a little while and then commented, 'I just don't understand why you don't line the pockets with the fur instead of putting it on the outside, then you could keep your hands warm.'

Mam'selle commented, 'We gave him a look of very respectful scorn.'

Unsurprisingly, Norman's autobiography has few such revealing details of his royal clients, or others. Although his second autobiography contains few authorised vignettes of his relationship with the royal ladies, they were not so sharply personal. This last volume of memoirs was never published.

Appraising Norman in 1955, Mam'selle remarked:

> Outwardly he changed, of course. He lost some of that wide-eyed look, grew much more suave in manner. He learned to dress elegantly, he became a little careful of what he ate. But our relationship remained the same. We were the same team, he imagining and I translating. We had great faith in each other. Often we argued and stormed, but never with ill feeling. If he designed a dress which I considered quite impossible, he would sometimes retreat gracefully and appear to agree with me. Then he would go across to another workroom and have it made there . . . He had learned to be a little crafty in the time that I was with him.[2]

One might qualify this by saying that he had necessarily learned to be more crafty from his birth on.

Being 'crafty' did not bring about better business for Norman. The pressure was mounting. In London John Cavanagh, Michael Sherard and Ronald Paterson were all making excellent day clothes, and in Paris Hubert de Givenchy was the latest to produce truly innovative designs. Norman made a speech to introduce Givenchy's London showing of his collection at this time. Amazingly, the well of Norman's inspiration never ran dry and he was not only able to produce beautiful collections but to create a simplified look for Queen Elizabeth, the Queen Mother on her visits to America and Canada in 1954. This extracted the essence of his less cluttered wartime designs for her, but updated the silhouette in a softly flattering way. The fringes and intricate drapes were discarded by day and by night the full-skirted dresses had a clean-cut elegance, whilst still glistening with embroideries. These were perhaps calculated to appeal to the taste of American women and received wide praise.

Ian Thomas remembered that

> the Queen Mother very often came to the House of Hartnell. She was always so very keen to please. Most dresses were described by her as 'delicious' . . . or 'delectable'. Nearly all her dresses had cross-over bodices – and on so many occasions I had tried to introduce a different bodice line or detail only for it to be turned down. Her evening dresses, usually worn over a crinoline petticoat, were works of art. They were dresses that couldn't possibly be worn by any other woman – at least under the age of twenty-five. But with her incredible panache and style she could get away with it.[3]

Norman also produced designs for the beautiful Vivien Leigh, a notable client of Victor Stiebel since the 1930s, and his theatrical work brought him other clients, such as the equally lovely Margaret Leighton and a younger generation including Susan Hampshire in the 1960s.

Norman's own highly personal touch of theatre came through the post each Christmas in the form of an embroidered Christmas card sent to clients and friends. These unique creations were the product of his embroideresses' lax moments during the summer. Each year brought forth a different design through the 1950s and 1960s, and continued in rather modified form after his death in 1979. By then the necessary embroideresses had dwindled to a few hands. The paillettes, beads and drops used in the cards can all be linked to various embroidered dresses designed during his career – his 1959 card used paillettes first seen on a 1932 evening dress. The vast stock of embroidery components outlasted the life of Norman's house housed in a small basement room on shelves containing small boxes dating back to the 1920s.

The cards also reflected another merchandising venture of 1955, the launch of the Norman Hartnell jewellery range under a separate company formed by George. Retailing from between 25s. to £10, all the pieces are excellent examples of mid-1950s taste. Using paste and semi-precious stones, Norman personally designed a few pieces but otherwise left everything to outside designers, often modifying sketches, much as he did with Ian's dress designs. Many of the pieces were bought from an Amsterdam supplier of both designs and finished products. The Jewellery Collection was launched in the salon on 25 July 1955 to great publicity and worn by the house mannequins, or models as they were increasingly referred to. Wearing black evening dresses, long gloves and hats, the costume jewellery was pinned over them by Norman and onto the velvet cushions they held, and Dolores and her cohorts were photographed in the salon and in the street. Income certainly resulted from jewellery, but only in a small way until 1960.

Wedding dresses continued to feature amongst the more lucrative of Hartnell's solid business activities. In 1956, the most widely publicised was that of Lady Anne Coke, the eldest daughter of the Earl of Leicester and a former Maid of Honour to the Queen at the Coronation in 1953. This was attended by Queen Elizabeth, the Queen Mother – suitably attired by Norman – and Princess Margaret. However, this was a less public country wedding and so unlike the pre-war London weddings dressed by Hartnell, which had attracted vast public crowds as at Margaret Whigham's to Charles Sweeny.

Now Duchess of Argyll, Norman was photographed with her, his client of a quarter of a century, in the autumn of 1955 together with her daughter Miss Frances Sweeny, who was in turn a young Hartnell client. Norman's clients were obviously all ageing with him and he needed their daughters for his next commissions. It was still a period when mothers and daughters dressed alike. In an interview with both women, it seemed as though the season remained fairly similar except for the absence of the Courts and lack of feathers and trains. It was a more regulated affair in 1955; in the 1930s, few people coordinated dinners and dances so that there had been five on one night and none the next. In 1955, a debutante, or deb, might be out every night of the week.[4] There seemed to be no question of the age groups looking at different designers: elegance and sophisticated glamour were still desired by the young women even into the era of the miniskirt.

Glamour was also the rule for stage performances. For Ascot 1954, Norman invited his old client Marlene Dietrich to stay at Lovel Dene and offered to design something for the Ascot meetings. As it was only two nights before her opening in London, Miss Dietrich regretfully declined – 'What a turn-up for the book it might have been.'[5] – and more successful for publicity than the deputation of women from the design studios of Leningrad's dress Houses in the following year.

Norman hated change and hated bidding farewell to long-established employees. In 1955, the great favourite of so many, who could transform an old sack into a luxurious garment had she chosen to, Dolores left Hartnell to live and marry in South Africa. According to the press, she had worn an estimated £3 million of clothes and £5 million of jewellery in her career, and walked thousands of miles showing them. South African newspapers speculated that Norman would follow and that Hartnell would soon have a South African House too. But this was to remain Norman's pipe dream.

Royal clothes filled his life and the British fashion press was not alone in finding much to write about. Princess Alexandra, daughter of Princess Marina, the Duchess of Kent, had ordered her first long dress from Norman and the French papers speculated that she might marry a foreign prince and become a Queen herself. 'Like a social A-bomb . . . she is bursting into the headlines'[6] was the most sensational headline. For Norman, it indicated hope with more work and publicity from a younger generation of clients.

He augmented his design capabilities for the Queen in 1956 by designing a special canopy for the Royal Tour of Nigeria in 1956. An aluminium canopy draped with red, white and blue velvet, nine feet square and twelve high to the tip of the surmounting crown, it was intended to be portable, carried by the ornamental corner poles. As a final Hartnell touch, eight suspended lamps illuminated it within and four corner ones outside. Apart from his own interior decorations, this was a rare foray into non-dress design. His only other much publicised essay in interior designs was for The Westbury hotel at the corner of Bond Street and Conduit Street. Designed by the architect Michael Rosenauer, the hotel gained a Norman Hartnell Suite.

Wakers was again called in to carry out Norman's ideas in pink and turquoise, with bamboo touches resembling exotic decorations in the Royal Pavilion, Brighton. There were wall lights made as ornamental birdcages with porcelain birds within, reflecting his own dovecote at Lovel Dene. When finished, the opening party on the terrace of the suite was an occasion for open-mouthed wonder. It proved no rival to Oliver Messel's Dorchester Penthouse

Suite but lasted for eight years until it was tactfully redecorated. Norman was not asked to submit ideas for a new suite.[7]

His packer Mrs Flo Smith had more constructive success on television by revealing the secrets of her packing skills, 'watching her wizard fingers twirl tissue paper in and out of the voluminous folds'.[8] Mrs Smith was sent to Brighton to pack the Latin American dolls during the war and remained with Hartnell until George sold the business.[9]

Norman's private life was the subject of carefully controlled scrutiny, a report on 'The Social Rise of the Dress Maker' noting the guests at his Ascot Gold Cup Day Party: 'the Aga Khan, the Begum, the Aly, the Bettina – Lord and Lady Hardwicke, Lady Orr-Lewis and Mrs John Ward'. It was noted that the Begum was so entranced by Norman's own bedroom curtains of rose-printed chintz, copying a design originally made for Beau Brummell, that she was going to use the copied design for her house near Cannes. 'From Beau to Begum – not bad,' said Norman, who was off to Monte Carlo for a holiday before returning to spend part of the winter in rooms rented in Albany from his old friend from Buenos Aires days, Captain Andrew Duncan.[10]

A further much-needed boost for the Hartnell coffers was expected from a new range of Norman Hartnell silk and nylon lingerie, with stockings produced by Walton Hosiery, and also from scent and jewellery. Norman should have profited but somehow did not, and into 1957 he was kept busy designing clothes for the State Visits to Portugal, France and Denmark.

Norman's health was giving more serious cause for concern, not least because his right shoulder was seizing up and he faced the very real possibility that he might lose the use of his right arm. Such a thing would be disastrous for a designer, especially for one who chose to ignore the prevalent H-line and the A-line and ploughed on with his own ideas, ignoring worldwide changing fashion.

Ominously a tiny paragraph in the Draper's Record had noted that 'Norman Hartnell Ltd, costumier [sic] 11 July, charge to Barclays Bank Ltd, securing all monies due or to become due to the bank charged on Lovel Dene and "The Lake" Lovel Hill both Winkfield nil 24 Aug 1954'.[11] Surprisingly, no newspaper sought further information on this and Norman was spared further embarrassment; enough had been caused by a supposed public row between Dawn Grant, 'The Hibiscus Queen', and Norman's reigning South African model Cynthia Oberholzer. The two were urged to publicly patch up their quarrel, which they did. It made good publicity in the women's pages of the time.

Such was the success of *Silver and Gold* that the producer-director Herbert Wilcox, husband of Anna Neagle, turned again to his suggestion that Norman's life be turned into a film and a short television series compèred by Norman or someone else. Although Norman found the idea 'most thrilling' he again unsurprisingly let the proposition lapse and must have again wondered what role Wilcox envisaged for Anna Neagle.[12] He was in greater demand than ever and went to a clutch of interesting parties at this time. One in the famously modern penthouse of Hans and Elsbeth Juda at 10 Palace Gate, Kensington brought the following thank-you letter:

> I was amused when I complimented you on your attractive home and you said, 'No, but it is not your taste is it?' But yours is certainly a very great taste, and if I had a house like yours I would decorate it just like that – if I had the taste.[13]

He did not and was even then redecorating Lovel Dene in a more extreme Gothick manner. His own bedroom was to have a Gothick bedstead and fitted wardrobe loosely based by Wakers on the Strawberry Hill Gothick which Norman loved. He simply ignored the rocky Hartnell finances and once more Micawber-like ploughed on with what might be seen as a fantasy whilst invitations poured in. He also became attached to Margaret Leighton and rented her small set at G3 Albany, with all the usual tenant's problems. 'You have no idea how practical I have been, you gorgeous actress,' he wrote. 'I got home one night to find your refrigerator is off – HARTNELL PUTS IT RIGHT.' The telephone and then electricity were cut off and he had to pay her bills. 'Hartnell doesn't mind because he is a homely creature . . . but oh! those thousands of stone steps!!'[14]

He turned down the request that he open the gardens at Lovel Dene under the National Gardens Scheme – 'My gardens are an absolute disgrace . . . the lawns, flower beds and sidewalks are riddled with the most obnoxious and ineradicable weeds. I should be ashamed.'[15]

Norman was in South Africa before the start of 1957 which was filled with royal orders. He needed sun and relaxation badly. During one spring after suffering flu he went with Ian Thomas to the hotel La Reserve at Beaulieu.

> We went for three weeks so N.H. could recuperate and I could perhaps get down to some sketching in peace and quiet. It was

early March when we arrived at Nice Airport and drove along the coast road to La Reserve, a most heavenly hotel on the waterfront . . . I would work in the mornings until lunchtime when we would have lunch in the dining room overlooking the water . . . it was exceptionally quiet. In the afternoon we would be driven around the surrounding countryside and I remember one particular spot that we were to visit time and time again. In a small orchard. The frail-looking cherry trees had, for disease protection, been sprayed with white lime. Their tiny flower buds of the clearest pale pink were burgeoning forth against the clear blue sky. On their white stems, they looked almost artificial. I often wondered if they had inspired N.H. many years later to design a blue chiffon evening dress embroidered with pink blossoms that the Queen wore in Japan.[16]

This is now considered one of his greatest creations.

The more immediate preoccupation was to design a dress for the Queen's appearance at the Paris Opera during her forthcoming 1957 State Visit to France, it had to be as breathtaking as the one he had achieved for her mother Queen Elizabeth in 1938. The two are completely different and the 1957 dress is perhaps finer, a reflection of his ever-evolving design skills. The bouffant-skirted design of ivory satin was in the fashionable idiom of the day, but with one of the integral masterly floating trains that Norman had so made his own in the 1920s and 1930s, this time with a slight hint of a crinoline. Although fitted with the shoulder straps necessary for the pinning of ribbon and orders, the effect was of a strapless gown perfectly fitted to the waist, below which a raised band of satin swept around the front and down the back to meet halfway along the raised train, where an enormous ruched bow forms the feature of the train. The idea was an advanced reworking of his 'Honey Blonde' design of Summer 1955 and carried out by his workrooms to perfection in the knowledge that French eyes would be hypercritical.

Seldom had the Queen appeared lovelier. The topaz, pearl, amber and gold embroideries were formed into the emblems of France and poppies, marguerites, acorns and sheaves of wheat represented 'the harvest', Napoleonic bees 'industry'. The dress is now in the V&A. Interestingly, an examination of the finish of the dress reveals that it does lack some of the attention given to such garments when Mam'selle was in the House. Some of the stitching around the interior of the hem is remarkably crude, almost like tacking. Norman was known to be rather negligent in such matters, not checking as well as he might (if at all). During the 1960s and 1970s construction and finish could be very poor, notably with the use of hideous zippers straight up the back of garments, which rather mocks his appearance on BBC TV at this time advising on dressmaking. This was never true of his pre-war garments, and not seen on the majority of post-war dresses until the late 1950s. But the dress was not about to set another new fashion and was worn only for this special occasion.[17]

Norman was in Paris to be at hand if needed for any reason by the Queen and to witness the triumph of his designs, as was Hardy Amies, who contributed to the Queen's wardrobe, notably with a day ensemble worn at Versailles. He conceded that Norman's clothes were the most spectacular and had the greatest success, but that he unexpectedly enjoyed the experience of sharing the visit and several conversations with him. Christian Dior again expressed his friendship and gave a cocktail party in honour of Norman during the Visit. Amies thought that Norman's design of the slim beaded silver dress worn by the Queen with a white fox cape for the journey by night on the Seine to be even better, and it aroused great acclaim amongst the crowds.[18] As the Queen's day clothes had been panned by the press on her arrival at Orly Airport, this was a triumphant reassertion of Norman's design capabilities.

Once home in mid-April, Norman became ill due to neuritis and went to bed at Lovel Dene, cancelling all his appointments. At the age of almost fifty-six and virtually a chain-smoker, he was almost forced to take life at a slower pace. He was touched during one of his spring illnesses that the Queen sent him a sheaf of daffodils from Windsor Castle to cheer him up with a hand-written note telling him that although they were not much she had picked them herself.[19]

Margaret Leighton had starred in the film *The Passionate Stranger* dressed by Norman, who wrote to her before his Paris trip. 'I thoroughly enjoyed your film. You looked beautiful and so did the dresses, but I don't think they have photographed them to their full value. Coming downstairs in the white coat was divine.'[20] The most glamorous silver evening ensemble with white fox designed for the film was later worn by her at a ball in Windsor Castle and is now in the collection of the Fashion Museum in Bath.

At the end of April 1957, Norman was severely ill and in the London Clinic for two operations to save his arm muscles. He could have been heartened by the glowing press reports of his designs for the Queen in Paris and possibly wondering why Lady Jebb, wife of the British Ambassador, wore dresses from French couturiers, for which she was roundly criticised by the *Daily Express*.[21] It was left to Norman to have the final word:

> I take it as a compliment that the French newspapers not once mentioned my name . . . they described in great detail what the Queen wore and how she looked. They listed what everyone else wore with the names of the French designers. But never in the tiniest type did my name appear . . . Dior threw a party for me and reserved a ground-floor suite at the Ritz so that I could watch the royal procession go by. The important thing is the tremendous triumph of the Queen. If I helped, I am glad.[22]

The contrast between Dior's largesse and Norman's financial predicament is obvious. Dior had excellent financial backers and took good advice, so that his name was prominently seen on an increasing number of fashion accessories around the world and his couture dresses were often exclusively licensed to manufacturers abroad. In this field, George was completely out of his depth and Norman had dismissed the advisors who could have put him into a similar position. With the patronage of the Queen and Royal Family, he had worldwide publicity that he could never have undertaken or paid for himself.

In May, the Queen undertook a State Visit to Denmark and wore a striking matching coat and skirt patterned with a green grape design, causing the usual press flurry of excitement. It was highly fashionable and becoming, as were her evening dresses by Norman and Hardy Amies, the former producing one with enormous embroidered circles centred by blue stones, worn again in 1960 for the State Opening of Parliament to magnificent effect. The popular press naturally dubbed the design a 'dartboard'.

Norman was also at the centre of the *Daily Mirror*'s exercise in attempting to create the Deb of the Year by means of a competition won by the attractive Jill Carter, a miner's daughter. With free publicity in mind, he created a full-blown romantic evening dress for her and also acquired a fee and necessary publicity for his Norman Hartnell stockings.

This was increasingly to be a pattern in Norman's life. 'Will Haute Couture Disappear?' ran a headline in June 1957 with the news that Digby Morton was not showing a couture collection but concentrating on 'country casuals'.[23] A phrase heard during the war, the profits from designer-created ready-to-wear was now to be taken as seriously as the headlines that 1930s fashions were on the way back.[24] Norman had not only lived through it before but had also helped to created it; now he had to reinvent it and himself again. The perceptive fashion journalist Ernestine Carter thought that London clothes were now more wearable than anything seen in Paris or Rome,[25] but soon even Norman was creating designs featuring 'the sack', which was not a 1930s idiom.

In October 1957, Dior unexpectedly died and Norman, sincerely moved, said:

> Above all else he will be remembered for the wonderful beauty he brought to a rather drab world. Dior was one of the few men I would ever go to for advice and help. For there was nothing small about him. No jealousy. He was a simple man. A shy one. A gentle one. But never a mean man.

There was a Requiem Mass for Dior at Notre Dame de France, Leicester Place, WC2H, which Norman attended wearing a black cravat and accompanied by Madame Jeanne. Dior's workforce from his small London House attended, as did clients such as the Duchess of Argyll and the designer Victor Stiebel, then chairman of IncSoc.[26] Norman's perceptive words about Dior could, of course, also be used to describe himself.

By the beginning of 1958, Yves St Laurent, Dior's protégé and successor, was making the headlines and James Laver was predicting that Audrey Hepburn, Givenchy's famous client, was the star to watch as she had the shape of the future. He was correct, but even then Norman was protesting about shorter skirts,[27] when there was no alternative for him now but to follow the general trend as best he could – for 'shake, rattle and roll' now began to determine the shape of women's clothes to come.

CHAPTER SEVENTEEN

Another go at it . . .

I n 1956, Phyllis (Topsy) had been designing pottery and a small show of her work was illustrated in *The Tatler*.[1] She and her husband were now in Teheran, where he was with John Mowlem & Co. Topsy wrote to her brother: 'My dear Normie, have been reading some interesting "gossips" about the collection – your rehash of a 1925 bead fringe, etc., described (rather acidly, I thought) as the yoke that fell flat. It seems more like the yoke that brings home the bacon to me!'

She was anxious about the whereabouts of her son Charles and her husband's career. 'But we have sunshine, good friends and both fit, hope you are too, dear. Now, please, where is our son??? Lots of love from Maudie.'[2]

Mrs Price was able to write back with the news that Charles was well and had seen his uncle who had been busy all day with a visit from Princess Margaret. By May, Topsy was dead and Norman's stepsister Nimbo wrote:

> I have not phoned you or written before today, because I've been
> very grieved about Phyllis and I am *sure* you have been too, Poor
> Normie! Only time will soften the blow. What a dreadful shock . . .
> I do wish I had seen Phyllis. On Monday, after the funeral, will
> you drive straight back to Lovel Dene? or would you like to come
> here? We should love you to come and there is always a warm wel-
> come waiting for you here, *always*, but you do just as you like, but
> I thought I would write and ask you . . . Excuse more, Normie
> darling, with fondest love to you and very deep sympathy, from
> your loving sister Nimbo.[3]

Topsy was buried next to her mother in the churchyard at Clayton, Sussex to be joined in the years to come by her husband and brother. Although they had fallen out over the running of Norman Hartnell Ltd, she and Norman had remained fond of one another. Various messages of sympathy reached him; that of Nimbo must have reminded him of how she had encouraged his very early attempts to produce drawings. As her letter reveals, she remained devoted to him. Queen Elizabeth, the Queen Mother, sent Norman a letter of sympathy that moved him and he sent a touching reply back. His own letter to the Queen on the death of her husband King George VI is also a masterful example of tactful sympathy.

Nearing sixty and without a truly steady companion in his life apart from the presence of George, Norman could be withdrawn and lonely.[4] Once used to Ian Thomas, he increasingly relied upon him as his design assistant and as a solid business companion with whom he could go out in the evening, but there was always the ritual of being 'home by 10.30' to await a mysterious visitor; Ian found this disconcerting and could only imagine an assignation. No further details were forthcoming, but Miss Godley's experience narrated at the beginning partly explains the situation.

There were occasional moments of cheer for Norman with Blake, still Chaplain of Bristol Prison. In February he had written:

> My dear Bish *AT LAST* the picture of the beloved Queen Mother (to be framed in *rich gold*!) Thank you so very much, I'd a feeling it (she) would arrive eventually! Such an enchantingly rich and appropriate gown she's wearing too . . . Oh, I *do* indeed realise how frighteningly busy *you* are . . . I accomplish quite a lot (in necessary letter writing *alone*).
>
> [By the way, a letter may arrive for me c/o yourself at 'BREW-TIN' street on Thursday, marked '*to be CURLED* for' so I may pop in, in the course of the morning to appropriate same, with your most gracious permission. . .] I thought 'Bank Leakage' for a thoroughly *wet* bank manager's wife simply dripped with sodden surrealist implication, sir! . . . As always, Blake.[5]

And on 11 July they were to attend the Magdalene Dinner – 'and so we will sit side by side. A pity Harry Warrender can't be there too! Yours Bish.'[6] To which the real Bish replied: 'This is being typed by my delicious dark-haired secretary because I am busy. I suppose you will call here sometime on Friday where you can change into my dinner jacket (jackets are worn boxy these days and three-quarter length sleeves are in) . . . Yours in haste.'[7]

Old friends were a solace. Beverley Nichols recorded his observations of a young woman asking first Oliver Messel and then Norman the facile question, 'Have you a favourite colour?'

> Norman is also a kindly and courteous man, but he was tired, he had been rushing around all day putting the finishing touches to his latest collection. So he answered rather abruptly, 'For a house. For a car? For a flower? For a dress?'
>
> The young woman blinked. 'Oh . . . for a dress, of course.'
>
> He frowned at her in mock severity. 'I don't know. But I can tell you this, young lady, I have certain very definite hates.'
>
> 'Such as?' she asked.
>
> 'Flax blue and rust, next to each other, or even worse . . . pink and yellow. Like those ghastly herbaceous borders where people plant African marigolds under Dorothy Perkins roses.'
>
> She giggled. 'It's lucky I put on my little black dress.'
>
> 'On the contrary, it's merely unimaginative.' There was a twinkle in his eye that robbed his words of any offence. 'With your colouring I would choose something totally different . . . However, you would refuse to wear it. I would suggest any one of the most beautiful group in the whole colour range . . . lilacs, wisterias, pale mauves, violet. I've been trying to get women to wear these colours for over twenty years, but they won't. Clever women, stupid women, women with taste, women without it. Ask them to wear any of those colours and in the vast majority of cases they dig in their heels and say no. Don't ask me why. It's one of the great mysteries of life . . . It's fatal to even mention them,' he said as the woman wandered off.[8]

The battle for colour waged by Norman had its counterpart in many facets of his designing. Twice a year, Norman and Ian went to Paris, and in the mid-1950s these visits were mainly concerned with choosing the hats to go with the collections. Claude Saint-Cyr had her main business in Paris; her Bruton Street branch was in the hands of trusted employees and visited only occasionally by Madame Saint-Cyr. There were always well-mannered fights over what Madame Saint-Cyr called, 'Norman's big 'ats.' Madame Saint-Cyr liked her way with the neat, trim styles, while Norman wanted to satisfy his passion for large hats and would usually end up with one in black straw, one in white and another in navy.[9]

But Norman had firm ideas on what was becoming, hence his famous remark deprecating short skirts. 'Most women's knees look like underdone rock cakes.'[10] He was equally uncompromising about the view of Tibor Reich's new drawing room in his modern house. 'Monstrous, without beauty or craftsmanship. Any view through that meanly constructed window would be more pleasing than the hideous room behind it,'[11] which suggests that he was being more than diplomatically polite when writing to Mr and Mrs Hans Juda and less a fan of modernism than he had been in his House at 26 Bruton Street.

Time was now catching up with the man who had once espoused modernity in his own House, if not in his own home. He was photographed with Godfrey Winn at a party to launch Beverley Nichol's reminiscences of the 1920s (*The Sweet and Twenties*) at Lady Aberconway's magnificent Mayfair house in South Street, It was suddenly remembered that he had been in business for almost forty years.

As the 'Sack' dress made its appearance and reminded columnists of the 1920s, so Norman's early days were remembered. Cecil Beaton wrote in British *Vogue* of July 1958 about his early days as a photographer, when English fashion was so limited that the magazine articles were on anything but fashion and it was a relief when Norman's wedding dresses made the news and he could photograph them and the young girls wearing Norman's evening dresses.

If Cecil Beaton was now describing Norman in terms of nostalgic affection, then Norman must surely have been worried. Of Norman's clothes for the State Visit to France in 1957, Cecil Beaton was most disparaging to Lady Jebb, wife of the British Ambassador. It was noted that Lady Jebb was dressed for all events by French couturiers, hardly calculated to spread the fame and talents of British designers, if a diplomatic nod to France. In her diary entry for 14 April 1957 she noted that Beaton wrote to her 'the Queen triumphed over Hartnell's bad taste', although Lady Jebb thought that the sheath dress worn for the trip down the Seine suited her beautifully.[12] In the years to follow, especially after the complexities he experienced in dressing the film *My Fair Lady*, Beaton's attitude mellowed considerably.

The fact that Norman was ageing was undeniably visible. In the early 1930s he had first designed for Mrs Hay Whigham and her daughter Margaret, later Mrs Charles Sweeny. Now enduring her second marriage she was Duchess of Argyll and her daughter Frances Sweeny became Duchess of Rutland wearing a pink tulle wedding dress cut on vaguely princess or New Look lines, but shorter in the front and the hem edged with ostrich fronds dipping at the rear. The reception at Claridge's was illustrated in most popular newspapers and society journals. Now Norman ranked as a star guest in his own right and was mentioned in the reports, along with another of his 'young' clients Lady Lewisham, daughter of the novelist Barbara Cartland, an early admirer and promoter of his work. Norman also designed the trousseau for the beautiful young duchess, who wrote to him from her honeymoon a charming letter of thanks for all his efforts – something few of his clients ever managed to do.

Again reinforcing his status as a survivor of the 1920s, Norman was asked to participate in the BBC's tribute to Jack Buchanan and recounted his story of designing all the costumes for *Battling Butler* and then taking his family to watch it in the high anticipation of seeing his name in the programme credits – only to be embarrassed and annoyed on finding that his name was not included. This retrospective view of his life was inevitably marred by sadness.

Kate Day has just told me of your sad loss. Please accept my deep and sincere sympathy. I remember Topsy when you were over the way and made the first tulles that revolutionised fashion and I know the help she was to you and how close you were. It is a terrible gap that is left but I am glad the illness was not prolonged.

My news, dear Norman, is that I am retiring at the end of the summer. My firm have been *very* kind. I must thank you for the gaiety and fun you have brought into my life as a fashion writer and thank you for many kindnesses to me personally. Affectionately yours, Joyce Reynolds.[13]

She had been latterly supportive as the fashion columnist of *Country Life*, and as a former editor of *Harper's Bazaar* had contributed to the 1935 booklet *The House of Hartnell* when Norman had moved into 26 Bruton Street. Norman replied:

How very sweet of you to write me a kind letter of sympathy.

Yes, you are one of the few that would remember sister and me when we started at no. 10 Bruton Street. She was a wonderful help to me.

I am afraid the days of floating tulles have given way to the endurance of 'sack cloths' – but I always have my royal dresses as an artistic outlet.

How lucky you are, dear Joycey, to be retiring at the end of the summer. I shall miss you, for truly you have always been most helpful and generous and I have always regarded you as a real friend, which is rare. My love to you.[14]

Norman's lack of generous employers to fund his own possible retirement, the growing disenchantment with the direction in which fashion was going and sadness at his sister's death were set against his enduring triumphs and pleasures in designing for his royal clients.

Nevertheless, his business was scarcely booming: the illusion of a prosperous Norman was retained and enhanced, but the facts were sadly different. A man approaching sixty with few assets, he had to reinvent himself, much as his client Marlene Dietrich had done, or the other highly publicised stage legend Noël Coward sought to do. Work for the stage did lead to further success for Norman with the younger generation of actresses. Margaret Leighton's clothes in Rattigan's *Variation on a Theme* were glorious and worn by her with distinction, but some critics considered them too dressy and extravagant for the times; the age of the Beatnik and Angry Young Man had arrived. Norman hated it.

Norman continued to attract well-known clients during the 1950s and 1960s. The wife of the holiday-camp entrepreneur, Mrs Billy Butlin, was one such client often mentioned by the press, as was Lady Docker, the flamboyant wife of Sir Bernard Docker, owner of BSA and Daimler, for which she designed eye-stopping car interiors and exterior trims displayed at the Earl's Court Motor Show. Barbara Cartland and her daughter Lady Lewisham, later Lady Dartmouth, also wore Norman's creations with great style, as did a bevy of stage and film stars, including the Hollywood superstar Elizabeth Taylor. There were never enough to bolster the Hartnell coffers as Norman and George desired.

When Norman attended the centenary dinner at the Dorchester on 25 July 1958 to mark the founding of the House of Worth he must have wondered at 'Morts', Mrs Mortimer, the elegant 81-year-old director, who had begun her career as a mannequin with Reville around 1900 and had still not retired.

As Norman noted: 'There are no grandmothers any more. They have completely vanished. Every woman nowadays is ageless. They all have very elegant dresses, tortured hair, made-up faces. They never seem to grow old. Do you remember when you last saw a comfortable grandmother?'

Whilst looking at Morts he might have reflected on Madame Jeanne in his salon with her violet rinse, cardigans, brooches and cigarettes held in a hand weighted by jingling bracelets. The youth craze was taking off and Norman had to keep up with the times.

The obvious answer was still sought in merchandising and sales of the Hartnell name abroad, so successful for other designers, but the company reports make as dispiriting reading today as they did then. George was no Pleydell nor yet a Bish, and the worst fears of Norman's former directors were coming to fruition.

In May 1956, Norman received a letter from George to the board of Norman Hartnell Ltd in which George asked for more salary. This was undoubtedly shown to Norman beforehand, who had discussed it the previous evening with the two other major shareholders, Major and Mrs Cecil Wills, both of whom were completely captivated by Norman and George. Mrs Gladys Wills was totally besotted by Norman and her letters to him are full of gratitude for the dresses he designed for her and her daughter, for which she naturally paid.

Norman's true estimation of his co-directors emerges in a typically flippant letter written to his old friend Sir Anthony Lindsay Hogg on 26 October 1955:

> Thank you very much for your kind invitation to cocktails . . . but it happens to be the evening of the Royal Film Command Performance to which I am going, occupying two seats to the value of 50 gns.
>
> My companion for the film is Mrs Cecil Wills, whom you have met, a very sweet little matron and I wondered if you would be so kind as to allow me to bring her with me to your soiree. I ask this for two reasons. I dislike going to a party alone, and both she and I could do nicely with a gin before bowing and curtsying to royalties.

The extraordinary devotion of Major and Mrs Wills is both touching and sad, for their investment in the company brought but small dividends.

In May 1956, George earned £2,000 per annum and had an expense allowance of £400. The combined total was then a considerable sum.

Mrs Wills said she would like to suggest Mr Mitchison's salary be increased to £3,000 per annum and that he be given an expense allowance of £1,000 per annum. Mr Hartnell suggested increasing Mr Mitchison's expense allowance to £1,200 per annum and giving him a service fee of 10% on the amount derived from the various franchises under Mr Mitchison's supervision.

Bob Fearnley-Whittingstall then pointed out that this arrangement would net George £1,050 and suggested a pro-rata figure, which was agreed. George himself suggested 2.5% on each franchise. This contrasts most strangely with Norman's own position. He wanted to liquidate monies owing by him on his director's account and to do so the board agreed that the company would buy the remainder of his possessions at 26 Bruton Street. Not only that, but Norman's royalties on *Silver and Gold* of the large amount of £19,503.1s.2d. were appropriated by the company.

> None of it was due to him personally by virtue of the fact that he
> had been authorised by the company to devote a considerable part
> of his time as managing director in the furtherance of these various
> projects and the company had borne the whole of the expenses.

This fiction is easily disproved for Norman had been so unwell when his autobiography was undertaken that Evans Brothers had utilised others to write large parts of it drawn from his notes. Norman therefore personally gave away his own income to maintain the company on the scale at which it was operating.

In 1954, the net profit on couture activities was merely £2,783.15s.0d. or 4.1% of turnover 10d. in the £1 of sale. This had led to Norman cashing in a life policy in 1955 and more seriously to an 'unpleasant interview' with the manager of Westminster Bank, Carlos Place. This went on to a second discussion at the head office. Poor Norman had asked that he might be accompanied by someone, 'either by some other member of the board, by the company's accountants or by the company's solicitors, but on both occasions, he was told that he was to come alone.' Only Mr Gilbert, manager at Carlos Place, went with him.

This underlines the terrifying chasm of insolvency yawning in front of Norman and so correctly predicted by Fred Smith, Medlam and Topsy. The bank now had a total stranglehold on the company and on Norman, who had ceased to be a Micawber and apparently made a Faustian pact with the all-consuming devil of his mismanaged business and private finances. He had traded in virtually all of his assets to satisfy the greed of Norman Hartnell Ltd and that of its demanding acolytes.

There is no simple answer to the question of why this had finally happened. Partly the situation must be ascribed to Norman's own vanity and continuing desire to bolster his fame and position as a universally accepted leading designer – and in Britain the major designer – with the kudos of his Royal Warrants. Had he himself had the time and capacity to pursue his franchise agreements with the close attention and vigour they deserved, he could have become an extremely rich man. Instead, he preferred to live in a state of creativity and near-suspension of reality, leaving this vital aspect of business to the untrained George to muddle through the international licensing mazes and traps created by far more astute businessmen than George could ever hope to become.

Norman also suffered from the serious handicap of trusting a man with whom he had only emotional ties and of allowing his own fetishistic fantasy life to become a powerful private need that lasted into old age. George was both Norman's protector against the ever-present threat of scandal and his equally self-serving guardian.

Of Norman's male friends and guests from the 1960s and 1970s, none interviewed have forgotten the nightly telephone calls from George to Norman, during which an account of his day's doings and the identity of whoever might be present was accounted for. The Cracknells, who had been installed at Lovel Dene by George and were regarded by him as trustworthy, were also questioned by him about Norman's guests and his activities. Norman admittedly felt the need of a strong male figure in background control of his life and George was this man until Norman died. It was also convenient that George was married and had a separate existence of his own, which Norman sometimes shared, sometimes at Christmas or on holiday in Seahouses, near Alnwick, Northumberland, from where George had come. There can be no doubt that Norman liked the dark element of control and menace emanating from the increasingly bulky form of the much taller figure of George; equally he could hardly expect to end the relationship without repercussions. But Norman had now left himself with only one great asset – his design talents.

Alone with Westminster Bank, Norman had to make the best of it. A report had been made by an assessor on the company's affairs at the instigation of the bank, and Norman asked to see this. Astonishingly 'this request had at first been absolutely refused, [then] he was told that a copy would be supplied to him after certain matters had been cut out of it . . . the attitude shown to him by the Head Office representatives had been one of somewhat contemptuous hostility.'

Norman asked if the bank would prefer to have the company accounts removed to another bank and unsurprisingly the reply was that if he would find such a bank, 'Westminster Bank Limited would do everything to facilitate its removal.' Remarkably, Major and Mrs Wills completely stood with Norman, who 'a few days after this unpleasant interview . . . had stayed the night with Mr Hugh Fraser, a multi-millionaire controlling the organisation known as the House of Fraser'

Luckily for Norman, the Cavendish Square branch of Barclays Bank took over the accounts at Fraser's instigation and allowed an overdraft of £30,000, but to be reduced to £20,000 as soon as possible. The Westminster Bank report was shown to the board with 'numerous excisions' causing 'astonishment' but the overdraft would not be paid for until submitted in full. Norman had once more been suspended over the abyss and, luckily for him, just pulled back - again. Fraser had, no doubt, reasons for helping Norman, who was to establish retail outlets in the major House of Fraser stores in the near future.

By March 1959, the company was again in debt, owing the bank £29,516, and Norman called a meeting to report the 'acute financial position'. Hugh Fraser gave a guarantee of £10,000 – but the overdraft limit remained at £30,000. Although sales amounted to a large £171,421, the expenses totalled an even larger £184,073, and the deficit of £13,652 was only reduced to £5,276 because of income from franchises – some of which had then ceased. The net loss was running at £100 per week.

It would have seemed inconceivable to the outsider that such a drastic situation could possibly exist behind the doors of the glamorous Hartnell building with its famous designer attending to so many distinguished clients' needs. The Royal Tours and State Visits of the Queen, Princess Margaret and the appearances of Queen Elizabeth, the Queen Mother were all enthusiastically commented upon, as were Norman's designs for them, his other clients and his House collections. However, behind the glitter of the salons and the luxurious reflections in the mirrors waited a real crisis.

According to company papers, George could only suggest that production costs in the workroom be examined more closely: 'Mr Hartnell said that, having listened with interest to the discussion, he would go into the matter very carefully with the stock-keeper in order to reduce the material content of each model. . .' There was also a brief mention of the extraordinary amount of travelling, entertaining, publicity and advertising expenses – £23,369 – more than four times the net trading loss for the year: 'Every possible step should be taken to reduce expenditure under these heads.'

The board echoed the very things so deprecated by Fred Smith that were still true nearly fifteen years later, and George could only feebly suggest that the downstairs salon should be leased out for £2,500 a year to a hairdresser. He was thus proposing to rid Hartnell of its invaluable and only showroom window onto the street.

The usual question was raised with Norman concerning the royal accounts, as his diffidence in dealing with such matters that annoyed both Palace officials and his own board had now led to '£10,000 owing on the royal accounts and Mr Hartnell said that he would take an early opportunity of speaking to Her Majesty's Private Secretary with a view to suggesting a substantial payment on account'.

Quite why Norman persisted in riling everyone concerned with these necessarily delicate matters is again a perplexing question as the correspondence clearly shows the procedures to be followed. Norman simply did not want to know about money – in interviews he frequently stated that he knew nothing about the prices of his clothes and that he left such matters to others. Whilst Miss Godley was there to carefully look after the administration of his personal accounts, all went well, but he extended this principle to company business too, only weighing in on the subject of fees, as previously with Berkertex.

With merchandising licences, neither he nor George had much control over the running of the businesses bearing the Hartnell name. In December 1959, when the company accountant asked for the balances owing from Norman Hartnell (Australia) Ltd and Norman Hartnell (South Africa) Ltd George had to reply that Jack Barregar had explained the accounts on a recent visit – 'had agreed them, but had not yet confirmed them in writing'. The debit on the company account now stood at £21,592.[15]

On the one hand Royal Tours and State Visits furthered the patronage of such influential clients and made Hartnell an ever-greater worldwide name. On the other hand, the same patronage entailed certain problems that a clever businessman might have overcome. When George VI died in 1952, turnover was affected because of large cancellations of orders – the royal ladies alone cancelled thirty orders – and

> some of [the] materials had been specially purchased and a number of garments were being worked upon, all of which constituted a loss . . . In 1953, coronation year, the coronation robes of the Queen, Queen Mother and Princess Margaret together with six for Maids of Honour, the Duchess of Kent and Princess Alexandra occupied so much of our staff that we had to refuse clients. Many of these customers were of course lost for ever.

Special prices and arrangements were made for the supply of garments to the Queen, the Queen Mother, Princess Margaret and the Duchess of Kent. During the five-year period from 1 August 1949 to 31 July 1954 it is estimated that these special concessions resulted in undercharges as follows, assuming rates had been fixed as to normal clients.

There followed a quantified list of the amounts applicable to:

> The Queen
> The Queen Mother
> Princess Margaret
> The Duchess of Kent

These made up a substantial annual average, but there was no record of Norman or his accountant ever having written to the Private Secretaries about these amounts. Indeed, they were written off as company losses.

The report went on:

> Nor must the fact that vendeuse and fitters go to the Palace be overlooked. In the period under review garments were supplied, assuming that each garment required two fittings (a fair average) this would have meant visits at (approximately X plus the taxi ride), the time of the people concerned would be more than double a normal fitting because of travelling time. Obviously no extra charge is involved in this respect as the vendeuse and fitter would

49

51

52

49 'In Love': a Hartnell scent promotion with a new dress c. 1953

50 Bergdorf Goodman, NYC, Hartnell's 'Silver and Gold Coronation Collection' in multiple window displays. 1953

51 NH, the Hartnell Jewellery Collection in-House c. 1956

52 Hartnell Jewellery Collection modelled l-r, Ruby, Emerald, Sapphire, Garnet c. 1957

54

52 NH, Madame Jeanne at Notre Dame de France, Soho,
Requiem Mass for Christian Dior 1957

53 NH, Madame Isabelle fitting Cassandra c. 1960

54 NH, most trusted employees, early 1960s

55

56

57

58

55 Madame Vera, Dolores, salon c. 1950

56 NH, HM Queen Elizabeth, The Queen Mother and HRH
Princess Margaret wear Hartnell. IncSoc Show 1958

57 Design for HM Queen Elizabeth II as Queen of Canada, worn 1959

58 Design for HM Queen Elizabeth II as Queen of Canada, worn 1957

62

61

59 Design for HRH Princess Margaret's wedding dress worn 1960

60 Design for HM Queen Elizabeth, The Queen Mother, worn
at the wedding of HRH Princess Margaret 1960

61 Film costume by Hartnell, Dame Anna Neagle : 'Maytime in Mayfair' 1949

62 NH, Hartnell Christmas Party, star guest Frances Day (r) sings 1948

63

65

64

67

66

63 NH, Valerie Hobson, Anne Todd and Jack Hawkins examine designs 1955
64 NH, the Duchess of Bedford on tv: 'What's My Line' 1962
65 Shirley Eaton, 'Bond Girl', models Hartnell lingerie c. 1960
66 NH, international star hairdresser Alexandre c. 1966
67 Effervescent Hartnell clients Mary, Lady Delamere and Barbara Cartland (r) c. 1960

68

69

70

71

68 NH, Owen Hyde Clarke design menswear,t 26 Bruton Street, Mayfair c. 1970
69 NH, John Packer of Reid & Taylor arrive for their show, Beirut. 1972
70 NH, Mara, John Packer, Kenneth Partridge and Felicity Rutland (front) c. 1972
71 NH, Cilla Black, Tommy Nutter c. 1975

72 NH, six designing decades. le petit salon, 26 Bruton Street, Mayfair c. 1972

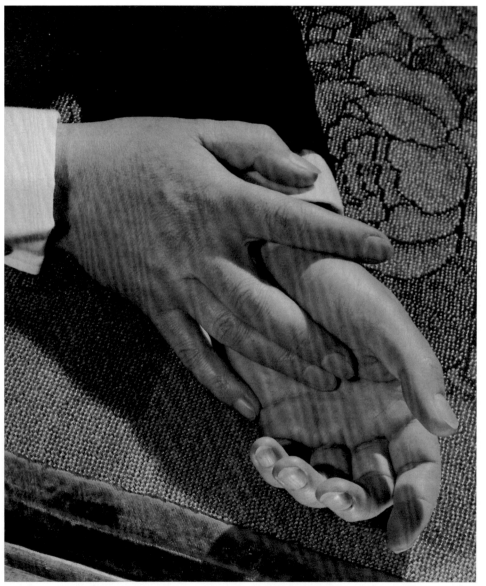

73 NH, the hands of a designer and artist c. 1953

have been paid whether or not BUT they would have been more gainfully occupied.

When fashion journalists such as Ernestine Carter and Prudence Glynn later wrote that Norman had entered a designing cul-de-sac with his role as a royal designer, they were more accurate than they guessed, in financial terms, but also wrong to expect a designer to keep pulling rabbits out of hats for the amazement of the world's fashion press and consumers of couture. In fact, he did have many tricks left up his sleeve and his royal clientele brought him the plum job of designing the wedding dress of Princess Margaret when she married Antony Armstrong-Jones in 1960.

John Cavanagh considered that this wedding dress was one of Norman's greatest designs, if not the greatest. To a younger designer trained notably at Molyneux in Paris, 'the sheer simplicity of the design and elegance of the line formed on a complicated structure in white layers of flimsy organza revealed the masterly hand of a man who truly understood how fabric behaves.' Although Norman was not a dressmaker himself, he knew from his experience over the decades just how every type of natural or artificial fabric could be shaped and cut to fulfil his own wishes. He relied on the competence of his workforce and increasingly on Ian Thomas, who noted:

> It was certainly not Mr Hartnell's idea of a wedding dress! He had come back from Clarence House after the initial discussions for the design of the dress with a small scrap of paper and on it a small pencil sketch of a wedding dress. It had a fitted bodice, long tight sleeves and a V neck – utterly plain – and it was suggested that the material should be organza. Apparently the sketch had been done by Antony Armstrong-Jones – who of course at one time had been a designer [sic]. The look on Mr Hartnell's face told all! No embroidery, no lace, no satin appliqué. 'It'll be nothing more than a nightgown,' he said. His passion for over-elaborate clothes would not be given its full rein.[16]

Miss Louie independently confirmed this initial suggestion for the design of the dress and she went to Clarence House with over twenty samples of white organza for the Princess to choose from.[17] This was not unusual when dealing with important clients. Lady Joubert, administrator of IncSoc in succession to Ann Ryan, was once with Norman in his room at Bruton Street when Miss Louie came in and extended an arm covered with a row of blue fabric snippets saying, 'Queen Elizabeth doesn't like these blues and wants another, but this is all we've got.'

'If Her Majesty wants another blue then she shall have it,' was all Norman said.[18]

Miss Louie stressed that the basis of the wide-skirted design lay in the six layers of the organza allowing the dress movement without any wrinkles. As Ian Thomas said:

> It was his genius that eventually gave it its beauty. The rouleaus of organza that would bind the dress together would be repeated on the fine silk tulle veil, giving it fluted scalloped beauty that it would never have had if it had just been tulle alone. Isabelle – the French fitter – made the dress and none of us during the making . . . realised what dramas there were to come! . . . The six layers of white silk organza were bound at the hem with a rouleau of the same material.
>
> All went well until the day before the wedding when the dress was receiving its final press. Due perhaps to the composition of the material, or the way that differing grains had been used, some of the layers started to shrink so badly that the night before the wedding the rouleau had to be taken off and the skirt redone. Stitching went on all night, but the result was well worth it. The dress was perfect for its setting in the Abbey and looking back now I remember Mr Hartnell's beaming face when praise was heaped upon him for this unexpectedly simple creation. He lapped it up! If only people had known his heartache when it was originally suggested![18]

The dress had a tight V-necked bodice and long sleeves, but with typical ingenuity echoing that of Queen Elizabeth's train to the dress worn to the 1947 Opening of Parliament in South Africa, it was made with a division at the back of the skirt so that on emerging from the Irish state coach the beautiful Princess Margaret was in an immaculate crease-free dress. On this occasion, the division was more subtle, as it was invisible.

Ian and others involved from Hartnell were invited to watch the departure of the Princess from the hall of Clarence House and to watch the procession returning up The Mall to Buckingham Palace. Ian had been Norman's assistant for almost eight years, but he thought this was the closest he had been to a member of the Royal Family, apart from seeing them in the House from a distance. Amazingly, he had also never met another member of IncSoc, with the exception of his initial meeting with Cavanagh and a single meeting with Victor Stiebel, who made the going-away clothes of the Princess appropriately in 'Sunshine Yellow'. It was generally thought that Stiebel would be asked to design the wedding dress, as the Princess had worn many of his designs, and it was believed to be the greatest disappointment of his career that he could not crown it with such a great success. He was, however, typically generous in his letter of congratulation to Norman.

The wedding provided Norman with the opportunity to design an outstanding full-length day dress for the Queen in turquoise, the plain silk front of the skirt enhanced with appliqued lace at the back and over the belted bodice. Worn with a lace bolero jacket and a superb hat of net crowned by two turquoise roses, the Queen wore matching long turquoise gloves with the three-quarter-length sleeves of the jacket. A necklace of pearls the size of pigeons' eggs and a diamond brooch and bracelets ensured that the Queen appeared to her best advantage in company with her sister, who literally dazzled Westminster Abbey with the Poltimore diamond tiara. Both Queen Elizabeth and the Duchess of Kent were in slim-fitting, rather restrained long dresses, but the bridegroom's mother, Norman's old friend of the 1920s, Lady Rosse, was in a short dress and coat – echoes of Madame Lebrun's predicament during the 1938 state visit.

Norman's triumphant reassertion of his genius as a designer was timely. He had already provided some interesting designs for Princess Margaret's Caribbean Tour and for the Queen's Tour of America and Canada in 1959, when he had produced another variation of the line first seen in the famous 1957 Paris Opera dress. With a fan-tail replacing the attenuated bow and train, Canada saw the Queen in a full-skirted dinner dress of jade green and turquoise. He had produced an intermediate version of this line for the State Visit to the Netherlands in 1958, the longer train of the Paris Opera design foreshortened and a bow acting as a sort of bustle. The slim line of the 1957 Paris Seine boat-trip dress was replicated in a simple sheath of citrus-yellow ribbon lace re-embroidered with 'diamonds', crystals and silver. He also designed another dress for Canada in 1959, of lavender and rose printed taffeta with a swathed bodice and elaborately tucked and draped fringed side panels, which stresses the fact that Norman was a designer capable of enhancing a variety of clients with individual styles of their own.

It is rare that two women could recall meeting another in 'the same Hartnell', although Bebe Daniels and Evelyn Laye had that experience at the Variety Artists Ball held in the Albert Hall in the early 1950s. Both women wore lemon yellow embroidered Hartnell dresses with 'diamonds' and gilded pearls and found themselves sitting at the same table. Norman wrote:

> I need not have worried so much for my morning mail contained two telegrams. One said: 'I hate you and I hate Evelyn Laye. Close my account at once. Signed Bebe Daniels.' The other said: 'I hate you and I hate Bebe Daniels. Close my account at once. Signed Evelyn Laye.[19]

Journalists often printed photographs of the Queen and Queen Elizabeth, the Queen Mother talking to Anna Neagle – 'all dressed by Hartnell and all in different individual styles'. Clients such as J. Stanleigh Turner and his wife Ann went to Norman for just such reasons. The Duke of Windsor had turned down a giant aquamarine as too large and expensive, but Mr Turner bought it and it was mounted as part of a diamond necklace, for which Norman designed a strapless ice-blue duchesse satin evening dress with navy stars embroidered on the bodice and down one side. In 1955 this dress cost £500.[20] Such commissions were sadly rare.

The making of Princess Margaret's wedding dress had not been difficult from the technical side alone. The unwanted and feared intrusion of the press had finally been able to crack the secrecy surrounding the Hartnell royal design. As James Brady recounts, he was asked to obtain this for his paper *W.W.D.*, which had formerly been so supportive of Norman and now wanted a real scoop. This time it worked – Brady visited George and was politely told nothing, but as most fine fabrics and accessories were bought by the London dressmakers in Paris, *W.W.D.*'s Paris fashion editor Thelma Sweetinburgh set to work and dredged around amongst the employees of the fabric houses. A rough sketch was made of the dress and Mr Brady took it to London showing it to George. 'Mitchison's moustache and mutton chops quivered with a proper disdain' and he took the drawing inside to show Norman, who would make no comment. George made none either, fearing yet another spat with

Commander Colville at the Palace. But Princess Margaret was upset that *W.W.D.* published a reasonable facsimile of her dress.[21]

The Cracknells were with Norman when this happened and he was distraught at the thought of possibly having to design another dress, through no fault of his own. As it was, the design had to be carefully reworked all through the night before the wedding because of the way the fabric now reacted to pressing. George Cracknell remembered Norman writing letters to Princess Margaret, the Queen and to Queen Elizabeth, which he then had to deliver, being sent off in Norman's car. The look of relief on Norman's face was palpable when he received a long, understanding letter from the Queen, and Cracknell remembered him waving four sheets of paper and saying that they all understood what had happened. Norman had to make his way to the house through the woods by the lake as the press were waiting for him in the front.[22] It was an occasion for more apologies to Commander Colville too, who was never particularly happy when having to answer questions about clothes.

For Norman, such moments of real pain were a far cry from the whimsical pieces often asked for by journalists. For example, *Woman's Own* asked him (as well as a dozen other famous people) for 'a line on any "miserly" habit . . . such as turning out the gas, saving this or that'.

George tellingly scribbled, 'I squeeze my toothpaste tube until I hear Mr Mclean screaming for mercy,' but this was not unnaturally replaced by Norman with 'I always bow to a full moon because she is so beautiful', although the former was undoubtedly more to his true taste, as was Blake's suggestion of an 'alternative last verse for you . . . of . . . the rollicking hymn "Through the Night of Doubt and Sorrow".

> Swift the hungry Swan and Edgar
> On the lake at Lovel Dene
> Munch the muffins soaked in Vodka
> While the un-chic ghost turns GREEN.[23]

Norman was a great giggler, so much so that in the mid-1950s the photographer Paul Tanqueray had a difficult time posing both George and Norman for their portraits and disliked the results to the extent that he asked them both to come back again separately.[24]

Scarcely had H.M.Y. *Britannia* left Tower Bridge on 6 May 1960 with the newly married princess and her husband than the New Norman Hartnell Cosmetic Range Fashion Tour took off on 8 May to tour the British Isles in a party including Norman, George, the remarkable Major Donald Neville-Willing (sometime London agent for Marlene Dietrich), Ann Price, Flo Smith and a chorus of model girls headed by Cynthia Oberholzer.

From London, the party flew to Glasgow, continued to Edinburgh, Newcastle, from where the whole party went for a day trip to Alnwick Castle, and the Lake District before going to Liverpool, Nottingham, Manchester and back to London on 21 May. They left on 22 May for Birmingham, including a show booked for Stoneleigh Abbey (then changed due to a fire), leaving next for Coventry and ending in Leeds on 27 May, where the itinerary ends: '9.45 p.m. fish and chips supper will be arranged at the local fish shop, WHERE SHOES NEED NOT BE WORN.'

Not unnaturally, following the royal wedding, press coverage and local interest was intense, especially as Norman appeared after each show and mingled with local worthies. The cosmetics certainly sold well and there were hopeful signs that the income would help the sick financial state of the company, especially as House of Fraser stores began to feature the new Hartnell range and Hugh Fraser wrote to Norman that he was personally encouraging this. Many of the shows, such as that in Coventry, were given in aid of charity, a form of show Norman had pioneered in the 1920s.

Of the many British shows that Hartnell gave, two were particularly memorable – one at Ascot in 1959 held in the Royal Enclosure with pouring rain outside and one at J. Paul Getty's house at Sutton Place in 1967, where the models were incredulous at the pay telephones they had to use and Norman found the drinks cabinet locked and a butler with no keys.[25] Shows were also put on at Highclere and Cliveden in 1962, which were televised. They were expensive for Hartnell to stage and internal correspondence reveals that whilst being excellent for publicity, they achieved little for the financial success of the company.

In 1960, Norman took a holiday in Vichy where he attended Dr Regnault's clinic, one of several annual visits, often with George. Norman also went to stay with Dr Regnault in his house in Casablanca. He went primarily to lose weight and to find some release from the pressures of his business life. Concerned with his increasingly aged looks, Miss Pugh of Alstons Corsetry supplied him with an 'Alston rubber reducing corset' and he went to Rebelle Coiffeur de Dames at 29 Berkeley Street, Mayfair, to have his hair dyed, something he had begun to do during the war. His crimped, wavy locks occasioned some surreal correspondence: 'Unfortunately in the summer the sun does have a tendency to lighten the colour and bring out the red shades. I do hope you will appreciate this difficulty and let us have another go at it, as I feel sure that we can get it under control.'[26] Plaintive letters from Rebelle begging forgiveness apparently went unanswered.

Towards the end of 1960, Norman was asked by Mr Cashman of *Woman's Mirror* for his opinion on what he thought was the most important event in 1960, the year in which Gagarin went into space, and he answered, 'As opposed to Russia's ready access into Heaven, the sight of H.R.H. the Princess Margaret approaching the altar for her wedding in Westminster Abbey.'

And to the enquiry as to what event had affected him personally, he wrote, 'The murder of the modest by the lascivious,' for he was increasingly disenchanted with developments in society and fashion.

On reflection, he crossed the comment out and wrote, 'After two years the relief of eventually launching my cosmetic range,' as usual displaying a typically astute flair for public relations and free advertising, whilst not dwelling on his own private life.

CHAPTER EIGHTEEN

But never mind!

The 1960s were a particularly difficult time for couture, whether in London, Paris – or anywhere. In London, the fashion press was still keen to report on the bi-annual London Collections but finding increasing difficulty with the glamorous image it had once conjured up as young women ceased to dress like their mothers and the latest dance crazes made Hartnell's favourite styles for evening dresses impractical. Wholesalers' fashionable clothes were now made for a younger market at easily affordable prices and the competitive quality of finished ready-to-wear garments was also extremely high. It became possible for young women to have several changes of clothing in their wardrobes and discard them more rapidly in favour of the next craze. All the London designers looked more closely at ready-to-wear. Digby Morton had already moved from couture into his country casuals and Hardy Amies was to carry on both facets of this with skill and success, having in the early 1950s established a ready-to-wear in-house department usually sourced from other suppliers ready-made.

Norman's wartime foray into Berkertex ready-to-wear had been followed post-war by licenses granted to South Africa and Australia, and there were licences in New Zealand and Canada for ready-to-wear clothing made to his designs. Apart from the very long running arrangement with *Woman's Day* in England, which featured a Hartnell dress on the cover and a pattern inside, Norman had also licensed a simple embroidery design to be featured in each issue, usually for a tea or tray cloth in simple cross-stitch worked in primary colours. Scent, stockings, lingerie and cosmetics were now sold under his name. In the 1960s, he also diversified this name into knitwear, mainly designed by Ian Thomas, who went abroad to examine the competition, seek ideas and suitable manufacturing sources. From Florence, he sent a typical letter:

. . .the stuff in the shops is most uninteresting, but the garments we are seeing now have a little more character . . . but of course anything new and exciting tends to be rather expensive . . . The cheap stuff is mainly in mohair and is rather bulky and hairy – of course it is hand knitted – (slave labour!). To me these things look rather 'rustic' or 'peasant' . . . not very 'Hartnell'. We saw a lovely collection of knitted garments outside Florence – it looks more like jersey . . . jacket, jumper or blouse and skirt. These are about £10.0s.0d. the ensemble here, making it rather pricey by the time it gets to England . . . I think this will conflict with our ready-to-wear – because the captain is always saying 'No skirts!' However, Kennerley-Edwards thinks this can be through another company of yours GVK. Well that's his responsibility – don't hold me to it! I personally thought we were here to buy a few sample knitwear garments and have a good look round – but Kennerley-Edwards is seeing jewellery, scarves, materials etc., etc. My only regret is that the trip was not properly organised and appointments made in advance . . .

I am leaving Florence . . . to Montreux. We are a little short of money so I thought it better if we start back soon . . . The rainwear is very poor – only very cheap things . . . The styles we designed for Ganex are way up on these! . . . Sorry no postcards – but we have no money.[1]

Apart from the not unusual confusion of Hartnell goals, ways and means, the letter is also interesting for the reference to the Ganex 'mac' for which Norman and Ian had designed new styles. These were to be a UK-wide sensation after Harold Wilson became Prime Minister and was photographed wearing one. Norman had remained on friendly terms with Harold and Mary Wilson since the former's post at the Board of Trade in the 1940s.

Ian Thomas's reference to lack of funds was as much a reflection of the currency controls in operation as to the paucity of Hartnell funding for others than Norman or George. However, writing to his lawyer David Jacobs in early 1961, inviting him to dinner, Norman added, 'Incidentally I have no cook at the moment – I am terribly fond of tins.'[2]

Jacobs had been instrumental in obtaining a loan for the cash-stricken House of Hartnell in 1960 and was another fount of useful, practical advice – when listened to. This did not stop Norman from carrying on with the latest redecoration of Lovel Dene, for which he was given a stuffed horse's head in preparation for turning one small room, later sometimes called the Black Room, into what was ostensibly solely a tiny museum of military items, including uniforms. His real enthusiasm for such things was also a conspicuous part of his success in always knowing the most suitable colours to be worn by members of the Royal Family on state occasions and on Royal Tours.[3]

But whilst the clothes for the Royal Tours and State Visits and other events continued to fill newspaper columns, they did not fill the Hartnell coffers. The establishment of ready-to-wear collections was an urgent priority, eventually resulting in the new Le Petit Salon on the ground floor and the establishment of in-house Hartnell salons all over the country in selected House of Fraser stores. Furthermore, influential observers such as Cecil Beaton still deplored much of his output for the Royal Family. In 1960, Beaton observed Queen Elizabeth in a 'hideous turquoise-green telephone cover. How *could* he?' Possibly, because she wanted it.

For the Queen's visit to Italy in 1961, Norman again designed elegant clothes. There is no doubt that the concurrent use of Hardy Amies designs for part of the wardrobe on each Royal Tour had the effect of sharpening Norman's pencil and avoiding too many of the over-lavish details he so revelled in. There was a greater coherence in both line and look, also affected by Ian Thomas's collaboration. The Queen looked truly fashionable, but in her own style.

For an historic meeting with the Pope, the Queen wore one of Norman's most dramatically simple designs. A slim, slightly bell-shaped dress of black lace worn with the obligatory black veil rising up from the head and cascading down on either side of the Russian fringe tiara, which won the day as the veil disappointingly failed to maintain the height as designed. Part of the problem in designing such grand dresses lay in the magnificence of so much of the jewellery worn by members of the Royal Family and it was not always known what exactly would be worn with a finished design. However, in the case of the relatively simple black lace dress, almost anything would have been seen to advantage. Because protocol suggested that black was appropriate in the presence of the Pope within the glories of the Vatican, the Queen was also able to wear a colour usually avoided because of its association with death and mourning.[4]

The Royal Tours of India and Pakistan in the same year had also necessitated a large wardrobe of clothes to be worn in a wide variety of climatic conditions. It was on this occasion that the Press Secretary, Richard Colville, who was often infuriated at the press attention focusing solely on the Queen's clothes, snapped that Her Majesty did not have dresses specially designed for clambering aboard elephants, though the dresses were quite suitable for ascending the steps of aeroplanes and the principle was the same. More serious were the complaints of the Queen herself about the construction of some of her dresses made under the supervision of Madame Isabelle, for some had net reinforcements attached in the usual way to both seams and hems, in spite of Miss MacDonald's instructions to the contrary, and the difficulty in moving and sitting elegantly in these ungiving cages can be imagined.

As the dresses were packed away in trunks for several weeks, it was Miss MacDonald's frustrating task to rapidly try and unpick these and some unwanted thick shoulder straps. This was another instance of lack of quality control before the finished articles left 26 Bruton Street, however the superb embroideries looked suitably magnificent – and at this date Norman was amongst the last London designers able to produce them under close secrecy in-house.

Norman was at hand in Rome whilst the Queen was there and also in India, where he was utilised as a judge in Bombay beauty contests, yet still managed to produce his Autumn–Winter 1961 show, writing to a friend, 'You are quite right, it is hard work producing a collection like that.'[5]

Ian Thomas noted:

> After a session in Paris (buying fabrics and accessories) it was all the more noticeable how difficult it was to produce a collection in London. Belt and button manufacturers almost non-existent here compared with Paris. If we wanted to see a belt collection in Paris, twenty delighted manufacturers would have been on our doorstep at the crack of dawn, with the most artistic and beautifully made collections. Anything could be changed – if a different colour was wanted, the chosen belt, in our colour would be delivered the following morning . . . the choosing of fabrics used to take about a week. Collections of fabrics would come over from Paris in about May for the winter collections and November for the spring of the following year.

Although Norman designed dresses in artificial fabrics for both Courtaulds in Britain and Du Pont in the USA, these were usually created solely for use in advertisements. Virtually all the fabrics used in-house were of natural fibres, some from Sekers or Ascher, most from abroad.

Louie . . . would arrange the piles of ranges in a fitting room and the three of us would go through the thousands of patterns. In a collection, by one manufacturer, or perhaps 300 or 400 cloths, we would perhaps choose half a dozen. It was not always that we could choose the most gorgeous of the fabrics. Some of them were almost too beautiful to be worn – and although N.H. liked his glamour, it was always the bread and butter numbers that paid the rent. Woollen coatings suitable for day would be teamed with a silk for the dress. Mr Bell the furrier would be consulted about a matching fur to a fabric – and perhaps a white fox would be tinted to match an evening coat.

The furrier's room produced the highest return in the building, as ever. But his job was simple compared to Norman's.

When all the models had been created, fitted on model girls, taken in one eighth of an inch here, let out half an inch there, hours spent in getting the garment just right, Mr H. would suddenly decide to put it on another girl, and the whole garment would, much to the fitter's disgust, which she would show quite plainly, be fitted all over again.

One can only marvel at Norman, then in his sixties with nearly forty years of a string of collections, battling on and on.

We always had the most awful rehearsals. It was always our intention to have one three or four days before a show but nearly always it was the day before. What a shambles it all was. It was always found that one model girl – one of the boss's favourites, had six dresses more than the next girl. We always hoped to have a rehearsal to ourselves but it never turned out that way. There were always two or three members of the press, who wanted to be in on the collection before their rivals.

Norman always got on well with the model girls, who generally adored him. After Dolores left, he and George, as well as Ian, were particularly fond of the beautiful blonde South African Cynthia Oberholzer. They all relished the humour of all the girls.

Once, some found boxes of Norman's 1940s platform shoes and gave themselves an impromptu show wearing them. Norman discovered the show in progress and asked for it to be repeated for him.[6]

Such moments were a relief from the nervous exhaustion of pre-collection days when, as Ian remembered

> the rehearsal was always attended by the saleswomen whose stony faces were never a joy to behold. They would never commit themselves to admiring anything in the new collection – they never seemed to have the courage of their convictions about a model – until perhaps they had sold it half a dozen times. Then it became 'ravishing' in their eyes – 'such a lovely dress – didn't I say it would sell?' It was only Mme Jeanne, the head vendeuse, who would come up and congratulate us, and not until the following day – or a diplomatic lapse of time – would she come up and discuss cleverly what had been left out or what should be put in.[7]

For Norman, the routine was only varied by the attempts to make ready-to-wear pay, and to this end he would go to a great variety of First Nights or dances, anything to help promoting Norman Hartnell. Quiet evenings were relished by him, as he claimed never to be lonely.

Mrs Cracknell remembered that at Lovel Dene he would sometimes just stand and stare into the distance and she realised he was thinking of a new design. At home, he drank little and ate simple things. She once found him boiling an egg in an electric kettle. 'Why not?' he said. But as the 1960s wore on, Mrs Cracknell thought him a 'lonely soul', and although friends such as Rex Sherren visited him, he seemed sometimes lost.

His neighbours, Mr and Mrs Kenneth Thornton (who had terrible problems with 'Norman the Neighbour' or 'Norman the Nuisance', as he called himself, when he had been forced to agree to George's scheme for a mink farm at Lovel Dene) found him rather morose until he had been enlivened by some scotch. On one occasion, they also had to lend him £5 in Windsor, when he was suddenly caught out without any cash in his pocket.

George Cracknell, George Mitchison's batman in Malaya, was initially grateful for the job but hated the smelly mink farm he had to look after. He also came to resent George and what he and his wife thought was his bad controlling influence over Norman, especially when Lovel Dene was sold. The subsequent CEOs of the Hardy Amies-Norman Hartnell company names were in turn also supportive of my work for this biography, Simon Petherick; Tim Maltin and Tony Yusuf. However, Timothy Tufnell considered that Norman was also afraid of them. They were both very fond of Norman and were fascinated by his guests and also the preparations Norman took for them. Although a friend of John and Fanny Cradock, for whom Norman made some glittering dresses to wear during her culinary displays, he really loved simple food. Red beef with the juice running out of it was more to his taste than 'crab diable au gratin' which he submitted to yet another journal wanting a star's favourite recipe.[8]

In spite of his taste for simple food, if not for alcohol, Norman developed gout, which caused him to miss many engagements in autumn 1961, including lunch with Lady Illingworth, owner of one of the last grand Mayfair houses at 44 Grosvenor Square, and drinks nearby with another old client Rafaelle, Duchess of Leinster. This really was the last of old London, as were the great shows put on by IncSoc in the presence of members of the Royal Family. In the 1950s, they had become a regular event, but in the early 1960s, it was the Duchess of Kent, Princess Marina, who reactivated a declining IncSoc by asking for one to be held in St James's Palace in 1961. The often lavishly staged shows included one held at Osterley in 1960, almost a swansong for the world for which couture and its then designers most wished design for, and after the official end of debutante Presentations to the Queen at Buckingham Palace in March 1958 so seldom enjoyed fully again.

The more memorable of the IncSoc shows were choreographed by Norman's old friend Robert Nesbitt and decorated by a new friend, the young Kenneth Partridge, who went to great lengths to provide an exotic setting for one held in Hanover Square, even borrowing antique furniture from Frank Partridge Ltd, the antique dealers in Bond Street.

As the old London Society way of life died and Presentations ceased, so couture began to fade along with its ageing clients and practitioners in the face of a younger generation no longer aspiring to dress like their mothers, or even grandmothers. To a young person joining Hardy Amies in the early 1960s, Norman Hartnell himself seemed antediluvian and his clothes verging on the absurd. Some of his publicity-driven show-stoppers certainly were, none more so than a crinoline skirt made of 1,000 real £5 notes as a prize for a Top Rank bingo competition in 1963, or his 'Carmen' dress for an IncSoc show of 1962 in the presence of Queen Elizabeth, held in the lavish bar of the Royal Opera House. 'Carmen' featured a dress composed of band over band of silk fringe and a cartwheel hat with similar decoration not unlike a vast lampshade. It made Norman's client, Marlene Dietrich, wearing outrageous Travis Banton clothes in *The Devil is a Woman*, seem underdressed.[9]

Norman's love of films, and glamorous films especially, never left him. He and Ian often went to the cinema in the evening, whereupon Norman would buy a huge bar of chocolate and eat it all by himself! Sometimes they would go to Claridge's Causerie for hot chocolate before Norman was left at 26 Bruton Street, but always by 10.30 pm. The Cracknells considered that Ian had become like a 'son' to Norman and that 'he had become not only used to him, but also depended upon him'[10]

Many of the fresher, more simple designs, such as a beaded checkerboard top to an evening dress in spring 1962 were more in the style of Ian than Norman, who chose the moment of the opening of the film *Star*, the musical biography of Gertrude Lawrence, to remake a 1935 dress he had designed for her. He put it unannounced into his winter 1968 collection and it attracted more press interest than anything else in the collection, although photographs reveal it as a rather shoddily made travesty of the real thing.

His early 1960s collections were full of well-made, simply cut and beautifully beaded or embroidered dresses that may be seen as marking the swan song of Norman's career. In 1962, he was asked how he compared British haute couture with that of France and Italy, answering:

> Well, you know, we suffer from this absurd naive modesty, it applies to everything. We just have no faith in things which emanate from this country. It applies particularly to fashion and it's about time we started to think differently. What we need most of all perhaps is a change of attitude in the home, where parents still look upon an artistic career as the pursuit of the academic failure. For the British, art is a second-rate thing. I get pathetic letters all the time, you know, my boy is a duffer at school, do you think he'll make a good dress designer! It's a terribly bad approach since today there are more opportunities than ever for anyone with a genuine flair for creative dress designing.

He did not think that fashion departments of art schools could necessarily produce good designers: 'Oh no, not as a matter of course. They can turn out good artisans, good workers. But a really good dress designer is born. You cannot be *trained* to be a good designer.'

He also deprecated the fact that mid-century fashion had no great contemporary recorders in the manner of Longhi, Goya, Fragonard, Lely or van Dyck, let alone Winterhalter and Sargent. Asked about John: 'No, not really, it's all sweaters and skirts with Augustus.'

He was probably also thinking of the unfinished portrait by John of Queen Elizabeth in one of his 1939 spangled tulle crinolines, which hung in Clarence House. He might have mentioned some of the more traditional artists such as Gunn or Kelly, or even some talented fashion illustrators like Eric (Carl Erickson), Francis Marshall or his friend Andrew Robb, but he believed the reason for a lack of such artists to be, 'Because nowadays artists are lazy. There's no craft, it's all craftiness.'[11]

He did admire what he saw as 'the youthful exuberance' of Mary Quant, in a letter to Christina Foyle accepting an invitation to a Literary Luncheon celebrating the publication of her biography *Quant on Quant*. He stressed this, even though it meant that he was supporting a fashion movement quite out of tune with his own talents and taste.

With the April 1963 wedding of the Queen's cousin Princess Alexandra to the Hon. Angus Ogilvy, Norman displayed his virtuosity in adapting to Miss Quant's challenge whilst retaining his own love of spectacle and decorative clothes. The bride was dressed by John Cavanagh in an elegantly simple dress, but Norman designed the dresses worn by the Queen, Queen Elizabeth the Queen Mother, Princess Margaret and Princess Marina. The latter was alone in not wearing a coat with her dress, a simple golden sheath open on one side and tied with the fashionably flat rectangular bow of the period above a contrasting fabric embroidered with gold and topaz beads.

The Queen's short green dress was embroidered with a lily-of-the-valley design over which was worn an open opaque organza coat of palest green. No doubt Norman remembered the disappointment of Hardy Amies during the 1957 state visit to France, when the short coat over the matching pale blue-grey silk with an embroidered bodice was kept firmly closed due to the chilly weather at Versailles. Norman's opaque design for the Queen's coat made this impossible.

Princess Margaret wore Norman's most interesting design of primrose yellow organza, her open coat covered entirely with tiny silk primrose heads. Each design has the fashionable lines of the period, even that of the Queen Elizabeth, for the simple outline was of the moment, yet all the designs express the individuality and personality of the wearer and Norman created an effective tableau once again. Norman had made his mark on another national occasion, reported worldwide. He now chose this opportune moment to open his new in-house 'Le Petit Salon.'

The inventive invitation card depicts the exterior of the 'shop' window on the ground floor of 26 Bruton Street and opens in the centre to reveal the printed invitation and a note from Norman:

> Dear Madam, for a long time now I have wanted to open a small salon in my house to provide Hartnell-designed garments to be sold at budget prices 'off the peg'. . . Day and evening dresses, coats, suits, etc. will be on sale in Le Petit Salon at prices starting from £25. So if you are looking for inexpensive and elegant clothes, including special dresses for cocktail parties, or the theatre, I hope you will find them to your liking in my new Salon. Yours faithfully . . .

He then expanded on what was on offer. 'This collection includes suits, coats, day dresses, dresses and jackets, cocktail dresses, evening dress, furs, fashion accessories and perfume, cosmetics, stockings, knitwear, hats by Madame Claude St-Cyr of Paris, shoes by Edward Rayne.'

A great deal of thought and effort went into designing the new Petit Salon created by Kenneth Alexander Partridge, by now well known for his displays in many shops and for IncSoc shows. The colour scheme was unlike that of the salon upstairs, for there clearly had to be a division between the couture and ready-to-wear. In effect, there were three separate areas based on what Norman called epinard green, cochineal pink and cat's-eye blue. The first room was in green and white with mustard silk furnishings. The second in pink, white, cerise and shades of pink as a sales area for coats, suits and dresses, and the third room was blue/green, white and mustard for the sale of millinery and sweaters.

'The three rooms are decorated by four white lattice columns to create a feeling of outdoors with inside luxury and Hartnell is typically represented here by the trio of magnificent Waterford chandeliers,' ran the press release. 'But wait, this is not all, for way beyond is a new "all white, all bright" Petit Salon fashion theatre. No gimmicks – no colours – only the perfect setting in which to choose beautiful clothes by Norman Hartnell.'[12]

The new venture was greeted with applause by all who saw it, including the textile supremo Miki Sekers, who unsurprisingly thought that his close friend 'Kenneth Partridge has done a terrific job', which he had. But it was at least ten years too late and widely regarded as a desperate gambit to keep the couture doors open. The opening of mini replicas in Fraser stores around the UK, then known in-house as shopettes, was seen as more innovative – Kenneth Partridge also designed many of these. Yet sales were never particularly good and the miniskirt soon made all Norman's clothes seem old hat to the under-forties generation.

'Creative people are never lonely or bored. Even when I'm on holiday I am creating. I redecorate my house, or gain inspiration from a beautiful building or a lovely tree. Life goes on, excitingly, all the time,' Norman told the *Daily Herald* in January 1963, in the wake of burst pipes in the ageing Bruton Street House. Expensive stocks of fabric and evening dresses were ruined. More tellingly, he finally publicly admitted, 'I'm not a millionaire, I just live like one.'[13]

The contrived illusion was maintained with increasing difficulty. Kenneth Partridge later chuckled over his memories of various nocturnal excursions with Norman in his creaking old chauffeured limousine car. Everything around Norman was ageing.

In 1962, Madame Jeanne died; another link with the most glorious days of his fading career. Royal and other clients wrote to console Norman, knowing of her great role front of house. Blake was one of the few still there to give Norman necessary companionship and laughter. He was invited to watch his friend at a fashion competition in the Albert Hall, but then Norman wrote again:

> On serious consideration and considered reflection, I do not think that the stupid fashion-riddled competition on Wednesday evening is your 'saucer of soup'.
>
> I know you would only be irritated and bored, and I feel that your impatience would put me off my judging stroke!
>
> Furthermore, I cannot, because of a previous appointment with Her Gracious Majesty Queen Elizabeth the Queen Mother, spare the whole ensuing day to go visiting romantic ruins. So, I think 'twere better if I called for you, say at the Ritz – then whisk away to the forest.
>
> Anyhow, I feel certain the weather next week will be chill and bitter and it would be better to be by the cosy fire-side at Lovel

Dene than motoring through the bleak wastes of Bucks or Berks. Please write and say you agree.[14]

Norman could at least share some of his problems with Blake and unburden himself of his worries. Apart from a surviving half-sister, his family links were disappearing. Topsy's husband James died, leaving just one son, Charles, but Norman saw Blake at frequent intervals.

> My dear Norman . . . *this* letter is to say what a joy 'twas to see you and, too, have your charming company all to myself for an entire evening . . . I trust you had a stimulating stay at bounteous Böoour-nemouth and were able to switch into the proper programmes at the 'say-col-logical' moments, sir! I loved the jolly tweeds show. I was so glad you could visit my chambers and see the stern-looking portrait and I look lovingly up at Albert, as he *longs* to pop (or poop?) behind those violet velvet coy-tins with their ample tassels, Hart*nell*! Nor have I, or *will* I, forget the more serious note struck just before we sallied forth for eggs, figs and kippers. *THIS* shall be in my most constant thoughts and prayers, *dear soul*. You are always bright and brave over your trials and worries and you (you and George) *do* so richly deserve to succeed.[15]

In July 1963, Norman was asked by L. Kingscote Billings, Head of English at a school in Devizes, to name a poem that inspired him. Bish turned to Blake for his usual knowledgeable advice. Blake replied on the Feast of Saint Bartholomew.

> My counsel is to avoid the obvious Shelley and Keats and insuf-ferable Shakespeare and pounce on reliable old Wordsworth and choose THIS sonnet of his: The World is too much with us, late and soon . . . etc. (Punctuation above is accurate in every respect, even the dash before 'Great God!') Proteus was Neptune's herds-man. Then Mr Spiffington-Kinghorn can get his class to write down all they know about PROTEUS AND TRITON, see!! . . . on Thursday I adventured into Gloucestershire in a friend's motor in his Austin-Healey proceeding at *between 70 to 90 miles ALL THE WAY*!!! I am still alive and I LOVED it, so there!

Blake also had the thrill of a magenta priest's stole enlivened with artificial amethysts or rubies or gold sequins in the Hartnell embroidery workroom,[16] but in February 1964 this became irrelevant to him and he was more than worried about Norman, who had been rushed to hospital in Windsor after suffering a heart attack. 'I hope you are resting peacefully and thinking only of the HAPPIEST events in your variegated life, dear Bish.'[17]

All the newspapers carried reports of Norman's illness and that he was to rest peacefully for two months. Amongst those writing was the designer Peter Russell, who had closed his House some years previously and after a time in Australia had finally retired to Kent. He urged Norman to give it all up and retire, as Victor Stiebel did. Norman knew that he could not, for his House and business were completely at the mercy of the bank and his personal assets negligible.

Shortly before his heart attack, an announcement had been made to the press on 22 January that 'Mr Ian Thomas, who has been Mr Hartnell's personal assistant since 1953, is now playing a major part in designing the collections.' Unlike Dior, who consciously took on Yves St Laurent as a possible replacement, Norman never publicly acknowledged Ian before this date. When Ian had received considerable press coverage in Australia, because of the great amount of designing he was doing for Barregar's franchise out there, the latter wrote to Norman on the inadvisability of weakening his image as 'sole designer'. Even in an interview with *The Studio* of December 1962, Norman stated that he was the only designer at Hartnell.

Once the fact that Norman was to be out of action for some time had publicly sunk in, attention again focused on Ian, but newspapers were told that Mr Hartnell would carry on designing from his convalescence, even though a flight to Cairo had to be cancelled whilst he stayed in the King Edward VII Hospital, Windsor. George Cracknell, naturally nicknamed Crackers by Norman, simply told the *Yorkshire Evening Post* that Norman had been in and out of bed because of a chill.[18]

In February 1964, he missed Peter Sellers' wedding to Britt Ekland, but was able to revel in the photographs of the startlingly beautiful 21-year-old marrying in his design of an up-to-the-minute barely knee-length white wild silk sheath with a wide band of silk petals around the hem and a matching hat. Huge crowds surrounded the door of Guildford Registry Office, in scenes not unlike the pre-war weddings he had dressed.

Norman naturally hoped for more young clients, having shown his abilities in the most modern idiom. Sellers was an enthusiastic fan of Norman and considered that the dress he designed for Britt to wear at the Royal Command Film Performance in 1964 was the most fabulous dress he had ever seen and wanted more of the same. He also put an idea into Norman's head when he wrote that if Norman ever decided to make men's clothes, then he would be one of the first clients for them. He then signed himself 'Dad'.[19]

Norman was still ill in June in spite of a holiday in Mandelieu-la-Napoule; when preparing for his annual Ascot party he had tonsillitis. Crackers helped with the flower arrangements, as did Ian, and each room at Lovel Dene was given a different arrangement according to a typed list specifying vases and flowers to be used. Covent Garden flower market was visited and then Norman's arranging began. Miss Louie generally kept the outside bar on these occasions, although the weather was often uncertain.

He also missed a fashion show at Woodhall Spa featuring his latest collection shown with new and old Rolls-Royces. As if this was not enough, Norman was asleep in his flat at 26 Bruton Street when on 16 July he was woken by telephone to be told that Lovel Dene was ablaze. The heat of the fire had operated an intercom connected with the Cracknells' flat and so the firemen were able to save much except for the Wedgwood Room, his dressing room with all his clothes, three bathrooms and two further bedrooms. As described earlier, Norman lost antique furniture, chandeliers, paintings and thirty suits. Damage from the smoke was extensive, as was water damage.

> Alas, [Norman wrote in an unfinished letter] I really have suffered loss – both sentimentally as well as the intrinsic value of many objects d'art which, as far back as a boy scouring places like Bath and Brighton, I collected and saved up my money for. And with Father Time advancing so rapidly, I feel I have not the impetus within me, nor sufficient years left ahead, to make it worthwhile searching for and seeking them anew.
>
> Now they have all gone like a lot of old friends who have suddenly died altogether and whose charred memory solely remains. But never mind! Making a virtue of necessity by facing life with a smile – I shall always.

Literally dusting himself down, he bounced back yet again. He had to buy ready-made clothes for a trip to America, but then Wakers was put to reconstructing the damaged areas as soon as the insurers settled the claim. Norman then ostensibly had a wonderful time visiting antique shops and supervising Wakers in his work. In fact, only a small amount of the compensation went into new furnishings or objects, but for once, cheques were paid immediately and the insurer's payment to Norman ensured that work went on at full speed. His former kindness to others also resulted in several generous presents, not least the roll of blue velvet from a solid supplier for remaking the Wedgwood Room curtains.

In February, he entertained Edward Molyneux and had drinks with him at Victor Stiebel's flat. Old friends and colleagues were increasingly important.

Norman's generosity was never purely self-serving. In 1964, Minnie Hogg, who had given him his first all-important press publicity, was elderly and living in a home in South Kensington when Gladys Boyd arranged with Norman for an outing to view his 1964 collection, which 'gave her immense pleasure'. Similarly, he kept in touch with another early admirer, Alison Settle, and continued writing to her to the end. Alice Delysia was another correspondent, married to a diplomat in the Canaries, and he tried to tempt her over. 'There are lots of elegant dresses that would suit the great DELYSIA superbly,' he wrote hopefully.

It was difficult for him to realise that he was over sixty and, considering his sedentary lifestyle, smoking and dietary habits, he made a remarkable recovery from his heart attack.

'Tweed suited and rosy-cheeked with a russet tie and ginger socks, he looked – discounting the heavy gold and platinum accessories – so very much more like a young farmer out on the spree than a middle aged couturiers with the weight of a fashion empire on his shoulders,' wrote a perceptive journalist before his illness.

He looked just as countrified afterwards. He attributed his youthful looks to

a truth so trite you'll be furious with me. No gland extracts, no elixirs, no *little* secrets for you to expose. It's simply that I was born without a trace of envy. Such an ageing, uglifying emotion! All that bile – so bad for the stomach. All those jealous looks – so hard on the face. People tell me that life is a rat race, but I am utterly unconscious of any little mice scampering along beside me. I *delight* in the successes of my competitors.

And there's worse to come. I actually love the human race. Isn't it awful! I have swans on my lake, peacocks strutting on my terrace, pigeons like a snow storm whenever I call, a house I adore, a Rolls-Royce and a Bentley purring in the garage plus peace and quiet and some very pretty china. I also have a sense of tremendous satisfaction and fulfilment. You see I've helped so many women to do their duty. Which is to decorate the passing scene. There's no excuse for ugliness these days. I don't even believe that every woman needs someone to look beautiful *for*. I was born under Gemini you know – so I'm utterly contradictory. I thrive on *colour* – conversely I could hardly be happier in a fog. All those beautiful misty greys and stark black trees without leaves. I think that's why I want to go to Japan . . . Not really. I've been around the world three times on business. That's surely enough for any man.

Norman also declared himself in favour of 'Teds' rather than 'Beatniks' as the former gave colour to street corners! Asked why he had never married, he lit a cigarette before replying (and his pose with a tilted cigarette was famous), 'I very nearly did once. But, darling, you cannot make a story out of that. It was long ago and she preferred another man.'

The interview would have been hugely famous if he had admitted that he also preferred another man. 'She's very, very happy – and so am I. Alone. Isn't it sad.'[20] And he roared with laughter. But according to the Cracknells and to others who knew him, this was indeed the truth.

In the late 1960s, Norman still enjoyed going to out-of-the-way ordinary pubs in the East End for a diversion. The much younger Kenneth Partridge once went with him and, having left the chauffeured Rolls-Royce nearby, they made their way to a nearly deserted pub, where a man shouted out, 'There 'e is, I told you 'e'd come!' The man had apparently won a bet. The surreal evening then progressed to a meeting with another man's aged mother in a basic flat on the Commercial Road where they drank cocoa with her.

Of all the many bizarre shared incidents, the strangest occurred in a pub in Southend where Norman was drenched by a pint of beer flung at him, whereupon the door opened and in walked a huge man. 'Tiny,' said Norman. 'Normie!' roared the man and promptly threw out the miscreant.[21] He appeared to be the driver of a tourists' bus and may have been the intended recipient of one of Norman's prize pieces of doggerel.

Ta-Ta To Tiny

I regret to put in writing
That I shall not be inviting
Musgrove – *you* to ever stay
with me again
For, my grudge against some men is
– who take up, then give up tennis –
That they've played their strokes
with balls that proved in vain
Both my lady loves admired you
At that time I could have fired you
For you couldn't differentiate
their names
Don't you realise that 'Madewell'
Is a lady friend that's payed well
And that Helen's just another
of these Dames?
What! – Moireen *Sells*? No
Moireen gives
(Whilst Mrs M collects the divs:)
There's quite a bit of difference
in those girls
Moireen tells me in the boudoir
How inept and very rude you are
Moireen sells – but not to pigs
who don't like pearls
So, if Musgrove can't be tactful
To his friend, whose life is packed full
of divergent virgins, beautiful
or plain
I now formulate a barrage – ban
Signed by his pal Jack Barregar
'Don't put your TINY foot in it
again!'

Who the hapless Musgrove was, or why he so aroused Norman's wrath, is now lost with other extraordinary details of Norman's life. Needless to say, George questioned Norman and especially Kenneth closely about their evenings out.

For a man of his time approaching his mid-sixties, Norman led an active life of unusual variety. In September 1964, he wrote to an author telling the story of Foyles Literary Luncheons: 'I apologise for the delay . . . you may know I have been ill. I had to go to France to recuperate and now my house in Windsor Forest has been burnt. And these unpleasant activities have occupied all my time.' He said that he had been to many enjoyable luncheons of which the one held in honour of *Silver and Gold* had been most extraordinary 'due to the fact that I was so nervous during the whole occasion I remember nothing of particular interest except . . . Ginette Spanier', who told of how she had asked him for a job when he first opened and he had told her that she was 'too young and rather raw'.

The joke was on him as she became the most celebrated Parisian vendeuse long associated with Pierre Balmain. 'This may interest you although it is rather a feeble little story,'[22] he said. However, the story is contradicted by Miss Spanier, who spoke at her own celebratory Foyles Luncheon on 18 December 1959 in honour of her first biography *It Isn't All Mink*. She said that he had asked her to work for him and she had 'said no, because at that time I was going off to America, so I did not work for him'![23] Both firmly believed themselves to be correct.

With the rapid waning of couture, there were some attempts by the old guard to stem the flow of customers. The venerable Morts had written to Norman after the wedding of Princess Alexandra and the ball given by the Queen at Windsor in honour of the event: 'I am sure you realised what a tremendous uplift in business this wedding and ball gave us all, if only the royalties could give a ball in early April to start off the season.'

Norman replied:

> If I see a Lady-in-Waiting I might talk seriously to her. On the other hand, I may have the honour of seeing Her Majesty within the next day or so and I could quite safely, I trust, tell the Queen how much the Windsor Ball has already given an uplift to London

haute couture and I feel convinced that my explanation will be well received.[24]

Whatever was or was not said had no effect, for London couture was now in free fall, although still fighting back.

Norman sent George to Las Vegas in his place for an international fashion festival at Wilbur Clark's Desert Inn in 1964, when Lady Joubert accompanied designers Ronald Paterson and Michael. Norman designed three of his most luxurious evening dresses for the occasion costing £500 and paid for by the organisers. It turned out to be an important event honouring Cyril Magnin, of the department store I. Magnin, and the American designer Oleg Cassini. This time Norman had the excuse of ill health preventing him from this important publicised occasion. However, he did sit as a judge on the panel choosing the University of Manchester's Rag Queen in 1965.

The redecoration of Lovel Dene absorbed him:

> Dear Mr Wakers,
>
> I enclose herewith the silhouette of the cornice in the Hall . . . As I told you the builders are leaping ahead with the rest of the house, but I do want your beautiful emerald green moiré drapes, etc., for the hall, and most importantly also for the grey glass and gold beading framing the grisaille panels in the drawing room.
>
> Also the little marble platforms, illuminated underneath with strip lights.
>
> Also the two low cocktail tables, similarly electrified underneath.
>
> And, of course, my beautiful lemon-yellow Mann and Fleming curtains, held up with the Hartnell golden eagles.
>
> Also the thrilling white globes, big and small. And the white tulip-shaped . . . Don't forget, dear Mr Wakefield, Ascot starts the second week in June and I would like to be completed by the middle of May.[25]

He sold a Victorian dentist's chair, a fashionable 'junk' foible of the period:

> I myself fell for its Victorian amusement – all in carrot-coloured velvet and black iron. Especially the cuspidor at its side! I bought it for a Victorian bathroom, but by the time I had specially furnished

the bathroom there was no room for the chair (it was either that or the bath). Anyhow I purchased the chair from an antique shop in Jermyn Street, where the proprietor told me that Mr Cary Grant and Mr Gregory Peck and 'Monsieur Maigret' were all after it but eventually Hartnell had it. With regard to the chair being sat upon by Her Majesty Queen Victoria, I am not at all certain on this point.[26]

It was all a diversion from the dreaded call of his bank manager in London to whom he wrote at the same time: 'I have been confined to my house in the country with various chills, including stomach upset, lumbago and finally gout on the knee-cap. All these things were hard to endure and kept me away from working in London.'[27] He was also looking for new staff at Lovel Dene, whilst at the house, A.J. Harris was taken on the payroll as an all-purpose clerk and security officer.

By October 1965, Norman Hartnell was listed in *Queen's* 'Society: The Index', which placed his company firm and others, such as the hairdresser Steiner, amongst a list of 'has-beens'. Criticism of the Queen's clothes had begun during the Royal Tour of North America in 1959, and many were said to be dowdy, unfashionable and downright ugly. Frequent letters arrived from members of the public suggesting to Norman various ideas about changing the regal style. Mr Steiner wrote to him that the editor of *Queen* Jocelyn Stevens had remarked that he could not care a damn about anybody, but Norman was disinclined to attach his name to a writ for damages. He knew that his private life would not stand a little investigative journalism if the matter were to be taken into court.[28]

Norman had agreed to design a new uniform for the Women's Police and had just been congratulated by Lady Jeanne Stonor on the wedding dress he had designed for her daughter's wedding, which Norman attended, and thanked him for making her own dress back in 1938. She asked him to attend a private mass at Stonor Park on 4 December, which Norman accepted with interest as he had, he said, little knowledge of a Catholic Mass.[29]

An even more pressing reason to keep in good odour with the press lay in the opening of more Petit Salons in 1965 and 1966 – none of them fated to last more than a few years. Fashion shows were given on their inauguration and Norman made his stock speech to encourage the local women of means.

Whilst this was in progress, George had acquired the lease of a block of flats in Faro, Portugal and was negotiating with a boutique owner and marble supplier – it was the great period of marble-topped coffee tables. His friend Olive Teague helped him to furnish the flats at Avenida Chico de Outubro. Unsurprisingly things soon went wrong with the finance and in addition, the Petit Salons barely covered their costs.

A link with the highly fashionable Parisian based international celebrity hairdresser Alexandre was next undertaken, with his salon occupying rooms on the second floor of 26 Bruton Street, the intention being to lure a captive clientele into the couture on the floor below and vice versa. This enjoyed initial but limited success, partly due to its location.

Norman was also disappointed that his attempt to design the dresses for *Star!*, the film of Gertrude Lawrence's life, was a failure although Saul Chaplin of Twentieth Century Fox had been sent *Silver and Gold* with a letter from Norman: 'I do realise that Captain Molyneux did most of her dresses, but I knew and dressed Gertie Lawrence right at the beginning and towards the end, including all her dresses for *Tonight at 8.30*.'[30]

Another of his pre-war clients happily still with him, Barbara Cartland, was frustrated at the stockroom people who would not allow customers of the Petit Salon to have clothes in different colours. Norman replied to this wide-spread complaint: 'a sensible girl like you must realise how difficult it is, within a ready-to-wear department, to make up certain garments in other materials, colours, etc. It all has to be re-matched and the price rearranged. And it sets the sales ladies and the stock-keepers agog with confusion.'[31]

Confusion was also apparent on the faces of young Parisians in October 1966 when they viewed the Norman Hartnell boutique in the Paris store Au Printemps – 'most of these clothes are for the middle aged' was a typical comment and his evening dresses were 'not chic at all' although Serena Sinclair reported: 'He's reversed the Norman Conquest.'[32]

Sadly, this did not last long. Nor did the sort of attention in Le Petit Salon that many clients demanded, and a stiff notice was sent down on 30 March 1966 to the effect that whilst existing stock remained on the rails '131 SPECIAL orders have been taken', which negated the effect of Le Petit Salon, when clients treated it as a cheaper version of the couture upstairs. Another attempt to revive flagging sales came when dresses were made incompletely finished with enough selvedge to adjust any garment to almost any size. It proved as unpopular as the existing stock.

As 1966 wore on and finances were perilously near an all-time low, Norman sold some of his collection of militaria. On 2 June he received Manny Silverman of Moss Bros with his principal, interested in the collection. Some twenty-five years later, Silverman and his associates, headed by Roy Dixon, were to buy the Norman Hartnell Ltd. from Norman's heir, George, and begin a spirited resurrection of the House. Norman would have undoubtedly been amused to know that guest designers including Gina Fratini and Murray Arbeid would design guest collections and that Marc Bohan, formerly designer at Dior, would be the last great name involved in the revival, cruelly cut short by the economic recession and the Gulf War.

In mid-1965, there was every hope that Ian Thomas would be able to carry on the business, much as Ken Fleetwood was relied on at Hardy Amies. However, when there was no money available to pay the staff one week, Ian was asked to speak to Bill Riley, who decades ago was in Footlights with Norman. Riley would only lend money if Ian had a stake in the company, to which Norman was agreeable, but George was obviously not.

It was in the spring of 1967 that Mrs Cracknell discovered Norman sitting on a sofa in the drawing room at Lovel Dene sobbing loudly. 'They've taken the house away from me,' he told her and remained in tears on the sofa for some time. All the successful times, the happy times, the parties for Ascot, the designing, in fact his life for thirty years had been bound up with Lovel Dene, the only real home he had known since his mother's death when he was a twenty-year-old up at Cambridge. The company had simply exhausted all possible credit and so the bank instructed Norman to sell the house, which had been transferred after the war to the company for tax and upkeep reasons, and then repay a large part of the loan. If Norman regretted his break with John Pleydell and subsequent dismissal of the sound advisors he had benefitted from in the past, then he never mentioned it. He had appealed to his solicitor David Jacobs and even to Harold Wilson for advice and help.

With Norman's consummate skill at being friendly with everyone possible, he had written to the new Prime Minister on 27 February 1963:

> Well, all I now want to do is to add my small voice of congratulations to you . . . I hope that there will be some reason for us to meet again soon. I trust that your wife, Mary, is well – I suppose a great strain will be put upon her also from now onwards, but I expect she is overwhelmingly happy about it all.

Norman maintained the contact fostered since 1947 and wrote to Mrs Wilson on 13 November 1964.

> I have of course been thinking a lot about you and Harold recently, having read the great news whilst I was in America – doing my best for Britain . . . I do not want to trouble your husband by bothering him with a letter, so would you be very sweet and convey to him my warmest congratulations on the wonderful eminence and great position he now so splendidly holds.
>
> Now, Mary, a sensible business talk. Busy as you must be, should you ever suddenly want something absolutely ready-to-wear, there is a most practical and inexpensive department here for day clothes, cocktail and sensible evening dress and I should always be very happy to see you, if you ever find the time or the need to pop in.

Non-committal, Mrs Wilson replied that she would bear this in mind.

It was sadly only a couple of years before Norman was writing to the Prime Minister about the desperate financial plight he found himself in and the threat of embarrassment should the House fail with such eminent clients as he had.

His hopes of closer ties with the House of Fraser were dashed when the group acquired Harrods, in a different league from Hartnell. Norman sent off another of his 'poems' to Hugh Fraser.

Breach of Promise

Mr Fraser, last year, to me with words parried
Said Norman, 'In Business we soon will be married.'
But now says this 'I've changed my mind, Norman'
And he's tarried and married a Harrod.
Oh I do so like coming to Glasgow
But I'm not having fun here. Alas, no.
H.F.'s fun, or is he?
He keeps me so bizzy
And just won't let a lad or a lass go.

As usual both Norman and George looked for a new direction and found that Serge Mirman was of great assistance. The husband of the milliner Simone Mirman, who had made hats for the Hartnell collections since October 1965, he was instrumental in helping the company's resourceful financial director John Royle in setting up a German company. Had this been done in the early 1950s on the back of the shows in Hamburg and Baden-Baden, there might have been a successful Hartnell Deutschland. As it was, the Hertie chain of stores was selling dresses for the sterling equivalent of £3.10s.00d, so down-market that even George balked at a business arrangement with a German company specialising in mass-produced clothing. He recognised the potential blow to the waning prestige of the Hartnell name, already given a severe blow by the retail of paper patterns and a mail-order outlet, for which Norman wrote the following blurb.

> The cool flowerlike elegance of the
> Hartnell Look
> was once only for the privileged few. Now
> it is reflected on every dress page of the
> Catalogue.
> Whatever you choose is now
> Hartnell – chosen too!

As Norman had written, Father Time was now rapidly marching on and he had few options left to enable the survival of Norman Hartnell Ltd.

CHAPTER NINETEEN

A few yards of satin . . .

O
n 14 April 1967, Norman moved out of Lovel Dene. The preceding March had brought the death of Major Cecil Wills, a major shareholder of great importance to the company and consequently to both Norman and George. The death of Charles Creed in that year continued the quickening pace of extinction amongst London's dwindling couture Houses, but Norman and George forged ahead with new plans. They had no other option. Luckily, as a result of the Rolls-Royce show, the cloth manufacturers Reid & Taylor were put in touch with Hartnell by the solicitor H. Bart-Smith, who introduced the dynamic young John Packer from the textile company to Norman. Not only did the two men get on immediately, but each saw the value of each other in forming a business relationship. The initiation menswear designs suggested to Norman by Peter Sellers now came to full fruition with Norman's designs using the superb cloth for which Packer's company was world famous.

Norman had designed men's shirts since the 1940s. Hardy Amies had the sense to link up with the retail menswear chain Hepworth's in the late 1950s and reap rewards from the early 1960s onwards, so Norman now created men's couture collections in styles largely of his own invention but always capturing the mood of the moment. Kenneth Partridge was involved with several of the lavish internationally staged fashion shows resulting from the collaboration and treasured a white silk evening shirt with a luxurious jabot consisting of layer upon layer of looped ruffles, each separate loop ending in a paste diamond. The 1960s were a wonderfully creative period for men's clothes and Norman proved again that he was an ideal designer for changing times.[1]

His most immediate problem of finding somewhere to live after his eviction from Lovel Dene was partly solved by his friend Timothy Tufnell. After showing him several tiny properties in the area of Ascot and Sunningdale, an arrangement was eventually made with Mr Tufnell that Norman would occupy a wing of his house White Walls, London Road, Sunninghill. Once again Norman had to redecorate his own quarters, but on a much-reduced scale. The move was emotionally and physically tiring for him. Nor was there much money for the work involved – during the quarter to March 1964, for example, Hartnell couture had made a loss of almost £10,000 for the business – and survived largely by swallowing the profits generated by Le Petit Salon.[2]

In the mid-1960s, Pierre Balmain told Norman and Ian that he was charging Madame Volterra the equivalent of £800 or £900 pounds for his grand embroidered dresses. Norman could barely charge £300 or £400 in London and his overheads were still greater than those of the Parisian couturier. Norman was reliant on merchandising his name more extensively and no doubt pondered this on his move to Sunninghill.

Ian Thomas observed the move:

> After Lovel Dene, this small lodging seemed almost unbearable. He had not the heart to decorate it himself so all his furniture was rather piled into it. When I heard that he was to spend a few days in Cornwall, I took it upon myself to do something about this sad state of affairs. With fellow workers from the firm, Ted, Jack and Walter, we made our way to Sunninghill armed with wallpaper, paint, fabrics and set to work. It was a labour of love and in no time the house started to become more 'Hartnell'. Everything seemed to slot in place and on the day that the boss was to arrive back, I bought flowers and plants, with my own money, and told Crackers his devoted butler to light the fire just before his arrival. It obviously all worked as the following day I received a charming letter:[3]

> West Wing, White Walls, Sunningdale

> Monday night, 15 May 1967

> Dear Ian,
>   Ian, dear friend – how very grateful I am to you for having done so much, so deftly and so quickly to make this new small dwelling of mine so charming and easy to live in . . . considering the difficult conditions under which I now live.

As I sit here, writing you this brief but sincere note of thanks, the whole room looks so enchanting – just as I would have liked it, and just as you – knowing me so well – knew that I would like it.

But I did not realise, whilst having a few days' careless respite in Cornwall that you were doing all this for me in my absence. It is one of the kindest acts of Christian friendship that any one person could do for another. Of late I have not been a very happy person – you understand I am sure – but now, at present, to be surrounded by such comfort and prettiness, a symposium of our mutual tastes, it is a great solace to me. For which I thank you very much indeed.

I hope that our artistic tendencies and our existences may be enjoyed for many years yet – but whatever the conditions of life may be, I want you to know that I shall always admire you, always be grateful to you and always be deeply very fond of you.

That's quite enough, isn't it? But before I pop into bed, I say to you Goodnight and God bless you always. N.H. with love.

Yet within a year Ian Thomas had left Norman Hartnell, his ambition always thwarted by George, or Mitch as he and others also called him, who could not allow Norman to nominate a successor not under George's direct control. Obviously, a new heir at Hartnell would want his own business advisor and would certainly be unwilling to tolerate George, and without Hartnell, George would be financially lost. Hence Ian's eventual backer had made it a condition of his cash injection that George should go.

Significantly, Norman's professional relationship with Ian Thomas had obviously led to a good personal friendship, and for many years Ian at his request signed his own fine completed sketches with a very good copy of Norman's distinctive signature. Ian knew that George quite often signed Norman's cheques for him, again with a startlingly accurate copy of Norman's signature – indeed George's own handwriting was so eerily similar to Norman's that the two are also not easy to dissemble on papers in the surviving archives. However, when Norman asked Ian to sign cheques with the famous Norman Hartnell signature, he balked at the idea and declined wondering at possible consequences. George knew the value of Ian to the business and to Norman, but was not about to lose any of his control over 'The Boss', yet trouble came again, as Blake might well have described it.[3]

Mrs Wills had died in 1964 and Major Wills in 1968. They held a considerable number of shares in the company, which were offered to Norman by their executors in an endeavour to settle the estate. Major Wills had 10,000 Redeemable Preference Shares of £1 each and 2,250 Preference 'B' shares of £1 each, and the Probate price of the shares was accepted by the Estate Duty Office in 1968 at 15/- each for 'A' shares and 7/6 for 'B' shares. Again and again, letters were sent to Hartnell, for Norman simply did not have the money available and found it impossible to find a purchaser for the shares. The seven heirs were left in a financial limbo, much as Norman found himself in, acutely embarrassed by the situation, for the main portion of the Wills' modest fortune had been invested in Norman Hartnell Ltd, from which they had received regular, if small, dividends. Yet in 1966, Norman, George, John Royle and Serge Mirman began to set up a Swiss company.

Norman himself became an extraordinary floating tenant, for when Timothy Tufnell sold White Walls to an ardent female admirer of Norman's, Mrs Martha Guinness, Norman in his little wing came with the house. Norman then paid a tiny rent and small proportion of the heat, light and fuel bills on the condition that he redesign the whole interior of White Walls for her. The house was usually described to the press as his house, but now Norman was again placed in a difficult position, because the ageing Mrs Guinness wanted to marry him.

In the years preceding their house-sharing, Mrs Guinness had been a good client and was often a useful companion for Norman at parties and first nights. But she often sat in the Bruton Street salon for hours waiting for a sight of Norman, who would peep through the dividing curtains from the model room and despairingly ask Miss Louie what he should do. Now in his sixties, it was as though the days at no. 10 Bruton Street were returning to haunt him, but now there was no big sister or anyone else to ask his suitor to leave, which was undoubtedly lucky for him in the long run. Once, at Rose Place (as his part of the house was known when the house was renamed) he was awakened by Mrs Guinness telephoning him for help as her bedroom had been invaded by a swarm of bluebottles. His suggestion was that she open the windows wide and turn off the lights! This form of summons was not unusual.

During these latter years, Norman used the 'bedsit', as he termed the part of the top floor of 26 Bruton Street made into a small flat, much as his father had advised in 1923 at 10 Bruton Street. He was often away. Without the lure and responsibility of Lovel Dene, his life tended at times to revert to his 1920s Mayfair existence of evenings with friends and theatres or cinemas.

To the outsider, the name Norman Hartnell signified glamour with a long history of internationally publicised dress designs for royal clients, world-famous women and stars of stage and screen. Every week seemed to find the name broadcast by the media. Hatnell was a British institution, apparently as permanent as any London landmark. Few knew the real financial situation of the business and of the man behind it.

Norman Hartnell was a very public figure. In the early 1960s, he had often been a companion of his old friend Blake Brown at Covent Garden performances of Wagner. Blake had become more frail and depressed than his old friend Bish, life in Bristol proving to be increasingly grim. On his birthday in 1961 he wrote peevishly:

> How easily you could have sent me a line or a TINY present; but you haven't . . . I have been ill for a week, but now I eat a cold supper in my salon, into which the golden sun is *POURING*! Tongue and chicken and apple pie and cream. Cocktails first; then a deliciously *WARMED* Burgundy! *Whose* company do I require but my own? If your Rolls-Royce were to draw up, I'd be delighted; but *it never will* . . . Good-night: Bish.
>
> PS Oh, how I *hate* Mozart's sickening operas: 'Must I forgo my pleasure?' A *HIDEOUS* song from *The Miscarriage of Pigaro* ! – so what? Oh, what a *SPLENDID* idea to have *Civil* War in France, with Offenbach's strains in the offing! and De Gaulle on stilts singing 'J'en ai meme' in the Place de la Discord!!

Other letters followed at intervals and Blake stayed from time to time with Norman, but by 1967 just before Norman's move, he wrote, 'Dear Norman, My legs grow weaker and more painful every day. I'm soon having a friend to share my flat, as it's *not* safe to be alone. Anything might happen. Do write again soon, please. As always Blake.'

A week before his move from Lovel Dene, Bish wrote back: 'Now I have received your rather "wobbly" and sad little letter and I think it is time your old pal came to cheer you up. It is terribly difficult and I cannot spare much time Blake, but . . .' He then proposed leaving on Saturday, 8 April and returning on the Sunday. 'I will send you a pre-paid reply tomorrow . . . I hope this will all work well and I enclose five glamorous £s to help you on your "wobbly" – but happy I hope – way . . . In horrid haste.'

Norman had been and remained a consistently loyal friend to his 'old chum' until Blake died, horribly burnt on falling over his electric fire, even when faced with the appalling collapse of his Lovel Dene life and everything it meant to him.

Whilst the Alexandre salon brought publicity and prestige (Princess Grace and Elizabeth Taylor were clients in Paris), it was not expensive for £3 a cut, shampoo and set by his top stylist M. Claude. The death of couturier Jacques Heim in January 1967 had again brought pessimistic headlines about the death of couture in Paris and its likely end with the current generation of designers – journalist Barbara Griggs terming Hardy Amies 'Old Indestructible'.[4]

All remaining members of IncSoc had other interests apart from haute couture to keep them going. Or as Shirley Flack wrote, 'London Fashion Week . . . as usual it turned out to be the non-event of the season. Even Hartnell yesterday was pretty but predictable. Says Mr Rayne, "Soldier on is our slogan of the day."'[5] Photographers concentrated on Mary Quant, mini-dresses and ready-to-wear. It was Hartnell's clients that now kept him in the headlines, such as Mrs Jack Lyons or Eileen Joyce, making a comeback:

> I'm very calm about the performance but I got into a terrible state about what to wear. I went back to Norman Hartnell and suggested a long skirt and a chiffon blouse. He said chiffon was for knickers and old ladies so he thought of something else, nicer. He said I should dye my hair to match – either goldfish pink or Scotch marmalade. I said do you mean whisky marmalade? He's got a very good sense of humour.[6]

After her performance at the Royal Albert Hall she went on to receive twenty bouquets from fans and a huge koala-bear mascot from Jeremy Thorpe.

Norman was always consulted for his opinions on dress and cosmetics and had firm ideas on miniskirts and women in trousers.

> If I were a housewife, scrubbing away in the kitchen sink or going out to do some gardening, I would wear a pair of nice warm pants. But, because my hindquarters – by nature's design – would stick

out in unattractive immensity, I would wear a nice long tweed coat to cover it.

This is where pants are splendid.

We all know the female form is divine, especially when carved completely nude in chilly marble, but the aforesaid posterior in human flesh is not so attractive when stretched between thick prickly tweeds. However . . . a cute, young girl in well-cut pants, even though the posterior sticks out in a pert, perky and provocative manner, looks most attractive.[7]

In his spring 1967 show, Norman showed a trouser evening dress named 'Best Foot Forward'. The man who had designed chiffon fox-fur-weighted trousers forty-five years earlier now showed a dress with one slim leg and one vast enveloping one that swirled around the other in an elegant manner. He also showed miniskirts in the following years, usually with a maxi coat, before settling on what he termed the 'Mixi' line, again incorporating swirling chiffons, kaftan-like dresses with shirred edging to batwing sleeves, trouser suits and fur trimmings, one suit having a monkey-fur waistcoat at a time when nobody used this fur anymore.[8] All these looks were preceded by statements that Norman would *not* use a particular line or look, just as he had initially rejected the New Look and the A, H or Trapeze Lines, yet eventually using variations of them all. It made good publicity to say 'no' and there was never any subsequent comment on his initial attitude – fashion journalism was only preoccupied with the latest news.

The only members of the Royal Family to follow the new lines almost as soon as they emerged were Princess Margaret and then Princess Anne, both of whom used Norman's designs increasingly sparingly. For the Queen, Norman continued with the slim look established during the State Visit to Paris in 1957, when the Queen wore the silver lace sheath dress for a voyage along the Seine. There were occasional variations on this thence, but the practicality of wearing and maintaining dresses with a simple outline made them a favourite on Royal Visits or Tours abroad. The cost of maintaining the embroidery workrooms was accounted for by not replacing retiring staff, and many Hartnell evening dresses were now unembroidered, with the exception of one or two 'star' models or special orders.

Jean Rook took Norman for a walk down Carnaby Street. His verdict was that, 'The men's clothes are marvellous – if I was seventeen and thin again I'd be in them.' When asked about the women's clothes, he diplomatically said, 'Very suitable in the right place.'[9]

He and Ian had already proven their versatility as designers on innumerable occasions when they were commissioned to design a new uniform for the Women's Police in London, Simone Mirman designing the cap. Ian also designed uniforms for East-West Airlines and together they tackled the uniform for reception at London Airport, all of which were judged successful.

'You don't change a uniform with Paris fashions,' was the comment of a police spokesman and Norman had ample experience of designing uniforms that were modern, dignified and likely to be suitable for some years to come.

With Norman's lukewarm interest in day clothes and great interest in uniforms, the results were polished up by Ian Thomas, indisputably the better artist, although Norman's sketches had more character. The policewomen received a smart pillbox cap and double-breasted boxy jackets over slim skirts, with a cape for bad weather. The tie was now a trim bow turned under the collar and the uniform was feminine and practical. A *Sunday Express* cartoon showed a football brawl subdued by women police in old-style uniforms whilst a Hartnell clad WPC holds up one hand to the caption 'Not in me new Norman 'Artnell, love!'

In the Winter 1962 magazine of No. 3 District Metropolitan Police, Norman was interviewed about the new uniform, which he stated was made of the same material as the previous uniform, but he added a nylon velvet collar. He also said that designing uniforms was more difficult than designing evening dresses, but he was obviously proud of the way in which the notebooks were hidden between the bust and hip-line in the natural curves of the body, which also explains the looser line of the jackets.

At Christmastime, when asked for the name of his favourite guest, Norman said, 'Cinderella – she's bound to be pretty and she would be sure to leave at midnight.'[10]

Until his death in 1979, journalists could always be sure of a good quip or an entertaining interview with Norman, as Anne Batt discovered. 'Mr Norman Hartnell,' he dictated to her in ringing tones, 'talked to me in his lemon-yellow Empire room wearing a suit of disappointed peacock blue with a peahen coloured stripe . . . I say . . . that's RATHER good . . . I say do put that bit in – only you simply must call me Norman.'

He was then asked about being in business for forty-five years. 'OH LEAVE OFF THAT YOU HORRIBLE GIRL,' he replied. 'You can ask me:

Am I currently making any clothes for Her Majesty . . . you can say that on your way in you saw Princess Marina, one of the most elegantly dressed ladies in England, walk in here.'

In fact, he had not seen her and rushed off, 'I've just *cut* Princess Marina. I rushed off to say I'm sorry, Your Highness, but she slipped into the Ladies and I nearly bumped my nose on the door . . . yes, you can mention my age if you put some nice remarks after it.'

They then discussed his menswear project and Norman neatly side-stepped the continual financial failure of his mass-production schemes.

> I have got to keep haute couture going because we need it for public entertainment and decorous diplomacy. Everyone gets a great frisson and thrill from beautiful clothes. They may not have the money to actually buy the clothes . . . But then to appreciate an art gallery you don't have to be able to buy the pictures.

Without actually stating that he needed *someone* to buy couture clothes, as he was not running a charitable institution, he then admitted to living in something of an ivory tower. 'I do have this nostalgia for the Edwardian times when many beautiful women wore beautiful clothes.'

As to his health, he avoided butter, bread and potatoes. 'And every day [I do] my daily dozen – I lie on my back and pedal a bicycle in the air very fast.'[11]

The year 1967 was when Norman's lifestyle was suddenly reduced to a few rooms, none of them large. He even had to take the train from Waterloo to Ascot on occasion as his chauffeured days were also restricted. However, he set off in November to a fashion contest in Munich run by the magazine *Für Sie*, part of the Hartnell company's long-drawn-out planning to market the name in Germany, which became linked to the Swiss company set up by John Royle and George. In September 1967, George had written to David Jacobs, their solicitor, asking if the registered office of the company could be transferred to Jacob's address 'in case the worst should happen and we have to put the company into voluntary liquidation'.[12] Norman had also asked for Jacob's advice on receiving a letter from his former friend and business associate John Pleydell concerning both the original ownership of Lovel Dene when it was bought in 1935 and the shares still held by Pleydell in Norman Hartnell Ltd and Hartnell Perfumes Ltd. Norman rebuffed all claims, yet in the coming years there was a rapprochement between the two men and Pleydell was to give Norman sound financial advice.

It is extraordinary that by 1968 the name Norman Hartnell was seen on thirty-one products and this number was then added to when a new range of handbags was launched selling from £7.10s to £250 for one in crocodile. A typical Norman touch of fantasy was found in one bag with a 'secret' front panel opening to reveal a mirror.

But for Norman the special event was undoubtedly the visit to Bruton Street of the Queen as his diary shows on 26 March ('H.M. the Queen visits HERE'). This was not usual, as we have seen, but it was not unusual for either the Queen or Princess Margaret to choose models from the current collection; the model was then withdrawn to avoid the unlikely event of two identical dresses meeting. The other major event of 1968 to be recorded reads bleakly 'Sunday, 3 November 1968 RBB RIP', the day after his second cousin Angela Goldsbrough's marriage, for which she wore a wedding dress designed by Yuki, Norman's innovative replacement for Ian Thomas.

Writing to a mutual old friend of Blake's death, Norman wrote:

> It is over now and upset me considerably at the time.
>
> I can tell you that he was found one morning by the fire brigade; he was on the floor having passed out from asphyxiation because his electric fire fell over. He was suffering from chronic arthritis, diabetes and vertigo and I daresay he fell down and could not get up.
>
> The only thing is he declined considerably and seemed very old and very unhappy. He often said he was longing to pass out.
>
> I went to the funeral in Bristol which was conducted by two eminent men, the Bishop of Southwark and the Bishop of Bristol, and I only hope that Blake (I called him by that name) is at last in peace, which he certainly wasn't during these last few weeks.
>
> Yes, as one gets older, life gets sadder, and all that is left are happy memories.[13]

Writing to the Bishop of Southwark, Mervyn Stockwood, whom Norman had first encountered in the gloom of a wartime station as they both made their way to visit Blake, Norman wrote: 'I did tell you briefly afterwards how much I appreciated all the things you said about our dear, good, naughty, mutual friend. In lovely and amusing words, you summed up his character, and I am sure he would have enjoyed every word you said about him.'[14]

The Bishop was to become friendlier with Norman in the following years and officiated at Norman's memorial service in 1979.

The resignation of Ian Thomas in 1968 was a severe blow to Norman, who had written to very many contacts in order to find a suitable replacement before finding the eminently suitable Japanese designer, Yuki- Gnyuki Torimaru.

Yuki went on to become a successful London-based designer. He had studied at the London College of Fashion and worked for the wholesalers Rembrandt, before going to Michael of Carlos Place, renowned for the fine cutting and tailoring that are also the basis for Yuki's designs. He was only with Norman from September 1968 until the middle of 1969, when he left to work for Pierre Cardin in Paris.

Godfrey Winn, in 1970, wrote asking for advice on setting up a business, about which Norman had no idea ('When this house started in 1923 things were different'), but suggested he had a word with Ian Thomas, who had by then started his own business, having worked temporarily for Wakers drawing perspectives.

In 1968, the successful Reid & Taylor connection led to shows in Brussels, Munich, Milan, Düsseldorf and Copenhagen from Thursday, 3 May to 4 May, the shows taking place on-board a new 707 with the seats removed down the centre to form a catwalk. In the coming seasons, shows were staged at Castle Howard, where a special train disgorged its merry passengers into a huge fleet of Rolls-Royces, some raked in from neighbouring CWS undertakers.

John Packer emerged in his Norman-designed suiting with frogged jacket in Portugal and Beirut. Norman was smitten by the moustachioed doorman at the Beirut hotel and had an amusing time searching the car with him for his 'lost' gloves. Kenneth Partridge also remembered him on hilarious form just before his personal appearance on the plane, asking the model girls, 'Are my seams straight and my hem level? Then push the old girl on,' before emerging from behind the curtains to take a bow on the catwalk. He had just become part of the 'Swinging Sixties', even if a headline gave his winter 1968 collection the thumbs down. 'A thirty-year-old yawn from Hartnell . . . Dull? This show was unbearably boring. Yawn-making . . . "*Diner à deux*" was the twee name for one of the numbers.'[15]

Norman was scarcely alone of his generation in carrying on their careers. Evelyn Laye took over Anna Neagle's role in the long-running *Charlie Girl*, which had already run for three and a half years, during which Anna Neagle had never missed a performance. She had also hit rock bottom financially, together with her husband Herbert Wilcox, but reinvented herself on stage – both she and Miss Laye were dressed for their parts by Norman and Miss Laye (then sixty-nine) did admit to cutting out one dance from the show – after all Anna Neagle was a mere 64-year-old. Both women had been Norman's clients for almost forty years and designs for their early clothes were on sale in June 1969 when Norman found a source of revenue amongst his design archive. Sketches for Gertrude Lawrence, Delysia, Jessie Matthews, Isabel Jeans and Mistinguett were all represented in the show that only included stage work or early designs for the fabulous Gaby Deslys made when he was a schoolboy.

In order to bring in more cash, he began writing a book called *Dress Sense* with Lady Ann Lambton, giving his ideas on dress for all occasions and some history of the company, together with amusing events. It was never published, but the idea was taken up by the journalist Zita Alden, who syndicated a Norman Hartnell column to the English press with great success throughout the early 1970s; Norman called her 'Ghostie'.

Norman's health was declining. His doctor prescribed two fifteen-minute walks a day preceded by a TNT pill under his tongue, no smoking, weight reduction of 10 lbs and cyclospasmol. Norman also regularly underwent colonic irrigation and for a man of his age appeared remarkably youthful and was still able to produce inventive designs. By 1969, he had helped to design clothes for over thirty state visits or royal tours abroad and an extraordinary number of royal occasions at home. It seemed effortless for him and he once again rose to the occasion of the the Investiture of H.R.H. Prince Charles as Prince of Wales at Caernarfon Castle on 1 July 1969.

The event was masterminded by Lord Snowdon as Constable of the Castle famously in a uniform he had designed himself. Norman was once more able to devise a tableau blending varied colours and fabrics for the dresses of royal ladies. Queen Elizabeth, The Queen Mother wore an apple-green dress with a shorter skirt than usual and an off-the-face hat reminiscent of those of thirty years before and decorated with dyed heron feathers. The Queen wore a pale yellow silk dress and coat with a 'Tudor' hat made by Simone Mirman to Norman's design of organza embroidered with pearls and beads. Unusually it brought a letter of congratulations from Cecil Beaton who thought it 'absolutely perfect for the setting – and didn't look like millinery'.[16]

Norman was clearly delighted:

Our two minds agree about the hat, it just did not have to be a fluffy milliner's confection and I felt that her medieval helmet was right in the end.

Words of praise from you are so welcome by someone like myself, and I reciprocate by saying how much I have admired everything you have ever photographed, written, drawn or spoken.[17]

This must have surprised Beaton, who had said some acidic things about both Norman and his designs over the decades. This new warmth seems to have been created by the highly successful retrospective exhibition of Beaton's photographs held at the National Portrait Gallery at the instigation of its perceptive director Dr Roy Strong, who also commissioned a photograph of Norman for the Gallery collection, although not taken by Beaton.

In the following year, Beaton cleverly arranged an exhibition at the V&A Museum ('Fashion – An Anthology by Cecil Beaton') which was the first truly comprehensive retrospective exhibition of twentieth-century clothing. Beaton had by then created the extensive wardrobe of costumes for the film *My Fair Lady* and had good experience of the demands put upon a designer. He wrote to Norman in May 1970 asking if he could help him to find some of his day dresses for the exhibition show, most of which was eventually to become part of the V&A's permanent collection. Norman replied:

I am extremely sorry to say that I have been sadly unsuccessful. I have asked many of my ageing clients (those who have not yet passed away!) and they all give the same reply – that they disposed of the dresses to poor relations, charity dress tea parties, gave them to their maids, or just burned them.

I did, however, broach the subject mentioning your name to H.M. the Queen Mother and she produced a black velvet afternoon dress and coat trimmed with jet, which I gather she may be sending you . . . I continue to go on dressmaking but it is not enjoyable these days, and I hope ere long to slide out of it. I do hope we shall have cause to meet sometime soon.

They did. Norman went to lunch at Beaton's house in Pelham Place.
Beaton replied that

it is just too silly of me not to have started this some time ago (30 years!). But we *must* be represented by something of yours, so please don't give up the search. I saw the Queen Mother on Thursday and said how much I admired her rose-mauve costume and she said it was yours. It was a marvellous colour and very simple and made her look her best. She has promised me something of her wardrobe – and I'd looked for a crinoline of sparklets . . . the whole collection would be incomplete without you. My sister has one of your ballroom dresses in tulle but it doesn't do you justice. With blessings, Cecil.

In the event, this dress of 1928 and the Flowers of the Field dress worn by the Queen at the Opera during the State Visit to France in 1957 together with a white satin dress of 1959 embroidered with aquamarines and turquoise flower frost beads were all that was seen of Norman's work. As the House held an extensive collection of what were known as 'back numbers', this is both sad and strange.

That Hartnell was still in business in 1971 was, however, due to both luck and a timely revival of trading. In December 1968, David Jacobs was found dead in his house. Once again Norman needed another legal advisor. However, by October 1969 he was writing again to the Prime Minister, his old acquaintance Harold Wilson:

Forgive me but, finding myself in distressed circumstances, I write to you personally and urgently, to enlist your sympathy and although I am not asking for any special favouritism, I do appeal for your intervention to obviate the calamity of my threatened position. If such intervention is impossible, I will readily understand.

My company has a high international reputation, but has run into certain difficulties because of the pressures of overheads on high fashion in this country and of the general financial shortage.

The Purchase Tax authorities were here yesterday and distrained on my company's assets for arrears of Purchase Tax amounting to £4,307, due July of this year. There is no question of my company's ability to pay, but large amounts are due to my business here and I have considerable difficulty in collecting these overdue sums and I fear this . . . may continue for some time.

Norman then outlined the fact that payments by instalments had been declined and that he had a week until furniture and fittings were to be removed. It was again a pitiable situation for him to have been placed in by the mismanagement of his company.

'I am prompted to appeal to you for your kindly help and to rescue me from the disgrace of this humiliation.' He then stressed how he had always promoted British fashion worldwide, participating in a wide variety of shows at his own expense and that he was even now engaged in licensing negotiations, which would bring money into Britain.

Norman received an immediate reply from an assistant stressing that the Prime Minister could not intervene personally but had passed on his letter to the Chancellor of the Exchequer and Norman was able to write a letter of thanks: 'Today we have heard from the Purchase Tax authorities to the effect that there will be no pantechnicon outside these premises on Monday next. You see, therefore, how very grateful I am to the Prime Minister and to your good self.'[18]

The news was received with relief by Norman, George and John Royle, who had concocted the original letter between them. The strain did nothing for Norman's health, and Mrs Guinness was genuinely so alarmed that she suggested a buzzer between the two parts of the house. Norman rejected this idea and had the telephone re-sited to his bed, but he began to consult the surgeon Sir Ronald Bodley Scott on a regular basis.

In 1971, Norman cooperated with Mary Cathcart Borer on another book, *Royal Courts of Fashion* published by Cassell. It covered the themes of high fashion through the ages that so appealed to him and is an interesting survey although without any references in the text indicating the source material, which the publisher Cassell should have corrected. It attracted good reviews, particularly from his new friend Prudence Glynn of *The Times*, one of the most respected British fashion editors, who wrote asking for exclusivity in return for giving him a page.

Norman replied: 'Dear Lady Windlesham, Madam Glynn (any relation to Elinor?) or Prudence, Thank you so much for your nice letter in which you say you have read and enjoyed my book . . . I have two sketches from *Silver and Gold* which depict those beautiful creatures Gertrude Lawrence and Isabel Jeans',[19] not mentioning that they had been drawn by Ian Thomas, now designing under his own name. Ian Thomas also designed for the Queen. As he well remembered, Miss MacDonald had telephoned him to say that the Queen wanted him to design for her and Thomas had replied, 'But what will Mr Hartnell say?' He was firmly told not to take any notice of what he said – '*THE QUEEN* wanted to see him'.

In his new book, Norman charted the use and decline of royal-inspired 'fashion' with the rise of new money after the First World War which swept away most of the Courts of Europe in its wake.

A friend wrote to him: 'I . . . feel you have come successfully through your "Ordeal by Questioning" by all the fashion writers. SS [Serena Sinclair, I suppose] of the *Telegraph* was a bit silly, I thought. What was she expecting? Some sort of Crawfie nonsense, I suppose.'

To his very old journalist friend Alison Settle, Norman wrote a forthright note about her review in *The Lady*: 'I am glad you enjoyed the book . . . Personally, I found it rather dull – but it has sold quite well. With old-fashioned love to you.'[20] The book was also well reviewed abroad followed by successful sales, especially in Australia.

Norman also received an admiring fan letter from an old friend the celebrated New York fashion public relations expert and journalist Eleanor Lambert Berkson, compiler of the annual International Best Dressed Poll which included the Queen in the 'Best Dressed Hall of Fame', and usually contained the name of at least one Hartnell client in its annual listing. Norman wrote a flattering letter back: 'How nice to receive your enthusiastic letter about my book.' Miss Lambert wanted to order several dozen copies to send to various editors and review it in her syndicated column. 'You, the clever, smart and elegant girl will get your copies before that.'[21]

Interestingly, the great American designer Oleg Cassini, Mrs Kennedy's 'court' designer, was to write in his autobiography of problems similar to those Norman experienced in his career – he suffered from being American in his own country and in refusing to open a business in Paris. As Cassini wrote, 'Half of the pull of Paris . . . lay in the beauty and culture of Paris, which drew journalists like a magnet, again and again. He turned down representation by Eleanor Lambert and it proved a huge mistake as he thought she never forgave him.'[22]

At seventy, Norman received many congratulations, not least from his former 'rival' Victor Stiebel:

Dearest Normie, when I read in *The Times* of your birthday, my thoughts were filled with affection and admiration. And so this belated note is to wish you, oh so *very* well on reaching with such 'spirit' your *70th*. Well done you. There must be many more please. Even this polluted (in every sense of the word) old London of ours could not do without its Hartnell decorations.

I work on Vol 2 of my memoirs – *The Thirties* and in it I have written an appreciation of my old pal. Rather over-written it is. Hope you won't mind. With affection and a cartload of good wishes.[23]

Increasingly smitten by illness, Stiebel's memoirs were never completed for publication and Norman was still left in the same harness of the early 1930s when Stiebel had first asked Norman for a job. Michael Sherard had also closed his doors and become a lecturer in fashion. Norman was to outlast almost all of his former IncSoc colleagues with the remarkable exception of the astute Hardy Amies – 'Hardly Amiable' as Norman dubbed him, but 'Hardy Perennial' to the fashion press.

Norman seems not only to have courted danger in his private and business life, but also in the number of fires in his houses. In 1970, just in time for New Year 1971, Mrs Guinness's central heating system exploded and enveloped her house in smoke and flames. She was rescued by her butler, the damaged house saved, and Norman's 'sniffy' quarters, as he described them to a friend, damaged by smoke. He increasingly spent time with George and eventually holidayed with Delta and Marcus Hartnell in Malta.

In 1973, he was not chosen to design the wedding dress of Princess Anne, although he had for a time designed for her including mini-skirted dresses, but both the Queen and Queen Elizabeth, the Queen Mother wore Norman's strikingly fashionable innovative designs. The Queen wore a heavy silk coat of sapphire-blue silk with unusual diamond-shaped inlets either side in front of the flared waistline. This fastened with four diamond-shaped silk-covered buttons over a dress of the same fabric and of similar design. The hat by Simone Mirman consisted of a bandeau of matching silk with a snood of gathered dark blue lace.

The same spare 1970s line was echoed in the coat and dress worn by the Queen Mother, the dress with a double diamond aperture through which a panel of beige and light brown chiffon was inserted to fall over the left shoulder, a remarkably pared down version of some of the fantastic dresses designed for her by Norman in the 1940s, but retaining great elegance. Unfortunately, this dress was invisible to the public under a beige and gold banded silk coat with three-quarter sleeves bordered with sable cuffs.

The Queen Mother remained his loyal client and Norman wrote to another client:

> It is most unusual – when a thing is perfect – to receive any thanks thereto, because most customers just take perfection for granted!
>
> Also you seem to be the only person, probably apart from H.M. the Queen Mother, who can, with sympathy, envisage the terrible difficulties I experience in getting my Maison de Couture going successfully. The suppliers of material are closing down . . . also belt makers, the flower makers . . . beads are nigh unprocurable, so are embroideresses. I used to have fifty-five embroidery girls – I now have five, three of which are part-time! We cannot get seam-stresses or tailorring [sic] hands.
>
> Materials are ten times the price – if we can get them. All wages are up, and the rent has been trebled! So you will understand the difficulties I am having in preparing my new autumn collection.[24]

In the early 1960s, he had entered into an admiring friendship with Violet Bonham Carter, who especially delighted in his Christmas cards. These were considered to be rather vulgar by Ian Thomas and others but were an original way of keeping embroideresses working in the summer months. In the 1960s, he sent out 750 each Christmas. People wrote to ask for them if left off the list and many people collected them to bring out each Christmas. His former mannequin Averil Anstruther sent a photograph of herself standing in front of their festive glory. This custom was dwindling, as were the embroideresses. Today, the surviving cards command high prices at auction having done ser-vice as Christmas decorations all over the world.

There were still new friends, such as Nicholas Haslam, who interviewed him for the paper *Ritz* and the decorator Robin Anderson who invited him to dine, as did the designer Bill Gibb. Generally, he had a much quieter life as his heart was weaker. He went on a cruise and hated it as much as Beverley Nichols, a fellow passenger, did. Afterwards they exchanged letters thanking one another for their mutual support and conversation.

In 1972, the shoemakers Bective brought out a range of Norman Hartnell women's shoes mainly designed and coordinated by Jean Matthew, who was an important designer at Rayne. The 7% return on sales proved too little for the impatient George, who also thought the product of insufficient quality for the Hartnell name. He broke the contract and took back the display rack in the ground-floor showroom in 1974 – yet another short-lived venture that had netted a small income disproportionate to the amount of effort put into it by many people.

Negotiations with Germany did not bring much joy either. Rumours flew about that Norman Hartnell would open a salon in Hamburg, but the reality turned out to be menswear, concentrating on shirts and ties for which George considerately submitted 'the badge which we now use for the ties' featuring a large monogram 'N.H.' with three stars above it and three beneath. The relationship with Schildmann and Company seems to have been one of frustration at the slowness with which matters were handled in London and the venture was again short-lived, having absorbed considerable amounts of time and generated the usual paper mountain.

How far Norman really absorbed himself with these projects is unclear, as he concentrated on relaunching 'In Love' and on the Australian and South African licences, trips to both countries undertaken in the 1960s.

Australia was particularly successful for publicity thanks to Margot Macrae, an adept journalist and publicist for Norman. As Countess of Buckinghamshire, she later included Norman in several events organised for charity in London.

Demands on Hartnell and Norman to aid charitable dances or raffles with fashion shows or presents for raffles were now usually refused as the cost was enormous for staging a show, and apart from the present of cosmetics there was little that the House could afford to offer. Norman was also increasingly loath to make personal appearances if they demanded a speech. He had never been fond of public speaking at the best of times, although usually available for radio or television interviews – he appeared on the popular Russell Harty Show and was even a panellist on the TV quiz *Call My Bluff*. He had a pleasant voice and the Cracknells had often heard him singing to himself at home. Furthermore, as Godfrey Winn and Beverley Nichols still carried on with their careers as survivors of another more glamorous era, so Norman with his *art moderne* salon was increasingly seen as an interesting character.

The late 1960s rediscovery of art deco by collectors was fostered by the books of Bevis Hillier and Martin Battersby so that when interest in Norman's pre-war designs was enhanced by the reissue of the recordings of his clients Evelyn Laye, Gertrude Lawrence or Jessie Matthews, he was again sought out by a younger audience.

The revolution that occurred in men's clothing was symptomatic of this, for the 1920s had witnessed the last important changes. In an interview with *Gentleman*, Norman was asked whether he had always been interested in men's clothing designs: he had not – his interest had only been in them as a background to the silhouette of designs for women, although he admired the craftsmanship of Savile Row.

> But my honest esteem was frequently mixed with the paralysing monotony of their achievements. Now and again I believed that . . . a change must come. I was interested in the fashions of Huntsman. But with curiosity and amusement I also followed the violent beginning of the future emancipation of post-war youth, i.e. the Rockers, the Teddies, the Carnaby Clique.

Norman claimed to have been won over to Reid & Taylor fabrics by 'the intoxicating colours. I always derived my inspiration from the material' and here he claimed that John Packer worked on him 'with the conviction of a missionary' although the fees received were never discussed in the interview. 'The wishes of Mr Packer did not . . . restrict my work.'

He also included classic designs in the collection. Norman also stressed that 'formerly it was women between thirty-five and forty-five years old who achieved maximum elegance . . . as she was only then worldly enough and possessed the necessary means.' Now the twenty and thirty age group of men and women was the fashion target and ideal.

Asked if he would ever wear long hair or bell-bottoms (he was then over seventy years old) Norman replied 'No, certainly not,' but he did see older men wearing colourful clothes with taste.[25] In 1975, he wrote to thank John Packer for

> our lovely evening out . . . at the Café Royal was more entertaining. I didn't think much of the 'mond' [sic] – and I thought the two cockney women announcing the Male Award Winners were dreadful! But that was not your fault – you, the usual charming, generous host . . . and I must add looking the most elegant person in the room in your stewed prune Hartnell, with your squashed beetle waistcoat.

I cannot help thinking that the fashion world is deteriorating lamentably and that it will soon be time to get out of it. But you are fortunate in your exquisite materials for gentlemanly wear clothing. So you see, I did find it all a most interesting and enjoyable evening – THANKS TO YOU.[26]

Yet Norman still had no option but to carry on keeping his name before the public as best as he could.

The perennial question of dress and its part in signifying a person's station in life was often put to Hartnell or linked to his name; even the 1956 film *The Man Who Knew Too Much* one of Hitchcock's characters remarks that even if Bud Flanagan were dressed by Hartnell he would not look like an aristocrat. It was this fame of being a 'household word' that had to be nurtured continuously in order to nurture Norman.

Partly with the idea of keeping his name before the public by holding another exhibition and partly for relaxation Norman began to paint his own forms of exotic birds.

He wrote to Mrs John Ellis:

> . . . expressing thanks to you for all the trouble you are taking with me and my painting. The special paper you sent me – which became hidden amongst a lot of magazines – I eventually found and it is now deposited safely down at Ascot . . . also I told you there is a smelly garage, half of which is being cleared out for my desk and me, and I hope sooner or later to squeeze a couple of tubes of oil paint and start dabbing away straight on to the inexpensive paper! I really do think you are a most charming and patient lady and it is wonderful the way you keep up your enthusiasm. It will be just as wonderful when I show a little enthusiasm and get down to work.[27]

Vera Ellis wrote him more encouraging letters urging him to try using a palette knife and sympathising with his fainting fits. Old friends kept in touch. To P. Joyce Reynolds, thanking her for mentioning Minnie Hogg in an article, Norman wistfully replied, 'It is so nice to hear from someone who appreciates the beauty of fashion that was and which is now fast fading. I envy you your walnut trees and the flowering bushes . . . with best wishes and again so many thanks for keeping in touch with me.'[28] Like so many people who have delighted in the company of older and wiser people, Norman had buried most of his friends and family.

Although the ever-ambitious George continued to have schemes for promoting and exploiting the Norman Hartnell name, he came to a full stop with his scheme to open a Mayfair Hartnell's Club in conjunction with Harry and Andrew Meadows of The Twenty-One Club. Possibly an ideal venture for George, the world of gaming clubs was scarcely in Norman's interest and could hardly have kept the Royal Warrants over his doors. But from 1964 to 1974 George persisted.

A further scheme was the Norman Hartnell International Academy of Deportment opened under the direction of two of Norman's most accomplished and well-known models Jane Chorley and Mara Levey. This further brainchild of George's also died virtually stillborn, much to the distress of the main names involved.

Financial salvation came from several other sources and was desperately needed again in 1974 when Mattli, involved with the manufacture of the new Norman Hartnell ready-to-wear collection, wrote to George that a GVK cheque in part payment had been returned by his bank and weekly payment was then demanded.[29] At one stage it was even proposed by Rae Rhavis, one of the final members to join IncSoc before its collapse, that their two businesses merge, which was given serious consideration for a week or two.

Norman cashed in Premium Bonds, cancelled subscriptions and had by June 1973 an overdrawn personal Ascot bank account of £1,098 against monies on deposit of £2,084 – £2,000 of which was held as a guarantee for the company. His London account was little better – even the cooperation with the Great Universal Stores catalogue brought in only enough money to assist in keeping 26 Bruton Street going.

Numerous alternative premises were suggested, but Norman clung on.[30] It was enough to bear that he had to use a garage of his tiny country house as a studio, a situation from which he had escaped in 1922 to found his own House with Topsy. To give up the prime symbol of his success would have been too much for him to bear unless he could have retired.

The sadness of his situation is underlined in his diary, for he was a man steeped in ceremony and dates. The entry for Saturday, 3 April 1971 is empty except for one word: 'Clayton', the location of his mother's and Topsy's graves. It was the fiftieth anniversary of his mother's death and Norman marked it as he had on the day following his first successful London show decades ago by visiting the grave.

In the few years left to Norman, he was greatly assisted by John Pleydell, whom he visited in his flat in Estoril, Portugal in 1972. Strangely, he had been living in Bish's old flat in Eastern Terrace, Kemptown, Brighton before settling abroad. Perhaps it was no coincidence as he became Norman's saviour yet again, having advised him to do something about his health.

On 7 January 1972 he wrote to Norman: 'I have left you £50,000. Of this £10,000 will be paid to you outright on my death and £40,000 will be invested to pay you the interest in your lifetime.' He also wrote in July that he would give him Christmas and birthday gifts of £2,000 each. In the meantime, he had stayed at Rose Place and Norman had taken him to the polo at Windsor and the Police Horse Show, two of his regular dates.

It must have been a strange feeling to be sharing life together for however brief a time after forty years and yet one can understand why Norman had felt claustrophobic in his company. 'Mr and Mrs Cracknell helped to make my stay enjoyable – they are priceless and devoted to you,' Pleydell wrote. Then enigmatically and significantly, 'I do hope that the "CRISE" with your friend has now past. Please *take very* great care not to become too *involved in any dangerous intrigue*. For the sake of your good name and business, you cannot and must not be involved in any scandal.' This was something Norman had flirted with for most of his adult life.

John Pleydell then suggested that Norman's chauffeur White, who had a terrifying record of accidents with Norman's aged Rolls-Royce, should be replaced. 'He is a very old and sick man . . . Mrs Guinness I thought looked very ill, so try to be patient with her so long as she is at Rose Place . . . my love to you.'[31]

Little was asked for in return, except an oil painting of 'Normie'. Norman replied that he was pleased by the letter and news but as he wrote, 'No, the cheque you left for Dorothy has not been cashed. I think instead of "utilising" my money I prefer that you gathered it all up and replaced it back where it came from at M. This is according to the suggestions of my advisers here.'

His typewritten version was more veiled, but on 30 July John Pleydell died of a heart attack in the early hours of the morning. Mutual friends were then helpful to Norman, but it later turned out that a subsequent will had been made and although Norman was in the first and the second, the latest version was incomplete so a legal problem ensued. Once again, Norman had his expectations dashed at the last minute.

By 1977, Norman's career had come full circle with the extensive publicity surrounding the Queen's Silver Jubilee Year of 1977. Although Hardy Amies' pink silk dress and coat attracted the most attention when worn to St Paul's Cathedral on the day itself, Norman was the one to receive a knighthood in the New Year's 1977 Silver Jubilee Honours List. He was dubbed by Queen Elizabeth the Queen Mother, and naturally was delighted at the fact that the honour was a personal one within the gift of the sovereign, and that it had been arranged by the Queen that he received it from the hands of the Queen Mother. Beforehand, he was worried that he might be glued by his gout to the dubbing stool, but all went smoothly.[32]

The knighthood cemented Norman's status as a significant dress designer and he did his best to reflect its status. In an interview, the garage at Sunninghill became 'a little cottage where he paints birds of paradise' and he said, 'It's a lot more fun than putting big busts and bigger bottoms into manure-brown coats and skirts.'[32]

Before the flood of congratulations and journalists bore down on him, he was able to stress that he had insisted on being a British *not* French designer. 'We broke that prejudice down. And every dressmaker in this country can thank us for that. You can put that down in your notebook.'

When asked about modern designers, he paused and said slowly, 'They design for their contemporaries, which is the best thing they can do.'[31]

On the day of his knighthood, Queen Elizabeth the Queen Mother had prepared a surprise for Norman, wearing a peacock-blue version of a dress he had designed for her in mauve. 'She had it secretly copied without my knowledge,' Norman told a journalist. 'She meant it to be a surprise for me at the investiture. She thought the colour would be a splendid contrast against the crimson background in the ballroom, and it was.'[33] No doubt she also knew that the colour was one of Norman's favourites. If he thought about his relatively humble place of birth and the Crown & Sceptre in Streatham Hill, he did not mention it, yet his journey to the status of Knight Commander of the Royal Victorian Order had been a long and magnificently distinguished one in which he had surprisingly often been his own worst enemy.

At Christmas 1976, Serena Sinclair reported that Norman had been watering the chrysanthemums on his mother's and three sisters' graves at Clayton. 'Don't like them, but what else can you get in December?' His mother and sister were always in his thoughts at moments of personal sorrow and rejoicing.

With typical modesty, he had been away on the weekend when the award was announced. 'I fled to Eastbourne – sorry it sounds so bourgeois – and simply walked alone on the beach and watched the foam foaming.'[33] His surviving stepsister, Lady Kilner, was to have accompanied him to the Palace but was too ill, so his friend Lady Diana Meston went with him and later wrote that the occasion now ranked with an Evening Court in 1939 as her most treasured occasion.

Yet Norman's design work still continued. A menswear-designing contract was made with the Japanese company Teijin Shoji Kaisha, which produced a lucrative, elegant collection of his clothes, assisted by the publicity around the State Visit of the Queen to Japan in 1975 and preceded the Emperor and Empress's European Tour in 1971. This belated entry into the Japanese market was still worthwhile.

His knighthood was marked by a lunch hosted at The Mirabelle on 27 January 1977 by his consistently faithful friend Edward Rayne – 'The Cobbler' as he signed himself to Norman, who termed himself in reciprocal cards and letters 'The Little Woman Round the Corner'. The guests represented were a virtual roll call of old friends and acquaintances: Ernestine Carter, Lady Hartwell, Jocelyn Stevens, Eric Crabtree, George, Prudence Glynn, Beatrix Miller, John Glover, Winefride Jackson, Lord Hayter, Lt Col Keown-Boyd, Serena Sinclair, Joyce Kirkman and Betty Kenward – the society columnist 'Jennifer' of *Harper's & Queen*, a consistently generous client and commentator on Norman's designs and collections.

Edward Rayne submitted his speech to Norman in advance so that he would not be surprised. Norman made an elegant speech in reply, particularly thanking the press representatives who can 'make or mar' a designer. He then mentioned his great gratitude to Minnie Hogg, *Vogue,* Alison Settle and even Cecil Beaton. He mentioned facets of his career and ended with the wish that he hoped to 'retire on Friday'. He could not, of course.

Hardy Amies telegrammed: 'So sorry not to be with you to drink the health of the first Frock Maker Knight. Please give my love to everybody and accept again my warmest and sincere congratulations. Hardy.' Edward Rayne would also be awarded a knighthood later on, as was Hardy Amies, the second designer to be so honoured by the Queen.

Ian Thomas had not been asked, but at the Ball to celebrate the Queen's

Jubilee later in the year he suddenly heard a familiar voice behind him say, 'Would you get me a whisky, dear boy?' and turned to see Sir Norman sitting in a chair. It was their first contact for years and Ian never knew if his usual Christmas and birthday cards to Norman were simply ignored or never reached him. They did reach him, but Sir Norman was particularly upset that Miss Louie, his stock-keeper for decades and one of his first employees, should have chosen to go with Ian rather than stay with him. She was fiercely loyal to both men but found the business atmosphere with Mitch at 26 Bruton Street less and less to her taste.

Norman was pleased that the entertainer Cilla Black asked him for designs, and she subsequently appeared in some of his elegant evening dresses. A hint of possible further rejuvenation of his clientele came with a wedding dress for a member of the Al-Ghanim Gulf family. But as with various other menswear projects, age and ill health made further progress with new contacts impossible over his remaining two years of life.

In March 1977, Norman opened the Chelsea Antiques Fair now mentioning Lady Clare Hartnell, 18th Mayor of Chelsea, (1939–41) as a fully fledged aunt. By April, Winefride Jackson had retired from the *Telegraph* after twenty-five years and wrote to Norman: 'How kind you always were when I was learning the job . . . I shall always treasure the replica panel of embroidery on the Queen's coronation dress.'[35]

It was Sir Norman's friend Andrew Robb, the illustrator for the *Daily Express*, who had the largest collection of such panels, usually given to him as the press waited at Bruton Street to hear the news of which design was being worn by the Queen on a particular occasion during a state visit or royal tour.

'These had all been mounted and framed, and now they hung there brilliantly illuminated, a coruscating galaxy of breathtaking beauty,' wrote Norman. 'They hang there not as a memoir of ephemeral fashion but as a reminder of the historic significance of all the great State visits, so dutifully undertaken by our beloved monarch Her Majesty the Queen,' he wrote in the introduction to *The Queen's Clothes*.[36]

Norman wrote back as usual thanking Winefride Jackson for her help to him over the years and saying that she should look after the embroidery, 'for there will be no new Hartnell collections for you to view'. He wished her luck with her projects for a new book: 'I have had many propositions . . . but I find myself too lazy to tackle the job!'[37]

He was preoccupied by memories, visiting Honiton to seek out his father's birthplace, as he wrote in May to his 'cousin' Grace Connor in America, and in July Beatrix Miller, Editor of British *Vogue*, gave him a celebratory lunch. His old confidential clerk and holder of many secrets Ivy Godley wrote to him: 'I meant to tell you yesterday that the two roses you gave us many years ago have blossomed wonderfully this year. They are Elizabeth of Glamis and Norman Hartnell – I think they must know it is jubilee year – oh I am sorry I mean Sir Norman,' she added, having begun with 'Dear Mr'.[38]

Business still called from abroad on various occasions, for example, a typical cable read 'For Mitchison Suggest Boss Immediately Give Interviews London Offices Australian Newspapers On Royal Tour Clothes. Stop. Amies Here Talking Big Regards TOM'.

By now, however, Norman could scarcely care less and in February 1978 he made an appointment with Sir Richard Bayliss, having the additional problem of a hernia after being rushed to the Princess Christian Hospital in Windsor in September 1977 where he remained for three weeks instead of at a health farm. His body was failing.

After X-rays he was prescribed Benoral to ease the stiffening of his joints, a condition from which Topsy had suffered. His diary became emptier and emptier as his health declined and over the next year he was noticeably frailer.

Ivy Godley wrote to him in July 1978: 'It was nice to see so many old friends again but, oh, I was sorry to see you looking so unlike your usual happy self . . . I shall hope to find you looking better, my love as always.'[39]

Around him all his old employees were also ageing fast.

'Cher petit Patron and Fayre Knight, I am still alive in spite of all the awful things that have happened to me . . . I hope that you are well and still making lots of nice dresses for our beloved Queen . . . Vera.'[40]

In September he wrote to Donald Neville-Willing:

> I want to go and see *Dracula* at the Shaftesbury. I don't care if it got bad notices – I want to see the costumes and scenery. If I called for you in a hired car, could you give me a small snack to eat before the theatre? Then we could drive to the theatre. Could you book me a stage box (with your professional influence) . . .
>
> Anthony Tancred has come to live near me. Is he a friend or an enemy?
>
> Mr Royle is dead.

I have got my spring show in half an hour.

If you are not in America . . .' [41]

Shades of the former Blake and Bish friendship are apparent here.

Norman never gave up hope. He was sustained by the knowledge that his talents continually triumphed over adversity, partly due to his deep religious faith and partly to his effervescent sense of humour, which made a mockery of unpleasant reality.

This is typified by his 1970 response to *Woman* magazine questioning a 'personality', as he had become, on, 'What I'd do with a windfall'. Not publicly known to have few financial resources left, he replied, '£5: "I'd buy lot's of flowers." £50: "Mm that would give me about half a suit or some shirts." £500: "I'd stock up the cellar." £50,000: "I don't know what I would do. I'm so rich already!" My honest answer, actually to all these WOMAN windfall questions is that I would put the whole lot in the bank. But if you insist that I spend it... Oh! I know: I'd rent a palace in Italy for five weeks, fully staffed. All right? Toodle-oo!'

On 14 December 1978, his faithful old client Jeanne Stourton, Lady Stonor, wrote to thank him for a party and complimented him on his elegance and the house on its loveliness, but over the next few weeks when staying with George he was far from well and eventually he needed a wheelchair to make the short journey from bedroom to bathroom and back, George helping him as best he could, whilst Norman had more dizzy spells and George became more and more alarmed.

On 8 June 1979, four days short of his seventy-eighth birthday, Norman died. George wrote to Jean Mathew that the local people had never seen so many flowers at their church in Clayton for the burial of one person. 'This in itself is a tribute to a wonderful gentleman.'[42]

The Bishop of Southwark, Mervyn Stockwood, officiated at the Memorial Service on 25 June in Southwark Cathedral for 'Sir Norman Hartnell, the brilliant designer and Bossy, a beloved, warm, affectionate human being', and both Robert Nesbitt and Barbara Cartland read lessons, the latter dressed in a violet creation designed by Norman. The Queen was represented by Sir Rennie Maudslay and Queen Elizabeth the Queen Mother by Lord Adam Gordon. The congregation consisted of over 1,000 people, including most of his major surviving clients and contemporaries.

The Bishop referred to their mutual friend Richard Blake Brown and later in his memoirs he was to mention a strange paranormal occurrence whilst staying the following March in Norman's former house, lent for the weekend by George, when a jade ornament fell from the end of the chimney piece on Friday evening. When sitting around the fire again on Sunday with the Bishops of Woolwich and Kingston, Stockwood mentioned the occurrence, whereupon the ornament fell off again. He thought that if it had not been caused by the fire, it was the sort of joke Blake would perpetrate with Norman's approval, just for the fun of it.[43]

The memorial service brought together so many of Norman's old employees, including Miss Louie, who was quoted as saying, 'There were no unhappy times with Hartnell. This is an opportunity for us to remember the happy times with an adorable boss.'[44] As the Bishop said, 'He was a true, perfect, gentle knight' – the last words being inscribed on Sir Norman's tombstone.

In fact, Norman wrote a better epitaph for himself in 1963:

> Women and wine are all very well, but companionship and cold water are much better for the health and the pocket. There is a song in one's heart, a song from the barrel organ, and a song in the tinkling of a successful till. The melodies of all these linger on.

Now, he lies in the same churchyard as his beloved mother and half-sisters, together with members of their families and 'Jugs' Stuart who lies with his wife Topsy in between the graves of Norman and his mother, beneath a spreading evergreen tree. His grave is already weathered, the words 'Dressmaker to the Queens of England' becoming fainter. His headstone has sunk and leans poignantly towards those of his dear mother and sister, as he did emotionally through all his long, distinguished life.

'A few yards of satin last longer than flesh and bones'
– Norman Hartnell.

APPENDIX I

Norman Hartnell and the Coronation of H.M. Queen Elizabeth II
1953
From *Silver and Gold* chapters thirteen and fourteen.

Plans for the Coronation were soon set into motion, and magnificently accomplished by His Grace the Duke of Norfolk. In the autumn, I visited the Earl Marshal's Office, in Belgrave Square, where Bluemantle, Pursuivant of Arms, explained that a new design was required for alternative dress to be worn by viscountesses and baronesses at the coronation.

The existing habiliment of these peeresses was a combination of two garments, comprising a kirtle of crimson velvet, bordered all round with a narrow edge of miniver pure, scalloped or straight in front, or gathered back in three festoons, each tied with a bow of golden tinsel. This kirtle is worn over the usual full Court dress, which should be white or slightly cream-coloured, with lace, embroidery, or brocade, according to taste. Gold and silver can be used but no colour may be introduced into it. With this is worn a mantle with a train, called a Robe (attached to and falling from the shoulders) also of crimson velvet and ermine.

There was considerable concern regarding the costliness of these robes which, hitherto, it had been imperative to wear for every Coronation ceremony in the Abbey. Bluemantle asked if I would undertake to evolve a design of one garment to replace the two separate ones, and thus help reduce the cost for those ladies who might not be as wealthy as the world imagined.

The same need for economy applied to the costly metallic coronet hitherto worn by peeresses. He asked if I would design an inexpensive and appropriate headgear, perhaps based on the design worn by barons before the days of Charles II and known as a Cap of State. The Robes of State and Coronets had not been altered since the reign of Queen Anne and for days I puzzled over the salient points. I wished to retain the form-fitting grace of the kirtle but to dispose of its ugly sleeves which were about nine inches long. Also, the kirtle stopped short in a hard, clumsy line at the feet. The Robe, of course, trailed elegantly on the floor, yet the cape of white fur adjoined at the shoulder was square and stumpy.

Eliminating the less attractive aspects of both kirtle and Robe, I chose the fitted line of the former, ignoring the sleeves, and reformed the square line of the short ermine cape of the latter into a graceful curve which, standing away from the back of the wearer, covered the tops of the arms – often the most unattractive part of the female form – and met in front, where it clasped like a broad cape collar in the high-waisted princess line. It was the most generally wearable and most flattering and feminine of all the six designs I had painted. I then designed and drew thirty ideas for the Cap of State. Meanwhile, I had to search for an inexpensive red velveteen and some cheap white pelts of the humble rabbit in an effort to affect the necessary economy.

When all was ready I returned to the Earl Marshal's office where I was most courteously received by Garter King of Arms, Sir George Bellew. Of the thirty Caps of State one was unanimously preferred. Estimates of the cost, which had turned out to be surprisingly low, were submitted to Garter and Bluemantle. The selling price had been reduced from £500 to a matter of £30.

Before I left Belgrave Square I was required to undertake the task of devising some form of head covering to be worn by those ladies who would attend the Abbey ceremony wearing, perhaps, day clothes if the short-skirted fashion were permitted. For those wearing long evening dress, tiaras were advised. Garter kindly drew for me a neat little sketch of the kind of headgear he imagined would be suitable, and after some days I returned again with a few dozen more.

It was finally agreed officially that 'those ladies attending the Coronation in short evening dress must wear a head covering which must not cover the face, but should be in the form of a veil, falling from the crown or back of the head as far as the shoulders, but not lower than the waistline. Any colour excepting black can be used and should be made in a suitably light material such as tulle, chiffon, organza or lace. This can be attached by a comb, jewelled pins, flower, or ribbon bows – but not with feathers.'

The little Cap of state, now made up in its right materials, looked gaily modern and attractive, and was described as a crimson velvet Cap enriched with narrow gold braid and bordered with a narrow strip of white fur. The Cap was made to fit the crown of the head and had to have a gold or gold-coloured tassel or other similar decoration which consisted of a knot of gold braid ending in drop pearls.

Later I was granted the honour of an audience at Buckingham Palace. Her Majesty was pleased to approve of everything submitted to her notice and I retired feeling less guilty of having interfered with fashions favoured in the reign of good Queen Anne.

One October afternoon in 1952, Her Majesty the Queen desired me to make for her the dress to be worn at her Coronation.

I can scarcely remember what I murmured in reply. In simple conversational tones the Queen went on to express her wishes. Her Majesty required that the dress should conform in line to that of her wedding dress and that the material should be white satin. It was almost exactly five years earlier that I had put the final touches to the dress which, as Princess Elizabeth, she had worn on the day of her wedding to the Duke of Edinburgh.

When my first exhilaration was over, I settled down to study exactly what history and tradition meant by a 'Coronation dress'. I visited the London Museum and the London Library and leafed through authoritative tomes.

The first Queen Elizabeth had an inborn love of splendour, and I had visions of the sort of thing I would have created if I had been a dress designer in the sixteenth century. She had worn a tiara-like headdress with flowers and jewels in her hair, a radiating and bejewelled ruff, heavy pearl ear-rings, a fur-trimmed cloak, puffings studded with more jewels, ruffles at the wrists and a fan of peacock feathers. Her skirt opened to disclose a kirtle diapered with jewels.

All this seemed a trifle ornate and I learned that the courtiers of the period were also rather gaudy fellows, wearing jackets slashed to reveal pull-outs of the wildest colours, and dripping with jewellery. I felt that the Tudors offered little help, beyond their Rose, which I certainly hoped to introduce into the Coronation dress of 1953.

Then I turned to the study of Queen Anne, who most unhappily was crippled with gout on the day of her Coronation. She wore a dress of gold tissue with a petticoat embroidered with jewels and gold lace, and a traditional mantle of crimson velvet trimmed with miniver. There was no mention of any Mistress of the Robes, which was remarkable. The first 'mistress' was actually a man and he called himself Groom of the Stole to Charles II. It was not until Queen Anne's day that the Groom became Mistress and she was none other than Lady Sarah Churchill, the wife of the Duke of Marlborough. This ambitious and dominating lady had created the title for herself and also became 'Keeper of the Privy Purse'. The rôle of Mistress of the Robes then disappeared until Queen Victoria came to the Throne. The pictorial evidence of the robe and dress worn by the young Queen seems a little conflicting and her own diaries were not very helpful.

'I took off my crimson robe and kirtle and put on my supertunica of cloth of gold, also in the shape of a kirtle, which was put over a singular sort of little linen gown trimmed with lace,' she wrote. I guessed that the latter would be the one on exhibition in the London Museum in Kensington Palace. More valuable were the pictures of the actual Coronation scene, showing the grouping of people around the Throne, notably the trainbearers, who, according to one witness, 'made the Queen look even smaller'.

After gathering all the factual material I could, I then retired to the seclusion of Windsor Forest and there spent many days making trial sketches. My mind was teeming with heraldic and floral ideas. I thought of lilies, roses, marguerites and golden corn; I thought of altar cloths and sacred vestments; I thought of the sky, the earth, the sun, the moon, the stars and everything heavenly that might be embroidered upon a dress destined to be historic.

Altogether, I created nine differing designs which began in almost severe simplicity and proceeded towards elaboration. I liked the last one best, but naturally did not express my opinion when I submitted these paintings to Her Majesty.

The *First* I showed to the Queen was an extremely simple style in lustrous white satin, lightly embroidered along the edge of the bodice and around the skirt's hem in a classic Greek-key design, somewhat similar to that worn by Queen Victoria.

The *Second* was modern line, slender and slimly fitting, embroidered in gold and bordered with the black-and-white ermine tails of Royal miniver.

The *Third* was a crinoline dress of white satin and silver tissue, encrusted with silver lace and sewn with crystals and diamonds.

The *Fourth* was emblazoned with a theme of Madonna and arum lilies tumbling with pendant pearls.

The *Fifth* depicted what might have been a flouting of tradition, for I had introduced a note of colour in the violets of modesty expressed in *cabochon* amethysts and in the rubies of the red roses that glittered and mingled in the waving design of wheat, picked out with opals and topaz. But Her Majesty eased my uncertainty by saying that the suggestion of colour was not inadmissible.

The *Sixth,* again of white satin, was of spreading branches of oak leaves, in a way emblematic, with knobbly acorns of silver bullion thread that dangled on small silver crystal stalks amidst the glinting leaves of golden and copper metals. This design met with gracious approval.

The *Seventh* introduced in bold character the Tudor Rose of England, each bloom padded and puffed in gold tissue against a white gloss of satin and shadowed and surrounded by looped fringes of golden crystals.

The *Eighth* sketch, which automatically suggested itself to me from the previous sketches with the emblem of the Tudor Rose, was composed of all the emblems of Great Britain. Therefore it included the Thistle of Scotland, the Shamrock of Ireland and the daffodil which, at that time, I thought to be the authentic national emblem of Wales. All these floral emblems, placed in proper positions of precedence on the skirt, were to be expressed in varying tones of white and silver, using small diamonds and crystals for pin point coruscation.

Her Majesty approved of this emblematic impression but considered that the use of all white and silver might too closely resemble her wedding gown. She liked the theme of the fifth design and suggested that I might employ the aid of colour in representing the four emblems.

I mentioned that the gown of Queen Victoria was all white, but Her Majesty pointed out that, at the time of her Coronation in 1838, Queen Victoria was only 18 years old and unmarried, whereas she herself was older and a married woman. Therefore, the restrictions imposed upon the gown of Queen Victoria did not apply to her own. I then drew a facsimile of the chosen sketch and enjoyed the pleasure, known to all artists, of painting the small rainbow touches of pastel colours into a pencilled black-and-white drawing.

Later, at another audience, the Queen made a wise and sovereign observation. It was, in effect, that she was unwilling to wear a gown bearing emblems of Great Britain without the emblems of all the Dominions of which she was now Queen.

I then drew and painted the *Ninth* design which proved more complicated than I had expected. A new design had to be provided and I found it necessary to raise up the three emblems of Scotland, Ireland and Wales to the upper portion of the skirt, thus contracting the space they occupied upon the satin background, to allow for more space below, where all the combined flowers of the Commonwealth countries could be assembled in a floral garland, each flower or leaf nestling closely around the motherly English Tudor Rose, placed in the centre.

Meanwhile, to confirm the accuracy of these emblems, I again consulted that amiable authority, Garter King of Arms, at the office of the Earl Marshal. He supplied me with a particularly decorative Tudor Rose, and the Thistle and the Shamrock proved simple. I then made the mistake of asking for the daffodil of Wales.

'A daffodil!' exclaimed Garter. 'On no account will I give you a daffodil. I will give you the correct emblem of Wales, which is the Leek.'

The leek I agreed was a most admirable vegetable, full of historic significance and doubtless of health-giving properties, but scarcely noted for its beauty. Could he not possibly permit me to use the more graceful daffodil instead?

'No, Hartnell. You must have the Leek,' said Garter, adamant.

My enthusiasm blunted, I went down to Windsor, greatly depressed. The fading afternoon light showed only barren trees, a lake glum and grey, and the whole landscape wrapped in November gloom. I went out to the vegetable garden, pulled up a leek and suddenly remembered the cap badge of the Welsh Guards. Perhaps, after all, something could be done with it. In the end, by using lovely silks and sprinkling it with the dew of diamonds, we were able to transform the earthy Leek into a vision of Cinderella charm and worthy of mingling with her sisters Rose and Mimosa in a brilliant Royal Assembly, and fit to embellish the dress of a queen.

Samples of the intended floral emblems had to be submitted to Her Majesty before the final decision was made. My embroidery rooms at once began to evolve these eleven motifs and we realised finally that the only satisfactory method of interpreting all the fine flowers was to use the silken stitchery, as well as jewels, sequins and beads, so that the despised Leek proved a real inspiration after all.

An appointment was made for some members of my staff and myself to visit Sandringham House. So, on a very cold Saturday morning, we motored up to Norfolk with two car loads of people and dresses. Apart from the now completed ninth sketch and the precious emblems, we took with us a generous collection of dresses for her tour of Australasia in the early part of the following year. These dresses were beautifully packed by the indispensable Florrie who accompanied us this time in the additional capacity of *habilleuse*.

The atmosphere of Sandringham is about as different from that of Buckingham Palace and Windsor Castle as could possibly be imagined, and I can well understand why successive generations of the Royal Family have such a great affection for this rambling Victorian country home and its encircling pinewoods.

After luncheon we staged the most informal dress show I have ever presented, for it took place in a large bedroom of old-fashioned charm. The mannequins entered through a door that led out of a capacious white bathroom. From this quaint display some dresses were chosen as the basis of the wardrobe for Australia.

It was then my duty to present to the Queen the final sketch together with the coloured emblems. Each of them had been mounted in a circular gilded wooden frame and I laid out the following emblems:

England. The Tudor Rose, embroidered in palest pink silk, pearls, gold and silver bullion and rose diamonds.

Scotland. The Thistle, embroidered in pale mauve silk and amethysts. The calyx was embroidered in reseda green silk, silver thread and diamond dewdrops.

Ireland. The Shamrock, embroidered in soft green silk, silver thread bullion and diamonds.

Wales. The Leek, embroidered in white silk and diamonds with the leaves in palest green silk.

Canada. The Maple Leaf, in green silk embroideries, bordered with gold bullion thread and veined in crystal.

Australia. The Wattle flower, in mimosa yellow blossom with the foliage in green and gold thread.

New Zealand. The Fern, in soft green silk veined with silver and crystal.

South Africa. The Protea, in shaded pink silk, each petal bordered with silver thread. The leaves of shaded green silk and embellished with rose diamonds.

India. The Lotus flower, in mother-of-pearl embroidered petals, seed pearls and diamonds.

Pakistan. Wheat, cotton and jute. The wheat was in oat-shaped diamonds and fronds of golden crystal, the jute in a spray of leaves of green silk and golden thread, and the cotton blossom with stalks of silver and leaves of green silk.

Ceylon. The Lotus flower, in opals, mother-of-pearl, diamonds and soft green silk.

Apart from the Irish Shamrock, which was judged a little too verdant in tone, the Queen was pleased to agree to the ensemble as my design for her Coronation Gown.

Her Majesty Queen Elizabeth the Queen Mother, who was sitting between the Queen and Her Royal Highness Princess Margaret, had been watching the display from a slender Victorian sofa at the end of an enormous bedstead. She was pleased to accept my design for her own gown which was to be of white satin bordered with gold tissue and embroidered in a feather design of crystal, gold and diamanté.

Princess Margaret then graciously ordered her dress from my sketch which depicted a white satin dress embroidered in open-worked design of broderie anglaise, strengthened with crystal, and with marguerites and roses worked in silver thread and shimmering with pearls.

The design I submitted for Her Majesty's trainbearers was also accepted. The interest of this design was concentrated mainly on the back of the skirt. Realising that the Maids of Honour, carrying the Queen's State Robes of imperial velvet, would show the backs of their dresses almost more than the front as they followed her up the aisle, I had arranged for the embroideries of small golden leaves and pearl white blossom to cascade down the backs of their billowing skirts of white satin.

The Maids of Honour were to be six beautiful young women, chosen from the noblest families in the land. They were Lady Jane Vane-Tempest-Stewart, Lady Anne Coke, Lady Moyra Hamilton, Lady Mary Baillie-Hamilton, Lady Jane Heathcote-Drummond-Willoughby and Lady Rosemary Spencer-Churchill.

I explained to the assembled royal ladies the predominant motifs of the dress I was designing for Her Royal Highness the Duchess of Kent and her daughter, the young Princess Alexandra, so that there should be no clash or confusion of colour in the dresses.

For the Duchess of Kent I designed a dress of white satin embroidered with perpendicular panels of golden mosaic design, and for the Princess a diaphanous garment of white lace and tulle lightly threaded with gold.

Two more gowns for the Coronation were commanded to be made by me in white and gold brocade of varying patterns for the Countess of Euston and the Countess of Leicester, Her Majesty's Ladies of the Bedchamber.

It had in truth been a crowded hour.

APPENDIX II

The following is a summary of Norman Hartnell's mid-twentieth-century fabric sources and provides a record of his fast vanishing world of suppliers and the manner in which Norman Hartnell selected from his inspirational sources. This was written for *Silver and Gold* and not included in the published book.

The first collection of woollen goods arrives. Four or five suitcases from the house of John G. Hardy are unstrapped and let loose countless swatches of masculine-looking suitings which, however, make up admirably for the ladies.

I am allowed to keep this collection for half a day only, as other houses are waiting their turn to see it.

Rival representatives pass each other on the staircase of my trade entrance, and I am pleased to see the collection of H. & S. Simons. Hundreds more tweeds are placed on another table. We go through these two collections quickly, comparing the various points of colour and weight.

A nut-brown partnership of thick wool and thin wool dyed to exactly matching colour may be chosen here, and there, possibly, a heavy velour of prune colour to go over, maybe, a dress of strawberry pink crepe which we shall have to find later amongst the silks.

The next travellers call round in the afternoon, representing Glendor Fabrics and D. Rankine Hamilton.

By now we have made a choice of about eight woollen samples and we have packed up the first two collections in their suitcases to make room for the new arrivals.

The afternoon is spent searching through all the patterns in every swatch and if another tan-coloured wool is found that is more suitable than the one of our first choice, then we promptly cancel the first one.

Mrs Burns leaves the lovely products of Heather Mills. All these are carefully scrutinised and compared again with the earlier collections, when the question is asked as to the varying prices of all these goods and the promised dates for delivery.

Sweetenburgh Fabrics pass under our professional eyes and Mr Stone of Rodier presents huge cases full of brilliant coloured woollen beauties from France.

By now I have spent about two or three days struggling through the heaviest of tweeds and am longing for the relief of choosing some lighter woollens from Messrs Wain and Shiell. This collection is always a delight to me. Little check woollens of, say, grey and white are teamed up with the plain woollens to match in similar grey, and there is a whole range of colourings from which to choose. We choose lots of these Shielana woollens and Mr Davis is very pleased.

Mr Boucher of Dumas & Maury is bringing a delectable selection of coat fabrics and jewel-coloured velours and duvetyns. These are for the dressy coats to be worn, perhaps, overdresses of dark satins or cocktail dress of chestnut and gold brocade.

Then Mr Hunt displays the treasures of Dormeuil Frères – many more lovely things from which to choose, although I must exercise a certain control, for by now I have chosen materials for many a model, and the collection must not become too overloaded with woollen coats to be made.

The Moreau collection is brought to me by the mannerly Mr Bennett, exquisitely soft cloths from which we select a cosy wool of mint green to be trimmed with beaver, a blood-red duvetyn to be weighted with black Persian lamb and a brilliant cherry wool to be collared and cuffed with snowy white mink, taking good care that when the model is finished the mannequin does not look too much like Father Christmas. For here in this winter collection the art of the furrier is combined with that of the dressmaker. I invite, therefore, my master furrier, Signor Belloni, known as Mr Bell, to estimate the cost of such luxurious pelts as embellishment to the ensembles and, of course, I receive the advice on furs that I need from so expert a man as he.

The next session then is with three masters: Mr Bell, and the famous tailors, Signor Rossi and Monsieur François, who help me select the correct quality of velvets for winter wearing.

The quality they will choose. The colouring I will.

So with the selection of velvets, the viewing of the silken goods has begun.

In small patterns, a few inches square, are all the velvet colours of a stained-glass window. Each one of these speak to me separately of the lovely coat or dress each one of them could make, but another voice – that of an unreasoning customer speaks also, saying:

'It's disgraceful that this expensive velvet dress should crease.'

They do, of course, crease, and they always will. But, too, there is surely always an iron?

The pastel shades of velvet are almost irresistible in palest turquoise, lilac and candy pink. But resisted eventually they are, for they would prove too costly for the young wearer and too enlargening for the mature.

The exquisite silks and satins from Ducharne are rippled out at our feet by Mr Clayton, an amiable fellow who has a sponge-coloured moustache and moustache-coloured hair.

With so much beauty here in Ducharne works of art, as in the like and lovely collections of Hurel, presented by Mr Busch, and of Chatillon-Mouly presented by Mr Gilling, and of Renel fabrics presented by Mr Evendon, one is overwhelmed to such an artistic extent that one's selective power becomes blunted. The temptation is to buy the whole lot, but common sense, callous to a point of unkindness to these gentlemen travellers and their superb goods, has to be employed to resist the rustling flower-strewn taffetas and rainbow-metal-threaded brocades that, in the flush of their costly glory, are often too rich in beauty for women to wear.

The avoidance of the extremely beautiful happens likewise in the showing of my dress collections when a woman will refuse the most beautiful dress, in preference for a little work-a-day number. Hence I can appreciate the disappointment felt by these merchants when I hastily brush aside their most sumptuous textiles.

Recklessly, however, I do order one or two of these glorious products, to be included in the collection merely for the sake of decoration.

Mr Sewel brings in the Bianchini tissues, equally gracious, and the same *embarras de richesse* confronts us – beauty upon beauty.

Mr Richardson, who can easily double for film star Bob Montgomery, represents the two houses of Soieries Nouveautes and Jean Page, from whom I always select many fascinating silks, both plain and patterned.

Coudurier's fabulous goods are brought in by courteous Mr Jackson, and Mr Bowdridge, ever attentive, deposits his brilliant fabrics from Bradford & Perier.

From the collection of C.I. Davis, Mr Andrew persuades me to model several of his rainbow-hued satins and taffetas, and Mr Hall explains the rich and varied Jacqmar stuffs.

Mr Garigue, looking like a French aristocrat whose long white neck had somehow cheated the blade of Madame Guillotine (although he was born in Manchester) gives us the exquisite products of Staron – taffetas and organzas printed in exactly the same design and vaporous gleaming gauzes.

The English house of A.C. Kay is always to be relied upon to have coloured crepes and lustrous satins, tinted to perfection. So does Frank Loynes, but as Mr Davies points out, their most popular products are their surahs and their silk organzas.

George Gray, everybody knows, exists in Bond Street, but everybody does not see the collection of special fabrics that Mr Gray shows to the couturiers exclusively.

Miss Magar brings round the interesting and ultra-modern prints from the resourceful house of Ascher, who were the first people far-sighted enough to ask Topolski, the famous artist, to design some of their most individual prints.

Philip Stamp supplies silks and haberdashery through the constant visits of Mr Turner. So does the helpful house of Friends, through Mr Arthur Friend himself.

And always I am pleased to see my old friend Mr Fraser of MacCulloch and Wallis, who supplies all the materials for all those linings, petticoats and underdresses and often the very lovely materials that make the glamorous overdress too.

Then come the laces. Firstly from Nottingham, and the courteous Colonel Birkin comes to discuss his famous samples of lace.

Usually they are based on well-known classic designs as have been woven on their looms for years, but they are always attractive. I always buy one black lace and one white lace from Birkin's, and always have much success with it.

The collection of laces by Racine present a formidable task to any selector. They are all so lovely, light as a tinted cobweb, or heavy with metal threads.

A moment later Mr Ray shows delightful laces from Daltroff.

That one cannot possibly order a lengthy yardage of these gorgeous laces is, I hope, easy to understand by explaining, for instance, that should I order just one yard of this opulent dentelle – costing £18 a yard of eighteen inches in width – I then cut that yard smartly in half. For only one of these half yards will be used to compose the sparse bodice of an evening dress, and the skirt of this dress will be clouds of drifting tulle, thus making economical necessity a virtue.

For tulles and nets I call first upon Playle's, maybe out of graceful memory to dear old Mr Ewelmes, whose place is now taken by the obliging Mr Cubitt: often I ponder on the miles and miles of transparent tulles that I must in my time have bought from the late Mr Ewelmes.

Heathcoat's, of course, are famous for their British nets, as Mr Fouracre well knows, and so is the house of McGregor. But however many bewildering materials may by now have been decided upon for this anticipated winter collection, the search is not yet over.

Belts and buttons have yet to be chosen, and most carefully chosen too, to complete 100 ensembles.

Personally I do not care for fussy or elaborate buttons on either dresses or coats, but when pretty little Susan of Paris House cajoles me it is hard to say no.

Mr Stevens is also a past master in the production of leather and stone buttons. Belts of supple leather are a speciality of Goodman's. Madam Crystal makes excellent belts, draped or neat, of dress material or suede, with which she supplies the matching gloves.

An establishment called Mayfair Accessories have a vast array of accessories for Mayfair dressmakers.

ACKNOWLEDGEMENTS

The author gratefully acknowledges:

Her Late Majesty Queen Elizabeth, The Queen Mother, for selecting a wide range of her historic Hartnell dresses and allowing the author to view and photograph them at Clarence House;

Her Late Royal Highness Princess Margaret, Countess of Snowdon, for memories of Hartnell and his influence;

Her Late Royal Highness Princess Alice, Duchess of Gloucester for providing extensive information on her patronage of Hartnell.

This biography intentionally followed my illustrated survey of Sir Norman Hartnell's creative work *Be Dazzled!*, lavishly published by Suzy Slesin of Pointed Leaf Press NYC, as Sir Norman Hartnell surely would have approved.

My thanks are due to Tom Perrin of Zuleika, my enthusiastic publisher of a new generation taking up the torch for those who have contributed so much to the cultural history of our Great Britain.

I am also grateful to Ellie Brown at Iconic Images.

I first began serious work on this biography in 1992, but first wrote about Sir Norman Hartnell in 1977. Very many of those who gave first-hand information have sadly died in the meantime and I hope that this will be a fitting testimony to their memories and insights.

I acknowledge with grateful thanks the influence of Gerald Lacoste, friend of Hartnell and acclaimed architect of his art moderne House and salon at 26 Bruton Street, Mayfair and of his country house Lovel Dene, Windsor Forest.

It was in a Lacoste designed house that my parents first met in 1938 and he suggested that I record Hartnell's life.

My late mother, a 1930s client of Hartnell, first enthused me with her memories of her clothes and life in inter-war London. The late Ian Thomas, then the third Dressmaker By Appointment to HM The Queen, kindly informed me in great detail of his days as Sir Norman's assistant and wrote pages of notes specifically for this book. Kenneth Partridge, friend and interior designer of the Hartnell Petit Salons and of various glamorous dress shows, added a multitude of memories and invaluable contacts. Mr and Mrs Emanuel Silverman and Roy Dixon, owners of the last full-scale incarnation of the House of Hartnell, commissioned me to completely renovate the building and encouraged my researches by giving me the remaining archive of papers before the business closed. Caroline Knox, then at John Murray, originally commissioned a biography before John Murray was sold. The subsequent CEOs of the Hardy Amies-Norman Hartnell company names were in turn also supportive of my work for this biography: Simon Petherick; Tim Maltin and Tony Yusuf. Eiji Takahatake has loyally supported me and the project with great determination and constant encouragement from the beginning, as has the Reverend Julian Browning, a son of the publisher of his autobiography *Silver & Gold*.

I am particularly indebted to the following past and present for many happy times sharing their memories and much laughter:

Miss Shirley Abicair; Sir Hardy Amies; Mr Geoffrey Angold; Mr Murray Arbeid; Margaret, Duchess of Argyll; M. Pierre Balmain; Mrs Pamela Barnet; Mr Beauregard Becquart; Ms Stella Beddoe; Ms Beatrice Behlen; Miss Lesley Blanche; Mr Hugo Bourcier; Mr and Mrs Bowen (Miss Louie); Miss Joyce Carey; Mrs Carmen Butler-Charteris; Ms Ernestine Carter; Dame Barbara Cartland; Mr John Cavanagh; Ms Jane Chorley; Mr and Mrs Hugh Clifford-Wing; Lady Diana Cooper; Mr and Mrs George Cracknell; Ms Thelma Cranston; Mr John Creswell; Mr James Darwood; Mrs Jack Dennis; Mr Roy Dixon; Mrs Margaret Donaldson; Mrs Mary Dubury; Mr Richard Dunn, Mrs Edwina Ehrman; Miss Evelyn; Mrs Daphne Fielding; Mr Kenneth Fleetwood; Mrs Christina Foyle; Mr Frederick Fox; Monsignor Alfred Gilbey; Mr Gareth Goodsir-Cullen; Ms Luci Gosling; Mrs Grace

Gray; Ms. Felicity Green; Dame Patricia Hambleden; Dr Paul Harlow; Miss Julie Harris; Miss Beryl Hartland; Professor Amy de la Haye; Mr Clifford Henderson; The Hon. David Herbert; Mr David and Lady Pamela Hicks; Mr Bevis Hillier; Caroline, Lady Hobart; Ms Minn Hogg; Geoffrey Houghton-Brown; Mr Peter Hope-Lumley; Sir Robin Janvrin; Mr Timothy Jones; Lady Joubert; Mrs Betty Kenward; Mrs James Knox; Lady Jane Lacey; Mr and Mrs Gerald Lacoste; Lady Ann Lambton; Rafaelle, Duchess of Leinster; Mrs Eleanor Lambert; Miss Evelyn Laye; Mrs Angela Loudon; Mr Robert Luck; Ms Ruth Lynam; Ms Eleri Lynn; Mrs Doreen McKillop; Ms Joanna Marschner; Mrs John Meares; Miss Murial Mitchell Henry; Mr Jon Moore; Timothy Morgan-Owen; Mr Desmond Morris; Dame Jean Maxwell Scott; Mrs Muriel Monson, Mr Geoffrey Munn; Ms Deirdre Murphy; Mr and Mrs Alec Murray; Mr Austin Mutti-Mewse; Mrs Brenda Naylor; Dame Anna Neagle; Mr Robert Nesbitt; Mr John Partridge; Mrs Rosemary Partridge; Mr Matthew Pel; Mr Ronald Paterson; Mrs Jan Pettigrew; Mr Simon Powell-Jones; Mr Alan Powers; Mrs Ann Price; Miss Raemonde Rahvis; Mr Nicholas Rayne; Mr Neil Roger; Anne, Countess of Rosse; Ms Ann Ryan; Mr Percy Savage; Miss Anne Scott-James; Mrs Prudence Seddon; Ms Dora Shackell; Mr Michael Sherard; Mr Peter Shoebridge; Mr Emanuel Silverman; Mr and Mrs Robin Sligh; Mrs Flo Smith; Miss Adrienne Spanier; Mrs Ginette Seidmann-Spanier; Professor Dr Gavin Stamp; Sir Jocelyn Stevens; Mrs Lew Stone; Sir Roy Strong; Mrs Tamara Talbot-Rice; Mr William Tallon; Mr and Mrs Kenneth Thornton; Mr Teddy Tinling; Mr Gnyuki Torimaru (Yuki); Mr Timothy Tufnell; Lady Freda Valentine; Mr Jan van Velden; Mr Hugo Vickers; Mrs Diana Vreeland; Mr Norris Wakefield; Professor Dr David Watkin; Miss Elizabeth Welch; Mrs Hugh Williams; Mr and Mrs Rick Williams; Mr Michael Whittaker and many others, including former employees of Norman Hartnell Ltd.

I am forever indebted to and wish to particularly thank the following for their great professional knowledge, expertise and skills: Mr Tom Williamson, Dr Jonathan Fluxman, Professor Jamil Mayet, Dr Iqbal Malik, Mr Andrew Chukwuemeka and the wonderful staff of the Wellington and Nuffield Hospitals.

BIBLIOGRAPHY

Amies, Hardy, 'Just So Far', Collins, London, 1954.

Amies, Hardy, 'Still Here', Weidenfeld & Nicolson, London. 1984.

Architecture Illustrated, 'New Show-room in Bruton Street, W1., For Messrs Hartnell Ltd.' London, December 1934.

Argyll, Margaret, Duchess of, 'Forget Not', W.H.Allen, London, 1975.

Attfield, Judy, 'Utility Reassessed: The Role of Ethics in the Practice of Design.' Manchester University Press,1999.

Baily, Leslie, 'Scrapbook for the Twenties.' Muller, London,1959.

Balmain, Pierre, 'My Years and Seasons', Cassell, London, 1964.

Bamford, T.W, 'Rise of the Public Schools A Study of Boy's Public Boarding Schools in England and Wales from 1870 to the Present Day', Nelson, London, 1967.

Bailey, Peter, 'Parasexuality and Glamour: The Victorian Barmaid as Cultural Prototype', Gender and History II, 1990.

Barnes, Alison, 'Royal Sisters Volumes', Pitkin. London, 1951.

Barrow, Andrew, 'Gossip: a History of High Society 1920-1970', Hamish Hamilton, London, 1978.

Barrow, Andrew, 'International Gossip: A History of High Society 1970-1980', Hamish Hamilton, London, 1983.

Beaton, Cecil, 'The Book of Beauty', Duckworth, London, 1930.

Beaton, Cecil, 'Scrapbook', Batsford, London, 1938.

Beaton, Cecil, 'My Royal Past', Batsford, London, 1939.

Beaton, Cecil; Quennel, Peter, 'Time Exposure', Batsford, London 1941.

Beaton, Cecil, 'Photobiography', Odhams, London, 1951.

Beaton, Cecil, 'The Glass of Fashion', Weidenfeld & Nicolson, London, 1954.

Beaton, Cecil, 'Royal Portraits', Weidenfeld & Nicolson, 1963.

Beaton, Cecil, 'Diaries' vols 1920s-1970s, Weidenfeld & Nicolson. London. 1961-1973.

Beaton, Cecil, 'The Best of Beaton', Weidenfeld & Nicolson, London, 1968.

Beaton, Cecil; Vickers, Hugo intro., 'Beaton in the Sxities', Weidenfeld & Nicolson, London, 2003.

Beauman, Nicola, 'Morgan; A Biography of E.M. Forster', Hodder & Stoughton, London, 1993.

Beaumont, Cyril W, 'Supplement to Complete Book of Ballets,' C.W. Beaumont, London. 1942.

Beckles, Gordon, 'The Coronation Souvenir Book',Daily Express, London, 1937.

Bell, Quentin, 'On Human Finery', Allison & Busby, London. 1992.

Berry, Jess, 'House of Fashion: Haute Couture and the Modern Interior', Bloomsbury Visual Arts, London, 2018.

Betsky, Aaron, 'Queer Space:

Architecture and Same-Sex Desire',
William Morrow, New York, 1997.

Birt, Catherine, 'Royal Sisters Volume
One', Pitkin, London.1949.

Blake Brown, Richard, 'Miss Higgs and
the Silver Flamingo', Duckworth,
London. 1931.

Blake Brown, Richard, 'The Apology
of a Young Ex-Parson', Duckworth,
London. 1932.

Blum, Dilys E., 'Shocking! The Art and
Fashion of Elsa Schiaparelli', Philadel-
phia Museum of Art, Yale University
Press, USA & London, 2004.

Bolitho, Hector ed., 'Coronation Book
Of Queen Elizabeth II', Odhams,
London, 1953.

Bradford, Sarah, 'Elizabeth: A Biography of Her Majesty the Queen',
William Heinemann Ltd, London.
1996.

Brady, Sean, 'Masculinity and Male
Homosexuality in Britain, 1861-1913',
Palgrave, Basingstoke, 2005.

Brendon, Piers and Whitehead, Phil-
lip, 'The Windsors: A Dynasty
Revealed',Hodder&Stoughton,
London. 1994.

Breward, Christopher; Conekin, Becky
and Cox Caroline, 'The Englishness
of English Dress', Berg, Oxford. 2002.

Breward, Christopher, 'Fashioning
London: Clothing and the Modern
Metropolis'. Berg, Oxford, 2004

Breward, Christopher; Ehrman, Edwina;
and Evans, Caroline,'The London
Look: Fashion from Street to Catwalk', Yale University Press- Museum
of London, 2004.

Britannia and Eve, 1923-1940.

Brown, Susanna, 'Cecil Beaton and
the iconography of the House of
Windsor', Photography and Culture,
London, 2011.

Bryan Bigham, Randy, 'Lucile: Her Life

by Design', MacEvie Press Group,
San Francisco, 2012.

Buckton, Henry (ed), 'By Royal Command', Peter Owen, London. 1997.

Byng, Douglas, 'As You Were', Duckworth, London, 1970.

Bystander, The, 1923-1940

Carter, Ernestine, '20th Century Fashion',
Eyre Methuen, London. 1975.

Carter, Ernestine, 'The Changing World
of Fashion', Weidenfeld & Nicolson,
London. 1977.

Carter, Ernestine; Ryan, Ann, 'With
Tongue in Chic.' Michael Joseph,
1974.

Cartland, Barbara, 'We Danced All
Night', Hutchinson, London.1971.

Cartland, Barbara, 'Scrapbook' Royal
Photographic Society, London, 1980.

Cassini, Oleg, 'In My Own Fashion',
Simon & Schuster, Riverside, NJ,
1987.

Channon, Sir Henry, 'Chips': the Diaries of', Weidenfeld & Nicolson, 1967.

Chadwick, Whitney; Latimer, Tirza
True, 'The Modern Woman Re-Vis-
ited: Paris Between the Wars', Rutgers
University Press, 2003.

Chase, Edna Woolman and Ilka,
'Always In Vogue', Gollancz. London.
1954.

Chevalier, Maurice, 'Dans la vie faut pas
s'en faire', Omnibus, Paris, 2012.

Clark, Brigadier S. F. 'The Royal Tour:
Parts One to Four,' Pitkins, London
1953-1954.

Cochran, Charles B, 'Cock-a-Doo-
dle-Do', Dent, London, 1941.

Collier, Richard, 'The Rainbow People',
Weidenfeld & Nicolson, London,
1984.

Costume 45: Ness, Caroline; Brooks,
Mary M, 'Rediscovering Mattli: A
Forgotten 1950s London Couturier.'
2011.

Country Life, London, 1923-1979.

Coxhead, Elizabeth, 'Constance Spry: A Biography', William Luscombe Publisher Ltd., London, 1975.

Creed, Charles, 'Maid to Measure', Jarrolds, London, 1961.

Croall, Jonathan, 'John Gielgud Matinee Idol to Movie Star', Methuen Drama, London, 2011.

Croft-Cooke, Rupert, 'The Altar In the Loft', Putnam, London. 1960.

Croft-Cooke, Rupert, 'The Numbers Came', Putnam, London. 1963.

Cullen, Oriole, 'Francis Marshall', V&A, London, 2018.

Daily Express, 21 November 1927 et seq.

Daily Express, 'Hartnell's India Wardrobe for the Queen', 1 February 1961.

Daily Mail, London 1923-1980.

Daily Mirror, 'Marquis's Son Weds', London, 28 October 1927.

Davies-Strodder, Cassie et al., 'London Society Fashion 1905-1925: The Wardrobe of Heather Firbank', V&A, London, 2015.

Dawnay, 'Model Girl', Weidenfeld & Nicolson, London, 1956.

Deans, Marjorie, 'Meeting at the Sphinx', Macdonald, London. 1946.

De Courcy, Anne, 'Debs at War 1939-1945', Weidenfeld & Nicolson, London, 2005.

De Courcy, Anne, 'The Last Season', Phoenix, London, 2003.

De Guitaut, Caroline,' The Royal Tour: A Souvenir Album', Royal Collection Publications. London. 2009.

de la Haye, Amy; Tobin, Shelley, 'Chanel: The Couturiere at Work', V&A, London, 1995

de la Haye, Amy (ed.), 'The Cutting Edge: Fifty Years of British Fashion.' V&A, London. 1996.

de la Haye, Amy; Taylor, Lou; Thompson, Eleanor, 'A Family of Fashion: The Messels. Six Generations of Dress', Philip Wilson, London, 2005.

de la Haye, Amy; Mendes, Valerie, 'Fashion Since 1910', Thames & Hudson, London, 2010.

de la Haye, Amy (ed.), 'London Couture', V&A, London, 2015.

De-La-Noy, Michael, 'Denton Welch: The Making of a Writer', Viking, London, 1984.

De-La-Noy, Michael, 'The Queen Behind the Throne', Cornerstone, London,1994.

Derrick, Robin; Muir, Robin (eds.), 'Unseen Vogue: The Secret History of Fashion Photography,' Little, Brown & Company, London. 2002.

Desmond, Florence, 'Florence Desmond by Herself', George Harrap, London 1953.

De Valois, Ninette, 'Invitation to the Ballet', John Lane., London. 1953.

Dior, Christian, 'Dior By Dior', Weidenfeld & Nicolson, London. 1957.

Donaldson, Frances, 'A Twentieth Century Life', Weidenfeld & Nicolson, London, 1992.

Dudley, Sandra, et al eds, 'Narrating Objects, Collecting Stories: Essays in Honour of Professor Susan M Pearce', Routledge, London, 2012.

Duff, David, 'George and Elizabeth', Collins, London, 1983.

Duff-Gordon, Lady, 'Discretions and Indiscretions' Frederick A Stokes & Co., New York, 1932.

Dundee Courier, The, 1930-1950

Eastoe, Jane, 'Elizabeth: Reigning In Style', Pavilion Books, London. 2012.

Edwards, Anne, 'Royal Sisters: Elizabeth and Margaret 1926-1956', Collins, London 1990.

Edwards, Anne, Robb, Andrew, 'The Queen's Clothes', Elm Tree Books, London. 1977.

Edwards, Arthur; Rae, Charles, 'The Queen Mum – Her First Hundred Years', HarperCollins London, 2000.

Elegante Welt, Heft 3, Duesseldorf. Maerz 1954.

Ellis, Jennifer,' The Duchess of Kent: An Intimate Biography', Odhams, London, 1952.

Era, The 1885-1920

Erte, 'Things I Remember: An Autobiography', Peter Owen, London, 1975.

Evans, Caroline, 'The Mechanical Smile: Modernism and the First Fashion Shows in France and America', Yale UP, New Haven and London, 2013.

Evening Standard, The, 'Always that warm smile...always that queenly style.' London, 4 August 1970.

Evening Standard, The, 'A birthday album of photographs', London, 4 August 1970.

Feaver, William (Ed.), 'Thirties - British Art and Design Before the War. an exhibition organised by the Arts Council of Great Britain in collaboration with the Victoria & Albert. Gallery, 25 October 1979-13 January 1980', Arts Council of Great Britain / Hayward Gallery 1979, London, 1979

Ferragamo, Salvatore, 'Shoemaker of Dreams', George G. Harrap Ltd, London. 1957.

Field, Leslie, 'The Queen's Jewels: The Personal Collection of Elizabeth II,' Weidenfeld & Nicolson, London. 1987.

Fielding, Daphne, 'Mercury Presides', Eyre & Spottiswoode, London, 1954.

Fielding, Daphne, 'The Nearest Way Home', Eyre & Spottiswoode, London, 1970.

Flanner, Janet, 'Paris Was Yesterday 1925-1939', Irving Drutman, New York, 1972.

Flanner, Janet, 'London Was Yesterday 1934-1939', Michael Joseph, London, 1973.

Fletcher, Richard, 'Lovel Dene', Decoration, London, 1936.

Fogg, Marnie, 'Boutique: A 60s Cultural Phenomenon', Mitchell Beasley. London. 2003.

Galt, Rosalind, 'Pretty: Film and the Decorative Image,' Columbia University press, New York, 2011.

Gardiner, James, 'Gaby Deslys: A Fatal Attraction', Sidgwick & Jackson, London, 1986.

Garland, Madge, 'The Indecisive Decade', Macdonald, London.1968.

Garland, Madge, 'Fashion: A Picture Guide To Its Creators and Creations.' Penguin, Harmondsworth. 1962.

Garland, Madge, 'The Changing Form of Fashion', Praeger, New York, 1970.

Garnier, Guillaume; Villien, Bruno, 'Pierre Balmain. 40 Annees De Creation', Musee De La Mode Et Du Costume, Paris, 1985.

Gibson, Robin; Roberts, Pam, 'Madame Yevonde: Colour, Fantasy and Myth', NPG, London, 1990.

Giroud, Francoise, 'Dior: Christian Dior 1905-1957.', Thames & Hudson, London. 1987.

Gladwyn, Lady Cynthia, 'The Diaries of Cynthia Gladwyn' Constable, London, 1995.

Gloucester, Princess Alice Duchess of, 'Memories of Ninety Years', Collins & Brown, London, 1991.

Glynn, Prudence, 'In Fashion: Dress In the Twentieth Century', George Allen & Unwin, London. 1978.

Glynn, Prudence, 'Tread softly for you tread on £29.', The Times, Thursday September 30, 1976.

Gorst, Frederick J., 'Of Cabbages and Kings', W.H.Allen, London, 1956.

Graves, Charles, 'The Cochran Story: A Biography of Sir Charles Blake Cochran', W.H. Allen, London, c 1952.

Graves, Robert, 'Goodbye to All That', Jonathan Cape, London, 1929.

Green, Martin, 'Children of the Sun: A

Narrative of "Decadence" in England After 1918', Basic Books, Inc., New York, 1976.

Greer, Howard, 'Designing Male', Robert Hale, London, 1952.

Guardian, The, 8 February 1992 Edward Rayne obituary.

Hamburger, Estelle, 'It's a Woman's Business', Victor Gollancz, London 1940.

Harper's Bazaar 1920s–1980.

Harpers & Queen 1960s–1980.

Hartnell, Norman, 'How Fashions Are Born', unidentified journal. 1938

Hartnell, Norman, 'Royal Courts of Fashion', Cassell, London, 1971.

Hartnell, Norman, 'Silver and Gold', Evans Brothers, London. 1955, V&A, 2019.

Hartnell, Norman, co-author, 'The Bedders Opera', unpublished for Footlights, Cambridge, 1920.

Haskell, Arnold 'Balletomania', Victor Gollancz. London. 1934.

Haskell, Arnold, 'Ballet to Poland', Adam and Charles Black, London 1940.

Haskell, Arnold, 'Ballet Panorama', B.T. Batsford, London. 1943.

Haskell, Arnold, 'Balletomane at Large', Heinemann, London.1972.

Hawes, 'Fashion is Spinach', Random House, New York, 1938.

Heald, Tim, 'A Peerage for Trade- a History of the Royal Warrant.'RWHA & Sinclair-Stevenson. 2001.

Henrey, Robert, 'The Siege Of London', Right Book Club, London, 1946.

Hewison, Robert, 'Footlights: A Hundred Years Of Cambridge Comedy', Methuen, London, 1983.

Hicks, Pamela, 'Daughter of Empire: Life as a Mountbatten', Weidenfeld & Nicolson, 2012.

Hirschfeld, Magnus, 'Berlins drittes Geschlecht', H. Seemann, Berlin und Leipzig, 1904.

Hole, Lawrence, 'The Goddesses: Portraits by Madame Yevonde', Darling, London, 2000.

Hope, Anthony, 'The Prisoner of Zenda', Penguin, London. 2008

Hope, Anthony, 'Rupert of Hentzau', Penguin, London, 2008.

Houlbrook, Matt, 'Queer London; Perils and Pleasures in the Sexual Metropolis, 1918-57', Chicago University Press, 2005.

House & Garden, Conde Nast, London.

Howell, Geraldine, 'Wartime Fashion: From Haute Couture to Homemade 1939-1945.' Berg, London, 2012.

Hutter, Joerg, 'Richard von Krafft-Ebing' in Homosexualität. Handbuch der Theorie- und Forschungsgeschichte (Rüdiger Lautmann ed.), Campus Verlag, Frankfurt and New York 1993.

Ideal Home, November 1947

Illustrated, 'Coronation Parade for the Queen', London, 6 December 1952

Independent, The: Edward Rayne obituary, 11 February 1992.

Janes, Dominic, 'Picturing The Closet: Male Secrecy and Homosexual Visibilty in Britain', Oxford University Press, 2015.

June, 'The Glass Ladder', Heinemann, London, 1960.

Keay, Douglas, 'Queen Elizabeth the Queen Mother', IPC, London, 1980.

Keenan, Bridget, 'The Women We Wanted to Look Like', Macmillan, London, 1977.

Kelly's, Post Office and Harrod & Co Directory, London, various.

Kennet, Frances et al., 'Norman Hartnell', Brighton & Bath, 1985.

King George's Jubilee Trust, 'Their Majesties Visit to Canada the United

States of America and Newfound-
land', Macmillan, London, 1939.

King George's Jubilee Trust, 'The
Royal Family In Wartime', Odhams,
London, 1945.

Krafft-Ebing, Richard v., 'Psychopathia
Sexualis: eine Klinisch-Forensische
Studie', F. Enke, Stuttgart, 1886.

Lady, The 1923–1979

Lambert, Angela, 'The Last Season
of Peace', Weidenfeld & Nicolson,
London, 1989.

Lambert, Eleanor, 'The World of Fashion: People, Places, Resources,' New
York & London, 1976.

Lancaster, Marie-Jacqueline (Ed.),
'Brian Howard: Portrait of a Failure',
Anthony Blond Ltd., London, 1968

Larkin, Colin, 'The Guinness Who's
Who of Stage Musicals', Guinness
World Records Limited, London,
1994.

Laver, James, 'Clothes', Burke, London,
1952.

Laver, James, 'Museum Piece', Andre
Deutsch, London, 1963.

Laver, James, 'Women's Dress in the
Jazz Age.' Hamish Hamilton, London,
1964.

Laye, Evelyn, 'Boo To My Friends',
Hurst & Blackett, London 1958.

Lewis-Crown, Peter, 'House of Lachasse:
The Story of a Very English Gentleman', Delancey Press, London. 2009.

London Collections, The, 'Silver Jubilee
1977', Fashion Promotions, London,
1977.

London Post Office, Street Directories,
1870–1930.

Lyall, Gavin, 'The Royal Tour of India
and Pakistan. State Visits to Nepal
and Iran', Pitkins, London, 1961.

Lynam, Ruth, 'Paris Fashion', Michael
Joseph, London, 1972.

MacCarthy, Fiona, 'Last Curtsey: the

End of the Debutantes', Faber &
Faber, London. 2006.

Marschner, Joanna & Behlen, Beatrice,
'Hats and Handbags: Accessories from
the Royal Wardrobe'. Historic Royal
Palaces. 2003.

Marshall, Francis, 'London West', The
Studio, London and New York. 1944.

Martin, Robert, K.; Piggford, George,
eds. 'Queer Forster', University of
Chicago Press, 1997.

Massingbred, Hugh, 'Her Majesty
Queen Elizabeth The Queen Mother,
Woman of the Century', Macmillan,
London, 1999.

Matthews, Jessie, 'Over My Shoulder',
W.H.Allen, London, 1974.

Mayhew, Henry, 'London Characters &
Crooks', the Folio Society, London.
1996.

Mathew, Jean, unpublished notes on
Rayne history circa 1987

McConathy, Dale; Vreeland, Diana,
'Hollywood Costume: Glamour! Glitter! Romance!', Abrams, NYC, 1976.

McDowell, Colin, 'A Hundred Years of
Royal Style', Muller Blond & White,
London. 1985.

McDowell, Colin, 'The Literary Companion to Fashion', Sinclair-Stevenson,
London. 1995.

McDowell, Colin, 'Forties Fashion
and the New Look', Introduction by
Hardy Amies. Bloomsbury.London.
1997.

McDowell, Colin, 'Shoes: Fashion and
Fantasy', London, 1989.

Mendes, Valerie D.; de la Haye, Amy,
'Lucile Ltd. London, Paris, New York
and Chicago 1892–1930s', V&A,
London, 2009.

Menkes, Suzy, 'The Royal Jewels', Grafton, London, 1985.

Miller, Ruby as Darewski, Madame
Max, 'Believe Me Or Not!', John
Long, London, 1933.

Miller, Ruby, 'Champagne From My Slipper', London-Herbert Jenkins, 1962.

Mistinguett, 'Toute ma vie', Juillard, Paris, 1954.

Molloy, John T., 'New Women's Dress For Success', Grand Central Publishing, NYC. 1976.

Morrah, Dermot, 'The Royal Family', Odhams, London, 1950.

Morrah, Dermot, 'The Royal Family in Africa', Hutchinson, London, 1947.

Munn, Geoffrey, 'Tiaras: A History of Splendour', ACC, London, 2002.

Muir, Robin, 'Norman Parkinson; Portraits In Fashion', Palazzo Editions, Bath. 2010.

Muir, Robin, 'Unseen VOGUE', Little, Brown. London. 2002.

Mulvagh, Jane, 'VOGUE: History of C20th fashion', Bloomsbury Books, London. 1988.

Mulvagh, Jane 'Costume Jewellery in Vogue', Thames & Hudson, London, 1988.

Nathan, Archie, 'Costumes by Nathan', Newnes: London, 1960.

Neagle, Anna, 'There's Always Tomorrow. An Autobiography', W.H.Allen, London, 1974.

New York Times, The, 'Elizabeth's Gown Set With Pearls', NYC, 20 November 1947.

New York Times, The, 'Astor Ballroom is Scene of Regal English Show', NYC, 21 April 1960.

New York Times, The, 'Hartnell Bares The Knee', NYC, 19 January 1966.

Nichols, Beverley, 'Oxford-London-Hollywood: An Omnibus', Jonathan Cape, London, 1931.

Nichols, Beverley, 'Crazy Pavements', Jonathan Cape, London, 1934.

Nichols, Beverley, 'The Fool Hath Said', Jonathan Cape, London, 1936.

Nichols, Beverley, 'The Sweet and Twenties', Weidenfeld & Nicolson, London, 1958.

Nicklas, C; Pollen, A eds, 'Dress History: New Directions in Theory and Practice', Bloomsbury Academic, London, 2015.

Nickolls, L.A., 'Royal Cavalcade: A Diary of The Royal Year', MacDonald, London, 1949.

Nickolls, L.A., 'The First Family: A Diary of the First Year', MacDonald, London, 1950.

Nickolls, L.A., 'The Royal Story: A Diary of the Royal Year', MacDonald, London, 1951.

North, Susan, 'Redfern Limited, 1892–1940', Costume No 43, London, 2009.

Observer, The, 'Her Majesty Isn't Naff, She's Avant-Garde', 23 November 2003.

O'Byrne, Robert, 'Style City: How London Became a Fashion Capital', Frances Lincoln Ltd., London, 2009.

Packard, Anne, 'The Royal Tour of Canada', Daily Graphic, London, 1951.

Page, Betty, 'On Fair Vanity', Convoy Publications Ltd, London. 1954.

Palmer, Alexandra, 'Couture and Commerce: The Transatlantic Fashion Trade in the 1950s', UBC Press with Royal Ontario Museum. 2001.

Palmer, Alexandra, 'Dior: A New look. A New Enterprise.' V&A Publishing. 2009.

Palmer, Alexandra, 'Christian Dior: History and Modernity, 1947–1957', Hirmer, Munich, 2019.

Parkinson, Norman, 'Would You Let Your Daughter', Weidenfeld & Nicolson, London. 1985.

Peacocke, Marguerite, 'Queen Mary: Her Life and Times', Odhams, London, 1953.

Pepper, Terence, 'Dorothy Wilding; The

Pursuit of Perfection', NPG, London, 1991.

Pick, Michael, 'Gerald Lacoste', Journal of the Thirties Society, London, 1982.

Pick, Michael, 'Royal Design, Loyal Style', The London Collections. 1977.

Pick, Michael, 'The English Room', Weidenfeld & Nicolson, London, 1985.

Pick, Michael, Lacoste and the Hartnell Salon, Antique Interiors, London, 199

Pick, Michael, 'Obituary: Michael Sherard'. The Independent. London,1 February 1999

Pick, Michael, 'Hardy Amies', AVENUE Magazine Inc., New York. April 1999.

Pick, Michael, 'The Queen's Coronation Dress', Daily Mail YOU, June 2002.

Pick, Michael, 'Be Dazzled !', Pointed Leaf Press, New York, 2007.

Pick, Michael, 'Hardy Amies', ACC Publications, London, 2012.

Pick, Michael, 'Shoes for Stars: Rayne', ACC Publications, London, 2016.

Picken, Mary; Miller, Dora, 'Dressmakers of France', Harper & Brothers, New York, 1956.

Picture Post, various issues, Hulton, London, 1938–1958.

Picture Post, 'Who Buys Our Best Clothes?', Hulton, London, 5 March 1949.

Picture Post, 'Hartnell and the Coronation', Hulton, London, 24 January 1953.

Picture Post, 'The Steps to a New Elizabethan Age', Hulton, London, 13 June 1953.

Picture Post, 'Picture Post, 'Adel Models Hartnell Nighties', Hulton, London, 18 March 1957.

Picture Post, 'Coronation Couturier', Hulton, London, 24 January 1953.

Pimlott, Ben, 'The Queen: Elizabeth II and the Monarchy'. Harper Collins, London. 2001.

Poiret, Paul, 'En habillant l'époque', Grasset, Paris, 1930.

Pope-Hennessey, James, 'Queen Mary', George Allen & Unwin, London. 1959.

Pratt, Lucy & Woolley, Linda, 'Shoes', V&A Publications, London. 2008.

Pringle, Colombe, 'Roger Vivier', Assouline, Paris. 2005.

Pringle, Margaret, 'Dance Little Ladies: The Days of the Debutante', Orbis, London. 1977.

Quant, Mary, 'Quant by Quant', Cassell, London. 1966

Queen, (The), 1930–1970.

Rasche, Adelheid; Thomson, Christina (Eds.) 'Christian Dior and Germany 1947–1957', Arnoldsche, Suttgart, 2007

Raverat, Gwen, 'Period Piece', Faber & Faber, London,1952.

Rayne, Edward, Unfinished draft for an autobiography. 1988.

Recorder, The, London, 1940s

Rhodes James, Robert (ed),' Chips The Diaries of Sir Henry Channon', Weidenfeld & Nicolson, London. 1967.

Ritz Magazine, 'Hartnell Interview with Nicky Haslam ' circa 1977.

Robb, Andrew; Edwards, Anne, 'The Queen's Clothes', Elm Tree Books, London. 1977.

Robb, Andrew, 'Lifestyle', Elm Tree Books, London, 1979.

Robinson, Julian, 'Fashion In the Forties', Academy, London.1976.

Robyns, Gwen, 'Barbara Cartland: An Authorised Biography', Sidgwick & Jackson, London, 1984.

Ross, Josephine, 'Society in Vogue', Conde Nast Books, London, 1992.

Rouff, Maggy, 'La philosophie de l'elegance', Éditions littéraires de France, Paris, 1942.

Sacher-Masoch, Leopold v., 'Venus im Peltz', Cotta, Stuttgart, 1870.

Saint Cyr, Claude, 'Le siècle en *cha-peaux: Claude Saint-Cyr*, Histoire d'une modiste'. Du May, Paris, 1991.

Saville, Margaret, 'Royal Sisters Volume One', Pitkin, London. 1949.

Saville, Margaret, 'Royal Sisters Volume Two', Pitkin, London. 1950.

Saville, Margaret, 'Royal Sisters Volume Five', Pitkin, London, 1953.

Savran, David, 'The sadomasochist in the closet', Contemporary Theatre Review, 1998.

Schiaparelli, Elsa, 'Shocking Life: The Autobigraphy of Elsa Schiaparelli', Dent, London, 1954.

Scott, Elizabeth, 'Royal Sisters Volume Four', Pitkin, London. 1952.

Scott-James, Anne, 'In the Mink', Michael Joseph, London, 1953.

Scott-James, Anne, 'Sketches from a Life', Michael Joseph, London, 1993.

Seebohm, Caroline, 'The Man Who Was Vogue: The Life and Times of Conde Nast', Weidenfeld & Nicolson, London. 1982.

Settle, Allison, 'London Can It Become a World Fashion Centre?', Picture Post, Hulton, London, 6 January 1945.

Shawcross, William, 'Queen Elizabeth The Queen Mother: The Official Biography', Macmillan, London, 2009.

Shawcross, William, 'Counting One's Blessings: The Selected Letters of Queen Elizabeth The Queen Mother', Macmillan, London, 2012.

Shephard, Sue, 'The Surprising Life of Constance Spry', Macmillan, London, 2010.

Sheridan, Lisa 'From Cabbages to Kings', Odhams, London, 1955.

Sheridan, Lisa, 'Our Princesses in 1942', John Murray, London, 1942.

Shew, Betty Spencer, 'Royal Wedding', MacDonald, London, 1947.

Shew, Betty Spencer, 'Queen Elizabeth the Queen Mother', Hodder & Stoughton, London, 1954.

Snagge, John, 'Princess Margaret: A Pictorial record of Her Life and Wedding', Odhams, London, 1960.

Spanier, Ginette, 'It Isn't All Mink', Collins, London, 1959.

Spooner, Catherine; McEvoy, Emma eds., 'The Routledge Companion to the Gothic' for 'Queer Gothic', Routledge, London, 2007.

Steele, Valerie, 'Shoes – A Lexicon of Style', Rizzoli. NYC. 1999.

Strasdin, Kate, 'Inside the Royal Wardrobe: A Dress History of Queen Alexandra', Bloomsbury Visual Arts, 2017.

Strong, Roy, 'Cecil Beaton: The Royal Portraits', Thames & Hudson, London. 1998.

Strong, Roy, 'The Roy Strong Diaries 1967–1987', Weidenfeld & Nicolson, London, 1997.

Sweeny, Charles, 'Sweeny: The Autobiography', Wingham Press Ltd, UK. 1991.

Talbot, Godfrey, 'The Royal Family', Country Life Books, Surrey. 1980.

Talbot, Godfrey, 'Queen Elizabeth The Queen Mother', Country Life Books. 1978.

Talbot, Godfrey, 'The Royal Family', Country Life Books, Surrey, 1980.

Talbot, Godfrey and Vaughan Thomas, Wynford, 'Royalty Annual no 3', Andrew Dakers, London, 1954.

Tatler, The, 1 Aug 1951 et seq

Telegraph, The Daily, 'Dressing as a Queenly Queen', London, 23 February 1961.

Thaarup, Aage, 'Heads and Tails', Cassell, London. 1956.

Theatre World, 1945 et seq.

Thomas, Wynford Vaughan, 'Royal Tour', Hutchinson, London, 1954.

Tiffany, John A., 'Still Here', Pointed Leaf Press, NYC, 2011.

'The Queen' Magazine, issues from 1930–1960

Thomas, Wynford Vaughan, 'Royal Tour: 1953–1954', Hutchinson, London. 1954.

Time, December 10, 1951, 'The British Look'.

Times, The, 'Dignified Simplicity of the Queen's Dress', London 6 May 1960

Times, The: Edward Rayne obituary 10 February 1992

Trewin, J.C., 'The Gay Twenties', Macdonald, London. 1958.

Trewin, J.C., 'The Turbulent Thirties', Macdonald, London. 1960.

Tyrrel, Rebecca, "The Face of British Fashion," in the Sunday Times Magazine (London), 16 October 1989.

V&A, 'Utility Collection of the Incorporated Society of London Fashion Designers, 1942', V&A, London, 1942.

Varney, Carleton, 'The Westbury's Hartnell Suite', Architectural Digest, January 2003.

Vickers, Hugo, 'Cecil Beaton: The Authorised Biography', Weidenfeld & Nicolson, London. 1985.

Vogue Magazine 1920–1980 Conde Nast, London, New York, Paris.

Waddell, Gavin, 'How Fashion Works: Couture, Ready-to-Wear and Mass Production,' Blackwell Science, Oxford, 2004.

Warwick, Christopher ed., 'Queen Mary's Photograph Albums', Sidgwick & Jackson, London, 1989.

Watt, Judith, 'The Penguin Book of Twentieth Century Fashion Writing', Viking, London.1999.

Waugh, Alec, 'The Loom of Youth', Grant Richards, London. 1917

Wheeler-bennet, John 'King George VI: His Life and reign',Macmillan, London, 1958

Wilcox, Claire; Mendes, Valerie, 'Modern Fashion In Detail', V&A Museum, 1991.

Wilcox, Claire (ed.) 'The Golden Age of Couture: Paris and London 1947 – 57.' V&A, London, 2008.

Wilding, Dorothy, 'In Pursuit of Perfection', Robert Hale, London, 1958.

Winn, Godfrey, 'The Young Queen: the Life Story of Her Majesty Queen Elizabeth II' Hutchinson, London 1952.

Winn, Godfrey, 'The Infirm Glory', Michael Joseph, London, 1967.

Withers, Audrey, 'LifeSpan', Peter Owen, London, 1994.

Women's Wear Daily: 1928–1979

Woodbridge, Nicola, 'Women In Business 1700–1850', Boydell and Brewer. 2006

Wulff, Louis, 'Queen Mary: An Authoritative Portrait', Sampson, Low, London. 1949.

Wulff, Louis, 'Elizabeth and Philip: Our Heiress and Consort', Sampson Low, London, 1947.

Wulff, Louis, 'Queen of Tomorrow', Sampson Low, London, 1947.

Wyndham, Francis, 'The Pearly King', Sunday Times magazine. London, 1968.

Wyndham, Francis, 'The Theatre of Embarrassment', Chatto & Windus, London, 1991.

Yevonde, Madame, 'In Camera', John Gifford, London, 1940.

Young, Sheila, 'The Queen's Jewellery', Ebury Press, London. 1969.

Yoxall, H. W., 'A Fashion of Life', William Heinemann Ltd., London. 1966.

Zilkha, Bettina, 'Ultimate Style: The Best of the Best Dressed List', Assouline, NYC, 2003.

A NOTE ON IMAGES

All images reproduced in this book are (unless otherwise specified) from The Michael Pick Collection. The author and publisher would be happy to correct any errors or omissions at the next possible opportunity.

NOTES

Chapter 1

1. As told to the author by Kenneth Partridge and Ian Thomas.
2. Hartnell, Norman, *Silver and Gold*, Evans Brothers Ltd, London. 1955.
3. Hartnell, Norman, typescript c1960.
4. *Daily Express*. Wednesday, 17 February 1960.
5. *Daily Express*. Wednesday, February 1960.
6. *Silver and Gold*, op. cit.
7. N.H. papers.
8. *Silver and Gold*, op. cit.
9. Croft-Cooke, Rupert: *The Numbers Came*, Putnam, New York, p.56–8. 1963.
10. N.H. to Grace Conner née Hartnell, Oklahoma City. 5 May 1972.
11. *The London Directory 1896*.
12. Conversations with former employees and the website on pub history https://pubshistory.com/KentPubs/Lee/LordNorthbrook.shtml includes the informative census returns as follows: 1861/Samuel Coulson/Licensed Victualler/39/Lincolnshire/Census; 1861/Mary Coulson/Wife/37/Lincolnshire/Census; 1861/Mary Coulson/Daughter/11/St Georges, Middlesex/Census; 1861/Susan Coulson/Daughter/9/St Georges, Middlesex/Census; 1861/Ann Coulson/Daughter/4/St Giles, Middlesex/Census; 1861/Elizabeth Coulson/Daughter/2/St Giles, Middlesex/Census.

Norman Hartnell's grandmother and Emma Mary Polley and her family of the Lord Northbrook public house at 116 Burnt Ash Road in Lee, London SE12 are indicated by the following census entries: 1881/Henry K .Polley/Licensed Victualer/46/Clerkenwell/Census ****; 1881/Emma M. Polley/Wife/43/Poplar/Census; 1881/Martha E. Spindler/Daughter/22/Bromley/Census; 1881/George S. Polley/Son/18/BromleyCensus; 1881/Emma M. Polley/Daughter/14/Bromley/Census; 1881/Alfred E. Polley/Son/11/Bromley/Census; 1881/Edward A. Polley/Son/7/Poplar/Census, 1881/Alexander J.S. Polley/Son/2/Lee, Kent/Census; 1881/Louisa C. Polley/Daughter/1/Lee, Kent/Census; 1881/John M. Spindler/Son in Law, Currier Leather Dresser/24/Bermondsey/Census; 1881/Kate E. Spindler/Grand Daughter/3/Bermondsey/Census; 1881/Jessie S. Spindler/Grand Daughter/1/Bermondsey/Census

13. Conversation with Mrs Angela Loudon, great-niece of Hartnell. October 1994.

14. Ibid.

15. Conversations with ex-workroom and showroom staff.

16. William Hickey.

17. Whitehead, Jack, *The Growth of St Marylebone and Paddington London*. 1989.

18. Ibid.

19. Ibid., p.16.

20. Ibid., p.17.

21. Brown, J. Hanley, *Bygone Streatham*, Mitchell, London. 1926. Additional information from John Creswell of The Streatham Society, February 1997.

22. *Streatham Pictures From the Past*, Streatham Society, London. 1983.

23. *Post Office Directory 1897*.

24. *The Suburban Directory 1909/10*.

25. *Silver and Gold*, op. cit.

26. Magdalene College, Cambridge, N.H.'s 'Application for Admission', 1920.

27. N.H. papers: an appeal for funds went unanswered. *Streatham News*. 19 February 1960.

28. Croft-Cooke, Rupert, Cities, Allan Wingate, London, p.105. 1954.

29. Harper, Charles G., *The Brighton Road*. 1905.

30. Baily, Leslie, *Scrapbook for 1914*, Frederick Muller Ltd, London, p.40. 1952.

31. *The Brighton Road*. Charles G Harper, Chapman & Hall Ltd., London, 1906.

32. Ibid. pp.38–60.

33. Ibid.

34. Ibid. pp.30–31.

35. Ibid. pp.32–3.

36. *Silver and Gold*, op. cit.

37. Vickers, Hugo, *Cecil Beaton: A Biography*, Weidenfeld & Nicolson, London. 1986.

38. Hampden-Cook, Ernest, *The Register of Mill Hill School 1807–1926*, Mill Hill School, London. 1926.

39. *Silver and Gold* original unedited MS

40 Brunskill, E.L., 'Suzette' of Cheltenham – owner of a 'small gown shop' for 25 years, letter. 1 January 1961.

41. Buck, Mrs Harold, St. Thomas Ontario, letter. 6 May 1958.

42. Allen, Marjorie (née Albery), Brighton, letter. 16 August 1958.

42. *Silver and Gold*, op. cit., p.16.

43. *Mill Hill Magazine*, vol. 105, no. 3, summer 1977, pp.94–5, letter from H.S. Sly, South Africa.

44. *Mill Hill Magazine*, vol. 47, no. 4, November 1919.

45 N.H. to Mrs Robert Beaty, 'A Man I'd Like to Meet – Norman Hartnell', broadcast. 25 April 1952.

46. Plummer, Alec F., letter. n.d.

47. Hartnell, Norman, letter. 27 September 1973.

48. Landless, E.H.M. Burnley. 20 November 1947

49. Hartnell, Norman. 4 December 1947

50. *Silver and Gold*, op. cit., p.15.

51. Ibid.

52. Ibid p.16.

53. Hartnell, Norman, letter to Neville Allen, Wargrave. 8 May 1950. The V&A Museum has a design for Mrs Whitmee dating from the early 1920s.

54. *Mill Hill Magazine*, op. cit.

55. *Silver and Gold*, op. cit., pp.17–18.

56. Ibid. p.16.

57. Ibid.

58. Bennett, Raymond A. 'Hatmaker to *The Queen*', *Housewife*. March 1956.

59. Letter from Kate Day to N.H. 21 November 1955.

60. Bewscher, D., Nobis, Blandford Press, London. 1979.

60. Spanier, Ginette, *It Isn't All Mink*, Collins, London. 1959.

61. Bewscher, D., *Nobis*, Blandford Press, London. 1979.

62. Hickey, William, 'This is Your Life you didn't see!', column in *Daily Express*. 17 February 1960.

63. *Mill Hill Magazine*, op. cit. pp.156–7.

Chapter 2

1. Forster, E.M., *The Longest Journey*, Abinger, p.ixviii. 1907.

2. Forster, E.M., *Goldsworthy Lowes Dickinson*, Edward Arnold, London, p.29. 1934.

3. Hartnell, Norman, 'Beauty and Fashion', press release. 31 October 1960. 'Night nursery' has become plain nursery and 'emphatic ginger cows' are 'brown'. *Silver and Gold*, p.15.

4. N.H. to Rt Hon. H. Willinck, Q.C. 2 July 1954.

5. *Post Office Directories*.

6. Magdalene College, Cambridge, N.H.'s 'Application for Admission', 1920.

7. N.H. to A.S. Ramsey. 22 February 1920.

8. N.H. to A.S. Ramsey. 30 September 1920.

9. Beaton, Cecil, diary, 1 June 1923, quoted in Vickers, Hugo, *Cecil Beaton*, p.34.

10. *Silver and Gold*, op. cit.

11. Brown, Richard Blake, letter to N.H. 5 pm 18 November 1955.

12. Brown, Richard Blake, coloured postcard of Magdalene c1958.

13. Croft-Cooke, Rupert, *The Altar in the Loft*, Putnam, London. 1960.

14. Brown, Richard Blake, *The Apology of a Young Ex-Parson: Extracts from his private diary of three years in Anglican Orders*, Duckworth, London, p.293. 1952.

15. Ibid. p.259.

16. Ibid. p.172.

17. *Silver and Gold*, op. cit., pp.19, 28.

18. Conversations with Angela Loudon. 1992–6.

19. Brown, Richard Blake, *The Apology of a Young Ex-Parson*, op. cit. p.100.

20. Ibid.

21. Croft-Cooke, Rupert, *The Altar in the Loft*, op. cit.

22. *Silver and Gold*, op. cit., p.18.

23. *Silver and Gold*, op. cit., p.10.

24. Rylands, George, quoted in Vickers, Hugo, *Cecil Beaton*, op. cit., p.28.

25. Rylands, George, letter to author. 27 April 1993.

26. 'A Man I'd Like to Meet – Norman Hartnell', op. cit.

27. N.H. to Gordon Gow, *Woman's Hour*. 11 April 1963.

28. Footlights Archive, Cambridge and information from Dr Harry Porter. 7 April 1993. Also in the cast was M.D. Lyon and J.C. Hogg father of Min Hogg (1939-2019) the founding editor of *World of Interiors*.

29. Rylands, George, letter to author. 27 June 1993.

30. 'A Man I'd Like to Meet – Norman Hartnell', op. cit.

31. N.H. and Gordon Gow, *Woman's Hour*, op. cit.

32. Anon. Letter to E. Vulliamy. 22 January 1921.

33. Ramsay, A. to Mrs Hough, 12 Victoria Park. 18 April 1921.

34. Ramsay, A. to N.H. 22 June 1921.

35. Croft-Cooke, Rupert, *The Altar in the Loft*, op. cit. p.85.

36. Gardiner, James, *Gaby Deslys: A Fatal Attraction*, Sidgwick & Jackson, London introduction. 1986

37. N.H. to A.S. Ramsey. 22 September 1921.

38. *Hammersmith Palais Dancing News.* April 1920.

39. Baily, Leslie, *Scrapbook for The Twenties*, Frederick Muller Ltd, London. 1959.

40. Lyrics of *The Bedder's Opera.*

41. Ibid.

42. Noakes, R.A., letter to *The Times*, 30 June 1987.

43. *Silver and Gold*, op. cit., p.19.

44. Anon Magdalene College Archives.

45. *Silver and Gold*, op. cit. p.19.

46. Anon, Magdalene College Archives, letter. 16 September 1922.

47. H.B., Magdalene College Archives, letter. 19 September 1922.

48. Ramsay, A., Magdalene College Archives, op. cit. 1 January 1923.

Chapter 3

1. *London Trade Directory 1902.*

2. *Kellys Directory 1966.*

3. *Silver and Gold*, op. cit. p.20.

4. Hogg, Minnie T., letter. 5 January 1966.

5. *Silver and Gold*, op. cit.

6. *Silver and Gold*, op. cit.

7. N.H. papers.

8. *Silver and Gold*, op. cit.

9. Melville, Alan to N.H., letter with script written at the meeting of 10 April 1950. 26 April 1958. It was recorded in the Aeolian Hall, Bond Street on 13 May 1958 and N.H. received 5 gns fee from the BBC!

10. Graves, Charles, *The Cochran Story*, W.H. Allen, London. n.d.

11. *Silver and Gold*, op. cit.

12. Bowan, Mrs Anne to N.H. 9 December 1953.

13. N.H. papers.

14. Baily, Leslie. Scrapbook for the Twenties, op. cit., p.35.

15. Laver, James, *Taste & Fashion*, Harrup, London. 1945.

16. Graves, Robert and Hodge, Alan, *The Long Weekend*, Faber & Faber, London. 1940.

17. Cunnington, C. Willett, *English Woman's Clothing in the Present Century*, Faber, London. 1922.

18. *Silver and Gold*, op. cit., p.23.

19. Kemp, Mrs Annie E. of Lewes to N.H. 26 April 1957.

20. Spanier, Ginette, *It Isn't All Mink*, op. cit.

21. Duff-Gordon, Lady, *Discretions and Indiscretions*, Jarrold, London. 1931.

22. *Silver and Gold*, op. cit. pp.23–5 et seq.

23. Etherington-Smith M. and Pilcher J., *The 'It' Girls*, Hamish Hamilton, London, pp.227–8. 1986.

24. Duff-Gordon, Lady, op. cit., quoted in *The 'It' Girls*, op. cit.

25. Nichols, Beverley, *The Sweet and Twenties*, Weidenfeld & Nicolson, London, p.133. 1958.

26. Croft-Cooke, Rupert, *The Numbers Came*, Putnam, London, p.56. 1963.

27. Conversations with Kenneth Partridge. 1992–2012.

28. Croft-Cooke, Rupert, op. cit.

29. *Silver and Gold*, op. cit. pp.25–6.

30. Trewin, J.C., *The Gay Twenties*, Macdonald, London, chapters 32 and 33. 1958.

31. *Silver and Gold*, op. cit.

32. Nichols, Beverley, *The Sweet and Twenties*, op. cit. pp.133–4.

33. *Silver and Gold*, op. cit. N.H. press release c1946–66.

34. Cartland, Barbara, *We Danced All Night*, p.43.

35. N.H. typescript draft. n.d.

36. Griffin, Ethel G. to N.H. 3 June 1953.

37. N.H. papers.

38. Brown, Richard Blake, *The Apology of a Young Ex-Parson*, op. cit. p.25.

39. Nichols, Beverley, *Crazy Pavements*.

40. Brown, Richard Blake, *The Apology of a Young Ex-Parson*, op. cit.

41. Croft-Coooke, Rupert, op cit

42. Bowen, Louise, Mrs, interviews with author

43 *Silver and Gold* op. cit.

44 N.H papers, unidentified press clippings

45 *Silver and Gold* op. cit.

46 *Silver and Gold* op.cit. and N.H Papers, various unidentified press clippings

47 Brown, Richard Blake, *The Apology of a Young Ex-Parson*, op. cit.

Chapter 4

1. McDowell, Colin, *A Hundred Years of Royal Style*, Muller, Blond & White, London. 1985.

2. Nichols, Beverley, *The Sweet and Twenties*, op. cit.

3. Cartland, Barbara, *We Danced All Night*, op. cit.

4. Bowen, Mrs Louise, interview. 11 April 1992.

5. Ibid.

6. *Silver and Gold*, op. cit. p.40.

7. Anon, press clipping. n.d.

8. Anon, press clipping. n.d.

9. *Evening News*. 16 March 1926.

10. *Morning Post*. 20 March 1926.

11. *The Referee*. 20 May 1926.

12. Anon, press cutting. n.d.

13. N.H. to Lady Rosse. 23 January 1977.

14. Rosse, Anne, Countess of to Norman Hartnell. 1985.
15. *Madras Mail*. 2 July 1926.
16. Chase, Edna Woolman and Chase, I., *Always in Vogue*, Gollancz, London, p.129. 1954.
17. Yoxall, H. W., *A Fashion of Life*, William Heinemann Ltd, London, pp.66–70. 1966.
18. *Silver and Gold*, op. cit., p.41.
19. *Silver and Gold*, op. cit., pp.40–41.
20. *East Anglia Daily Times*. 8 August 1927.
21. *The Sun*. 5 August 1927.
22. *New York Herald*. 8 August 1927.
23. *Westminster Gazette*. 19 August 1927.
24. *Silver and Gold*, op. cit., p.44.
25. *Westminster Gazette*. September 1927.
26. Fielding, Daphne, *Mercury Presides*, Eyre & Spottiswoode, London, p.124. 1954.
27. *Sunday Herald*. 25 September 1927.
28. Beaton, Cecil – unpublished diaries
29. *Evening Standard*.
30. *Daily Chronicle*. 22 November 1927.
31. *Daily Chronicle*. 9 November 1927.
32. *The Star*. 24 November 1927.
33. Various newspapers and *Sheffield Independent*. 24 November 1927.
33. *Newcastle Daily Journal*. 3 December 1927.
34. Ibid.
35. *Sunday Express*. 18 September 1927.
36. *Daily News*. 24 January 1928.
37. Ibid.
38. *The Lady*. 13 October 1927.
39. *Northern Echo*. 10 October 1927.
40. *Vogue*. Oct 1928.
40. *Yorkshire Post*. 18 February 1928.
41. *Morning Post*. 13 June 1928.
42. *Silver and Gold*, op. cit., pp.68–70.
43. Interviewer.
44. Eve. 21 December 1927.
45. Brown, Richard Blake, *The Apology of a Young Ex-Parson*, op. cit.
46. Meyrick, Kate, *Secrets of the 43 Club*, J. Long, London. 1933.
47. *New Yorker*, 'On & Off the Avenue'. 22 September 1928.

Chapter 5

1. *Daily Mail*. 8 October 1928.
2. Stayne, Mrs B.M. (née Rich), letter to N.H. 11 January 1956.
3. *Daily Express*. 9 October 1928.
4. *Silver and Gold*, op. cit., pp.45–6.
5. Conversation with Mrs Doreen May McKillop née Bell. 8 April 1992.
5. Fairchild International. n.d. (1929)
6. *New York Herald*.
7. Bedwell, Bettina, 'Liberty'. 30 March 1929.
7. *Daily Telegraph*. 25.04.1929.
8. Nichols, Beverley, op. cit., p.126.
9. Beaton, Nancy, newspaper article. n.d.
10. Brighton Exhibition catalogue, p.12.
11. *The Times*. 11 May 1929.
12. *W.W.D.* 2 May 1929.
13. *Paris Times*, no. 1, 793.
14. *Daily Mirror*. n.d.
15. N.H. to Barbara Cartland. 4 July 1969.

16. *Daily Express*. 23 June 1929.

17. Sketch. 10 July 1929.

18. N.H. to Mrs L. Hart, Toronto. 28 June 1966.

19. Price, Ann to Peter Balean, Roxburghshire, 3 August 1977. In 1997 this would be about £2,500.

20. *Daily Mail*, Paris. 1 August 1929.

21. *W.W.D.* August 1929 various dates.

22. *New York Times*. 25 August 1929.

23. Lewis, Mary of Best & Co, letter 30.10.29.

24. Chase, E.W. and I., *Always in Vogue*, op. cit., p.215.

25. *New York Times*. 3 November 1929.

Chapter 6

1. *Vogue*. November 1930.

2. *Evening News*. 22 Janaury 1930.

3. *Daily Telegraph*. 11 January 1930.

4. *Daily Herald*. 18 February 1930.

5. *Evening Standard*. 25 February 1930.

6. *Daily News*. 11 February 1930.

7. *Daily Express*. 24 February 1930.

8. Ibid.

9. Anon, newspaper. n.d.

10. *Daily Mail*. 4 July 1930.

11. Settle, Alison. 30 April 1957.

12. *Daily Express*.

13. Minute Book.

14. Author conversation with Margaret, Duchess of Argyll,.

15. Author conversation with Dame Barbara Cartland.

16. *Harper's Bazaar*. February 1930.

17. *Silver and Gold*, op. cit., p.59.

18. Ibid.

19. *Sunday News*. 1 February 1930.

20. Pick, Michael, 'Gerald Lacoste', *The Thirties Society Journal*. 1986. Based on interviews with G.L.

21. *Daily Express*. 21 April 1931.

22. Brown, Richard Blake, *Miss Higgs and Her Silver Flamingo*, Duckworth, London, p.64. 1931.

23. Ibid, p.240.

24. Ibid, p.241.

25. *Sunday Graphic*. 20 September 1931.

26. *Harper's Bazaar*. November 1931.

27. *Sunday Graphic*, 22 November 1931.

28. *Silver and Gold*, op. cit., p.65.

28 Author conversation with Mrs Doreen May McKillop née Bell about January 1932. 8 April 1992.

29. *W.W.D.* 10 February 1932.

30. *The Queen*, March 1932.

31. *Silver and Gold*, op. cit., p.49.

32. *Yorkshire Post*. 27 January 1932.

33. *Daily Mail*. 10 May 1932.

34. *The Times*. 3 March 1932.

35. *Daily Sketch*. 3 March 1932.

36. *The Sphere*. 24 September 1932.

37. Author conversations with Margaret, Duchess of Argyll. 1970s–80s.

38. *Silver and Gold*, op. cit., p.63.

39. Home Notes. 5 February 1933.

40. *Silver and Gold*, op. cit., pp.48–9.

41. *Silver and Gold*, op. cit., p.49.

42. Conversations with various former employees.

Chapter 7

1. N.H. unpublished MS.
2. *Silver and Gold*, op. cit., pp.49–50.
3. *Silver and Gold*, op.cit., p50.
4. Wyndham, Francis, *The Pearly King. Sunday Times magazine* 1968, reprinted in *The Theatre of Embarrassment*. 1991.
5. *The Sun*. 24 October 1964.
6. N.H. 1960s. n.d.
7. Chase, Edna Woolman and Chase, I., *Always in Vogue*, op. cit. pp.238–9.
8. *Vogue*. April 1935.
9. *Harper's Bazaar*. February 1935.
10. *Yorkshire Evening Press*. 14 February 1935.
11. Author conversations with former staff employees.
12. Brown, Richard Blake, *My Aunt in Pink*, Seeker. 1936.
13. Croft-Cooke, Rupert, *The Wild Hills*, op. cit., p.89.
14. N.H., fragments of 3pp text for interview. n.d. c1935.
15. *Birmingham Gazette*. 10 May 1935.
16. Letter from former employee.
17. Bystander.
18. N.H., private ledger. 1936. The Retail Price Index gives the purchasing value of £1 as being £67 in 2019 values.
19. Maxwell-Scott, Dame Jean, letter.
20. N.H. unpublished dis. 1954. In 1997 Mrs Daphne Fielding still remembered the velvet model which she often wore and the borrowed furs.
21. Princess Alice, *The Memoirs of Princess Alice, Duchess of Gloucester*, Collins, London, p.106. 1983.
22. *Silver and Gold*, op. cit., pp.71,89.
23. *Sunday Dispatch*. 6. October 1935.
24. *Manchester Guardian*. 2 October 1935.
25. Evening Gazette, Reading. 7 October 1935.
26. *Sunday Dispatch*. 13 October35
27. Yevonde, *In Camera*, The Woman's Book Club, London, pp.201–2. 1940.
28. Maxwell-Scott, Dame Jean, letter to author.
29. Author conversation with Mrs L. Bowen. 11 April 1992.
30. *Silver and Gold*, op. cit., pp.90–91.
31. Bowen, Mrs L., op. cit.
32. *Silver and Gold*, op. cit.
33. Ibid.
34. N.H. papers and company records.

Chapter 8

1. Author conversation with Mrs Muriel Monson née Wilkins. 13 May 1992.

2. Bowen, Mrs Louise, (Miss Louie) op. cit.

3. Monson, Mrs Muriel née Wilkins, op. cit.

4. Nichols, Beverley, *The Sweet and Twenties*, op. cit., pp.128–9.

5. Monson, Mrs Muriel née Wilkins, op. cit.

6. Taylor, Mrs Grace, letter. 6 April 1992.

7. Monson, Mrs Muriel née Wilkins, letter 7 March 1992.

8. Gray, Mrs Grace née Harbour, letter. 20 March 1992.

9. Donaldson, Mary, letter. 1 March 1992.

10. *Silver and Gold*, op. cit., p.61.

11. Author conversation with John Cavanagh.

12. Cartland, Barbara, *We Danced All Night*, op. cit. p.181.

13. Author conversation with Dame Barbara Cartland.

14. N.H. interview. n.d.

15. Cavanagh, John, op cit.

16. *Silver and Gold*, op. cit., pp.56–8.

17. N.H., unpublished MS.

18. Conversation with Peter Shoebridge. April 1992.

19. Conversation with Mr and Mrs George Cracknell. April 1992.

20. Conversations with Kenneth Partridge, op cit.

21. Conversations with Ian Thomas. 1992–3.

22. Conversation with Major Timothy Tufnell, M.C. 1994.

23. Conversations with Norris Wakefield and Mr and Mrs George Cracknell.

24. Conversations with Ian Thomas and Kenneth Partridge, Peter Shoebridge and Mr and Mrs G. Cracknell.

25. I am indebted to the eminent forensic psychiatrist and Jungian analyst Dr Paul Harlow MA MRCPsych, for his informative opinion on Norman's sexual behaviour and referring me to the works of Havelock Ellis, where the reader will find pertinent analysis of various facets of fetishistic behaviour.

26. N.H., unpublished MS.

27. The Observer. 8 Novemebr 1936.

28. Newspaper. n.d.

29. Sherard, Michael, conversation. April 1992.

Chapter 9

1. Hartnell, Norman, *Coronation Collection 1937*, booklet.

2. Cartland, Barbara, The Isthmus Years, Hutchinson, London. 1942.

3. N.H. unpublished MS. n.d. (1960s).

4. Coronation Collection 1937, op. cit.

5. *W.W.D.* 10.03.37.

6. *New York Journal-American.* 22 March 1937.

7. *Silver and Gold*, op. cit., pp.93–4. See also the account in the authorised biography George VI by John Wheeler-Bennett.

8. Maurois, André, *Memoirs 1885–1967*, Harper & Row, London, pp.179–80. 1970.

9. *Silver and Gold*, op. cit., p.95.

10. N.H. unpublished MS. 1954.

11. *Silver and Gold*, op. cit., p.92.

12. N.H. official descriptions for press. 1938.

13. *Silver and Gold*, op. cit., pp.95–9.

14. *New York Herald Tribune*. 21 July 1938.

15. *L'Illustration*, no. 4978. 30 July 1938.

16. *Silver and Gold*, op. cit., p.99.

17. Cavanagh, John, interview with author. 27 June 1991.

18. Monson, Mrs Muriel née Wilkins, interview with author. 13 May 1992.

19. *Silver and Gold*, op. cit., pp.98–9.

20. Nichols, Beverley, *News of England*, J. Cape, London. 1938.

21. Sloane, Hilde to N.H. 18 May 1960.

22. Williams, Mrs Hugh, conversation with author.

23. *Silver and Gold*, op. cit., p.74.

24. Ibid. p.76.

25. Thomas, Ian, conversations.

26. Bowen, Mrs Louie, op. cit.

27. *Silver and Gold*, op. cit., pp.73–96.

28. Smail, Beatie Cameron, *Canadian Home Journal*, no. 7, p.17. 1938.

29. *Daily Mail*. July 1938.

30. Stewart, Peter, *Women's Illustrated*, no. 9, p.9. 1938.

31. *Daily Telegraph*. Jan/July 1938.

32. *Tatler*. 30 July 1938.

33. 'Barbara', *Sussex Daily News*. 31 August 1938.

34. *Liverpool Daily Post*. 14 November 1938.

35. *Vogue*. October 1938.

36. *Sunday Referee*. 20 November 1938.

37. *The Sun*, 'New York World Telegram'. 5 August 1939.

38. Gunn, Eleanor.

39. *L'Illustration*. 1 April 1939.

40. Kee, Robert, *The World We Left Behind: A Chronicle of the Year 1939*, Weidenfeld & Nicolson, London, 1984. This gives a full account of the visit in its historical setting.

41. Lambert, Angela, *The Last Season of Peace*, Weidenfeld & Nicolson, London. 1989.

42. Balmain, Pierre, *My Years and Seasons*, Cassell, London, pp.56–7. 1964.

Chapter 10

1. Beaton, Cecil, *The Wandering Years*, Weidenfeld & Nicolson, London, pp.372–7. 1961. ('Because,' twinkled the Queen, 'I expect he had visions of his lovely dresses appearing again.')

2. N.H. n.d.

3. *The Queen*, pp.4,11. 2 August 1939.

4. *The Queen*, 13 September 1939.

5. N.H. papers.

6. Pleydell, John to N.H. 10 May 1967.

7. N.H. to John Pleydell.

8. Mitchell, Carmelita. n.d.

9. Normand Habans, Mme Jeanne in interview, New York. 1940.

10. *NewsWeek*. 8 April 1940.

11. Gays Mills (Wisc) *Independent*. 4 April 1940.

12. *Time*. 11 August 1940.

13. *Harper's Bazaar*. n.d. (autumn 1940).

14. Settle, Alison, *Observer*. 17 November 1940.

15. Middleton, *Yevonde*, op.cit.

16. *Silver and Gold*, op. cit., pp.106–7.

17. Ibid. p.102.

18. N.H. papers.

19 Chase, Edna Woolman, op. cit. pp.293–4.

20. Yoxall, H. W., *A Fashion of Life*, op. cit. p.72.

21. N.H.. 19 November 1941.

22. N.H., papers.

23. N.H., papers. 20 August 1942.

24. N.H., papers. 13 September 1942.

25. Conversations with Tamara Talbot Rice.

26. Réalités. 1943.

27. Gerson, Madame Gyliana B., letter. March 1943.

28. Ibid.

29. N.H. to Mrs Mary Lloyd. 29 May 1942.

30. Godley, Ivy to Edward Higham., 3 June 1942.

31. Gillard, E.G. to N.H., 11 June 1942. N.H. to Gillard. 1 July 1942.

32. N.H. 29 June 1942.

33. N.H., speech. 6 October 1942.

34. Holmes, H.A. to N.H. 16 October 1942.

35. N.H. 16 November 1942.

36. Clarendon, Lord to V. Vivian. 28 November 1942.

37. Vivian, V. to N.H. 1 December 1942.

38. N.H. to Lady Willingdon. 9 February 1943.

39. N.H. 15 October 1943.

40. N.H. correspondence and papers.

41. Ibid.

42. *Silver and Gold*, op. cit., pp.103–5.

43. Fletcher, Richard to Sir Shane Leslie. 18 December 1944.

44. Delaney, Bernard O.P. to R. Fletcher. 22 July 1943.

45. Hewit, Ernest to Richard Fletcher. 3 August 1943.

46. N.H. correspondence.

47. N.H. to Hans Juda. 2 January 1944.

48. N.H. to M.W. Elphinstone. 18 February 1944.

49. N.H. papers. October 1961.

50. Author conversations with Mrs Brenda Naylor. 1992–96.

51. Fletcher, Richard to Miss Ivy Godley. 2 July 1944.

52. N.H. to Mrs Price, n.d. (July 1944).

53. Dartmouth, Lady Ruby. 6 July 1944.

54. Price, Anne (Mrs L.E.M.) to Lady Dartmouth, 9 July 1944.

55. Panter-Downes, Mollie, London *War Notes*.

56. *Silver and Gold*, op. cit., pp.101–2.

57. Beaton, Cecil, *Photobiography*, Odhams, London. 1952.

58. N.H. notes to *Vogue* for profile. 1964.

59. Rhodes James, Robert (ed.), Chips: *The Diaries of Sir Henry Channon*, Weidenfeld & Nicholson, London. 1967

60. N.H. to George Mitchison. 1 February 1944.

61. N.H. to Daphne Barker. 21 January 1944. She *modelled* (for *Picture Post*) Iris Lockwood's dresses for press

photographs and was herself a revue artiste.

62. N.H. to Lord Rothermere. 8 February 1944 to 22 March 1944.

63. N.H. to Messrs Water and Barnard. 22 March 1944.

64. Godley, Ivy to N.H. 18 April 1944.

65. N.H. salary chits. May and June 1944.

66. Godley, Ivy to N.H. 19 May 1944.

67. N.H. to Ivy Godley. 24 May 1944.

68. Godley, Ivy to N.H. 3 July 1944.

69. N.H. to Ivy Godley. 30 June 1944.

70. N.H. to Ivy Godley. n.d.

71. Godley, Ivy to N.H. 6 July 1944.

72. N.H. to Hugh Fraser. 22 August 1944.

73. Anon, press clipping. June 1944.

74. *Evening Word.* 1 May 1944.

75. Brenda Naylor, conversation. 1996.

76. *Nottingham Evening Post.* 2 November 1944.

77. *West Lancashire Evening Gazette.* 28 November 1944.

78. N.H. 7 December 1944.

79. N.H. to Eric Barker. 28 December 1944.

Chapter 11

1. Croft-Cooke, Rupert, *The Numbers Came*, op. cit., pp.1956–7.

2. N.H. to Neville Allen. 23 October 1944.

3. Fletcher, Richard to Lady Kenmare. 23 January 1945.

4. de Casteele, Madeleine to N.H. 18 February 1945

5. Stuart, James to G.A.M. Brown, Peshawar. 20 November 1945.

6. Anon to Lady Willingdon. 14 December 1945.

7. N.H. to Kate Day. 23 March 1945.

8. N.H. to Lady Sheila Birkenhead. 11 May 1945.

9. N.H. papers.

10. Smith, F.W. to H.B. Hartnell. 18 April 1944.

11. N.H. to F.W. Smith. 1 August 1944.

12. N.H. to Mrs Price. 19 August 1945.

13. N.H. to Mrs Price. Wednesday ? August 1945.

14. Price, Mrs Anne to N.H. 21 August 1945.

15. N.H. to Miss C.B. Arlow. 5 April 1945.

16. N.H. papers and *Silver and Gold*, op. cit., pp.109–11.

17. Price, Mrs Anne to Mrs Verna Welby. 29 May 1946.

18. Stuart, Mrs Phyllis to Mrs Ann Price. n.d.

19. N.H. papers.

20. *Silver and Gold*, op. cit., p.110.

21. Henderson, J. to N.H. 13 June 1946 and 3 July 1946.

22. *Silver and Gold*, op. cit., pp.110–11.

23. Parrot, Dorothy M. to N.H. 28 June 1946.

24. N.H. to Mrs Stuart. 1 July 1946.

25. Thaarup, Aage, *Heads and Tails*, Cassell, London, pp.145–7. 1956.

26. N.H. to Richard Blake Brown. 20 February 1946.

27. Price, Mr A. to Richard Blake Brown. 17 July 1946.

28. N.H. papers.

29. Thaarup, Aage, op. cit., p.155–6.

30. Wheeler-Bennett, John, *George VI*, Macmillan, London. 1958.

31. Morrah, Dermot, *The Royal Family In Africa*, Hutchinson, London. 1942.

32. *Silver and Gold*, op. cit., p.116.

Chapter 12

1. *Evening Standard*. 4 February 1947.

2. N.H. papers.

3. N.H. to Captain Andrew Duncan. 1 July 1947.

4. *La Derniere Heure*. 24–27 Juin 1947.

5. N.H. papers.

6. Ibid.

7. Ibid.

8. Ibid and quoted by Spencer Shew, Betty, *Royal Wedding*, MacDonald & Evans, London, p.106. 1947.

9. *Silver and Gold*, op. cit., p.113.

10. Ibid., p.114.

11. N.H. papers.

12. *Evening Standard*. 29 January 1948. Author conversations with Brenda Naylor. 1991–2015.

13. *Woman's Journal*, p.35. February 1948.

14. N.H. papers.

15. In conversation with author and subsequently in a newspaper interview. *Sunday Telegraph*.

16. Cottenham, Lady Patricia to N.H. 17 January 1948.

17. Brown, Richard Blake to N.H. 6 December 1946.

18. Brown, Richard Blake to N.H. 17 January 1948.

19. N.H. to D.C. Ordess. 16 April 1948.

20. N.H. to Mrs Jane Hartnell. 30 April 1948.

21. *Yorkshire Evening Post*. 25 May 1948.

22. Medlam, Henry to F.W. Smith. 29 November 1947.

23. Mitchison, George to F.W. Smith. 14 September 1948.

24. Smith, F.W. to N.H. October 1948.

25. Price, Mrs Ann to Miss Lonsdale. 26 May 1949.

26. N.H. to F.W. Smith. 6 April 1950.

27. Smith, F.W. to G. Mitchison. 13 February 1948.

28. N.H. to F.W. Smith. 8 October 1949.

29. De-la-Noy, Michael (ed.) *Journals of Denton Welch*.

30. F.W. Smith to N.H. 11 October 1949.

31. F.W. Smith to N.H. 8 November 1949.

32. *Daily Graphic*. 23 June 1949.

33. *Silver and Gold*, op. cit., pp.106–8.

34. *Irish Times*. 14 June 1949.

35. *Daily Herald*. 14 June 1949.

36. Lamond, Sylvia, Western *Daily Mail*. 26 July 1949.

37. *Beacon News* (syndicated). 28 November 1949.

38. *Silver and Gold*, op. cit., p.112.

39. *Observer*. 9 October 1949.

40. Music teacher. January 1950.

41. Conversation with Mr and Mrs George Cracknell, 1992.

42. N.H. to Richard Blake Brown. 7 January 1949.

43. Brown, Richard Blake to N.H. February 1950.

44. *News Chronicle.* 6 March 1950.

45. *Fashion Trade Weekly.* 27 April 1950.

Chapter 13

1. *Maclean's Magazine.* 1 January 1951.

2. Various Australian newspapers.

3. N.H. papers.

4. *Life.* 8 October 1951

5. Stuart, Mrs Phyllis to N.H. 27 June 1950.

6. Stuart, Mrs Phyllis to N.H. 15 August 1950.

7. Stuart, Mrs Phyllis to N.H. 15 November 1950.

8. Fearnley-Whittingstall, Bob to N.H. 24 January 1951.

9. *Vogue* and various newspapers.

10. Amies, Sir Hardy, *Still Here*, Weidenfeld & Nicolson, London, pp.84–5. 1984.; Pick, Michael, Hardy Amies, ACC, Woodbridge. 2012.

11. Amies, Hardy, Just So Far, Collins, London, p.165. 1954; Pick, Michael, Hardy Amies, op. cit.

12. Economist. August 1951.

13. Creed, Charles to N.H. 26 April 1951.

14. Picture Post. 29 September 1951.

15. Stewart, Mrs Phyllis to N.H. 2 September 1951.

16. N.H. to Mrs Hughes-Smith. 8 May 1950.

17. N.H. to Mrs Whitaker. 23 October 1950.

18. N.H. to Gerald Hervey. 15 November 1950.

19. *Silver and Gold*, op. cit., p.118.

20. Ibid., pp.119–20.

21. Ibid., p.121.

Chapter 14

1. *Silver and Gold*, op. cit., pp.121–2.

2. Ibid., pp.123–4.

3. Hartnell press release.

4. A song sheet.

5. MS and notes prepared and given to the author by the late Ian Thomas for publication in this biography.

6. Demoronex, Jacqueline, *Le Siècle en Chapeaux – Claude Saint-Cyr – Histoire d'une modiste*, Du May, Paris. 1991

7. Notes prepared and given to the author by the late Ian Thomas for publication in this biography.

8. *Silver and Gold*, op. cit., p.124.

9. Ibid., p.128.

10. Notes prepared and given to the author by the late Ian Thomas for publication in this biography.

11. Ibid.

12. Ibid., p.131 and 1991 interview with Lady Jane Rayne, subsequently Lady Jane Lacey.

13. Ibid., p.131–2.

14. N.H. papers.

15. Ibid.

Chapter 15

1. Hartnell papers.
2. Amies, Hardy. *'Still Here'*, op. cit. p.32; Pick, Michael, Hardy Amies, op. cit.
3. *Woman's Illustrated*. n.d.
4. Ibid.
5. *The People*. 18 November 1950.
6. Anon, undated journal, p.18.
7. Driberg, Tom, *News Chronicle*. 23 January 1954.
8. Thomas, Ian. March 1992.
9. Ibid.
10. Ibid.; Bowen, Mrs L., N.H. papers.
11. Thomas, Ian. March 1992.
12. N.H. papers.
13. *Daily Express*. 2 March 1953.
14. *Daily Telegraph*. 30 July 1953.
15. Pick, Michael, *'Rayne Shoes for Stars'* op. cit.; *Sunday Dispatch*. 2 August 1953.
16. *Daily Sketch*. 12 August 1953.
17. The most accurate, if jumbled, reference work remains Edwards, Anne, *The Queen's Clothes*, with a foreword by Sir Norman Hartnell, KCVO, Express/Elm Tree Books, London. 1977.
18. Nickolls, L.A., *The Queen's World Tour*, MacDonald, London. 1954.
19. *News Chronicle*, June 1953.
20. N.H. papers. n.d. (1954 and 1947).
21. N.H. to Dr Dunlop. 31 March 1954.
22. N.H. to Max Shapiro. 1 September 1954.
23. N.H. papers.
24. Pick, Michael, *Hardy Amies*, op. cit.

Chapter 16

1. Thomas, Ian, conversations. March 1992.
2. Miles, Mrs Germain, Cape Argus. 23 April 1955.
3. Thomas, Ian, conversations. March 1992.
4. *Picture Post*. 6 August 1955.
5. *Newcastle Journal*. 1 June 1954.
6. Cathcart, Helen, *Trinidad Guardian*.
7. Wakefield, Norris, conversations. 1999.
8. *Johannesburg Star*. 7 March 1956.
9. Smith, Mrs Flo, conversation. 1995.
10. *Iraq Times*. 17 November 1956.
11. *Drapers Record*. 27 August 1955.
12. Wilcox, Herbert to N.H.. 17 January 1956; N.H. in reply. 27 January 1956.
13. N.H. to Hans Juda. 18 January 1956.

14. N.H. to Margaret Leighton. 17 June 1957.

15. N.H. to Miss M Raphael. 6 February 1957.

16. Thomas, Ian, conversations. March 1992. Mr Cracknell was told by Hartnell that one proposal to him resembled the 1923 wedding dress of Queen Elizabeth the Queen Mother. Interview 1992.

17. Edwards, Anne, *The Queen's Clothes*, op. cit. pp.72,73; Wilcox, C. and Mendes, V., *Modern Fashion in Detail*, V&A, London, p.102.

18. Amies, Hardy, *Still Here*, op. cit., p.99.

19. N.H. MS (unpublished).

20. N.H. to Margaret Leighton. 26 March 1957.

21. *Daily Express*. 12 April 1957.

22. *Sunday Graphic*. 14 April 1956.

23. *Express and Star*, Wolverhampton. 25 June 1957.

24. *Yorkshire Post*. 26 July 1957.

25. *Sunday Times*. 28 July 1957.

26. *Daily Express*. 24 October 1957.

27. *Bolton Evening News*. 30 January 1958.

Chapter 17

1. *The Tatler*. 20 June 1956.

2. Stuart, Mrs James. 27 February 1958.

3. to N.H. 16 May 1958.

4. Conversation with Mr and Mrs George Cracknell, 1992.

5. Brown, Richard Blake to N.H. 11 February 1958

6. Brown, Richard Blake to N.H. 30 June 1958.

7. N.H. to Richard Blake Brown. 9 July 1958.

8. Nichols, Beverley, *My World*, 19 February 1958.

9. Thomas, Ian, conversations. March 1992.

10. *Housewife*. 1 April 1958.

11. *Sunday Dispatch*. 13 April 1958.

12. Jebb, Miles (ed.), *The Diaries of Cynthia Jebb*. Constable, London, p.206. 1996.

13. Reynolds, P. Joyce to N.H. 30 May 1958.

14. N.H. to P. Joyce Reynolds. 12 June 1958.

15. N.H. papers.

16. Bowen, Mrs Louise, op. cit.

17. Conversation with Lady Joubert. February 1997.

18. Thomas, Ian, conversations. March 1992.

19. *Silver and Gold*, op. cit., p.53.

20. Morgan-Owen, Timothy. 21 February 1992.

21. Brady, James, *Superchic*, Little, Brown and Company, pp.20–22. 1974.

22. Cracknell, George. 25 April 1992.

23. Brown, Richard Blake to N.H. 20 March 1959.

24. Tanqueray, Paul to N.H. 19 April 1947.

25. Bowen, Mrs Louie, op. cit.

26. Frederick of Rebelle's to N.H.

Chapter 18

1. Thomas, Ian to N.H. n.d.
2. N.H. to David Jacobs. 10 February 1961.
3. N.H. to Champion and Wilson. 10 February 1961.
4. One notable exception was a black velvet crinoline dress worn for a 1950s Royal Command Film Performance, an echo of the famous 1940s Hartnell–Beaton collaboration for Queen Elizabeth.
5. N.H. to S. Stocks. 27 July 1961.
6. Norton, Felicity, letter. 1992.
7. Thomas, Ian, conversations. March 1992.
8. Conversation with Mr and Mrs George Cracknell. 1992.
9. Conversations with Robert Nesbitt, Kenneth Partridge, Lady Joan Joubert and Geoffrey Angold. 1992–7.
10. Conversation with Mr and Mrs George Cracknell. 1992.
11. N.H. to Mervyn Levy, 'The Studio'. December 1962.
12. Hartnell press releases and Kenneth Partridge.
13. N.H. *Daily Herald*. 17 January 1963.
14. N.H. Richard Blake Brown. 27 February 1962.
15. Brown, Richard Blake to N.H. 5 October 1962.
16. Brown, Richard Blake to N.H. 23 August 1963.
17. Brown, Richard Blake to N.H. 11 November 1963 and 28 February 1964.
18. *Yorkshire Evening Post*. 12 February 1964.
19. Sellers, Peter to N.H. 2 February 1965.
20. *Sunday Express*, Veronica Papworth. 21 January 1962.
21. Conversations with Kenneth Partridge, op. cit.
22. N.H. to Sam Heppner. 21 August 1964.
23. Spanier, Ginette. 18 December 1959.
24. Mortimer Mrs C. to N.H. 29 April 1963; N.H. to Mrs Mortimer ('Morts'). 1 May 1963.
25. N.H. to Noris Wakefield. 13 April 1965.
26. N.H. to Mrs M. Chapman. 30 April 1965.
27. N.H. to Mr R. Broxup. 23 April 1965.
28. Steiner, H.D. to N.H. et seq. 29 October 1965–15 November 1965.
29. Stonor, Lady Jeanne to N.H. November 1965.
30. N.H. to Saul Chaplin. 19 January 1966.
31. N.H. to Mrs Hugh McCorquodale. 18 March 1966.
32. *Daily Telegraph*. 30 September 1966.
33. N.H. papers.

Chapter 19

1. N.H. papers.
2. N.H. papers.
3. Thomas, Ian, conversations. March 1992.

4. *Evening Standard.* 11 January 1967.

5. *Daily Sketch.* 19 January 1967.

6. *Sunday Times.* 26 February 1967.

7. N.H. 14 September 1966.

8. For the significance of this refer to pp.187.

9. *Daily Sketch.* 19 July 1967.

10. *Yorkshire Evening Post.* 22 December 1967.

11. *Daily Express.* 27 October 1967.

12. N.H. papers.

13. N.H. to Mrs M. Smyth. 28 November 1968.

14. N.H. to Mervyn Stockwood. 14 November 1968.

15. *Liverpool Daily Post.* 18 July 1968.

16. Beaton, Cecil to N.H. 2 July 1969.

17. N.H. to Cecil Beaton. 4 July 1969.

18. N.H. to Harold Wilson. 22 October 1969; 24 October 1969.

19. N.H. to Prudence Glynn (Lady Windlesham). 26 September 1971.

20. N.H. to Alison Settle. 9 May 1972.

21. N.H., Eleanor Lambert Berkson. 18 January 1972.

22. Cassini, Oleg, *In My Own Fashion*, Simon & Schuster, London, p.218. 1987.

23. Stiebel, Victor to N.H. 16 June 1971.

24. N.H. to Mrs Congreve. 3 August 1972.

25. N.H. interview. n.d. c1972.

26. N.H. to John Packer. 6 March 1975.

27. N.H. to Mrs (John) Vera Ellis. 16 April 1975.

28. N.H. to P. Joyce Reynolds. 9 October 1975.

29. Taylor, Gilbert of Mattli to G.M. 25 March 1974.

30. N.H. papers.

31. Pleydell, John to N.H. 26 May 1975.

32. *The Guardian*, 2 March 1977.

33. The *Daily Telegraph*, clippings. n.d.

34. N.H. papers.

35. Jackson, Winefride. 14 April 1977.

36. Edwards, Anne and Robb, Andrew, *The Queen's Clothes*, Elm Tree Books, London, p.9. 1977.

37. N.H. to Winefride Jackson. 20 April 1977.

38. Godley, Ivy to N.H. 4 July 1977.

39. Godley, Ivy to N.H. 26 June 1978.

40. Madame Vera. 15 July 1978.

41. N.H. to Major Donald Neville Willing.

42. Mitchison, George to Jean Matthews. 16 June 1979.

43. Stockwood, Mervyn, *Chanctonbury Ring*, Hodder & Stoughton, London, p.178. 1982.

44. Bowen, Mrs Louise, newspaper clipping n.d.

INDEX

Aberconway, Lady Christabel 382
Abrahams, Sir Adolphe 264
A C Gill & Co 330
Ackerley, J R 187
A Cottle & Sons 307
Adams, Mrs 306
ADC Theatre 41
Adrian 213, 230, 240
Aga Khan 372
Aga Khan, Aly 372
Aga Khan, Begum 316, 372
Airlie, Countess of 199
Albert Hall 394, 409
Alden, Zita 'Ghostie' 434
Alexandra, HM Queen 207, 249
Alexandra, HRH Princess 341, 344, 371, 390, 416
Alexandre 418-419
Algar NH butler 283
Al-Ghanim family 448
Alhambra Glasgow 170
Alice in Wonderland 358
Alice, Madame 341
Alistair 21
Allan, Mrs Neville 240
Allen, Marjorie nee Albery 19
Alpar, Gitta 189, 190
Alstons Corsetry 396
Altman's NYC 265
Aly Khan, Bettina 372
Amies, Sir Hardy 49, 188, 196, 198, 216, 226, 230, 234, 238, 260, 282, 329, 330, 337, 347, 349, 359, 362, 363, 365, 375, 376, 399, 401, 405, 407, 420, 423, 428, 439, 447, 449
Anderson, Joan 337
Anderson, John Murray 56
Anderson, Robin 440
Andree, Madame 144

Anglo-Brazilian Society 269
Anne, HRH Princess 429
Anne, HM Queen 333, 334
Ansell, Gracie 63, 64
Anstruther, Averil 212, 226, 440
Antoine 148
Antrim, Lady 200
Apollo Theatre 111
Arbeid, Murray 419
Arden, Elizabeth 190, 272
Archibald, Miss 108
Arlow, Miss 270
Armelin, Cressie 176
Armstrong, Eliza 13
Armstrong-Jones, Antony 391, 434
Arnaud, Yvonne 54, 131, 309
Arnold, Miss Marie Louise 243-244
Aschers fabrics 402
Ashley, Lady Sylvia 107, 140
Atkinson 330
Atlee, Clement 279
Auchinleck, Field Marshal Sir Claude John 253
Auer, Mischa 212
Au Printemps 331, 419
Auriol, President et Madame 312
Austin, Mrs J 14
Austin 7 226
Austin Healey 410
Austin Sheerline 297, 357
Australian Newspapers Ltd 268
Ava, Earl of 126
'Babes in the Wood' 272
Baker, Josephine 282
Ballard, Flora 286
B. Altman & Co NYC 102
Balmain, Pierre 22, 57, 198, 211, 221, 294, 348, 351, 416, 424

Baldwin, Mrs Stanley 137

Bankhead, Tallulah 64, 83, 101

Banti, Madame 145

Banton, Travis 96, 163, 315, 329, 405

Bakst 21

Barclay, Miss Helen Lee

Barclays Bank Ltd 372, 388

Barkers 59

Barnett, Constance 7, 19, 79

Barraclough, Judy 317

Barregar, Jack 316, 363, 389, 411, 416

Barrie, Sir James 131

Bart-Smith, H 423

Bath, Marquess of

Bath, Fashion Museum 375

Batsfords 247

Batt, Anne 430

Battersby, Martin 441

Bauer, Mr 145

Bauhaus 148

Baumer, Lewis 125

Bavaria, King Ludwig of 32, 41

Baylis, Dame Lilian 72

Bayliss, Sir Richard 449

BBC 189

Beardsley, Aubrey 42, 62

'Beatniks' 414

Beauchamp, Earl 82

Beaton, Baba 142-143

Beaton, Sir Cecil 16, 29, 32, 36, 37, 42, 67, 82, 89, 90, 98, 99, 105, 110, 134, 140, 143, 198, 218, 223, 238, 248, 252, 312, 330, 342, 382, 401, 434-436, 447

Beaton, Nancy 98, 110, 115, 140

Beardsley, Aubrey 42, 62

Bective 440

Beddington-Behrens, Major E 261

Behar family 132

Behar, Miss 132

Belgium, King of 208

Bell, Miss 108

Bell, Mr furrier 403

Bellenger, Captain 254

Bendix, Mrs Carl 98,

Benson, E F 113

Bentley 413

Berard, Christian 'Bebe' 198,

Berker, Leslie 230, 232-233, 269, 296, 331, 349

Berkertex 230, 242, 244, 260, 283, 295, 331, 399

Berners, Lord 215

Bernhardt, Sarah 261

Berry, Hon Eileen 127

Berry, Miss Sheila 159

Berthe, Madame 198

Bessboroough, Lady 214

Best & Co. NYC 106-107, 117, 118

Best Dressed Hall of Fame 438

Best, Edna 107, 111, 135

Bethell, Lord 79

Bingham, Lady Rose 101, 141

Birkenhead, Lady 266-267

Birkenhead, Lord 159

Bishop, John Gilbert 19

Black, Cilla 448

Black, George 227, 230, 248, 254

Blackman, Saul and his Band 66

Blair, George 243

Blaxhall, Mr Stanley 145

Bloomsbury Set 27

Boadicea, Queen 62

Board of Trade 230, 232, 298, 400

Bocher, Main 88, 159

Bockridge 293

Bodley Scott, Sir Ronald 437

Bohan, Marc 419-420

Bonham Carter, Lady Violet 440

Bon Marche, Brixton 233

Bosdari, Countess Babe 113

Botticelli 126, 286

Bourne & Hollingsworth 68

Bowen, Mrs Louise 'Miss Louie' 72, 79, 99, 152, 169, 173, 176, 187, 220, 259, 391-392, 403, 412, 426, 448, 451

Bowes-Lyon, Lady Elizabeth 193

Bowes-Lyon, Mrs 303

Boyd, Gladys 413

Bracknell, Lady 100

Brady, James 394

Bradley, Mr 65

Bradleys 145-146

Braemar Games 295

Braganza, TIH Princesses of 271

Braithwaite, Lilian 105
Brandt, Edgar 56
Brialix (Paris) 87
Britannia 395
British Colour Council 246
British Film Week 282
Brooke, Miss Jean 85
Brougham and Vaux, Lady 140
Brougham and Vaux, Lord 132
Brown, Donald 34
Brown, Lincoln 34, 72
Brown, Richard Blake 'Blake' 29, 32-33, 35, 36, 38, 39, 44, 50, 53, 66, 67, 69, 71, 75, 87, 99, 130, 134, 162, 178, 184, 263, 276, 293, 298, 313, 380, 395, 409, 410-411, 426, 427, 432, 450
Browne, Coral 269, 292
Browning, John 365
Brummel, Beau 372
BSA 384
Buchanan, Jack 51, 52, 101, 292, 383
Buccleuch, Duchess of 202
Buccleuch, Duke of 165, 168
Buccleuch, Mary Duchess of 165
Buckley, Pat 292
Buckmaster, Captain 332
Burghley, Lord 34
Buonaccorso, Niccolo 91
Burton, Sir Montague 290
Butlin, Mrs Billy 384
Butt, Dame Clara 59
Cafe Royal 442
Calico Printers Association 246
Cambridge, Lady Mary 78
Campbell, Miss 233
Campbell, Mrs Patrick 32
Campbell-Walter, Fiona 351
Canadian Broadcasting Corporation 261
Candide 105
Caravella Club 257
Cardin, Pierre 433
Cardus, Neville 313
Carisbrooke, Lady Irene 113
Carnaby Clique 442
Carol, King of Romania 273
Carter, Ernestine 377, 390, 447
Carter, Jill 376

Cartier 264
Cartland, Dame Barbara 63, 79, 80, 85, 89, 90, 109, 113, 128, 174, 181, 196-197, 383, 385, 419, 450
Cashman, Mr 397
Cassell NH publisher 437
Cassini, Oleg 438
Castle, Marjorie 188
Castlerosse, Lady Doris 113
Cathcart Borer, Mary 437
Cavanagh, John 180, 331, 337, 356, 368, 391, 393, 407
Cecil, Hugh 83
Cezard, Mr 175
Chamberlain, Lady 214
Chambers, Miss 'Miss Potts' 338-339
Chambre Syndicale 238, 281
Champcommunal, Elspeth 87, 147, 148
Chanel, Mlle Coco 54, 81, 89, 94, 95, 102, 106, 107, 120, 124, 155, 197, 221
Chanel No 5 156
Channon, Sir Henry 'Chips' 112, 203, 252
Chaplin, Mr 13
Chaplin, Saul 419
Chapman, Mrs 32
Charlot, Andre 56
Chase, Edna Woolman 86, 157, 228, 233
Chateau de Madrid au Bois 116
Chelsea 235
Cheruit 102
Chorley, Jane 331, 350, 444
Christian, Linda 311
Churchill, Mr Randolph 127
Churchill, Mr Winston 244
Churchill, Mrs Winston 214
Cinderella 139, 152, 340, 430
Circus Party, The 102
Ciro's 257, 313
Clare-Clare, Mrs 249
Claridge's 137, 148, 261
Claridge's Causerie 406
Clarke, Arundell 227
Clark Minor, Lady 108
Claude, Monsieur 428
Cleopatra, Queen 97
Coates, Wells 295, 331

Cochran, Charles B 53, 55, 125, 134, 140, 189-190, 215
Cockney 253
Coke, Lady Anne 370
Coleridge-Taylor, Avril 294
Collins, Frank 56
Collins, Miss Jose 21, 38, 100-101, 130
Colville, Commander Richard 312, 395, 401
Comedy, Haymarket 212
Conde Nast 234
Connor, Grace 449
Cooper, Lady Diana 64, 79, 92, 126, 127, 130, 214, 215
Cooper, Dame Gladys 68, 105
Copacabana Palace Hotel 271-272, 273, 274
Corbusier, Le 148
'Corisande', 45, 49, 53, 57, 91
Coronation Dress 202, 335, 448
Corrigan, Mrs James 149
Cottenham, Patricia Countess of 292
Coulson 7, 14
Coulson, George 10
Coulson, John Harmston 10
Coulson, Mrs John 9
Coulson, Sam 263
Coulson, Samuel John 10
Courtaulds fabrics 402
Courtneidge, Ciceley 174, 228
Courtois & Detrois 108
Coward, Sir Noel 28, 55, 78, 99, 164, 181, 182-183, 190, 384
Coyle, John 316
Cox, Mabel 67
Crabtree, Eric 297, 331, 362, 447
Cracknell, Mr 'Crackers' & Mrs 185, 313, 387, 395, 404, 406, 411, 412, 414, 420, 424, 441, 445
Cradock, Fanny and John 405
Crane, Lady 240
Crane, Walter 15
Cranston, Thelma 331
'Crawfie' 438
Crawford, Joan 213
Crawford's Advertising Agency 230
Creed, Charles 228, 238, 282, 310, 331, 423
Creed (Paris) 87, 103
Crillon, Hotel de 221, 224

Criterion Theatre 309
Croft-Cooke, Rupert 33-34, 35, 52, 60, 72, 263
Cunard, Lady Emerald 90,
Cunnington, C Willet 55
Curtis Brothers Dairy 14
Curzon, Lady 130
Daimler 297, 384
Dalys Theatre 45, 48, 84
Dane, Ted NH driver 342
Daniels, Bebe 261, 394
Dannhom, John 290
Dare & Bishop 8
Darnieres, Miss 261
Dartmouth, Lady 250
Dartmouth, Lady Raine 384
Dashwood, Lady 214
David Jones Sydney 265, 295, 318
Davide, Madame Germaine 'Mam'selle' 70, 73, 81, 102, 123, 144-145, 170, 173, 177, 229, 245, 365-368, 374
Davies, Brian 43
Day, Doreen 292
Day, Miss Edith 261
Day, Frances 101, 214, 227, 261
Day, Kate 22-23, 266, 330, 349
Debroy Somers Quintet 226
Dean, Basil 226
Dean Paul, Brenda 101, 115
Debenham Son & Freebody 92
De Boisson, Miss 312
De Casteele, Madame Madeleine 174, 176, 178, 179, 203, 265
Deferment Board 258
De Gaulle, President Charles 427
De Givenchy, Hubert 368-369
De Hooch, 330
Delanghe, Angele 278, 282
Del Rio, Dolores 282
Delysia, Alice 130, 140-141, 153, 164, 180, 181, 182-183, 213, 413, 434
De Meyer, Baron 86, 110, 124, 129, 131, 150
Denmark, King and Queen of 329
Denise, Madame 129
D'Erlanger, Baron 92
D'Erlanger, Robin 92
De Oliveira, HE Ambassador Regis 199

De Pompadour, Madame 108, 116
De Rivoli, Madame 155
Derry, Mr and Mrs 13
Derwent, Lady 214
Desiree, Madame 50, 52, 67
Deslys, Gaby 1, 21, 22, 41, 130, 434
Desmond, Florence 170, 180
Devonshire, Mary Duchess of 342
De Wolkoff, Anna 216
Dezengremel, Miss 108
Diaghilev School 21
Dick, Douglas 331
Dick, Sir Reid 207
Dietrich, Marlene 159, 188, 190, 245, 261, 315, 329, 370-371, 384, 405
Dior, Christian 198, 210, 260, 277-278, 281, 285, 291, 294, 298, 299, 311, 312, 314, 352-354, 359, 360, 362, 374, 376, 377, 411, 420
Dixon, Adele 189, 214
Dixon, Dorothy 101
Dixon, Roy 419
Doble, Frances 99
Docker, Sir Bernard & Lady 384
Dodero, Madame Alberto 274
Doherty, Miss 70, 73
Dolly Sisters, The : Jenny and Rosie 56
Dolores, Epstein model 73, 74
'Dolores' mannequin 212, 282, 331, 370, 371, 403
Dominican Order, Father Provincial of the 246
Donaldson, Margaret 179
Donegal, Marchioness of 244
Doniville, Lady 89
Doolittle, Eliza 13
Dorchester Hotel 228, 257, 371
Drawbell, J W 365
Drew, Jane 295
Driberg, Tom 354
Dubury, Mrs Mary 176
Dudley, Lord and Lady 250, 289
Dudman, H Curtis 19, 20, 22
Duff, Lady Juliet 115, 130, 244
Dufferin and Ava, Marquess of 126
Duff-Gordon, Lady Lucy 'Lucile' 57, 58, 59, 68, 87, 338
Duley, Miss Edie 259, 341
Duncan, Captain Andrew 270, 275, 282, 372

Dunlop, Dr J K 361
Du Pont USA fabrics 402
Durling, Violet 67
Dyas, Mr 305
Eaden, Lilley & Co, Messrs 42
East-West Airlines 430
Ecktachrome 247
Edward VII 16, 63
Edward VII Hospital Windsor 411
Edward VIII 169, 187, 189, 191, 194, 200
Egerton, Lady Alice 329
Eileen mannequin 87, 144
Ekland, Britt 411
Elgar 313
Elisack, Mr 145
Eliza (Pygmalion) 13
Elizabeth, Empress of Austria 32, 41, 200
Elizabeth, HRH Princess 3, 21, 142, 168, 174, 193, 229, 236, 246, 260, 261, 275-277, 278-279, 284, 286, 287, 294, 298, 299, 311, 314, 325, 329, 332, 349, 367
Elizabeth I, HM Queen 93
Elizabeth II, HM Queen 5, 7, 64, 105, 112, 328, 333, 334, 335-336, 338, 340, 341, 342, 343, 347, 348-349, 351, 358, 367, 370, 371, 374-376, 389, 390, 393, 394, 395, 401-402, 405, 407, 416, 418, 429, 432, 434, 436, 437, 438, 439, 446, 448, 450
Elizabeth, HM Queen, later Queen Mother 38, 65, 77, 90, 91, 103, 105, 163, 165, 191, 193-194, 197, 199, 200-201, 202, 203, 206, 207, 208, 213, 215-216, 218-219, 221, 223-224, 227, 228, 230, 236, 240, 242, 243, 246, 251, 252, 268-269, 273, 275, 278-280, 283, 287, 289, 293-294, 295, 296, 299, 311, 312, 314, 315-316, 317, 322, 328, 332, 333, 336, 338, 340, 343-345, 354, 358-360, 363, 369, 370, 380, 388, 390, 392-393, 394, 395, 401, 405, 407, 409, 434, 435, 439-440, 446, 450
Ellis, Mrs John 443
Elphinstone, Hon M W 247
Elsie, Lily 105
Ely, Marchioness of 199
Epstein, sculptor 73
Erickson, Carl 'Eric' 407
Erte 21, 41

Esther, Madame 62
Ettinger, Miss 247
Eugenie, Empress 200
Euston, Countess of 341
Evans Brothers 365, 386
Mrs Evans 68
Evans, Edith 61
Evans, Kathleen 19
Father Time 422
Faust 387
Fearnley-Whittingstall, R 'Bob' 317-325, 361, 386
FIC Fashion Industries Club 290-291, 331, 357
Fellowes, Mrs Reginald 230
Ferguson, A C 43
Ferragamo, Salvatore 285
Festival de Bruxelles 282
Festival of Britain 290
Fields, Gracie 214
Filene's Boston 294
Fisher, Mrs 250, 282
Flack, Shirley 428
Flanagan, Bud 443
Fleckheimer, Richard see Fletcher, Richard 264
Fleetwood, Kenneth 420
Fleming, Ronald 112-113
Fletcher, Richard 8, 59, 60, 61, 63, 72, 73, 87, 90, 103, 112, 114, 151, 158, 159, 239, 240, 256-257, 244, 245, 246, 248, 249, 250, 259, 260, 261, 263, 264, 276, 347, 350
Follett's 229
Footlights 28, 35, 36, 38, 39, 43, 184, 185, 190, 293, 420
Ford, Miss Avis 276
Ford, Helen 111
Forster, E.M 27, 33
Fortnum & Mason 238
Foster of Ships, Miss 290
Foyle, Christina & Literary Luncheons 124, 407, 416
Fox Films 163
Fox-Pitt, Mrs 107
Fragonard 406
Franck, Cesar 313
Frank Partridge Ltd 405
Fraser, Sir Hugh 259-260, 363, 388, 396, 421

Fratini, Gina 419
French, Valerie 113, 132
Frere, A S 236
'Fritzi (e)' Mrs Hilde Lincoln Leven, 203, 212
Fry, Maxwell 295
Fuad, King of Egypt 93
F W Woolworth, 127
Fyffes, Messrs 17
Gagarin, Yuri 397
Gainer, Lady 271
Galitzine, Princess Vera 234
Galsworthy, John 22
Gamages 124
Gandarillas, Antonio 244
Ganex mac 400
Garbo, Greta 240
Gardiners of Ipswich 331
Garlands Norwich 331
Garnier, Charles 209
Garrick Theatre 292
Garson, Greer 190
Garter King of Arms 333, 339
Gasque, Miss Maysie 127
Gay, John 42, 43
George V 16, 91, 111, 146, 147, 157, 168, 169, 187, 191, 199, 206, 207, 209, 242
George VI 65, 77, 169, 199, 200, 206, 209, 223, 227, 252, 275-276, 279, 293-294, 295, 310, 322, 332, 336, 344, 368, 380, 390
Gerson, Madame Gyliana B
'Gert and Daisy'253, 355
Getty, J Paul 396
Gibb, Bill 440
Gibson Girl 17
Gielgud, Sir John 215
Gilbert, Mr 301-301, 386
Gina mannequin 177
Gingold, Hermione 313
Girl Guides 248, 310
Gladys Cooper's Beauty Preparations 128
Gloucester, HRH Prince Henry Duke of 131, 165, 193,
Gloucester, HRH Duchess of 193, 197, 199, 203, 217, 236, 246, 252, 277, 344, 367
Glover, John 447
Glyn, Elinor 58

Glynn, Prudence, Lady Windlesham 391, 437, 447

Godley, Miss Ivy 1-3, 176, 234, 249, 250, 258-259, 261, 306, 380, 389, 449

Goebbels, Joseph 219

Goetze, Sigismund 223

'Golden Arrow', 97

Goldsbrough, Angela, Mrs George Loudon 11, 328, 432

Goldscheider 245

Goossens, Sidonie 73

Gordon, Lord Adam 450

Gordon, Helene 198

Gorell Barnes, Mr F 38

Goya 406

Grace, Princess 428

Grant, Cary 417

Grant, Dawn 372

Granta 32

Graves, Robert 55

Gray, Mrs Grace 'Ruby ' 178

Gray, Mr 179

Great Universal Stores 444

Greece, Prince Christopher of 101

Green, Sergeant 179

Greenaway, Kate 58

Greer, Howard, 58, 96

Greig, Sir Louis 211

Gres, Madame 155

Grey, Anne 135

Grieg 313

Griffin, Miss Ethel 67, 68

Griggs, Barbara 428

Grossmith &Sons, Messrs 305

Guedalla, Philip 246

Guinan, Texas 101

Guinness, Mrs Bryan 110

Guinness, Mrs and Mrs Bryan

Guinness, Mr Ernest 111

Guinness, Lady Evelyn 107

Guinness, Lady Honor 112

Guinness, Mrs Loel (nee Joan Yarde-Buller) 141

Guinness, Mrs Martha 424, 437, 439, 445

Guinness, Maureen 113, 126

Guinness, Miss Oonagh 111, 113, 114, 126, 127, 200

Gunn, Sir Herbert John 407

Gunters 247

Gurr, Tom 268, 316, 363, 449

Gustave, Madame 245

GVK 444

Gwynne, Nell 358

Haddon, Peter 190

Haig, Lady Victoria 116

Hale, Binnie 226

Halsey, Lt T E 85

H & M Rayne Ltd 287-288, 311, 359, 361

Hambrook, Miss Harriet 9

Hammer, Dr Reginald 34

Handley-Seymour Ltd, Madame 77, 98, 165, 193-194, 197, 202, 336

Handsworth School 164

Haneker, David 337

Hard, Arnold 290

Hardwicke, Lady 372

Hardwicke, Lord 113, 372

Harper, Miss 62

Harper, 'Mr' 62

Harris, A J 418

Harrods Buenos Aires 273, 274

Harrods 92, 230, 233, 421

Hart, Mrs L 115

Hart-Davis, Deirdre 127

Hartley, Rex 96

Hartnell, Bishop Bishop 9

Hartnell, Lady Clare 144, 234, 244, 448

Hartnell, Elizabeth nee Clegg 8

Hartnell, Emma Mary 7, 11, 12, 14, 17, 19, 37, 46-47, 74, 185, 379, 444-445, 446-447, 451

Hartnell, George 8

Hartnell George Bishop 9

Hartnell, Henry Bishop 'Bish' 7, 8, 9, 12, 16, 17, 18, 29, 37, 46, 47, 51, 63, 65, 66, 69, 72, 79, 87, 103, 112, 118, 119, 120, 126, 128, 144-145, 149, 184, 215, 225, 229, 231, 235-236, 246, 261, 263, 268, 357, 367, 385

Hartnell, Mrs Jane (second wife of 'Bish')133, 263, 293, 295, 348

Hartnell, Henry John 30

Hartnell, Mr and Mrs Marcus 439

Hartnell, Miss Maude 30
Hartnell, Phyllis Maude 'Topsy' 1, 12, 14, 18,
    18, 19, 51, 59, 62, 63, 65, 66, 69, 70, 72, 79,
    87, 112, 133, 102, 103, 108, 115, 118, 119, 120,
    126, 137, 143, 161, 176, 250, 259, 263, 265, 270,
    272, 274, 295, 304,
325-328, 331, 348-349, 361, 366, 379, 383, 386,
    444, 446-447, 449, 451
Harty, Russell show 441
Harvey Nichols 92, 362
Harwood, H M, 124
Haslam, Nicholas 440
Hathaway, Anne 155
Havinden, Mrs Ashley 230
Hay Wrightson 170
Hayter, Sir George 199
Hayter, Lord 447
Heifetz, 160
Heim, Jacques 428
Helena Victoria, HRH Princess 137, 200
Henderson, J 273
Heneker, Captain 240
Hepburn, Audrey 377
Hepworths 423
Hereford, Viscount 156
Herrmann, Otto 286
Hervey, Gerald 332
Hevren, Mr 232
Hibiscus Queen Festival 363, 372
Higham, Edward 'Teddy', 22, 23, 93, 240
Hildyard, C 67
Hillier, Bevis 441
Hill-Wood, The Hon Anne
Hippodrome 214, 227, 242
Hitchcock, Alfred 188, 443
Hitler, Adolf 219
Hogarth, William 43
Hogg, Miss Minnie 49, 50, 51, 57, 58, 63, 73,
    99, 272, 413, 443, 447
Holford, Lady Susan 89
Holiday, Mrs 177
Hollenden, Lord 290-291,
Holliday, Misses 67
Holmes, H A 241
Home Guard 236
Hampshire, Susan 369

Hertie 422
Hope, Anthony 185
Hopkins, Miriam 190
Hordern's Sydney 318
Hore-Belisha, Mr Leslie 221
Horney, Brigitte 188, 190
Horrockses 359, 362
Hotel Atlantic Hamburg 361
Hough, Mrs 32, 40
House of Fraser 388, 396, 401, 421
Hoyningen-Huene, Baron 107, 109, 132
Howard, Brian 113, 115
Hubbard, P C 24
Hughes, Mrs 53
Hugo, Victor 239
Hulbert, Claude 38
Hutch 115
Hutchison, Percy 117
Hyder, Lilian 181, 291
Illingworth, Margaret, Lady 405
IncSoc 109, 230, 281, 286, 290, 291, 328, 331, 332,
    351, 359, 377, 391, 405, 408, 428, 439, 444
Indian Red Cross & St John's 283
Ingillson, Mrs Florence 17
'In Love' 337, 441
Innes-Ker, Lord Robert 101
International Calico Printers 234
Irene 285
Isabelle, Madame 341, 402
Isobel, Madame 98, 136
IT (International Textiles) 247
Jack NH employee 424
Jackson, Mrs 174
Jackson, Winefride 447, 448
Jacobs, David 225, 400, 420, 431, 436
Jacqmar 282
Jacques Heim 153
James, Charles 110, 283
James, Edward 151
Japan, Imperial Princesses 362
Jay's 54
Jean, Ronald 181
Jeans, Isabel 109-110, 124, 125, 140, 164, 190,
    227, 434, 437
Jebb, Lady 376, 382
Jersey, Earl of 136

John XXIII, Pope 401
John, Augustus 407
John Lewis 68, 69
John Mowlem & Co 379
Jolliffe, William 132
Joubert de la Ferte, Lady Joan 391, 417
Joyce, Eileen 294, 313, 428
Juda, Mr and Mrs Hans 247, 285, 373, 382
Juliana, Queen of the Netherlands 329
Jungman, Miss 'Baby' 127, 132
Kagi, Mr and Mrs 215, 263
KCVO 446
Keane, Doris 21
Keats 410
Kelly, Sir Gerald 209, 407
Kelly, Renee 117
Kelso 332
Kelvin Hall 363
Kenmare, Enid, Lady 244, 264
Kennedy, Mrs Jacqueline 438
Kennedy, Mrs Joseph 218
Kennedy, Mrs P G 93
Kennerley-Edwards, Mr 400
Kent, HRH Prince George Duke of 153, 157
Kenward, Betty 'Jennifer' 447
Keowan-Boyd, Lt Col 447
Kerman, Isidore 269
Keys, Nelson 113
Khan, Price Aly 141
Kilner, Hew 59
Kilner, Lady 447
Kimberley, Lady 73
Kindersley, Mr Philip 111, 114
Kindersley, Mrs Philip 126
Kingscote Billings, L 410
Kingston, Bishop of 451
Kirkman, Joyce 447
Knatchbull-Hugessen, Sir Hughe 237, 282
Knight, Miss Paula 130
Knoblock, Edward 248
Korda, Alexander 159, 190, 194
Kurhaus Baden-Baden 361
Lachasse 188, 196, 216, 228, 233, 329, 348
Lacoste, Gerald 131-132, 139, 140, 144, 146, 148,
    150-151, 159, 173, 216, 295, 316
Lagonda 221-222, 226, 229, 231, 241, 295

La Maison du Diable 221
Lana mannequin 331
Lambert, Eleanor 438
Lambton, Lady Ann
Lancaster, Marie-Jacqueline 113
Lancaster, Osbert 291
'Lancastrian' 271
Lane, Lupino 215
Lane, Miss 44
Langley Moore, Doris 314
Lanvin, Jeanne 21, 54, 68, 81, 103, 116, 138, 155,
    156
Lanz, Rudolf 198
La Reserve Beaulieu 373
Lascelles, Viscount
Laszlo, Vasco 220
Latin American Exhibition 258
Laver, James 55, 211, 244, 260, 286, 351, 377
Lavery, Lady Hazel 73
Lawrence builders 145
Lawrence, Gertrude 99, 135, 137, 158, 164, 181, 182-
    83, 189, 227, 253, 406, 419, 434, 437, 441, 442
Laye, Evelyn 174, 178, 228, 261, 309, 394, 433-
    434, 442
Leach, Mrs 67
Lebrun, Monsieur et Madame 219, 293, 312,
    393
Leeds, Duke of 101
Leicester, Countess of 341
Leicester, Earl of 370
Leigh, Viven 369
Leighton, Margaret 369, 373, 375, 384
Leinster, Rafaelle, Duchess of 405
Lelong 81, 102, 238
Lely 407
Lennon, Dennis 295
Leon, H Cecil 43
le petit salon 401, 407-408, 418-419, 424
Leslie, Sir Shane 244, 245, 246
Leslie, Sylvia 51
Leveson-Gower, Miss Elizabeth 221
Levey, Mara 444
Lewis, Rosa 101
Lewisham, Lady Raine 383
Liberty & Co 252
Liddell-Hart, Captain Basil 93

Lillie, Bea 218
Lindbergh, Charles 92
Lindsay Hogg, Sir Anthony 101, 113, 385
Linlithgow, Lady Vicereine of India 215, 272
Lloyd, Marie 261
Lohr, Dame Marie 61,
Logan, Jacqueline 130
London Airport uniform 430
London College of Fashion 433
London Films 159, 190, 194
Longhi 406
Lonsdale, Frederick 137, 291
Losch, Tilly 114
Loudon, Mrs George nee Angela
    Goldsbrough 37
Louis XIV, King 111
Louise mannequin 177
Louise, Queen of Sweden 78
Lowson, Mrs Denys 328
Lucile, see Duff-Gordon, Lady Lucy
Lupescu, Madame Magda Elena 273
Lutyens, Eva 175, 216
Lyautey, Marechal 200-201
Lygon, Lady Lettice 82
Lygon, Lady Mary 213
Lygon, Lady Sibell 89, 90
Lynn, Olga 'Oggie' 64
Lyon, Beverley 45
Lyon, M D 'Dar' 34, 43, 44, 53, 168
Lyon, Mrs 45
Lyons, Mrs Jack 428
MacClean, Miss Catherine 210
MacDonald, Miss 'Bobo' 335, 356, 402, 437-438
MacDonald, Jeanette 136
Macrae, Margot Countess of Buckingham-
    shire 441
Macy's NYC 227
Madonna, The 111
Magnin, Cyril 417
I Magnin 268, 417
Maigret 417
Mainbocher 88, 138, 198
Maison Arthur, 124
Manchester, Duke of 101
Mandel Brothers 283-284
Mandel, Mrs and Mrs Leon 283

Mann, Mrs Dolly 112-113, 151, 160
Mann & Fleming 417
Manners, Lady Ursula 214
Manpower Board 236
Mappin Sao Paulo 274
Marcel 44
March, Iris 190
Marcus, Stanley 284
Margaret, HRH Princess 168, 169, 174, 193,
    236, 246, 275, 278-280, 287, 288, 291, 311,
    312, 314, 317, 325, 328, 329, 330, 333, 340, 344,
    351, 355, 367, 370, 379, 388, 390, 392-393, 394,
    395, 397, 407, 429, 432
Marguerite, 176
Marie Antoinette, Queen 93, 136
Marie Louise, HRH Princess 137
Marina, HRH Princess of Greece, HRH
    Duchess of Kent 153, 157, 165, 176, 187, 202,
    314, 351
210, 246, 250, 252, 270, 292, 329, 341, 344, 348,
    355-356, 371, 390, 393, 405, 407, 431
Marlowe Society 34, 36, 75
Marsh, Sir Edward 27
Marshall Field 268
Marshall, Francis 407
Mary, HRH Princess Royal 54, 90, 165, 310,
    344
Mary, HM Queen 50, 77, 78, 91, 105, 111,
    137, 146, 165, 168, 170, 178, 194, 202, 203,
    204-207, 209, 242, 246, 276, 277, 288-289,
    293, 344
Maschwitz, Eric 43, 44, 293
Massereene and Ferrard, Lady 73
Massey, Raymond 189
Massigli, Madame 312, 314
Masters, Auntie Agnes 347
Mata-Hari 282
Mathew, Jean 440-441, 450
Matthews, Jessie 132, 211, 434, 442
Mattli 348, 444
Maudslay, Sir Rennie 450
Maugham, Mrs Syrie 138, 143
Maugham, Somerset 215
Maurois, Andre 200-201
Mayfair Club 257
Mayfair Hartnell's Club 444

McCaig, Rev Prof Archibald 14
McClure, Sir John 19, 23, 30, 32
McCord, Mary 116
McCorquodale, Alistair 85, 90
McCorquodale, Raine 174
McKillop, Mrs 137
Mclean, Mr 395
McMullin, John 157
Meadows, Harry & Andrew 444
Medlam, solicitor 232
Medlam, Henry 'Tito' 295, 301, 308, 357, 361, 386
Melville, Alan 52-53
Mendelssohn, Felix 155
Messel, Anne later Countess of Rosse 85, 110, 214, 226, 393
Messel, Oliver 85, 131, 158, 214, 215, 371, 381
Meston, Lady Diana 447
Metropolitan Police uniform 430
Meyer Emporium Melberne 295
Meyrick, Mrs Kate 101
MGM 230
Micawber 358, 373, 387
Michael of Carlos Place 417, 433
Milford Haven, Marchioness of 199
Miller, Beatrix 447, 449
Miller, Lee 246-247,
Miller Mundy, Mrs 225
Mill Hill School, Headmaster of 349
Millington-Drake, Lady Effie 245
Milne, Oswald 148
Ministry of Information 237, 239, 243, 246, 282
Ministry of Labour 236
Mirabelle 447
Mirman, Serge 421, 426
Mirman, Simone 421, 430, 434, 439
Mistinguett 131, 153, 163, 434
Mitchison, Clare
Mitchison, Doris 187, 309
Mitchison, George 'Mitch' 186, 187, 220, 224, 226, 228, 229, 234-235, 244, 250, 253, 254-256, 268, 269, 270-271, 276-277, 282, 283, 285, 290-291, 294, 295-297, 299-309, 312, 316-325, 331, 332, 338, 347, 357-358, 361-362, 363, 367, 370, 372, 376, 384, 385-386, 387-389,

394, 396, 400, 403, 410, 415, 416, 419, 421, 423, 425-426, 431, 437, 439, 441, 444, 447, 448, 449, 450-451
Mitchison, Norman 309
Mitford, Nancy 90, 114-115
Moheitoh Japan 362
Mole, Madame 67, 68, 70
Molyneux, Edward, 57, 68, 70, 81, 87, 88, 97, 99, 102, 103, 107, 120, 123, 125, 136-137, 138-139, 140, 143, 147, 148, 153, 156, 157, 174, 180, 181, 187, 198, 210, 211, 216, 226, 228, 229, 233, 234, 235, 243, 260, 270, 276-277, 281, 282, 310, 311, 329, 338, 342, 347, 391, 413, 419
Moniz de Aragão, Dona Isabel 244, 270
Moniz de Aragão, HE Senhor S J 270
Monkman, Phil 293
Monson, Mrs Muriel, 174, 175, 178
Montagu Douglas Scott, Lady Alice 131, 165, 166, 167, 168, 169, 174
Montagu Douglas Scott, Mr Claud Andrew 116
Moore-Brabazon, Colonel 131
Mortimer, Mrs 'Morts' 384, 416
Morton, Digby 188, 196, 216, 228, 230, 233, 260, 329, 376, 399
Mosca, Bianca 230, 282
Moss Bros 419
Motley 153
Mountbatten, Lady Louis 101, 126, 130, 255-256,
Mountbatten, Lady Tatiana 199
Mountbatten, HRH Prince Philip, Duke of Edinburgh 284, 294, 325, 332, 345
Mount Temple, Lady 332
Mozart, Wolfgang Amadeus 7, 427
Mulholland, Miss 145
Musée des Arts Décoratifs Paris 270
Museum of London 152
Musgrave, Clifford 340
Musgrove, 'Tiny' 414-415
Mussolini, Benito 188
MVO 347
NAAFI 226, 255
Nanty Inc NYC 268, 284, 311
Nash, John 211
National Portrait Gallery 435

Naylor, Brenda 'Dear Girl' 249, 261, 266-267, 283, 291, 338, 356

Neagle, Dame Anna 195, 200, 290, 358, 373, 433-434

Neiman Marcus Fashion Award 284-285, 288

'Nell Gwynne' 195

Neptune 410

Nesbitt, Mrs Robert (Iris) 'Paige' 140, 213, 248, 271-272

Nesbitt, Robert 227, 243, 254, 271-272, 405, 450

Neville-Willing, Major Donald 396, 449

Nevinson, C R W 125

'Nevvie' 264

Newnes and Pearson, 365

New York Revellers, 101

Nichols, Beverley 28, 59, 63, 64, 71, 79, 110, 115, 178, 211, 381, 382, 440, 441

Nicotine, Madame 181

Nimbo, NH step-sister 379

Norfolk, Duchess of 202

Norfolk, Duke of 101, 333

Normand Habans, Madame Jeanne 174, 179, 203, 217, 227, 254, 283, 288, 353, 355, 377, 384, 404, 409

Northesk, Lord 113

Norton, Hon Kay 130

Norton, Hon Mrs Richard 126

Norwich Union 234

Novello, Ivor 99, 105, 113, 115, 130, 164, 227, 351

Nunburnholme, Lord 90

Oberholzer, Cynthia 372, 403

Oberon, Merle 134, 153

Obolensky, Princess Irena 261

Offenbach 427

Ogilvy, Hon Angus 407

Ogilvy, David 34

Oldfield, Colonel 24

Oliver, Eric 298

Olivier, Sir Laurence 264

Olympic Games London 292

Ordess, D C 293

Ordre de les Palmes Academiques 354

Orleans-Braganza, HIH Prince Pedro de 272

Orleans-Braganza, Princess Esperanza 272

Orleans-Braganza, Princess Teresa 272

Orr-Lewis, Lady 372

O'Shea, Tessie 303

Ospovat 92, 130

Ouida 32

Oxford and Asquith, Lady Margot 73, 83, 92, 103, 213

Packer, John 423, 433, 442

Page NH chauffeur 282

Page, William Bishop 29

Paget, Lady Elizabeth 214

Paget, Lady Victor 107, 130

Palladium theatre 231

Palmer, Lilli 227

Panter-Downes, Mollie 125, 251

Paper Economy Committee 246

Parfums Hartnell, Les 268, 284

Paris Trades 164

Parker, Percival 126

Parrot, Dorothy 274

Paquin (London) 61, 62, 215, 228, 230, 311

Partington, Denis 71

Partridge, Kenneth Alexander 184, 185, 186, 405, 408-409, 414-415, 423, 433

Passavant, Helen 18'

'Pat', Princess, Patricia of Connaught 137

Paterson, Ronald 331, 356, 368, 417

Patou 81, 95, 102, 116, 123, 130, 138, 180, 219

Pay, Colonel 230

Payne, Mrs E 10

Peacock, Kim 135

Peck, Gregory 417

Pelly, Mr Dennis 115

Peron, Eva 274

Peter Robinson 68

Phelps, Mrs Elspeth 107

Phillips, Captain 92

Phipps, Lady Sybil 166

Phipps, Sir Eric 87

Pick 13

Pierre Hotel NYC 229

Pilgrim, C G 66

Pilkington glass 149, 150

Platt, Suzanne 213

Pless, Daisy Princess of 32, 293

Pleydell, John 144-145, 149, 152, 156, 158, 159, 160, 164, 165, 168, 170, 174, 180, 184, 186,

189, 196, 214, 217, 220-221, 224-225, 235-236, 268, 296, 325, 357, 367, 385, 431-432, 445-446
Plummer, May 20
Plunkett, Dorothy 113
Poiret, Paul 17, 62, 81, 116
Polley, Alfred 11, 12
Polley, Henry Killick 9
Polley, Margot 12
Polley, Jim 12
Poltimore tiara 393
'Pompadour' 209
Pompadour Products 286
Ponsonby, Lady Elizabeth 115
Pontings 59
Portarlington, Lady 131
Poulett, Lady Bridget 110, 142, 217
Power, Tyrone 311
Pratts, Streatham 13
Princess Christian Hospital 449
Price, Mrs Ann 99, 115, 240, 248, 250, 259, 269, 271, 272, 274, 276, 296, 350, 379
Proteus 410
P S Gimbles Philadelphia, 118
Pugh Bros 151
Pugh, Miss 396
Quaglino's 130
Quant, Mary 407, 428
Queen Alexandra's Royal Army Nursing Corps 310
Queen Charlotte's Ball 265
Queen Elizabeth 285
Queen Mary 189

Rahvis, Dora 216
Rahvis, Raemonde 216, 230, 444
Ramsay, Lady Patricia 137
Ramsey, A S 30-32, 40, 47
Raphael 167
Rasmussen, Steen Eiler 13
Ravensdale, Baroness 244
Raverat, Gwen 27
Rattigan, Terence 351, 384
Rawlings, Mrs H E 115
Rayne, Edward 103, 220, 288, 290, 316, 408, 428, 447

Rayon Design Centre 295
'Rebecca' film 227
Rebelle Coiffeur 396-397
Recamier 274
Redfern 103, 125
Redfern Gallery 291
Regnault, Dr 396
Reich, Tibor 382
Reid & Taylor 423, 433, 442
Rembrandt company 433
Rembrandt, Mdme 155
Rendigs, Charles 284-285, 304
Renoir, Mdme 155
Reville & Rossiter 54, 59, 61, 92, 98, 384
Reville-Terry 77, 126, 136, 156, 350
Revillon Freres 138, 145-146
Reynolds, P Joyce 151, 383-384, 443
Rice, F A 65
Richards, Miss 246
Richards, Miss Patricia 136
Riley, Bill 420
Ritz Hotel London 213, 214, 269, 409
Robb, Andrew 407, 448
Robinson, Hugh 291
Robinson, John 127
Rochester, Bishop of 34
Rockers 442
Rogez, Marcelle 163, 197
Rolls-Bentley 297
Rolls-Royce 282, 357, 412, 413, 414, 423, 427, 433, 445
Romania, King Carol of 201, 208, 216
Romania, Prince Nicholas of 101
Rook, Jean 429
Roosevelt, Mrs Franklin Delano Jr 228
Rose, Nola 351
Rosenauer, Michael 371
Rosse, Anne, Countess of see Messel, Anne
Rosse, Earl of 115
Rossi, Mr 338-339
Rothermere, Lady 328
Rothermere, Lord 228, 257, 266-267
Rothschild 210
Rottenberg, H 38, 43, 44
Rouff, Maggy 147, 226
Royal Command Film 351, 411

Royal Opera House 405, 427
Royal Train 252
Royal Warrant 202, 219, 311, 387
Royle, John 421, 426, 431, 437, 449
Roxburghe, Duchess of 202
Russeks Fifth Avenue NYC 117, 197
Russell, Peter 106, 125, 140, 196, 216, 228, 230, 238, 277, 282
Ruthven Twins, The 113, 114-115
Rutland, Duchess of 202
Rutland, Frances Duchess of nee Sweeny 383
Ryan, Ann 392
Rylands, Dr George 'Dadie' 36-37, 39, 45, 66
Saint Bartholomew 410
Saint-Cyr, Claude 330, 339, 361, 381-382, 408
Saks Fifth Avenue 268, 311
Salter, Myra(h) 44, 53
Sarawak, Rajah of 85
Sargent 407
Savoy, The 181, 314
Savoy Grill 293
Scarafia, Marla 351
Schiaparelli, Elsa 138, 147, 153, 157, 175, 189, 198, 213, 221, 226, 311, 362
Schiaparelli, Signorina 213
Schildmann & Co 441
Schofield, A M B 44
Scott, Lady Angela166
Scott, Lady Elizabeth, 221
Scott, Lady Victoria 132
Scottish Industries Fair 363
Seadom Marks, Mrs Marguerite 214
Sefton, Lord 101
Sekers fabrics 402
Sekers, Miki 408
Selfridge, Gordon 56, 241, 242
Selfridge's 230, 241
Sellers, Peter 411-412, 423
Servat, Madame Emilienne 175, 341
Settle, Alison 127, 151, 241, 413, 438, 447
Seyler, Athene 83
Shanks, Alec 227
Shaftesbury Theatre 227, 449
Shakespeare 410
Shaw, George Bernard 13, 22
Shearer, Norma 230

Sherard, Michael 190, 349-350, 368
Sherren, Rex 229, 404
Schenck, Joseph 153
Shelley 410
Shirley mannequin 87
Silver Jubilee 1977 446
Silverman, E 'Manny' 268, 419
Simpson, Mrs Ernest 89, 175, 176, 187, 189, 200
Sinclair, Serena 438, 446, 447
Sitwell, Osbert 244
Sitwell, Sacheverell 244
Skeffington, Derek 188
Sly, H S 19
Smiley, Sir Hugh 140
Smith, Lady Eleanor 113, 140
Smith, Mrs Flo 'Florrie' 340, 372
Smith, Francis Walter 'Fred' 119, 126, 128, 144-145, 260, 263, 268-269, 270, 272, 284, 295, 296-309, 357, 361, 386, 389
Snow, Mrs Carmel 228, 277
Snowdon, Lord see Armstrong-Jones
Sonia, mannequin 140
Spanier, Adrienne 'Didi'
Spanier, Ginette 22, 57, 416
Spencer-Churchill, Lady Sarah 221
Spry, Constance 138
SSAFA 240, 242, 243, 265
St Laurent, Yves 377, 411
St Rose of Lima 245
Stanleigh Turner, Mr and Mrs J 394
Stark, Miss Freya 291
Stallite, Stella 131
Stead, W T 13
Steinberg, J 290
Steiner, Mr 418
Stephenson, Miss Dorothy 'Dolores' 212
Stevens, Jocelyn 418, 447
Stewart, Muriel 96
Stiebel, Victor 29, 55, 71, 86, 126, 128, 138-139, 142, 147, 158, 164, 190, 216, 226, 228, 233, 282, 356 311, 337, 347-348, 349, 369, 377, 393, 411, 413, 438-439
Stockwood, Mervyn Bishop of Sothwark 432-433, 450-451
Stone, Mrs Lew 257
Stonor, Lady Jeanne 418, 450

Stourton, Jeanne 142

Strand Theatre 67

Strassner, Joe 188, 190, 243,

Strathmore, Earl and Countess of 65, 112, 208, 216

Streatham Hill Theatre 189

Street, Helen 'Nellie' 271

Street, Kathleen 176

Strong, Sir Roy 435

Stuart, Charles 265, 379, 410

Stuart, Mrs James see Hartnell, Phyllis 161

Stuart, James; 'Jim' or 'Jugs' 128, 161, 265, 379, 410, 451

Stuart, Jeanne 139, 257

Studio Lisa 252

Sutherland, Duchess of 82

Swan&Edgar, Piccadilly store 62, 92

Swan & Edgar, swans at Lovel Dene 316, 395

Sweeny, Charles 141, 370

Sweeny, Frances 370, 383

Sweetinburgh, Thelma 394

Swinburne, Algernon 36

'Swinging Sixties'433

Talbot Rice, Tamara 237

Tancred, Anthony 449

Tanqueray, Paul 395

Tappe, Herman Patrick 88

Tate Gallery 246

Tate, Sir Henry

Tattersall's 214

Taylor, Elizabeth 384, 428

Taylor, Mrs 177

Tchaikovsky 313

T. Eaton & Co Canada 110, 265, 292

Ted, NH employee 424

Teddies 442

'Teds' 414

Teijin Shoji Kaisha 447

Tennyson, Lady 155

Terry, Ellen261

Thaarup, Aage 158, 251, 275, 279, 292

Thalberg, Irving 230

Thatcher, Dorothy 91

Thatcher, Heather 164, 291

Theatre de la Mode, Le 270

Thesiger, Ernest 115

Thistlethwayte, Mr T 127

Thomas, Ian 120, 152, 186, 329, 330, 350, 355-357, 365, 369, 373-374, 380-381, 392-393, 399-400, 401, 402, 403-4, 406, 411, 420, 424-425, 430, 432, 433, 437-438, 440, 447-448

Thomas Shirts USA 284, 363

Thornton, Mr and Mrs Kenneth 404

Thorpe, Jeremy 428

Thynne, Lady Mary 90, 91, 165, 167

Tiepolo 167

Titmuss, Phyllis 51

Todd, Dorothy 86

Todd, Miss Nellie 67

Tofield, Mrs 177

Torimaru, Gnyuki, designer Yuki 432, 433

Travers, Captain Dudley 137

Treble, Sepha 190

Tredegar, Lord (Evan Morgan) 87

Trollope & Sons 145, 151

Truman, Hanbury, Buxton & Co Ltd 11

Tufnell, Mrs Sibyl 266

Tufnell, Major Timothy 276, 404, 423-424, 426

Tussaud, Bernard 245

Twentieth Century Fox 419

Twenty-One Club 444

Tyrwitt, Dame Mary 310

Underdown, Mrs 8

Usherwood, Professor Sydney 14

V-1 & V-2 rockets 249, 261

V&A Museum 147, 211, 374

Van Cleef & Arpels 11

Van Dyck 407

Variety Artists Ball 394

Vaughan, Henry vii

Vaughan Williams 313

Vauxhall 226, 234, 241

Vera, Madame 449

Victoria, HM Queen 101, 199, 207, 221, 336, 358, 417

Vionnet, Madeleine 89, 94, 116, 138

Vivex Process 168-169

Vivian, Daphne 61, 78, 89, 92, 164, 165

Vivian, Lt Col V 242

Vivian Smith, The Hon R H 242

Volterra, Madame 424

Vyner, Margaret 'Bunch of Flowers' or 'Michael' 211, 214, 218, 219
Wagner, Richard 28, 32, 41, 130, 427
Wagner, Mrs 155
Wakefield, Norris 'Wakers' 151, 160, 186, 332, 373, 412, 417, 433
Waldorf Astoria 182
Wales, HRH Prince of, Charles 294, 434
Wales, HRH Prince of, Edward 141, 169, 175
Walsh, Jane 227
Walter NH employee 424
Walton Hosiery 372, 376
Ward, Mr F 225, 268, 302
Ward, Mrs John 372
Warrender, Harold 'Harry'34, 66, 130, 380
Warrender, Lady Maud 62, 63
Warwick, Earl of 141
Waterhouse, Alfred 27
Waters, Elsie and Doris 253, 254-255, 355
Waugh, Evelyn 36, 184
Wavell, Lady Vicereine of India 235
Wedgwood 213, 220, 267, 412-413
Welch, Denton 298
Welch, Elizabeth 243
Weller, Miss 203, 204
Welles, Sumner 228
Welsby, Miss 272
West, Mae 315, 329
Westbury Hotel, NH Suite 371
Westminster Bank 307, 357, 386-388
Westminster, Duchess of 214, 303
Weymouth, Lady 91, 96, 158, 165, 215
Weymouth, Lord 61, 215
W & G Foyle 124
Whigham, Mr and Mrs George Hay 142, 383
Whigham, Miss Margaret ;Mrs Charles Sweeny; Margaret, Duchess of Argyll 101, 121, 134, 141-142, 217, 261, 370, 377, 383
Whistler, Rex 160
Whitehead, A J 13
White NH chauffeur 445
'White Train' 279
Whitmee, H J 21, 22
Whitmee, Mrs 22
Whittaker, Michael 363
Wilbur Clark's Desert Inn 417

Wilcox, Herbert 290, 358, 373, 434
William Hickey column 12
Williams, Hugh 212
Williams, Sidney 18
Williamson, David 23
Willingdon, Marie, Dowager Marchioness of 243, 244, 265-266
Willink, Sir Henry Urmston 28-29
Wills, Major Cecil and Mrs Gladys 250, 270, 318-325, 327, 385-386, 388, 423, 426
Wilson & Co 143
Wilson, Mr and Mrs Harold 292, 400, 420-421, 436-437,
Windsor, Duchess of 198
Winn, Godfrey 28, 382, 433, 441
Winnie, Miss 79
Winterhalter, Franz Xaver 200-201, 210, 407
Withers, Googie 309
Women's Police uniform 430
Women's Royal Army Corps 310
Wood, Jane 99
Wooley-Hart, Mrs 140, 218
Woolwich, Bishop of 451
Wordsworth 410
Worth, Charles Fredrick 61, 209
Worth (London) 61, 125, 147, 156, 178, 228, 230, 260, 348, 384
Worth(Paris) 81, 87, 103, 116, 203
Wray, Fay 158
Wyndham, Francis 182
Wyndham, Miss Olivia 115
Wyndham's Theatre 64, 190
Wynyard, Diana 189
Yankee Clipper 225
Yevonde, Madame 83, 168, 229
York, Duchess of see Elizabeth, Queen
York, Duke of see George VI
Yoxall, Harold 233
Yugoslavia, Prince Paul 210
Yugoslavia, Princess Paul, Princess Olga of Greece, 210, 314
Yuki 422, 423
Zinkeisen, Doris 248
Zulnie David 272, 274

Later: 1946 .....

Heartily endorsed 15 years

"Blake", in
pensive but
boyish
vein!
...